Yocto Project Customization for Linux

The Essential Guide for
Embedded Developers

Rodolfo Giometti

Yocto Project Customization for Linux: The Essential Guide for Embedded Developers

Rodolfo Giometti
LUCCA, Italy

ISBN-13 (pbk): 979-8-8688-1434-1   ISBN-13 (electronic): 979-8-8688-1435-8
https://doi.org/10.1007/979-8-8688-1435-8

Copyright © 2025 by Rodolfo Giometti

Managing Director, Apress Media LLC: Welmoed Spahr
Acquisitions Editor: James Robinson-Prior
Editorial Project Manager: Jacob Shmulewitz

Distributed to the book trade worldwide by Springer Science+Business Media New York, 1 New York Plaza, New York, NY 10004. Phone 1-800-SPRINGER, fax (201) 348-4505, e-mail orders-ny@springer-sbm.com, or visit www.springeronline.com. Apress Media, LLC is a Delaware LLC and the sole member (owner) is Springer Science + Business Media Finance Inc (SSBM Finance Inc). SSBM Finance Inc is a **Delaware** corporation.

For information on translations, please e-mail booktranslations@springernature.com; for reprint, paperback, or audio rights, please e-mail bookpermissions@springernature.com.

Apress titles may be purchased in bulk for academic, corporate, or promotional use. eBook versions and licenses are also available for most titles. For more information, reference our Print and eBook Bulk Sales web page at http://www.apress.com/bulk-sales.

Any source code or other supplementary material referenced by the author in this book is available to readers on GitHub. For more detailed information, please visit https://www.apress.com/gp/services/source-code.

If disposing of this product, please recycle the paper

To Mauro and Aleandro. You know why.

Table of Contents

xi

About the Author

Rodolfo Giometti is an engineer, IT specialist, embedded GNU/Linux expert, and Software Libre evangelist. He has over 20 years of experience with GNU/Linux Embedded on x86, ARM, MIPS, and PowerPC-based platforms, and he is the maintainer of the LinuxPPS projects (Linux's Pulse Per Second subsystem). Rodolfo still actively contributes to the Linux source code, contributing several patches and new device drivers for industrial application devices.

About the Technical Reviewer

Antonio Tringali a freelance electronic engineer, develops cutting-edge hardware and software solutions with a focus on cybersecurity.

Acknowledgments

I would like to express my deepest gratitude to Giacomo Vianelli for his support and suggestions.

Heartfelt thanks to my technical reviewer, Antonio Tringali, for his suggestions and critical reading of what is reported in this book.

This book would not be the same without the intuition of James Robinson-Prior and the support of Gryffin Winkler and Shobana Srinivasan.

Finally, to my family for their unwavering support throughout this journey. To my spouse Valentina and my children Romina and Raffaele, who supported me during the time of writing this book.

Introduction

Embedded computers have become very complex in the last few years since they are called to solve plenty of complex problems that humans did by themselves before. This complexity has involved hardware and software, and embedded systems now need very complex OSes in order to work as expected.

The Yocto OS is now the effective standard for the most part of the embedded systems around the world. This is due to its robustness, high configuration, high availability of software packages, and the ability to support several hardware platforms with common mechanisms so that developers may deploy their systems with minor effort even on different machines.

This book shows how the Yocto build system (i.e., the Yocto Project's machine to build binary images from sources) works and how developers may easily (and quickly) move from the demo Yocto distributions that silicon vendors relay for their development kits to their final product. It accompanies developers from the demo Yocto distribution to their final Yocto distribution by explaining how the build system works and by doing practical examples.

What This Book Covers

This book talks about the Yocto Project, but it is not yet another book talking about the Yocto Project. In fact, its main goal is not to explain how the Yocto Project works (even if something must be explained anyway, and this is done in the second part of this book), but it talks instead about how developers can alter an already functional Yocto distribution (which has usually been developed for a development kit from a silicon vendor) to support their embedded system which is (typically) derived from those development kits!

So, this book has a first part where I briefly introduce some common embedded terms and where I present the embedded kit I'm going to use in this book to effectively test my example code on real hardware (I know perfectly that I cannot cover all possible hardware configuration all my readers may work on; that's why I have tried to write all examples in the most generic form I could, so that, even if you have a different hardware configuration, you may hopefully use these examples on your systems).

In this first part, I also explain how to get Yocto sources and how to set up a possible host machine configuration to be able to recompile a Yocto image from scratch.

Below is a brief introduction of each chapter related to this first part:

- *Chapter 1 – Setting Up the Building Environment* starts by introducing some common terms of the embedded programming world, then it presents the development kit used in this book: the EDIMM 2.0 STARTER KIT by Engicam. And, after a brief introduction of the board, it sets up both serial and Ethernet communication channels in order to be able to supply commands and code on real hardware. Finally, it explains how to install a complete developing system on a GNU/Linux-based host system (on both real and emulated machines).

- *Chapter 2 – Installing the Sources* shows how to download Yocto sources and how to set up a fully functional build environment. Then it shows how to build a Yocto image from scratch and how to install it on our embedded kit. In the end, some notes about how to fix up the network connection on the new image are provided with some notes about how to update the code.

The second part follows, and it can be considered as the theoretical part of this book. In fact, in this part, I will explain some theory about how the Yocto build system works and how developers can use available tools to properly manage the sources to fit their needs. This is not a complete manual (there is already one very well-written and complete manual on the Internet at `https://docs.yoctoproject.org/ref-manual/index.html`, where the readers can find whatever about the theory is not covered here), but I present and explain such concepts that we are going to use in this book so that it can be used as a practical reference text.

A brief introduction of each chapter of this theoretical part is as follows:

- *Chapter 3 – Yocto Project Basics* introduces the Yocto Project's basic information, which every Yocto developer should know in order to better understand how it works. To begin, I will explain what the Yocto Project is and its basic concepts. Next I will present the main Yocto components starting from its main configuration files and the variables they hold.

- *Chapter 4 – Yocto Tools* introduces most used Yocto commands such as BitBake, recipetool, devtool, etc. All these commands are then used in the next chapters to create or manage recipes.

- *Chapter 5 – BitBake Internals* shows how the Yocto Project's main component, named BitBake, works, how it uses variables, and how it executes its tasks. BitBake has its syntax which has similarities to several other programming languages. But it also provides some unique features, and we need to understand how BitBake interprets these objects in order to be able to write effective recipes and/or manage the Yocto distribution.

- *Chapter 6 – Recipes* shows how recipes can be written and how they work, for example, which variables and tasks we can put in them and how we can use them to create packages or root filesystem.

In the end, the third part follows, and it can be considered as the practical part of this book. In fact, I'm going to show here how to effectively write or modify recipes or how to define a new layer or machine, and I'll present some possible best practices and configurations that developers may use to improve their projects.

A brief introduction of each chapter of this practical part is as follows:

- *Chapter 7 – Generating and Managing Layers* explains how a new layer can be added to an existent Yocto build system. In this manner, developers may add their customizations and recipes within a private layer where they have a total control of the newly developed Yocto system.

- *Chapter 8 – Adding New Hardware* shows how new machines can be derived from the already defined ones, in such a way to reduce the developing time needed to define new custom hardware. Techniques explained in this chapter will reduce the time to market of new hardware!

- *Chapter 9 – C Application Recipes* focuses the attention on recipes for programs written in C (or C++). Several examples of user space and libraries are presented, along with a kernel space project.

- *Chapter 10 – Python Application Recipes* explains how to generate recipes for Python-based projects by proposing two different ways to do so (via setuptools3 or via pypi).

- *Chapter 11 – Miscellaneous Recipes* covers various common problems in embedded computing which don't fit into the previous two chapters, for example, how to get a newer program release, how to add a system service, or how to deploy native packages (i.e., for the host machine).

- *Chapter 12 – Image Recipes* explains how to write recipes to generate root filesystem images, that is, how to group together several package recipes to have a running root filesystem for our embedded machines.

- *Chapter 13 – Optimizations and Best Practices* reports some final suggestions about how to properly configure our Yocto build system to save all sources or (for example) about having the ability to build a development or production release easily, etc.

What You Need for This Book

The following are the prerequisites for efficient learning.

Software Prerequisite

Regarding the software, you should have some knowledge of a non-graphical text editor such as vi or nano. Even though the graphical interface can be used by directly connecting an LCD, a keyboard, and a mouse to embedded kits. In this book, we assume that you can do little modifications to text files by using a text editor only.

The host computer, that is, the computer you will use to cross-compile the code and/or to manage your embedded systems, is assumed to run a GNU/Linux-based distribution. My host PC is running an Ubuntu 22.04, but you can also use a newer Ubuntu Long-Term Support (LTS) or a Debian-based system too with little modifications. Alternatively, you may use another GNU/Linux distribution but with a little effort from you, mainly regarding the needed tools' installation, library dependencies, and package management.

Foreign systems such as Windows, macOS, or similar are not covered in this book.

The knowledge of how a C/C++ compiler works and how to manage a Makefile is required. This book will also present some kernel programming techniques, but these must not be taken as a kernel programming course. You need a proper book for such a topic! However, each example is well documented, and you will find several suggested resources.

As a final note, I suppose that you know how to connect a GNU/Linux-based board on the Internet to download a package or a generic file.

Hardware Prerequisite

In this book, all code is developed and tested on the EDIMM 2.0 STARTER KIT developed by Engicam, but you can use another embedded kit due to the fact that the code is portable. It should compile for different systems without any issue. However, some minor modifications may be required in order to properly move binary images on these systems and when deriving new machines from an existing one.

Conventions

In this book, you will find many text styles that distinguish between different kinds of information. Here are some examples of these styles and an explanation of their meaning.

Long Outputs, Codes, and Command Lines

When I need to show part of long outputs (or file contents), I may remove non-relevant text by replacing it with three dots, leaving untouched the important content, as in the example below:

```
$ cat very_long_file.txt
Line 1
Line 2
Line 3
...
Line 999
Line 1000
...
```

In the above output, lines after Line 3 until Line 999 have been removed, as well as lines after Line 1000.

Code words in text, folder names, filenames, file extensions, path names, dummy URLs, and user input are shown as follows: "To get the preceding kernel messages, we can use both the dmesg and tail -f /var/log/kern.log commands."

A block of code is set as follows:

```
#include <stdio.h>
int main(int argc, char *argv[])
{
        printf("Hello World!\n");
        return 0;
}
```

where the indentation can be composed of eight or four spaces in order to get the best readability.

Any command-line input or output given on my host computer as a non-privileged user is written as follows:

```
$ cat /etc/lsb-release
```

When I need to give a command as a privileged user (root) on my host computer, the command-line input or output is then written as follows:

```
# systemctl restart schroot
```

You should notice that all privileged commands can be executed by a normal user too by using the sudo command with the form

```
$ sudo <command>
```

So the preceding command can be executed by a normal user as

```
$ sudo systemctl restart schroot
```

Note also that due to space reasons in the book, you may read very long command lines as follows:

```
$ sudo apt install man python-is-python3 wget git gpg bzip2 chrpath cpio
diffstat file gcc g++ gawk gcc make zstd lz4 xz-utils python3-distutils
```

However, generally, for better readability, I'll break the command line as below:

```
$ sudo apt install man python-is-python3 wget git gpg bzip2 \
  chrpath cpio diffstat file gcc g++ gawk gcc make zstd lz4 \
  xz-utils python3-distutils
```

However, in some special cases you can find broken output lines as follows:

```
$ ssh root@192.168.32.132
The authenticity of host '192.168.32.132 (192.168.32.132)' can't be esta
blished.
RSA key fingerprint is SHA256:EJPYPkw+lcPowlZnJosrrJMLO8QKCekVzJo62FBdLs
g.
...
```

Unfortunately, these lines cannot be easily reported into a printed book, so you should consider them as a single line.

Yocto Tools' Usage Messages

Regarding the Yocto tools, I usually prefer to show the tool's usage message which can be displayed by using the -h (or --help) option argument, as shown below:

```
$ devtool -h
NOTE: Starting bitbake server...
usage: devtool [--basepath BASEPATH] [--bbpath BBPATH] [-d] [-q]
               [--color COLOR] [-h]
               <subcommand> ...

OpenEmbedded development tool

options:
  --basepath BASEPATH   Base directory of SDK / build directory
  --bbpath BBPATH       Explicitly specify the BBPATH, rather than
getting it from the metadata
  -d, --debug           Enable debug output
  -q, --quiet           Print only errors
  --color COLOR         Colorize output (where COLOR is auto, always,
                        never)
  -h, --help            show this help message and exit

subcommands:
  Beginning work on a recipe:
    add                     Add a new recipe
    modify                  Modify the source for an existing recipe
...
```

Most tools, however, have several subcommands (as shown above), so to get specific usage messages for these subcommands you have to invoke them with the -h (or --help) option argument too:

```
$ devtool add -h
NOTE: Starting bitbake server...
usage: devtool add [-h] [--same-dir | --no-same-dir] [--fetch URI]
          [--npm-dev] [--version VERSION] [--no-git]
          [--srcrev SRCREV | --autorev] [--srcbranch SRCBRANCH]
          [--binary] [--also-native] [--src-subdir SUBDIR]
          [--mirrors] [--provides PROVIDES]
          [recipename] [srctree] [fetchuri]
```

```
Adds a new recipe to the workspace to build a specified source tree. Can
optionally fetch a remote URI and unpack it to create the source tree.

arguments:
  recipename           Name for new recipe to add (just name - no
                       version, path or extension). If not specified,
                       will attempt to auto-detect it.
  srctree              Path to external source tree. If not specified, a
                       subdirectory of
                       /home/giometti/yocto/imx-yocto-bsp/imx8mp-build/
                       workspace/sources will be used.
  fetchuri             Fetch the specified URI and extract it to create
                       the source tree

options:
  -h, --help           show this help message and exit
  --same-dir, -s       Build in same directory as source
...
```

However, I'm going to explain all these aspects when they are used in the book.

Yocto Syntax Changes Across Releases

The Yocto Project has several releases, and most of the earlier releases are still actively used at the time of the writing of this book (in the embedded world, the time passes slowly than in the real world), so you should pay attention to this note.

Before the Yocto Project 3.4 Release (codename Honister), and more precisely before BitBake 1.52, the syntax for OVERRIDES (explained in detail in Section 5.3) used the underscore character instead of the colon used starting from the Honister release. This means that a variable assignment that was earlier written as reported below:

```
SRC_URI_mx8m = "file://somefile"
SRC_URI_append = " file://somefile"
SRC_URI_append_mx8m = " file://somefile2"
```

from the Honister release becomes

```
SRC_URI:mx8m = "file://somefile"
SRC_URI:append = " file://somefile"
SRC_URI:append:mx8m = " file://somefile2"
```

since `mx8m`, `append`, and the composite form `append:mx8m` are all what Yocto developers call an override.

This applies to any use of override syntax, as shown below:

```
SRC_URI_remove_mx8m = "file://somefile3"
SRC_URI_prepend_mx8m = "file://somefile4 "
FILES_${PN}-tools = "${bindir}/someprog"
IMAGE_CMD_tar = "tar"
SRCREV_pn-bash = "somerev"
BB_TASK_NICE_LEVEL_task-compile = '0'
```

that would now become

```
SRC_URI:remove:mx8m = "file://somefile3"
SRC_URI:prepend:mx8m = "file://somefile4 "
FILES:${PN}-tools = "${bindir}/someprog"
IMAGE_CMD:tar = "tar"
SRCREV:pn-bash = "somerev"
BB_TASK_NICE_LEVEL:task-compile = '0'
```

However, since a lot of old code and documentation are still present around the world, you may still find a lot of code and documentation using _append, _prepend, _remove, and other old override syntax. But now you are warned about it, and you can easily move from one to another to make things work properly as expected.

File Modifications

When modifying a text file, I'm going to use the unified context **diff** format, since this is a very efficient and compact way to represent a text modification. This format can be obtained by using the `diff` command with the `-u` option argument or by using the `git diff` command.

As a simple example, let's consider the following text as `file1.txt`:

```
This is the first line
This is the second line
This is the third line
...
This is the last line
```

Suppose we have to modify the third line, as highlighted in the following snippet:

```
This is the first line
This is the second line
This is the new third line modified by me
...
This is the last line
```

You can easily understand that reporting each time the whole file for a simple modification is quite obscure and space consuming. However, by using the unified context diff format, the preceding modification can be written as follows:

```
--- a/file1.txt
+++ b/file1.txt
@@ -1,5 +1,5 @@
 This is the first line
 This is the second line
-This is the third line
+This is the new third line modified by me
 ...
 This is the last line
```

Now the modification is obvious and written in a compact form! It starts with a two-line header where the original file is preceded by `---` and prefixed with the a/ string, and the new file is preceded by +++ and prefixed with the b/ string. The header then follows one or more change hunks that contain the line differences in the files. The preceding example has just one hunk where the unchanged lines are preceded by a space character, while the lines to be added are preceded by a + character, and the lines to be removed are preceded by a – character (note that the above output is not exactly what the `diff -u` or `git diff` commands return, but it is still in the unified context diff format).

Still, for space reasons, most patches reported in this book have reduced indentation to fit the printed page width; however, they are still perfectly readable in a correct form.

For the real patch, you should refer to the files provided on GitHub.

Serial and Network Connections

In this book, I'm going to mainly use two different kinds of connections to interact with the embedded kit used to run our examples: the serial console and an SSH terminal over an Ethernet connection.

The serial console is mainly used to manage the system from the command line, and it's largely used to monitor the system, especially to take under control the booting messages.

An SSH terminal is quite similar to the serial console, even if it is not the same (e.g., booting messages from the bootloader or the kernel messages do not automatically appear on a terminal). However, it can be used in the same manner as a serial console to give commands and to edit files from the command line.

In Section 1.3, I'm going to explain in detail how you may use these connections to interact with your embedded kit from a Linux-based host machine. Regarding the target, even if they are obviously referred to my embedded kit, they can be easily applied with minor effort on every embedded machine running the Yocto Project.

Other Conventions

New terms and important words are shown in **bold** or *italic*. Words that you see on the screen, for example, in menus or dialog boxes, appear in the text like the `Clicking the Next button moves you to the next screen` string.

Warnings or significant notes appear in a box like this:

Tips and tricks appear like this.

CHAPTER 1

Setting Up the Building Environment

In this chapter, we are going to define some common terms used in this book which are relative to the embedded world (a skilled reader may safely skip it), then we'll present an overview of the embedded device we will use in this book (of course, a different one can be used, but the readers should adapt command settings presented here to their machines).

A useful section about how to set up the target machine is then proposed. This part is quite generic, even if all settings are obviously related to our embedded device.

The last sections of this chapter are about how to set up the host system – the readers can use it to set up a GNU/Linux-based working machine or a dedicated virtual one – and about how to install a Yocto building environment. This part is obviously related to our embedded device, but it can be easily adapted for other systems.

1.1 Embedded World Terms

Before putting our hands on our embedded system with the Yocto Project, it is recommended that the readers acquaint themselves with some terms that an embedded developer should know to avoid misunderstandings.

© Rodolfo Giometti 2025
R. Giometti, *Yocto Project Customization for Linux*,
https://doi.org/10.1007/979-8-8688-1435-8_1

People who have already worked with GNU/Linux embedded systems may skip this part, even if we suggest taking a look at it anyway (the readers may still learn something new!).

Term	Description
Target	The **target** system is the embedded computer that we wish to manage. Usually, it is an ARM platform, but this is not a fixed rule. In fact, PowerPC and MIPS are other (less) common platforms. Even the x86 platform (a standard PC) can be an embedded computer.
Host	The **host** system is the computer we will use to manage the target system. Often, it is a normal PC (x86 platform with 32 or 64 bits) or MAC, but even other platforms can be used. Normally, the host system is more powerful than the target one, since it's usually used for heavy compiling tasks that the target cannot perform at all or for tasks that it takes a long time to perform.
Serial console	This is the most important communication port in an embedded system. Using the **serial console**, the user has complete control of the system, even if it's not correctly set up. In fact, the serial console is not only indispensable for debugging but is also the last resort if, by chance, the operating system files are messed up and the board refuses to boot (actually this is not entirely true since every modern CPU has several ways to recover messed booting code – first and foremost, the *serial downloader* – however, for the embedded developer, it's a must-have!).

(continued)

Term	Description
Compiler (or native compiler) and the cross-compiler	The native compiler runs on a machine (host or target) and builds the code for itself; that is, the compiler running on a PC builds the code for the PC, like the one running on an ARM machine builds the code for the ARM machine itself, while the cross-compiler is just a compiler that builds the code for a foreign machine (i.e., a cross-compiler can run on a PC to generate binaries for an ARM machine).
Distribution	Distribution (or Linux distribution, often called **distro** for short) is an operating system made from a software collection based on Linux (the kernel) and many software packages (most from the GNU project or based on some Libre Software license) usually managed by a package management system. There are various distributions, and they are available for a wide variety of systems, ranging from embedded devices (OpenWrt or, in our case, the **Yocto Project**) and personal computers (**Ubuntu** or **Debian**) to powerful supercomputers.
Root filesystem	The root filesystem (or **rootfs** for short) is the filesystem contained on the same partition on which the root directory is located. This is the most important filesystem in a UNIX system, and it's the first one to be mounted by the kernel. All other filesystems (if any) are mounted on it.

(continued)

3

Term	Description
System-on-Module	A *System-on-Module* (**SoM**) is a board-level circuit that integrates a system in a single module or board; a typical application is in the area of embedded systems.
	A SoM serves a special function like a *system-on-a-chip* (SoC for short – which usually is a CPU with peripherals on the same chip) but with more external peripherals, even if it still requires a high level of interconnection. Simply speaking, a SoM is a cross between a SoC and a single-board computer; in fact, usually a SoM is a SoC with some basic peripherals (such as the RAM, a storage device such as eMMC or flash memories, and maybe a Wi-Fi module, EEPROM memories, etc.) which is mounted on a specific carrier to become a fully functional system.
Carrier board (carrier for short)	SoMs often need to be mounted on a **carrier** board (or *baseboard*) which breaks the bus out to standard peripheral connectors and provide proper power sources (such as power supplies or batteries).
	Frequently, carriers also provide more peripherals to have a flexible way to add or remove peripherals (typically, we use one SoM with different carriers to deploy different systems).

Now that some important terms have been pointed out, we are ready to step into the next section.

1.2 Target System Overview

In this book, we are going to use the **EDIMM 2.0 Starter Kit** developed by **Engicam**. This embedded system is based on a SOM equipped with the **i.MX8M-Plus CPU** by **NXP** and a carrier with several exported peripherals specifically designed by Engicam.

An image of the SOM is reported in Figure 1-1.

Figure 1-1. *The SoM i.Core MX8M Plus by Engicam*

All documentation and support for this SoM (System-on-Module) can be retrieved from `https://www.engicam.com/vis-prod/101684/EDIMM-SOM-based-on-NXP-iMX-8M-Plus`.

The carrier board where this SoM is mounted is the **EDIMM 2.0 Form Factor Capacitive Evaluation Board**; together they form the **EDIMM 2.0 Starter Kit** by Engicam. A rearview of the carrier board is reported in Figure 1-2.

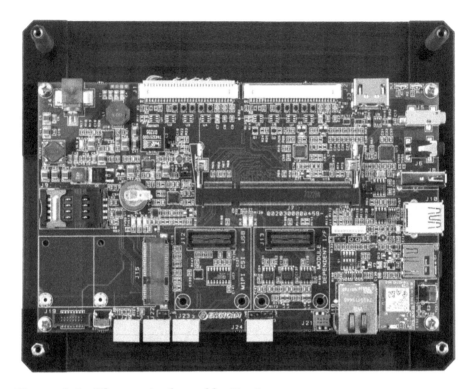

Figure 1-2. *The carrier board by Engicam*

All documentation and support for this starter kit can be retrieved at
https://www.engicam.com/vis-prod/101366/EDIMM-2-0-
STARTER-KIT-EDIMM-2-0-Form-Factor-Capacitive-
Evaluation-Board. A registration may be required for full access.

Engicam provides both the Yocto Project and Android OSes for this
machine, and on board we have the following peripherals:

- LCD 7" with capacitive touch screen

- 1 x HDMI interface (Module Dependent)

- 2 x LVDS interface up to FULL HD

- 1 x Gb Ethernet (second interface on demand)

- 1 x Audio interface

- 1 x USB3.0 (Module Dependent)

- 3 x USB2.0

- 1 x microSD

- 1 x RS485

- 1 x RS232

- 1 x Console (RS232)

- 2 x CAN BUS (Module Dependent)

- Wi-Fi interface

- Mini PCIe (Module Dependent)

- 1 x MIPI CSI

Readers who are interested in using this board can ask directly to Engicam at `https://www.engicam.com`.

1.3 Setting Up the Target Machine

Now it's time to set up our target machine. Of course, we are going to present all commands and settings related to the Engicam board presented above, but the readers may adapt our job to their systems since these procedures are quite usual for every embedded system.

1.3.1 Serial Connection

In order to have full control of our embedded device, we need to correctly set up the serial console over the serial connection.

Each embedded system based on the GNU/Linux OS has a dedicated serial port callcd **serial console**, which developers can use to debug and manage the system even with a reduced environment (just a single terminal!).

Note that it is almost frequently that the serial console is not implemented via the usual serial RS232 connection, but via USB. In this last case, the embedded system still uses a serial port, but its data goes over a USB connection using a Serial-to-USB converter as the one supplied with the Engicam development kit (see Figure 1-3).

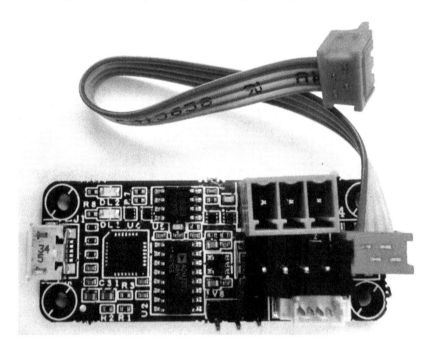

Figure 1-3. *The Serial-to-USB converter by Engicam*

The readers should carefully read the user manual from Engicam in order to correctly plug the serial console adapter connector. Otherwise, the output in the serial terminal may be garbled, and the readers may not understand why.

So, once connected to our development kit, we can verify that the USB connection is ready by taking a look at the kernel messages of our host computer via the dmesg command, as shown below:

```
$ sudo dmesg -w
...
usb 1-9: new full-speed USB device number 6 using xhci_hcd
usb 1-9: New USB device found, idVendor=10c4, idProduct=ea60, bcdDevice
=1.00
usb 1-9: New USB device strings: Mfr=1, Product=2, SerialNumber=3
usb 1-9: Product: CP2102N USB to UART Bridge Controller
usb 1-9: Manufacturer: Silicon Labs
usb 1-9: SerialNumber: 567bb04d5a89eb11a614c5809693f7bc
usbcore: registered new interface driver cp210x
usbserial: USB Serial support registered for cp210x
cp210x 1-9:1.0: cp210x converter detected
usb 1-9: cp210x converter now attached to ttyUSB0
...
```

Note that dmesg is a typical GNU/Linux command, and it should be available on every desktop GNU/Linux distribution. If the readers are using a non-GNU/Linux host machine (and they should not...), then they have to check their system's user manual to get an equivalent command.

On some systems, the product can be reported as Engicam USB-to-Serial with the manufacturer as Engicam. Of course, this is not a problem at all.

In the above messages, we see that the *Serial-to-USB* converter is attached to the ttyUSB0 device, so we can use it on every serial terminal emulator to get access to the serial console. In our case, we use the very popular serial communication program called **Minicom**, as reported below:

```
$ minicom -o -c on -D /dev/ttyUSB0
```

Note that if the minicom command is not available, we can install it on any Ubuntu-like OS, just by using the command below:

```
$ sudo apt install minicom
```

If the program is correctly installed, we should get something as in Figure 1-4.

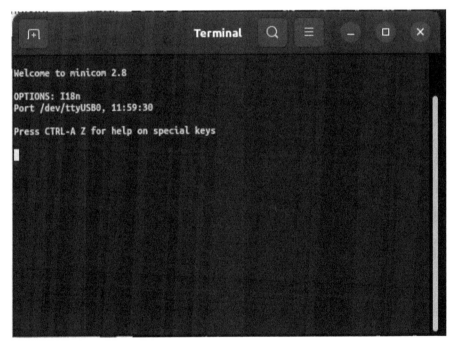

Figure 1-4. *The* minicom *output*

Now, to be sure that our minicom is correctly set up, we should press the CTRL-a and o key sequence to get the configuration menu, where we have to select the Serial port setup entry (by using the arrow keys). If everything has been done correctly, we should get the settings window reported in Figure 1-5.

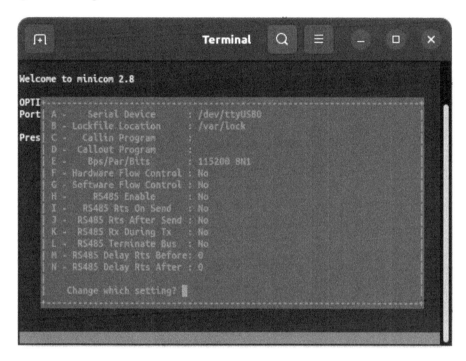

Figure 1-5. *The minicom settings window*

Now we should check that every setting in our system is as shown in Figure 1-5 and then save the current configuration as the default to have the right setting on every running of the minicom tool (we can use the Save setup as dfl entry in the previous menu which is reached back by pressing the Enter key).

After we save the configuration as default, we shall exit the menu and restart the board. This can be done by pulling the plug off and on the socket or by pushing the reset button near the board power supply plug. Then, we should get the following messages:

```
U-Boot SPL 2021.04+fslc+g480445efe5 (Feb 13 2023 - 15:13:15 +0000)
DDRINFO: start DRAM init
DDRINFO: DRAM rate 4000MTS
DDRINFO:ddrphy calibration done
DDRINFO: ddrmix config done
SECO:  RNG instantiated
Normal Boot
WDT:   Not found!
Trying to boot from BOOTROM
image offset 0x8000, pagesize 0x200, ivt offset 0x0
NOTICE:  BL31: v2.4(release):lf-5.15.5-1.0.0-0-g05f788b9b
NOTICE:  BL31: Built : 05:49:10, Mar  2 2022
...
```

These messages are referred to the SPL (Secondary Program Loader) prebootloader, while below are the ones referred to the U-Boot bootloader:

```
...
U-Boot 2021.04+fslc+g480445efe5 (Feb 13 2023 - 15:13:15 +0000)

CPU:   i.MX8MP[8] rev1.1 1600 MHz (running at 1200 MHz)
CPU:   Industrial temperature grade (-40C to 105C) at 27C
Reset cause: POR
Model: Engicam i.MX8MPlus iCore
DRAM:  4 GiB
MMC:   FSL_SDHC: 1, FSL_SDHC: 2
Loading Environment from MMC... OK
Fail to setup video link
In:    serial
Out:   serial
Err:   serial
SECO:  RNG instantiated
...
```

In these messages, we can notice that our system is the Engicam
i.MX8MPlus iCore equipped with 4GB of RAM. Then U-Boot continues
as below:

```
...
BuildInfo:
  - ATF 05f788b
switch to partitions #0, OK
mmc2(part 0) is current device
flash target is MMC:2
Net:   eth1: ethernet@30bf0000 [PRIME]
Fastboot: Normal
Normal Boot
Hit any key to stop autoboot:  0
## Error: "distro_bootcmd" not defined
Running BSP bootcmd ...
switch to partitions #0, OK
mmc2(part 0) is current device
Failed to load 'boot.scr'
30792192 bytes read in 95 ms (309.1 MiB/s)
Booting from mmc ...
58643 bytes read in 1 ms (55.9 MiB/s)
Moving Image from 0x40480000 to 0x40600000, end=423f0000
## Flattened Device Tree blob at 43000000
   Booting using the fdt blob at 0x43000000
   Using Device Tree in place at 0000000043000000, end 0000000043011512
...
```

Once U-Boot has finished loading the *fitimage* (named above as
Flattened Device Tree blob) holding the kernel and its **DTB** (i.e.,
the kernel's device tree blob), then it starts the kernel producing the
following output:

```
...
Starting kernel ...

[    0.000000] Booting Linux on physical CPU 0x0000000000 [0x410fd034]
[    0.000000] Linux version 5.15.5+g2da4fc0a5923 (oe-user@oe-host) (aa
rch64-poky-linux-gcc (GCC) 11.2.0, GNU ld (GNU Binutils) 2.37.20210721)
#1 SMP PREEMPT Wed Feb 1 08:46:51 UTC 2023
[    0.000000] Machine model: Engicam i.Core i.MX8MPlus
...
```

Again, we can see that the machine model is `Engicam i.Core i.MX8MPlus`, and following the next messages, we can also retrieve the kernel command line:

```
...
[    0.000000] Kernel command line: console=ttymxc1,115200 root=/dev/mm
cblk2p2 rootwait rw
...
```

Once the boot process is finished, we should get the login prompt as shown below:

```
...
[  OK  ] Started Weston, a Wayland ...mpositor, as a system service.
[  OK  ] Reached target Graphical Interface.
         Starting Record Runlevel Change in UTMP...
[  OK  ] Finished Record Runlevel Change in UTMP.

NXP i.MX Release Distro 5.15-honister imx8mp-icore-4gb ttymxc1

imx8mp-icore-4gb login:
```

Here, after entering the `root` user, we can just press the `Enter` key to get the root prompt:

```
root@imx8mp-icore-4gb#
```

Great! Through the serial console, we have verified that the system is up and running.

Now we can move to the next section to set up a more practical network connection via SSH.

The prompt may vary according to the system characteristics.

1.3.2 Network Connection

Establishing a network connection is quite an easy task when a Yocto OS is running on an embedded system. Firstly, we have to connect an Ethernet cable to our system, and on the serial console we should get something as below:

```
IPv6: ADDRCONF(NETDEV_CHANGE): eth0: link becomes ready
imx-dwmac 30bf0000.ethernet eth0: Link is Up - 100Mbps/Full - flow contr
ol rx/tx
```

Now we can use the `ip` command to assign an IP address to the `eth0` interface as below:

```
# ip address add 192.168.32.132/24 dev eth0
```

Then we can test the connection by using the `ping` command to send a ping message to another machine on our LAN, as shown below:

```
# ping 192.168.32.2
PING 192.168.32.2 (192.168.32.2) 56(84) bytes of data.
64 bytes from 192.168.32.2: icmp_seq=1 ttl=64 time=0.698 ms
64 bytes from 192.168.32.2: icmp_seq=2 ttl=64 time=0.360 ms
^C
```

However, this method is not reliable since at the next reboot the network configuration will be lost, nor will we have a default gateway setting to allow a remote Internet connection. So, the best solution can be by using a proper configuration file to set up a static network connection, which will be established at every boot of the system.

To do so, let's create a new file under the `/etc/systemd/network/` directory as below:

```
# cat > /etc/systemd/network/50-eth0.network <<__EOF
[Match]
Name=eth0

[Network]
Address=192.168.32.132/24
Gateway=192.168.32.2
DNS=192.168.32.2
__EOF
```

Of course, the readers should replace all the above IP addresses with their addresses in order to get a functional Internet connection.

Then we have to restart the systemd-networkd service:

```
# systemctl restart systemd-networkd
```

Now, to check if everything is working, we can do as below:

```
# ip addr show dev eth0
2: eth0: <BROADCAST,MULTICAST,DYNAMIC,UP,LOWER_UP> mtu 1500 qdisc mq st
ate UP group default qlen 1000
    link/ether 9c:53:cd:0d:8f:78 brd ff:ff:ff:ff:ff:ff
    inet 192.168.32.132/24 brd 192.168.32.255 scope global eth0
       valid_lft forever preferred_lft forever
    inet6 fe80::9e53:cdff:fe0d:8f78/64 scope link
       valid_lft forever preferred_lft forever
# ip route
default dev eth0 scope link
default via 192.168.32.2 dev eth0 proto static
192.168.32.0/24 dev eth0 proto kernel scope link src 192.168.32.2
```

OK, everything seems to be in place now. We just need to test if we can enter in the system via **SSH**, so on the host machine we can try to execute the next command:

```
$ ssh root@192.168.32.132
The authenticity of host '192.168.32.132 (192.168.32.132)' can't be est
ablished.
RSA key fingerprint is SHA256:EJPYPkw+lcPowlZnJosrrJMLO8QKCekVzJo62FBdL
sg.
This key is not known by any other names
Are you sure you want to continue connecting (yes/no/[fingerprint])?
```

Now we can continue by entering the string yes, and we should get an output as shown below:

```
Warning: Permanently added '192.168.32.132' (RSA) to the list of known
hosts.
```

Great! Now we can also use an SSH connection to get logged on our embedded system, so we can move ahead to see how we can set up the developers' host machines.

1.4 Setting Up the Host Machine

To get a running Yocto system, we need a functional building environment on a host machine. The host machine we decide to use could be a normal PC or a virtualized one, and we can use alternative solutions to achieve this goal as reported in the Yocto Project Documentation site at `https://docs.yoctoproject.org/` where, in Section 1.3, we can get a list of supported OSes.

At the time of writing this book, we can read the list of OSes reported in Figure 1-6.

Figure 1-6. *The supported Linux distribution by the Yocto Project*

By taking a look at the screenshot in Figure 1-6, it's obvious that the only available building environment is a desktop Linux–based distro! So other OSes are not allowed.

In this scenario, Yocto developers can choose their preferred desktop Linux–based distro from the list.

In this book, we are going to use the **Ubuntu** OS; however, developers having different Linux-based OSes can easily follow the examples in this book because, once the Yocto Project is installed, the used commands are quite distro independent.

An important note here is that the supported Linux distribution list depends on the Yocto release we decide to use on our embedded system, and the screenshot in Figure 1-6 is referred to *Mickledore 4.2.999*. If we have to use a different release, we can refer to it by changing the selection at the top of the page of section *1 System Requirements* (see `https://docs.yoctoproject.org/ref-manual/system-requirements.html`), as shown in Figure 1-7.

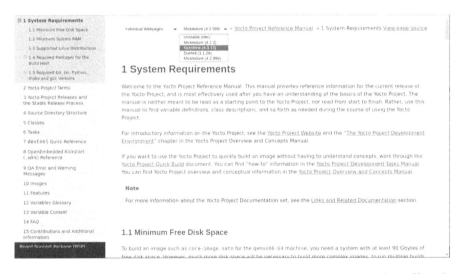

Figure 1-7. *How to select a different Yocto release within the official documentation*

In this book, we are going to use Yocto version **Kirkstone 4.0.13**, and the supported Linux distributions are

- Ubuntu 20.04 (LTS)

- Ubuntu 22.04 (LTS)

- Fedora 37

- Debian GNU/Linux 11.x (Bullseye)

- AlmaLinux 8.8

So in this book, we are going to use **Ubuntu 22.04** as our building OS.

When this book is published, a new Yocto version would be available: the Yocto **Scarthgap 5.0.5**. All next explanations and examples will be ported as is to the new release, and, when necessary, all needed modifications or important new commands will be reported.

1.4.1 Building on Virtual Machines

A simple (and everywhere functional) solution to get a machine running a Linux-based OS is to use a virtual machine running on a proper virtual engine. In this case, we can use our preferred virtualization system, for example, VirtualBox or VMWare where we have to install our Ubuntu 22.04 LTS.

Even if this is the easiest way to get a building machine, good developers should consider using a real machine as a building system; this is because a real machine is much more efficient than an emulated one and since building the Yocto image is quite hardware resource consuming, and emulated PCs may not be the best to use if we need a quick compiling system. The readers should consider that compiling a Yocto image from scratch would require several hours on a real PC, so they can imagine how much time it may take on an emulated machine!

As stated, to install a building system on a generic blank machine (real or emulated, it's not the point), the first step is to know where the Ubuntu 22.04.3 LTS (Jammy Jellyfish) OS can be downloaded. The readers can find it at https://releases.ubuntu.com/jammy/, while Figure 1-8 shows a screenshot of the page.

Figure 1-8. *The Ubuntu 22.04.3 LTS download page*

Then click the *Desktop image* link, and, once the corresponding ISO image is downloaded, we can go further and install it on our preferred host machine.

If we decide to create a new emulated image, we can just select the downloaded ISO image as the booting image; otherwise, for a real PC, the preferred way to install the OS is by creating a bootable USB stick. On Ubuntu, the needed utility to do so is named **Startup Disk Creator**, and the readers may find tons of examples on the Internet about how to use it.

1.4.2 Building by Using schroot (and debootstrap)

In the case where we already have a functional GNU/Linux system as the main system OS, but it's not an Ubuntu 22.04, we can avoid installing a virtual machine by using a *chrooted environment*, as the one provided by the **schroot** tool.

Installing schroot is quite trivial on every desktop GNU/Linux system which provides precompiled packages, but the hard task could be getting the Ubuntu 22.04's root filesystem if your OS doesn't provide a tool named debootstrap. In fact, this last tool can be used to create a Debian/Ubuntu base system from scratch by downloading .deb files from a mirror site and carefully unpacking them into a directory where we can *chroot* into.

With the term *chroot* we mean an operation on Unix-like operating systems that changes the apparent root directory for the current running process and its children. The program that is run in such a modified environment cannot see nor access files in the parent directories.

On an Ubuntu- or Debian-based system, we can simply resolve the problem by using the command below:

```
$ sudo apt install schroot debootstrap
```

For non-Ubuntu users, they can use the packaging management tool provided by their Linux-based OS similarly.

Note that this solution will only work if the running system is a 64-bit PC (usually named amd64 or identified as x86_64 by the command uname -i).

Now if we already have an Ubuntu 22.04 root filesystem, we can put it in a dedicated directory (in our example, `/srv/chroot/ubuntu-jammy-amd64`); otherwise, we can create a new one by using `debootstrap` with the following commands:

```
$ sudo mkdir /srv/chroot && cd /srv/chroot
$ sudo debootstrap --verbose jammy ubuntu-jammy-amd64
```

If everything goes well, we should see an output as reported below:

```
I: Retrieving InRelease
I: Checking Release signature
I: Valid Release signature (key id F6ECB3762474EDA9D21B7022871920D1991B
C93C)
I: Retrieving Packages
I: Validating Packages
I: Resolving dependencies of required packages...
I: Resolving dependencies of base packages...
I: Checking component main on http://archive.ubuntu.com/ubuntu...
I: Retrieving adduser 3.118ubuntu5
I: Validating adduser 3.118ubuntu5
I: Retrieving apt 2.4.5
I: Validating apt 2.4.5
...
```

When the command ends, the root filesystem should be in place:

```
$ ls /srv/chroot/ubuntu-jammy-amd64
bin   dev  home  lib32  libx32  mnt  proc  run   srv  tmp  var
boot  etc  lib   lib64  media   opt  root  sbin  sys  usr
```

Now the next step is to configure the `schroot` tool to correctly enter into our new chrooted system. To do so, we have to add a new file into the `schroot`'s configuration directory, as shown below:

```
$ sudo bash -c 'cat > /etc/schroot/chroot.d/ubuntu-jammy-amd64 <<__EOF__
[ubuntu-jammy-amd64]
description=Ubuntu Jammy (arm64)
directory=/srv/chroot/ubuntu-jammy-amd64
users=giometti
#groups=sbuild
#root-groups=root
#aliases=unstable,default
type=directory
```

```
profile=desktop
personality=linux
preserve-environment=true
__EOF__'
```

Note that the `cat` command is surrounded by two tick (') characters.

Note also that the `directory` parameter is set to the path holding our new root filesystem and that the `users` parameter is set to `giometti`, which is my username (this is a comma-separated list of users that are allowed access to the chroot environment – see the related man pages on `man schroot.conf`).

Looking at the above settings, we see that the `profile` parameter is set to `desktop`; this means that it will be considering all files in the `/etc/schroot/desktop` directory. In particular, the `fstab` file holds all the mount points we would like to be mounted into our system.

So, we should verify that it holds at least the following lines:

```
$ cat /etc/schroot/desktop/fstab
# fstab: static file system information for chroots.
# Note that the mount point will be prefixed by the chroot path
# (CHROOT_PATH)
#
# <file system> <mount point>   <type>  <options>       <dump>  <pass>
/proc           /proc           none    rw,bind         0       0
/sys            /sys            none    rw,bind         0       0
/dev            /dev            none    rw,bind         0       0
/dev/pts        /dev/pts        none    rw,bind         0       0
/home           /home           none    rw,bind         0       0
/tmp            /tmp            none    rw,bind         0       0

# If you use gdm3, uncomment this line to allow Xauth to work
#/var/run/gdm3  /var/run/gdm3   none    rw,bind         0       0
# For PulseAudio and other desktop-related things
/var/lib/dbus   /var/lib/dbus none    rw,bind         0       0

# It may be desirable to have access to /run, especially if you wish
# to run additional services in the chroot.  However, note that this
```

```
# may potentially cause undesirable behaviour on upgrades, such as
# killing services on the host.
#/run           /run           none    rw,bind        0       0
#/run/lock      /run/lock      none    rw,bind        0       0
#/dev/shm       /dev/shm       none    rw,bind        0       0
#/run/shm       /run/shm       none    rw,bind        0       0
```

Now everything is in place, and we have only to restart the schroot service:

```
$ sudo systemctl restart schroot
```

If everything has been done correctly, we should list all available chrooted environments by asking them to schroot with the following command line:

```
$ schroot -l
Chroot:ubuntu-jammy-amd64
```

OK, everything is running well, and we can enter into the chrooted Ubuntu 22.04 system with the command below executed from our home directory:

```
$ cd
$ schroot -c ubuntu-jammy-amd64
$ cat /etc/lsb-release
DISTRIB_ID=Ubuntu
DISTRIB_RELEASE=22.04
DISTRIB_CODENAME=jammy
DISTRIB_DESCRIPTION="Ubuntu 22.04 LTS"
```

Note that it is important to execute the schroot command within our home directory (or at least within a directory that our chrooted environment system can get access to); otherwise, we will get a warning message as shown below:

```
$ cd /srv/chroot/
$ schroot -c ubuntu-jammy-amd64
W: Failed to change to directory '/srv/chroot': No such file or directo
ry
I: The directory does not exist inside the chroot.  Use the --directory
 option to run the command in a different directory.
W: Falling back to directory '/home/giometti'
```

At this point, our new Ubuntu 22.04 is functional, but it's still not ready to go because it's very minimal. This can be verified by taking a look at the file /etc/apt/sources.list:

```
$ cat /etc/apt/sources.list
deb http://archive.ubuntu.com/ubuntu jammy main
```

This file holds references to all Ubuntu repositories where precompiled packages are stored and ready to be installed. All Ubuntu users know that many sources are missing, and a well-configured system should have at least the following settings:

```
$ cat /etc/apt/sources.list
deb http://archive.ubuntu.com/ubuntu/ jammy main universe restricted mu
ltiverse
deb http://security.ubuntu.com/ubuntu jammy-security main universe rest
ricted multiverse
deb http://archive.ubuntu.com/ubuntu/ jammy-updates main universe restr
icted multiverse
```

Note that the above settings are referring to the main Ubuntu sites, but we may also use mirrors (please surf the Internet to find them). For example, for Italy we have the URL http://it.archive.ubuntu.com/ubuntu/.

After the file /etc/apt/sources.list is well configured, we have to execute the following command to read and set up the new sources:

```
$ sudo apt update
```

If everything has been done correctly in the end, we should get a message as below:

```
98 packages can be upgraded. Run 'apt list --upgradable' to see them.
```

To update these packages, we can use the command:

```
$ sudo apt upgrade
```

Now we are ready to install all the basic tools we are going to use in this book, and to see how we have to move to the next section.

1.5 Installing the Building Environment

Now, in order to be sure that all needed commands are correctly installed within our new Ubuntu system (in both the real and virtual cases), we should try to install some packages.

So, let's use the following command:

```
$ sudo apt install man gawk gpg bzip2 wget git diffstat unzip \
        texinfo gcc g++ build-essential chrpath socat cpio \
        python-is-python3 python3-distutils python3 python3-pip \
        python3-pexpect xz-utils debianutils iputils-ping \
        python3-git python3-jinja2 libegl1-mesa libsdl1.2-dev \
        python3-subunit mesa-common-dev zstd liblz4-tool file \
        locales libacl1
$ sudo locale-gen en_US.UTF-8
```

Another important tool we require for our development system is the **repo** command, which is the main tool to easily download and set up all needed Yocto resources.

In a freshly installed system, it is quite usual that this command is not installed, so we can do it by using the *package management system* of our OS. In the case of Ubuntu, we can do it with the command below:

```
$ sudo apt install repo
```

If we use this solution, we may get the following warning message:

```
... A new version of repo (2.50) is available.
... New version is available at: /home/giometti/yocto/imx-yocto-bs
p/.repo/repo/repo
... The launcher is run from: /usr/bin/repo
!!! The launcher is not writable.  Please talk to your sysadmin or
 distro
!!! to get an update installed.
```

In this case, we have to resolve the issue by manually overwriting the repo program or by continuing to use the older version.

Otherwise, we can do the same by grabbing repo directly from Google's site, as shown below:

```
$ sudo wget https://storage.googleapis.com/git-repo-downloads/repo \
       -O /usr/local/bin/repo
$ sudo chmod a+x /usr/local/bin/repo
```

If everything has been done correctly, we should be able to execute the following command:

```
$ repo --help
usage: repo COMMAND [ARGS]

repo is not yet installed.  Use "repo init" to install it here.

The most commonly used repo commands are:

  init      Install repo in the current working directory
  help      Display detailed help on a command

For access to the full online help, install repo ("repo init").

Bug reports: https://issues.gerritcodereview.com/issues/new?component=1
370071
```

We may get something like the following error message:
```
bash: repo: command not found
```

If so, we need to verify that the directory /usr/local/bin/repo is correctly set up within the PATH variable as shown below:

```
$ echo $PATH
/usr/sbin:/usr/bin:/sbin:/bin:/usr/games:/usr/local/games:/snap/bi
n:/snap/bin
```

Here, the directory /usr/local/bin/repo is missing, and we can fix it by doing as shown below:

```
$ PATH="/usr/local/sbin:/usr/local/bin:$PATH"
```

27

If we try to relaunch the command now, it should work.

As a final note, in order to make this change permanent, we can add an export to our `.bashrc` (or similar).

OK, now all the needed commands should be ready, so we can move on to the next chapter where we are going to see how to install Yocto sources.

1.6 Summary

In this chapter, we reviewed some terms from the embedded world, and we have presented the embedded kit we will use throughout this book. We also discovered how to get connected to it via both a serial console and an SSH connection.

Then we set up our host machine (in both real and chrooted versions) to get a fully functional building system.

Now we can move further to see how to install Yocto sources on our host machine.

CHAPTER 2

Installing the Sources

Once the building environment is up and running, we will have to get all
the needed Yocto sources. To do so, we should keep in mind which is the
target system where our new system should run. In fact, even if the Yocto
OS supports different architectures from several CPU vendors, it's quite
common that each vendor has forked its tree to support its products. This
is not typically a problem since whatever we are going to present in this
book is generic and (maybe the last 5% of) the customizations can be
easily adapted for each development kit we have to work on.

Our embedded system is i.MX8 based, so we have to download and
install the Yocto OS developed by NXP, and in this book we are going to
do so. The readers who have a different system can easily do the same by
using a standard Yocto Project or the version released and suggested by
their hardware vendor.

In this chapter, the readers should execute all commands as is (or
by applying the modifications needed for their embedded kits), since all
explanations about what we are doing will be deeply described in the next
chapters.

2.1 Downloading the Repositories

Now we are ready to start the downloading of needed sources, so
within our building system we need to move to a dedicated directory
(we are going to use the yocto directory under the giometti's home

© Rodolfo Giometti 2025
R. Giometti, *Yocto Project Customization for Linux*,
https://doi.org/10.1007/979-8-8688-1435-8_2

directory – i.e., the /home/giometti/yocto directory) and then execute the
repo command as reported below:

```
$ mkdir imx-yocto-bsp && cd imx-yocto-bsp
$ repo init -u https://github.com/nxp-imx/imx-manifest \
        -b imx-linux-kirkstone -m imx-5.15.71-2.2.0.xml
$ repo sync
```

The **repo** tool is the most used method to easily download and set
up all the needed Yocto resources. The above commands get the source
revision *imx-linux-kirkstone* from https://github.com/nxp-imx/imx-
manifest, and they can do so by using the file imx-5.15.71-2.2.0.xml as
the default manifest file.

To install the Scarthgap version, we can use the repo
command below:

```
$ repo init -u https://github.com/nxp-imx/imx-manifest \
        -b imx-linux-scarthgap -m imx-6.6.52-2.2.0.xml
```

A **manifest file** is just a list of repositories to be downloaded in order to
have a working Yocto build system for our embedded board.

When executing the repo, we may get the following warning
message:

```
... A new version of repo (2.39) is available.
... New version is available at: /home/giometti/yocto/imx-yocto-bs
p/.repo/repo/repo
... The launcher is run from: /usr/local/bin/repo
!!! The launcher is not writable.  Please talk to your sysadmin or
 distro
```

We can easily fix it by simply doing what the message suggests, that
is, by copying the new repo version file over the current one in /usr/
local/bin/repo (or whenever suggested in the reader's message).

However, if we keep running the older version, everything should
continue to work correctly.

If everything goes well, we should get our working directory populated
as below:

```
$ ls
imx-setup-release.sh  README  README-IMXBSP  setup-environment  sources
```

wherein the `sources` directory should be placed all Yocto Project's
layers (in the next chapter, we are going to explain what a *layer* is):

```
$ ls sources/
base                meta-freescale-3rdparty    meta-openembedded    poky
meta-browser        meta-freescale-distro      meta-qt6
meta-clang          meta-imx                   meta-timesys
meta-freescale      meta-nxp-demo-experience   meta-virtualization
```

In most cases, this should be enough to obtain whatever we need to
start Yocto compilation; however, in this special case, we need to add
another layer (i.e., more source code) which is provided by Engicam. We
have to do so to have all the needed code to support our embedded kit.

This must be done in the source directory, where all layers relay, by
using the commands reported below:

```
$ cd sources
$ git clone https://github.com/engicam-stable/meta-engicam-nxp.git \
      -b kirkstone
```

In this manner, we clone all sources from `https://github.com/`
`engicam-stable/meta-engicam-nxp.git` at branch *kirkstone*.

At the end, we'll get the new layer reported as below:

```
$ ls meta-engicam-nxp/
conf            README.md               recipes-core
COPYING.MIT     recipes-bsp             recipes-images
note.txt        recipes-connectivity    recipes-kernel
```

OK, now we are ready to start! So let's go back to the working directory above using the `cd` command as shown below:

```
$ cd ..
```

Then we can move to the next section to see how to start the building process.

2.2 Setting Up the Build Directory

Now that everything is in place, we can start to compile our new Yocto image for the embedded system we have to work on. However, before starting the real compilation stage, we must set up the build directory and whatever we need into our environment to properly execute all compiling tools.

Usually, to do so, the first step is to source a special file named `setup-environment` which creates a proper environment to correctly compile all needed tools and, obviously, the desired code.

When we try to execute it, we get a useful usage message, as reported below:

```
$ ./setup-environment
-e
Usage: MACHINE=<machine> DISTRO=<distro> source setup-environment <buil
d-dir>
Usage:                                 source setup-environment <buil
d-dir>
    <machine>     machine name
    <distro>      distro name
    <build-dir>   build directory

The first usage is for creating a new build directory. In this case, the
script creates the build directory <build-dir>, configures it for the
specified <machine> and <distro>, and prepares the calling shell for run
ning bitbake on the build directory.

The second usage is for using an existing build directory. In this case,
the script prepares the calling shell for running bitbake on the build
directory <build-dir>. The build directory configuration is unchanged.
```

```
...
Examples:

- To create a new Yocto build directory:
  $ MACHINE=imx6qdlsabresd DISTRO=fslc-framebuffer source setup-environ
ment build

- To use an existing Yocto build directory:
  $ source setup-environment build
```

At the beginning, we can read that we have two usage modes to execute this script:

- The first one is for creating a new build directory.

  ```
  $ MACHINE=<machine> DISTRO=<distro> \
          source setup-environment <build-dir>
  ```

  The command sets up the build directory `<build-dir>` (where all generated files are placed with our desired Yocto images) and configures it for the specified `<machine>` and `<distro>`. Moreover, it prepares the calling shell to be able to properly run the command `bitbake` (and all other commands available in the build system).

  When executed for the first time, this command generates a configuration file where `MACHINE` and `DISTRO` variables are recorded.

- The second usage is for (re)using an already existing build directory. The usage is

  ```
  $ source setup-environment <build-dir>
  ```

  The command prepares the calling shell for running `bitbake` (and its siblings) on the build directory `<build-dir>`, while the environment configuration is obtained by reading the configuration file generated with the first usage mode.

In the next section, we are going to present in detail this configuration file, which is located in `conf/local.conf`.

All these considerations are always true, but in this case, we are using a special Yocto release by NXP. NXP's developers decided to add a supplemental initial script (which in turn calls the `setup-environment` script) called `imx-setup-release.sh`, so we have to use it to properly set up our building environment.

If we execute it by adding the usual -h option argument, then we can read its usage message, as reported below:

```
$ ./imx-setup-release.sh -h
-e
Usage: source imx-setup-release.sh
    Optional parameters: [-b build-dir] [-h]

    * [-b build-dir]: Build directory, if unspecified script uses 'buil
d' as output directory
    * [-h]: help

To return to this build environment later please run:
    source setup-environment <build_dir>
```

So the command we have to execute for the first time is the following:

```
$ DISTRO=fsl-imx-xwayland MACHINE=imx8mp-icore source \
        imx-setup-release.sh -b imx8mp-build
```

Note that by altering the name supplied with the -b option argument, we can use different building directories for several systems.

Furthermore, the readers should keep in mind that next time they want to return to the Yocto environment, they must execute the following command within the `imx-yocto-bsp` directory, as shown below:

```
$ cd imx-yocto-bsp
$ source setup-environment imx8mp-build
```

Once executed, the command will start displaying the following message:

```
Build directory is  imx8mp-build
/home/giometti/yocto/imx-yocto-bsp

Some BSPs depend on libraries and packages which are covered by NXP's
End User License Agreement (EULA). To have the right to use these binar
ies in your images, you need to read and accept the following...

LA_OPT_NXP_Software_License v39 August 2022
IMPORTANT.  Read the following NXP Software License Agreement ("Agreeme
nt") completely. By selecting the "I Accept" button at the end of this
page, or by downloading, installing, or using the Licensed Software, you
indicate that you accept the terms of the Agreement, and you acknowledge
that you have the authority, for yourself or on behalf of your company,
...
(a)     to use and reproduce the Licensed Software (and its Derivative
Works prepared under the license in Section 2.2(b)) solely in combinati
On with a NXP Product; and
--More--(11%)[Press space to continue, 'q' to quit.]
```

Then we just have to press the SPACE key until we get the question:

```
Do you accept the EULA you just read? (y/n)
```

Let's press the y key so we can finally move within the build directory (i.e., imx8mp-build), and finally we get the message:

```
EULA has been accepted.

Welcome to Freescale Community BSP

The Yocto Project has extensive documentation about OE including a
reference manual which can be found at:
    http://yoctoproject.org/documentation

For more information about OpenEmbedded see their website:
    http://www.openembedded.org/

You can now run 'bitbake <target>'

Common targets are:
    core-image-minimal
    meta-toolchain
    meta-toolchain-sdk
    adt-installer
    meta-ide-support
```

```
Your build environment has been configured with:

    MACHINE=imx8mp-icore
    SDKMACHINE=i686
    DISTRO=fsl-imx-xwayland
    EULA=
BSPDIR=
BUILD_DIR=.
meta-freescale directory found
```

The content of the newly created directory is shown below:

```
$ ls
conf
```

As we can see (for the moment), we just have the conf directory with the following content:

```
$ ls conf/
bblayers.conf       local.conf       local.conf.sample
bblayers.conf.org   local.conf.org   templateconf.cfg
```

Note that the local.conf file above is the one generated at the first attempt of imx-setup-release.sh execution, as said above.

Now we have to modify the bblayers.conf to add the Engicam layer to our Yocto sources. Usually, this step is not needed, but in this special case we have to do it since Engicam's developer didn't provide a proper repo manifest to automatically download all needed sources with the repo command above.

Honestly speaking, Engicam developers provided a similar way to automatically get all the needed software, even if in a not usual way. In fact, they suggest their customers use a dedicated script to download and set up their latest BSP (Board Support Package) release at the link https://github.com/engicam-stable/engicam-bsp-scripts.

The readers should check the documentation of their embedded systems to know if their manifest is complete or if they require more steps before starting the compilation.

In Section 13.4, we are going to explain how to add a complete repo manifest, taking this special case as an example. Furthermore, in Chapter 7, we will see how to add our custom meta layer.

To do so, we need to execute the command below:

```
$ bitbake-layers add-layer ../sources/meta-engicam-nxp
NOTE: Starting bitbake server...
NOTE: Your conf/bblayers.conf has been automatically updated.
```

Now, if we take a look at the conf/bblayers.conf file, we can verify that Engicam's layer has been added, and it is now ready to be used:

```
$ cat conf/bblayers.conf
...
BBLAYERS = " \
  ${BSPDIR}/sources/poky/meta \
  ${BSPDIR}/sources/poky/meta-poky \
...
BBLAYERS += "${BSPDIR}/sources/meta-qt6"
BBLAYERS += "${BSPDIR}/sources/meta-virtualization"
BBLAYERS += "/home/giometti/yocto/imx-yocto-bsp/sources/meta-engicam-nx
p"
```

As we can see in more detail within Section 3.4.4, the variable BBLAYERS lists the layers to enable during the build. So by using the above syntax, in the last line we add the directory where the Engicam layer resides.

After doing this, we are ready to start compiling our first Yocto image; however, before continuing, it is better to take a closer look at the conf/local.conf file to take a first look at its content.

Here, we are going to give the readers a basic introduction to this configuration file. A more complete reference is in Section 3.4.

2.3 Understanding Basic Configuration Settings

As stated above, in this section we will explain the minimal settings that the readers should know to have a basic idea about what we are doing to set up our Yocto build system in order to fit our needs.

If we take a look at the current content of the file, we should see the following settings:

```
$ cat conf/local.conf
MACHINE ??= 'imx8mp-icore'
DISTRO ?= 'fsl-imx-xwayland'
PACKAGE_CLASSES ?= 'package_rpm'
EXTRA_IMAGE_FEATURES ?= "debug-tweaks"
USER_CLASSES ?= "buildstats"
PATCHRESOLVE = "noop"
BB_DISKMON_DIRS ??= "\
    STOPTASKS,${TMPDIR},1G,100K \
    STOPTASKS,${DL_DIR},1G,100K \
    STOPTASKS,${SSTATE_DIR},1G,100K \
    STOPTASKS,/tmp,100M,100K \
    HALT,${TMPDIR},100M,1K \
    HALT,${DL_DIR},100M,1K \
    HALT,${SSTATE_DIR},100M,1K \
    HALT,/tmp,10M,1K"
PACKAGECONFIG:append:pn-qemu-system-native = " sdl"
CONF_VERSION = "2"

DL_DIR ?= "${BSPDIR}/downloads/"
ACCEPT_FSL_EULA = "1"
```

The MACHINE and DISTRO variables are used to identify the hardware machine and its related distribution settings we are going to use to build the Yocto image. Since, as the first step, we will build from scratch an Engicam image for their embedded kit named imx8mp-icore using a Freescale Wayland–based distribution, we can leave these variables untouched.

Regarding the PACKAGE_CLASSES, we decided to set it to package_ipk since we wish to have **IPKG** (Itsy Package Management) packages instead of the **RPM** (Red Hat Package Manager) ones.

The readers should refer to Section 3.4.1 for further information about the differences between the IPKG and RPM package formats.

Also, note that on some systems the variable PACKAGE_CLASSES can be set to package_deb instead of package_rpm. We can safely reset to package_ipk anyway.

Then we also add the package-management string within EXTRA_IMAGE_FEATURES to have a package management system to easily install extra packages at runtime within our final image (i.e., the IPKG packages). Simply speaking, we should add the lines to our file:

```
# Switch to IPKG packaging and include package-management in the image
PACKAGE_CLASSES = "package_ipk"
EXTRA_IMAGE_FEATURES += "package-management"
```

Other variables can be left untouched, while some words must be spent on the DL_DIR variable. As explained later in this book, this variable specifies the download directory used by the build process to store all downloads, and by default it points to the downloads directory within the build directory. We can leave it as is, or we can decide to move it outside the build directory to get two advantages:

1. If we decide to remove the build directory, all downloaded sources will not be removed either.

2. We can share the downloaded sources with different Yocto Project's image builds and then save disk space and possibly accelerate the build process.

In our system, we decided to set this variable to point to the directory /home/giometti/Projects/DL_ARCHIVES/yocto where we have some already downloaded sources (it is up to the readers to choose a proper location).

Then we should verify that the variable ACCEPT_FSL_EULA is set to "1" to inform the Freescale/NXP layers that we have accepted their EULA license (or some code will not be compiled!).

This variable is related to the Freescale's code, and it's quite usual that on non-Freescale Yocto distributions it is not needed at all, even if something similar may be present anyway.

At this point, our local.conf file should look as reported below:

```
$ cat conf/local.conf
MACHINE ??= 'imx8mp-icore'
DISTRO ?= 'fsl-imx-xwayland'
PACKAGE_CLASSES ?= 'package_rpm'
EXTRA_IMAGE_FEATURES ?= "debug-tweaks"
USER_CLASSES ?= "buildstats"
PATCHRESOLVE = "noop"
BB_DISKMON_DIRS ??= "\
    STOPTASKS,${TMPDIR},1G,100K \
    STOPTASKS,${DL_DIR},1G,100K \
    STOPTASKS,${SSTATE_DIR},1G,100K \
    STOPTASKS,/tmp,100M,100K \
    HALT,${TMPDIR},100M,1K \
    HALT,${DL_DIR},100M,1K \
    HALT,${SSTATE_DIR},100M,1K \
    HALT,/tmp,10M,1K"
PACKAGECONFIG:append:pn-qemu-system-native = " sdl"
CONF_VERSION = "2"

DL_DIR = "/home/giometti/Projects/DL_ARCHIVES/yocto/"
ACCEPT_FSL_EULA = "1"

# Switch to IPKG packaging and include package-management in the image
PACKAGE_CLASSES = "package_ipk"
EXTRA_IMAGE_FEATURES += "package-management"
```

Now our `local.conf` file is almost ready, but before starting the compilation, we should consider the next two steps too.

The first one is about the fact that we are using an Engicam embedded kit with 4GB of RAM, while, by default, the Engicam layer is set to 2GB memory layout. We need to alter the file `imx8mp-icore.conf` in the Engicam layer as below:

```
--- sources/meta-engicam-nxp/conf/machine/imx8mp-icore.conf
+++ sources/meta-engicam-nxp/conf/machine/imx8mp-icore.conf
@@ -14,7 +14,7 @@
 "

 UBOOT_CONFIG_BASENAME = "imx8mp_icore"
-UBOOT_CONFIG ??= "2gb"
+UBOOT_CONFIG ??= "4gb"
 UBOOT_CONFIG[1gb] = "${UBOOT_CONFIG_BASENAME}_1gb_defconfig,sdcard"
 UBOOT_CONFIG[2gb] = "${UBOOT_CONFIG_BASENAME}_defconfig,sdcard"
 UBOOT_CONFIG[4gb] = "${UBOOT_CONFIG_BASENAME}_4gb_defconfig,sdcard"
```

This setting is just to obtain a running Yocto image for our embedded kit, but during normal Yocto development, we should avoid altering the original layers in this way.

A better and more reliable way to do so will be explained starting from Chapter 7 in this book.

The second step is about the possibility to add another two special settings to the `local.conf` file to avoid a slowdown of our machine during the image building. This is because the Yocto Project may strongly impact hardware resources in terms of required disk space and RAM (and possibly CPU overheating).

The Yocto Project uses several parallel threads to speed up the compilation, but each building thread will require a dedicated amount of RAM that can easily rise above 3GB! So, for example, to safely run eight building threads, we should plan to have 3 or 4GB of RAM for each thread,

41

which means to have in total 32GB of RAM. Since such an amount of RAM is not always available, we can forcibly reduce the number of building threads by setting the variable BB_NUMBER_THREADS within the conf/local.conf to something like available RAM in GB divided by 4. This is because this variable is used to set the maximum number of tasks the build system should run in parallel at any one time, and, by default, it is equal to the number of cores on the build system. Even if this could seem a reasonable value, the RAM usage issue presented above should move developers to using a lower value.

Moreover, the variable PARALLEL_MAKE, which is used to set the maximum number of parallel threads, a make, ninja, or more specific build engines (like the Go language) will launch during the compilation.

This variable is usually in the form -j <N>, where <N> represents the maximum number of parallel threads such engines can run. By default, the build system automatically sets this variable to be equal to the number of cores the build system uses, so it is better to set it to a lower value (in our example, we decided to use the value 2).

Just to give an example of what happens if the system is overloaded during Yocto building, we report below some typical errors due to low memory conditions:

```
collect2: fatal error: ld terminated with signal 9 [Killed]
compilation terminated.
```

Another possible error message can be

```
ERROR: Worker process (23011) exited unexpectedly (-9), shutting down...
```

or

```
fatal error: Killed signal terminated program
compilation terminated.
```

Whenever some of the above messages are displayed during the building, we should consider lowering the values in BB_NUMBER_THREADS and PARALLEL_MAKE variables.

___

In the end, typical settings for an 8GB RAM system can be as follows:

```
# Limiting HW resources
BB_NUMBER_THREADS = "4"
PARALLEL_MAKE = "-j 2"
```

Finally, with these last settings, our local.conf file should look as below:

```
$ cat conf/local.conf
MACHINE ??= 'imx8mp-icore'
DISTRO ?= 'fsl-imx-xwayland'
PACKAGE_CLASSES ?= 'package_rpm'
EXTRA_IMAGE_FEATURES ?= "debug-tweaks"
USER_CLASSES ?= "buildstats"
PATCHRESOLVE = "noop"
BB_DISKMON_DIRS ??= "\
    STOPTASKS,${TMPDIR},1G,100K \
    STOPTASKS,${DL_DIR},1G,100K \
    STOPTASKS,${SSTATE_DIR},1G,100K \
    STOPTASKS,/tmp,100M,100K \
    HALT,${TMPDIR},100M,1K \
    HALT,${DL_DIR},100M,1K \
    HALT,${SSTATE_DIR},100M,1K \
    HALT,/tmp,10M,1K"
PACKAGECONFIG:append:pn-qemu-system-native = " sdl"
CONF_VERSION = "2"

DL_DIR = "/home/giometti/Projects/DL_ARCHIVES/yocto/"
ACCEPT_FSL_EULA = "1"

# Switch to IPKG packaging and include package-management in the image
PACKAGE_CLASSES = "package_ipk"
EXTRA_IMAGE_FEATURES += "package-management"

# Limiting HW resources
BB_NUMBER_THREADS = "4"
PARALLEL_MAKE = "-j 2"
```

Great! Now let's move to the next section and then start the build!

2.4 Doing the Build

Now we can start building our first Yocto image, which can be the default Engicam's evaluation image for our embedded system named engicam-evaluation-image-mx8, so we can execute the command below:

```
$ bitbake engicam-evaluation-image-mx8
```

We may get the following error message:

```
ERROR:  OE-core's config sanity checker detected a potential misco
nfiguraction.
    Either fix the cause of this error or at your own risk disable
 the checker (see sanity.conf).
    Following is the list of potential problems / advisories:

    Your system needs to support the en_US.UTF-8 locale.

Summary: There was 1 ERROR message, returning a non-zero exit code.
```

If so, we can resolve the problem in two ways:

1) The quick-and-dirty way is by using the following command:

```
$ sudo locale-gen en_US.UTF-8
```

2) Or we can use the command below:

```
$ sudo dpkg-reconfigure locales
```

This will open a menu as in Figure 2-1 where we can add all requested locales (and more) and then select en_US.UTF-8 as the default.

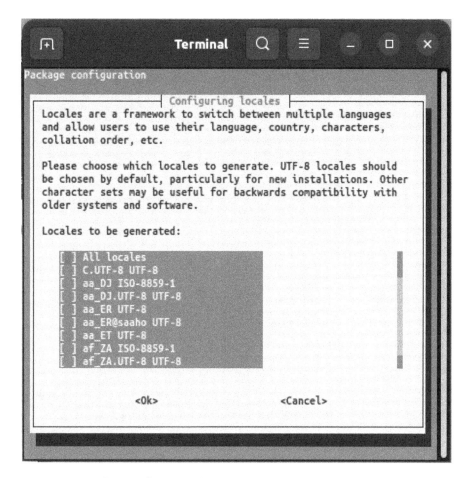

Figure 2-1. *The configuring locale menu*

If everything works well, we should see that the system is building our Yocto image, then we can take our preferred cup of tea or coffee and start reading a book, since it will take a long time...

Just for reference, we report below a screenshot of the messages displayed by the building system as shown on our system:

```
$ bitbake engicam-evaluation-image-mx8
Loading cache: 100% |###################################| Time: 0:00:05
Loaded 4754 entries from dependency cache.
Parsing recipes: 100% |###################################| Time: 0:00:01
```

45

Parsing of 3208 .bb files complete (3206 cached, 2 parsed). 4756 target
s, 295 skipped, 3 masked, 0 errors.
NOTE: Resolving any missing task queue dependencies
NOTE: Multiple providers are available for runtime linux-mfgtool-base (
linux-fslc-lts-mfgtool, linux-fslc-mfgtool, linux-imx-mfgtool)
Consider defining a PREFERRED_RPROVIDER entry to match linux-mfgtool-ba
se
NOTE: Multiple providers are available for runtime linux-mfgtool-image
(linux-fslc-lts-mfgtool, linux-fslc-mfgtool, linux-imx-mfgtool)
Consider defining a PREFERRED_RPROVIDER entry to match linux-mfgtool-im
age
NOTE: Multiple providers are available for runtime linux-mfgtool-image-
image (linux-fslc-lts-mfgtool, linux-fslc-mfgtool, linux-imx-mfgtool)
Consider defining a PREFERRED_RPROVIDER entry to match linux-mfgtool-im
age-image

```
Build Configuration:
BB_VERSION           = "2.0.0"
BUILD_SYS            = "x86_64-linux"
NATIVELSBSTRING      = "universal"
TARGET_SYS           = "aarch64-poky-linux"
MACHINE              = "imx8mp-icore"
DISTRO               = "fsl-imx-xwayland"
DISTRO_VERSION       = "5.15-kirkstone"
TUNE_FEATURES        = "aarch64 armv8a crc crypto"
TARGET_FPU           = ""
meta
meta-poky            = "HEAD:24a3f7b3648185e33133f5d96b184a6cb6524f3d"
meta-oe
meta-multimedia
meta-python          = "HEAD:744a4b6eda88b9a9ca1cf0df6e18be384d9054e3"
meta-freescale       = "HEAD:c82d4634e7aba8bc0de73ce1dfc997b630051571"
meta-freescale-3rdparty = "HEAD:5977197340c7a7db17fe3e02a4e014ad997565a
e"
meta-freescale-distro = "HEAD:d5bbb487b2816dfc74984a78b67f7361ce404253"
meta-bsp
meta-sdk
meta-ml
meta-v2x             = "HEAD:9174c61f4dc80b14e0bfdaec9200ed58fb41615f"
meta-nxp-demo-experience = "HEAD:52eaf8bf42f8eda2917a1c8c046003c8c2c8f6
29"
meta-chromium        = "HEAD:e232c2e21b96dc092d9af8bea4b3a528e7a46dd6"
meta-clang           = "HEAD:c728c3f9168c8a4ed05163a51dd48ca1ad8ac21d"
meta-gnome
meta-networking
meta-filesystems     = "HEAD:744a4b6eda88b9a9ca1cf0df6e18be384d9054e3"
```

```
meta-qt6               = "HEAD:ed785a25d12e365d1054700d4fc94a053176eb14"
meta-virtualization    = "HEAD:9482648daf0bb42ff3475e7892542cf99f3b8d48"
meta-engicam-nxp       = "kirkstone:983ed77473c8567045d88165a33c81c4ac8b4
e89"
```

```
Initialising tasks: 100% |###############################| Time: 0:00:04
Sstate summary: Wanted 3196 Local 0 Mirrors 0 Missed 3196 Current 643 (
0% match, 16% complete)
NOTE: Executing Tasks
WARNING: brcm-patchram-plus-1.0-r0 do_package_qa: QA Issue: Recipe LICE
NSE includes obsolete licenses GPLv2 [obsolete-license]
WARNING: linux-engicam-5.15.71+gitAUTOINC+ac58548817-r0 do_package_qa:
QA Issue: Recipe LICENSE includes obsolete licenses GPLv2 [obsolete-lic
ense]
Setscene tasks: 3839 of 3839
Currently  1 running tasks (8898 of 8909)   99% |###################### |
0: engicam-evaluation-image-mx8-1.0-r0 do_rootfs - 7m27s (pid 2601500)
 81% |# |
```

At the time the readers are trying to do this build, it may fail because of some packages switching their main branch from *master* to *main*, for example, **cracklib**; if so, we can change the SRC_URI within the file meta/recipes-extended/cracklib/cracklib_2.9.8.bb in the poky meta layer to

```
--- a/meta/recipes-extended/cracklib/cracklib_2.9.8.bb
+++ b/meta/recipes-extended/cracklib/cracklib_2.9.8.bb
@@ -9,7 +9,7 @@ DEPENDS = "cracklib-native zlib"

 EXTRA_OECONF = "--without-python --libdir=${base_libdir}"

-SRC_URI = "git://github.com/cracklib/cracklib;protocol=https;bran
ch=master \
+SRC_URI = "git://github.com/cracklib/cracklib;protocol=https;bran
ch=main \
            file://0001-packlib.c-support-dictionary-byte-order-de
pendent.patch \
            file://0002-craklib-fix-testnum-and-teststr-failed.pat
ch \
            "
```

This follows the GitHub's and other proposals of 2020 for branch *master* to *main* rename, so should be repeated for other similar issues.

In the above output, we can notice that we are almost at the end of the compilation. In fact, a task numbered 8898 is running over 8909 tasks to complete, and the building system is building the root filesystem image (usually named *rootfs*) of our new Yocto image.

Another interesting thing to notice in the above output message is the list of the current layers used for the compilation. For each layer, the building system shows the current HEAD of the corresponding git repository.

Regarding the warning messages we see above (and reported below):

```
WARNING: brcm-patchram-plus-1.0-r0 do_package_qa: QA Issue: Recipe
 LICENSE includes obsolete licenses GPLv2 [obsolete-license]
WARNING: linux-engicam-5.15.71+gitAUTOINC+ac58548817-r0 do_package
_qa:
QA Issue: Recipe LICENSE includes obsolete licenses GPLv2 [obsolet
e-license]
```

These warnings are related to some issues with the LICENSE variable for packages brcm-patchram-plus and linux-engicam. This variable is used to list the packages' licenses, and the ones set for these packages are obsolete; however, these are just warnings and the compilation should continue (all these concepts will be explained in detail in the next chapters of this book, the readers should go on without worries).

When finished and everything ended without errors, we can take a new look at the current building directory (which is imx8mp-build) to see what has changed. We should have the following:

```
$ ls
bitbake-cookerdaemon.log  cache  conf  sstate-cache  tmp
```

New directories are present, and under the directory tmp/deploy we should have the following entries:

```
$ ls tmp/deploy/
images  ipk  licenses
```

Here, we have all the generated files for the target system; particularly under images, we have all the binary images we can use on our embedded system:

```
$ ls tmp/deploy/images/imx8mp-icore/
Image
Image--5.15.71+git0+ac58548817-r0-imx8mp-icore-20231114154828.bin
Image-imx8mp-icore.bin
bl31-imx8mp.bin
Engicam-evaluation-image-mx8-imx-imx-boot-bootpart.wks
...
```

while within the directory ipk we have all the packages, divided per architecture, in the IPKG format that we can install on our embedded system:

```
$ ls tmp/deploy/ipk/
all  armv8a  armv8a-mx8mp  imx8mp_icore
$ ls tmp/deploy/ipk/imx8mp_icore/
alsa-state-dbg_0.2.0-r5_imx8mp_icore.ipk
alsa-state-dev_0.2.0-r5_imx8mp_icore.ipk
alsa-state_0.2.0-r5_imx8mp_icore.ipk
alsa-states_0.2.0-r5_imx8mp_icore.ipk
base-files-dbg_3.0.14-r89_imx8mp_icore.ipk
base-files-dev_3.0.14-r89_imx8mp_icore.ipk
base-files-doc_3.0.14-r89_imx8mp_icore.ipk
base-files_3.0.14-r89_imx8mp_icore.ipk
...
```

At this point, we can test our new Yocto image by using a microSD card in order not to rewrite the onboard eMMC because if something went wrong, we can brick our new development kit! On the other hand, if we put a nonfunctional image on the microSD, we can easily recover the system by simply removing or replacing it.

As every good embedded programmer knows, the sentence *if something went wrong we can brick our new development kit* is not entirely correct. This is because every system has the ability to recover from a not running image and restore a functional system even if the onboard storage image is corrupted.

For example, CPUs by Freescale/NXP can use the uuu utility to do such recovery (see `https://github.com/nxp-imx/mfgtools`). However, using an external microSD is a good way to speed up every development activity without touching the current onboard software.

OK, to proceed, we need a microSD (at least 8GB) inserted within our host system, and then we can use the command below to write the new image:

```
$ cd tmp/deploy/images/imx8mp-icore
$ zstdcat engicam-evaluation-image-mx8-imx8mp-icore.wic.zst | \
        sudo dd of=<disk> bs=8M conv=fdatasync status=progress
```

where the readers should replace the <disk> string with their block device that is connected with the microSD (in our case, we have to use of=/dev/sdd).

Once the image has been written, then we have to put the microSD into the embedded kit and then select the boot from the microSD by closing the JM1 (Boot CFG) jumper (see Figure 2-2).

Figure 2-2. *The JM1 (Boot CFG) jumper closed*

Now, if we turn on the system, we should get the following output on the serial console:

```
U-Boot SPL 2022.04-master+g05dea559b9 (Oct 26 2023 - 13:17:23 +0000)
DDRINFO: start DRAM init
DDRINFO: DRAM rate 4000MTS
DDRINFO:ddrphy calibration done
DDRINFO: ddrmix config done
SECO:  RNG instantiated
Normal Boot
Trying to boot from BOOTROM
Boot Stage: Primary boot
image offset 0x8000, pagesize 0x200, ivt offset 0x0
NOTICE:  BL31: v2.6(release):automotive-13.0.0_1.1.0-0-g3c1583ba0
NOTICE:  BL31: Built : 11:00:38, Nov 21 2022
...
```

Here, we see that our code is currently running just by looking at the date of the build. Then the booting stage continues with U-Boot as below:

```
...
U-Boot 2022.04-master+g05dea559b9 (Oct 26 2023 - 13:17:23 +0000)
CPU:    i.MX8MP[8] rev1.1 1600 MHz (running at 1200 MHz)
CPU:    Industrial temperature grade (-40C to 105C) at 18C
Reset cause: POR
Model: Engicam i.MX8MPlus iCore
DRAM:   4 GiB
...
switch to partitions #0, OK
mmc1 is current device
...
```

In the above messages, the interesting part to notice is the fact that during our first boot the current device was mmc2 (i.e., the eMMC), while now we got that the current device is the mmc1 (i.e., the microSD), as it should be.

Then the boot continues until the kernel starts, and we report below the kernel command line where there are other interesting information:

```
...
[    0.000000] Kernel command line: console=ttymxc1,115200 root=/dev/mm
cblk1p2 rootwait rw
...
```

Again, we notice that this time the root device is /dev/mmcblk1p2 instead of /dev/mmcblk2p2 as in our first boot in Section 1.3.

OK, now the building system is up, running, and successfully tested! So we can move to the next section where we are going to do some minor settings to have proper settings useful to easily exchange data with our embedded system via a network connection.

2.5 Checking the Network Connection

Now that the new image is up and running, we should check if the network connection works as expected; otherwise, we have to fix it to be able to easily exchange data with our embedded kit. This behavior will be widely used in the next chapters to send new packages to be tested on real hardware, so it's important we set it up before continuing.

Let's take a look at the network interface settings by using the `ip` command on the serial console:

```
# ip addr
1: lo: <LOOPBACK,UP,LOWER_UP> mtu 65536 qdisc noqueue state UNKNOWN gro
up default qlen 1000
    link/loopback 00:00:00:00:00:00 brd 00:00:00:00:00:00
    inet 127.0.0.1/8 scope host lo
       valid_lft forever preferred_lft forever
    inet6 ::1/128 scope host
       valid_lft forever preferred_lft forever
2: can0: <NOARP,ECHO> mtu 16 qdisc noop state DOWN group default qlen 10
    link/can
3: can1: <NOARP,ECHO> mtu 16 qdisc noop state DOWN group default qlen 10
    link/can
4: eth0: <BROADCAST,MULTICAST,UP,LOWER_UP> mtu 1500 qdisc mq state UP g
roup default qlen 1000
    link/ether 6a:53:3f:e2:98:65 brd ff:ff:ff:ff:ff:ff
    inet6 fe80::6853:3fff:fee2:9865/64 scope link
       valid_lft forever preferred_lft forever
5: wlan0: <BROADCAST,MULTICAST> mtu 1500 qdisc noop state DOWN group de
fault qlen 1000
    link/ether 00:25:ca:7c:27:27 brd ff:ff:ff:ff:ff:ff
```

OK, in our case, we have no valid IP address assigned to the eth0 interface, so we can reuse the settings done in Section 1.3.2 and then restart the `systemd-networkd` service to have a similar network configuration. Needed commands are reported below:

```
# cat > /etc/systemd/network/50-eth0.network <<__EOF
[Match]
Name=eth0

[Network]
Address=192.168.32.132/24
Gateway=192.168.32.2
DNS=192.168.32.2
__EOF
# systemctl restart systemd-networkd
# ip addr show dev eth0
```

```
4: eth0: <BROADCAST,MULTICAST,UP,LOWER_UP> mtu 1500 qdisc mq state UP g
roup default qlen 1000
    link/ether 6a:53:3f:e2:98:65 brd ff:ff:ff:ff:ff:ff
    inet 192.168.32.132/24 brd 192.168.32.255 scope global eth0
       valid_lft forever preferred_lft forever
    inet6 fe80::6853:3fff:fee2:9865/64 scope link
       valid_lft forever preferred_lft forever
```

The output of the above ip command tells us that now the network connection is restored as before, then we can retry an SSH connection from our host machine:

```
$ ssh root@192.168.32.132
@@@@@@@@@@@@@@@@@@@@@@@@@@@@@@@@@@@@@@@@@@@@@@@@@@@@@@@@@@@@@@@@@@@@
@    WARNING: REMOTE HOST IDENTIFICATION HAS CHANGED!     @
@@@@@@@@@@@@@@@@@@@@@@@@@@@@@@@@@@@@@@@@@@@@@@@@@@@@@@@@@@@@@@@@@@@@
IT IS POSSIBLE THAT SOMEONE IS DOING SOMETHING NASTY!
Someone could be eavesdropping on you right now (man-in-the-middle atta
ck)!
It is also possible that a host key has just been changed.
The fingerprint for the RSA key sent by the remote host is
SHA256:Jrn/CrOBAPjZwXNK2IJZqISSDKQ3lX8S4jkT7OZzmpw.
Please contact your system administrator.
Add correct host key in /home/giometti/.ssh/known_hosts to get rid of t
his message.
Offending ED25519 key in /home/giometti/.ssh/known_hosts:102
  remove with:
  ssh-keygen -f "/home/giometti/.ssh/known_hosts" -R "192.168.32.132"
Host key for 192.168.32.132 has changed and you have requested strict c
hecking.
Host key verification failed.
```

The warning message is something expected because we have installed a new image, which in turn will generate new SSH keys. So let's remove the offending keys on the host and retry the connection:

```
$ ssh-keygen -f "/home/giometti/.ssh/known_hosts" -R "192.168.32.132"
# Host 192.168.32.132 found: line 102
/home/giometti/.ssh/known_hosts updated.
Original contents retained as /home/giometti/.ssh/known_hosts.old
$ ssh root@192.168.32.132
The authenticity of host '192.168.32.132 (192.168.32.132)' can't be est
ablished.
```

```
RSA key fingerprint is SHA256:Jrn/CroBAPjZwXNK2IJZqISSDKQ3lX8S4jkT7OZzm
pw.
This key is not known by any other names
Are you sure you want to continue connecting (yes/no/[fingerprint])? yes
Warning: Permanently added '192.168.32.132' (RSA) to the list of known
hosts.
root@imx8mp-icore-cy:~#
```

OK, looking at the above prompt, we can see that now we are in the same condition as in the previous chapter when we do the boot from the eMMC.

Now before moving to the next section, we should take a look at how we can update the Yocto code we've downloaded before, just in case we wish to grab new features or bug fixes from NXP or Engicam.

2.6 Updating (and Inspecting) the Code

In case we need to update one or more layers, maybe just in case we need to fix some bugs, or we need new features, we can use several ways to do so. However, the readers should follow some best practices before proceeding.

In fact, embedded developers should avoid updating or changing the layers defined by their hardware suppliers; this is because we should always work on well-fixed releases. If a bug fix or a new feature is needed, we should try to do it in our custom layer (as presented later in this book). So if we need support from the hardware manufacturer, we can refer to its release and then specify the changes done within our layer. This way of working allows the manufacturer to easily reproduce the problem and to quickly provide a possible bug fix. However, this is not a fixed rule, and, sporadically, we may have to update a layer from the hardware supplier or even from the Yocto main project. In this case, we proceed by trying to download well-fixed releases or tags in such a way that every change can be documented in some way.

For all these reasons, in this section, we are going to introduce this topic by using Engicam's layer as an example to give an idea about what we have to do to get software updates. Then we show what to do if we need to update the code by using the repo command.

Since all meta layers are usually stored as git repositories, to update a single layer, we can use the git command as usual with the pull subcommand as shown below:

```
$ git -C sources/meta-engicam-nxp pull origin
Already up to date.
```

Here, we asked git to check if some updates are available, and the answer was that everything is up to date. The readers should note that, since the meta-engicam-nxp layer is not managed by the current manifest, using this method is the only way to update this layer.

This will be fixed in Section 13.4 where we move this layer within a proper repo manifest.

On the other hand, when the meta layers composing our Yocto distribution are in a repo manifest, we can use the repo command to update all of them at once as shown below:

```
$ cd ..
$ ls -ld .repo
drwxrwsr-x 7 giometti giometti 4096 Nov 24 09:27 .repo
$ repo sync
Fetching: 28% (4/14) 0:05 | 2 jobs | 0:00 meta-virtualization @ source..
```

Note that to correctly execute the repo command, we need to move into the parent directory where the hidden directory .repo has been created during the installation of the source (see Section 2.1).

By using the repo sync command, we ask the repo to scan all repositories defined within the current manifest and then to check for updates.

When finished, we should get something with the following output:

```
Fetching: 100% (14/14), done in 7.426s
repo sync has finished successfully.
```

This means that the update has been done successfully.

However, repo has several useful subcommands, as we can see by just executing it with the -h option argument, as shown below:

```
$ repo -h

Usage: repo [-p|--paginate|--no-pager] COMMAND [ARGS]

Options:
  -h, --help            show this help message and exit
  --help-all            show this help message with all subcommands and
 exit
  -p, --paginate        display command output in the pager
  --no-pager            disable the pager
...
The most commonly used repo commands are:
  abandon       Permanently abandon a development branch
  branch        View current topic branches
  branches      View current topic branches
  checkout      Checkout a branch for development
  cherry-pick   Cherry-pick a change.
  diff          Show changes between commit and working tree
  diffmanifests Manifest diff utility
  download      Download and checkout a change
  grep          Print lines matching a pattern
  info          Get info on the manifest branch, current branch or unm
erged branches
  init          Initialize a repo client checkout in the current direc
tory
  list          List projects and their associated directories
  overview      Display overview of unmerged project branches
  prune         Prune (delete) already merged topics
  rebase        Rebase local branches on upstream branch
  smartsync     Update working tree to the latest known good revision
  stage         Stage file(s) for commit
  start         Start a new branch for development
  status        Show the working tree status
  sync          Update working tree to the latest revision
  upload        Upload changes for code review
See 'repo help <command>' for more information on a specific command.
See 'repo help --all' for a complete list of recognized commands.
```

```
Bug reports:
https://issues.gerritcodereview.com/issues/new?component=1370071
```

By using the info subcommand, we can get information about the manifest branch (or other ones) as shown below:

```
$ repo --no-pager info

Manifest branch:
Manifest merge branch: refs/heads/imx-linux-kirkstone
Manifest groups: default,platform-linux
---------------------------
Project: fsl-community-bsp-base
Mount path: /home/giometti/yocto/imx-yocto-bsp/sources/base
Current revision: 60f79f7af60537146298560079ae603260f0bd14
Manifest revision: 60f79f7af60537146298560079ae603260f0bd14
Local Branches: 0
---------------------------
...
Project: meta-virtualization
Mount path: /home/giometti/yocto/imx-yocto-bsp/sources/meta-virtualizat
ion
Current revision: 9482648daf0bb42ff3475e7892542cf99f3b8d48
Manifest revision: 9482648daf0bb42ff3475e7892542cf99f3b8d48
Local Branches: 0
---------------------------
Project: poky
Mount path: /home/giometti/yocto/imx-yocto-bsp/sources/poky
Current revision: 24a3f7b3648185e33133f5d96b184a6cb6524f3d
Manifest revision: 24a3f7b3648185e33133f5d96b184a6cb6524f3d
Local Branches: 0
---------------------------
```

The option argument --no-pager has been used to disable the pager to obtain a simple continuous output (instead of a paged one) for the book purposes.

Here, we can check, for instance, if the current branch is the same as the manifest one. However, a better output could be achieved by adding the -d option argument, as reported below:

```
$ repo --no-pager info -d

Manifest branch:
Manifest merge branch: refs/heads/imx-linux-kirkstone
Manifest groups: default,platform-linux
---------------------------
Project: fsl-community-bsp-base
Mount path: /home/giometti/yocto/imx-yocto-bsp/sources/base
Current revision: 60f79f7af60537146298560079ae603260f0bd14
Manifest revision: 60f79f7af60537146298560079ae603260f0bd14
Local Branches: 0
Local Commits: 0 (on current branch)
---------------------------
Remote Commits: 0
---------------------------
...
Project: meta-virtualization
Mount path: /home/giometti/yocto/imx-yocto-bsp/sources/meta-virtualizat
ion
Current revision: 9482648daf0bb42ff3475e7892542cf99f3b8d48
Manifest revision: 9482648daf0bb42ff3475e7892542cf99f3b8d48
Local Branches: 0
Local Commits: 0 (on current branch)
---------------------------
Remote Commits: 0
---------------------------
Project: poky
Mount path: /home/giometti/yocto/imx-yocto-bsp/sources/poky
Current revision: 24a3f7b3648185e33133f5d96b184a6cb6524f3d
Manifest revision: 24a3f7b3648185e33133f5d96b184a6cb6524f3d
Local Branches: 0
Local Commits: 0 (on current branch)
---------------------------
Remote Commits: 0
---------------------------
```

The readers should notice the sequence of the option arguments used in the above command. In fact, --no-pager is an option argument of the repo command, while -d is about the info subcommand. So the writing order is important!

In this output, we have more information than before about the local commits.

To have a quick view about the status of the working tree, we can use the status subcommand, and in the case our working tree is not perfectly clean, we may get an output as reported below:

```
$ repo status

project sources/base/                             (*** NO BRANCH ***)
 -m     setup-environment
project sources/meta-openembedded/                (*** NO BRANCH ***)
 -m     meta-oe/recipes-support/devmem2/devmem2_2.0.bb
project sources/poky/                             (*** NO BRANCH ***)
 -d     meta-skeleton/recipes-skeleton/service/service/COPYRIGHT
 -d     meta-skeleton/recipes-skeleton/service/service/skeleton_test.c
 -m     scripts/buildhistory-collect-srcrevs
```

Note that the output may vary.

Here, we can easily notice that files setup-environment and meta-oe/recipes-support/devmem2/devmem2_2.0.bb have been modified, while files COPYRIGHT and skeleton_test.c within the directory meta-skeleton/recipes-skeleton/service/service have been deleted. Now to see the differences in the project sources/meta-openembedded/, we can do as shown below:

```
$ repo diff sources/meta-openembedded/

project sources/meta-openembedded/
diff --git a/meta-oe/recipes-support/devmem2/devmem2_2.0.bb b/meta-oe/r
ecipes-support/devmem2/devmem2_2.0.bb
index aee6bfe3d..07f99e43c 100644
--- a/meta-oe/recipes-support/devmem2/devmem2_2.0.bb
+++ b/meta-oe/recipes-support/devmem2/devmem2_2.0.bb
@@ -1,4 +1,4 @@
-SUMMARY = "Simple program to read/write from/to any location in memory"
```

```
+SUMMARY = "Program to read/write from/to any location in memory"
 LICENSE = "GPL-2.0-or-later"
 LIC_FILES_CHKSUM = "file://devmem2.c;endline=38;md5=a9eb9f3890384519f43
5aedf986297cf"
```

Of course, if we execute the `repo diff` command without specifying any projects, we get the differences within all projects in the manifest.

Since the `meta-engicam-nxp` layer is not in the manifest file, we cannot get information for it, and we have to use the normal Git command to inspect possible modifications. In Section 7.4.4, we are going to propose a possible solution for these special conditions.

The readers now should have an idea about how they can use the `repo` command to inspect their Yocto build systems.

2.7 Summary

In this chapter, we have downloaded all the needed sources to be able to compile our own Yocto image on the host machine we set up in the first chapter of this book. Then we've configured the build directory where we are going to do all our tests and modifications to create new recipes, as explained later in this book, and we've verified that the build system is fully functional by generating our first runnable Yocto image. This new Yocto image can now be used to test all example settings, recipes, and packages we will present in the following chapters.

Furthermore, by having the Yocto sources within our machine, we can study how it works and verify and test every topic we are going to explain further in this book.

CHAPTER 3

Yocto Project Basics

In previous chapters, we set up our host machine, and we downloaded Yocto sources, so now we are ready to start looking deep in them.

In this chapter (and in the next ones until Chapter 6), we are going to introduce the Yocto Project's basic information which every Yocto developer should know in order to better understand how it works. Then, after explaining what the Yocto Project is and its basic concepts, we will present the main components of the Yocto Project, starting with its configuration files and the variables they hold. In the next chapters, we will continue this presentation by explaining how to use the Yocto Project's main tools and by looking deeper into what the Yocto Project's recipes are.

The readers who don't know Yocto internals very well should read this chapter (and maybe the next ones), while the readers that want to start modifying their Yocto sources can directly move to Chapter 7 and use these chapters as reference.

3.1 What Is the Yocto Project

About the question *"what is the Yocto Project?"* the answer is simple, and the best definition can be read directly from the Yocto Project (YP) main page at `https://yoctoproject.org`:

> *The Yocto Project (YP) is an open-source collaboration project that helps developers create custom Linux-based systems regardless of the hardware architecture.*

© Rodolfo Giometti 2025
R. Giometti, *Yocto Project Customization for Linux*,
https://doi.org/10.1007/979-8-8688-1435-8_3

The project provides a flexible set of tools and a space where embedded developers worldwide can share technologies, software stacks, configurations, and best practices that can be used to create tailored Linux images for embedded and IOT devices, or anywhere a customized Linux OS is needed.

The Yocto Project, in these last years, has been de facto the most important distribution in the embedded world, since every CPU, SOM, and embedded manufacturer uses the Yocto Project as base (or demo) distribution for its embedded development kits.

Surfing within the Yocto Project site and especially within its documentation pages, the readers may notice both the terms **OpenEmbedded** and **Poky**.

Without going deeper and to keep the explanation simple, we can say that

- *OpenEmbedded* is a build automation framework (which is a proper cross-compile environment for the platform to work on) which is used to create Linux distributions for embedded devices.

- *Poky* is the name of the Yocto Project's reference distribution that contains the OpenEmbedded build system as well as a set of *metadata* (see below) to allow developers to be able to build their own distributions.

The Yocto Project relies on both of them, and the image reported in `https://docs.yoctoproject.org/dev/_images/key-dev-elements.png` well explains this interdependence.

The main advantage for all developers having an embedded kit derived from the Board Support Package (or BSP) of their hardware manufacturer is that they can easily generate a fully functional OS ready to be used for their specific applications by doing a few modifications. These modifications, instead of having been done on the original code, are applied by overriding and/or appending information (these concepts will be better explained later in this book). This can effectively reduce the time to market, and it is the main reason why it's so important to know how to customize the Yocto Project with these techniques!

3.2 The Layer Model

In order to be able to do effective and reliable Yocto customizations, we have to understand what the **Yocto Project's Layer Model** is. Simply speaking, it is a development model based on the concept of **layer**, which simultaneously supports collaboration and customization. In fact, with the term *layer*, we intend a repository that contains related sets of instructions that tell the build system what to do.

These layers can depend on other layers, and they are applied according to a sort of priority. Usually, a Yocto distribution has several layers, each of them specific for a particular purpose. Some are basic layers which are present in every Yocto distribution, while others are hardware specific and may change if we change the hardware we have to work with.

The strength of the concept of *layer* is that developers can collaborate, share, and reuse layers and, in this case, produce new layers to add new functionalities and support. This can be done since layers can contain changes to previous instructions or settings that allow developers, by overriding what is already written, to customize previously supplied collaborative (or community) layers to suit their product requirements.

We can simplify this concept (and this is a massive simplification of it!) by considering the structure of (squared) onion peels, reported in Figure 3-1.

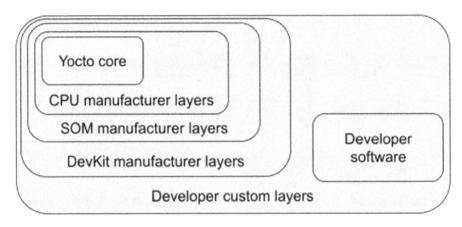

Figure 3-1. *The layers of interdependencies as (squared) onion peels*

This feature is significant since we can easily adapt an already functional Yocto image to a custom board, which in turn usually differs from a devkit just for a few characteristics!

Later in this book, when we see how we can add our custom layer, we'll notice that it is quite usual that a Yocto Project's layer is named with the `meta-` prefix. We can see a real example by taking a look at the directory `sources` within Yocto sources:

```
$ ls imx-yocto-bsp/sources/
base                meta-freescale            meta-openembedded
meta-browser        meta-freescale-3rdparty   meta-qt6
meta-clang          meta-freescale-distro     meta-timesys
meta-cy             meta-imx                  meta-virtualization
meta-engicam-nxp    meta-nxp-demo-experience  poky
```

The readers should consider that the name of the directory holding all meta layers of their Yocto sources is not all the time set to `sources`. They may find names as `meta` or `layers` or even find no dedicated directory at all, and all meta layers are simply placed within the root directory of Yocto sources!

We can see that this is not a fixed rule (in fact, rare exceptions exist as the layer poky in the output above); however, following this layer naming convention can save us trouble later when Yocto components or tools *assume* our layer name begins with the `meta-` prefix.

The **meta** word is because a layer holds recipes (i.e., a set of configurations for the build tool – see later in this book), configuration files, and other information that refers to the build instructions themselves. As well as the data used to control what things get built and the effects of the build, and all these things are generically called with the term **metadata**. Metadata also includes commands and data used to indicate what versions of software are used, from where they are obtained, and changes or additions to the software itself (patches or auxiliary files) that are used to fix bugs or customize the software for use in a particular situation.

Apart from the naming, we can identify three types of layers:

- Software layers: Containing user-supplied recipe files (files having the `.bb` suffix in the name), patches, and append files (files having the `.bbappend` suffix in the name).

  A good example of a software layer might be the `meta-qt5` layer (see `https://layers.openembedded.org/layerindex/branch/master/layer/meta-qt5`), which is for version 5.0 of the popular Qt cross-platform application development framework for desktop, embedded, and mobile.

- Machine BSP layer(s): Usually one (but sometimes more) specific *Board Support Package* (BSP) layer providing machine-specific configurations. These types of layers hold specific information about a particular target architecture or development kit.

  Typically, these layers are the ones holding the `machine.conf` files, that is, the specific machine configuration files (see Section 3.4.2) and the recipes to build the kernel, the bootloader(s), and other hardware-specific recipes.

  For example, in this book, we are going to use the `meta-freescale` layer (see `https://github.com/Freescale/meta-freescale`).

- Distribution layers (or Distro layers): These layers hold policy configuration for the images being built for a particular distribution.

  Typically, these layers are the ones which hold the `distro.conf` files, that is, the specific machine configuration files (see Section 3.4.3).

  For example, in this book, we are going to use the `meta-freescale-distro` (see `https://github.com/Freescale/meta-freescale-distro`) which provides support for Freescale's Demonstration images for use with the Yocto Freescale's BSP layer above.

Even with the minor differences reported above, usually all layers have a similar structure. They all contain a licensing file (if the layer is to be distributed), a `README` file, a `conf` configuration directory, and recipe directories (all of them named with the `recipes-` prefix).

All layers are parsed by the **BitBake** tool, which is the main tool within the Yocto build environment described in the next chapter, that uses the `bblayers.conf` file (which is part of the user configuration – see Section 3.4.5) to find what layers it should be using as part of the build.

However, all these aspects will be widely presented in the next chapters. For the moment, let's take a look at the Yocto Project's core components.

3.3 The Core Components

The core Yocto components can be summarized in the next simple list:

- The `bitbake` task executor, which handles the parsing and execution of data files as

- **Recipes**, which provide details about particular pieces of software

- **Classes**, which abstract common build information (for instance, how to build a Linux kernel or bootloader)

- **Configuration data**, which defines machine-specific settings, image policies, and so forth. Configuration data acts as the glue to bind everything together.

The `bitbake` tool, by reading the configuration files, knows how to combine classes and recipes together to produce an image and refers to each data source as a layer.

Before introducing BitBake, it is better to spend some words pointing out what a recipe, class, or configuration data are, even if in this section we are going to give just an introduction to these concepts, while a more detailed explanation will take place in the next chapters.

3.3.1 Recipes

As already introduced above, a **recipe** is a file that has the `.bb` suffix in the name, and it contains information about a single piece of software.

This information includes the location from which to download the unaltered source and any patches we wish to be applied to that source. A recipe also includes the configuration options to apply during the compilation, how to compile the source files, and how to package the compiled output with the needed configuration files (if there are).

For example, a basic recipe is the one regarding the uFTP program:

```
$ cat sources/meta-openembedded/meta-networking/recipes-support/uftp/uf
tp_5.0.bb
DESCRIPTION = "Encrypted UDP based FTP with multicast"
HOMEPAGE = "https://sourceforge.net/projects/uftp-multicast"
SECTION = "libs/network"
LICENSE = "GPL-3.0-only"
LIC_FILES_CHKSUM = "file://LICENSE.txt;md5=d32239bcb673463ab874e80d47fa
e504"

UPSTREAM_CHECK_URI = "https://sourceforge.net/projects/uftp-multicast/f
iles/source-tar/"

SRC_URI = "${SOURCEFORGE_MIRROR}/uftp-multicast/source-tar/uftp-${PV}.t
ar.gz"
SRC_URI[sha256sum] = "562f71ea5a24b615eb491f5744bad01e9c2e58244c1d6252d
5ae98d320d308e0"

DEPENDS = "openssl"

do_install () {
        oe_runmake install DESTDIR=${D}
}
```

Even if we have explained nothing about the recipes, just by reading the above recipe, we can easily understand what it does. In fact, the heading part with the variables DESCRIPTION, HOMEPAGE, etc., is a descriptive part, while the center part with the variable SRC_URI is responsible for locating the sources. Then the recipe tells us that it depends on the OpenSSL package (or recipe), and in the end we can see how the program files are installed within the final image by executing the make command with a special command line (we will see in the next chapters that the oe_runmake is just a useful wrapper for the make command).

Even if a recipe can be located within just one file, sometimes it may happen that several recipes share common code; in such cases, we can use one or more include files (which are files having the .inc suffix in the name). These files are not recipes, but they can be included in recipes (or even in classes or even in other .inc files – see below), and they work almost the same way as include headers in the C programming language.

They are essentially used to avoid duplication in recipes; in fact, in the .bb files we should specify only the differences between the recipes, while the common parts are placed in one (or more if needed) .inc file (usually) in the same folder, and that file is used by both recipes.

To include a file within a recipe file, we can use the include or require directive. Their effect is almost the same, but when we use require, and the specified file doesn't exist, that generates a fatal error and stops the build. When we use include, the build will continue even if the specified file doesn't exist (see Section 5.4 for further information about these directives).

An example of a recipe, including another file, is the one to build the Vim tool, but in its *tiny* form:

```
$ cat sources/poky/meta/recipes-support/vim/vim-tiny_9.0.bb
require vim.inc

SUMMARY += " (with tiny features)"

PACKAGECONFIG += "tiny"

do_install() {
    install -D -m 0755 ${S}/src/vim ${D}/${bindir}/vim.tiny
}

ALTERNATIVE_PRIORITY = "90"
ALTERNATIVE_TARGET = "${bindir}/vim.tiny"
```

This recipe is fascinating because it shows how it requires some other instructions from the file `vim.inc`, and then it adds some special settings. That is, it appends the string (`with tiny features`) to the SUMMARY variable which describes the package, and it adds the `tiny` option to the PACKAGECONFIG variable which instructs the build system about how to compile the package, then it just installs the `vim.tiny` application which is the tiny version of the main (and famous) Vim application.

Another essential aspect regarding recipes is that they can be implemented by also using append files (which have the `.bbappend` suffix in the name). These special recipe files (named **append files**) are used to append metadata to other recipes with the same name; for example, we can append metadata to the `myrecipe.bb` file by using the `myrecipe.bbappend` file.

To be more precise, append files must have the same root names as their corresponding recipes. For example, the append file `myrecipe_2.3.bbappend` must apply to `myrecipe_2.3.bb` file. This means the original recipe and append filenames are version number specific, so if the corresponding recipe is renamed to update to a newer version, the corresponding `.bbappend` file must be renamed as well.

A way not to worry about versions is by using the wildcard % character to instruct BitBake that the append file `myrecipe_%.bb` applies to all versions or that the append file `myrecipe_2.%.bb` applies to all `2.x` software versions.

Within the Yocto build environment, it is common practice that the `.bbappend` files are used to make additions or changes to the content of another layer's recipe without having to copy the other recipe into each layer. Even in this book, we will create .bbappend files which reside within our layer, while the main .bb recipe files to which we are appending metadata reside in a different layer.

Being able to append information to an existing recipe not only avoids duplication but also automatically applies recipe changes in a different layer to our layer. If we were copying recipes, we would have to manually merge changes as they occur!

As a simple example of the .bbappend file, we can consider the following:

```
$ cat sources/meta-freescale-3rdparty/recipes-bsp/mc-utils/mc-utils_git
.bbappend
FILESEXTRAPATHS:append:lx2160acex7 := "${THISDIR}/${PN}-lx2160acex7:"

SRC_URI:append:lx2160acex7 = "\
        file://0001-lx2160acex7-add-8x10G-dual-40G-and-dual-100G-DPL-DP
C.patch \
"

MC_FLAVOUR:lx2160acex7 = "CEX7"
```

In the above recipe, we should know that the form FILESEXTRAPATHS :append:lx2160acex7 means that bitbake must append the path name ${THISDIR}/${PN}-lx2160acex7 (where THISDIR and PN are special variables explained later in this book) to the variable FILESEXTRAPATHS when the special machine name lx2160acex7 is used. This is needed because, when machine lx2160acex7 is used, in SRC_URI we have to append a patch file which is needed to support some specified hardware. So, the original recipe is untouched, but in the special case where machine lx2160acex7 is used, bitbake should do something more. So powerful! Isn't it?

A better explanation about what a syntax as FILESEXTRAPATHS:ap pend:lx2160acex7 means will be done in Section 5.3.

A final note on recipes is about the fact that they can hold instructions to build a single package or instructions to generate a complete Yocto image, which in turn is made by a list of packages. As seen in the above recipes, all instructions were about how to compile a specific package; however, the recipe below is just for describing how to build a final Yocto image (i.e., a root filesystem):

```
$ cat sources/poky/meta/recipes-core/images/core-image-minimal.bb
SUMMARY = "A small image just capable of allowing a device to boot."

IMAGE_INSTALL = "packagegroup-core-boot ${CORE_IMAGE_EXTRA_INSTALL}"

IMAGE_LINGUAS = " "

LICENSE = "MIT"

inherit core-image

IMAGE_ROOTFS_SIZE ?= "8192"
IMAGE_ROOTFS_EXTRA_SPACE:append = "{@bb.utils.contains$("DISTRO_FEATURES
", "systemd", " + 4096", "", d)}"
```

In the above recipe, all packages to be installed in the root filesystem are reported in `IMAGE_INSTALL`. This list is specified by using a package group named `packagegroup-core-boot` (we'll see later what a packagegroup is in Section 11.4) and another variable called `CORE_IMAGE_EXTRA_INSTALL` used to specify more packages by configuration files (we are going to see this feature in Section 12.2).

3.3.2 Classes

Class files have the `.bbclass` suffix in the name, and they contain information that is useful to share between recipe files. When a recipe inherits a **class** (by using the `inherit` directive – see Section 5.4 for further information on this directive), it takes on the settings and functions for that class.

For example, the autotools class contains common settings for any application that is built with the GNU Autotools as shown below:

```
$ cat sources/poky/meta/classes/autotools.bbclass
...
CONFIGUREOPTS = " --build=${BUILD_SYS} \
                  --host=${HOST_SYS} \
                  --target=${TARGET_SYS} \
                  --prefix=${prefix} \
                  --exec_prefix=${exec_prefix} \
                  --bindir=${bindir} \
                  --sbindir=${sbindir} \
                  --libexecdir=${libexecdir} \
                  --datadir=${datadir} \
                  --sysconfdir=${sysconfdir} \
                  --sharedstatedir=${sharedstatedir} \
                  --localstatedir=${localstatedir} \
                  --libdir=${libdir} \
                  --includedir=${includedir} \
                  --oldincludedir=${oldincludedir} \
                  --infodir=${infodir} \
                  --mandir=${mandir} \
                  --disable-silent-rules \
                  ${CONFIGUREOPT_DEPTRACK} \
                  ${@append_libtool_sysroot(d)}"
...
oe_runconf () {
    # Use relative path to avoid buildpaths in files
    cfgscript_name="`basename ${CONFIGURE_SCRIPT}`"
    cfgscript=`python3 -c "import os; print(os.path.relpath(os.path.dir
name('${CONFIGURE_SCRIPT}'), '.'))"`/$cfgscript_name
    if [ -x "$cfgscript" ] ; then
        bbnote "Running $cfgscript ${CONFIGUREOPTS} ${EXTRA_OECONF} $@"
        if ! CONFIG_SHELL=${CONFIG_SHELL-/bin/bash} ${CACHED_CONFIGUREV
ARS} $cfgscript ${CONFIGUREOPTS} ${EXTRA_OECONF} "$@"; then
            bbnote "The following config.log files may provide further
information."
            bbnote `find ${B} -ignore_readdir_race -type f -name config
.log`
            bbfatal_log "configure failed"
            fi
    else
        bbfatal "no configure script found at $cfgscript"
    fi
}
...
```

In the above piece of code, we can see that, for example, the variable CONFIGUREOPTS is properly configured in order to be called during the configuring stage within the oe_runconf() function. Furthermore, in the file we can see the following:

```
...
autotools_do_compile() {
        oe_runmake
}
autotools_do_install() {
        oe_runmake 'DESTDIR=${D}' install
        # Info dir listing isn't interesting at this point so remove it i
f it exists.
        if [ -e "${D}${infodir}/dir" ]; then
                rm -f ${D}${infodir}/dir
        fi
}
...
```

These are the actions bitbake should do during the compiling and installing stages when the GNU Autotools are used.

Another interesting example about classes is the kernel class, which contains instructions for compiling the Linux kernel. For example, in this class file, we can find the following:

```
$ cat sources/poky/meta/classes/kernel.bbclass
...
PROVIDES += "virtual/kernel"
DEPENDS += "virtual/${TARGET_PREFIX}binutils virtual/${TARGET_PREFIX}gc
c kmod-native bc-native bison-native"
DEPENDS += "${@bb.utils.contains("INITRAMFS_FSTYPES", "cpio.lzo", "lzop
-native", "", d)}"
DEPENDS += "${@bb.utils.contains("INITRAMFS_FSTYPES", "cpio.lz4", "lz4-
native", "", d)}"
DEPENDS += "${@bb.utils.contains("INITRAMFS_FSTYPES", "cpio.zst", "zstd
-native", "", d)}"
...
```

Here, we can see that all kernel packages will provide the virtual package virtual/kernel (further information about these virtual packages are reported later in this book) and that they will depend on some packages providing file compressors according to the type of the *initramfs* image the developers wish to use (which is specified within the `INITRAMFS_FSTYPES` variable – see Section 6.5.3).

Moreover, within the file `kernel.bbclass` we can find the following code:

```
...
kernel_do_configure() {
    # fixes extra + in /lib/modules/2.6.37+
    # $ scripts/setlocalversion . => +
    # $ make kernelversion => 2.6.37
    # $ make kernelrelease => 2.6.37+
    touch ${B}/.scmversion ${S}/.scmversion

    if [ "${S}" != "${B}" ] && [ -f "${S}/.config" ] && [ ! -f "${B}/.co
nfig" ]; then
        mv "${S}/.config" "${B}/.config"
    fi

    # Copy defconfig to .config if .config does not exist. This
    # allows recipes to manage the .config themselves in
    # do_configure:prepend().
    if [ -f "${WORKDIR}/defconfig" ] && [ ! -f "${B}/.config" ]; then
        cp "${WORKDIR}/defconfig" "${B}/.config"
    fi

    ${KERNEL_CONFIG_COMMAND}
}

do_savedefconfig() {
    bbplain "Saving defconfig to:\n${B}/defconfig"
    oe_runmake -C ${B} savedefconfig
}
do_savedefconfig[nostamp] = "1"
addtask savedefconfig after do_configure
...
```

where we can see which commands are executed during the kernel configuration stage and that, for each kernel package, we have a special function called do_savedefconfig() which executes after the do_configure(), and that can be used to save the default kernel configuration within the defconfig with the usual command make savedefconfig (every kernel developer should perfectly know this command and how it is very useful in order to obtain a compact version of the current kernel configuration settings). All these things are available for all the packages belonging to this class.

However, besides these interesting (and important) class files (especially the latter), the really most important class file is the base. bbclass class file located in the poky layer within the file meta/ classes/base.bbclass. This class is special since it is always included automatically for all recipes and classes, and it contains definitions for standard basic tasks such as fetching, unpacking, configuring, compiling, installing, and packaging, as shown below:

```
$ cat sources/poky/meta/classes/base.bbclass
...
oe_runmake_call() {
        bbnote ${MAKE} ${EXTRA_OEMAKE} "$@"
        ${MAKE} ${EXTRA_OEMAKE} "$@"
}

oe_runmake() {
        oe_runmake_call "$@" || die "oe_runmake failed"
}
...
```

Above, we can see where the function oe_runmake() is defined, and, if we continue reading through the file, we can find the definition of basic functions for compiling or installing a package:

```
...
addtask compile after do_configure
do_compile[dirs] = "${B}"
base_do_compile() {
        if [ -e Makefile -o -e makefile -o -e GNUmakefile ]; then
                oe_runmake || die "make failed"
        else
                bbnote "nothing to compile"
        fi
}
```

```
addtask install after do_compile
do_install[dirs] = "${B}"
# Remove and re-create ${D} so that is it guaranteed to be empty
do_install[cleandirs] = "${D}"

base_do_install() {
        :
}

base_do_package() {
        :
}
...
```

Functions `base_do_install()` and `base_do_package()`, having just the colon (`:`) character as body, are empty functions which return *true*, due to the fact that this character is a built-in shell that is basically equivalent to the `true` command.

These tasks (and others) are often overridden or extended by other classes added during the project development process, since, by default, the configuring, installing, and packaging tasks are defined empty, while the compiling task just runs any `Makefile` present as we can see above.

3.3.3 Configurations

The configuration files have the `.conf` suffix in the name, and they define various configuration variables that govern the Yocto build process.

Several **configuration files** which cover several areas exist: some configuration files define machine configuration options, other distribution configuration options, compiler tuning options, general common configuration options, and other user configuration options.

These files are usually located within directories named `conf` within each layer and also in the build directory.

The content of the `conf/local.conf` file has already been introduced in Section 2.3.

Since these files are crucial, in the next section we are going to show the most important (and used) ones, so in this section we do not report their content, and we just spend some words explaining how these files are parsed.

The first thing `bitbake` will do is parse the project's `bblayers.conf` file (which is located in the build directory at `conf/bblayers.conf`) to determine via the variable BBLAYERS which layers must be used to build the sources, then it parses all `layer.conf` files (one from each layer) and the `bitbake.conf` file.

As we can see in Section 7.2, the `layer.conf` file in each layer is used to construct key variables such as BBPATH and BBFILES, which are used, the former, to search for configuration and class files within the `conf` and `classes` subdirectories of each layer and, the latter, to locate both recipe (`.bb` files) and recipe append (`.bbappend`) files.

Note that if there is no `bblayers.conf` file, then `bitbake` assumes the user has set both variables BBPATH and BBFILES directly in the environment.

Once the BBPATH variable has been constructed, it is used to locate the `bitbake.conf` file, which in turn may also include other configuration files using the `include` or `require` directives or via the command line or the environment (see Section 4.1.3).

OK, for the moment we can stop the discussion here and move to the next section where we go deep into each configuration file to see which variables they hold and what these variables do.

3.4 Main Configuration Files

After an overview of what the Yocto Project is and which are its main components, it's time to start learning the Yocto Project more deeply by taking a look at one of the most important parts of it, that is, its configuration files. This is because all Yocto Project's components use these files, and understanding who they are and what they do is the first step to take.

3.4.1 The local.conf File

The local.conf configuration file contains user-defined variables that affect every build, and it is located within the build directory in the conf subdirectory, as already seen in Section 2.3.

For example, the target machine selection, controlled by the MACHINE variable, is defined here with the DISTRO variable which controls the distribution policies. Moreover, it holds the download directory where all sources are stored by defining the DL_DIR variable, the definition of the packaging format controlled by the PACKAGE_CLASSES variable, etc.

This file, if not present, when we start the build, is created from the local.conf.sample file when we source the top-level build environment setup script (usually setup-environment as seen in Section 2.2).

In this section, we will give the readers the most exhaustive list of possible variables they can find within this configuration file, and to do so we can take a look at the local.conf.sample file which is located in the meta-poky layer. Below is its content:

```
$ cat sources/poky/meta-poky/conf/local.conf.sample
...
#
# Machine Selection
#
# You need to select a specific machine to target the build with. There
# are a selection of emulated machines available which can boot and run
```

```
# in the QEMU emulator:
#
#MACHINE ?= "qemuarm"
#MACHINE ?= "qemuarm64"
#MACHINE ?= "qemumips"
...
#
# This sets the default machine to be qemux86-64 if no other machine is
# selected:
MACHINE ??= "qemux86-64"
...
```

The MACHINE variable specifies the target device for which the image is built. The variable corresponds to a machine configuration file of the same name, through which machine-specific configurations are set. Thus, when MACHINE is set to beaglebone-yocto, the corresponding beaglebone-yocto.conf machine configuration file is read from the conf/machine subdirectory in one layer (see Section 3.4.2 where we show such file in detail).

The readers should notice that in the Yocto Project there are several ways to assign a value to a variable, and the operators ?= and ??= are two of them. We can take a look at Section 5.1.2 for further information; however, for the moment the important thing to know is that the operation MACHINE ?= "qemuarm" means *assign the qemuarm value to the MACHINE variable if not already set; otherwise, leave it alone*, while the operation MACHINE ??= "qemux86-64" means *assign the qemux86-64 value to the MACHINE variable if not already set with any other method*.

Then the file continues with the following relevant content:

```
...
#
# Where to place downloads
#
```

```
# During a first build, the system will download many different source
# code tarballs from various upstream projects. This can take a while,
# particularly if your network connection is slow. These are all stored
# in DL_DIR. When wiping and rebuilding you can preserve this directory
# to speed up this part of subsequent builds. This directory
# is safe to share between multiple builds on the same machine too.
#
# The default is a downloads directory under TOPDIR which is the build
# directory.
#
#DL_DIR ?= "${TOPDIR}/downloads"
...
```

As reported in the comment above, the DL_DIR variable specifies the download directory used by the build process to store downloads, and by default this points to the downloads directory within the build directory.

Note that usually, in the Yocto Project, the build directory is defined by the TOPDIR variable.

Still looking in the comment, we should consider that a basic image may require several gigabytes of data from upstream project releases, so if we have multiple builds on our machine, then by default each will have a downloads directory with very similar (duplicated) content. Furthermore, if we remove the build directory to test a clean build, then the Yocto Project will need to redownload everything!

In these scenarios, we can reduce build times by having a machine global download directory that all builds can make use of. This is simple to achieve by setting the DL_DIR variable to a path outside the build directory.

An important note to point out is about the fact that, by default, DL_DIR gets files suitable for mirroring everything except Git repositories. If we want tarballs of git repositories, we have to add the BB_GENERATE_MIRROR_TARBALLS variable to our local.conf as below:

```
BB_GENERATE_MIRROR_TARBALLS = "1"
```

By doing the above settings, we instruct the Yocto build system to create an archive for each source that it checks out and place that archive in the downloads directory. For subsequent builds, if the source is needed, it will first look in the directory pointed to by DL_DIR for an archive before attempting to fetch it from the Internet, so by using a suitable global directory for DL_DIR and by enabling BB_GENERATE_MIRROR_TARBALLS we can improve the building time by reducing the amount of time taken to obtain sources from the Internet.

This effectively is an offline build, which greatly improves the reliability and reproducibility of builds due to the fact that it's not that uncommon for a remote URL to be temporarily unavailable (or hosted on a slow server).

Moreover, keep reading the local.conf.sample file where we read the following:

```
...
#
# Where to place shared-state files
#
# BitBake has the capability to accelerate builds based on previously
# built output.
# This is done using "shared state" files which can be thought of as
# cache objects and this option determines where those files are placed.
#
# You can wipe out TMPDIR leaving this directory intact and the build
# would regenerate from these files if no changes were made to the
# configuration. If changes were made to the configuration, only shared
# state files where the state was still valid would be used (done using
# checksums).
#
# The default is a sstate-cache directory under TOPDIR.
#
#SSTATE_DIR ?= "${TOPDIR}/sstate-cache"
...
```

As reported in the comment above, the bitbake command (i.e., the core of the Yocto build system) can accelerate builds by using these *shared state* files which are stored within the directory address by the SSTATE_ DIR variable. By default, this directory is named sstate-cache, and it's located within the build directory (i.e., by default, set to ${TOPDIR}/ sstate-cache).

As for the downloads directory, also data within this directory may take several gigabytes of disk space, so, much like the DL_DIR, the shared state cache can also be moved outside of the build directory to a machine-wide directory that can be shared by all builds. This can significantly improve the speed of a build (and reduce disk space).

However, the readers should notice what is written in the comment above, that is:

> ... *(we) can wipe out TMPDIR (the temporary directory – see below) leaving this directory intact and the build would regenerate from these files if no changes were made to the configuration. If changes were made to the configuration, only shared state files where the state was still valid would be used (done using checksums).*

Without going deep in the Yocto build system internals, the above statement means that if we wipe out the TMPDIR directory without touching the SSTATE_DIR, bitbake will be able to regenerate the build from the sstate-cache, and this is another good reason why we should consider moving this directory outside the build directory.

All these benefits are because when bitbake identifies that there is a *sstate-cache* for a given task, it will substitute the task with an alternative (named *setscene* – not covered in this book) which will replicate the final result of the substituted task (e.g., by copying the cached build artifacts to the expected location) with the final result of speeding up the image building.

Again, in the `local.conf.sample` file, we can find the specifications for the TMPDIR:

```
...
#
# Where to place the build output
#
# This option specifies where the bulk of the building work should be.
# done and where BitBake should place its temporary files and output.
# Keep in mind that this includes the extraction and compilation of many
# applications and the toolchain which can use Gigabytes of hard disk
# space.
#
# The default is a tmp directory under TOPDIR.
#
#TMPDIR = "${TOPDIR}/tmp"
...
```

The variable TMPDIR is used to specify where all temporary files, apart from the shared state cache generated by the Yocto Project's build system, are placed. By default, this directory is named tmp, and it's located within the build directory (i.e., by default, ${TOPDIR}/tmp).

This directory can be left within the build directory, since even if we move it as for DL_DIR and SSTATE_DIR we do not benefit from the advantage of sharing generated files. However, if we decide to move it, we must take care of the filesystem used by TMPDIR which must have standard filesystem semantics (that must support mixed-case filenames, POSIX file locking, and persistent *inodes*). For example, due to various issues with NFS (Network File System) and bugs in some implementations, NFS does not meet this minimum requirement, so TMPDIR cannot be on NFS!

Another important variable in the `local.conf.sample` is DISTRO:

```
...
#
# Default policy config
#
# The distribution setting controls which policy settings are used as
# defaults.
# The default value is fine for general Yocto project use, at least
# initially.
```

```
# Ultimately when creating custom policy, people will likely end up
# subclassing these defaults.
#
DISTRO ?= "poky"
...
```

As for the MACHINE variable, the DISTRO one is essential during the build of a Yocto image. This corresponds to a distribution configuration file whose filename is the same as the variable's argument with the .conf suffix. For example, the distribution configuration file for the Poky distribution is named poky.conf, and it's located in the meta-poky/conf/distro directory of the source directory (see Section 3.4.3 where we explain this file in detail).

The readers should notice that the file holds the following notes about the DISTRO variable:

```
# As an example of a subclass there is a "bleeding" edge policy
# configuration where many versions are set to the absolute latest
# code from the upstream source control systems. This is just
# mentioned here as an example, its not useful to most new users.
# DISTRO ?= "poky-bleeding"
```

So we can use this bleeding-edge distribution to get the Poky default distribution that includes the most up-to-date versions of packages.

By continuing to read the sample file, we arrive at the following content, which is essential in the case we wish to use a package management system in our Yocto Project:

```
...
#
# Package Management configuration
#
# This variable lists which packaging formats to enable. Multiple
# package backends can be enabled at once and the first item listed in
# the variable will be used to generate the root filesystems.
# Options are:
#  - 'package_deb' for debian style deb files
```

```
#  - 'package_ipk' for ipk files are used by opkg (a debian style
#    embedded package manager)
#  - 'package_rpm' for rpm style packages
# E.g.: PACKAGE_CLASSES ?= "package_rpm package_deb package_ipk"
# We default to rpm:
PACKAGE_CLASSES ?= "package_rpm"
...
```

As written in the variable's comment, PACKAGE_CLASSES specifies the package manager the Yocto build system uses when packaging data. We can provide one or more of the available arguments for the variable, but, in this case, the build system will use only the first argument in the list as the package manager when creating our image, while all packages will be created using any additional packaging classes we specify.

The readers should note that the chosen package manager affects the build-time performance and has space ramifications. In general, building a package with IPKG (or the *Itsy Package Management* system, a lightweight package management system designed for embedded devices that resembles Debian's DPKG – the latter selected with package_deb) takes about 30% less time as compared to using RPM (the Red Hat Package Manager) to build the same or similar package. That's why we might consider setting PACKAGE_CLASSES to package_ipk if we wish to build smaller systems.

After the packaging system, we find the extra image configuration defaults:

```
...
#
# Extra image configuration defaults
#
# The EXTRA_IMAGE_FEATURES variable allows extra packages to be added to
# the generated images. Some of these options are added to certain image
# types automatically. The
# variable can contain the following options:
#  "dbg-pkgs"      - add -dbg packages for all installed packages
#                    (adds symbol information for debugging/profiling)
#  "src-pkgs"      - add -src packages for all installed packages
#                    (adds source code for debugging)
```

```
#  "dev-pkgs"       - add -dev packages for all installed packages
#                     (useful if you want to develop against libs in the
#                     image)
#  "ptest-pkgs"     - add -ptest packages for all ptest-enabled packages
#                     (useful if you want to run the package test
#                     suites)
#  "tools-sdk"      - add development tools (gcc, make, pkgconfig etc.)
#  "tools-debug"    - add debugging tools (gdb, strace)
#  "eclipse-debug"  - add Eclipse remote debugging support
#  "tools-profile"  - add profiling tools (oprofile, lttng, valgrind)
#  "tools-testapps" - add useful testing tools (ts_print, aplay, arecord
#                     etc.)
#  "debug-tweaks"   - make an image suitable for development
#                       e.g. ssh root access has a blank password
# There are other application targets that can be used here too, see
# meta/classes/image.bbclass and meta/classes/core-image.bbclass for
# more details.
# We default to enabling the debugging tweaks.
EXTRA_IMAGE_FEATURES ?= "debug-tweaks"
...
```

Variable EXTRA_IMAGE_FEATURES is used to add extra packages to the generated images, but putting in one or more of the above keywords. For example, consider the following setting:

```
EXTRA_IMAGE_FEATURES = "debug-tweaks tools-profile dbg-pkgs"
```

With debug-tweaks, we ask the build system to make an image suitable for development, for example, by allowing root logins and logins without passwords (including root ones). With tools-profile, we ask to add to our image some profiling tools such as OProfile, LTTng, and Valgrind. While using dbg-pkgs, we ask bitbake to add -dbg packages (we are going to spend more words on this special packages class on Section 6.3.4) for all installed packages whose add symbol information for debugging and profiling.

OK, there are several other variables in the local.conf.sample file and others we can put into the local.conf file, but we prefer to stop their listing here for space reasons. However, we are going to introduce them later in this book when we need one of them for some setting.

3.4.2 The machine.conf File

If we try to find a file with this name, we'll fail. In fact, here, the string `machine` is just a placeholder for the target board we are preparing our images for. For example, in our case in Section 8.1, we are going to use the name `imx8mp-icore-cy.conf` for the configuration file in the `conf/machine` directory for our custom layer, and we can select it by specifying the setting `MACHINE = "imx8mp-icore-cy"` in the configuration file `conf/local.conf` presented above.

Since all the machine-specific configurations are done in this file, we need to have some basic understanding of its contents in case we need to modify it.

As done in the previous section, and in order to have a non-exhaustive example of these configuration settings, we can take a look at the file `conf/machine/beaglebone-yocto.conf` in the `poky/meta-yocto-bsp` directory layer:

```
$ cat sources/poky/meta-yocto-bsp/conf/machine/beaglebone-yocto.conf
#@TYPE: Machine
#@NAME: Beaglebone-yocto machine
#@DESCRIPTION: Reference machine configuration for http://beagleboard.o
rg/bone and http://beagleboard.org/black boards
...
```

At the top of the file, there are just some useful remarks about the configuration file content, then it continues as follows:

```
...
PREFERRED_PROVIDER_virtual/xserver ?= "xserver-xorg"
XSERVER ?= "xserver-xorg \
           xf86-video-modesetting \
           "
...
```

This is a section where the graphical system is defined.

The PREFERRED_PROVIDER variable is used when multiple recipes provide the same item; this variable determines which recipe is preferred and thus provides the item. To do so, we must always suffix this variable with the name of the desired item (virtual/xserver in the example above), and we should define the variable using the preferred recipe's name (in the example, xserver-xorg).

The trick here is simple, but an example may explain it better. The variable PROVIDES holds a list of aliases by which a particular recipe can be known. By default, this variable holds the recipe's name (which is held in PN), but we may add other names to it as the eudev_3.2.10.bb recipe does:

```
$ cat sources/poky/meta/recipes-core/udev/eudev_3.2.10.bb
...
PROVIDES += "udev"
...
```

Now, within the variable PROVIDES for this recipe, we have the list "eudev udev". All these additional aliases are synonyms for the recipe and can be useful for satisfying dependencies of other recipes during the build, as specified by the DEPENDS variable. This variable is used to list a recipe's build-time dependencies, so if a recipe needs eudev it must specify the following:

```
DEPENDS += "eudev"
```

However, it's quite common that this recipe needs a generic package which provides the *udev functionalities*, and not specifically eudev, so the recipe should specify the following:

```
DEPENDS += "udev"
```

In this manner, if another package provides such generic *udev functionalities* and the eudev package is not available in our Yocto Project, we have good chances that everything will continue to work.

However, we can still *suggest* to the Yocto build system which is our preferred *udev functionalities* package by using the PREFERRED_ PROVIDER variable as shown below:

```
PREFERRED_PROVIDER_udev = "eudev"
```

In this manner, if there are more packages which provide the udev functionalities, the build system will follow the PREFERRED_ PROVIDER setting.

The XSERVER variable specifies the packages that should be installed to provide an X server and drivers for the current machine, assuming our image target recipe directly includes packagegroup-core-x11-xserver or, perhaps indirectly, includes x11-base in the IMAGE_FEATURES variable (see Section 6.5 for further information about this variable).

Then, our example machine.conf file continues with the following:

```
MACHINE_EXTRA_RRECOMMENDS = "kernel-modules kernel-devicetree"

EXTRA_IMAGEDEPENDS += "virtual/bootloader"
...
```

The MACHINE_EXTRA_RRECOMMENDS variable affects only images based on packagegroup-base, which does not include the core-image-minimal or core-image-full-cmdline images, and is used to specify a list of machine-specific packages to install as part of the final image being built that are not essential for booting the machine; in the above example, we ask to add kernel modules and the device-tree files to the final image.

Note that the image being built has no build dependency on this list of packages, that is, the image that will build even if one or more packages in this list are not found. This is different from MACHINE_EXTRA_RDEPENDS which does the same, but the image will not build if something is not found.

The readers can see Section 11.4 for further information about the packagegroup-base package group and about package groups in general, while core-image-minimal and core-image-full-cmdline images are generic Yocto Project's images defined in the poky layer, respectively, in the recipe files meta/recipes-core/images/core-image-minimal.bb and meta/recipes-extended/images/core-image-full-cmdline.bb.

As the readers can learn by themselves within each recipe file, the former is just a small image just capable of allowing a device to boot, while the latter is a console-only image with more full-featured Linux system functionality installed.

The EXTRA_IMAGEDEPENDS variable is used to specify a list of recipes to build that do not provide packages for installing into the root filesystem. In the example, this is the virtual/bootloader package (used to compile the bootloader, then it doesn't provide any file for the root filesystem) which in turn is selected by the PREFERRED_PROVIDER_virtual/bootloader setting (see below in this section).

Another interesting part of the beaglebone-yocto.conf is shown below:

```
...
SERIAL_CONSOLES ?= "115200;ttyS0 115200;ttyO0 115200;ttyAMA0"
SERIAL_CONSOLES_CHECK = "${SERIAL_CONSOLES}"
...
```

This group of variables are used to define a serial console to be enabled by using getty (a program which manages a terminal line and its connected terminal – see man getty for further information on this tool).

As shown above, we can provide for SERIAL_CONSOLES one or multiple devices separated by spaces, a value that specifies the baud rate followed by the TTY device name separated by a semicolon.

The variable SERIAL_CONSOLES_CHECK is present for backward compatibility, since in recent Yocto Project releases it is no longer necessary. In fact, all consoles listed in SERIAL_CONSOLES are checked for their existence before a getty is started on them.

Keep reading in this example file; we can also find a section related to the kernel to be used for the machine:

```
...
PREFERRED_PROVIDER_virtual/kernel ?= "linux-yocto"
PREFERRED_VERSION_linux-yocto ?= "5.15%"

KERNEL_IMAGETYPE = "zImage"
KERNEL_DEVICETREE = "am335x-bone.dtb am335x-boneblack.dtb am335x-bonegr
een.dtb"
KERNEL_EXTRA_ARGS += "LOADADDR=${UBOOT_ENTRYPOINT}"
...
```

Again, the PREFERRED_PROVIDER variable is used to specify which kernel recipe to use when we refer to the virtual/kernel recipe, while the PREFERRED_VERSION variable is used to instruct the Yocto build system which version should be given preference if there are multiple versions of a recipe available.

As for PREFERRED_PROVIDER, we must always suffix the variable with the package name we want to select (linux-yocto in the above example), and we should specify the package version accordingly (the 5.15% string above).

In the Yocto Project, we can use the wildcard % character to match any number of characters, which can be useful when specifying versions that contain long revision numbers that potentially change. In our example, we can match any version that starts with the string 5.15.

The readers should take care of the fact that the use of the % character is limited in that it only works at the end of the string, so we cannot use the wildcard character in any other location of the string!

More information about the usage of the wildcard % character can be retrieved when we talk about the PV variable within Section 3.4.4.

In some machine configuration files, we may find PREFERRED_VERSION defined with one or more overrides to set a machine-specific value, as below (see Section 5.3.1 for further information about overrides):

```
PREFERRED_VERSION_linux-yocto:qemux86 = "5.0%"
```

The readers should note that if a recipe with the specified version is not available, a warning message will be shown. On the other hand, if we want this to be an error, we can use the REQUIRED_VERSION variable as below:

```
REQUIRED_VERSION_linux-yocto:qemux86 = "5.0%"
```

If both REQUIRED_VERSION and PREFERRED_VERSION are set for the same recipe, the REQUIRED_VERSION value applies.

The variable KERNEL_IMAGETYPE sets the type of kernel to build for a device, which defaults to zImage (so in the above example, it could have been unspecified). This variable is used when building the kernel and is passed to make as the target to build (so its value depends on the kernel used).

We can build additional kernel image types in addition to the image type specified in KERNEL_IMAGETYPE by using KERNEL_IMAGETYPES where we can list additional types of kernel images to be built.

The variable KERNEL_DEVICETREE specifies the name of the generated Linux kernel device tree (the .dtb) file. It is preferred to provide just the .dtb files separated by spaces; therefore, legacy support for specifying the full path to the device tree also exists.

In order to use this variable, the kernel-devicetree class must be inherited in the recipe (usually this is already done by the kernel.bbclass file, and we aren't concerned about this).

In the end, the variable KERNEL_EXTRA_ARGS is used to specify additional make command-line arguments the Yocto build system passes on when compiling the kernel (as for KERNEL_IMAGETYPE, its setting depends on the kernel used).

If we continue reading the file, we will get the bootloader section:

```
...
PREFERRED_PROVIDER_virtual/bootloader ?= "u-boot"

SPL_BINARY = "MLO"
UBOOT_SUFFIX = "img"
UBOOT_MACHINE = "am335x_evm_defconfig"
UBOOT_ENTRYPOINT = "0x80008000"
UBOOT_LOADADDRESS = "0x80008000"
...
```

This part of the file is about the bootloader settings. As the first step is to define the recipe for the bootloader with the usual PREFERRED_PROVIDER mechanism, then special settings for U-Boot compilation are provided. These settings are managed by the poky/meta/classes/uboot-config.bbclass file where SPL_BINARY is used to address the name of the binary file of the *Secondary Program Loader* (SPL), UBOOT_SUFFIX to specify which is the suffix of the U-Boot binary image (which is defined as UBOOT_BINARY?="u-boot.${UBOOT_SUFFIX}"), UBOOT_MACHINE to specify the U-Boot default configuration file to be used during the building (see Section 8.2 for further information), and UBOOT_ENTRYPOINT with UBOOT_LOADADDRESS to specify which are the U-Boot entry point and load address to be used for the machine.

Then in the file, we can read the following:

```
...
MACHINE_FEATURES = "usbgadget usbhost vfat alsa"
...
```

This variable specifies the list of hardware features the machine addressed by MACHINE is capable of supporting. A non-exhaustive list of hardware features supported by the Yocto Project is reported below (the complete list can be retrieved at https://docs.yoctoproject.org/ref-manual/features.html#machine-features):

- alsa: The machine has ALSA (Advanced Linux Sound Architecture) audio drivers.

- bluetooth: The machine has integrated Bluetooth devices.

- keyboard: The machine has a keyboard.

- rtc: The machine has a real-time clock.

- serial: The machine has serial support.

- usbgadget: The machine is USB gadget device capable.

- usbhost: The machine is USB host capable.

- vfat: The machine has a FAT filesystem.

- wifi: The machine has integrated Wi-Fi.

The variable MACHINE_FEATURES is combined with the DISTRO_FEATURES (see the next section for further information about this variable) to specify which support we want in our distribution for various features, and both of them are required to provide feasible support on the final system.

For example, to provide feasible Bluetooth support on the final system, we must be sure that `bluetooth` was present in both `MACHINE_FEATURES` and `DISTRO_FEATURES`; in fact, if we have added `bluetooth` in `MACHINE_FEATURES` but not in `DISTRO_FEATURES`, applications used by the Yocto image will be built without Bluetooth support, while if we have added `bluetooth` in `DISTRO_FEATURES` but not in `MACHINE_FEATURES`, modules and applications needed for the Bluetooth will not be installed, though the operating system has support for Bluetooth.

OK, for the moment we can stop this explanation here; however, before moving to the next section, we have to spend a few words about the following setting at the beginning of the file:

```
...
DEFAULTTUNE ?= "cortexa8hf-neon"
include conf/machine/include/arm/armv7a/tune-cortexa8.inc
...
```

This is needed to include in the configuration file all the settings needed to specify the build for Cortex-A8 machines. The file is located under the `sources/poky/meta` directory layer.

Within the `machine.conf` file, there may exist other variables, but due to space reasons, as done before, we are going to introduce them later in this book when they are needed for the discussion.

3.4.3 The distro.conf File

As for `machine.conf`, if we try to find a file with this name, we'll fail. In fact, even here, `distro` is just a placeholder for the target root name we are preparing our images for. The readers can refer again to Section 8.1 where we will use the file `fsl-imx-xwayland.conf` in the `conf/distro` directory of the layer under the `sources/meta-imx/meta-sdk` directory; we will select it by specifying the setting `DISTRO="fsl-imx-xwayland"` in our `conf/local.conf` file.

All the distribution-specific configurations are done in this file. As for the `machine.conf`, we need to have some basic understanding of its contents just in case we need to modify it.

In order to have a non-exhaustive example of these configuration settings, we can take a look at the file `conf/distro/poky.conf` in the `poky/meta-poky` directory layer as reported below:

```
$ cat sources/poky/meta-poky/conf/distro/poky.conf
DISTRO = "poky"
DISTRO_NAME = "Poky (Yocto Project Reference Distro)"
#DISTRO_VERSION = "3.4+snapshot-${METADATA_REVISION}"
DISTRO_VERSION = "4.0.4"
DISTRO_CODENAME = "kirkstone"
SDK_VENDOR = "-pokysdk"
SDK_VERSION = "${@d.getVar('DISTRO_VERSION').replace('snapshot-${METADA
TA_REVISION}', 'snapshot')}"
SDK_VERSION[vardepvalue] = "${SDK_VERSION}"

MAINTAINER = "Poky <poky@lists.yoctoproject.org>"

TARGET_VENDOR = "-poky"

LOCALCONF_VERSION = "2"
...
```

All the above variables are used to describe the distribution, while a more interesting part is what follows:

```
...
# Override these in poky based distros
POKY_DEFAULT_DISTRO_FEATURES = "largefile opengl ptest multiarch waylan
d vulkan"
POKY_DEFAULT_EXTRA_RDEPENDS = "packagegroup-core-boot"
POKY_DEFAULT_EXTRA_RRECOMMENDS = "kernel-module-af-packet"

DISTRO_FEATURES ?= "${DISTRO_FEATURES_DEFAULT} ${POKY_DEFAULT_DISTRO_FE
ATURES}"
...
```

The variable DISTRO_FEATURES (which is defined by combining POKY_DEFAULT_DISTRO_FEATURES, POKY_DEFAULT_EXTRA_RDEPENDS, and POKY_DEFAULT_EXTRA_RRECOMMENDS) is used to specify the support we want in our distribution features. Usually, the presence or absence of a feature in DISTRO_FEATURES is translated to the appropriate option supplied to the configure script during the configuration task for recipes that optionally support the feature.

A non-exhaustive list of these distribution features is reported below (while the complete list can be retrieved at https://docs.yoctoproject.org/ref-manual/features.html#ref-features-distro):

- alsa: The distribution has Advanced Linux Sound Architecture support.

- bluetooth: The distribution has Bluetooth support.

- keyboard: The distribution has keyboard support, and keymaps can be loaded during booting.

- opengl: Includes the Open Graphics Library.

- pam: The distribution has Pluggable Authentication Module (PAM) support.

- ppp: The distribution has PPP dial-up support.

- pulseaudio: The distribution has support for PulseAudio.

- systemd: The distribution has Systemd support.

- systemd-resolved: Includes support and uses systemd-resolved as the main DNS name resolver in glibc Name Service Switch (this is a DNS resolver daemon from systemd suite).

- usbgadget: Includes USB Gadget Device support.

- `usbhost`: Includes USB host support.

- `usrmerge`: Merges the /bin, /sbin, /lib, and /lib64 directories into their respective counterparts in the /usr directory to provide better packaging and application compatibility.

- `wayland`: Includes the Wayland display server protocol and the library that supports it.

- `wifi`: The distribution has Wi-Fi support.

- `x11`: Includes the X server and libraries.

The readers should notice that just enabling `DISTRO_FEATURES` alone doesn't enable feature support for packages. In fact, mechanisms such as making `PACKAGECONFIG` track `DISTRO_FEATURES` are used to enable/disable package features (see Section 6.3.3 for further information about this topic).

Continue reading the `poky.conf` file, and we can read the following:

```
...
PREFERRED_VERSION_linux-yocto ?= "5.15%"
PREFERRED_VERSION_linux-yocto-rt ?= "5.15%"
...
```

As said in the previous section, these are `PREFERRED_VERSION` settings for the `linux-yocto` and `linux-yocto-rc` packages regarding the default kernel to be used (of course, we can decide to use a different kernel package).

Then we find the following:

```
...
DISTRO_EXTRA_RDEPENDS += "${POKY_DEFAULT_EXTRA_RDEPENDS}"
DISTRO_EXTRA_RRECOMMENDS += "${POKY_DEFAULT_EXTRA_RRECOMMENDS}"
...
```

The variable DISTRO_EXTRA_RDEPENDS specifies a list of distro-specific packages to add to our image packagegroup-base, while DISTRO_EXTRA_ RRECOMMENDS specifies a list of distro-specific packages to add to our images if the packages exist; otherwise, no errors will be reported.

Other settings are available in the distro.conf file, but, as before, we stop here for space reasons, and we refer the readers later in this book when one of these variables will be used in the discussion.

3.4.4 The bitbake.conf File

This is BitBake's configuration file, and it is parsed first, and then the rest of the configuration files listed in it are parsed. It is located under the sources/poky/meta/conf directory, and unlike other configuration files presented here, we (usually) don't have to modify it! However, it is useful to know what it includes to better understand other configuration files and how default values are assigned.

By taking a look at this file, the readers can verify that it is not a small file at all; it contains more than 900 lines of configuration and metadata, so we cannot go through it line by line. However, we'll report here some pieces of it that are useful to well understand how important variables are defined by default.

So, let's start with the variables presented in the previous sections as DL_DIR, SSTATE_DIR, and TMPDIR which are defined at their default values in this file as shown below:

```
...
TMPDIR ?= "${TOPDIR}/tmp"
...
DL_DIR ?= "${TOPDIR}/downloads"
SSTATE_DIR ?= "${TOPDIR}/sstate-cache"
...
```

Moreover, standard target filesystem paths used in recipes are defined here (note the export keyword which states that such variables can be used within developer shell scripts – see Section 5.1.1):

```
...
# Path prefixes
export base_prefix = ""
export prefix = "/usr"
export exec_prefix = "${prefix}"

root_prefix = "${@bb.utils.contains('DISTRO_FEATURES', 'usrmerge', '${e
xec_prefix}', '${base_prefix}', d)}"

# Base paths
export base_bindir = "${root_prefix}/bin"
export base_sbindir = "${root_prefix}/sbin"
export base_libdir = "${root_prefix}/${baselib}"
export nonarch_base_libdir = "${root_prefix}/lib"

# Architecture independent paths
export sysconfdir = "${base_prefix}/etc"
export servicedir = "${base_prefix}/srv"
export sharedstatedir = "${base_prefix}/com"
export localstatedir = "${base_prefix}/var"
export datadir = "${prefix}/share"
export infodir = "${datadir}/info"
export mandir = "${datadir}/man"
export docdir = "${datadir}/doc"
export systemd_unitdir = "${nonarch_base_libdir}/systemd"
export systemd_system_unitdir = "${nonarch_base_libdir}/systemd/system"
export nonarch_libdir = "${exec_prefix}/lib"
export systemd_user_unitdir = "${nonarch_libdir}/systemd/user"

# Architecture dependent paths
export bindir = "${exec_prefix}/bin"
export sbindir = "${exec_prefix}/sbin"
export libdir = "${exec_prefix}/${baselib}"
export libexecdir = "${exec_prefix}/libexec"
export includedir = "${exec_prefix}/include"
export oldincludedir = "${exec_prefix}/include"
localedir = "${libdir}/locale"
...
```

We won't need to change these variables, but we should reference these while developing recipes. So, in order to get an idea of their typical usage, here is a short reminder table with the most commonly used variables (Table 3-1).

Table 3-1. *The default most commonly used variables*

Variable Name	Typical Value
base_prefix	empty
prefix	/usr
exec_prefix	/usr
base_bindir	/usr/bin
base_sbindir	/usr/sbin
base_libdir	/usr/lib
sysconfdir	/etc
servicedir	/srv
localstatedir	/usr/share/info
datadir	/usr/share
systemd_unitdir	/usr/lib/systemd
systemd_system_unitdir	/usr/lib/systemd/system
bindir	/usr/bin
sbindir	/usr/sbin
libdir	/usr/lib

The base paths base_bindir, base_sbindir, and base_libdir have been reported here (even if poorly used in recipes) just to address the fact that they can be different from their architectural independent counterparts according to the usrmerge feature in the DISTRO_FEATURES variable (as seen in the previous section).

Other useful variables used in configuring the Yocto image can be the following, which are also self-explanatory:

```
...
# Root home directory
ROOT_HOME ??= "/home/root"

# If set to boolean true ('yes', 'y', 'true', 't', '1'), /var/log links
# to /var/volatile/log.
# If set to boolean false ('no', 'n', 'false', 'f', '0'), /var/log is on
# persistent storage.
VOLATILE_LOG_DIR ?= "yes"
...
```

The architecture-dependent build variables used for compilation and other building tasks that are all the variables prefixed with BUILD_, HOST_, and TARGET_ are defined as follows:

```
...
BUILD_ARCH := "${@os.uname()[4]}"
BUILD_OS := "${@os.uname()[0].lower()}"
BUILD_VENDOR = ""
BUILD_SYS = "${BUILD_ARCH}${BUILD_VENDOR}-${BUILD_OS}"
BUILD_PREFIX = ""
BUILD_CC_ARCH = ""
BUILD_LD_ARCH = ""
BUILD_AS_ARCH = ""
BUILD_EXEEXT = ""

HOST_ARCH = "${TARGET_ARCH}"
HOST_OS = "${TARGET_OS}"
HOST_VENDOR = "${TARGET_VENDOR}"
HOST_SYS = "${HOST_ARCH}${HOST_VENDOR}-${HOST_OS}"
HOST_PREFIX = "${TARGET_PREFIX}"
HOST_CC_ARCH = "${TARGET_CC_ARCH}"
```

```
HOST_LD_ARCH = "${TARGET_LD_ARCH}"
HOST_AS_ARCH = "${TARGET_AS_ARCH}"
HOST_EXEEXT = ""
...
TARGET_ARCH = "${TUNE_ARCH}"
TARGET_OS = "linux${LIBCEXTENSION}${ABIEXTENSION}"
TARGET_VENDOR = "-oe"
TARGET_SYS = "${TARGET_ARCH}${TARGET_VENDOR}-${TARGET_OS}"
TARGET_PREFIX = "${TARGET_SYS}-"
TARGET_CC_ARCH = "${TUNE_CCARGS}"
TARGET_LD_ARCH = "${TUNE_LDARGS}"
TARGET_AS_ARCH = "${TUNE_ASARGS}"
...
```

The readers should notice the immediate expansion used for BUILD_
ARCH and BUILD_OS variables.

These variables are widely used in recipes during the configuration or compilation stages, and their names should be self-explanatory too (at least for every C programmer). The readers who like to have further information about the real meaning and usage of these variables are invited to take a look at the Yocto Project's documentation at https://docs.yoctoproject.org/3.1.29/ref-manual/ref-variables.html.

The date/time or the package default variables which are extensively used in recipes or to create timestamps or filenames are defined as follows:

```
...
DATE := "${@time.strftime('%Y%m%d', time.gmtime())}"
TIME := "${@time.strftime('%H%M%S',time.gmtime())}"
DATETIME = "${DATE}${TIME}"
...
```

Again, the readers should notice the immediate expansion used for DATE and TIME (see Section 5.1.1); in fact, if not used, we may get different values for both of them!

Another important set of variables are the following ones which are used to define the package and recipe's name (PN), version (PV), and other important data (see Chapter 6 in order to see how we can use these variables) as shown below:

```
...
PN = "${@bb.parse.vars_from_file(d.getVar('FILE', False),d)[0] or 'defa
ultpkgname'}"
PV = "${@bb.parse.vars_from_file(d.getVar('FILE', False),d)[1] or '1.0'
}"
PR = "${@bb.parse.vars_from_file(d.getVar('FILE', False),d)[2] or 'r0'}"
PE = ""
PF = "${PN}-${EXTENDPE}${PV}-${PR}"
EXTENDPE = "${@['','${PE}_'][int(d.getVar('PE') or 0) > 0]}"
P = "${PN}-${PV}"
...
```

Then the definition of basic variables used in every recipe to describe the relative package, which usually are replaced by proper values as described in Chapter 6:

```
...
SECTION = "base"
PRIORITY = "optional"
SUMMARY ?= "${PN} version ${PV}-${PR}"
DESCRIPTION ?= "${SUMMARY}."
...
LICENSE ??= "INVALID"
MAINTAINER = "OE-Core Developers \
<openembedded-core@lists.openembedded.org>"
HOMEPAGE = ""
...
```

In Chapter 6, we will also see that each recipe usually generates a main package followed by *sibling* packages that can be used to install package sources or binaries for debugging purposes, documentation, etc. These sibling packages have the same name as the main package plus a suffix as -src for sources, -dbg for debugging, and -doc for documentation as defined below still within the bitbake.conf file:

```
...
# The following two are commented out because they result in a recursive
# definition of the variable in some corner cases.  These are left in
# to illustrate the intended behavior.
#SUMMARY:${PN} ?= "${SUMMARY}"
#DESCRIPTION:${PN} ?= "${DESCRIPTION}"

SUMMARY:${PN}-src ?= "${SUMMARY} - Source files"
DESCRIPTION:${PN}-src ?= "${DESCRIPTION}  \
This package contains sources for debugging purposes."

SUMMARY:${PN}-dbg ?= "${SUMMARY} - Debugging files"
DESCRIPTION:${PN}-dbg ?= "${DESCRIPTION}  \
This package contains ELF symbols and related sources for debugging \
purposes."

SUMMARY:${PN}-dev ?= "${SUMMARY} - Development files"
DESCRIPTION:${PN}-dev ?= "${DESCRIPTION}  \
This package contains symbolic links, header files, and \
related items necessary for software development."

SUMMARY:${PN}-staticdev ?= "${SUMMARY} - Development files (Static \
Libraries)"
DESCRIPTION:${PN}-staticdev ?= "${DESCRIPTION}  \
This package contains static libraries for software development."

SUMMARY:${PN}-doc ?= "${SUMMARY} - Documentation files"
DESCRIPTION:${PN}-doc ?= "${DESCRIPTION}  \
This package contains documentation."
...
```

Another interesting group of variables in this configuration file that will be reused in Chapter 6 are the ones related to the FILES variable as below:

```
...
FILES:${PN} = "${bindir}/* ${sbindir}/* ${libexecdir}/* \
            ${libdir}/lib*${SOLIBS} \
            ${sysconfdir} ${sharedstatedir} ${localstatedir} \
            ${base_bindir}/* ${base_sbindir}/* \
            ${base_libdir}/*${SOLIBS} \
            ${base_prefix}/lib/udev ${prefix}/lib/udev \
            ${base_libdir}/udev ${libdir}/udev \
            ${datadir}/${BPN} ${libdir}/${BPN}/* \
            ${datadir}/pixmaps ${datadir}/applications \
            ${datadir}/idl ${datadir}/omf ${datadir}/sounds \
            ${libdir}/bonobo/servers"
```

```
FILES:${PN}-bin = "${bindir}/* ${sbindir}/*"

FILES:${PN}-doc = "${docdir} ${mandir} ${infodir} ${datadir}/gtk-doc \
              ${datadir}/gnome/help"
SECTION:${PN}-doc = "doc"

FILES_SOLIBSDEV ?= "${base_libdir}/lib*${SOLIBSDEV} ${libdir}/lib*${SOLIBSDEV}"
FILES:${PN}-dev = "${includedir} ${FILES_SOLIBSDEV} ${libdir}/*.la \
                ${libdir}/*.o ${libdir}/pkgconfig ${datadir}/pkgconfig \
                ${datadir}/aclocal ${base_libdir}/*.o \
                ${libdir}/${BPN}/*.la ${base_libdir}/*.la \
                ${libdir}/cmake ${datadir}/cmake"
SECTION:${PN}-dev = "devel"
ALLOW_EMPTY:${PN}-dev = "1"
RDEPENDS:${PN}-dev = "${PN} (= ${EXTENDPKGV})"

FILES:${PN}-staticdev = "${libdir}/*.a ${base_libdir}/*.a \
                ${libdir}/${BPN}/*.a"
SECTION:${PN}-staticdev = "devel"
RDEPENDS:${PN}-staticdev = "${PN}-dev (= ${EXTENDPKGV})"

FILES:${PN}-dbg = "/usr/lib/debug /usr/lib/debug-static /usr/src/debug"
SECTION:${PN}-dbg = "devel"
ALLOW_EMPTY:${PN}-dbg = "1"
...
```

We should also note other special settings such as SECTION (used to define a section a package belongs to) and ALLOW_EMPTY which is used to signal the build system that those packages can be empty (otherwise, an error arises due to the fact that, by default, a package cannot be empty!).

Finally, we report below other useful variables related to the directories where the generated packages and images are deployed:

```
...
# Setting DEPLOY_DIR outside of TMPDIR is helpful, when you are using
# packaged staging and/or multimachine.
DEPLOY_DIR ?= "${TMPDIR}/deploy"
DEPLOY_DIR_TAR = "${DEPLOY_DIR}/tar"
DEPLOY_DIR_IPK = "${DEPLOY_DIR}/ipk"
DEPLOY_DIR_RPM = "${DEPLOY_DIR}/rpm"
DEPLOY_DIR_DEB = "${DEPLOY_DIR}/deb"
DEPLOY_DIR_IMAGE ?= "${DEPLOY_DIR}/images/${MACHINE}"
DEPLOY_DIR_TOOLS = "${DEPLOY_DIR}/tools"
...
```

The last argument regarding this configuration file is the one about the ordering of how all configuration files are read. We have already introduced this topic, but here is the demonstration! In fact, if we keep reading the `bitbake.conf` file (which is the first one to be read), we can see

```
...
################################################################
# Include the rest of the config files.
################################################################

require conf/abi_version.conf
include conf/site.conf
include conf/auto.conf
include conf/local.conf
require conf/multiconfig/${BB_CURRENT_MC}.conf
include conf/machine/${MACHINE}.conf
include conf/machine-sdk/${SDKMACHINE}.conf
include conf/distro/${DISTRO}.conf
include conf/distro/defaultsetup.conf
include conf/documentation.conf
include conf/licenses.conf
require conf/sanity.conf
...
```

This is how other configuration files are included in the list.

The readers may now well understand that the `bitbake.conf` file is a fascinating place where we can find useful information in order to understand how the Yocto build system in general, and `bitbake` in particular, works.

Due to space reasons, we have to stop here, but curious readers are encouraged to keep reading this file.

3.4.5 The bblayers.conf

The `bblayers.conf` file tells `bitbake` what layers we want considered during the build. When we get a Yocto distribution, layers in this file include the ones minimally needed by the build system at which we can add any custom layers we have created, as we are going to explain in this book in Section 7.2, or how we have already done in Section 2.2.

As per `local.conf`, if `bblayers.conf` is not present when we start the build, it is created from the `bblayers.conf.sample` file when we source the top-level build environment setup script (usually `setup-environment`).

In this file, three important variables are defined, as we can see in the file we are currently using in our build system:

```
$ cat imx8mp-build/conf/bblayers.conf
...
BBPATH = "${TOPDIR}"
BSPDIR := "${@os.path.abspath(os.path.dirname(d.getVar('FILE', True)) +
'/../..')}"

BBFILES ?= ""
BBLAYERS = " \
  ${BSPDIR}/sources/poky/meta \
  ${BSPDIR}/sources/poky/meta-poky \
...
  ${BSPDIR}/sources/meta-freescale \
  ${BSPDIR}/sources/meta-freescale-3rdparty \
  ${BSPDIR}/sources/meta-freescale-distro \
"

# i.MX Yocto Project Release layers
BBLAYERS += "${BSPDIR}/sources/meta-imx/meta-bsp"
BBLAYERS += "${BSPDIR}/sources/meta-imx/meta-sdk"
...
BBLAYERS += "${BSPDIR}/sources/meta-qt6"
BBLAYERS += "${BSPDIR}/sources/meta-virtualization"
BBLAYERS += "/home/giometti/yocto/imx-yocto-bsp/sources/meta-engicam-nx
p"
```

Variable BBPATH is a colon-separated list used by `bitbake` to locate `.bbclass` files and `.conf` files. This variable can be considered as analogous to the PATH variable for Bash, which is why we must be sure to set BBPATH to point to the build directory in case we are trying to execute `bitbake` from a directory outside of the build directory. To do so, we can do the following:

```
$ export BBPATH="<path_to_build_directory>"
```

The BBFILES is a space-separated list of available recipe files bitbake uses to build software. Usually, in bblayers.conf it is set to the empty string, and its setting is to demand file layer.conf in each meta layer (see the next section). However, when specifying recipe files, we can pattern match using wildcards as shown below:

```
BBFILES += "${LAYERDIR}/recipes-*/*/*.bb \
            ${LAYERDIR}/recipes-*/*/*.bbappend"
```

Finally, the BBLAYERS variable lists the layers to enable during the build, and, as we can see above, when we added the Engicam layer in Section 2.2, this file had been modified by adding the last line reported above with the meta-engicam-nxp layer reference.

Even if we can modify this file by hand, typically it is modified using the tool bitbake-layers as shown in Section 4.2.

3.4.6 The layer.conf

This is the main configuration of a Yocto meta layer. Once a meta layer has been added to the BBLAYERS variable, the file layer.conf within its conf subdirectory is read by bitbake in order to get basic information about the layer.

In order to see what this file holds, we can read the layer.conf file from Engicam's meta layer:

```
$ cat sources/meta-engicam-nxp/conf/layer.conf
# We have a conf and classes directory, add to BBPATH
BBPATH .= ":${LAYERDIR}"

# We have recipes-* directories, add to BBFILES
BBFILES += "${LAYERDIR}/recipes-*/*/*.bb \
            ${LAYERDIR}/recipes-*/*/*.bbappend"

BBFILE_COLLECTIONS += "meta-engicam-nxp"
BBFILE_PATTERN_meta-engicam-nxp = "^${LAYERDIR}/"
BBFILE_PRIORITY_meta-engicam-nxp = "6"

LAYERDEPENDS_meta-engicam-nxp = "core"
LAYERSERIES_COMPAT_meta-engicam-nxp = "kirkstone"
```

The BBPATH variable is the same as in the bblayers.conf file, and in the above example we just append the current LAYERDIR to it.

The readers should note here that both operators .= and += append data to a variable, but they do it differently. In the former case, the variable expansion happens immediately, while in the latter case the variable is expanded when it is actually referenced. In Section 5.1.3, these concepts are fully explained.

Note also that when the variable LAYERDIR is used inside the layer.conf configuration file, this variable provides the path of the current layer, and its references are expanded immediately when parsing of the file completes; otherwise, it is not available.

Furthermore, the BBFILES variable is the same as in the bblayers.conf file and, as already stated in the section above, defines the location for all recipes in the layer.

The BBFILE_COLLECTIONS variable establishes the current layer through a unique identifier that is used throughout the Yocto build system to refer to the layer. So, in our example, Engicam's developers set the identifier meta-engicam-nxp as the representation for the container layer named meta-engicam-nxp.

This unique identifier is used to override the variables BBFILE_
PATTERN, BBFILE_PRIORITY, etc. So, if Engicam's developers
have chosen the name engicambsp, the above settings should be
rewritten as below:

```
$ cat sources/meta-engicam-nxp/conf/layer.conf
...
BBFILE_COLLECTIONS += "engicambsp"
BBFILE_PATTERN_engicambsp = "^${LAYERDIR}/"
BBFILE_PRIORITY_engicambsp = "6"

LAYERDEPENDS_engicambsp = "core"
LAYERSERIES_COMPAT_engicambsp = "kirkstone"
```

The variable BBFILE_PATTERN, which must be suffixed, expands
immediately during parsing to provide the directory of the layer, while
BBFILE_PRIORITY (with the suffix) sets a priority to use for recipes in the
layer when the Yocto build system finds recipes of the same name in
different layers. The higher the number, the higher the priority.

In the end, we have variables LAYERDEPENDS with the (not listed above)
LAYERVERSION and LAYERSERIES_COMPAT (all of them must be suffixed
when defined). The first one lists the layers, separated by spaces, on which
this recipe depends (if any). Optionally, we can specify a specific layer
version for a dependency by adding it to the end of the layer name, as is
the example below:

```
LAYERDEPENDS_engicambsp = "core (=3)"
```

In this case, version 3 of core is requested, and it can be defined within
the core meta layer by using the LAYERVERSION as a single number as
shown below:

```
LAYERVERSION_core = 3
```

An error is produced if any dependency is missing or the version
numbers (if specified) do not match exactly.

In the end, `LAYERSERIES_COMPAT` lists the Yocto versions for which a layer is compatible. The variable gives the system a way to detect when a layer has not been tested with new releases of the Yocto Project, and more than one release can be specified, as below:

```
LAYERSERIES_COMPAT_engicambsp = "kirkstone mickledore"
```

Note that setting `LAYERSERIES_COMPAT` is required by the Yocto Project version 2, and the build system produces a warning if the variable is not set for any given layer.

3.5 Summary

In this chapter, we have learned what the Yocto Project is, how it is composed (by several meta layers), and which are its core components.

Then we took a more in-depth look at the Yocto main configuration files, so now we know which variables they hold, and then we are ready to see the Yocto tools and how they can be used. In the next chapter, we are going to learn in detail how BitBake works.

CHAPTER 4

Yocto Tools

After we have understood what the Yocto Project is and where its variables are located and what they mean, it's time to look at the Yocto Project's main tools.

In this chapter, we are going to introduce the most used Yocto commands, while in the next chapters we will explain more how they can properly create our custom Yocto image, eventually by adding our custom recipes.

4.1 bitbake

BitBake is a core component of the Yocto Project and is used by the build system to build packages and images.

By using the `bitbake` command, we can run shell and Python tasks efficiently and in parallel while working within complex inter-task dependency constraints. To instruct BitBake in doing so, we use recipes written in a specific format to perform sets of tasks. All these aspects will be explained in detail in Chapter 5; for the moment, we will just introduce the tool by showing its usage message and some basic usages.

To get the `bitbake` usage message, we can execute it by adding the usual `-h` option argument as shown below:

```
$ bitbake -h
Usage: bitbake [options] [recipename/target recipe:do_task ...]

    Executes the specified task (default is 'build') for a given set of
    target recipes (.bb files).
```

© Rodolfo Giometti 2025
R. Giometti, *Yocto Project Customization for Linux*,
https://doi.org/10.1007/979-8-8688-1435-8_4

It is assumed there is a conf/bblayers.conf available in cwd or in BBPATH which will provide the layer, BBFILES and other configuration information.

```
Options:
  --version       show program's version number and exit
  -h, --help      show this help message and exit
  -b BUILDFILE, --buildfile=BUILDFILE
                  Execute tasks from a specific .bb recipe directly.
                  WARNING: Does not handle any dependencies from other
                  recipes.
  -k, --continue  Continue as much as possible after an error. While the
                  target that failed and anything depending on it cannot
                  be built, as much as possible will be built before
                  stopping.
  -f, --force     Force the specified targets/task to run (invalidating
                  any existing stamp file).
  -c CMD, --cmd=CMD
                  Specify the task to execute. The exact options
                  available depend on the metadata. Some examples might
                  be 'compile' or 'populate_sysroot' or 'listtasks' may
                  give a list of the tasks available.
...
```

The usage message is quite long, so it has been truncated due to space reasons.

At the very beginning, we can notice that a conf/bblayers.conf should be available in the current working directory or in BBPATH environment variable which will provide the layer, BBFILES, and other configuration information (as already introduced in Sections 3.4.5 and 3.4.6). In fact, if we wish to run bitbake from a directory outside the build directory, we must be sure to set BBPATH to point to the build directory. For example:

```
$ export BBPATH="/path/to/our/build/directory"
$ bitbake target
```

Readers may notice that there are plenty of options we can use with `bitbake`, and in this section we are going to show the most important ones, then, later in this book, we will show more useful usage modes (for a complete reference of the `bitbake` command, refer to BitBake's user manual at `https://docs.yoctoproject.org/bitbake/2.6/index.html`).

4.1.1 Executing Tasks

Keep looking at the above usage message; we can see how to execute a task for a given set of target recipes. Even if we still don't know what a recipe is in detail nor what a task is (these concepts will be explained in detail, respectively, in Chapter 6 and in Section 5.3), we can easily imagine that a recipe is just a list of tasks (or rules) which must be executed in order (according to their interdependencies) to obtain a package. The last task to be executed is called `build` (or `do_build`).

So `bitbake`'s usage message tells us that if we specify a recipe name as below, the default task `build` for `my_recipe` will be executed:

```
$ bitbake my_recipe
```

The default task, when none is specified (e.g., with the `-c` command-line option – see below), is specified by the `BB_DEFAULT_TASK` variable without the `do_` prefix (in fact, the default `do_build` task is specified as `BB_DEFAULT_TASK="build"`).

On the other hand, executing specific tasks for a single recipe file is relatively simple; we just have to specify the file in question, and `bitbake` parses it and executes the specified task. To specify a task besides the default one, we can use the `-c` option argument as shown below:

```
$ bitbake -b foo.bb -c clean
```

The above command runs the do_clean() (or clean) task for the foo. bb recipe file.

We can also specify different tasks for individual targets when we specify multiple targets. For example, we ask bitbake to execute the do_fetch task for recipe foo and then the task do_clean for recipe bar:

```
$ bitbake foo:do_fetch bar:do_clean
```

We can use the special task do_listtasks to have a detailed list of all tasks available within a specific recipe. For example, the command below shows all tasks for the i2c-tools recipe:

```
$ bitbake -c listtasks i2c-tools
...
do_build                Default task for a recipe - depends on all othe
r normal tasks required to 'build' a recipe
do_checkuri             Validates the SRC_URI value
do_clean                Removes all output files for a target
do_cleanall             Removes all output files, shared state cache, a
nd downloaded source files for a target
do_cleansstate          Removes all output files and shared state cache
for a target
do_compile              Compiles the source in the compilation directory
do_configure            Configures the source by enabling and disabling
 any build-time and configuration options for the software being built
...
do_pydevshell           Starts an interactive Python shell for developm
ent/debugging
do_unpack               Unpacks the source code into a working directory
NOTE: Tasks Summary: Attempted 1 tasks of which 0 didn't need to be rer
un and all succeeded.
```

We should note here that all tasks are displayed with a little note about what they do. All this information is stored in sources/poky/meta/conf/ documentation.conf by using the variable flags below (see Section 5.1.4 for further information about variable flags):

```
$ cat sources/poky/meta/conf/documentation.conf
# this file holds documentation for known keys, possible values and
# their meanings. Please update, correct and extend this documentation.
# Mail your changes to openembedded-devel@openembedded.org
```

```
# DESCRIPTIONS FOR TASKS #


do_bootimg[doc] = "Creates a bootable live image"
do_build[doc] = "Default task for a recipe - depends on all other norma
l tasks required to 'build' a recipe"
do_bundle_initramfs[doc] = "Combines an initial ramdisk image and kerne
l together to form a single image"
do_checkuri[doc] = "Validates the SRC_URI value"
do_clean[doc] = "Removes all output files for a target"
do_cleanall[doc] = "Removes all output files, shared state cache, and d
ownloaded source files for a target"
do_cleansstate[doc] = "Removes all output files and shared state cache
for a target"
do_compile[doc] = "Compiles the source in the compilation directory"
do_compile_kernelmodules[doc] = "Compiles loadable modules for the Linu
x kernel"
do_compile_ptest_base[doc] = "Compiles the runtime test suite included
in the software being built"
do_configure[doc] = "Configures the source by enabling and disabling an
y build-time and configuration options for the software being built"
do_configure_ptest_base[doc] = "Configures the runtime test suite inclu
ded in the software being built"
do_deploy[doc] = "Writes deployable output files to the deploy director
y"
do_pydevshell[doc] = "Starts an interactive Python shell for developmen
t/debugging"
do_devshell[doc] = "Starts a shell with the environment set up for deve
lopment/debugging"
do_diffconfig[doc] = "Compares the old and new config files after runni
ng do_menuconfig for the kernel"
do_fetch[doc] = "Fetches the source code"
do_install[doc] = "Copies files from the compilation directory to a hol
ding area"
...
```

The other two interesting ways to execute a task are by using the -f option argument and by using the -C option argument. Let's see what they do.

By looking at the bitbake usage message, we get

```
...
  -f, --force     Force the specified targets/task to run (invalidating
                  any existing stamp file).
...
```

```
-C INVALIDATE_STAMP, --clear-stamp=INVALIDATE_STAMP
                Invalidate the stamp for the specified task such as
                'compile' and then run the default task for the
                specified target(s).
```
...

Their usage is quite similar, but by using -f we ask bitbake to force the execution of the specified targets/tasks even if its stamp file suggests skipping it (similarly as the make command does when it considers a target file out of date) because any existing stamp file is invalidated. While using -C, we invalidate the stamp file for the specified task only, and then we run the default task for the specified target.

For example, we can force a rerun of the task unpack for a recipe by using the following command line:

```
$ bitbake -c unpack -f recipe
```

Or we can force the execution of the do_compile task of a recipe, as in the next command-line example:

```
$ bitbake -C compile -c compile recipe
```

When we build a Yocto image, it may be useful using the -k option argument as below:

```
$ bitbake -k image-recipe
```

In this manner, we ask bitbake to continue the build process as much as possible after an error.

Even if it will not produce any image, it will do so in such a way that whatever is not dependent on the failing target will be built before stopping. In fact, by default, bitbake stops when a task fails, even if it may continue building other tasks. By using such option arguments, we ask bitbake to continue as long as it can, so when we have found a fix for the failing target, we can resume and speed up the image building by just compiling the remaining tasks depending on the previous failure task.

Before closing this panoramic on the bitbake command line, .
we should take a look at the -v (--verbose) and -D (--debug) option
arguments; they can be very useful during a recipe debugging. In fact, in
the usage message we can read

```
...
  -v, --verbose   Enable tracing of shell tasks (with 'set -x'). Also
                  print bb.note(...) messages to stdout (in addition to
                  writing them to ${T}/log.do_<task>).
  -D, --debug     Increase the debug level. You can specify this more
                  than once. -D sets the debug level to 1, where only
                  bb.debug(1, ...) messages are printed to stdout; -DD
                  sets the debug level to 2, where both bb.debug(1, ...)
                  and bb.debug(2, ...) messages are printed; etc.
                  Without -D, no debug messages are printed. Note that
                  -D only affects output to stdout. All debug messages
                  are written to ${T}/log.do_taskname, regardless of the
                  debug level.
...
```

With the -v option argument, we can display more information notes
on the standard output, while with the -D option argument we can display
debugging messages too.

As it's easily understood, the bb.note() and bb.debug() functions
are used to display notes or debugging messages in the various
tasks, while the readers should notice that regardless of the debug
level, all debug messages are written to ${T}/log.do_taskname.

Readers should remember that ${T} refers to a temporary directory
inside the hierarchy of the build directory (in our case, it should be
tmp/work/imx8mp_icore-poky-linux/engicam-evaluation-
image-mx8/1.0-r0/temp).

Also, it's important to know that we can easily inspect all logs by
looking within the file bitbake-cookerdaemon.log placed in the
building directory.

4.1.2 Using More Configuration Files

In Section 3.4, we have shown several configuration files, and especially in Section 3.4.1 we looked at in detail one of the most important configuration files we have to manage; however, these are not the only configuration files read by bitbake. In fact, all configurations set in the conf/local.conf file can also be set in the conf/site.conf and conf/auto.conf configuration files.

These two files are not created by the environment initialization script, so we need to create them by ourselves, and they can be used as follows:

- site.conf: Used to configure multiple build directories. For example, if we have many build environments, and they share some common features, we can set these default build properties here (typically the variable PACKAGE_CLASSES can be set here).

- auto.conf: Usually, it holds the same variables held in conf/local.conf or the conf/site.conf files, but it is created and written to by a *Continuous Integration System* (CI) or an *Autobuilder* (AB).

When we launch bitbake, it reads the configuration files in a specific order: site.conf, auto.conf, and local.conf (see Section 3.4.4).

In addition to these files, we can supply more configuration files by using -r (or --read=) and/or -R (or --postread) option arguments. So, as reported within the usage message (duplicated below), if we use -r PREFILE we ask bitbake to read the specified file before bitbake.conf, while with -R POSTFILE we ask bitbake to read the specified file after bitbake.conf:

```
...
  -r PREFILE, --read=PREFILE
                      Read the specified file before bitbake.conf.
  -R POSTFILE, --postread=POSTFILE
                      Read the specified file after bitbake.conf.
...
```

In this manner, we can alter the `bitbake` configuration file from the command line by simply prepending or appending some variable redefinitions (see Section 12.4 for a practical example).

In any case, a good way to get an idea of both the configuration settings used in our execution environment and which configuration files are read (and in which order) is by running the following bitbake command:

```
$ bitbake -e
```

At the top of the output message, we can see the many configuration files used in the execution environment, as shown below:

```
#
# INCLUDE HISTORY:
#
# /home/giometti/yocto/imx-yocto-bsp/imx8mp-build/conf/bblayers.conf
# /home/giometti/yocto/imx-yocto-bsp/sources/poky/meta/conf/layer.conf
# /home/giometti/yocto/imx-yocto-bsp/sources/poky/meta-poky/conf/layer.
conf
# /home/giometti/yocto/imx-yocto-bsp/sources/meta-openembedded/meta-oe/
conf/layer.conf
...
```

Above, we can see that the first file read is `bblayers.conf`, and then all `layer.conf` files for each defined layer are read until the one within the Engicam's layer:

```
...
# /home/giometti/yocto/imx-yocto-bsp/sources/meta-engicam-nxp/conf/laye
r.conf
...
```

At this point, `bitbake` starts including other configuration files as said above:

```
...
# conf/bitbake.conf includes:
#    /home/giometti/yocto/imx-yocto-bsp/sources/poky/meta/conf/abi_versi
on.conf
#    conf/site.conf
#    conf/auto.conf
#    /home/giometti/yocto/imx-yocto-bsp/imx8mp-build/conf/local.conf
```

```
#    /home/giometti/yocto/imx-yocto-bsp/sources/poky/meta/conf/multiconf
ig/default.conf
#    /home/giometti/yocto/imx-yocto-bsp/sources/meta-engicam-nxp/conf/ma
chine/imx8mp-icore.conf includes:
#       /home/giometti/yocto/imx-yocto-bsp/sources/meta-engicam-nxp/conf/
machine/include/imx8mp-engicam.inc includes:
#         /home/giometti/yocto/imx-yocto-bsp/sources/meta-freescale/conf/
machine/include/imx-base.inc includes:
#           /home/giometti/yocto/imx-yocto-bsp/sources/meta-freescale/con
f/machine/include/fsl-default-settings.inc
...
```

In the above output, we can see that both `site.conf` and `auto.conf` are not defined, but if we define one of them with another custom configuration file, we can do the following:

```
$ echo 'MY_CUSTOM_VAR="value 1"' > conf/auto.conf
$ echo 'MY_CUSTOM_VAR="value 2"' > conf/my_conf_file.conf
```

We add a custom variable in both `auto.conf` and in a generic `my_conf_file.conf`, then we can execute `bitbake` as follows:

```
$ bitbake -e -r conf/my_conf_file.conf
#
# INCLUDE HISTORY:
#
# conf/my_conf_file.conf
# /home/giometti/yocto/imx-yocto-bsp/imx8mp-build/conf/bblayers.conf
...
#   conf/site.conf
#   /home/giometti/yocto/imx-yocto-bsp/imx8mp-build/conf/auto.conf
...
```

Now the first configuration file read is `my_conf_file.conf`, instead of `bblayers.conf`, and the `auto.conf` files are now read with the path name /home/giometti/yocto/imx-yocto-bsp/imx8mp-build/conf/auto.conf. And not only that! If we go through the output, we can see how `bitbake` assigns the final value to our custom variable; in fact, we can read:

```
...
#
# $MY_CUSTOM_VAR [2 operations]
#   set /home/giometti/yocto/imx-yocto-bsp/imx8mp-build/conf/my_conf_fi
```

```
le.conf:1
#      "value 2"
#    set /home/giometti/yocto/imx-yocto-bsp/imx8mp-build/conf/auto.conf:1
#      "value 1"
# pre-expansion value:
#    "value 1"
MY_CUSTOM_VAR="value 1"
...
```

which is the expected value due to the sequence of configuration files read. On the other hand, if we use the command line below, we should expect a different behavior:

```
$ bitbake -e -R conf/my_conf_file.conf
#
# INCLUDE HISTORY:
#
# /home/giometti/yocto/imx-yocto-bsp/imx8mp-build/conf/bblayers.conf
...
#    conf/site.conf
#    /home/giometti/yocto/imx-yocto-bsp/imx8mp-build/conf/auto.conf
...
#    /home/giometti/yocto/imx-yocto-bsp/sources/poky/meta/conf/sanity.co
nf
# conf/my_conf_file.conf
# /home/giometti/yocto/imx-yocto-bsp/sources/poky/meta/classes/base.bbc
lass includes:
#    /home/giometti/yocto/imx-yocto-bsp/sources/poky/meta/classes/patch.
bbclass includes:
...
```

Now the my_conf_file.conf file is read as the last configuration file; in fact, the base.class file is parsed after it (and other class files follow), then the final value for MY_CUSTOM_VAR is now set as shown below:

```
...
#
# $MY_CUSTOM_VAR [2 operations]
#    set /home/giometti/yocto/imx-yocto-bsp/imx8mp-build/conf/auto.conf:1
#      "value 1"
#    set /home/giometti/yocto/imx-yocto-bsp/imx8mp-build/conf/my_conf_fi
le.conf:1
#      "value 2"
```

```
# pre-expansion value:
#   "value 2"
MY_CUSTOM_VAR="value 2"
...
```

which is correct.

Another interesting example to see about variable setting is the one regarding the PACKAGE_CLASSES variable we altered in the conf/local. conf file as in Section 2.3. Readers should remember that we did the following:

```
$ cat conf/local.conf
MACHINE ??= 'imx8mp-icore-cy'
#MACHINE ??= 'imx8mp-icore-cy'
DISTRO ?= 'fsl-imx-xwayland'
PACKAGE_CLASSES ?= 'package_rpm'
...
# Switch to IPKG packaging and include package-management in the image
PACKAGE_CLASSES = "package_ipk"
EXTRA_IMAGE_FEATURES += "package-management"
...
```

And if we check in the bitbake -e output, we can see what is reported below:

```
...
#
# $PACKAGE_CLASSES [4 operations]
#   set? /home/giometti/yocto/imx-yocto-bsp/imx8mp-build/conf/local.con
f:3
#     "package_rpm"
#   set /home/giometti/yocto/imx-yocto-bsp/imx8mp-build/conf/local.conf
:23
#     "package_ipk"
#   set? /home/giometti/yocto/imx-yocto-bsp/sources/poky/meta/conf/dist
ro/defaultsetup.conf:16
#     "package_ipk"
#   set /home/giometti/yocto/imx-yocto-bsp/sources/poky/meta/conf/docum
entation.conf:312
#     [doc] "This variable specifies the package manager to use when pa
ckaging data. It is set in the conf/local.conf file in the Build Direct
ory."
```

```
# pre-expansion value:
#    "package_ipk"
PACKAGE_CLASSES="package_ipk"
...
```

In the above output, we see how the variable PACKAGE_CLASSES is set in
the several configuration files read by bitbake, and especially within our
conf/local.conf it first does a set? assignment and then a set one (these
are two different kinds of variable assignment that are well explained in
Section 5.1.2). Furthermore, it sets the [doc] flag for PACKAGE_CLASSES
variable as specified in the documentation.conf file as introduced in
Section 4.1.1.

Before continuing, the readers should notice that executing bitbake
with the -e option argument is just a tricky way to display the value a
specific variable assumes within the Yocto build system. In fact, we can do
as below to easily get the PACKAGE_CLASSES value:

```
$ bitbake -e | grep 'PACKAGE_CLASSES='
PACKAGE_CLASSES="package_ipk"
```

Note the equal sign (=) at the end of the regular expression. This can be
used to select just the variable assignment and discard noise.

4.1.3 Passing Variables from the Command Line

Another interesting way to use BitBake is the possibility to pass special
settings via environment variables. In fact, before parsing configuration
files, the command bitbake looks at certain variables:

- BB_ENV_PASSTHROUGH specifies the internal list of
  variables to allow from the external environment into
  the bitbake environment. By default, the value of this
  variable is not specified, and then the following list is
  used: BBPATH, BB_PRESERVE_ENV, BB_ENV_PASSTHROUGH,
  and BB_ENV_PASSTHROUGH_ADDITIONS.

- BB_ENV_PASSTHROUGH_ADDITIONS specifies an additional set of variables (on top of the internal list set via BB_ENV_PASSTHROUGH) to allow from the external environment to the bitbake environment.

- BB_PRESERVE_ENV disables environment filtering, and all variables are allowed in from the external environment into the bitbake environment.

- BB_ORIGENV contains a copy of the original external environment (before any filtration) in which bitbake was run.

- BITBAKE_UI is used to specify the User Interface (UI) module to use when running bitbake (this variable is equivalent to the -u command-line option).

Apart from BB_ORIGENV, all the above variables must be set in the external environment for them to work, and they are used to pass some data within bitbake and then in the Yocto build system; however, we may be interested in passing more variables than these, and to do so we can use at least two ways.

Before continuing, it is better to underline the fact that passing external variables to bitbake is not the common way to work in the Yocto Project; that's why bitbake usually filters its execution environment before starting its job. However, there may exist some special circumstances where this rule can be ignored; that's why we are going to report these techniques.

The simplest way is by using BB_PRESERVE_ENV, but this method is not the best to do due to the fact that all variables are passed to bitbake, and also this is an error-prone method. So we simply don't consider it as a valid method.

So, the real first method, and the real natural way to solve our problem, is by using the BB_ENV_PASSTHROUGH variable since it has been introduced for this task. To show how we can use it, let's define a custom variable to be passed to bitbake as below:

```
$ export MY_CUSTOM_VAR="some value"
```

Note that the export keyword is needed in Bash to address variables to be exported to all child processes.

Now, if we check the bitbake environment, we can verify that MY_CUSTOM_VAR is not defined:

```
$ bitbake -e | grep MY_CUSTOM_VAR= || echo "not found"
not found
```

On the other hand, if we use BB_ENV_PASSTHROUGH as below, the variable is now found:

```
$ export BB_ENV_PASSTHROUGH="MY_CUSTOM_VAR"
$ bitbake -e | grep MY_CUSTOM_VAR= || echo "not found"
MY_CUSTOM_VAR="some value"
```

Within BB_ENV_PASSTHROUGH, we can put a white space separated list of variables to be passed to bitbake as done by the Yocto build system with the variable BB_ENV_PASSTHROUGH_ADDITIONS, as shown below:

```
$ bitbake -e | grep BB_ENV_PASSTHROUGH_ADDITIONS=
BB_ENV_PASSTHROUGH_ADDITIONS="ALL_PROXY BBPATH_EXTRA BB_LOGCONFIG BB_NO_
NETWORK BB_NUMBER_THREADS BB_SETSCENE_ENFORCE BB_SRCREV_POLICY DISTRO FT
PS_PROXY FTP_PROXY GIT_PROXY_COMMAND HTTPS_PROXY HTTP_PROXY MACHINE NO_P
ROXY PARALLEL_MAKE SCREENDIR SDKMACHINE SOCKS5_PASSWD SOCKS5_USER SSH_AG
ENT_PID SSH_AUTH_SOCK STAMPS_DIR TCLIBC TCMODE all_proxy ftp_proxy ftps_
proxy http_proxy https_proxy no_proxy "
```

Since BB_ENV_PASSTHROUGH_ADDITIONS is used by the Yocto build system, it is better not to use it for our variables' management.

Another more sophisticated way to pass an environment variable is by using BB_ORIGENV in a recipe, as shown below:

```
MY_VAR = d.getVar("BB_ORIGENV", False).getVar("MY_VAR", False)
```

This is because, as stated above, bitbake saves a copy of the original environment into the variable BB_ORIGENV, and then we can read it by using a Python function (for the moment, we cannot test this behavior, but in Section 5.1.5 we are going to test it).

While there is nothing wrong with these methods, readers should remember that bitbake does accept a --postread argument, as explained above. That means that we can write as many bitbake variables as we want to some temporary configuration file and have it read after bitbake.conf by specifying the name of the file on the command line.

```
For example:
$ cat > conf/my_conf_file.conf <<__EOF__
MY_CUSTOM_VAR="some value"
__EOF__
$ bitbake -e --postread=conf/my_conf_file.conf | grep MY_CUSTOM_VAR=
MY_CUSTOM_VAR="some value"
```

This method can be a valid alternative to the two methods presented above. In fact, in the next chapters of this book, we are going to see that this last method is the preferred one.

4.2 bitbake-layers

The bitbake-layers command handles common meta layer tasks as reported by its usage message:

```
$ bitbake-layers -h
NOTE: Starting bitbake server...
usage: bitbake-layers [-d] [-q] [-F] [--color COLOR] [-h] <subcommand>
...

BitBake layers utility
```

```
options:
  -d, --debug           Enable debug output
  -q, --quiet           Print only errors
  -F, --force           Force add without recipe parse verification
  --color COLOR         Colorize output (where COLOR is auto, always,
                        never)
  -h, --help            show this help message and exit

subcommands:
  <subcommand>
    show-layers         show current configured layers.
    show-overlayed      list overlayed recipes (where the same recipe
                        exists in another layer)
    show-recipes        list available recipes, showing the layer they
                        are provided by
    show-appends        list bbappend files and recipe files they apply
                        to
    show-cross-depends  Show dependencies between recipes that cross
                        layer boundaries.
    layerindex-fetch    Fetches a layer from a layer index along with
                        its dependent layers, and adds them to
                        conf/bblayers.conf.
    layerindex-show-depends
                        Find layer dependencies from layer index.
    add-layer           Add one or more layers to bblayers.conf.
    remove-layer        Remove one or more layers from bblayers.conf.
    flatten             flatten layer configuration into a separate
                        output directory.
    create-layer        Create a basic layer

Use bitbake-layers <subcommand> --help to get help on a specific command
```

As we can see above, by using, for example, the subcommand show-layers, we can show all configured layers. If we try to execute this subcommand on already installed Yocto sources, we get something as reported below:

```
$ bitbake-layers show-layers
NOTE: Starting bitbake server...
layer                 path                                              priority
========================================================================
meta       /home/giometti/yocto/imx-yocto-bsp/sources/poky/meta        5
meta-poky  /home/giometti/yocto/imx-yocto-bsp/sources/poky/meta-poky    5
...
```

133

```
meta-bsp   /home/giometti/yocto/imx-yocto-bsp/sources/meta-imx/meta-bsp 8
...
meta-v2x   /home/giometti/yocto/imx-yocto-bsp/sources/meta-imx/meta-v2x 9
...
meta-qt6   /home/giometti/yocto/imx-yocto-bsp/sources/meta-qt6         5
...
```

Here, we can see all the layer names, their path names, and, as the last parameter, their priority. This parameter establishes a priority to use for recipes in the layer when the Yocto build system finds recipes of the same name in different layers. A larger value for priority results in higher precedence.

To specify a desired priority for a new layer, we can use the --priority option argument within the subcommand create-layer that we can use to add a new layer to our current Yocto sources. Below is the subcommand usage message:

```
$ bitbake-layers create-layer -h
NOTE: Starting bitbake server...
usage: bitbake-layers create-layer [-h] [--layerid LAYERID]
                                   [--priority PRIORITY]
                                   [--example-recipe-name EXAMPLERECIPE]
                                   [--example-recipe-version VERSION]
                                   layerdir

Create a basic layer

positional arguments:
  layerdir               Layer directory to create

options:
  -h, --help             show this help message and exit
  --layerid LAYERID, -i LAYERID
                         Layer id to use if different from layername
  --priority PRIORITY, -p PRIORITY
                         Priority of recipes in layer
  --example-recipe-name EXAMPLERECIPE, -e EXAMPLERECIPE
                         Filename of the example recipe
  --example-recipe-version VERSION, -v VERSION
                         Version number for the example recipe
```

This command creates a new meta layer within the `layerdir` path name, but to effectively add it to our Yocto Project, we have to use the `add-layer` subcommand as reported below:

```
$ bitbake-layers add-layer -h
NOTE: Starting bitbake server...
usage: bitbake-layers add-layer [-h] layerdir [layerdir ...]

Add one or more layers to bblayers.conf.

positional arguments:
  layerdir    Layer directory/directories to add
...
```

To remove a layer, we can use the `remove-layer` subcommand:

```
$ bitbake-layers remove-layer -h
NOTE: Starting bitbake server...
usage: bitbake-layers remove-layer [-h] layerdir [layerdir ...]

Remove one or more layers from bblayers.conf.

positional arguments:
  layerdir    Layer directory/directories to remove (wildcards allowed, enclose
in quotes to avoid shell expansion)
...
```

Another interesting subcommand (even if less used) is `flatten`, which can be used to combine any specified layers, or all layers, into a single layer:

```
$ bitbake-layers flatten -h
NOTE: Starting bitbake server...
usage: bitbake-layers flatten [-h] [layer ...] outputdir

Takes the specified layers (or all layers in the current layer
configuration if none are specified) and builds a "flattened" directory
containing the contents of all layers, with any overlayed recipes removed
and bbappends appended to the corresponding recipes. Note that some manual
cleanup may still be necessary afterwards, in particular:

* where non-recipe files (such as patches) are overwritten (the flatten
  command will show a warning for these)
* where anything beyond the normal layer setup has been added to
  layer.conf (only the lowest priority number layer's layer.conf is used)
* overridden/appended items from bbappends will need to be tidied up
```

```
* when the flattened layers do not have the same directory structure (the
  flatten command should show a warning when this will cause a problem)
```

Warning: if you flatten several layers where another layer is intended to
be used "inbetween" them (in layer priority order) such that recipes /
bbappends in the layers interact, and then attempt to use the new output
layer together with that other layer, you may no longer get the same
build results (as the layer priority order has effectively changed).

```
positional arguments:
  layer      Optional layer(s) to flatten (otherwise all are flattened)
  outputdir  Output directory
...
```

Readers may notice from the usage message above that this subcommand can be useful, but it may require some human help.

Another useful usage of this command is to inspect recipes within layers by using the show-recipes, show-appends, and show-overlayed subcommands. By using show-recipes, we can list available recipes among the layers they belong to. For example, we can do the following:

```
$ bitbake-layers show-recipes u-boot-engicam
...
=== Matching recipes: ===
u-boot-engicam:
  meta-engicam-nxp      2022.04
```

In this example, we obviously find just one recipe within the Engicam's meta layer. But we can also use wildcards with an entirely different result:

```
$ bitbake-layers show-recipes u-boot-*
...
=== Matching recipes: ===
u-boot-boundary:
  meta-freescale-3rdparty 2022.04 (skipped: incompatible with machine i
mx8mp-icore (not in COMPATIBLE_MACHINE))
u-boot-engicam:
  meta-engicam-nxp      2022.04
u-boot-fslc:
  meta-freescale        2022.07 (skipped: PREFERRED_PROVIDER_virtual/boo
tloader set to u-boot-engicam, not u-boot-fslc)
u-boot-fslc-mfgtool:
  meta-freescale        2022.07+gitAUTOINC+a21d7668eb
```

```
u-boot-fslc-mxsboot:
  meta-freescale       2022.07 (skipped: incompatible with machine imx8
mp-icore (not in COMPATIBLE_MACHINE))
u-boot-imx:
  meta-bsp             2022.04 (skipped: PREFERRED_PROVIDER_virtual/boo
tloader set to u-boot-engicam, not u-boot-imx)
  meta-freescale       2022.04 (skipped: PREFERRED_PROVIDER_virtual/boo
tloader set to u-boot-engicam, not u-boot-imx)
u-boot-imx-mfgtool:
  meta-bsp             2022.04
  meta-freescale       2022.04
u-boot-imx-tools:
  meta-bsp             2022.04
...
```

This time, the output is quite longer, and we can notice that some recipes are skipped due to a PREFERRED_PROVIDER setting and others due to COMPATIBLE_MACHINE settings (see Section 6.3.3 for further information on this variable). Other recipes as u-boot-imx-mfgtool are from more than one layer, and, in this case, they are listed with the preferred version first. To get a list of all overlayed recipes and the available versions in each layer, with the preferred version first, we can use the show-overlayed subcommand.

In the end, the show-appends subcommand is more interesting:

```
$ bitbake-layers show-appends -h
NOTE: Starting bitbake server...
usage: bitbake-layers show-appends [-h] [pnspec ...]

Lists recipes with the bbappends that apply to them as subitems.

positional arguments:
  pnspec      optional recipe name specification (wildcards allowed, en
close in quotes to avoid shell expansion)
...
```

This subcommand can be used to display the append files (which will be explained in detail in Chapter 6) of one or more recipes, that is, all .bbappend files as in the example below:

```
$ bitbake-layers show-appends imx-boot
...
=== Matched appended recipes ===
imx-boot_1.0.bb:
  /home/giometti/yocto/imx-yocto-bsp/sources/meta-engicam-nxp/recipes-b
sp/imx-boot/imx-boot_1.0.bbappend
  /home/giometti/yocto/imx-yocto-bsp/sources/meta-imx/meta-bsp/recipes-
bsp/imx-mkimage/imx-boot_1.0.bbappend
imx-boot_1.0.bb:
  /home/giometti/yocto/imx-yocto-bsp/sources/meta-engicam-nxp/recipes-b
sp/imx-boot/imx-boot_1.0.bbappend
  /home/giometti/yocto/imx-yocto-bsp/sources/meta-imx/meta-bsp/recipes-
bsp/imx-mkimage/imx-boot_1.0.bbappend
```

In the above output, we can see that there are two recipes for imx-boot, and both of them have two append files; the two recipes can be located as above with the show-recipes subcommand:

```
$ bitbake-layers show-recipes imx-boot
...
=== Matching recipes: ===
imx-boot:
  meta-bsp              1.0
  meta-freescale        1.0
```

Most of these commands will be extensively explained and used in Chapter 7.

4.3 recipetool

This utility can be used to handle common recipe tasks. In fact, if we take a look at its usage message, we get the following output:

```
$ recipetool -h
NOTE: Starting bitbake server...
usage: recipetool [-d] [-q] [--color COLOR] [-h] <subcommand> ...

OpenEmbedded recipe tool

options:
  -d, --debug      Enable debug output
  -q, --quiet      Print only errors
```

```
  --color COLOR   Colorize output (where COLOR is auto, always, never)
  -h, --help      show this help message and exit

subcommands:
  setvar          Set a variable within a recipe
  newappend       Create a bbappend for the specified target in the
                  specified layer
  create          Create a new recipe
  edit            Edit the recipe and appends for the specified target.
                  This obeys $VISUAL if set, otherwise $EDITOR,
                  otherwise vi.
  appendfile      Create/update a bbappend to replace a target file
  appendsrcfiles  Create/update a bbappend to add or replace source
                  files
  appendsrcfile   Create/update a bbappend to add or replace a source
                  file
Use recipetool <subcommand> --help to get help on a specific command
```

This tool is extensively used in this book, especially in Chapter 9 and following; however, in these pages we will introduce its main usages.

Using the subcommand create as shown below, we can automate creation of base recipes based on the source files (locally or remotely):

```
$ recipetool create -h
NOTE: Starting bitbake server...
usage: recipetool create [-h] [-o OUTFILE] [-p PROVIDES] [-m]
                         [-x EXTRACTPATH]
                         [-N NAME] [-V VERSION] [-b] [--also-native]
                         [--src-subdir SUBDIR] [-a | -S SRCREV]
                         [-B SRCBRANCH]
                         [--keep-temp] [--npm-dev] [--mirrors]
                         source

Creates a new recipe from a source tree

arguments:
  source                  Path or URL to source

options:
  -h, --help              show this help message and exit
  -o OUTFILE, --outfile OUTFILE
                          Specify filename for recipe to create
  -p PROVIDES, --provides PROVIDES
                          Specify an alias for the item provided by the
                          recipe
```

```
-m, --machine          Make recipe machine-specific as opposed to
                       architecture-specific
-x EXTRACTPATH, --extract-to EXTRACTPATH
                       Assuming source is a URL, fetch it and extract
                       it to the directory specified as EXTRACTPATH
-N NAME, --name NAME   Name to use within recipe (PN)
-V VERSION, --version VERSION
                       Version to use within recipe (PV)
-b, --binary           Treat the source tree as something that should
                       be installed verbatim (no compilation, same
                       directory structure)
--also-native          Also add native variant (i.e. support building
                       recipe for the build host as well as the target
                       machine)
--src-subdir SUBDIR    Specify subdirectory within source tree to use
-a, --autorev          When fetching from a git repository, set SRCREV
                       in the recipe to a floating revision instead of
                       fixed
-S SRCREV, --srcrev SRCREV
                       Source revision to fetch if fetching from an SCM
                       such as git (default latest)
-B SRCBRANCH, --srcbranch SRCBRANCH
                       Branch in source repository if fetching from an
                       SCM such as git (default master)
...
```

Note the `--also-native` option argument, which can be used to add the native variant of the recipe for the build host (as well as for the target machine). See Section 11.6 for further information about this kind of recipe.

First, we should note that sources can be located both locally and remotely, that is, sources can be within a directory on the local host, or they can be located on a remote host. The parameter source can be a filename:

```
$ recipetool create hello.c
```

or a URL, and in this case, it is better to provide the -o option argument to specify the recipe name to use:

```
$ recipetool create -o zlib_1.2.8.bb http://zlib.net/zlib-1.2.8.tar.gz
```

It can also be a Git repository where we ask for a specific branch with the -B option argument:

```
$ recipetool create -B master https://github.com/bast/cmake-example.git
```

A last note is about the fact that we can also specify a local Git repository by using the following command within the directory where the repository is located:

```
$ recipetool create git://$(pwd)
```

Moreover, this utility can also be used to create an append file (i.e., .bbappend) for an existing recipe by using the subcommand newappend as specified in the next usage message:

```
$ recipetool newappend -h
NOTE: Starting bitbake server...
usage: recipetool newappend [-h] [-e] [-w] destlayer target

arguments:
  destlayer               Base directory of the destination layer to write
                          the bbappend to
  target                  Target recipe/provide to append

options:
  -h, --help              show this help message and exit
  -e, --edit              Edit the new append. This obeys $VISUAL if set,
                          otherwise $EDITOR, otherwise vi.
  -w, --wildcard-version
                          Use wildcard to make the bbappend apply to any
                          recipe version
```

This command is really useful since, as we can see in the next chapters, we can easily alter a recipe to fix a configuration setting or to support our hardware. Furthermore, all these steps can be done within our custom layer, which highly increases customization and better code readability.

Using the edit subcommand, we can edit a recipe and all its append files at once (depending on the system editor):

```
$ recipetool edit -h
NOTE: Starting bitbake server...
usage: recipetool edit [-h] target

arguments:
  target        Target recipe/provide to edit
...
```

In fact, if we recall that for the recipe imx-boot we have two append files in our Yocto sources (in the previous section, we used the command bitbake-layers show-appends imx-boot to find it), then we can edit both the recipe and appends files by using the command below:

```
$ EDITOR=gedit recipetool edit imx-boot
```

We have set EDITOR to gedit to call this editor instead of the default one (we use vim) in order to get a new window as in Figure 4-1.

Figure 4-1. *The* imx-boot *recipe and its append files edited at once*

In the new window, we have the imx-boot recipe and its append files (the two imx-boot_1.0.bbappend files in the meta-engicam-nxp and meta-imx layers) edited at once!

Another interesting way to use recipetool is by using the setvar subcommand to add, delete, or update a variable in a recipe (or within an included file):

```
$ recipetool setvar -h
NOTE: Starting bitbake server...
usage: recipetool setvar [-h] [--recipe-only] [--patch] [--delete]
                         recipefile varname [value]

Adds/updates the value a variable is set to in a recipe

arguments:
  recipefile          Recipe file to update
  varname             Variable name to set
  value               New value to set the variable to

options:
  -h, --help          show this help message and exit
  --recipe-only, -r   Do not set variable in any include file if present
  --patch, -p         Create a patch to make the change instead of
                      Modifying the recipe
  --delete, -D        Delete the specified value instead of setting it
```

The usage is trivial, and we demand curious readers to see Section 11.3.3 for practical example usages.

Then, the last two subcommands (honestly, they are three, but two of them have almost the same usage) are appendfile and appendsrcfiles which require some more words to be better explained.

Regarding appendfile, its usage message is reported below:

```
$ recipetool appendfile -h
NOTE: Starting bitbake server...
usage: recipetool appendfile [-h] [-m MACHINE] [-w] [-r RECIPE]
                             DESTLAYER targetpath newfile

Creates a bbappend (or updates an existing one) to replace the specified
file that appears in the target system, determining the recipe that
packages the file and the required path and name for the bbappend
automatically. Note that the ability to determine the recipe packaging a
```

particular file depends upon the recipe's do_packagedata task having
already run prior to running this command (which it will have when the
recipe has been built successfully, which in turn will have happened if
one or more of the recipe's packages is included in an image that has
been built successfully).

```
arguments:
  DESTLAYER              Base directory of the destination layer to write
                         the bbappend to
  targetpath             Path to the file to be replaced (as it would
                         appear within the target image, e.g. /etc/motd)
  newfile                Custom file to replace the target file with

options:
  -h, --help             show this help message and exit
  -m MACHINE, --machine MACHINE
                         Make bbappend changes specific to a machine only
  -w, --wildcard-version
                         Use wildcard to make the bbappend apply to any
                         recipe version
  -r RECIPE, --recipe RECIPE
                         Override recipe to apply to (default is to find
                         which recipe already packages the file)
```

As we can read within the comment above, we can use the
subcommand to create (or update) a .bbappend for the recipe to replace
a file that appears in the target system, and the command will be able to
autodetect which is the recipe that packages the file and the required path
and name for the append file.

This is a fascinating behavior because it is not trivial to find out which
is the recipe that packages a file. So, once we have generated the final
image for our embedded system, and we need to alter, for example, a
configuration file within the root filesystem, we can use this command to
do it in a while.

Note that, according to what is reported in the usage message, *the
ability to determine the recipe packaging a particular file depends
upon the recipe's do_packagedata( ) task having already run prior
to running this command (which it will have when the recipe has*

been built successfully, which in turn will have happened if one or more of the recipe's packages is included in an image that has been built successfully).

So, the command is subject to fail in case the task do_packagedata for the package holding the desired file is not successfully executed.

On the other hand, the usage message for the appendsrcfiles subcommand is shown below:

```
$ recipetool appendsrcfiles -h
NOTE: Starting bitbake server...
usage: recipetool appendsrcfiles [-h] [-m MACHINE] [-w] [-W]
                                 [-D DESTDIR]
                                 DESTLAYER RECIPE FILE [FILE ...]

Creates a .bbappend (or updates an existing one) to add or replace the
specified file in the recipe sources, either those in WORKDIR or those
in the source tree. This command lets you specify multiple files with a
destination directory, so cannot specify the destination filename. See
the appendsrcfile command for the other behavior.

arguments:
  DESTLAYER             Base directory of the destination layer to write
                        the bbappend to
  RECIPE                Override recipe to apply to
  FILE                  File(s) to be added to the recipe sources
                        (WORKDIR or S)

options:
  -h, --help            show this help message and exit
  -m MACHINE, --machine MACHINE
                        Make bbappend changes specific to a machine only
  -w, --wildcard-version
                        Use wildcard to make the bbappend apply to any
                        recipe version
  -W, --workdir         Unpack file into WORKDIR rather than S
  -D DESTDIR, --destdir DESTDIR
                        Destination directory (relative to S or WORKDIR,
                        defaults to ".")
```

Readers should easily check that the appendsrcfile (without the last s) is almost a specified version of this subcommand; that's why it is not used in this book. However, we state here that appendsrcfile must be used in place of its multiple counterpart when we wish to specify the destination filename we'd like to have in the final root filesystem.

This subcommand can be used to create (or update) a .bbappend for a recipe to add or replace a specified file in the recipe sources. The new files are unpacked by default within the sources' directory (addressed by the S variable) or directly in the directory where packages are built (addressed by the WORKDIR variable) if they are not sources but just files to be installed in the root filesystem (e.g., if they are binaries, images, etc.).

Readers should move to Section 11.3 for practical usage examples of these commands.

4.4 devshell (and pydevshell)

When debugging certain commands or even when just editing packages, the devshell command utility can be very useful. To invoke the devshell, we have to use bitbake in the following form where <target> is a recipe name:

```
$ bitbake -c devshell <target>
```

Doing so, we ask bitbake to execute all tasks up to and including do_patch for the target recipe; then, a new terminal is opened, and we are placed in the directory addressed by the S variable (i.e., the source directory).

146

In the new terminal, all the Yocto build-related environment variables are still defined, so you can use commands such as configure and make to build code for the target as if the build system were executing them. Consequently, working this way can be helpful when debugging a build or preparing software to be used with the Yocto build system.

Let's do an example that uses devshell on a target named devmem2:

```
$ bitbake -c devshell devmem2
```

It may happen that when we execute the above command, the following error occurs:

```
ERROR: devmem2-2.0-r0 do_devshell: No valid terminal found, unable
 to open devshell.
Tried the following commands:
        tmux split-window -c "{cwd}" "do_terminal"
        tmux new-window -c "{cwd}" -n "OpenEmbedded Developer Shel
l" "do_terminal"
        xfce4-terminal -T "OpenEmbedded Developer Shell" -e "do_te
rminal"
        terminology -T="OpenEmbedded Developer Shell" -e do_termin
al
        mate-terminal --disable-factory -t "OpenEmbedded Developer
 Shell" -x do_terminal
        konsole --separate --workdir . -p tabtitle="OpenEmbedded D
eveloper Shell" -e do_terminal
        gnome-terminal -t "OpenEmbedded Developer Shell" – do_term
inal
        xterm -T "OpenEmbedded Developer Shell" -e do_terminal
        rxvt -T "OpenEmbedded Developer Shell" -e do_terminal
        tmux new -c "{cwd}" -d -s devshell -n devshell "do_termina
l"
        screen -D -m -t "OpenEmbedded Developer Shell" -S devshell
 do_terminal
...
```

This is because, as we can read in the error message, `bitbake` cannot find a valid terminal emulator program to execute; to resolve this issue, we just need to install one of the above attempted commands. For example, to use the program `screen` as a terminal emulator, we have to use the following installation command:

```
$ sudo apt install screen
```

For `tmux`, we can use the following:

```
$ sudo apt install tmux
```

If we prefer a graphical emulator as `rxvt`, we can do

```
$ sudo apt install rxvt-unicode
```

Then we have to re-execute BitBake.

If everything works well, a new terminal will be opened to the working directory of package devmem2:

```
$ echo $PWD
/home/giometti/yocto/imx-yocto-bsp/imx8mp-build/tmp/work/armv8a-poky-li
nux/devmem2/2.0-r0/git
$ ls
devmem2.c  LICENSE  README.md
```

Moreover, the environment of the new emulator has all the needed settings to compile the code for the target; in fact, we have, for example, the following environment variables:

```
$ echo $CC
aarch64-poky-linux-gcc -march=armv8-a+crc+crypto -fstack-protector-stro
ng -O2 -D_FORTIFY_SOURCE=2 -Wformat -Wformat-security -Werror=format-se
curity --sysroot=/home/giometti/yocto/imx-yocto-bsp/imx8mp-build/tmp/wo
rk/armv8a-poky-linux/devmem2/2.0-r0/recipe-sysroot
$ echo $CFLAGS
-O2 -pipe -g -feliminate-unused-debug-types -fmacro-prefix-map=/home/gi
ometti/yocto/imx-yocto-bsp/imx8mp-build/tmp/work/armv8a-poky-linux/devm
em2/2.0-r0=/usr/src/debug/devmem2/2.0-r0 -fdebug-prefix-map=/home/giome
tti/yocto/imx-yocto-bsp/imx8mp-build/tmp/work/armv8a-poky-linux/devmem2
```

```
/2.0-r0=/usr/src/debug/devmem2/2.0-r0 -fdebug-prefix-map=/home/giometti
/yocto/imx-yocto-bsp/imx8mp-build/tmp/work/armv8a-poky-linux/devmem2/2.
0-r0/recipe-sysroot= -fdebug-prefix-map=/home/giometti/yocto/imx-yocto-
bsp/imx8mp-build/tmp/work/armv8a-poky-linux/devmem2/2.0-r0/recipe-sysro
ot-native= -DFORCE_STRICT_ALIGNMENT
```

Readers may have a more complete idea about what is defined within our new environment by just using the env command.

Simply speaking, in the spawned terminals, the following occurs:

- The PATH variable includes all the cross-toolchain tools needed to compile code for the target.

- The pkgconfig variables find the correct .pc files.

- The configure command finds all necessary files to correctly compile the code for the target.

In this scenario, we can execute any compiling command by hand, or we can try to run a specific bitbake task by running the corresponding script in the ${WORKDIR}/temp directory prefixed with the prefix string run.do_.

For example, since we have no Makefile nor configure script to compile the program devmem2, we can try to execute the script run.do_compile to do the same steps bitbake will do to compile the code. Unfortunately, there are no run.do_compile scripts in the temp directory:

```
$ ls ../temp/run.do_*
../temp/run.do_devshell
../temp/run.do_devshell.2561711
../temp/run.do_fetch
../temp/run.do_fetch.2561654
../temp/run.do_patch
../temp/run.do_patch.2561690
../temp/run.do_prepare_recipe_sysroot
../temp/run.do_prepare_recipe_sysroot.2561663
../temp/run.do_qa_patch.2561690
```

```
../temp/run.do_qa_unpack.2561662
../temp/run.do_terminal.2561711
../temp/run.do_unpack
../temp/run.do_unpack.2561662
```

Note that any `run.do_` file that does not have a numeric extension (which is the PID of the executing task) is a symbolic link (symlink) to the most recent version of that file.

To create the missing task, we have to run it outside the `devshell`, so let's exit by using the `exit` command to terminate the `devshell` and then execute:

```
$ bitbake -c compile devmem2
```

Then re-enter the `devshell`, and we should get the following:

```
$ ls
devmem2  devmem2.c  LICENSE  README.md
$ ls ../temp/run.do_compile*
../temp/run.do_compile  ../temp/run.do_compile.2564184
```

Now the `run.do_compile` script exists, and we can execute it to recompile the code until we have finished our job.

```
$ ../temp/run.do_compile
devmem2.c: In function 'main':
devmem2.c:120:66: warning: format '%d' expects argument of type 'int',
but argument 3 has type 'size_t' {aka 'long unsigned int'} [-Wformat=]
  120 |    sprintf(fmt_str, "Read at address  0x%%08lX (%%p): 0x%%0%dlX
\n", 2*data_size);
...
```

Now we can fix all warnings as suggested below:

```
--- devmem2.c
+++ devmem2.c
@@ -117,7 +117,7 @@
                    fprintf(stderr, "Illegal data type '%c'.\n", acc
ess_type);
                    exit(2);
```

```
        }
-        sprintf(fmt_str, "Read at address  0x%%08lX (%%p): 0x%%0%dlX\n"
, 2*data_size);
+        sprintf(fmt_str, "Read at address  0x%%08lX (%%p): 0x%%0%ldlX\n
", 2*data_size);
    printf(fmt_str, (unsigned long)target, virt_addr, read_result);
    fflush(stdout);

@@ -145,8 +145,8 @@
                        read_result = *((uint64_t *) virt_addr);
                        break;
                }
-               sprintf(fmt_str, "Write at address 0x%%08lX (%%p): 0x%%
0%dlX, "
-                       "readback 0x%%0%dlX\n", 2*data_size, 2*data_siz
e);
+               sprintf(fmt_str, "Write at address 0x%%08lX (%%p): 0x%%
0%ldlX, "
+                       "readback 0x%%0%ldlX\n",      2*data_size, 2*
data_size);
                printf(fmt_str, (unsigned long)target, virt_addr,
                        write_val, read_result);
                fflush(stdout);
```

When finished, we can re-execute the compiling script to check if everything is OK:

```
$ ../temp/run.do_compile
```

Now we should get no warning messages from the command.

Note that the execution of a `run.do_<cmd>` script and `bitbake`'s execution of a task are identical. In other words, running the script reruns the task just as it would be run using the `bitbake -c <cmd>` command.

Now it's easy to understand that in this manner we have a valid and powerful tool to check all `bitbake` tasks used to generate a package!

Similar to working in a development shell as just described above, we can also spawn and work within an interactive Python development shell as shown below:

```
$ bitbake -c pydevshell devmem2
```

If everything works well, a terminal is opened as shown in Figure 4-2.

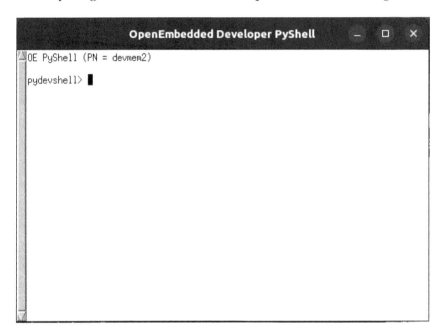

OpenEmbedded Developer PyShell

```
OE PyShell (PN = devmem2)

pydevshell>
```

Figure 4-2. *The pydevshell for the recipe devmem2*

As for `devshell` when we invoke the `pydevshell` task, all tasks up to and including `do_patch` are run for the specified target. However, instead of the `devshell` case, the key Python objects and code are available in the same way they are to BitBake tasks – in particular, the environment variable d (named data store or **internal data dictionary**; see Section 5.1.5 for further information about this variable).

So, commands such as the following are useful when exploring the data store and running functions:

```
> d.getVar("S")
'/home/giometti/yocto/imx-yocto-bsp/imx8mp-build/tmp/work/armv8a-poky-l
inux/devmem2/2.0-r0/git
> d.setVar("FOO", "bar")
> d.getVar("FOO")
'bar'
> bb.build.exec_func("do_compile", d)
```

```
devmem2.c: In function 'main':
devmem2.c:120:66: warning: format '%d' expects argument of type 'int',
but argument 3 has type 'size_t' {aka 'long unsigned int'} [-Wformat=]
 120 |          sprintf(fmt_str, "Read at address  0x%%08lX (%%p): 0x%%0
%dlX\n", 2*data_size);
...
```

As we can see, the commands execute just as if the Yocto build system were executing them or as if we were executing them from the devshell as done above.

To exit devshell, we can use the exit() command (note the parentheses) or just type the CTRL-D (i.e., EOF – end-of-file) key combination.

4.5 devtool

As recipetool, this command-line tool can be used to automate the generation of new recipes, but it can also be used to help the building, testing, and packaging software.

In the same manner as recipetool, the devtool command employs a number of subcommands that allow us to add, modify, and upgrade recipes.

The usage message is reported below:

```
$ devtool -h
NOTE: Starting bitbake server...
usage: devtool [--basepath BASEPATH] [--bbpath BBPATH] [-d] [-q]
               [--color COLOR] [-h]
               <subcommand> ...

OpenEmbedded development tool

options:
  --basepath BASEPATH   Base directory of SDK / build directory
  --bbpath BBPATH       Explicitly specify the BBPATH, rather than
                        getting it from the metadata
  -d, --debug           Enable debug output
  -q, --quiet           Print only errors
  --color COLOR         Colorize output (where COLOR is auto, always,
                        never)
  -h, --help            show this help message and exit
```

```
subcommands:
  Beginning work on a recipe:
    add                      Add a new recipe
    modify                   Modify the source for an existing recipe
    upgrade                  Upgrade an existing recipe
  Getting information:
    status                   Show workspace status
    latest-version           Report the latest version of an existing
                             recipe
    check-upgrade-status     Report upgradability for multiple (or all)
                             recipes
    search                   Search available recipes
  Working on a recipe in the workspace:
    build                    Build a recipe
    rename                   Rename a recipe file in the workspace
    edit-recipe              Edit a recipe file
    find-recipe              Find a recipe file
    configure-help           Get help on configure script options
    update-recipe            Apply changes from external source tree to
                             recipe
    reset                    Remove a recipe from your workspace
    finish                   Finish working on a recipe in your workspace
  Testing changes on target:
    deploy-target            Deploy recipe output files to live target
                             machine
    undeploy-target          Undeploy recipe output files in live target
                             machine
    build-image              Build image including workspace recipe
                             packages
  Advanced:
    create-workspace         Set up workspace in an alternative location
    extract                  Extract the source for an existing recipe
    sync                     Synchronize the source tree for an existing
                             recipe
    import                   Import exported tar archive into workspace
    menuconfig               Alter build-time configuration for a recipe
    export                   Export workspace into a tar archive
Use devtool <subcommand> --help to get help on a specific command
```

This is another tool which is extensively used in this book, especially in Chapter 9 and following; however, as done above, in the following pages we are going to introduce its main usages.

4.5.1 Adding and Modifying Recipes in the Workspace

When we use the subcommand add, a recipe is automatically created similarly as seen above for recipetool, but when we use the subcommand modify, the specified existing recipe is used to determine where to get the source code and how to patch it. In both cases, a private environment is set up so that, when we build the recipe, a source tree that is under our control is used to generate the package. By using a private environment, we can make all desired changes to the source and test it without changing the original source.

This new environment is created in the workspace directory (generically named the *workspace*), usually located under the build directory, and to see what it holds we can use the subcommand status as reported below:

```
$ devtool status
NOTE: Starting bitbake server...
INFO: Creating workspace layer in /home/giometti/yocto/imx-yocto-bsp/im
x8mp-build/workspace
INFO: No recipes currently in your workspace - you can use "devtool mod
ify" to work on an existing recipe or "devtool add" to add a new one
```

In the above example, since we haven't used devtool yet, a clean environment is created under the workspace directory within our build directory:

```
$ ls workspace
README   conf
```

Within the README file, there is some useful information about the devtool's workspace works and how it should be used by Yocto developers; we report its content below since it's fascinating:

```
$ cat workspace/README
This layer was created by the OpenEmbedded devtool utility in order to
contain recipes and bbappends that are currently being worked on. The
idea is that the contents is temporary - once you have finished working
```

155

on a recipe you use the appropriate method to move the files you have
been working on to a proper layer. In most instances you should use the
devtool utility to manage files within it rather than modifying files
directly (although recipes added with "devtool add" will often need
direct modification.)

If you no longer need to use devtool or the workspace layer's contents
you can remove the path to this workspace layer from your
conf/bblayers.conffile (and then delete the layer, if you wish).

Note that by default, if devtool fetches and unpacks source code, it
will place it in a subdirectory of a "sources" subdirectory of the
layer. If you prefer it to be elsewhere you can specify the source
tree path on the command line.

Apart from these considerations, we should take a look at the file
layer.conf under the above conf directory to well understand how the
workspace plays its role within the Yocto build system:

```
$ cat workspace/conf/layer.conf
# ### workspace layer auto-generated by devtool ###
BBPATH =. "${LAYERDIR}:"
BBFILES += "${LAYERDIR}/recipes/*/*.bb \
            ${LAYERDIR}/appends/*.bbappend"
BBFILE_COLLECTIONS += "workspacelayer"
BBFILE_PATTERN_workspacelayer = "^${LAYERDIR}/"
BBFILE_PATTERN_IGNORE_EMPTY_workspacelayer = "1"
BBFILE_PRIORITY_workspacelayer = "99"
LAYERSERIES_COMPAT_workspacelayer = "${LAYERSERIES_COMPAT_core}"
```

If we remember what was discussed in Section 3.4.6, the above
content is just the definition of a new layer; in fact, if we take a look at our
bblayers.conf, we get the following content:

```
$ cat conf/bblayers.conf
...
BBLAYERS += "${BSPDIR}/sources/meta-virtualization"
BBLAYERS += "/home/giometti/yocto/imx-yocto-bsp/sources/meta-engicam-n
xp"
BBLAYERS += "/home/giometti/yocto/imx-yocto-bsp/imx8mp-build/workspace"
```

As we can see, a new line has been added at the end of the file to add the new workspace to the BBLAYERS list. In this manner, we tell the Yocto build system to consider all recipes added in the devtool's workspace, which ultimately is a new layer.

Readers should notice that this new layer has the priority set to 99, which is the highest, and so, in this manner, any recipe placed here is used to generate the new images.

In order to better understand how the workspace works and what it holds, let's add some example recipes; for example, with the add subcommand we add a new recipe (which should not exist) to the workspace:

```
$ devtool add -h
NOTE: Starting bitbake server...
usage: devtool add [-h] [--same-dir | --no-same-dir] [--fetch URI]
                   [--npm-dev] [--version VERSION] [--no-git]
                   [--srcrev SRCREV | --autorev] [--srcbranch SRCBRANCH]
                   [--binary] [--also-native] [--src-subdir SUBDIR]
                   [--mirrors] [--provides PROVIDES]
                   [recipename] [srctree] [fetchuri]

Adds a new recipe to the workspace to build a specified source tree. Can
optionally fetch a remote URI and unpack it to create the source tree.

arguments:
  recipename            Name for new recipe to add (just name - no
                        version, path or extension). If not specified,
                        will attempt to auto-detect it.
  srctree               Path to external source tree. If not specified,
                        a subdirectory of /home/giometti/yocto/imx-yocto
                        -bsp/imx8mp-build/workspace/sources will be
                        used.
  fetchuri              Fetch the specified URI and extract it to create
                        the source tree

options:
  -h, --help            show this help message and exit
  --same-dir, -s        Build in same directory as source
  --no-same-dir         Force build in a separate build directory
  --fetch URI, -f URI   Fetch the specified URI and extract it to create
                        the source tree (deprecated - pass as positional
                        argument instead)
```

```
--npm-dev               For npm, also fetch devDependencies
--version VERSION, -V VERSION
                        Version to use within recipe (PV)
--no-git, -g            If fetching source, do not set up source tree as
                        a git repository
--srcrev SRCREV, -S SRCREV
                        Source revision to fetch if fetching from an SCM
                        such as git (default latest)
--autorev, -a           When fetching from a git repository, set SRCREV
                        in the recipe to a floating revision instead of
                        fixed
--srcbranch SRCBRANCH, -B SRCBRANCH
                        Branch in source repository if fetching from an
                        SCM such as git (default master)
--binary, -b            Treat the source tree as something that should
                        be installed verbatim (no compilation, same
                        directory structure). Useful with binary
                        packages e.g. RPMs.
--also-native           Also add native variant (i.e. support building
                        recipe for the build host as well as the target
                        machine)
--src-subdir SUBDIR     Specify subdirectory within source tree to use
--mirrors               Enable PREMIRRORS and MIRRORS for source tree
                        fetching (disable by default).
--provides PROVIDES, -p PROVIDES
                        Specify an alias for the item provided by the
                        recipe. E.g. virtual/libgl
```

The command is quite complex and complete, but to make a simple example about how to add a new recipe, we can take a public project as NetTest at https://github.com/giometti/nettest. This is a simple project implementing a couple of client/server programs to test and analyze network connectivity and loops; the two programs are named nettestc (the client) and nettests (the server).

To add this code into our workspace, we can use the command below:

```
$ devtool add nettest https://github.com/giometti/nettest.git
NOTE: Starting bitbake server...
INFO: Fetching git://github.com/giometti/nettest.git;protocol=https;bra
nch=master...
...
Build Configuration:
BB_VERSION          = "2.0.0"
```

```
BUILD_SYS              = "x86_64-linux"
NATIVELSBSTRING        = "universal"
TARGET_SYS             = "aarch64-poky-linux"
MACHINE                = "imx8mp-icore"
DISTRO                 = "fsl-imx-xwayland"
DISTRO_VERSION         = "5.15-kirkstone"
TUNE_FEATURES          = "aarch64 armv8a crc crypto"
TARGET_FPU             = ""
meta
meta-poky              = "HEAD:24a3f7b3648185e33133f5d96b184a6cb6524f3d"
meta-oe
meta-multimedia
meta-python            = "HEAD:744a4b6eda88b9a9ca1cf0df6e18be384d9054e3"
...
meta-engicam-nxp       = "kirkstone:983ed77473c8567045d88165a33c81c4ac8b4
e89"
workspace              = "<unknown>:<unknown>"
...
INFO: Using default source tree path /home/giometti/yocto/imx-yocto-bsp
/imx8mp-build/workspace/sources/nettest
INFO: Using source tree as build directory since that would be the defa
ult for this recipe
INFO: Recipe /home/giometti/yocto/imx-yocto-bsp/imx8mp-build/workspace/
recipes/nettest/nettest_git.bb has been automatically created; further
editing may be required to make it fully functional
```

As we can see, the devtool output is quite similar to the bitbake one
where we have an abstract of the current build configuration and source
status (in the next outputs, we do not report all these stuff due to space
reasons).

The devtool add command may not automatically determine the
correct recipe name or release. In this case, the rename subcommand is
useful, as reported within its usage message:

```
$ devtool rename -h
NOTE: Starting bitbake server...
usage: devtool rename [-h] [--version VERSION] [--no-srctree]
                      recipename [newname]

Renames the recipe file for a recipe in the workspace, changing the name
or version part or both, ensuring that all references within the
workspace are updated at the same time. Only works when the recipe file
itself is in the workspace, e.g. after devtool add. Particularly useful
when devtool add did not automatically determine the correct name.
```

```
arguments:
  recipename              Current name of recipe to rename
  newname                 New name for recipe (optional, not needed if you
                          only want to change the version)

options:
  -h, --help              show this help message and exit
  --version VERSION, -V VERSION
                          Change the version (NOTE: this does not change
                          the version fetched by the recipe, just the
                          version in the recipe file name)
  --no-srctree, -s        Do not rename the source tree directory (if the
                          default source tree path has been used) -
                          keeping the old name may be desirable if there
                          are internal/other external references to this
                          path
```

On the other hand, by using the subcommand modify, we can alter the source for an existing recipe by extracting the source being fetched by the recipe into a Git tree, so we can work on it:

```
$ devtool modify -h
NOTE: Starting bitbake server...
usage: devtool modify [-h] [--wildcard] [--extract | --no-extract]
                      [--same-dir | --no-same-dir] [--branch BRANCH]
                      [--no-overrides] [--keep-temp]
                      recipename [srctree]

Sets up the build environment to modify the source for an existing
recipe. The default behaviour is to extract the source being fetched by
the recipe into a git tree so you can work on it; alternatively, if you
already have your own pre-prepared source tree you can specify
-n/--no-extract.

arguments:
  recipename              Name of existing recipe to edit (just name - no
                          version, path or extension)
  srctree                 Path to external source tree. If not specified,
                          a subdirectory of /home/giometti/yocto/imx-yocto
                          -bsp/imx8mp-build/workspace/sources will be
                          used.

options:
  -h, --help              show this help message and exit
  --wildcard, -w          Use wildcard for unversioned bbappend
  --extract, -x           Extract source for recipe (default)
```

160

```
--no-extract, -n       Do not extract source, expect it to exist
--same-dir, -s         Build in same directory as source
--no-same-dir          Force build in a separate build directory
--branch BRANCH, -b BRANCH
                       Name for development branch to checkout (when
                       not using -n/--no-extract) (default "devtool")
--no-overrides, -O     Do not create branches for other override
                       configurations
--keep-temp            Keep temporary directory (for debugging)
```

A usage command can be the following, where we ask devtool to modify the existing recipe devmem2:

```
$ devtool modify devmem2
...
INFO: Source tree extracted to /home/giometti/yocto/imx-yocto-bsp/imx8m
p-build/workspace/sources/devmem2
INFO: Using source tree as build directory since that would be the defa
ult for this recipe
INFO: Recipe devmem2 now set up to build from /home/giometti/yocto/imx-
yocto-bsp/imx8mp-build/workspace/sources/devmem2
```

Readers should note two interesting option arguments. The first is --no-extract (or -n) which can be used to specify that we expect the source code to already exist, instead of the default behavior of checking out a fresh copy. For example:

```
$ devtool modify --no-extract devmem2 ~/develop/devmem2
```

Here, we specify that sources for devmem2 are already present under the ~/develop/devmem2 directory, so the build system has nothing to extract.

The second fascinating option argument is --same-dir (or -s) which can be used to force the build directory to be the same as the source one.

To verify that all recipes have been imported in the workspace, we can use the status subcommand:

```
$ devtool status
NOTE: Starting bitbake server...
devmem2: /home/giometti/yocto/imx-yocto-bsp/imx8mp-build/workspace/sour
ces/devmem2
nettest: /home/giometti/yocto/imx-yocto-bsp/imx8mp-build/workspace/sour
ces/nettest (/home/giometti/yocto/imx-yocto-bsp/imx8mp-build/workspace/
recipes/nettest/nettest_git.bb)
```

For the package devmem2 is reported the directory where sources
are located, while for nettest we also have (between parentheses) the
location of the newly created recipe. This information can also be retrieved
by taking a look at the new files created within the workspace subdirectory:

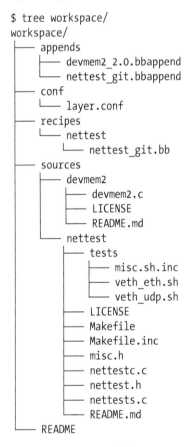

```
$ tree workspace/
workspace/
├── appends
│   ├── devmem2_2.0.bbappend
│   └── nettest_git.bbappend
├── conf
│   └── layer.conf
├── recipes
│   └── nettest
│       └── nettest_git.bb
├── sources
│   ├── devmem2
│   │   ├── devmem2.c
│   │   ├── LICENSE
│   │   └── README.md
│   └── nettest
│       ├── tests
│       │   ├── misc.sh.inc
│       │   ├── veth_eth.sh
│       │   └── veth_udp.sh
│       ├── LICENSE
│       ├── Makefile
│       ├── Makefile.inc
│       ├── misc.h
│       ├── nettestc.c
│       ├── nettest.h
│       ├── nettests.c
│       └── README.md
└── README

8 directories, 19 files
```

The above output shows perfectly the workspace directory structure:

- attic (actually not reported here, but that we can see further in this book) is a backup directory created by devtool when it needs to preserve anything when the command devtool reset has been used.

- conf is the configuration directory that contains the layer.conf file.

- appends is the directory that contains the append files (.bbappend) which point to the external sources.

- recipes is the directory containing recipes, a folder for each directory added whose name matches that of the added recipe. devtool places the corresponding recipe file (.bb) within that subdirectory.

- sources is the directory containing a working copy of the source files used when building the recipe, a folder for each set of source files matched to a corresponding recipe (note that, as reported in the usage messages, this is the default directory used as the location of the source tree when we do not provide a source tree path).

Remembering the output of subcommands add and modify, we can see that under the sources directory there are the two directories named nettest and devmem2, where the sources have been placed. Then under appends there are the two directories where the append files which define the external sources are placed. If we take a look at what these files hold, we can see something as follows:

```
$ cat workspace/appends/devmem2_2.0.bbappend
FILESEXTRAPATHS:prepend := "${THISDIR}/${PN}:"
FILESPATH:prepend := "/home/giometti/yocto/imx-yocto-bsp/imx8mp-build/w
orkspace/sources/devmem2/oe-local-files:"
# srctreebase: /home/giometti/yocto/imx-yocto-bsp/imx8mp-build/workspac
e/sources/devmem2
```

```
inherit externalsrc
# NOTE: We use pn- overrides here to avoid affecting multiple variants
in the case where the recipe uses BBCLASSEXTEND
EXTERNALSRC:pn-devmem2 = "/home/giometti/yocto/imx-yocto-bsp/imx8mp-bui
ld/workspace/sources/devmem2"
EXTERNALSRC_BUILD:pn-devmem2 = "/home/giometti/yocto/imx-yocto-bsp/imx8
mp-build/workspace/sources/devmem2"

# initial_rev: 5b395a946894eb4f4ef5d07c80a50a88573a541e
```

These files use the variables FILESEXTRAPATHS and FILESPATH to extend the search path the Yocto build system uses when looking for files and patches when it processes recipes and append files (see Section 5.3.4 for further information about these variables). Moreover, variables EXTERNALSRC and EXTERNALSRC_BUILD (with the special overriding pn- described in Section 5.3.1), defined in the class externalsrc, are used to support building software from source code that is external to the Yocto build system.

Building software from an external source tree means that the build system's normal fetch, unpack, and patch process is not used, which is the case when we use devtool's workspace.

As we can see further in Chapter 6, by default, the Yocto build system uses the S and B variables to locate unpacked recipe source code and to build it, respectively. However, when our recipe inherits the externalsrc class, then we use the EXTERNALSRC and EXTERNALSRC_BUILD variables in place of S and B, respectively.

By default, the B directory is set as ${WORKDIR}/${BPN}-{PV}/, which is separate from the source directory S. On the other hand, this class expects the source code to support recipe builds that use the B variable to point to the directory in which the Yocto build system places the generated objects built from the recipes.

As a last note, we should see that under `recipes` there is only the newly created recipe for `nettest`, while there is no recipe for `devmem2`. This is because `devtool` uses the original recipe. To prove it, we can use the subcommand `edit-recipe` to alter devmem2's recipe and verify that, in this case, the original recipe is modified. The usage message for the `edit-recipe` subcommand is reported below:

```
$ devtool edit-recipe -h
NOTE: Starting bitbake server...
usage: devtool edit-recipe [-h] [--any-recipe] recipename

Runs the default editor (as specified by the EDITOR variable) on the
specified recipe. Note that this will be quicker for recipes in the
workspace as the cache does not need to be loaded in that case.

arguments:
  recipename          Recipe to edit

options:
  -h, --help          show this help message and exit
  --any-recipe, -a  Does nothing (exists for backwards-compatibility)
```

So we can invoke it as shown below:

```
$ devtool edit-recipe devmem2
```

If everything works well, we should see something as below:

```
SUMMARY = "Simple program to read/write from/to any location in memory"
LICENSE = "GPL-2.0-or-later"
LIC_FILES_CHKSUM = "file://devmem2.c;endline=38;md5=a9eb9f3890384519f43
5aedf986297cf"

SRC_URI = git://github.com/denix0/devmem2.git;protocol=https;branch=mai
n"
SRCREV = "5b395a946894eb4f4ef5d07c80a50a88573a541e"

S = "${WORKDIR}/git"

CFLAGS += "-DFORCE_STRICT_ALIGNMENT"

do_compile() {
    ${CC} -o devmem2 devmem2.c ${CFLAGS} ${LDFLAGS}
}
```

```
do_install() {
    install -d ${D}${bindir}
    install devmem2 ${D}${bindir}
}
```

Now we can alter a bit the recipe, for example, by dropping the `Simple` word from the SUMMARY variable as below:

```
SUMMARY = "Program to read/write from/to any location in memory"
```

If we save the file with this modification, we can check that the recipe under the layer `meta-openembedded/meta-oe` has been modified:

```
$ git -C ../sources/meta-openembedded/meta-oe/ diff
diff --git a/meta-oe/recipes-support/devmem2/devmem2_2.0.bb b/meta-oe/r
ecipes-support/devmem2/devmem2_2.0.bb
index aee6bfe3d..07f99e43c 100644
--- a/meta-oe/recipes-support/devmem2/devmem2_2.0.bb
+++ b/meta-oe/recipes-support/devmem2/devmem2_2.0.bb
@@ -1,4 +1,4 @@
-SUMMARY = "Simple program to read/write from/to any location in memory"
+SUMMARY = "Program to read/write from/to any location in memory"
 LICENSE = "GPL-2.0-or-later"
 LIC_FILES_CHKSUM =
"file://devmem2.c;endline=38;md5=a9eb9f3890384519f435aedf986297cf"
```

In this case, if we alter the original recipe, and we wish to keep all modifications within a separate layer (e.g., our layer), we can do a `.bbappend` file where we put all modifications.

4.5.2 Inspecting Recipes

Besides `add` and `modify`, to work on a recipe, we can also use the `upgrade` subcommand:

```
$ devtool upgrade -h
NOTE: Starting bitbake server...
usage: devtool upgrade [-h] [--version VERSION] [--srcrev SRCREV]
                       [--srcbranch SRCBRANCH] [--branch BRANCH]
                       [--no-patch]
                       [--no-overrides] [--same-dir | --no-same-dir]
                       [--keep-temp] [--keep-failure]
                       recipename [srctree]
```

Upgrades an existing recipe to a new upstream version. Puts the upgraded recipe file into the workspace along with any associated files, and extracts the source tree to a specified location (in case patches need rebasing or adding to as a result of the upgrade).

arguments:
```
  recipename              Name of recipe to upgrade (just name - no
                          version, path or extension)
  srctree                 Path to where to extract the source tree. If not
                          specified, a subdirectory of  /home/giometti/yoc
                          to/imx-yocto-bsp/imx8mp-build/workspace/sources
                          will be used.
```

options:
```
  -h, --help              show this help message and exit
  --version VERSION, -V VERSION
                          Version to upgrade to (PV). If omitted, latest
                          upstream version will be determined and used, if
                          possible.
  --srcrev SRCREV, -S SRCREV
                          Source revision to upgrade to (useful when
                          Fetching from an SCM such as git)
  --srcbranch SRCBRANCH, -B SRCBRANCH
                          Branch in source repository containing the
                          revision to use (if fetching from an SCM such as
                          git)
  --branch BRANCH, -b BRANCH
                          Name for new development branch to checkout
                          (default "devtool")
  --no-patch              Do not apply patches from the recipe to the new
                          source code
  --no-overrides, -O      Do not create branches for other override
                          configurations
  --same-dir, -s          Build in same directory as source
  --no-same-dir           Force build in a separate build directory
  --keep-temp             Keep temporary directory (for debugging)
  --keep-failure          Keep failed upgrade recipe and associated files
                          (for debugging)
```

The usage is quite trivial, and we suggest seeing Section 11.2 for some usage examples. However, strictly related to this subcommand are the latest-version and check-upgrade-status ones, where the former can be used to inspect for new releases of a package:

```
$ devtool latest-version -h
NOTE: Starting bitbake server...
usage: devtool latest-version [-h] recipename

Queries the upstream server for what the latest upstream release is (for
git, tags are checked, for tarballs, a list of them is obtained, and one
with the highest version number is reported)

arguments:
  recipename  Name of recipe to query (just name - no version, path or
              extension)
...
```

This subcommand can be used to inspect a single recipe, as shown in the example below:

```
$ devtool latest-version dropbear
...
INFO: Current version: 2020.81
INFO: Latest version: 2022.83
```

while with check-upgrade-status we can inspect more than one recipe:

```
$ devtool check-upgrade-status -h
NOTE: Starting bitbake server...
usage: devtool check-upgrade-status [-h] [--all] [recipe ...]

Prints a table of recipes together with versions currently provided by
recipes, and latest upstream versions, when there is a later version available

arguments:
  recipe     Name of the recipe to report (omit to report upgrade info
             for all recipes)

options:
  -h, --help  show this help message and exit
  --all, -a   Show all recipes, not just recipes needing upgrade
```

An example usage to check two recipes is reported below:

```
$ devtool check-upgrade-status -a dropbear i2c-tools
...
INFO: dropbear   2020.81    2022.83   Yi Zhao <yi.zhao@windriver.com>
INFO: i2c-tools  4.3        MATCH     Anuj Mittal <anuj.mittal@intel.com>
```

Note that without the -a option argument, then just the `dropbear` entry will be displayed due to the fact the `i2c-tools` package is already at its latest release.

Readers should note that at the time they read this text the tool can be released in a new version, and it means that the above output may vary.

To search for available recipes by matching on recipe name, package name, description, and installed files, we can use the `search` subcommand:

```
$ devtool search -h
NOTE: Starting bitbake server...
usage: devtool search [-h] keyword

Searches for available recipes. Matches on recipe name, package name,
description and installed files, and prints the recipe name and summary
on match.

arguments:
  keyword     Keyword to search for (regular expression syntax allowed,
              use quotes to avoid shell expansion)
...
```

For example, a simple usage to search for something related to the I2C bus is reported below:

```
$ devtool search i2c
...
linux-libc-headers    Sanitized set of kernel headers for the C library
's use
libinput              Library to handle input devices in Wayland compos
itors
imx-test              Test programs for i.MX BSP
powertop              Power usage tool
i2c-tools             Set of i2c tools for linux
...
```

Note that this command is really basic, and to do better file searches within recipes is better using the command `oe-pkgdata-util` explained in the next section.

Once a recipe name has been found, we can use the `find-recipe` subcommand to locate the relative recipe file:

```
$ devtool find-recipe i2c-tools
...
/home/giometti/yocto/imx-yocto-bsp/sources/poky/meta/recipes-devtools/i
2c-tools/i2c-tools_4.3.bb
```

Then we can go into the recipe's directory to inspect it.

4.5.3 Building and Testing the Code

We have already seen the `edit-recipe` subcommand to alter the recipe file for a package; however, when all needed modifications are in place, we can use the `build` subcommand to try to build our new package:

```
$ devtool build -h
NOTE: Starting bitbake server...
usage: devtool build [-h] [-s] [-c] recipename

Builds the specified recipe using bitbake (up to and including
do_populate_sysroot, do_packagedata)

arguments:
  recipename            Recipe to build

options:
  -h, --help            show this help message and exit
  -s, --disable-parallel-make
                        Disable make parallelism
  -c, --clean           clean up recipe building results
```

So, for example, to build the NetTest tools, we can use the following command:

```
$ devtool build nettest
...
NOTE: nettest: compiling from external source tree /home/giometti/yocto
/imx-yocto-bsp/imx8mp-build/workspace/sources/nettest
NOTE: Tasks Summary: Attempted 730 tasks of which 722 didn't need to be
 rerun and all succeeded.
```

If we take a look at the sources' directory, we notice two special directories named oe-workdir and oe-logs:

```
$ cd /home/giometti/yocto/imx-yocto-bsp/imx8mp-build
$ ls workspace/sources/nettest
LICENSE        README.md  nettestc    nettestc.o  nettests.d  oe-workdir
Makefile       misc.h     nettestc.c  nettests    nettests.o  tests
Makefile.inc   nettest.h  nettestc.d  nettests.c  oe-logs
```

Within oe-logs we find all log files generated during the build, while within oe-workdir we can find all building results. However, in this example, we can note that something goes wrong; in fact, under oe-workdir there are no executables, and the only ones are located within the sources' directory:

```
$ find -L workspace/sources/nettest -executable -a -name 'nettest?'
workspace/sources/nettest/nettests
workspace/sources/nettest/nettestc
```

Moreover, by looking carefully, we also notice that they are in the wrong format:

```
$ file workspace/sources/nettest/nettest?
workspace/sources/nettest/nettestc: ELF 64-bit LSB pie executable, x86-
/home/giometti/yocto/imx-yocto-bsp/imx8mp-build
64, version 1 (SYSV), dynamically linked, interpreter /lib64/ld-linux-x
86-64.so.2, BuildID[sha1]=1265dff47c9e15a019fa7dc6c92b4783519a6687, for
 GNU/Linux 3.2.0, with debug_info, not stripped
workspace/sources/nettest/nettests: ELF 64-bit LSB pie executable, x86-
64, version 1 (SYSV), dynamically linked, interpreter /lib64/ld-linux-x
86-64.so.2, BuildID[sha1]=b0ae20314e4bb412bf40237fba1a8b8f0f14876a, for
 GNU/Linux 3.2.0, with debug_info, not stripped
```

So we have to fix the recipe! To do so, we have to use the `edit-recipe` subcommand as explained above:

```
$ devtool edit-recipe nettest
```

The recipe must be changed as below to do a proper executables' installation, or nothing will be moved into `oe-workdir`:

```
--- workspace/recipes/nettest/nettest_git.bb
+++ workspace/recipes/nettest/nettest_git.bb
@@ -30,8 +30,7 @@
 }

 do_install () {
-        # NOTE: unable to determine what to put here - there is a Makefile
            but no
-        # target named "install", so you will need to define this yourself
-        :
+        install -d ${D}${bindir}
+        install nettestc nettests ${D}${bindir}/
 }
```

However, this is not enough; in fact, if we try to build the code, an error will occur telling us that the wrong machine format has been generated. The error should be something as below:

```
Subprocess output:aarch64-poky-linux-objcopy: Unable to recognize the f
ormat of the input file `/home/giometti/yocto/imx-yocto-bsp/imx8mp-buil
d/tmp/work/armv8a-poky-linux/nettest/1.0+git999-r0/package/usr/bin/nett
estc'
```

To resolve this issue, we have to alter the NetTest's sources as reported below:

```
--- a/Makefile.inc
+++ b/Makefile.inc
@@ -3,8 +3,6 @@ all: $(TARGETS)
 VERSION := $(shell git describe --tags --abbrev=10 \
                          --dirty --long --always 2> /dev/null || \
                                echo "v0.0.0")
-CC := $(CROSS_COMPILE)gcc
-AR := $(CROSS_COMPILE)ar
 CFLAGS += -O2 -Wall -D_GNU_SOURCE -D__VERSION=\"$(VERSION)\"
 CFLAGS += -MMD     # automatic .d dependency file generation
 ifneq ($(DYNAMIC),y)
```

> Readers should not worry about what these steps do in detail, since this is just an introduction to `devtool`. All these aspects will be better explained starting from Chapter 9 and following.

Now, before recompiling the code, it is better to clean up the preceding building results by using the `-c` option argument, as shown below:

```
$ devtool build -c nettest
```

This will remove all files in the wrong format, and then we have to recompile again with the usual `build` subcommand. Now everything should be in the right place and in the right format; in particular, we have the structure under `oe-workdir` reflecting whatever should be installed in the final root filesystem image:

```
$ tree workspace/sources/nettest/oe-workdir/image/
workspace/sources/nettest/oe-workdir/image/
└── usr
    └── bin
        ├── nettestc
        └── nettests

2 directories, 2 files
```

These files can now be moved within our development kit to be executed. However, in order to be sure to pull whatever is needed in the right place, we can still use `devtool` to deploy all package files directly on the target over SSH with the `deploy-target` subcommand:

```
$ devtool deploy-target -h
NOTE: Starting bitbake server...
usage: devtool deploy-target [-h] [-c] [-s] [-n] [-p] [--no-check-space]
                             [-e SSH_EXEC] [-P PORT] [-I KEY]
                             [-S | --no-strip]
                             recipename target

Deploys a recipe's build output (i.e. the output of the do_install task)
to a live target machine over ssh. By default, any existing files will
be preserved instead of being overwritten and will be restored if you
run devtool undeploy-target. Note: this only deploys the recipe itself.
```

and not any runtime dependencies, so it is assumed that those have been
installed on the target beforehand.

```
arguments:
  recipename              Recipe to deploy
  target                  Live target machine running an ssh server:
                          user@hostname[:destdir]

options:
  -h, --help              show this help message and exit
  -c, --no-host-check     Disable ssh host key checking
  -s, --show-status       Show progress/status output
  -n, --dry-run           List files to be deployed only
  -p, --no-preserve       Do not preserve existing files
  --no-check-space        Do not check for available space before
                          deploying
  -e SSH_EXEC, --ssh-exec SSH_EXEC
                          Executable to use in place of ssh
  -P PORT, --port PORT    Specify port to use for connection to the target
  -I KEY, --key KEY       Specify ssh private key for connection to the
                          target
  -S, --strip             Strip executables prior to deploying (default:
                          False).
                          The default value of this option can be
                          controlled setting the strip option in the
                          [Deploy] section to True or False.
  --no-strip              Do not strip executables prior to deploy
```

This command is powerful, and it will be extensively used in Chapter 9.

On the other hand, to remove all deployed files from the target and to
restore the target as before, we can use (as already suggested within the
above message) the undeploy-target:

```
$ devtool undeploy-target -h
NOTE: Starting bitbake server...
usage: devtool undeploy-target [-h] [-c] [-s] [-a] [-n] [-e SSH_EXEC]
                               [-P PORT] [-I KEY]
                               [recipename] target
```

Un-deploys recipe output files previously deployed to a live target
machine by devtool deploy-target.

```
arguments:
  recipename              Recipe to undeploy (if not using -a/--all)
  target                  Live target machine running an ssh server:
                          user@hostname
options:
  -h, --help              show this help message and exit
  -c, --no-host-check     Disable ssh host key checking
  -s, --show-status       Show progress/status output
  -a, --all               Undeploy all recipes deployed on the target
  -n, --dry-run           List files to be undeployed only
  -e SSH_EXEC, --ssh-exec SSH_EXEC
                          Executable to use in place of ssh
  -P PORT, --port PORT    Specify port to use for connection to the target
  -I KEY, --key KEY       Specify ssh private key for connection to the
                          target
```

Readers should notice here that to correctly use these commands, two requirements must be accomplished:

1) For new recipes (that are not added in the workspace by the modify subcommand), we must be sure all building dependencies are present within our Yocto Project. These dependencies must be added in the DEPENDS variable as shown in several parts of Chapter 9 and following.

2) For recipes having runtime dependencies, we must be sure that these packages exist on the target hardware before attempting to run the application (e.g., by using the deploy-target subcommand). If dependent packages (as libraries, for instance) do not exist on the target, our application will fail when run.

The advantage of using these two commands, instead of moving all files by hand, is that in this manner we mimic whatever the build system will do when the tool will be installed into a Yocto image, and then we are sure that everything is done correctly.

In the case where we cannot simply deploy our package on the target by moving files (e.g., because we are modifying the kernel or the bootloaders), we can use the `build-image` subcommand:

```
$ devtool build-image -h
NOTE: Starting bitbake server...
usage: devtool build-image [-h] [-p PACKAGES] [imagename]

Builds an image, extending it to include packages from recipes in the
workspace

arguments:
  imagename               Image recipe to build

options:
  -h, --help              show this help message and exit
  -p PACKAGES, --add-packages PACKAGES
                          Instead of adding packages for the entire
                          workspace, specify packages to be added to the
                          image (separate multiple packages by commas)
```

The usage of this command is trivial, and readers may take a look at Sections 8.2 and 8.4 for several usage examples; however, we should note the -p option arguments which can be used to specify a comma-separated list of packages to be added to the newly generated image. This can be very useful in the case that not all packages of our workspace are ready to be tested or compiled, and we prefer not to include them in the building.

4.5.4 Finalizing the Job

Once our job is finished, we can remove a recipe from the workspace and simply drop all modifications (maybe because we are not happy about what we have done), by using the `reset` subcommand:

```
$ devtool reset -h
NOTE: Starting bitbake server...
usage: devtool reset [-h] [--all] [--no-clean] [--remove-work]
                     [recipename ...]

Removes the specified recipe(s) from your workspace (resetting its state
                     back to that defined by the metadata).

arguments:
  recipename         Recipe to reset

options:
  -h, --help         show this help message and exit
  --all, -a          Reset all recipes (clear workspace)
  --no-clean, -n     Don't clean the sysroot to remove recipe output
  --remove-work, -r  Clean the sources directory along with append
```

On the other hand, if we are happy about what we have done, we can save our job within the original layer or in a new one, maybe by using the --append option argument to create an append file into our another layer (this technique will be widely used later in this book due to the fact that it allows to encapsulate all customization within our custom layer), by using the update-recipe subcommand:

```
$ devtool update-recipe -h
NOTE: Starting bitbake server...
usage: devtool update-recipe [-h] [--mode MODE] [--initial-rev INITIAL_REV]
                             [--append LAYERDIR] [--wildcard-version]
                             [--no-remove] [--no-overrides] [--dry-run]
                             [--force-patch-refresh]
                             recipename

Applies changes from external source tree to a recipe
(updating/adding/removing patches as necessary, or by updating SRCREV).
Note that these changes need to have been committed to the git
repository in order to be recognised.

arguments:
  recipename           Name of recipe to update

options:
  -h, --help           show this help message and exit
  --mode MODE, -m MODE Update mode (where MODE is patch, srcrev, auto;
                       default is auto)
```

```
--initial-rev INITIAL_REV
                     Override starting revision for patches
--append LAYERDIR, -a LAYERDIR
                     Write changes to a bbappend in the specified
                     layer instead of the recipe
--wildcard-version, -w
                     In conjunction with -a/--append, use a wildcard
                     to make the bbappend apply to any recipe version
--no-remove, -n      Don't remove patches, only add or update
--no-overrides, -O   Do not handle other override branches (if they
                     exist)
--dry-run, -N        Dry-run (just report changes instead of writing
                     them)
--force-patch-refresh
                     Update patches in the layer even if they have
                     not been modified (useful for refreshing patch
                     context)
```

As we can read within the usage message above, all our changes need to have been committed to the Git repository to be recognized. In fact, if we take a look at the nettest working directory in the workspace, we should note that a new devtool branch has been created:

```
$ cd workspace/sources/nettest/
$ git status
On branch devtool
nothing to commit, working tree clean
```

Furthermore, a new tag devtool-base is used to mark the latest original commit:

```
$ git log --decorate --oneline -1
faf8744 (HEAD -> devtool, tag: v1.0, tag: devtool-base, origin/master, o
rigin/HEAD, master) Add README file
```

All these marks are used by devtool to detect all modifications we wish to add to a source code so that it can create a patch set once we use the update-recipe subcommand (see Chapter 8 and following for practical usages).

Readers should note that in the case the remote kernel is patched by supplemental patches added to the SRC_URI variable, then the tag devtool-patched is also used to keep track of these modifications. For example, in the case we have the linux-renesas.bb recipe holding the following setting:

```
KERNEL_URL="git://github.com/renesas-rz/rz_linux-cip.git"
SRC_URI = " \
    ${KERNEL_URL};protocol=https;nocheckout=1;branch=${BRANCH} \
    file://touch.cfg \
    file://0001-arm64-renesas-add-support-for-HCE-Engineering-A55-
VA.patch \
    "
Then, once we execute the devtool modify linux-renesas command we
get the following tags:
$ git log --oneline
ebe7ce7bd (HEAD -> rz-5.10-cip41, tag: devtool-patched) arm64 rene
sas: add support for HCE Engineering A55-VAL board
eeca3e330 (grafted, tag: devtool-base, origin/rz-5.10-cip41, devto
ol) drm: rcar-du: rcar_du_crtc: add condition for RZ/G2L's PLL set
ting
...
```

Here, the devtool-base tag is placed at the Git repository HEAD, while the devtool-patched tag is placed on the last applied .patch file.

However, even if it is better to know that these tags exist and what they are used for, all these aspects are masked by the devtool update-recipe subcommand, and developers may overlook them.

If we have to commit changes to a specified layer, we can also use the `finish` subcommand that, as we can see below, is equivalent to an update-recipe followed by the `reset` subcommand:

```
$ devtool finish -h
NOTE: Starting bitbake server...
usage: devtool finish [-h] [--mode MODE] [--initial-rev INITIAL_REV]
                      [--force]
                      [--remove-work] [--no-clean] [--no-overrides]
                      [--dry-run] [--force-patch-refresh]
                      recipename destination

Pushes any committed changes to the specified recipe to the specified
layer and remove it from your workspace. Roughly equivalent to an
update-recipe followed by reset, except the update-recipe step will do
the "right thing" depending on the recipe and the destination layer
specified. Note that your changes must have been committed to the git
repository in order to be recognised.

arguments:
  recipename              Recipe to finish
  destination             Layer/path to put recipe into. Can be the name
                          of a layer configured in your bblayers.conf, the
                          path to the base of a layer, or a partial path
                          inside a layer.
                          devtool finish will attempt to complete the path
                          based on the layer's structure.

options:
  -h, --help              show this help message and exit
  --mode MODE, -m MODE    Update mode (where MODE is patch, srcrev, auto;
                          default is auto)
  --initial-rev INITIAL_REV
                          Override starting revision for patches
  --force, -f             Force continuing even if there are uncommitted
                          changes in the source tree repository
  --remove-work, -r       Clean the sources directory under workspace
  --no-clean, -n          Don't clean the sysroot to remove recipe output
  --no-overrides, -O      Do not handle other override branches (if they
                          exist)
  --dry-run, -N           Dry-run (just report changes instead of writing
                          them)
  --force-patch-refresh
                          Update patches in the layer even if they have
                          not been modified (useful for refreshing patch
                          context)
```

By providing a specific `destination` (i.e., a name of a layer in `bblayers.conf`, a partial path inside a layer, or a complete path name), we can commit our changes in a custom layer (see Chapter 9 and following for practical usages).

4.5.5 Configuring the Code

If the software we are altering uses a configuration tool as GNU autoconf or the Linux's `menuconfig` tool, etc., the subcommand `configure-help` or `menuconfig` can be used to properly configure the code.

In order to understand how they can be used, we have to add new packages to our workspace. The first one is the Point-to-Point Protocol daemon:

```
$ devtool modify ppp
...
INFO: Adding local source files to srctree...
INFO: Source tree extracted to /home/giometti/yocto/imx-yocto-bsp/imx8m
p-build/workspace/sources/ppp
INFO: Using source tree as build directory since recipe inherits autoto
ols-brokensep
INFO: Recipe ppp now set up to build from /home/giometti/yocto/imx-yoct
o-bsp/imx8mp-build/workspace/sources/ppp
```

Note that the `autotools-brokensep` class is for recipes where a separate build directory doesn't work, while standard autotools supports this.

This tool uses the `configure` script, and we can see how the Yocto build system will call it during the configuration stage (i.e., the `do_configure` task), by using the `configure-help` subcommand as shown below:

```
$ devtool configure-help --no-pager ppp
...
configure information for ppp
-----------------------------------------

Arguments currently passed to the configure script:

--build=x86_64-linux --host=aarch64-poky-linux --target=aarch64-poky-li
nux --prefix=/usr --exec_prefix=/usr --bindir=/usr/bin --sbindir=/usr/s
bin --libexecdir=/usr/libexec --datadir=/usr/share --sysconfdir=/etc --
sharedstatedir=/com --localstatedir=/var --libdir=/usr/lib --includedir
=/usr/include --oldincludedir=/usr/include --infodir=/usr/share/info --
mandir=/usr/share/man --disable-silent-rules --with-libtool-sysroot=/ho
me/giometti/yocto/imx-yocto-bsp/imx8mp-build/tmp/work/armv8a-poky-linux
/ppp/2.4.9-r0/recipe-sysroot --disable-strip --disable-static
...
Some of those are fixed. The ones that are specified through EXTRA_OECO
NF (which you can change or add to easily):

--disable-strip --disable-static

The ./configure --help output for ppp follows.
-----------------------------------------
Support for Linux has not been included
in this distribution.  Sorry.
Unable to locate kernel source
```

The --no-pager above has been used to get a suitable output for
this book; readers may avoid using it and just enable their pager tool.

First, the command gives us the arguments currently passed to the
configure script (the fixed ones and the ones we can specify through
the EXTRA_OECONF variable) and then the output of the execution of
./configure --help. Now we can add other options and see the relative
output by using the --arg option argument as below:

```
$ devtool configure-help --no-pager ppp --arg --my-opt1 --my-opt2
...
The ./configure --my-opt1 --my-opt2 output for ppp follows.
-----------------------------------------
Support for Linux has not been included
in this distribution.  Sorry.
Unable to locate kernel source
```

The `configure` script provided by the ppp package is not standard; that's the weird output.

To see how the `menuconfig` subcommand works, we have to modify another recipe that supports the `make menuconfig` command to start a Linux-like configuration menu; so let's install the BusyBox tool:

```
$ devtool modify busybox
...
INFO: Adding local source files to srctree...
INFO: Source tree extracted to /home/giometti/yocto/imx-yocto-bsp/imx8m
p-build/workspace/sources/busybox
WARNING: SRC_URI is conditionally overridden in this recipe, thus sever
al devtool-override-* branches have been created, one for each override
 that makes changes to SRC_URI. It is recommended that you make changes
 to the devtool branch first, then checkout and rebase each devtool-ove
rride-* branch and update any unique patches there (duplicates on those
 branches will be ignored by devtool finish/update-recipe)
INFO: Using source tree as build directory since that would be the defa
ult for this recipe
INFO: Recipe busybox now set up to build from /home/giometti/yocto/imx-
yocto-bsp/imx8mp-build/workspace/sources/busybox
```

The warning about the conditional overrides for the SRC_URI variable (see Section 5.3 to know what an override is) is due to the fact that it has, for example, this override in the recipe:

```
SRC_URI:append:libc-musl = " file://musl.cfg "
```

So, if this override is applied, we get different sources. The tool takes into account all these possibilities just by adding a different branch for each override as shown below:

```
$ git -C workspace/sources/busybox/ branch
* devtool
  devtool-no-overrides
  devtool-override-libc-musl
  devtool-override-toolchain-clang
  master
```

183

We can also ask devtool to not create branches for other override configurations by using the -O (or --no-overrides) option argument. This can save us from possible errors in executing the above modify subcommand.

Now if we execute the following command, the configuration menu should appear in a new window as in Figure 4-3:

```
$ devtool menuconfig busybox
```

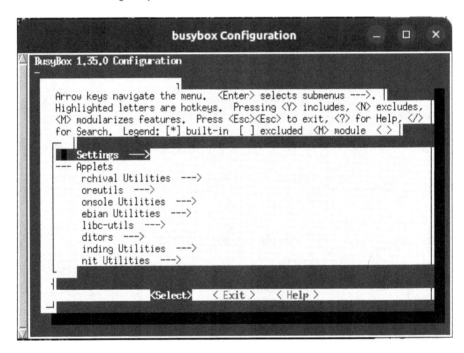

Figure 4-3. *The BusyBox's configuration menu*

Now if we try to alter the configuration (e.g., by adding the CATV feature), at the exit the above command should say the following:

```
...
INFO: Updating config fragment /home/giometti/yocto/imx-yocto-bsp/imx8m
p-build/workspace/sources/busybox/oe-local-files/devtool-fragment.cfg
```

And in the new file, we have the new configuration fragment:

```
$ cat workspace/sources/busybox/oe-local-files/devtool-fragment.cfg
# Tue Mar 19 12:39:55 2024
CONFIG_FEATURE_CATV=y
```

which is precisely the modification we have just done in the configuration.

4.5.6 Miscellaneous Commands

If we are interested in just taking a look at the code for a particular recipe, we can use the extract subcommand:

```
$ devtool extract -h
NOTE: Starting bitbake server...
usage: devtool extract [-h] [--branch BRANCH] [--no-overrides]
                       [--keep-temp]
                       recipename srctree

Extracts the source for an existing recipe

arguments:
  recipename            Name of recipe to extract the source for
  srctree               Path to where to extract the source tree

options:
  -h, --help            show this help message and exit
  --branch BRANCH, -b BRANCH
                        Name for development branch to checkout (default
                        "devtool")
  --no-overrides, -O    Do not create branches for other override
                        configurations
  --keep-temp           Keep temporary directory (for debugging)
```

It can be used on every recipe enabled in the build system even if it is not yet in the workspace; for example, to see the source code of the i2c-tools package, we can use the following command:

```
$ devtool extract i2c-tools /tmp/i2c-tools
...
INFO: Source tree extracted to /tmp/i2c-tools
```

We can also use the `sync` subcommand which is similar to the `extract` command, except it fetches the synced and patched branch to an existing git repository. This enables developers to keep tracking the upstream development while maintaining their local git repository at the same time:

```
$ devtool sync -h
NOTE: Starting bitbake server...
usage: devtool sync [-h] [--branch BRANCH] [--keep-temp] recipename
                    srctree

Synchronize the previously extracted source tree for an existing recipe

arguments:
  recipename              Name of recipe to sync the source for
  srctree                 Path to the source tree

options:
  -h, --help              show this help message and exit
  --branch BRANCH, -b BRANCH
                          Name for development branch to checkout
                          (default: devtool)
  --keep-temp             Keep temporary directory (for debugging)
                          (default: False)
```

If we wish to archive whatever we are doing to our `workspace` directory, we use the `export` subcommand:

```
$ devtool export -h
NOTE: Starting bitbake server...
usage: devtool export [-h] [--file FILE] [--overwrite]
                      [--include INCLUDE [INCLUDE ...] |
                      --exclude EXCLUDE [EXCLUDE ...]]

Export one or more recipes from current workspace into a tar archive

options:
  -h, --help              show this help message and exit
  --file FILE, -f FILE  Output archive file name
  --overwrite, -o       Overwrite previous export tar archive
  --include INCLUDE [INCLUDE ...], -i INCLUDE [INCLUDE ...]
                          Include recipes into the tar archive
  --exclude EXCLUDE [EXCLUDE ...], -e EXCLUDE [EXCLUDE ...]
                          Exclude recipes into the tar archive
```

Then we can restore them (or move to another workspace) by using the
import subcommand:

```
$ devtool import -h
NOTE: Starting bitbake server...
usage: devtool import [-h] [--overwrite] FILE

Import tar archive previously created by "devtool export" into workspace

arguments:
  FILE               Name of the tar archive to import

options:
  -h, --help         show this help message and exit
  --overwrite, -o    Overwrite files when extracting
```

Finally, if we don't have a workspace yet, and we wish to specify where
the workspace should be located, we can use the create-workspace to
locate it:

```
$ devtool create-workspace -h
NOTE: Starting bitbake server...
usage: devtool create-workspace [-h] [--create-only] [layerpath]

Sets up a new workspace. NOTE: other devtool subcommands will create a
workspace automatically as needed, so you only need to use devtool
create-workspace if you want to specify where the workspace should be
located.

arguments:
  layerpath      Path in which the workspace layer should be created

options:
  -h, --help     show this help message and exit
  --create-only  Only create the workspace layer, do not alter
                 configuration
```

In any case, as we can read in the message above and as already seen
at the beginning of this section, devtool subcommands will create a
workspace automatically as needed, and then this command is useful only
if we wish to change the default behavior.

4.6 oe-pkgdata-util

Another widely used command in this book is the oe-pkgdata-util which can be used to handle common target package tasks. Below, its usage message is reported:

```
$ oe-pkgdata-util --help
usage: oe-pkgdata-util [-h] [-d] [-p PKGDATA_DIR] <subcommand> ...

OpenEmbedded pkgdata tool - queries the pkgdata files written out during
do_package

options:
  -h, --help              show this help message and exit
  -d, --debug             Enable debug output
  -p PKGDATA_DIR, --pkgdata-dir PKGDATA_DIR
                          Path to pkgdata directory (determined
                          automatically if not specified)

subcommands:
  lookup-pkg              Translate between recipe-space package names and
                          runtime package names
  list-pkgs               List packages
  list-pkg-files          List files within a package
  lookup-recipe           Find recipe producing one or more packages
  package-info            Show version, recipe and size information for
                          one or more packages
  find-path               Find package providing a target path
  read-value              Read any pkgdata value for one or more packages
  glob                    Expand package name glob expression
Use oe-pkgdata-util <subcommand> --help to get help on a specific command
```

Readers should notice that the message says *queries the pkgdata files written out during do_package,* which means that we can inspect all packages which the do_package task has been executed for. If not, we get an error as below:

```
$ oe-pkgdata-util list-pkg-files devmem2
devmem2:
ERROR: Unable to find any built recipe-space package named devmem2
```

To know which are the built packages, we can use the `list-pkgs`
subcommand:

```
$ oe-pkgdata-util list-pkgs -h
usage: oe-pkgdata-util list-pkgs [-h] [-r] [-p RECIPE] [-u]
                                 [pkgspec ...]

Lists packages that have been built

arguments:
  pkgspec               Package name to search for (wildcards * ?
                        allowed, use quotes to avoid shell expansion)
options:
  -h, --help            show this help message and exit
  -r, --runtime         Show runtime package names instead of
                        recipe-space package names
  -p RECIPE, --recipe RECIPE
                        Limit to packages produced by the specified
                        recipe
  -u, --unpackaged      Include unpackaged (i.e. empty) packages
```

If we don't specify any package, we get the complete list; otherwise, we
can get a subset, as in the following example:

```
$ oe-pkgdata-util list-pkgs '*i2c*'
i2c-tools
i2c-tools-dbg
i2c-tools-dev
i2c-tools-doc
i2c-tools-misc
i2c-tools-src
i2c-tools-staticdev
```

Note the quotes to avoid shell expansion.

The most used subcommands for the `oe-pkgdata-util` tool are
definitely `list-pkg-files` and `find-path`. The first one is used to list files
within a package:

```
$ oe-pkgdata-util list-pkg-files -h
usage: oe-pkgdata-util list-pkg-files [-h] [-r] [-p RECIPE] [-u] [-l]
                                      [pkg ...]
```

Lists files included in one or more packages

```
arguments:
  pkg                       Package name to report on (if -p/--recipe is not
                            specified)

options:
  -h, --help                show this help message and exit
  -r, --runtime             Specified package(s) are runtime package names
                            instead of recipe-space package names
  -p RECIPE, --recipe RECIPE
                            Report on all packages produced by the specified
                            recipe
  -u, --unpackaged          Include unpackaged (i.e. empty) packages (only
                            useful with -p/--recipe)
  -l, --long                Show more information per file
```

For example, to see all installed files for the i2c-tools package with their sizes, we can use the following command line:

```
$ oe-pkgdata-util list-pkg-files -l i2c-tools
i2c-tools:
        /usr/lib/libi2c.so.0                    15
        /usr/lib/libi2c.so.0.1.1                9992
        /usr/sbin/eeprog                        18400
        /usr/sbin/i2cdetect.i2c-tools           18488
        /usr/sbin/i2cdump.i2c-tools             22584
        /usr/sbin/i2cget.i2c-tools              22584
        /usr/sbin/i2cset.i2c-tools              22584
        /usr/sbin/i2ctransfer.i2c-tools         18496
```

The second command, find-path, is used to do the inverse search, that is, to find a package providing a target path name:

```
$ oe-pkgdata-util find-path -h
usage: oe-pkgdata-util find-path [-h] targetpath

Finds the recipe-space package providing the specified target path

arguments:
  targetpath  Path to find (wildcards * ? allowed, use quotes to avoid
              shell expansion)
...
```

As an example, let's try to find which is the package providing the /usr/sbin/eeprog file in the target:

```
$ oe-pkgdata-util find-path /usr/sbin/eeprog
i2c-tools: /usr/sbin/eeprog
```

Another interesting usage for oe-pkgdata-util is with the lookup-recipe subcommand:

```
$ oe-pkgdata-util lookup-recipe -h
usage: oe-pkgdata-util lookup-recipe [-h] [-c] pkg [pkg ...]

Looks up the specified runtime package(s) to see which recipe they were
produced by

arguments:
  pkg                 Runtime package name to look up
...
```

Since in the Yocto Project it is possible that a recipe will produce more than one package (as we can see in Section 9.3), we need a way to determine which is the recipe that produces a package. For example, if we take a look at the built Python3 packages, we get quite a long list:

```
$ oe-pkgdata-util list-pkgs 'python3*'
python3-2to3
python3-asyncio
...
python3-debugger
...
python3-misc
...
python3-numpy
...
```

And if we try to find the recipe which produces, for instance, the python3-numpy, we can do as below:

```
$ find sources/ -name 'python3-numpy_*.bb'
sources/poky/meta/recipes-devtools/python/python3-numpy_1.22.3.bb
```

However, if we try to do the same for the python3-debugger package, we will find nothing:

```
$ find sources/ -name 'python3-debugger*.bb'
```

So, what can we do? To easily resolve the task, we can use the command below:

```
$ oe-pkgdata-util lookup-recipe python3-debugger
python3
```

This means that the package is generated by the python3 recipe, which is located in

```
$ find sources/ -name 'python3_*.bb'
sources/poky/meta/recipes-devtools/python/python3_3.10.7.bb
```

If we remember that by using the bitbake -e we can inspect variables, then to verify that this is the right recipe, we can check for the PACKAGES settings within the recipe as done below:

```
$ bitbake -e python3 | grep 'PACKAGES='
PACKAGES="python3-tests python3-2to3 python3-asyncio python3-audio pyth
on3-codecs python3-compile python3-compression python3-core python3-cry
pt python3-ctypes python3-curses python3-datetime python3-db python3-de
bugger python3-difflib python3-distutils-windows python3-distutils pyth
...
python3-locale python3 python3-misc python3-man"
```

And the python3-debugger is on the list.

Readers should take a look at Section 10.3 for some practical usage examples.

The other two useful subcommands we can use to inspect package information are package-info and read-value. These commands can be used to get information saved within the tmp/pkgdata/${MACHINE}/ directory in the build directory. In our case, the directory is named tmp/pkgdata/imx8mp-icore/, and if we try to read a file in the runtime subdirectory, we can see the following:

```
$ cat tmp/pkgdata/imx8mp-icore/runtime/i2c-tools
PN: i2c-tools
PV: 4.3
PR: r0
PKGV: 4.3
PKGR: r0
LICENSE: GPL-2.0-or-later
DESCRIPTION: The i2c-tools package contains a heterogeneous set of I2C
tools for Linux: a bus probing tool, a chip dumper, register-level SMBu
s access helpers, EEPROM decoding scripts, EEPROM programming tools, an
d a python module for SMBus access. All versions of Linux are supported
, as long as I2C support is included in the kernel.
SUMMARY: Set of i2c tools for linux
RDEPENDS:i2c-tools: update-alternatives-opkg glibc (>= 2.35)
SECTION: base
PKG:i2c-tools: i2c-tools
...
```

In the next chapters of this book, we are going to explain most of these variables. Moreover, curious readers about what holds the pkgdata directory and its subdirectories can take a look at the Yocto Project Documentation site at https://docs.yoctoproject.org/overview-manual/concepts.html#yocto-project-concepts.

Subcommand package-info returns by default the variables PKGV, PKGE, PKGR, PN, PV, PE, PR, and PKGSIZE, while by using read-value we can specify which variable we wish to read:

```
$ oe-pkgdata-util read-value -h
usage: oe-pkgdata-util read-value [-h] [-f FILE] [-n] [-u]
                                  valuenames [pkg ...]

Reads the named value from the pkgdata files for the specified packages

arguments:
  valuenames            Name of the value/s to look up (separated by
                        commas, no spaces)
  pkg                   Runtime package name to look up
```

```
options:
  -h, --help              show this help message and exit
  -f FILE, --file FILE    Read package names from the specified file
                          (one per line, first field only)
  -n, --prefix-name       Prefix output with package name
  -u, --unescape          Expand escapes such as \n
```

For example, we can get at once the short description and the license for the i2c-tools package by using the command below:

```
$ oe-pkgdata-util read-value SUMMARY,LICENSE i2c-tools
Set of i2c tools for linux GPL-2.0-or-later
```

However, it is usually used to get the runtime dependencies for a package:

```
$ oe-pkgdata-util read-value RDEPENDS i2c-tools
update-alternatives-opkg glibc (>= 2.35)
```

In this manner, we know that to install the i2c-tools package, we need the update-alternatives-opkg and glibc packages.

4.7 Summary

In this chapter, we have learned a lot about the Yocto tools. Now we know what the command bitbake is and how we can use it to build our code and generate packages we can install on our custom machines.

We also have learned about the bitbake-layers utility to manage the Yocto Project's meta layers, and we have seen how we can add or modify recipes by using recipetool and devtool. Then we have taken a look at other useful utilities; however, before starting to customize our Yocto Project, we require some other basic information about how bitbake manages its variables and tasks and about how a recipe is structured. That's why it's time to move on to the next chapter, where we will see more in detail how bitbake works (then in Chapter 6 we will start talking about recipes).

CHAPTER 5

BitBake Internals

In the previous chapter, we have seen an introduction of the most used (and useful) Yocto Project's tools, and we introduced the usage of the command `bitbake`. Now it's time to go deeply in understanding how this fundamental command works and how it uses its variables and how it executes its tasks.

In fact, each variable or task defined within a configuration or class file, and managed by BitBake, has its syntax which has similarities to several other languages but also has some unique features. Because the target of this book is to learn how we can customize a Yocto image by defining a new machine, adding or modifying recipes and other important actions within the Yocto environment, we need to understand how bitbake interprets these files.

5.1 Variable Management

As already seen in previous chapters, variables are the first object that every Yocto developer should know, but another significant aspect of variables is about how they can be assigned and manipulated.

However, to do so we need to execute some BitBake code easily, and to do so we can create a basic recipe where we can execute our examples. This new recipe can be placed within the Engicam layer as shown below:

```
$ cd sources/meta-engicam-nxp/recipes-core
$ mkdir cy-test
$ cat > cy-test/cy-test_0.1.bb <<__EOF__
```

© Rodolfo Giometti 2025
R. Giometti, *Yocto Project Customization for Linux*,
https://doi.org/10.1007/979-8-8688-1435-8_5

```
DESCRIPTION = "Recipe created to run simple code"
LICENSE = "MIT"
# Do not change above this line!

do_show_result() {
    bbplain "Hello World!"
}

# Do not change below this line!
do_show_result[nostamp] = "1"
addtask show_result
__EOF__
```

This will create an example recipe which simply displays the Hello World! message. If we remember what we said in the previous chapter about the bitbake command (see Section 4.1), we should know that by using the command below we execute the task do_show_result in the cy-test target recipe:

```
$ bitbake -c show_result cy-test
...
NOTE: Executing Tasks
Hello World!
NOTE: Tasks Summary: Attempted 1 tasks of which 0 didn't need to be rer
un and all succeeded.
```

Without going into detail for the moment, it's obvious that the bbplain command just prints a string on the standard output, and then we can use it to display useful messages to test our code.

Regarding the settings do_show_result[nostamp] = "1" and addtask show_result, they are needed (the latter) to define a new task within the bitbake environment and (the former) to force its execution each time we use the bitbake command to execute the task multiple times.

These concepts will be well explained later in this chapter.

Now we have an excellent tool to verify what we are going to explain in the next sections!

5.1.1 Basic Assignments and Expansion

The following example sets VARIABLE to value. This assignment occurs immediately as the statement is parsed. It is called a **hard assignment**.

```
VARIABLE = "value"
```

As expected, if we include leading or trailing spaces as part of an assignment, the spaces are retained:

```
VARIABLE = " value"
VARIABLE = "value "
```

The readers should pay attention to this space character retention since it is widely used within Yocto configuration files to specify lists of files, values, configuration settings and so on.

As the readers may imagine, setting VARIABLE to "" sets it to an empty string, while setting the variable to " " (just one blank character) sets it to a blank space, which is not the same setting!

Another important thing to point out is that we can use single quotes instead of double quotes when setting a variable's value. Doing so allows us to use values that contain the double quote character:

```
VARIABLE = 'this is a special "value" for VARIABLE'
```

Bourne shell users should notice that in BitBake's syntax single quotes work identically to double quotes in all other ways, that is, they do not suppress variable expansions.

In order to check the actual value of a variable value, we can use the bitbake command below (as already introduced in Section 4.1.2):

```
$ bitbake -e | grep 'ARCH_DEFAULT_KERNELIMAGETYPE='
ARCH_DEFAULT_KERNELIMAGETYPE="zImage"
```

This command displays variable values after the configuration files have been parsed.

If we look at the output of the bitbake -e command above, we can also notice that some variables are prefixed with the keyword export, as shown below:

```
$ bitbake -e | grep 'CC='
export BUILD_CC="gcc "
export CC="aarch64-poky-linux-gcc  -march=armv8-a+crc+crypto -fstack-pr
otector-strong  -O2 -D_FORTIFY_SOURCE=2 -Wformat -Wformat-security -Wer
ror=format-security --sysroot=/home/giometti/yocto/imx-yocto-bsp/imx8mp
-build/tmp/work/armv8a-poky-linux/defaultpkgname/1.0-r0/recipe-sysroot"
```

These variables are exported to the environment of running tasks; this means that they are *visible* inside tasks' bodies. To well understand how this mechanism works, let's consider the following example:

```
export VAR1
VAR1 = "value 1"
VAR2 = "value 2"

do_show_result() {
    VAR1="$VAR1 + data"
    bbplain "var1 = $VAR1"
    bbplain "var1 = ${VAR1}"
    bbplain "var2 = $VAR2"
    bbplain "var2 = ${VAR2}"
}
```

The piece of code above can be placed in the Engicam's meta layer until we have our own meta layer. So we can put the code below into a file named cy-test_0.1.bb in the directory meta-engicam-nxp/recipes-core/cy-test/, as shown below:

```
$ cat meta-engicam-nxp/recipes-core/cy-test/cy-test_0.1.bb
DESCRIPTION = "Recipe created to run simple code"
LICENSE = "MIT"
# Do not change above this line!

export VAR1
VAR1 = "value 1"
VAR2 = "value 2"

do_show_result() {
    VAR1="$VAR1 + data"
    bbplain "var1 = $VAR1"
    bbplain "var1 = ${VAR1}"
    bbplain "var2 = $VAR2"
    bbplain "var2 = ${VAR2}"
}

# Do not change below this line!
do_show_result[nostamp] = "1"
addtask show_result
```

The readers should alter the above recipe file by replacing the code between the two comments # Do not change above this line! and # Do not change below this line! and take the other code, as the keyword addtask or the variable flag do_show_result[nostamp], as is since it will be explained later. Moreover, in the following examples, because of space reasons, we are going to report just the code to be placed in the recipe file and not the whole file anymore.

If we execute the task do_show_result as explained above, we get the following output:

```
$ bitbake -c show_result cy-test
...
NOTE: Executing Tasks
var1 = value 1 + data
var1 = value 1
var2 =
var2 = value 2
NOTE: Tasks Summary: Attempted 1 tasks of which 0 didn't need to be rerun and
all succeeded.
```

Starting from here, still because of space reasons, we will not report anymore the `bitbake -c show_result cy-test` command nor the `NOTE:` messages, but just `bbplain` output.

Since only VAR1 is exported (and it is not relevant whether export VAR1 appears before or after assignments to VAR1, or we use a combined form as `export VAR1 = "value 1"`), while VAR2 is not, the $VAR1 form is replaced within the task body with the value held in the VAR1 variable, while $VAR2 results in an empty string.

The readers should carefully note here that `bitbake` does not expand $VAR1 because it lacks the obligatory curly braces ({}); rather, it is expanded by the shell. In fact, we can reassign the VAR1 content within the task by doing `VAR1="$VAR1 + data"`. On the other hand, `bitbake` expands ${VAR1}; that's why in the first line we get the string `value 1 + data`, while in the second one we just get `value 1`, which is the actual value of the exported variable.

The same considerations can be done to expand $VAR2 and ${VAR2}, and that's why we get a different output in the third and fourth lines.

In any case, we can find changes to a given variable in a specific recipe, by using the following command line:

```
$ bitbake recipename -e | grep 'VARIABLENAME='
```

This command checks the actual value of variable VARIABLENAME when the recipe `recipename` is built.

Variables can reference the contents of other variables using a syntax that is like variable expansion in Bourne shells. For example, if we look within our `conf/local.conf` file, we can see that variable BB_DISKMON_DIRS is set as reported below:

```
$ cat conf/local.conf
...
BB_DISKMON_DIRS ??= "\
    STOPTASKS,${TMPDIR},1G,100K \
    STOPTASKS,${DL_DIR},1G,100K \
```

```
STOPTASKS,${SSTATE_DIR},1G,100K \
STOPTASKS,/tmp,100M,100K \
HALT,${TMPDIR},100M,1K \
HALT,${DL_DIR},100M,1K \
HALT,${SSTATE_DIR},100M,1K \
HALT,/tmp,10M,1K"
```
...

However, if we ask bitbake to display its actual value, we get the following output:

```
$ bitbake -e | grep 'BB_DISKMON_DIRS='
BB_DISKMON_DIRS="    STOPTASKS,/home/giometti/yocto/imx-yocto-bsp/imx8m
p-build/tmp,1G,100K    STOPTASKS,/home/giometti/DL_ARCHIVES/yocto/,1G,
100K    STOPTASKS,/home/giometti/yocto/imx-yocto-bsp/imx8mp-build/ssta
te-cache,1G,100K    STOPTASKS,/tmp,100M,100K    HALT,/home/giometti/y
octo/imx-yocto-bsp/imx8mp-build/tmp,100M,1K    HALT,/home/giometti
 DL_ARCHIVES/yocto/,100M,1K    HALT,/home/giometti/yocto/imx-yocto-bsp
/imx8mp-build/sstate-cache,100M,1K    HALT,/tmp,10M,1K"
```

Note that when specifying path names, we should not use the tilde (~) character as a shortcut for our home directory. Doing so might cause bitbake to not recognize the path, since it does not expand this character in the same way a shell would. Instead, provide a fuller path name as above.

We have said that unlike in Bourne shells, the curly braces are mandatory, that is, only ${VAR} and not $VAR is recognized as an expansion of variable VAR. Furthermore, in BitBake, the equal-to operator (=) does not immediately expand variable references on the right-hand side. Instead, expansion is deferred until the variable assigned to is actually used. The result depends on the current values of the referenced variables. We can contrast this behavior by using the **immediate variable expansion operator** (:=), which results in a variable's contents being expanded immediately, rather than when the variable is actually used.

Another important thing to keep in mind is that if the variable expansion syntax is used on a variable that does not exist, the string is kept as is. For example, given the following assignment, VAR expands to the literal string "${FOO}" as long as FOO does not exist:

```
VAR = "${FOO}"
```

This behavior contrasts with GNU Make, where undefined variables expand to nothing.

To prove it, we can use our cy-test recipe, so let's put the above setting in it as shown below:

```
VAR = "${FOO}"

do_show_result() {
    bbplain "var = ${VAR}"
}
```

Then execute bitbake with the -e option argument to see how VAR is expanded:

```
$ bitbake -e -c show_result cy-test | grep '^VAR='
VAR="\${FOO}"
```

Note that if we execute the do_show_result task, as done above, we get the following output:

```
var =
```

This is because, when executed, the shell does the expansion to an empty string.

5.1.2 Setting Default Values

If we take another look at our conf/local.conf file, we can see the following code:

```
$ cat conf/local.conf
MACHINE ??= 'imx8mp-icore-cy'
DISTRO ?= 'fsl-imx-xwayland'
...
```

The **default value** operator ?= used for the DISTRO variable above achieves a **softer assignment** for the variable. This type of assignment allows us to define a variable if it is undefined when the statement is parsed, but to leave the value alone if the variable has a value. In the above example, if DISTRO is set at the time this statement is parsed, the variable retains its value, but if DISTRO is not set the variable is set to fsl-imx-xwayland.

The above assignment is immediate. Consequently, if multiple ?= assignments to a single variable exist, the first of those ends up getting used.

On the other hand, the **weak default value** operator ??= used for the MACHINE variable is the value which that variable will expand to if no value has been assigned to it via any of the other assignment operators. This operator takes effect immediately, replacing any previously defined weak default value. That is, if MACHINE is not set at all, the variable is set to imx8mp-icore-cy, but if the variable has been already set via any of the other assignment operators, then it retains its actual value.

The difference between ?= and ??= is that the latter is like ?= except the value is assigned at the end of the parsing process. In fact, if we use the following settings:

```
VAR ?= "value 1"
VAR ?= "value 2"
VAR = "value 3"
```

```
do_show_result() {
    bbplain "var = ${VAR}"
}
```

and we execute `bitbake`, we get the following output:

```
$ bitbake -c show_result cy-test
var = value 3
```

which is expected because as last assignment we use =; however, if we remove it:

```
VAR ?= "value 1"
VAR ?= "value 2"

do_show_result() {
    bbplain "var = ${VAR}"
}
```

now the assigned value changes as shown below:

```
var = value 1
```

since the second ?= assignment doesn't take effect. On the other hand, if we do the same with ??= as reported below:

```
VAR ??= "value 1"
VAR ??= "value 2"
VAR = "value 3"

do_show_result() {
    bbplain "var = ${VAR}"
}
```

the assigned value is value 3 as expected, but if we remove the last assignment:

```
VAR ??= "value 1"
VAR ??= "value 2"

do_show_result() {
    bbplain "var = ${VAR}"
}
```

the assigned value is value 2; that is the last one.

5.1.3 Appending, Prepending, and Removal

Other operators which are widely used within the Yocto Project's configuration files are the appending and prepending ones. In bitbake, we have several of them:

- Appending (+=) and prepending (=+) with spaces: These operators take immediate effect during parsing, and they insert a space between the current value and a prepended or appended one.

- Appending (.=) and prepending (=.) without spaces: These operators take immediate effect during parsing, and they do not insert a space between the current value and prepended or appended value.

The readers should take care of this difference since, as already stated, adding a space or not may cause an error or a wrong configuration during recipe parsing!

- Appending and prepending by the override style syntax: We can also append and prepend a variable's value using an override style syntax, as in the example below:

```
FOO = "foo"
FOO:append = " appended"
BAR = "bar"
BAR:prepend = "prepended-"
```

The variable FOO becomes "foo appended", and BAR becomes "prepended-bar" (override style syntax will be well explained in this chapter in Section 5.3.1). Note that when we use this syntax, no spaces are inserted!

Moreover, these operators differ from the :=, .=, =., +=, and =+ operators in that their effects are applied at variable expansion time rather than being immediately applied. This implies that, for example, if a class foo.bbclass that needs to add the value val to the variable FOO, and a recipe that uses foo.bbclass as follows:

```
inherit foo
FOO = "initial"
```

If foo.bbclass uses the form FOO += " val", then the final value of FOO will be initial, which is not what is desired because when the class file is parsed the += operator takes effect immediately and FOO is set to val, then the = operator is parsed, and the previous value is overwritten by the initial string.

To test it, we can do as follows by creating a simple .bbclass file within the meta-engicam-nxp layer directory as shown below:

```
$ mkdir classes
$ cat > classes/foo.bbclass <<__EOF__
FOO += " val"
__EOF
```

Then we can put the above code within our cy-test recipe:

```
inherit foo
FOO = "initial"

do_show_result() {
    bbplain "foo = '${FOO}'"
}
```

Now if we execute the do_show_result task, we get what we expected:

```
$ bitbake -c show_result cy-test
...
foo = 'initial'
```

On the other hand, if foo.bbclass uses the FOO:append = " val" form, then the final value of FOO will be "initial val", as intended to be because the variable expansion is done when the = operator is processed, and then the appending is done.

So let's alter the foo.bbclass code as reported below:

```
$ cat classes/foo.bbclass
FOO:append = " val"
```

Then we re-execute the task, we get the following output:

```
foo = 'initial val'
```

Another useful operator we can use within a configuration file is the removal override style syntax, which can be used to remove values from lists.

As already said, within Yocto recipes we may find lists defined as below:

```
FOO = "123 456 789 123456 123 456 123 456"
```

And in case we wish to remove some items in the list, for example, the string 123, we can use the syntax below:

```
FOO:remove = "123"
```

In fact, specifying a value for removal causes all occurrences of that value to be removed from the variable. In our example, FOO becomes "456 789 123456 456 456" (note the initial space and the double ones between 123456 and the two instances of 456).

We can also remove several items at once, as shown below:

```
BAR = " abc def ghi abcdef abc def abc def def"
BAR:remove = " \
    def \
    abc \
    ghi \
"
```

In this case, BAR becomes " abcdef " (note the initial and ending spaces).

Unlike the above operators :append and :prepend, there is
no need to add a leading or trailing space to the value, but like
:append and :prepend operators, :remove is applied at variable
expansion time.

To test these operators, we can use our cy-test recipe by putting the
following code within it:

```
FOO = "123 456 789 123456 123 456 123 456"
FOO:remove = "123"
BAR = " abc def ghi abcdef abc def abc def def"
BAR:remove = " \
    def \
    abc \
    ghi \
"

do_show_result() {
    bbplain "foo = '${FOO}'"
    bbplain "bar = '${BAR}'"
}
```

Then, if we execute the do_show_result task as above, we get the
following output:

```
foo = ' 456 789 123456  456  456'
bar = '     abcdef      '
```

The resulting strings are precisely what we expected.

5.1.4 Unsetting Variables and Flags

Variable flags are BitBake's implementation of variable properties or
attributes. It is a way of tagging extra information onto a variable. We have
already seen, for example, a usage of these flags within the file sources/
poky/meta/conf/documentation.conf in Section 4.1.1 where there are
some settings as the ones below:

```
do_build[doc] = "Default task for a recipe - depends on all other norma
l tasks required to 'build' a recipe"
do_clean[doc] = "Removes all output files for a target"
```

So variable flags are in the form

```
variable_name[flag_name] = "value"
```

We can define our own variable flags; however, it is quite usual to use the ones already defined in the Yocto build system; in fact, BitBake has a defined set of variable flags available for recipes and classes. Moreover, tasks support several flags which control various functionality of the task, as seen above in our cy-test recipe, that is the setting:

```
do_show_result[nostamp] = "1"
```

Doing this, we ask BitBake to not generate a stamp file for the task, which implies the task should always be executed.

Another widely used variable flag is noexec:

```
do_show_result[noexec] = "1"
```

It marks the task as being empty, and then it is not executed. There are several other flag variables (see Section 5.2.2), but here two interesting flags are presented: postfuncs and prefuncs. They can be used as shown below:

```
do_fetch[postfuncs] += "fixup_distcc_mirror_tarball"
do_configure[prefuncs] += "copy_pci_source_from_kernel"
```

They list functions to call after and before the completion of the task. In the above example, the function fixup_distcc_mirror_tarball is executed after the do_fetch, and copy_pci_source_from_kernel is executed before the do_configure.

The readers should note that we can define, append, and prepend values to variable flags as in the above example, so all the standard syntax operations previously mentioned work for variable flags except for override style syntax (i.e., :prepend, :append, and :remove).

In the end, we have to say that it is possible to completely remove a variable or a variable flag from BitBake's environment by using the unset keyword as below:

```
unset FOO
unset BAR[doc]
```

These two statements remove the FOO variable and the BAR[doc] flag variable.

5.1.5 Using Inline Python Variable Expansion

In some recipes (or more frequently in Yocto classes), we may need to use inline Python variable expansion to set variables to computed values.

For example, the next assignment results in the CURR_DATE variable being set to the current date:

```
CURR_DATE = "${@time.strftime('%Y%m%d', time.gmtime())}"
```

To test it, we can use our cy-test recipe:

```
CURR_DATE = "${@time.strftime('%Y%m%d%H%M%S', time.gmtime())}"

do_show_result() {
    bbplain "date = '${CURR_DATE}'"
}
```

Then when we execute the do_show_result task, we should get an output as below:

```
date = '20240322175040'
```

Note that in the following assignment, the function foo() is called each time the variable FOO is expanded:

```
FOO = "${@foo()}"
```

while, by using the following immediate assignment, the function foo() is only called once as soon as the assignment is parsed:

```
FOO := "${@foo()}"
```

This may lead to errors.

However, the most common use of this feature is to extract the value of variables from BitBake's environment (which is also named **internal data dictionary** or *Datastore Variables* and addressed as d.). The following code selects the DISTRO_NAME or DISTRO variable content (if the first variable is not defined):

```
CURR_DISTRO = "${@d.getVar('DISTRO_NAME') or d.getVar('DISTRO')}"
```

Note that to read flag variables, we have to use a slightly different syntax:

```
DOBUILD_DOC = "${@d.getVarFlag('do_build', 'doc', False)}"
```

The method getVar("VAR", expand) returns the value of variable VAR or None if it does not exist (using expand=True expands the value), while getVarFlag("VAR", flag, expand) returns the value of flag variable VAR[flag] or None if either the variable VAR or the named flag does not exist (using expand=True expands the value).

There are several other functions for accessing the *Datastore Variables*; a complete list is at https://docs.yoctoproject.org/bitbake/2.2/bitbake-user-manual/bitbake-user-manual-metadata.html#functions-for-accessing-datastore-variables.

To test these functions, we can still use the `cy-test` recipe as shown below:

```
CURR_DISTRO = "${@d.getVar('DISTRO_NAME') or d.getVar('DISTRO')}"
DOBUILD_DOC = "${@d.getVarFlag('do_build', 'doc', False)}"

do_show_result() {
    bbplain "distro = '${CURR_DISTRO}'"
    bbplain "doc = '${DOBUILD_DOC}'"
}
```

When we execute the task in the recipe, the output should be something as reported below:

```
distro = 'NXP i.MX Release Distro'
doc = 'Default task for a recipe - depends on all other normal tasks re
quired to 'build' a recipe'
```

Now we can test what was suggested in Section 4.1.3, that is, we can put the following code within the `cy-test` recipe:

```
BAR := "${@d.getVar('BB_ORIGENV', False).getVar('BAR', True)}"

do_show_result() {
        bbplain "BAR = '${BAR}'"
}
```

Note the `:=` assignment above; if we had used `=`, an error would arise!

Then, the way to pass some information from the command line is as shown below:

```
$ BAR="some value" bitbake -c show_result cy-test
...
BAR = 'some value'
```

Another widely used example of inline Python functions is reported below, where we can check whether a variable contains a specific string or not by using the `bb.utils.contains()` method:

```
CHK_DEBUG = "${@bb.utils.contains("IMAGE_FEATURES", \
                    "debug-tweaks", "debug", "no-debug", d)}"
```

If the variable IMAGE_FEATURES contains the string debug-tweaks, then the function returns debug; otherwise, it returns no-debug. To test it, we can use the following code in the cy-test recipe:

```
CHK_DEBUG = "${@bb.utils.contains("IMAGE_FEATURES", \
                    "debug-tweaks", "debug", "no-debug", d)}"

do_show_result() {
        bbplain "IMAGE_FEATURES = '${IMAGE_FEATURES}'"
        bbplain "CHK_DEBUG = '${CHK_DEBUG}'"
}
```

When we execute the task, we should get the following:

```
IMAGE_FEATURES = ' debug-tweaks package-management'
CHK_DEBUG = 'debug'
```

We can find many other functions that can be called from Python by looking at the source code of the BitBake module, which is in the poky/bitbake/lib/bb directory. For example, poky/bitbake/lib/bb/utils.py includes the newly tested function bb.utils.contains().

5.1.6 Using Anonymous Python Functions

The anonymous Python functions are special functions we can define within a recipe file to set variables, or perform other operations programmatically, during parsing. For example, the following conditionally sets VAR2 based on the value of VAR1 variable:

```
VAR1 = "value1"

do_show_result() {
        bbplain "var1 = ${VAR1}"
        bbplain "var2 = ${VAR2}"
}
```

```
python () {
    if d.getVar('VAR1') == 'value1':
        d.setVar('VAR2', 'value2')
}
```

If we put the above code within our example recipe, we should get the following output:

```
...
var1 = value1
var2 = value2
...
```

while, if we set VAR1 to value3, and we rerun the test, we should get another output:

```
...
var1 = value3
var2 =
...
```

Note that an equivalent way to mark a function as an anonymous function is to give it the name __anonymous, rather than no name. So, the example above can be written as

```
python __anonymous() {
    if d.getVar('VAR1') == 'value1':
        d.setVar('VAR2', 'value2')
}
```

An important thing to keep in mind with the anonymous Python functions is that they always run at the end of parsing, regardless of where they are defined, and if a recipe contains many anonymous functions, they run in the same order as they are defined within the recipe.

Particularly, overrides and override-style operators such as append, prepend, etc., are applied before anonymous functions run. This can be verified by using the following code:

```
VAR = "var "
VAR:append = " from outside"
```

```
do_show_result() {
        bbplain "var = ${VAR}"
}

python __anonymous() {
    d.setVar("VAR", "var from anonymous")
}
```

If we execute the cy-test recipe, we should verify that VAR ends up in the string var from anonymous, as shown below:

```
$ bitbake -f -c show_result cy-test
...
var = var from anonymous
...
```

So the function can be used to fix some settings at the end of the parsing. However, another interesting usage of these functions is reported in the poky layer within the file meta/recipes-core/meta/cve-update-db-native.bb:

```
$ cat poky/meta/recipes-core/meta/cve-update-db-native.bb
...
python () {
    if not bb.data.inherits_class("cve-check", d):
        raise bb.parse.SkipRecipe("Skip recipe when cve-check class is
not loaded.")
}
...
```

Here, the anonymous function is used to check if the class cve-check has been inherited and to raise a warning in case. This is to underline that these functions are not only to set variables but to do special actions at the end of parsing.

5.1.7 Exporting Variables

Occasionally, it may be useful to use BitBake's variables within a shell script; to do so, we have to export variables to the environment of running tasks by using the export keyword. For example, we can rewrite our cy-test recipe as below:

```
export CURR_DATE = "${@time.strftime('%Y%m%d%H%M%S', time.gmtime())}"

do_show_result() {
    bbplain "date = '$CURR_DATE'"
}
```

In this case, BitBake does not expand CURR_DATE in the show_result's body because it lacks the obligatory {}, but the shell expands it.

The readers should pay attention to this concept! In Section 5.2.1, we demonstrate that in this case the do_show_result function is expanded as

```
do_show_result() {
    bbplain "date = '$CURR_DATE'"
}
```

while in the previous one, it is expanded as

```
do_show_result() {
    bbplain "date = '20240325141632'"
}
```

So, by using export we can define a new variable which can be used within each shell function at execution time.

Note that it is also possible to define the variable and then export it (or vice versa); in both cases, we get the same results. In the output of bitbake -e, variables that are exported to the environment are preceded by export keyword, as we can easily verify below:

```
$ bitbake -e cy-test | grep 'CURR_DATE='
export CURR_DATE="20240325141652"
```

The readers should note here that a more accurate command line to get the content for a BitBake's variable could be the following:

```
bitbake -e cy-test | grep '^(export )?VARIABLE='
```

This will work in both cases where VARIABLE is exported or not.

5.2 Tasks

Now that we should know everything about BitBake's variables, we have to look more in detail about tasks. Together with variables, they are important to understand how recipes can convert the source code into a package or into a Yocto image.

5.2.1 Defining New Tasks

Tasks are units of execution for BitBake, and they can either be shell functions or Python functions (in the BitBake style) that have been promoted to tasks by using the addtask command, as already seen above when we defined our show_result task.

The first argument to addtask is the name of the function to promote a simple BitBake function into a task, and optionally some dependencies between the task and other tasks may follow, as in the example below:

```
python do_printdate() {
    import time
    bb.plain(time.strftime('%Y%m%d%H%M%S', time.gmtime()))
}
addtask printdate after do_fetch before do_build
```

The new task do_printdate will execute between the tasks do_fetch and do_build according to the current execution task list (see below). Tasks are only supported in recipe and class files (i.e., in .bb or .bbclass files and files included or inherited from these files).

Note that if the name does not start with the do_ prefix, then it is implicitly added, which enforces the convention that all task names start with the do_ string. Note also that instead of using the usual print() Python function, we used the bb.plain() function to print the current time, similarly as we did above for our show_result (or do_show_result task – starting from this point, these names are interchangeable). So, for example, a Python version of our testing task can be the following:

```
CURR_DATE = "${@time.strftime('%Y%m%d%H%M%S', time.gmtime())}"

python do_show_result() {
    curr_date = d.getVar('CURR_DATE', True)
    bb.plain("date = '%s'" % (curr_date))
}
```

Note that in this version we used four-space indentation instead of eight; if not, everything will work anyway, but we will get a warning as shown below:

```
WARNING: python should use 4 spaces indentation, but found tabs in
  example_0.1.bb, line 8
```

If we put that code within our cy-test recipe, and we execute it, we should get something as below:

```
date = '20240325135835'
```

An interesting note to point out here is about what we get if we replace the True argument within the d.getVar() function with a False, as shown below:

```
--- recipes-core/cy-test/cy-test_0.1.bb
+++ recipes-core/cy-test/cy-test_0.1.bb
@@ -5,7 +5,7 @@
 CURR_DATE = "${@time.strftime('%Y%m%d%H%M%S', time.gmtime())}"

 python do_show_result() {
-    curr_date = d.getVar('CURR_DATE', True)
+    curr_date = d.getVar('CURR_DATE', False)
     bb.plain("date = '%s'" % (curr_date))
 }
```

Doing so, the output of bitbake execution will be as reported below:

```
date = '${@time.strftime('%Y%m%d%H%M%S', time.gmtime())}'
```

This time, we get the content of CURR_DATE without expanding it. This different behavior is because, for shell tasks, BitBake writes a shell script to ${T}/run.do_taskname and then executes the script. The generated shell script contains all the exported variables, and the shell functions with all variables expanded as shown in the example below:

```
$ cat tmp/work/armv8a-poky-linux/cy-test/0.1-r0/temp/run.do_show_result
...
do_show_result() {
    bbplain "date = '20240325141632'"
}
...
```

while for Python tasks, BitBake executes the task internally, and then we can decide whether to do an expansion. If we look at the generated file ${T}/run.do_taskname now, we have the following code:

```
$ cat tmp/work/armv8a-poky-linux/cy-test/0.1-r0/temp/run.do_show_result
def do_show_result(d):
    curr_date = d.getVar('CURR_DATE', False)
    bb.plain("date = '%s'" % (curr_date))

do_show_result(d)
```

Looking at the expanded functions in the run file and the output in the log files (named ${T}/log.do_taskname) is a useful debugging technique.

Remember that to get the value of T, we can use the following command line:

```
$ bitbake -e -c show_result cy-test | grep '^T='
T="/home/giometti/yocto/imx-yocto-bsp/imx8mp-build/tmp/work/armv8a
-poky-linux/cy-test/0.1-r0/temp"
```

Now we can demonstrate the differences between using or not the keyword export. We have seen above that without it, the function is expanded as

```
$ cat tmp/work/armv8a-poky-linux/cy-test/0.1-r0/temp/run.do_show_result
...
do_show_result() {
    bbplain "date = '20240325141632'"
}
...
```

while if we use export, we get the following code:

```
$ bitbake cy-test
...
date = '20240326161459'
...
$ cat tmp/work/armv8a-poky-linux/cy-test/0.1-r0/temp/run.do_show_result
...
export CURR_DATE="20240326161459"
...
do_show_result() {
    bbplain "date = '$CURR_DATE'"
}
...
```

In the former code, we have a do_show_result task with a fixed body, while in the latter code we have a new variable CURR_DATE we can refer to another task than the do_show_result.

5.2.2 Understanding Task Execution

In order to understand how tasks are executed by BitBake, let's alter a bit our cy-test recipe as shown below:

```
--- cy-test_0.1.bb
+++ cy-test_0.1.bb
@@ -9,5 +9,4 @@
 }
```

```
 # Do not change below this line!
-do_show_result[nostamp] = "1"
-addtask show_result
+addtask show_result after do_fetch before do_build
```

We have already seen before that by using addtask specifying no
dependencies (assuming dependencies have not been added through
some other means), the only way to run the task is by explicitly selecting
it with the BitBake's -c option argument, as done until now. In fact, if
we try out this new example, we might see that the do_show_result task
is automatically run in the correct order within the current execution
task list:

```
$ bitbake cy-test
...
NOTE: Executing Tasks
date = '20240325153915'
Setscene tasks: 177 of 177
Currently  2 running tasks (735 of 747)  98% |######################## |
0: cy-test-0.1-r0 do_prepare_recipe_sysroot - 3s (pid 811992)
1: cy-test-0.1-r0 do_patch - 3s (pid 812000)
```

However, as before, the task is executed only the first time we build
the recipe; this is because BitBake considers the task up to date after that
initial run; on the other hand, we have already seen that if we want to force
the task to always be rerun for experimentation, we can use the nostamp
variable flag:

```
do_show_result[nostamp] = "1"
```

But now we have removed such a line, so we can still explicitly mark
the task for execution by providing the -f option argument to bitbake as
follows:

```
$ bitbake -f -c show_result cy-test
...
NOTE: Tainting hash to force rebuild of task /home/giometti/yocto/imx-y
octo-bsp/sources/meta-engicam-nxp/recipes-core/cy-test/cy-test_0.1.bb,
do_show_result
```

```
WARNING: /home/giometti/yocto/imx-yocto-bsp/sources/meta-engicam-nxp/re
cipes-core/cy-test/cy-test_0.1.bb:do_show_result is tainted from a forc
ed run
...
NOTE: Executing Tasks
date = '20240325155712'
NOTE: Tasks Summary: Attempted 2 tasks of which 1 didn't need to be rer
un and all succeeded.

Summary: There was 1 WARNING message.
```

As already introduced in a previous section, there are several flag variables we can use to customize task execution and behavior. Below is a list of the most used tasks' flags (refer to https://docs.yoctoproject. org/bitbake/2.6/bitbake-user-manual/bitbake-user-manual-metadata.html#variable-flags for a complete list):

- cleandirs: This flag empties directories that should be created before the task runs. Directories that already exist are removed and recreated to empty them.

- depends: This flag controls inter-task dependencies. For example:

  ```
  do_compile[depends] += "u-boot:do_deploy rcw:do_deploy uefi:do_de
  ploy"
  ```

  Here, all do_deploy tasks for u-boot, rcw, and uefi recipes must have completed before the do_compile task can execute.

- deptask: This flag controls task build-time dependencies. For example:

  ```
  do_configure[deptask] = "do_populate_sysroot"
  ```

  Here, the do_populate_sysroot task must complete before do_configure can execute.

- `rdepends` and `rdeptask`: These flags are similar
  to `depends` and `deptask` above but about runtime
  dependencies. The `PACKAGES` variable lists runtime
  packages, and each of these can have `RDEPENDS`
  and `RRECOMMENDS` runtime dependencies. An
  example can be

  ```
  do_package_write[rdeptask] = "do_package"
  ```

  In the above setting, we specify that the do_package
  task of each item in `RDEPENDS` must be completed
  before do_package_write can execute.

- `dirs`: This flag is used to list directories that should be
  created before the task runs. Directories that already
  exist are left as is, and the last directory listed is used as
  the current working directory for the task. For example:

  ```
  do_deploy[dirs] = "${DEPLOYDIR} ${B}"
  ```

  Here, `bitbake` creates the directory addressed in
  `DEPLOYDIR` and B variables before the do_deploy task
  runs and also sets the current working directory of
  do_deploy to the directory in B.

- `network`: When this flag is set to 1, it allows a task
  to access the network. In fact, by default, only the
  do_fetch task is granted network access (best practices
  say that recipes shouldn't access the network outside
  do_fetch).

- `noexec`: When this flag is set to 1, it marks the task as
  being empty, so no execution is required. Usually, this
  flag is used to disable tasks defined elsewhere that are
  not needed in a particular recipe or to set up tasks as
  dependency placeholders.

223

- `nostamp`: When this flag is set to 1, it tells BitBake to not generate a stamp file for a task, which implies the task should always be executed. However, we should keep in mind that any task that depends (possibly indirectly) on such a marked task will always be executed as well. So we should be careful to avoid unnecessary rebuilding.

- `postfuncs` and `prefuncs`: List of functions to call after and before the completion of the task. For example:

  ```
  do_fetch[postfuncs] += "fixup_distcc_mirror_tarball"

  do_configure[prefuncs] += "copy_pci_source_from_kernel"
  ```

  Here, `fixup_distcc_mirror_tarball` is executed after the `do_fetch`, and `copy_pci_source_from_kernel` is executed before the `do_configure`.

Another interesting feature about task execution is about the possibility to define multiple tasks as dependencies when calling `addtask`. For example:

```
addtask package_write_tar before do_build \
                     after do_packagedata do_package
```

Here, the `package_write_tar` task has to wait until both of the `do_packagedata` and `do_package` tasks complete.

In general, the order in which BitBake runs the tasks is controlled by its task scheduler, which can be configured or even redefined with custom implementations for specific use cases.

Even if these settings are out of the scope of this book, we can say that to select the name of the scheduler to use for the scheduling of BitBake tasks we can use the BB_SCHEDULER variable (see `https://docs.yoctoproject.org/bitbake/2.8/bitbake-user-manual/bitbake-user-manual-ref-variables.html#term-BB_SCHEDULERS`).

5.2.3 Prepending, Appending, and Redefinition

As per variable, we can append, prepend, or completely redefine a task. And we can easily explain how just by doing some examples.

Let's consider our original cy-test_0.1.bb recipe:

```
$ cat meta-engicam-nxp/recipes-core/cy-test/cy-test_0.1.bb
DESCRIPTION = "Recipe created to run simple code"
LICENSE = "MIT"
# Do not change above this line!

do_show_result() {
    bbplain "Hello World!"
}

# Do not change below this line!
do_show_result[nostamp] = "1"
addtask show_result
```

If we add a .bbappend file as below, and we try to execute the recipe, we should see that the output will change from the usual Hello World!:

```
$ cat meta-engicam-nxp/recipes-core/cy-test/cy-test_0.1.bbappend
do_show_result:prepend() {
    bbplain "------------"
}

do_show_result:append() {
    bbplain "I'm alive!!!"
    bbplain "------------"
}
```

When we execute the task, we should get

```
$ bitbake -c show_result cy-test
...
------------
Hello World!
I'm alive!!!
------------
...
```

225

It's obvious now that in this manner we can easily add some extra actions to tasks, which can be very useful to customize our recipes!

The readers should note that appends and prepends operators are cumulative, just like +=, =+, etc., so all appends/prepends are applied in the order they're seen while parsing.

On the other hand, we can also completely redefine a function just by rewriting its body. If we add another .bbappend file as below, we redefine the task's body:

```
$ cat meta-engicam-nxp/recipes-core/cy-test/cy-test_%.bbappend
do_show_result() {
    bbplain "Ciao ragazzi"
}
```

Note that we add the file cy-test_%.bbappend, which applies to every release number of the cy-test's recipe, just to be able to specify a different filename within the cy-test directory. Usually, we can do the same by specifying a cy-test_0.1.bbappend file in another layer.

In fact, if we execute again BitBake as above, now we should get the following output:

```
$ bitbake -c show_result cy-test
...
------------
Ciao ragazzi
I'm alive!!!
------------
...
```

which demonstrates that the task do_show_result has been correctly replaced.

5.2.4 Deleting a Task

As well as being able to add tasks, we can delete them. To do so, we can use the `deltask` command. For example, to delete the task used in the previous sections, you would use

```
deltask do_show_result
```

There is nothing more to say about this topic, but the fact that if we delete a task using the `deltask` command and the task has dependencies, the dependencies are not reconnected!

For example, consider the following setting:

```
addtask task1
addtask task2 after do_task1
addtask task3 after do_task2
```

Here, `do_task3` depends on `do_task2`, which depends on `do_task1`. Given this scenario, we can use `deltask` to delete `do_task2` as shown below:

```
deltask do_task2
```

Doing so, the implicit dependency relationship between `do_task3` and `do_task1` through `do_task2` no longer exists, and `do_task3` dependencies are not updated to include `do_task1`. Thus, it is not guaranteed that `do_task3` will be executed after `do_task1`.

To avoid this, if we want dependencies such as these to remain intact, we can use the `noexec` flag variable to disable the task instead of using the `deltask` command to delete it:

```
do_task2[noexec] = "1"
```

In this manner, `do_task2` is not executed, and the dependency relationship is still in place.

5.3 Conditional Syntax (a.k.a. Overrides)

The concept of conditional syntax, which is widely also named **overrides**, is a BitBake mechanism that allows variables (or tasks) to be selectively overridden at the end of parsing.

It is an essential concept that every Yocto developer should understand well. That's why we are dedicating a complete section to it.

5.3.1 Understanding the Overrides

By using the OVERRIDES variable, we can tell bitbake to conditionally select a specific version of a variable and to conditionally append or prepend the value of a variable. The OVERRIDES variable is a colon character–separated list that contains items for which we want to satisfy conditions. An example can be

```
OVERRIDES = "foo:bar:xyz"
```

Here, the OVERRIDES variable lists three overrides: foo, bar, and xyz. Thus, if we have a variable that is conditional on bar, then the bar-specific version of the variable is used rather than the non-conditional version.

Note that overrides can only use lowercase characters, digits, and dashes. Since colons are used to separate overrides from each other and from the variable name, they are not permitted in override names.

Above, we have set OVERRIDES as

```
OVERRIDES = "foo:bar:xyz"
```

Now let's consider the TEST variable set as below:

```
TEST = "default"
TEST:foo = "default for foo"
```

The variable TEST by itself has a default value of default, but we select the foo-specific version of the TEST variable thanks to the OVERRIDES settings.

Overrides apply in sequence, so if we have

```
OVERRIDES = "foo:bar:xyz"
TEST = "default"
TEST:foo = "default foo"
TEST:bar = "default bar"
```

then variable TEST will be set to "default bar".

We can also append and prepend operations to variable values based on whether a specific item is listed in OVERRIDES. Below is an example:

```
OVERRIDES = "foo:bar:xyz"
TEST = "default"
TEST:append:foo = " for foo"
TEST:prepend:bar = "bar "
```

Here, all overrides apply in sequence, so the TEST variable will be set to "bar default foo".

While we can set OVERRIDES by ourselves, the normal usage is to use the default value of OVERRIDES which includes several default values as reported within the bitbake.conf file as shown below:

```
$ cat sources/poky/meta/conf/bitbake.conf
...
# Overrides are processed left to right, so the ones that are named
# later take precedence.
# You generally want them to go from least to most specific. This means
# that:
# A variable '<foo>:arm' overrides a variable '<foo>' when
# ${TARGET_ARCH} is arm.
# A variable '<foo>:qemuarm' overrides '<foo>' and overrides '<foo>:arm'
# when ${MACHINE} is 'qemuarm'.
# If you use combination ie '<foo>:qemuarm:arm', then
# '<foo>:qemuarm:arm' will override '<foo>:qemuarm' and then '<foo>'
# will be overriden with that value from '<foo>:qemuarm'.
# And finally '<foo>:forcevariable' overrides any standard variable,
# with the highest priority.
# This works for functions as well, they are really just variables.
#
```

```
OVERRIDES = "${TARGET_OS}:${TRANSLATED_TARGET_ARCH}:pn-${PN}:${MACHINEO
VERRIDES}:${DISTROOVERRIDES}:${CLASSOVERRIDE}${LIBCOVERRIDE}:forcevaria
ble"
LIBCOVERRIDE ?= ""
CLASSOVERRIDE ?= "class-target"
DISTROOVERRIDES ?= "${@d.getVar('DISTRO') or ''}"
MACHINEOVERRIDES ?= "${MACHINE}"

FILESOVERRIDES = "${TRANSLATED_TARGET_ARCH}:${MACHINEOVERRIDES}:${DISTR
OOVERRIDES}"
...
```

As we can see above, there are several automatic settings done in this special variable; in particular, we have

- TARGET_OS specifies the target's operating system, and it can be usually set to linux for glibc-based systems based on GNU C Library, while it is usually set to linux-musl for Musl libC (other values are possible).

- TRANSLATED_TARGET_ARCH is a variable used where the system architecture (i.e., the one specified in TARGET_ ARCH) is needed in a value where underscores are not allowed as within package filenames (in this case, dash characters replace any underscore characters).

- pn-${PN} is a special setting which results in the prefix pn- followed by the target recipe name (see Section 6.1 for further information about the PN variable). Below in this section, we are going to show some usage examples.

- MACHINEOVERRIDES is a colon-separated list of machine overrides that apply to the current machine and its compatible architectures. Obviously, by default, this list includes the value of MACHINE.

- For example, on our system we have the following settings which represent all the machine types compatible with our target imx8mp-icore:

```
$ bitbake -e | grep 'MACHINEOVERRIDES='
MACHINEOVERRIDES="aarch64:armv8a:use-nxp-bsp:imx-generic-bsp:imx-
nxp-bsp:imxdrm:imxvpu:imaged:imxgpu2d:imxgpu3d:imxvulkan:mx8-gene
ric-bsp:mx8-nxp-bsp:mx8m-generic-bsp:mx8m-nxp-bsp:mx8mp-generic-
bsp:mx8mp-nxp-bsp:imx8mp-icore"
PRISTINE_MACHINEOVERRIDES="aarch64:armv8a:use-nxp-bsp:mx8mp:imx8m
p-icore"
```

- DISTROOVERRIDES is a colon-separated list of overrides specific to the current distribution. As we can see above, this list is initially set by BitBake to DISTRO (or to an empty value), but it can be modified later.

- CLASSOVERRIDE specifies the special class override that should currently apply (e.g., class-target, class-native, and so forth). As we can see above, this variable gets its default class-target value from the bitbake.conf file.

Even if Yocto classes are not fully covered in this book, a special note about a possible usage must be reported. In fact, in some recipes we may need an override that allows us to install extra files, but only when building for the target (addressed with the class-target):

```
do_install:append:class-target() {
    install target.conf ${D}${sysconfdir}
}
```

or when building for the host (addressed with the class-native):

```
do_install:append:class-native() {
    install native.conf ${D}${sysconfdir}
}
```

See Section 11.6 for an example about how to use target and native classes.

- LIBCOVERRIDE specifies some special libC overrides. By default, it is set to null, but it may be set to libc-musl or libc-newlib according to the several libC implementations used.

- The forcevariable override is the strongest override possible, and it can be used to specify some forced value.

A final note about overriding is related to the fact that override syntax, which is often used for machine- and distro-specific variable modification, has been changed from older releases (before Yocto Honister 3.4).

The previous syntax was something like

```
PACKAGECONFIG_append_machine = " pkgfeature"
```

This old style has been changed so that colons are used as override separators instead of underscores:

```
PACKAGECONFIG:append:machine = " pkgfeature"
```

In some releases, the current BitBake supports both syntaxes by doing a character replacement during variable processing, but in the next BitBake releases such support for the underscore syntax will be dropped. In these cases, a script to facilitate this transition is provided into sources/poky/scripts/contrib/convert-overrides.py. We may then run this on our meta layer as shown below:

```
$ sources/poky/scripts/contrib/convert-overrides.py our-meta-layer
```

In order to do a simple override example, we can still use our cy-test_0.1.bb recipe by using the following code:

```
TEST = "val"
TEST:pn-cy-test = "val example"

do_show_result() {
    bbplain "TEST = '${TEST}'"
}
```

Now if we try to build our cy-test package we should get something as below:

```
$ bitbake -c show_result cy-test
...
TEST = 'val example'
...
```

Note that if we try to build any other recipe, then TEST will be set to val.

5.3.2 Machine and Distros Overriding

We have seen above that the underlying mechanism behind both MACHINEOVERRIDES and DISTROOVERRIDES is simply that they are included in the default value of OVERRIDES. So we can use them to add extra overrides that should apply to a machine or to a distro.

A typical usage of these variables is to define a list of common attributes or features a machine or distro should inherit; for example, above we got that our machine, that is, based on the iMX8 processor, defines the following:

```
MACHINEOVERRIDES="aarch64:armv8a:use-nxp-bsp:imx-generic-bsp:imx-nxp-
bsp:imxdrm:imxvpu:imxgpu:imxgpu2d:imxgpu3d:imxvulkan:mx8-generic-bsp:mx8-
nxp-bsp:mx8m-generic-bsp:mx8m-nxp-bsp:mx8mp-generic-bsp:mx8mp-nxp-
bsp:imx8mp-icore"
```

Then by using several settings as below (included in file `sources/meta-freescale/conf/machine/include/imx-base.inc`), we can easily define a proper machine firmware according to the fact that our machine `imx8mp-icore` is compatible with the `mx8mp-generic-bsp` machine, etc.:

```
# Firmware
MACHINE_FIRMWARE ?= ""
...
MACHINE_FIRMWARE:append:mx53-generic-bsp   = " firmware-imx-vpu-imx53 f
irmware-imx-sdma-imx53"
MACHINE_FIRMWARE:append:mx51-generic-bsp   = " firmware-imx-vpu-imx51 f
irmware-imx-sdma-imx51"
MACHINE_FIRMWARE:append:mx8mm-generic-bsp  = " linux-firmware-imx-sdma-
imx7d"
MACHINE_FIRMWARE:append:mx8mn-generic-bsp  = " linux-firmware-imx-sdma-
imx7d"
MACHINE_FIRMWARE:append:mx8mp-generic-bsp  = " linux-firmware-imx-sdma-
imx7d firmware-imx-easrc-imx8mn firmware-imx-xcvr-imx8mp firmware-sof-i
mx"
MACHINE_FIRMWARE:append:mx8mq-generic-bsp  = " linux-firmware-imx-sdma-
imx7d"
MACHINE_FIRMWARE:append:mx8qm-generic-bsp  = " firmware-imx-vpu-imx8"
MACHINE_FIRMWARE:append:mx8qxp-generic-bsp = " firmware-imx-vpu-imx8"
MACHINE_FIRMWARE:append:mx8dx-generic-bsp  = " firmware-imx-vpu-imx8"
MACHINE_FIRMWARE:append:imx-mainline-bsp   = " linux-firmware-imx-sdma-
imx6q linux-firmware-imx-sdma-imx7d firmware-imx-vpu-imx6q firmware-imx
-vpu-imx6d"
```

Such kind of machine overrides are widely used across all Yocto sources! In fact, this mechanism is basic to easily modify variables to support different machines.

Suppose we have a layer named `meta-mach` that adds support for building a machine named `mach1` and another one named `mach2`. If both machines need a dependency to package `foo` but just `mach1` depends also on package `bar`, we can use the following code:

```
DEPENDS = "foo"
DEPENDS:append:mach1 = " bar"
```

In this manner, `DEPENDS` will be set to "foo bar" when we compile for machine `mach1`, while it will be set to "foo" otherwise.

Since our development kit is based on the Freescale's Yocto build system, we spend few words by introducing the MACHINEOVERRIDES_EXTENDER variable, which can be used to easily group different settings for similar platforms:

```
$ cat sources/meta-freescale/classes/machine-overrides-extender.bbclass:
#
# This allow to grouping of different settings for similar
# platforms.
#
# To indicate that a SoC contains following set of overrides, you
# can use:
#
# MACHINEOVERRIDES_EXTENDER:soc = "group1:group2"
#
# However to indicate that an override replaces a set of other
# overrides, you can use:
#
# MACHINEOVERRIDES_EXTENDER_FILTER_OUT:override = "group1 group2"
...
```

This special syntax is used, for example, within the meta-imx layer as shown below:

```
$ cat meta-bsp/conf/machine/include/imx-base-extend.inc as below:
...
# i.MX 8M Plus UltraLite
MACHINEOVERRIDES_EXTENDER:mx8mpul:use-nxp-bsp = "imx-generic-bsp:i
mx-nxp-bsp:imxfbdev:mx8-generic-bsp:mx8-nxp-bsp:mx8m-generic-bsp:m
x8m-nxp-bsp:mx8mpul-generic-bsp:mx8mpul-nxp-bsp"
MACHINEOVERRIDES_EXTENDER:mx8mpul:use-mainline-bsp = "imx-generic-
bsp:imx-mainline-bsp:mx8-generic-bsp:mx8-mainline-bsp:mx8m-generic
-bsp:mx8m-mainline-bsp:mx8mpul-generic-bsp:mx8mpul-mainline-bsp"
...
```

This means that for mx8mpul (i.e., the i.MX 8M Plus UltraLite CPU) if we set

```
MACHINEOVERRIDES .= ":use-mainline-bsp"
```

235

we select at once all the machine overrides defined by
MACHINEOVERRIDES_EXTENDER:mx8mpul:use-mainline-bsp.

As we can see, this feature is quite useful, but we remark that it is
not portable! So we can't use it on other implementations.

Regarding DISTROOVERRIDES, there are a very few usages of this
mechanism; however, if we look at the definition of the poky-tiny distro,
we can read the following:

```
$ cat sources/poky/meta-poky/conf/distro/poky-tiny.conf
# Distribution definition for: poky-tiny
...
# Poky-tiny is intended to define a tiny Linux system comprised of a
# Linux kernel tailored to support each specific MACHINE and busybox.
# Poky-tiny sets some basic policy to ensure a usable system while still
# keeping the rootfs and kernel image as small as possible.
...
require conf/distro/poky.conf
require conf/distro/include/gcsections.inc

DISTRO = "poky-tiny"
DISTROOVERRIDES = "poky:poky-tiny"
TCLIBC = "musl"
```

So we can use the following code to selectively set a dependency:

```
DEPENDS:append:poky-tiny = "foo"
```

As of the writing of this book, there are no usages of this kind of
overriding for the poky-tiny distro.

5.3.3 Overriding by Tasks

Another (less used but sometimes useful) overriding is about the possibility to set a variable within BitBake's environment just for the duration of a single task. To easily understand what we are saying, we can do a simple example by rewriting our cy-test_0.1.bb recipe as below:

```
TEST = "val"
TEST:task-show-result = "val_1"
TEST:task-show-another-result = "val_2"

do_show_result() {
    bbplain "TEST = '${TEST}'"
}

do_show_another_result() {
    bbplain "TEST = '${TEST}'"
}

# Do not change below this line!
addtask show_result
do_show_result[nostamp] = "1"
addtask show_another_result
do_show_another_result[nostamp] = "1"
```

Note that we have added the new task show_another_result, and the override names are built by using the task- prefix followed by the task name, where all underscore (_) characters have been replaced with minus (-) characters!

Now if we execute the show_result task, we get the following output:

```
$ bitbake -c show_result cy-test
...
TEST = 'val_1'
...
```

while if we execute the show_another_result task, we get

```
$ bitbake -c show_another_result cy-test
...
TEST = 'val_2'
...
```

However, this behavior is really useful when used with the standard tasks as configure, compile, build, etc.; in these cases, we can use the following:

```
TEST:task-configure = "val_1"
TEST:task-compile = "val_2"
TEST:task-build = "val_3"
```

Now TEST has the value val_1 while the do_configure task is executed, the value val_2 while the do_compile task is executed, and val_3 during do_build.

This syntax is also widely used with other combinations (i.e., :prepend, :append, and :remove) as below:

```
EXTRA_OEMAKE:prepend:task-compile = "${PARALLEL_MAKE} "
```

In the above settings, EXTRA_OEMAKE will be prepended by the ${PARALLEL_MAKE} settings during the do_compile task only.

5.3.4 File Overriding

Among variable overriding, in BitBake, file overriding also exists. This kind of overriding is fascinating, and it can simplify the developer's job. In fact, by using it, for example, we can specify different files to be put in the root filesystem according to the machine name.

As before, to understand what we are saying, let's consider the case where we have to install two different /etc/fstab files according to the case we are generating the root filesystem for the machine mach_foo or for the machine mach_bar. To do so, we can create a recipe where we specify this special file within the SRC_URI variable (see Section 6.3.2 for a complete explanation about this variable) as below:

```
SRC_URI += "file://fstab"
```

In this manner, when we execute bitbake, it will try to get the fstab file from the files subdirectory within the recipe's directory (actually it searches in other several directories too, as we are going to show below, but for the moment it's not so relevant for this explanation). However, thanks to the file overriding mechanism, it also will try to find the fstab files within the files/${MACHINE} directory too! So if we use the directory structure reported below, we can have general and machine-specific configurations:

```
$ tree files/
files/
├── mach_bar
│   └── fstab
├── mach_foo
│   └── fstab
└── fstab

2 directories, 3 files
```

Given this scenario, if MACHINE is set to mach_foo this will cause the build system to use the file files/mach_foo/fstab, while if MACHINE is set to mach_bar, then the build system will use the file files/mach_bar/fstab. Finally, for any machine apart from mach_foo and mach_bar, the build system will use the file files/fstab.

This mechanism is directed by the FILESPATH variable, which in turn is created by whatever we set within the FILESOVERRIDES variable. In fact:

- FILESPATH is a colon-separated list specifying the default set of directories the Yocto build system uses when searching for patches and files specified by each file:// URI in a recipe's SRC_URI statements for a given recipe (see Section 6.3.2).

It is set by default in the file sources/poky/meta/
classes/base.bbclass as follows:

```
$ cat sources/poky/meta/classes/base.bbclass
...
FILESPATH = "${@base_set_filespath(["${FILE_DIRNAME}/${BP}", "${F
ILE_DIRNAME}/${BPN}", "${FILE_DIRNAME}/files"], d)}"
...
```

The FILESPATH variable is automatically extended
using the overrides from the FILESOVERRIDES variable
because the function base_set_filespath() is defined
as below:

```
$ cat sources/poky/meta/classes/utils.bbclass
...
def base_set_filespath(path, d):
    filespath = []
    extrapaths = (d.getVar("FILESEXTRAPATHS") or "")
    # Remove default flag which was used for checking
    extrapaths = extrapaths.replace("__default:", "")
    # Don't prepend empty strings to the path list
    if extrapaths != "":
        path = extrapaths.split(":") + path
    # The ":" ensures we have an 'empty' override
    overrides = (":" + (d.getVar("FILESOVERRIDES") or "")).split(
":")
    overrides.reverse()
    for o in overrides:
        for p in path:
            if p != "":
                filespath.append(os.path.join(p, o))
    return ":".join(filespath)
...
```

- The FILESOVERRIDES variable is a colon-separated list
  to specify a subset of OVERRIDES to be used by the Yocto
  build system for creating FILESPATH which defaults to

```
FILESOVERRIDES = "${TRANSLATED_TARGET_ARCH}:${MACHINEOVERRIDES}:$
{DISTROOVERRIDES}"
```

However, there are two important notes about these variables to be considered:

1) We have to avoid hand-edit the FILESPATH nor the FILESOVERRIDES variables; if we want bitbake to look in directories apart from the defaults, we can extend the FILESPATH variable by using the FILESEXTRAPATHS variable.

2) Be aware that the default FILESPATH directories do not map to directories in custom layers where append files (.bbappend) are used. Again, if we want bitbake to find patches or files that reside with our append files, we need to use the FILESEXTRAPATHS variable again.

As readers may imagine, FILESEXTRAPATHS is a widely used variable in several recipes and especially in several append files! It is a colon-separated list of path names used to extend the search path, and best practices dictate that we should use the FILESEXTRAPATHS variable from within a .bbappend file as follows:

```
FILESEXTRAPATHS:prepend := "${THISDIR}/${PN}:"
```

In the above example, bitbake first looks for files in a directory that has the same name as the corresponding append file. In fact, THISDIR is the directory in which the file bitbake is currently parsing is located and PN is the recipe's filename (see Section 6.1 for further information about the PN variable).

An interesting real example is within the meta-engicam layer about the psplash package:

```
$ tree meta-engicam-nxp/recipes-core/psplash
meta-engicam-nxp/recipes-core/psplash
├── files
│   └── psplash-poky-img.h
└── psplash_git.bbappend

1 directory, 2 files
```

241

In the append file, we just have the following setting:

```
$ cat meta-engicam-nxp/recipes-core/psplash/psplash_git.bbappend
FILESEXTRAPATHS:prepend := "${THISDIR}/files:"
```

In this manner, we can specify the custom splash image in the file `psplash-poky-img.h` which will be overwritten by the default one during the package compilation.

Note that when extending `FILESEXTRAPATHS`, we must be sure to use the immediate expansion (`:=`) operator in order that `bitbake` evaluates `THISDIR` at the time the directive is encountered rather than at some later time when expansion might result in a directory that does not contain the files we need. Moreover, we have to include the trailing separating colon character (`:`) on prepending, which is necessary because we are directing `bitbake` to extend the path by prepending directories to the search path (similarly as done for the Bash's `PATH` variable).

Another usage of the `FILESEXTRAPATHS` is

```
FILESEXTRAPATHS:prepend := "path_1:path_2:path_3:"
```

To add more paths or, as in this last example, to extend the search path by using a MACHINE-specific override:

```
FILESEXTRAPATHS:prepend:mach_foo := "${THISDIR}/${PN}:"
```

However, the previous statement is not commonly used for machines but for BSPs instead, as done in the `.bbappend` file for the `wpa-supplicant` package as shown below:

```
$ cat meta-imx/meta-bsp/recipes-connectivity/wpa-supplicant/wpa-supplica
nt_%.bbappend
FILESEXTRAPATHS:prepend:imx-nxp-bsp := "${THISDIR}/${PN}:"

DEPENDS += "readline"
```

In this example, all machines compatible with the `imx-nxp-bsp` will apply the prepend (see in Section 11.3 the usage of this technique to prepend paths in `.bbappend` files that will be used for practical examples).

5.4 Including, Requiring, and Inheriting a File

In previous chapters, we have noted that within some recipe or configuration files there are some pieces of code as below:

```
inherit cmake pkgconfig
```

or as below:

```
require conf/machine/include/imx-base.inc
```

This is because BitBake allows for these files to share common functionalities or settings through inclusion of class files (.bbclass) or include files (.inc). For example, above, we tell the bitbake program that our recipe will use CMake and pkg-config tools to compile the code. Then it has to read the cmake.bbclass and pkgconfig.bbclass files, where the support for those tools resides. In the second example, we tell bitbake to read the file under conf/machine/include/imx-base.inc and consider its contents as it was written within the calling file (and to generate an error if it doesn't exist).

This section presents the mechanisms BitBake provides to allow us to share functionality between recipes and configuration files. Specifically, the mechanisms include the include, inherit, INHERIT, and require directives.

Note that BitBake uses the BBPATH variable to locate the include and class files, and then it searches the current directory. This behavior, as per FILESEXTRAPATHS, works similarly as done for the Bash's PATH variable.

5.4.1 The include and require Directives

This directive, as the #include for C, causes bitbake to insert the file specified at that location. The path specified on the include line is a relative path, and BitBake locates the first file it can find within BBPATH or the current directory.

About the require directive, we can say that it works exactly as include does, but it produces an error when the file cannot be found, while include does not. Consequently, it is recommended that if the file we are including is expected to exist, we should use require instead of the include directive. Simply speaking, we can say that require is processed at the start of the recipe, so it is for critical dependencies. Otherwise, include is typically used for configuration files which might not be available for different builds.

A typical usage is the one in the imx8mp-icore.conf file we have already seen in Section 2.3:

```
$ cat meta-engicam-nxp/conf/machine/imx8mp-icore.conf
#@TYPE: Machine
#@NAME: NXP i.MX 8M Plus i.core
#@SOC: i.MX8MP
#@DESCRIPTION: Machine configuration for Engicam imx8mp-icore SOM
#@MAINTAINER: <support@engicam.com>

require include/imx8mp-engicam.inc
...
```

By doing so, we can be sure that when BitBake parses the file, it will also parse the include file, or an error will arise preventing us from having wrong settings for our machine.

5.4.2 The inherit Directive

The inherit directive is used to add one or more functionalities contained in class files that a recipe requires. For example, as already said, if we put in our recipe file the statement inherit cmake pkgconfig, we tell BitBake to read the cmake.bbclass and pkgconfig.bbclass files where the support for the tools CMake and pkg-config resides.

Note that there are some differences between this directive and the include (or require) one:

1) We can specify more than one class file to be inherited, and we omit the .bbclass extension since it applies to class files only.

2) BitBake only supports this directive when used within recipes (.bb file) or class files (.bbclass file).

3) BitBake still searches the inherited .bbclass files by using the BBPATH variable, but within the classes subdirectory for each entry specified.

4) We can inherit class files conditionally by using a variable expression after the inherit statement. For example:

```
VARNAME = "default_class"
VARNAME:class_override = "overrided_class"
inherit ${VARNAME}
```

Note that if VARNAME is not defined, the inherit directive will produce an error as below:

```
ERROR: ParseError at /home/giometti/yocto/imx-yocto-bsp/sources/me
ta-engicam-nxp/recipes-bsp/u-boot-engicam/u-boot-engicam_2022.04.b
b:25: Could not inherit file classes/${VARNAME}.bbclass
ERROR: Parsing halted due to errors, see error messages above
```

It's clear now that the require and include directives previously described are a more generic method of including functionality as compared to the inherit directive. This directive is restricted to load class files only and to be used within recipe or class files only. These two generic directives are applicable for any other kind of shared or encapsulated functionality or configuration that does not suit a class file.

Before closing this section, we should note that we can conditionally inherit class files not only by using an override but also by using anonymous Python code, as reported below:

```
inherit ${@'classname' if condition else ''}
```

With the above code, we ask BitBake to inherit the class named classname if condition is true; in fact, if the expression is false, and it evaluates to an empty string, the statement does not trigger a syntax error because it becomes a no-op.

An example of the above usage can be found in the poky layer, as reported below:

```
$ cat poky/meta/recipes-devtools/btrfs-tools/btrfs-tools_5.16.2.bb
...
inherit autotools-brokensep pkgconfig manpages
inherit ${@bb.utils.contains('PACKAGECONFIG', 'python', 'setuptools3-ba
se', '', d)}
...
```

The classes autotools-brokensep, pkgconfig, and manpages are inherited unconditionally, while the class setuptools3-base is inherited if the variable PACKAGECONFIG holds the python setting only.

5.4.3 The INHERIT Directive

If the inherit directive has restricted functionalities, the INHERIT one is even more limited! In fact, it is not the capital version of inherit, it's a variable, and it can be used only to inherit a class when used within a configuration file (.conf).

A widely used usage of this directive is, for example, about enabling the build history, which causes the Yocto build system to collect build output information and commit it as a single commit to a Git repository.

This feature is disabled by default, and to enable it we have to add the `INHERIT` statement and set the `BUILDHISTORY_COMMIT` variable to 1 at the end of our `conf/local.conf` as reported below:

```
INHERIT += "buildhistory"
BUILDHISTORY_COMMIT = "1"
```

See Section 13.2 for further information about this topic.

As `inherit` counterpart, if we want to use the directive to inherit multiple classes, we can provide them on the same line as below:

```
INHERIT += "class1 class2"
```

5.5 Summary

In this chapter, we have seen how BitBake works; we looked at how variables can be set and unset or how they can be appended and prepended. We discovered what tasks are and how BitBake executes them and in which order, then we discovered the power of conditional syntax, and we learned about overrides which are widely used within the Yocto Project's recipes and configuration files. In the end, we learned about several inclusion directives we can use to write more efficient and more readable recipes.

Now we are ready to learn how to write the Yocto Project's recipes, so we can move on to the next chapter.

CHAPTER 6

Recipes

Recipes contain instructions about how to configure, compile, and deploy a given piece of software. Moreover, they contain the location of the source code and all patches to be applied to it to adapt the final package to the Yocto Project. In a few words, these files completely describe how to generate a software package from scratch!

In this chapter, we are going to take an in-depth look at what these files can hold and how we should write them to have a functional recipe file. In particular, this chapter will explain how recipes can be made and what they can hold, then starting from Chapter 9, we will also provide some practical examples in order to fix all the concepts presented here.

So let's start learning how to write recipe files.

6.1 Locating and Naming Conventions

As we already saw in Section 3.4.4 (and previously during the source's installation), during the configuration phase BitBake will have set the `BBFILES` variable which defines the list of recipe files (`.bb`) to parse, along with any append files (`.bbappend`) to apply. So, the `bitbake` program parses these files and stores the values of various variables they define into its data store.

We can name and locate these recipe files as we wish, but in general, they should follow the naming convention `recipes-category/name/name_version.bb`. For example, if we take a look at the

© Rodolfo Giometti 2025
R. Giometti, *Yocto Project Customization for Linux*,
https://doi.org/10.1007/979-8-8688-1435-8_6

meta-networking layer (within the meta-openembedded directory), we see the following structure:

```
$ ls sources/meta-openembedded/meta-networking/
COPYING.MIT  files                recipes-devtools  recipes-netkit
MAINTAINERS  licenses             recipes-extended  recipes-protocols
README       recipes-connectivity recipes-filter    recipes-support
classes      recipes-core         recipes-irc
conf         recipes-daemons      recipes-kernel
```

Here, we have several recipe categories as recipes-filter, recipes-protocols, recipes-daemons, etc., and, for example, in this last directory we find the following:

```
$ ls sources/meta-openembedded/meta-networking/recipes-daemons/
atftp        iscsi-initiator-utils  openhpi  pure-ftpd  vsftpd
autofs       keepalived             opensaf  radvd
cyrus-sasl   lldpd                  postfix  squid
igmpproxy    ncftp                  proftpd  tftp-hpa
ippool       networkd-dispatcher    ptpd     vb
```

Here, embedded developers should recognize several networking daemons. Then, for example, the corresponding recipe is located within the vsftpd directory with all the needed files to build the vsftpd package:

```
$ cd sources/meta-openembedded
$ tree meta-networking/recipes-daemons/vsftpd/
meta-networking/recipes-daemons/vsftpd/
├── files
│   ├── change-secure_chroot_dir.patch
│   ├── init
│   ├── volatiles.99_vsftpd
│   ├── vsftpd.conf
│   ├── vsftpd.ftpusers
│   ├── vsftpd.service
│   └── vsftpd.user_list
├── vsftpd-3.0.5
│   ├── 0001-sysdeputil.c-Fix-with-musl-which-does-not-have-utmpx.patch
│   ├── makefile-destdir.patch
│   ├── makefile-libs.patch
│   ├── makefile-strip.patch
│   ├── nopam.patch
│   ├── nopam-with-tcp_wrappers.patch
```

```
    ├── vsftpd-2.1.0-filter.patch
    │   └── vsftpd-tcp_wrappers-support.patch
    └── vsftpd_3.0.5.bb
```

2 directories, 16 files

The readers should notice that the recipe file, which is the one with the
`.bb` extension, is named `vsftpd_3.0.5.bb` because the available recipe is
for the release 3.0.5 of the vsftpd daemon (the very secure FTP daemon).

The readers should also notice that in the directory `meta-networking`
all recipes for related projects (in the above example, all networking
daemons' recipes) may share the same recipe directory (i.e., `recipes-daemons`).

Note that recipes' names and categories may contain hyphens, but
hyphens are not allowed in versions since they are used to space the
package's name from the package's version!

So, the usual name for recipe files is *name_version*`.bb` where *version*
usually has the form *XX.YY.ZZ*. However, this is not a fixed rule, and a
special note must be done for projects tracked by revision control tools,
for instance, the Git tool. In this case, the recipe does not correspond to a
released version of the software, so *version* is set to the string `git`, and the
recipe file is named *name_git*`.bb`.

This rigid structure is used within BitBake's environment to generate
the PN and PV variables. The former is used to hold the recipe name
(or the resulting package name – see below for further information),
while the latter holds the version of the recipe, and both are extracted
from the recipe filename. In the above example, the recipe is named
`vsftpd_3.0.5.bb`, then PN will be set to `vsftpd`, while the default value of
PV will be `3.0.5`.

However, about PN, this is not a fixed rule; in fact, there are special cases (not covered in this book) where the name stored in PN may also contain a special suffix or prefix. In fact, as specified by the Yocto Project's Reference Manual at `https://docs.yoctoproject.org/ref-manual/variables.html?highlight=srcrev#term-PN`, when we are using Bash to build packages for the native machine, PN is set to `bash-native`, while when we are using `bash` to build packages for the target and for Multilib (used for the creation of distros with libraries for different architectures originating from the same sources, for example, 32- and 64-bit libraries), PN would be `bash` and `lib64-bash`, respectively.

Note also that PV is generally not overridden within a recipe unless it is building an unstable (or development) version from a source code repository as Git or Subversion. In this case, it is rewritten as in the Netperf's recipe within the meta-openembedded layer, as shown below:

```
$ grep '^PV' meta-networking/recipes-support/netperf/netperf_git.bb
PV = "2.7.0+git${SRCPV}"
```

In this example, the recipe addresses the Netperf release 2.7.0 and adds the `+git` string followed by the content of the SRCPV variable, which holds the version string of the current package extracted from the Git repository (usually the commit ID). For Netperf, we have

```
bitbake -e netperf | grep PV=
PV="2.7.0+gitAUTOINC+3bc455b23f"
SRCPV="AUTOINC+3bc455b23f"
```

while for vsftpd, we get

```
$ bitbake -e vsftpd | grep PV=
PV="3.0.5"
```

All these special cases will be more clear and better explained in the next sections of this book.

6.2 Understanding Version Policies

Once we have understood how recipes should be named and where they should be placed, a significant thing to know is how the Yocto Project manages packages' versions. If we take a look at the file sources/poky/meta/classes/package_ipk.bbclass where the code is placed to build IPKG packages, we may get an idea about how packages' versions are defined:

```
...
    pe = d.getVar('PKGE')
    if pe and int(pe) > 0:
        fields.append(["Version: %s:%s-%s\n", ['PKGE', 'PKGV', 'PKGR']])
    else:
        fields.append(["Version: %s-%s\n", ['PKGV', 'PKGR']])
...
```

that is, by composing the variables PKGE, PKGV, and PKGR. These variables are, respectively, the epoch, the version, and the revision of each package built by the recipes, and they default to the variables PE, PV, and PG. In particular, we have the following:

- PE is the epoch of the recipe, and, by default, this variable is unset. This variable is used to make upgrades possible when the versioning scheme changes in some backward-incompatible way (it can only have an integer value).

- PV is the version of the recipe, and it is normally extracted from the recipe filename. For example, as in the example from the previous section, the recipe name is vsftpd_3.0.5.bb, then the default value of PV will be 3.0.5.

- PR is the revision of the recipe, and it defaults to r0. Subsequent revisions of the recipe conventionally have the values r1, r2, and so forth. It should reset to r0 when PV increases.

253

As already introduced in the previous section, PV is generally not set within a recipe unless it is built from a source code repository managed by git (or any other versioning tool). In such cases, a special setting should be used for PV, especially in the case that does not correspond to a released version of software (i.e., not a tagged version); the PV variable should include the git revision as shown below:

```
PV = "version+git${SRCPV}"
```

Here, version should be the most recently released version of the software from the current source revision (we can use the git describe command to determine this), and SRCPV is the version string of the current package. It is generated by the bitbake program according to the tool used to manage the source's repository.

This format is also useful when using the AUTOREV variable to set the recipe to increment source control revisions automatically within the SRCREV variable, during development, as shown below:

```
SRCREV = "${AUTOREV}"
```

In the next sections, we'll see a common usage of these variables during development. For the moment, the readers should note that SRCREV applies to Subversion and Git (and Mercurial and Bazaar too), and, when used, it causes a query on the remote repository every time BitBake parses our recipe. So, if we want to build a fixed revision and to avoid performing the query, we should specify a full revision identifier as the Netperf's recipe does:

```
$ grep SRCREV meta-networking/recipes-support/netperf/netperf_git
.bb
SRCREV = "3bc455b23f901dae377ca0a558e1e32aa56b31c4"
```

The readers should also note that if SRCREV is set to ${AUTOREV} the devtool modify command may fail. So be sure to not have this special setting before using devtool on a recipe!

Apart from these considerations, for normal recipes, we usually set PV (or bitbake does it for us by reading the recipe's name) to select our desired software release.

Finally, some words must be spent on PR and PE.

About PR, we should consider that it becomes significant when a package manager dynamically installs packages on an already built image. In this case, PR (and in turn PKGR) may help the package manager to distinguish which package is the most recent one in cases where many packages have the same version (PV and PKGV). A typical usage of this mechanism is when we have several packages with the same PV, but with different PR values. It means that all of them install the same upstream version, but the latest PR values may include, for instance, some bug fixes.

Values for PR had to be set manually, but, in most cases, these can now be set and incremented automatically by a *PR Server* connected with a package feed. However, this behavior is not covered in this book, and the readers may get further information in the *Working With a PR Service* section in the Yocto Project Development Tasks Manual at `https://docs.yoctoproject.org/3.2.3/dev-manual/dev-manual-common-tasks.html#working-with-a-pr-service`.

On the other hand, a typical usage of PE is when PV changes in such a way that it does not increase in respect to the previous value. So we can use PE to ensure package managers will upgrade it correctly. In fact, when PE is set to a value greater than 0, the package's name is composed of

```
${PN}-${PE}_${PV}-${PR}
```

instead of the usual:

```
${PN}-${PV}-${PR}
```

All these considerations are about the fact that recipe versions should always compare and sort correctly so that upgrades work as expected. In fact, usually conventional versions such as 1.4 upgrading to 1.5 happen naturally, but some versions don't. For example, 1.5rc2 (i.e., version 1.5 Release Candidate 2) sorts before 1.5, and upgrades from feeds won't happen correctly!

For version comparisons, in the case of IPK packages, the `opkg-compare-versions` program from the `opkg-utils` package can be useful when attempting to determine how two version numbers compare to each other.

In this special example, there are two ways to solve this problem:

1) We can set PE to 1, or a higher value, to force our ordering method.

2) We can use the tilde (~) operator, which sorts before the empty string, within PV as

   ```
   PV = "1.5~rc2"
   ```

In this manner, release `1.5~rc2` comes before release `1.5`.

There is a historical syntax which may be found where PV is set as a combination of the prior version plus the pre-release version, for example:

```
PV = "1.4+1.5rc2".
```

This is a valid syntax, but the tilde form is preferred.

6.3 Recipe Structure

Once we have understood how a recipe file and packages should be named and how to manage software versioning, we are now ready to take a look at how a recipe file is structured, that is, which variables we should use within it, when and where we can include files or inherit classes, etc.

Each time we write a recipe file, we should follow the general order below (when possible):

- General description: In this section, we find all variables which describe the recipe contents and code.

- Source code information: Here, we list all sources (local or remote) where the code must be taken from.

- Building rules: Here, we must add all rules needed to convert courses into executables or data.

- Packaging information: We put here all information needed to group built files into valid Yocto Project's packages ready to be installed into a target.

A practical example of what we are saying is reported within the poky meta layer in the `meta-skeleton/recipes-skeleton` directory, which holds several useful example recipes:

```
$ tree sources/poky/meta-skeleton/recipes-skeleton/hello-single/
sources/poky/meta-skeleton/recipes-skeleton/hello-single/
├── files
│   └── helloworld.c
└── hello_1.0.bb

1 directory, 2 files
```

This is a fully functional recipe where all needed files are stored locally. The recipe `hello_1.0.bb` looks like below:

```
$ cd sources/poky
$ cat meta-skeleton/recipes-skeleton/hello-single/hello_1.0.bb
DESCRIPTION = "Simple helloworld application"
```

```
SECTION = "examples"
LICENSE = "MIT"
LIC_FILES_CHKSUM = "file://${COMMON_LICENSE_DIR}/MIT;md5=0835ade698e0bc
f8506ecda2f7b4f302"

SRC_URI = "file://helloworld.c"

S = "${WORKDIR}"

do_compile() {
        ${CC} ${LDFLAGS} helloworld.c -o helloworld
}

do_install() {
        install -d ${D}${bindir}
        install -m 0755 helloworld ${D}${bindir}
}
```

The general description section holds the following settings:

```
DESCRIPTION = "Simple helloworld application"
SECTION = "examples"
LICENSE = "MIT"
LIC_FILES_CHKSUM = "file://${COMMON_LICENSE_DIR}/MIT;md5=0835ade698e0bc
f8506ecda2f7b4f302"
```

while the source code information section holds the following:

```
SRC_URI = "file://helloworld.c"
```

then the building rules section:

```
S = "${WORKDIR}"

do_compile() {
        ${CC} ${LDFLAGS} helloworld.c -o helloworld
}

do_install() {
        install -d ${D}${bindir}
        install -m 0755 helloworld ${D}${bindir}
}
```

In this recipe, there is no packaging information section due to the fact that the Yocto build system has some implicit rules to create packages (and to do many other tasks, as we can see below in this book), so no additional rules are needed to complete the job.

Note that the variable `COMMON_LICENSE_DIR` points to the directory `meta/files/common-licenses` in the poky layer, which is where generic license files reside.

6.3.1 General Descriptions

As already stated, in this section we can find general information about the package, and to do so the following variables can be used:

- `SUMMARY`: A one-line description (72 characters or fewer) of the binary package for packaging systems such as opkg, rpm, or dpkg.

- `DESCRIPTION`: The extended description of the binary package, possibly with multiple lines (i.e., the extended version of `SUMMARY`). We can omit it, and, in this case, it defaults to `SUMMARY`.

- `HOMEPAGE`: The URL to the upstream project's home page, if exists.

- `BUGTRACKER`: The URL upstream project's bug tracking website, if exists. The Yocto build system does not use this variable, but it could be useful for bug reporting.

- `SECTION`: Specifies the section in which packages should be categorized. This information is not needed to build the code, but the package management utilities can make use of this variable to group packages.

Usual values specified here are

- `base`: Packages which are part of a base system, for example, init scripts, core utilities, standard system daemons. etc.

- `doc`: Documentation packages as man pages and sample configuration files.

- `libs`: Runtime libraries (not used for development – see `devel`). It may have subsections as `libs/network`, `libs/multimedia`, etc., for better library categorization.

- `utils`: Generic utilities.

- `network`: Networking-related packages.

- `devel`: Development-related packages such as compilers, headers, debuggers, etc. It may have subsections as `devel/libs` (named also `libdevel`) used to store development libraries, `devel/python` for Python development code, etc.

- `shell`: Shell packages as `bash`, `zsh`, etc.

- `console`: Packages holding applications which run on the console, with no GUI-related libraries or interfaces to run. It may have subsections as `console/utils`, `console/network`, `console/editors`, `console/multimedia`, `console/network`, etc.

- `kernel`: Kernel-related packages. Frequently used subsections are `kernel/modules` (out-of-tree kernel modules) and `kernel/userland` (kernel tool to be executed within the user space).

   –   bootloaders: Packages holding the applications to
be used to load the kernel after the boot.

   –   x11: Packages related to the X11 (or graphic)
applications. Usually, its subsections are used
instead: x11/base, x11/libs, x11/utils, x11/
network, etc.

   –   Other sections as fonts, games, etc.

To get a basic idea about what sections are, we can take a look
within the bitbake.conf file:

```
$ grep SECTION sources/poky/meta/conf/bitbake.conf
SECTION = "base"
SECTION:${PN}-doc = "doc"
SECTION:${PN}-dev = "devel"
SECTION:${PN}-staticdev = "devel"
SECTION:${PN}-dbg = "devel"
SECTION:${PN}-src = "devel"
```

As we can see, by default, BitBake defines several packages for each
recipe, each of them well fixed within a proper section.

   •   LICENSE and LIC_FILES_CHKSUM: The former is used
to list the licenses that apply to the sources, while
the latter holds the checksums of the files holding
such licenses (see below in this section for further
information about what we can put into these
variables).

A typical layout for this general description section can be seen within
the recipe for the z-shell (zsh) located in the file zsh_5.8.bb within the
meta-openembedded layer, which is reported below:

```
$ cat sources/meta-openembedded/meta-oe/recipes-shells/zsh/zsh_5.8.bb
SUMMARY = "UNIX Shell similar to the Korn shell"
DESCRIPTION = "Zsh is a shell designed for interactive use, although \
               it is also a powerful scripting language. Many of the \
               useful features of bash, ksh, and tcsh were \
               incorporated into zsh; many original features were \
               added."
HOMEPAGE = "http://www.zsh.org"
SECTION = "base/shell"

LICENSE = "zsh"
LIC_FILES_CHKSUM = "file://LICENCE;md5=1a4c4cda3e8096d2fd483ff2f4514fec"
...
```

What is interesting to note here is about the last two variables. In fact, as we can see, LIC_FILES_CHKSUM holds information to check the license text and to track changes in it by using a checksum. If the license text changes, then the building will fail, and we have the opportunity to review such changes.

Unless LICENSE is set to CLOSE, we must specify a proper value for LIC_FILES_CHKSUM as in the above example for the Zsh's license. By using the settings above for LIC_FILES_CHKSUM, we tell the Yocto build system that the text of the license is held in the file LICENCE in the source's directory, and its MD5 checksum value is 1a4c4cda3e8096d2fd483ff2f4514fec.

There are different syntax we can use within the LIC_FILES_CHKSUM variable, and below there is an example:

```
LIC_FILES_CHKSUM = " \
    file://COPYING;md5=xxxxxxxxxxxx \
    file://licfile1.txt;beginline=5;endline=29;md5=yyyyyyyyyyyyyyyyy \
    file://source.c;endline=50;md5=zzzzzzzzzzzzzzzz \
...
```

First, note that we can specify several license files at once, and by using the beginline and endline keywords (values are considered inclusive), we can limit the check within a file. This is useful when the license text is written within a file among the code. For example, if we have the following file content:

```
$ cat -n helloworld.c
     1      /*
     2       * Copyright 2024 Rodolfo Giometti <giometti@enneenne.com>
     3       *
     4       * Permission is hereby granted, free of charge, to any
     5       * person obtaining a copy of this software and associated
     6       * documentation files (the "Software"), to deal in the
     7       * Software without restriction, including without
     8       * limitation * the rights to use, copy, modify, merge,
     9       * publish, distribute, sublicense, and/or sell copies of
    10       * the Software, and to permit persons to whom the Software
    11       * is furnished to do so, subject to the following
    12       * conditions:
    13       *
    14       * THE SOFTWARE IS PROVIDED "AS IS", WITHOUT WARRANTY OF ANY
    15       * KIND, EXPRESS OR IMPLIED, INCLUDING BUT NOT LIMITED TO
    16       * THE WARRANTIES OF MERCHANTABILITY, FITNESS FOR A
    17       * PARTICULAR PURPOSE AND NONINFRINGEMENT. IN NO EVENT SHALL
    18       * THE AUTHORS OR COPYRIGHT HOLDERS BE LIABLE FOR ANY CLAIM,
    19       * DAMAGES OR OTHER LIABILITY, WHETHER IN AN ACTION OF
    20       * CONTRACT, TORT OR OTHERWISE, ARISING FROM, OUT OF OR IN
    21       * CONNECTION WITH THE SOFTWARE OR THE USE OR OTHER DEALINGS
    22       * IN THE SOFTWARE.
    23       */
    24
    25      #include <stdio.h>
    26
    27      int main(void)
    28      {
    29              printf("Hello world!\n");
    30
    31              return 0;
    32      }
```

then within LIC_FILES_CHKSUM we should put the following:

```
LIC_FILES_CHKSUM = " \
    file://helloworld.c;beginline=1;endline=23;md5=yyyyyyyyyyyyyyyy \
    "
```

Note that if beginline is 1, it can be omitted.

Regarding what we can use within the LICENSE variable, we must follow the following rules:

- Do not use spaces within individual license names. So, for example, the license *GPL version 2.0 or later* can be specified with the string GPL-2.0-or-later.

- Recipes can specify more than one license name by separating them with the pipe character (|) when there is a choice between licenses or with the ampersand character (&) when there are multiple licenses for different parts of the source. For example:

  ```
  LICENSE = "LGPL-2.1-only | GPL-3.0-only"
  LICENSE = "MPL-1.0 & LGPL-2.1-only"
  ```

  The first line in the example states that the user may choose to distribute under either the LGPL version 2.1 or GPL version 3, while the second line states that the two licenses cover different parts of the source code.

  For standard licenses, we can use the names of the files within the poky layer in the meta/files/common-licenses directory or the SPDXLICENSEMAP flag names defined within the file meta/conf/licenses.conf:

  ```
  $ cat sources/poky/meta/conf/licenses.conf
  ...
  SPDXLICENSEMAP[AGPL-3.0] = "AGPL-3.0-only"
  SPDXLICENSEMAP[AGPL-3.0+] = "AGPL-3.0-or-later"

  # BSD variations
  SPDXLICENSEMAP[BSD-0-Clause] = "0BSD"
  ```

```
# GPL variations
SPDXLICENSEMAP[GPL-1] = "GPL-1.0-only"
SPDXLICENSEMAP[GPL-1+] = "GPL-1.0-or-later"
SPDXLICENSEMAP[GPLv1] = "GPL-1.0-only"
SPDXLICENSEMAP[GPLv1+] = "GPL-1.0-or-later"
...
```

- For recipes which define more than one package having different licenses, we can specify licenses on a per-package basis. For example, a piece of software whose code is licensed under GPLv2 but has accompanying documentation licensed under the GNU Free Documentation License 1.2 could be specified as follows:

```
LICENSE = "GFDL-1.2 & GPL-2.0-only"
LICENSE:${PN} = "GPL-2.0.only"
LICENSE:${PN}-doc = "GFDL-1.2"
```

See Section 6.3.4 to know how to manage multiple package information or Section 9.1 for a practical example.

- In the case of proprietary packages, we should use the keyword CLOSED, which doesn't need any other specifications.

6.3.2 Source Code Information

In this section, we provide information about how to get the code, which release and what is needed to get it compiled. To do so, we can use the following variables:

- DEPENDS: Lists the build-time dependencies for the recipe. These kinds of dependencies are other recipes whose contents (i.e., headers and/or shared libraries) are needed by the recipe at build time.

In the Yocto Project, it is important to understand the differences between build-time dependencies and runtime dependencies, which can be specified by using the RDEPENDS variable. See below in this section for a complete explanation of these concepts.

- PROVIDES: Holds a list of aliases by which a particular recipe can be known within the Yocto build system.

- By default, the value in PN is implicitly already in this list. Therefore, it does not need to be added, but we can add alias names here when it could be useful for satisfying dependencies of other recipes during the build (see below in this section for some examples).

As for DEPENDS and RDEPENDS, PROVIDES also has the RPROVIDES counterpart, which is used to specify package names to satisfy such runtime dependencies requested by RDEPENDS.

- PV: As already seen above, this variable stores the version of the recipe which is normally extracted from the recipe filename unless it is building from a source code repository (in that case, we have to properly set it as already shown above and how we will do below in this book).

- Note also that PV is the default value of the PKGV variable introduced above.

- SRC_URI: The list of source files. To give an exhaustive explanation of this variable is really complex, so it will be done below in this section; for the moment, we can say that it is the variable which tells BitBake which files to pull for the build and how and where to pull them.

- For example, if we need to fetch a tarball, apply two patches, and include a custom file, we can properly set the SRC_URI variable that specifies all those sources!

- SRCREV: As already introduced above, it is the revision of the source code used to build the package, and it is used with Subversion, Git, Mercurial, and Bazaar only.

- S: This points to the location in the build directory where unpacked recipe source code resides, and it defaults to ${WORKDIR}/${BPN}-${PV} (BPN is the base recipe name – see below). It's important to keep in mind that if the source tarball extracts the code to a directory named anything besides ${BPN}-${PV} or if the source code is fetched from a repository (Git, Subversion, etc.), then we must set S in the recipe so that the build system knows where to locate the unpacked source (see below).

Now that an introduction of these variables has been done, we need to spend more words on some of them and propose some examples to better understand how to use them.

Let's start with DEPENDS and consider a recipe named foo that contains the following assignment:

```
DEPENDS = "bar foo-native"
```

The practical effect of this assignment is that all files installed by the bar package will be available in the appropriate staging directory by the time the do_configure task for foo runs. And all files installed by the native version of recipe foo, which is named foo-native, will be ready to be invoked by the time the do_build task for the recipe foo runs.

While it's quite intuitive that by specifying bar as foo's dependency we say to the build system that to compile foo we need before compiling bar, the foo-native specification could lead to more ambiguous results. However, it will become clear if we consider foo-native as the package that holds, for example, a code generator we need to run before starting the foo compilation. In fact, that code generator may produce some files required by the compiler to produce foo. So, by specifying the foo-native dependency, we tell the build system we need to compile the native version of foo (i.e., the code that runs on the host) before compiling the version of foo for the target (an example is reported in Section 11.6.1).

In this latter case, that is, when some foo-native application is invoked, we may have to specify more path names in the host's PATH variable to allow proper execution on the host. By specifying the following, we can add the path names ${STAGING_BINDIR_NATIVE}/foo and ${STAGING_BINDIR_NATIVE}/bar at the beginning of PATH:

EXTRANATIVEPATH = "foo bar"

where STAGING_BINDIR_NATIVE usually points to the /usr/bin subdirectory of the sysroot directory for the build system on the host.

It's now clear, by the above example, that DEPENDS is not just a list of recipe names, but it is a list of PROVIDES names, which typically match recipe names. Moreover, these dependencies are valid during the building of the package due to the fact that they do not add any runtime dependencies between the packages produced by the two recipes.

For further information about runtime dependencies, the readers should see the RDEPENDS and RPROVIDES variables in Section 6.3.4.

Regarding PROVIDES, it is used to specify a list of aliases by which a particular recipe can be known. For example, let's take a look at the two recipes eudev_3.2.10.bb and systemd_250.5.bb within the sources/ poky/meta/recipes-core directory:

```
$ cat sources/poky/meta/recipes-core/udev/eudev_3.2.10.bb
SUMMARY = "eudev is a fork of systemd's udev"
HOMEPAGE = "https://wiki.gentoo.org/wiki/Eudev"
DESCRIPTION = "eudev is Gentoo's fork of udev, systemd's device file manager for
the Linux kernel. It manages device nodes in /dev and handles all user space
actions when adding or removing devices."
...
PROVIDES = "udev"
...
$ cat sources/poky/meta/recipes-core/systemd/systemd_250.5.bb
require systemd.inc

PROVIDES = "udev"
...
```

In both recipes, PROVIDES is set to udev, so both recipes can be aliased with the common name of udev.

This is useful when more than one package provides a generic functionality, and we wish to request a dependency to that functionality instead of the name of the package that implements it.

When we build a package, the recipe name PN is always implicitly prepended to PROVIDES, so the above settings with the sign = are perfectly functional; however, to avoid confusion, we should use the more intuitive sign +=.

In the example, the generic functionality is udev which is provided by both eudev and systemd packages, so a third recipe which requires the udev functionality can use the following DEPENDS settings instead of specifying a package name:

```
DEPENDS = "udev"
```

Then developers can determine which recipe is preferred and thus provides the requested functionality by using the PREFERRED_PROVIDER variable in a configuration file as below:

```
PREFERRED_PROVIDER_udev = "systemd"
```

This allows developers to detach functionalities from the packages that implement them (this will be more clear starting from Chapter 8 and following).

In addition to providing recipes under alternate names, the PROVIDES mechanism is also used to implement virtual targets. These virtual targets have been already introduced in Section 3.4.2 when we mentioned the virtual/xserver or virtual/kernel targets, where they correspond to some particular functionality (in the example, the X server and Linux). Recipes that provide the functionality in question list the virtual targets in PROVIDES, while recipes that depend on the functionality in question can include the virtual targets in DEPENDS to leave the choice of provider open. As above, the PREFERRED_PROVIDER variable is used to select which particular recipe provides a virtual target.

Now, as the last argument of this section, we should take a more in-depth look at the SRC_URI variable. We already said that this variable tells BitBake which files to pull for the build and how to pull them. However, it is time to do some examples in order to well understand how we can use it.

> To keep the explanation simple and focused on the major usage modes, we do not report all possible combinations available for the SRC_URI variable. The readers can look at `https://docs.yoctoproject.org/bitbake/2.6/bitbake-user-manual/bitbake-user-manual-ref-variables.html#term-SRC_URI` for a complete reference.

Within the SRC_URI variable, we can specify a list of possible URI protocols that BitBake must use to fetch the code. Here is a list of the most used protocols (and also used in this book):

- `file://`: Fetches files from the local machine where the recipe resides (usually a subdirectory in the recipe's main directory)

- `ftp://`, `sftp://`, `http://`, and `https://`: Fetch files from the Internet using respectively the FTP, SFTP, HTTP, or HTTPS protocol

- `git://`: Fetches files from a Git revision control repository

Depending on the selected protocols (or, as named in the Yocto Project, *fetcher*), various URL parameters can be specified, and below we will report some examples (again, for a complete list, the readers can look at `https://docs.yoctoproject.org/bitbake/2.6/bitbake-user-manual/bitbake-user-manual-fetching.html#fetchers`).

With `file://` we can specify a relative or absolute filename as below:

```
SRC_URI = "file://relative_filename"
SRC_URI = "file:///path/to/absolute_filename"
```

If the filename is relative, that is, specified with two slashes (/) after file:, the contents of the FILESPATH variable are used in the same way PATH is used to find executables. The build system searches, in order, from the following directories, which are assumed to be subdirectories of the directory in which the recipe file (.bb) or append file (.bbappend) resides. Several names are searched by default (i.e., are already present in FILESPATH):

- ${BPN}: The base recipe name without any special suffix or version numbers

- ${BP}-${BPN}-${PV}: The base recipe name and version but without any special package name suffix

- files: A directory named files alongside the recipe or append file

If the file cannot be found, it is assumed that it is available in the directory specified by the DL_DIR variable. Otherwise, if the filename is absolute, that is, specified with three slashes (/) after file:, we have no alternatives and the file must be placed as specified or error.

Note that if we specify a directory, the entire directory is then unpacked!

Using ftp://, sftp://, http://, and https:// is quite obvious, and some examples are below:

```
SRC_URI = "ftp://example.com/tarball.lz"
SRC_URI = "sftp://host.example.com/dir/path.file.txt"
SRC_URI = "http://example.com/tarball.zip"
SRC_URI = "https://host.example.com/dir/path.file.xz"
```

With the above fetcher, we can also specify the parameter downloadfilename that allows the fetcher to store the downloaded file in a specified custom filename in the DL_DIR directory. This is useful for avoiding collisions in DL_DIR when dealing with multiple files that have the same name. Two simple examples are below:

```
SRC_URI = https://somewhere.org/example/1.0.0/example;downloadfilename=
some-example-1.0.0.tgz"
SRC_URI = "http://www.netlib.org/benchmark/linpackc.new;downloadfilenam
e=linpacknew.c"
```

The former renames the downloaded file example into a more suitable (and useful) some-example-1.0.0.tgz, while the latter renames the silly linpackc.new name into more proper linpacknew.c.

Because URL parameters are delimited by semicolons, this can introduce ambiguity when parsing URLs that also contain semicolons, for example:

```
SRC_URI = "https://gcc.gnu.org/git/gitweb.cgi?p=gcc/gcc.git;a=snapshot;
h=bd5e88"
```

This URL should be modified by replacing semicolons with ampersand characters (&) as shown below:

```
SRC_URI = "https://gcc.gnu.org/git/gitweb.cgi?p=gcc/gcc.git&a=snapshot&
h=bd5e88"
```

In most cases, this should work, but due to the nature of the URL, we may have to specify the name of the downloaded file as well:

```
SRC_URI = "https://gcc.gnu.org/git/gitweb.cgi?p=gcc/gcc.git&a=snapshot&
h=bd5e88;downloadfilename=gcc-2.1.bz2"
```

As already stated before, if we address an archive in the fetcher, and it extracts the code to a directory named anything besides ${BPN}-${PV} (let's suppose it extracts to dir), then S should be set accordingly (as in the example):

```
S = "${WORKDIR}/dir"
```

Furthermore, in special circumstances we can specify a username and password in the SRC_URI as below:

```
SRC_URI = "https://giometti:password@www.enneenne.com/secret/data.gz"
```

The general form for a fetcher is

```
SRC_URI = "<fetcher>://[user:[password]@]<location>/<path>;<param
s>"
```

Note also that for the `sftp://` fetcher the password in the URI is not supported; use SSH keys to authenticate.

Moreover, if the variable BB_CHECK_SSL_CERTS is set to 0, then SSL certificate checking will be disabled. Of course, this variable defaults to 1.

Downloading a file from the Web is not reliable, and file integrity is of key importance for reproducing builds. In this case, the fetcher code can verify SHA-256 and MD5 checksums to ensure the archives have been downloaded correctly. We can specify these checksums by using some SRC_URI[] flag variables, as reported below:

```
SRC_URI[md5sum] = <value>
SRC_URI[sha256sum] = <value>
```

or directly within the SRC_URI variable (similarly to LIC_FILES_CHKSUM) as shown below:

```
SRC_URI = "http://example.com/foo.tgz;md5sum=4a8e0f237e961fd7785d19d07f
db994d"
```

This is useful when multiple URIs exist; however, in this case, it can also specify the checksums by naming the URLs as shown below:

```
SRC_URI = "http://example.com/foo.tgz;name=foo"
SRC_URI[foo.md5sum] = 4a8e0f237e961fd7785d19d07fdb994d
```

If `BB_STRICT_CHECKSUM` is set, then any download without a checksum triggers an error message.

The `git://` fetcher gets code from the Git source control system and creates a bare clone of the remote into the `GITDIR` directory, which is usually `DL_DIR/git2`. This bare clone is then cloned into the work directory during the unpack stage when a specific tree is checked out.

This fetcher supports several parameters, and below are the most used ones (see the full list at `https://docs.yoctoproject.org/bitbake/2.6/bitbake-user-manual/bitbake-user-manual-fetching.html#git-fetcher-git`):

- `protocol`: It is used to specify the protocol to be used to fetch the files. The default is `git` when a hostname is set, while if not set, it defaults to `file`. Other valid values are `http`, `https`, `ssh`, and `rsync`.

- `destsuffix`: Specifies the name of the directory in which to place the checkout. It defaults to `git/` (see below for an example where this parameter can be useful).

- `branch`: Specifies the branch (or branches – see below) of the Git tree to clone. It defaults to `master`.

- `tag` or `rev`: Specifies a tag to use for the checkout. Note that, to correctly resolve tags, BitBake must access the network, so tags are often not used.

- `nobranch`: When fetching source from a Git repository, BitBake will validate the `SRCREV` value against the specified branch; however, if we need to bypass this check (in the case we are fetching a revision corresponding to a tag that is not on any branch), we can add the setting `nobranch=1`.

275

Typical examples of this fetcher are below:

```
SRC_URI = "git://git.yoctoproject.org/git/poky;protocol=http"
SRC_URI = "git://github.com/asciidoc/asciidoc-py;protocol=https;branch=
main"
```

A special note must be done for the `ssh` protocol. In fact, the URL expected in SRC_URI differs from the one that is typically passed to the `git clone` command. For example, to clone the mesa repository over SSH, we should use the command below:

```
$ git clone git@gitlab.freedesktop.org:mesa/mesa.git
```

However, in SRC_URI we should specify the following:

```
SRC_URI = "git://git@gitlab.freedesktop.org/mesa/mesa.git;branch=main;p
rotocol=ssh;..."
```

Note that the colon (`:`) character changed into a slash (`/`) before the path to the project.

As already stated before, when using the `git://` fetcher, the `S` variable should be set accordingly:

```
S = "${WORKDIR}/git"
```

And when we have more than one repository to download, we can do something as the `tvm_0.7.0.bb` recipe does, as shown below:

```
$ cat sources/meta-imx/meta-ml/recipes-libraries/tvm/tvm_0.7.0.bb
...
SRCBRANCH = "lf-5.15.71_2.2.0"
TVM_SRC ?= "git://github.com/nxp-imx/eiq-tvm-imx.git;protocol=https"
SRC_URI = "${TVM_SRC};branch=${SRCBRANCH}\
            git://github.com/dmlc/dlpack;protocol=https;nobranch=1;d
estsuffix=${S}/3rdparty/dlpack;name=dlpack \
            git://github.com/dmlc/dmlc-core;protocol=https;nobranch=
1;destsuffix=${S}/3rdparty/dmlc-core;name=dmlc-core \
            git://github.com/agauniyal/rang;protocol=https;nobranch=
1;destsuffix=${S}/3rdparty/rang;name=rang \
            git://github.com/apache/incubator-tvm-vta;protocol=https
```

```
;nobranch=1;destsuffix=${S}/3rdparty/vta-hw;name=vta-hw \
                file://0001-tvm-CMakeLists.txt-Use-CMAKE-variables-for-l
ibs-inst.patch \
                file://tvm_runtime.pc.in \
"

SRCREV = "32c38730216147966f8d65f99b0c2d814fb8509b"
SRCREV_dlpack = "3ec04430e89a6834e5a1b99471f415fa939bf642"
SRCREV_dmlc-core = "6c401e242c59a1f4c913918246591bb13fd714e7"
SRCREV_rang = "cabe04d6d6b05356fa8f9741704924788f0dd762"
SRCREV_vta-hw = "87ce9acfae550d1a487746e9d06c2e250076e54c"

S = "${WORKDIR}/git"
...
```

In this example, we specify several Git repositories to fetch from, and by using the destsuffix parameter we will get a directory structure for the sources as below:

```
$ tree -L 1 tmp/work/armv8a-poky-linux/tvm/0.7.0-r0/git/3rdparty/
tmp/work/armv8a-poky-linux/tvm/0.7.0-r0/git/3rdparty/
├── cma
├── compiler-rt
├── dlpack
├── dmlc-core
├── libcrc
├── picojson
├── rang
└── vta-hw

8 directories, 0 files
```

Note also the SRCREV_<name> variables used to specify the different commit IDs for each repository.

In the end, some words about authentication. Specifying passwords directly in git:// URLs is not supported for security reasons, and SSH keys, ~/.netrc and ~/.ssh/config files, can be easily used as alternatives (the readers may get further information about these options within the SSH documentation).

6.3.3 Building Rules

The building rules are used to specify all information needed to build the sources. In this section, belong proper variables, we can specify some `inherit` directives to load specific supporting classes (see Section 5.4.2) and building tasks as do_configure or do_compile, etc., which are introduced below but explained in the dedicated section, Section 6.4.

Regarding the variables, they depend on the inherited build classes, so we report here the most used ones:

- EXTRA_OECONF: Used for additional configure script options when Autotools are used.

- EXTRA_OEMAKE: Used for additional GNU make options. It defaults to the empty string.

- EXTRA_OECMAKE: Used for additional CMake options. It defaults to the empty string.

- PACKAGECONFIG_CONFARGS: Used for additional configure options. It is not used directly, but by using PACKAGECONFIG.

- PACKAGECONFIG: By using it, we can enable or disable features of a recipe on a per-recipe basis. Usage of this variable (and its related flag variables) is powerful and explained below.

- COMPATIBLE_MACHINE: It contains a regular expression, matched against MACHINEOVERRIDES (see Section 5.3.1), that resolves to one or more target machines with which a recipe is compatible.

So, this variable can be used to stop recipes from being built for machines with which the recipes are not compatible (as an example for kernels or bootloader recipes).

The PACKAGECONFIG variable is used to specify a space-separated list of the features to enable. Then several flag variables specify the behavior of each feature by providing up to six order-dependent arguments, which are separated by commas. Each argument has the following meaning:

1) Extra arguments that should be added to the configure script argument list (EXTRA_OECONF or PACKAGECONFIG_CONFARGS) if the feature is enabled

2) The same as 1 but when the feature is disabled

3) Additional build dependencies that should be added to DEPENDS if the feature is enabled

4) The same as 3 but for RDEPENDS

5) Additional runtime recommendations that should be added to RRECOMMENDS (see below) if the feature is enabled

6) Any conflicting (i.e., mutually exclusive) PACKAGECONFIG settings for this feature

---

We can omit any argument we like, but must retain the separating commas until the last argument. For example:

```
PACKAGECONFIG[shared] = "--enable-shared"
PACKAGECONFIG[strip] = ",--disable-stripping"
```

In the former example, we just set the first argument, and no commas must be specified, while in the latter we set the second argument, so at least the first comma is needed.

A skeleton for this setting can be the following:

```
PACKAGECONFIG ??= "f1 f2 ..."
PACKAGECONFIG[f1] = "\
    --with-f1, --without-f1, \
    build-deps-for-f1, \
    runtime-deps-for-f1, runtime-recommends-for-f1, \
    packageconfig-conflicts-for-f1"
PACKAGECONFIG[f2] = "\
    --with-f2, --without-f2, \
...
```

However, to better understand how it works, a real example is the best, so we can look within the `cups-filters` recipe within the `meta-openembedded` layer, as shown below:

```
$ cat meta-openembedded/meta-oe/recipes-printing/cups/cups-filters.inc
...
PACKAGECONFIG[jpeg] = "--with-jpeg,--without-jpeg,jpeg"
PACKAGECONFIG[png] = "--with-png,--without-png,libpng"
PACKAGECONFIG[tiff] = "--with-tiff,--without-tiff,tiff"

PACKAGECONFIG ??= "${@bb.utils.contains('DISTRO_FEATURES', 'zeroconf',
'avahi', '', d)}"

PACKAGECONFIG[avahi] = "--enable-avahi,--disable-avahi,avahi"
PACKAGECONFIG[dbus] = "--enable-dbus,--disable-dbus,dbus"
...
```

If we specify (maybe by an append file) the following:

```
PACKAGECONFIG = "jpeg tiff"
```

then the configuration arguments passed to `configure` are

```
--with-jpeg --without-png --with-tiff --disable-avahi --disable-dbus
```

And in `DEPENDS` we get both the `jpeg` and `tiff` strings.

Note also that the recipe can auto-enable the `avahi` support by looking into `DISTRO_FEATURES` with the `bb.utils.contains()` function (see Section 5.1.5).

This mechanism is compelling, and, usually, if we want to change an existing PACKAGECONFIG block, we can do it in two ways:

- By creating an append file for the recipe and then setting or appending the value of PACKAGECONFIG:

```
PACKAGECONFIG = "f4 f5"
PACKAGECONFIG:append = " f4"
```

- By using a configuration file as local.conf or a specific distro.conf file by using a recipe override (see Section 5.3.1). If we suppose that the recipe is named myrecipe, we can do as below:

```
PACKAGECONFIG:pn-myrecipe = "f4 f5"
PACKAGECONFIG:append:pn-myrecipe = " f4"
```

Regarding the COMPATIBLE_MACHINE variable, it is better to do a real example. Within the Jailhouse recipe in the meta-imx layer, we can see the following setting:

```
$ cat meta-imx/meta-sdk/recipes-extended/jailhouse/jailhouse_0.2.bb
...
COMPATIBLE_MACHINE = "(mx8m-nxp-bsp|mx8ulp-nxp-bsp|mx93-nxp-bsp)"
...
```

In this manner, we prevent compiling this recipe for machines incompatible with mx8m-nxp-bsp, mx8ulp-nxp-bsp, or mx93-nxp-bsp ones.

After the settings of the above variables, in this building rules section we should also put the recipe's tasks, as do_compile, do_install, etc. A good example is reported within the avahi recipe in the poky layer:

```
$ cat poky/meta/recipes-connectivity/avahi/avahi_0.8.bb
...
do_configure:prepend() {
    # This m4 file will get in the way of our introspection.m4 with
    # special cross-compilation fixes
    rm "${S}/common/introspection.m4" || true
}
```

```
do_compile:prepend() {
    export GIR_EXTRA_LIBS_PATH="${B}/avahi-gobject/.libs:${B}/avahi-com
mon/.libs:${B}/avahi-client/.libs:${B}/avahi-glib/.libs"
}
...
do_install() {
        autotools_do_install
        rm -rf ${D}/run
        rm -rf ${D}${datadir}/dbus-1/interfaces
        test -d ${D}${datadir}/dbus-1 && rmdir --ignore-fail-on-non-empty
 ${D}${datadir}/dbus-1
        rm -rf ${D}${libdir}/avahi

        # Move example service files out of /etc/avahi/services so we
      # don't advertise ssh & sftp-ssh by default
        install -d ${D}${docdir}/avahi
        mv ${D}${sysconfdir}/avahi/services/* ${D}${docdir}/avahi
}
...
```

In the above example, we have a complete redefinition of the do_
install task, while the do_configure task and the do_compile task are
prepended with special code.

However, since most common tasks have default bodies, most recipes
simply don't specify anything here (while it's quite common for a recipe to
append, prepend, or rewrite one or more tasks). Since this is an essential
topic to understand writing good recipes, we will discuss it in detail in
Section 6.4.

Now let's go ahead to see the packaging information section for
a recipe.

6.3.4 Packaging Information

In this last section, we can put all the information needed to create all
the packages holding the programs and related data needed to execute a
specific task. The variables we can find here are listed below:

- PACKAGES: Holds the list of packages the recipe creates. It defaults to the following list, so in normal cases we can leave this variable as is (in Section 9.3, we are going to show how to use it):

```
${PN}-src ${PN}-dbg ${PN}-staticdev ${PN}-dev ${PN}-doc
${PN}-locale ${PACKAGE_BEFORE_PN} ${PN}
```

These packages are automatically generated by the Yocto build system, and they can be used for debugging purposes (-dev, -dbg, and -src), for development (-dev and -staticdev), for documentation (-doc), etc.

By using PACKAGE_BEFORE_PN, we can specify packages to be created before the default package named PN, so that those added packages can pick up files that would normally be included in it.

- FILES: It holds the list of files and directories that are placed in a package. The readers should notice that it can't be used directly, but by providing a package name override that identifies the resulting package only. For example:

```
FILES:${PN} = "${bindir}/foo"
FILES:${PN}-libs += "${libdir}/libfoo ${libdir}/libdir/libfoobar"
```

When specifying files or paths, we can use Python's glob syntax to match multiple files.

- ALTERNATIVE: Sometimes, the same command is provided in multiple packages. In this scenario, the build system needs to use the alternative system

283

to create a different binary naming scheme, so the commands can coexist. In this variable, we can list commands in a package that need such a scheme.

As FILES, to use this variable, we must provide a package name override that identifies the resulting package. For example, the tar recipe has the following alternative setting:

```
$ cat poky/meta/recipes-extended/tar/tar_1.34.bb
...
PACKAGES =+ "${PN}-rmt"
FILES:${PN}-rmt = "${sbindir}/rmt*"

inherit update-alternatives

ALTERNATIVE_PRIORITY = "100"
ALTERNATIVE:${PN} = "tar"
ALTERNATIVE:${PN}-rmt = "rmt"
...
```

Here, we define a special package tar-rmt, and then we can see an example of ALTERNATIVE settings for both tar and tar-rmt packages (see below for better explanation about how to use this alternative scheme).

- CONFFILES: Identifies configuration files that are part of a package and that the **package management system** (PMS) should consider special; in other words, these files can change after installation, and we would rather not reset them during the package update process; we'd like to be warned before the PMS overwrites them during the update process.

  A possible usage of CONFFILES is reported below:

```
CONFFILES:${PN} += " \
    ${sysconfdir}/file1.conf \
    ${sysconfdir}/file2.conf \
"
```

There is a relationship between the CONFFILES
and FILES variables. In fact, all files listed within
CONFFILES must also be present within FILES, since
configuration files are simply marked so that the
PMS will not overwrite them.

- RPROVIDES: Specifies a list of package name aliases
  that a package also provides to satisfy runtime
  dependencies of other packages, both during the
  build and on the target (as specified by RDEPENDS – see
  below). By default, a package's own name is implicitly
  already in the list.

  As with all package-controlling variables, we must
  always use the variable with a package name
  override:

  ```
  RPROVIDES:${PN}-mkimage = "u-boot-mkimage"
  ```

- RDEPENDS: Specifies a list of runtime dependencies of
  a package. It also must always be used with a package
  name override; however, the most common types
  of package runtime dependencies are automatically
  detected and added, then most recipes do not need to
  set RDEPENDS (see below for better explanations):

  ```
  RDEPENDS:${PN}-tftpd += "xinetd"
  ```

- RRECOMMENDS: Used with a package name override; it
  specifies a list of packages that extends the usability
  of a package being built. Packages listed here are not
  runtime dependencies for a package (there is RDEPENDS
  to do so), but rather it uses them for extended usability.

An interesting note for this variable is that it supports the following format:

```
RRECOMMENDS:${PN} = "package (operator version)"
```

where operator can be =, <, >, <=, or >=. For example, the following sets up a recommend on version 4.2 or greater of the package foo:

```
RRECOMMENDS:${PN} = "foo (>= 4.2)"
```

- RSUGGESTS: Specifies a list of additional packages that a recipe suggests for installation by the package manager at the time a package is installed (note that not all package managers support this functionality!):

```
RSUGGESTS:${PN} = "useful_package1 useful_package2"
```

- RCONFLICTS: Specifies a list of packages that conflict with packages, so a package cannot be installed if conflicting packages are not first removed:

```
RCONFLICTS:${PN} = "conflicting_package1 conflicting_package2"
```

This variable supports versioning as RRECOMMENDS.

- BBCLASSEXTEND: Allows Yocto developers to extend a recipe so that it builds variants of the software. For example, it can be used to build a native version of the recipe, which is a copy of the recipe specifically built to run on the build system (we are going to see how to manage such recipes in Section 11.6).

As seen in a section above for PROVIDES and DEPENDS, RDEPENDS and RPROVIDES variables work in the same manner. In fact, in the same recipes in the above example, we can also see

```
$ cat poky/meta/recipes-core/udev/eudev_3.2.10.bb
SUMMARY = "eudev is a fork of systemd's udev"
HOMEPAGE = "https://wiki.gentoo.org/wiki/Eudev"
```

```
DESCRIPTION = "eudev is Gentoo's fork of udev, systemd's device file man
ager for the Linux kernel. It manages device nodes in /dev and handles a
ll user space actions when adding or removing devices."
...
RPROVIDES:${PN} = "hotplug udev"
...
$ cat poky/meta/recipes-core/systemd/systemd_250.5.bb
require systemd.inc
...
RPROVIDES:udev = "hotplug"
```

Both recipes specify to the Yocto build system that they provide the hotplug functionality at runtime. So when a package specifies hotplug as its RDEPENDS setting, then the build system will correctly continue if at least one of the above packages is available.

Note that RDEPENDS:${PN}-dev automatically includes ${PN} by default, so we must be careful not to accidentally remove ${PN} when modifying RDEPENDS:${PN}-dev. To do so, we should use the += operator rather than the = operator in our recipes.

Regarding the alternative scheme, we have observed that it depends on the ALTERNATIVE variables, but not only that; in fact, a good example is within the systemd recipes (still in the poky layer) as shown below:

```
$ cat poky/meta/recipes-core/systemd/systemd_250.5.bb:
...
ALTERNATIVE:${PN} = "halt reboot shutdown poweroff runlevel ${@bb.utils
.contains('PACKAGECONFIG', 'resolved', 'resolv-conf', '', d)}"

ALTERNATIVE_TARGET[resolv-conf] = "${sysconfdir}/resolv-conf.systemd"
ALTERNATIVE_LINK_NAME[resolv-conf] = "${sysconfdir}/resolv.conf"
ALTERNATIVE_PRIORITY[resolv-conf] ?= "50"

ALTERNATIVE_TARGET[halt] = "${base_bindir}/systemctl"
ALTERNATIVE_LINK_NAME[halt] = "${base_sbindir}/halt"
ALTERNATIVE_PRIORITY[halt] ?= "300"

ALTERNATIVE_TARGET[reboot] = "${base_bindir}/systemctl"
ALTERNATIVE_LINK_NAME[reboot] = "${base_sbindir}/reboot"
ALTERNATIVE_PRIORITY[reboot] ?= "300"
```

```
ALTERNATIVE_TARGET[shutdown] = "${base_bindir}/systemctl"
ALTERNATIVE_LINK_NAME[shutdown] = "${base_sbindir}/shutdown"
ALTERNATIVE_PRIORITY[shutdown] ?= "300"

ALTERNATIVE_TARGET[poweroff] = "${base_bindir}/systemctl"
ALTERNATIVE_LINK_NAME[poweroff] = "${base_sbindir}/poweroff"
ALTERNATIVE_PRIORITY[poweroff] ?= "300"

ALTERNATIVE_TARGET[runlevel] = "${base_bindir}/systemctl"
ALTERNATIVE_LINK_NAME[runlevel] = "${base_sbindir}/runlevel"
ALTERNATIVE_PRIORITY[runlevel] ?= "300"
...
```

Firstly, we should notice how we can dynamically set the variable according to some special settings in PACKAGECONFIG, then we can see that for each alternative name we can specify the following flag variables:

- ALTERNATIVE_LINK_NAME: Used to map duplicated commands to actual locations. A good example to clarify this concept is about the bracket command, which can be provided by both the Coreutils and BusyBox packages. In this case, we must use the ALTERNATIVE_LINK_NAME variable to specify the actual location, as shown below:

```
ALTERNATIVE_LINK_NAME[bracket] = "${bindir}/["
```

If not specified, it defaults to ${bindir}/name.

- ALTERNATIVE_TARGET: Used to create default link locations for duplicated commands. A good example is within the bash recipe:

```
$ cat sources/poky/meta/recipes-extended/bash/bash.inc:
...
ALTERNATIVE:${PN} = "bash sh"
ALTERNATIVE_LINK_NAME[bash] = "${base_bindir}/bash"
ALTERNATIVE_TARGET[bash] = "${base_bindir}/bash"
ALTERNATIVE_LINK_NAME[sh] = "${base_bindir}/sh"
ALTERNATIVE_TARGET[sh] = "${base_bindir}/bash.${BPN}"
ALTERNATIVE_PRIORITY = "100"
...
```

Here, we define two alternatives for the package bash, and for both of them we define an ALTERNATIVE_LINK_NAME and an ALTERNATIVE_TARGET. Note that since for the bash alternative name the ALTERNATIVE_LINK_NAME and ALTERNATIVE_TARGET are the same, then the target for ALTERNATIVE_TARGET[bash] has the .${BPN} string automatically appended to it thanks to the build system (that's why for sh we have to do so by hand).

If ALTERNATIVE_TARGET is not defined, then it defaults to the ALTERNATIVE_LINK_NAME variable.

Available syntax forms for this variable are:

```
ALTERNATIVE_TARGET = "target"
ALTERNATIVE_TARGET[name] = "target"
ALTERNATIVE_TARGET_pkg[name] = "target"
```

With the last form, we mean something as below:

```
ALTERNATIVE_TARGET_${PN}     = "${bindir}/foo"
ALTERNATIVE_TARGET_${PN}-lib = "${libdir}/libfoo"
```

- ALTERNATIVE_PRIORITY: Used to create default priorities for duplicated commands. The available syntax forms for this variable (as for ALTERNATIVE_TARGET) are:

```
ALTERNATIVE_PRIORITY = "priority"
ALTERNATIVE_PRIORITY[name] = "priority"
ALTERNATIVE_PRIORITY_pkg[name] = "priority"
```

Before ending this section, we should mention the -dbg packages and explain something that may result useful, especially during the development stages. By default, the Yocto build system strips symbols from the binaries it packages, then, during the development, this behavior may result in some difficulties in using some debugging tools. We can prevent that by setting the INHIBIT_PACKAGE_STRIP variable to 1 in our local.conf configuration file; however, this setting will noticeably increase the size of our image!

However, we should note that for each package the build system produces also the -dbg counterpart, which holds the same executables of the main package but with all debugging symbols. So we can manually install debug (-dbg) packages for the applications we are going to debug and save space on the system.

We can also ask the build system to auto-add the specific -dbg packages to the current image by appending each debugging package to IMAGE_INSTALL or by adding all debug packages via the image feature dbg-pkgs to the EXTRA_IMAGE_FEATURES variable in local.conf. For example, in our conf/local.conf file we can do something as shown below:

```
--- conf/local.conf
+++ conf/local.conf
@@ -23,6 +23,7 @@
 # Switch to Debian packaging and include package-management in the image
 PACKAGE_CLASSES = "package_ipk"
 EXTRA_IMAGE_FEATURES += "package-management"
+EXTRA_IMAGE_FEATURES += "dbg-pkgs"

 # Limiting HW resources
 BB_NUMBER_THREADS = "4"
```

Note that this setting will noticeably increase the size of the final image, so we will need a larger microSD to be able to successfully write the whole image on it. For example, with the dbg-pkgs feature enabled, when we try to write the usual 8GB microSD we got

```
$ zstdcat tmp/deploy/images/imx8mp-icore-cy/engicam-evaluation-ima
ge-mx8-imx8mp-icore-cy.wic.zst | sudo dd of=$DISK bs=8M conv=fdata
sync status=progress
8025341952 bytes (8,0 GB, 7,5 GiB) copied, 14 s, 573 MB/s
dd: error writing '/dev/sdd': No space left on device
...
```

So the readers should consider not enabling it in their `local.conf` or getting a larger microSD.

Additionally, we can also specify how to split up and package debug and source information when creating debugging packages to be used, for example, with the GNU Project Debugger (GDB). We can use the `PACKAGE_DEBUG_SPLIT_STYLE` variable in the `local.conf` configuration file with the following options:

- `.debug`: With this option, all debugging and source information is placed in a single `-dbg` package file. All debug symbol files are placed within a `.debug` directory near the binaries so that if a binary is installed into `/bin`, then the corresponding debug symbol file is installed in `/bin/.debug` (source files are installed under `/usr/src/debug` instead). This is the default behavior if nothing is defined (however, it is usually set by the Poky distro – see below).

Note the dot character (`.`) at the beginning of the option name.

- `debug-file-directory`: This option works as above, but now all debug symbol files are placed entirely under the directory `/usr/lib/debug` and separated by the path from where the binary is installed. Now, if a binary is installed in `/bin`, then the corresponding debug symbols are installed in `/usr/lib/debug/bin`.

291

- `debug-with-srcpkg`: With this option, all debugging info is placed in the standard `-dbg` package as with the `.debug` option, while source is placed in a separate `-src` package. This is the default setting for this variable, as defined in Poky's `bitbake.conf` file.

- `debug-without-src`: This option is the same as above, but no source files are packaged at all.

6.4 The Building Tasks

If variables are used to enable or disable and to set or unset functionalities, the entities that actually do something (as generating packages or binary images) are tasks. In previous chapters, we have seen how to create a task and how to run it, but now it's time to see which are the basic tasks that are automatically created each time we start BitBake. This is to generate a package or, better, a Yocto image.

In this book, we don't analyze all such tasks (the complete list can be retrieved at `https://docs.yoctoproject.org/ref-manual/tasks.html#normal-recipe-build-tasks`), but we focus on the most important ones we may need to customize to create a new recipe. In fact, all basic tasks have default bodies which already do something standard, but we may need to alter such defaults to fit the needs of the software we are going to package.

All default bodies (and task execution ordering) are all defined within the **base class** in the file `sources/poky/meta/classes/base.bbclass`, and the readers should refer to this file in order to well understand how the Yocto Project works.

In this book, we will show several parts of this file to demonstrate how each basic task is defined; however, as a brief introduction we should note that usually a class function is defined with the following layout:

```
addtask taskname after do_taskdepends

# Flag variables
do_taskname[flag1] = "value1"
do_taskname[flag2] = "value2"
...

# Body
classname_do_taskname() {
    # Do some default actions
    ...
}
```

Firstly, we should note that all tasks' functions are named with the class name prefix followed by the do_ and then a proper name. Next, the class may specify some task's special behaviors by using one or more flag variables for the task, and then it uses the addtask directive to create the task and eventually to specify the interdependencies with other tasks.

The function name has a special layout because of how a class can export its function in BitBake. In fact, to export a function defined in a class, BitBake uses the EXPORT_FUNCTIONS directive, so when in the .bbclass file we have the following statement, the recipe which inherits the class will see a new do_taskname task:

```
EXPORT_FUNCTIONS do_taskname
```

In the EXPORT_FUNCTIONS directive, we can specify more than one class function to export. For example, within the bass.bbclass we can find

```
EXPORT_FUNCTIONS do_fetch do_unpack do_configure do_compile do_ins
tall do_package
```

If desired, our recipe can add code at the beginning or at the end of the function by using the prepend or append operations, or it can redefine the function completely (as explained in Section 5.2.3). However, if it redefines the function, there is no means for it to call the class version of the function. Here is where the EXPORT_FUNCTIONS directive comes to play its role: it provides a mechanism that enables the recipe's version of the function to call the original version of the function.

The class defines the function in the form classname_taskname; in our example, we have base_do_taskname, then, in the class file, we do

```
EXPORT_FUNCTIONS do_taskname
```

Now, if our recipe needs to call the class version of the task, it should call base_do_taskname. We can also conditionally call the class version of the function as follows:

```
do_foo() {
    if [ condition ] ; then
        # Call he do_taskname in base class
        base_do_taskname
    else
        # Do something else
        ...
    fi
}
```

By using this mechanism, a single recipe can freely choose between the original function, as defined in the class file, and the modified function in our recipe.

Now we can move forward and take a more in-depth look at the tasks defined in the base class.

6.4.1 The do_fetch Task

This is the task that fetches the source code by using the SRC_URI variable (and its argument's prefix to determine the correct fetcher module). It is defined as shown below:

```
addtask fetch

do_fetch[dirs] = "${DL_DIR}"
do_fetch[file-checksums] = "${@bb.fetch.get_checksum_file_list(d)}"
do_fetch[file-checksums] += " ${@get_lic_checksum_file_list(d)}"
do_fetch[vardeps] += "SRCREV"
do_fetch[network] = "1"
```

```
python base_do_fetch() {
    src_uri = (d.getVar('SRC_URI') or "").split()
    if not src_uri:
        return

    try:
        fetcher = bb.fetch2.Fetch(src_uri, d)
        fetcher.download()
    except bb.fetch2.BBFetchException as e:
        bb.fatal("Bitbake Fetcher Error: " + repr(e))
}
```

Usually, we don't need to redefine this task, but it may be useful to know how it works to introduce some useful task settings and to consider if we may need to append commands in our custom recipes.

The addtask directive just creates the task without ordering (this is the first task to be executed to create a package, so other tasks follow), while in the flag variables section we have

- do_fetch[dirs] = "${DL_DIR}": Since this task fetches some code, we ask to create the main downloading directory (subdirectories will be created by the fetcher object).

- do_fetch[file-checksums] = "...": This setting is used to specify (by the fetcher object according to the SRC_URI settings) a list of files to be checked during the checksums' computation (explaining in detail these concepts is out of the scope of this book, and curious readers may take a look at BitBake's user manual).

- do_fetch[vardeps] += "SRCREV": It is used to specify a dependency of the task to the value of the SRCREV variable. In particular, the task will be re-executed if the value of the variable changes.

- do_fetch[network] = "1": Specifies that the task can get access to the network (by default, tasks cannot do so).

295

Then the task just reads the value in SRC_URI and, in this case, calls the proper functions to download the sources.

6.4.2 The do_unpack Task

This is the task that unpacks the source code into the WORKDIR (working) directory, and it is defined as reported below:

```
addtask unpack after do_fetch

do_unpack[dirs] = "${WORKDIR}"
do_unpack[cleandirs] = "${@d.getVar('S') if os.path.normpath(d.getVar('
S')) != os.path.normpath(d.getVar('WORKDIR')) else os.path.join('${S}',
 'patches')}"

python base_do_unpack() {
    src_uri = (d.getVar('SRC_URI') or "").split()
    if not src_uri:
        return

    try:
        fetcher = bb.fetch2.Fetch(src_uri, d)
        fetcher.unpack(d.getVar('WORKDIR'))
    except bb.fetch2.BBFetchException as e:
        bb.fatal("Bitbake Fetcher Error: " + repr(e))
}
```

First, we should note that now we have a task ordering in the addtask directive, and, in particular, the do_unpack task runs after do_fetch. Then, as above, we specify that WORKDIR must be created before the task runs, but now we also say that a new empty directory should be created before the task runs, that is, the S directory (if it already exists, it will be removed and recreated to empty it).

Then, in the task's body, we can see that both do_fetch and do_unpack tasks work together to fetch the source files and unpack them into the build directory.

This task, as per do_fetch, is usually used as is and, eventually, appended.

6.4.3 The do_configure Task

This task configures the source by enabling and disabling any build-time and configuration options for the software being built, and it is defined as reported below:

```
addtask configure after do_patch

do_configure[dirs] = "${B}"

base_do_configure() {
    if [ -n "${CONFIGURESTAMPFILE}" -a -e "${CONFIGURESTAMPFILE}" ]; th
en
        if [ "`cat ${CONFIGURESTAMPFILE}`" != "${BB_TASKHASH}" ]; then
            cd ${B}
            if [ "${CLEANBROKEN}" != "1" -a \( -e Makefile -o -e makefi
le -o -e GNUmakefile \) ]; then
                oe_runmake clean
            fi
            # -ignore_readdir_race does not work correctly
            # with -delete; use xargs to avoid spurious
            # build failures
            find ${B} -ignore_readdir_race -name \*.la -type f -print0
| xargs -0 rm -f
        fi
    fi
    if [ -n "${CONFIGURESTAMPFILE}" ]; then
        mkdir -p `dirname ${CONFIGURESTAMPFILE}`
        echo ${BB_TASKHASH} > ${CONFIGURESTAMPFILE}
    fi
}
```

The task's dependency is to run after do_patch, and the directory B is its working directory, while regarding its body, it may look complicated; however, its default behavior is to run the oe_runmake clean command if a Makefile, makefile, or GNUmakefile file is found and CLEANBROKEN is not set to 1. On the other hand, if no such file is found or the CLEANBROKEN variable is set to 1, the do_configure task does nothing.

The CLEANBROKEN variable can be used to specify that the make clean command does not work for the software being built, and now it's quite obvious how it is used.

It should be noted that we discussed whether to run or not the make clean command in the do_configure task, but in the body we have the oe_runmake clean command (see Section 3.3.2).

As with all previous tasks, even this task is not usually redefined; instead, it is usually driven by setting the EXTRA_OEMAKE variable (which is empty by default) or by redefining it by inheriting another class as the CMake class (defined into cmake.bbclass file in the poky meta layer). In this last case, the task is defined as follows:

```
cmake_do_configure() {
    if [ "${OECMAKE_BUILDPATH}" ]; then
        bbnote "cmake.bbclass no longer uses OECMAKE_BUILDPATH.  The de
fault behaviour is now out-of-tree builds with B=WORKDIR/build."
    fi

    if [ "${S}" = "${B}" ]; then
        find ${B} -name CMakeFiles -or -name Makefile -or -name cmake_i
nstall.cmake -or -name CMakeCache.txt -delete
    fi

    # Just like autotools cmake can use a site file to cache result that
    # need generated binaries to run
    if [ -e ${WORKDIR}/site-file.cmake ] ; then
        oecmake_sitefile="-C ${WORKDIR}/site-file.cmake"
    else
        oecmake_sitefile=
    fi

    cmake \
      ${OECMAKE_GENERATOR_ARGS} \
      $oecmake_sitefile \
      ${OECMAKE_SOURCEPATH} \
      -DCMAKE_INSTALL_PREFIX:PATH=${prefix} \
      -DCMAKE_INSTALL_BINDIR:PATH=${@os.path.relpath(d.getVar('bindir')
, d.getVar('prefix') + '/')} \
```

```
        -DCMAKE_INSTALL_SBINDIR:PATH=${@os.path.relpath(d.getVar('sbin\di
r'), d.getVar('prefix') + '/')} \
        -DCMAKE_INSTALL_LIBEXECDIR:PATH=${@os.path.relpath(d.getVar('libe
xecdir'), d.getVar('prefix') + '/')} \
        -DCMAKE_INSTALL_SYSCONFDIR:PATH=${sysconfdir} \
        -DCMAKE_INSTALL_SHAREDSTATEDIR:PATH=${@os.path.relpath(d.getVar('
sharedstatedir'), d.  getVar('prefix') + '/')} \
        -DCMAKE_INSTALL_LOCALSTATEDIR:PATH=${localstatedir} \
        -DCMAKE_INSTALL_LIBDIR:PATH=${@os.path.relpath(d.getVar('libdir')
, d.getVar('prefix') + '/')} \
        -DCMAKE_INSTALL_INCLUDEDIR:PATH=${@os.path.relpath(d.getVar('incl
udedir'), d.getVar('prefix') + '/')} \
        -DCMAKE_INSTALL_DATAROOTDIR:PATH=${@os.path.relpath(d.getVar('dat
adir'), d.getVar('prefix') + '/')} \
      -DPYTHON_EXECUTABLE:PATH=${PYTHON} \
      -DPython_EXECUTABLE:PATH=${PYTHON} \
      -DPython3_EXECUTABLE:PATH=${PYTHON} \
      -DLIB_SUFFIX=${@d.getVar('baselib').replace('lib', '')} \
      -DCMAKE_INSTALL_SO_NO_EXE=0 \
      -DCMAKE_TOOLCHAIN_FILE=${WORKDIR}/toolchain.cmake \
      -DCMAKE_NO_SYSTEM_FROM_IMPORTED=1 \
      -DCMAKE_EXPORT_NO_PACKAGE_REGISTRY=ON \
      -DFETCHCONTENT_FULLY_DISCONNECTED=ON \
      ${EXTRA_OECMAKE} \
      -Wno-dev
}
```

Again, if we use this class, we don't need to redefine the task, but we should use the variables used in its body to properly drive its job. However, usually, the only used variable in the recipes is EXTRA_OECMAKE.

Furthermore, if our software doesn't need to be configured, we can force this task to do nothing by defining it as below directly within our recipe file:

```
do_configure () {
    :
}
```

The readers should remember that for Bash the colon (:) character is equivalent to the true command.

6.4.4 The do_compile Task

This task just compiles the source code. Its definition is reported below:

```
addtask compile after do_configure

do_compile[dirs] = "${B}"

base_do_compile() {
    if [ -e Makefile -o -e makefile -o -e GNUmakefile ]; then
        oe_runmake || die "make failed"
    else
        bbnote "nothing to compile"
    fi
}
```

Nothing special to say here, apart from the fact that it runs after do_configure. Its working directory is the B directory, and its default behavior is to run the oe_runmake function if a Makefile, makefile, or GNUmakefile file is found. Otherwise, it does nothing.

This task can be redefined by using the CMake class as below:

```
# To disable verbose cmake logs for a given recipe or globally config
# metadata e.g. local.conf add following
#
# CMAKE_VERBOSE = ""
#

CMAKE_VERBOSE ??= "VERBOSE=1"


# Then run do_compile again
cmake_runcmake_build() {
    bbnote ${DESTDIR:+DESTDIR=${DESTDIR} }${CMAKE_VERBOSE} cmake --buil
d '${B}' "$@" -- ${EXTRA_OECMAKE_BUILD}
    eval ${DESTDIR:+DESTDIR=${DESTDIR} }${CMAKE_VERBOSE} cmake --build
'${B}' "$@" -- ${EXTRA_OECMAKE_BUILD}
}

cmake_do_compile()  {
    cmake_runcmake_build --target ${OECMAKE_TARGET_COMPILE}
}
```

Since our software may not use neither make nor cmake, it's quite common that this task is redefined within recipes. For example, within the recipe for the devmem2 tool, we can read the following setting:

```
$ cat meta-openembedded/meta-oe/recipes-support/devmem2/devmem2_2.0.bb
...
CFLAGS += "-DFORCE_STRICT_ALIGNMENT"

do_compile() {
    ${CC} -o devmem2 devmem2.c ${CFLAGS} ${LDFLAGS}
}
...
```

And it works because variables CC, CFLAGS, and LDFLAGS are properly set by the Yocto build system when the task is executed.

Note the += operator used to add a flag for the compiler instead of using the equal to character (=); otherwise, all Yocto CFLAGS will be overwritten!

6.4.5 The do_install Task

This task copies files that are to be packaged into the holding area pointed to by the D variable. Note that this task runs with the current working directory set to B, which is the compilation directory, and then it moves generated files into D.

The do_install task is defined as shown below:

```
addtask install after do_compile

do_install[dirs] = "${B}"
# Remove and re-create ${D} so that is it guaranteed to be empty
do_install[cleandirs] = "${D}"

base_do_install() {
    :
}
```

Here, we see that do_install is executed after do_compile and that, by default, the task does nothing, so it's quite usual that it is overwritten by every recipe. However, this is not entirely true in the case a recipe inherits a class that does it for it; in fact, if we inherit the CMake class, we get the following default body:

```
cmake_do_install() {
    DESTDIR='${D}' cmake_runcmake_build --target ${OECMAKE_TARGET_INSTA
LL}
}
```

Note that both cmake_do_compile and cmake_do_install tasks use the internal function cmake_runcmake_build().

Furthermore, we can use EXTRA_OECMAKE (and other related variables) to instruct cmake to do its job. However, a usual form for the do_install task, when redefined into a recipe, can be seen in the devmem2_2.0.bb recipe file:

```
$ cat meta-openembedded/meta-oe/recipes-support/devmem2/devmem2_2.0.bb
...
do_install() {
    install -d ${D}${bindir}
    install devmem2 ${D}${bindir}
}
```

Note that, since D is always recreated empty, we have to create each subdirectory where we wish to install our files. In the above example, before installing the executable devmem2 we have to create the bindir directory in D.

When installing files, we should be careful not to set the owner and group IDs of the installed files to unintended values; in fact, some methods of copying files (as the cp command) can preserve the UID and/or GID of the original file, which is usually not what we want. Some safe methods for installing files according to this note are the following:

- Use the `install` utility as in the above example as the preferred method.

- If we wish to use the `cp` command, we should always use the `--no-preserve=ownership` option.

- If we need to use the `tar` command, we should always use the `--no-same-owner` option and do so for any other archive tool we wish to use.

An interesting usage of the above last method is the one within the **bin-package class**, located in the file `bin_package.bbclass` in the poky meta layer. It looks like this:

```
$ cat sources/poky/meta/classes/bin_package.bbclass
...
# Common variable and task for the binary package recipe.
# Basic principle:
# * The files have been unpacked to ${S} by base.bbclass
# * Skip do_configure and do_compile
# * Use do_install to install the files to ${D}
#
# Note:
# The "subdir" parameter in the SRC_URI is useful when the input package
# is rpm, ipk, deb and so on, for example:
#
# SRC_URI = "http://foo.com/foo-1.0-r1.i586.rpm;subdir=foo-1.0"
#
# Then the files would be unpacked to ${WORKDIR}/foo-1.0, otherwise
# they would be in ${WORKDIR}.
#

# Skip the unwanted steps
do_configure[noexec] = "1"
do_compile[noexec] = "1"

# Install the files to ${D}
bin_package_do_install () {
    # Do it carefully
    [ -d "${S}" ] || exit 1
    if [ -z "$(ls -A ${S})" ]; then
        bbfatal bin_package has nothing to install. Be sure the SRC_URI
 unpacks into S.
```

```
    fi
    cd ${S}
    install -d ${D}${base_prefix}
    tar --no-same-owner --exclude='./patches' --exclude='././.pc' -cpf -
. \
        | tar --no-same-owner -xpf - -C ${D}${base_prefix}
}

FILES:${PN} = "/"

EXPORT_FUNCTIONS do_install
```

This is a tiny class, but it is full of good examples! As reported in the header, this class is designed to manage binary packages easily, that is, when we have to just install binaries without any compilation; in fact, both the do_configure and do_compile tasks are inhibited from executing by setting the noexec flag variable to 1.

The subdir option within SRC_URI is used to properly set the directory name where the binaries will be exploded. The do_install task is then redefined in such a way it will install all files (but whatever is placed in ./patches and ././.pc directories) into the directory pointed to by ${D}${base_prefix} with proper owner settings. The task uses both install and tar commands (the latter with the --no-same-owner option).

The readers may see Section 11.5 for an example about how to use this class.

As a final note, we have to mention the installation of C libraries. In fact, in this case, a usual way to do so is shown below:

```
do_install () {
    install -d ${D}${libdir}
    install -Dm 0755 ${B}/libleak.so ${D}${libdir}/libleak.so
}
```

However, it is better to use the oe_soinstall() function, which also checks for the soname setting. In fact, in the file sources/poky/meta/classes/utils.bbclass, where the function is defined, we can see

```
oe_soinstall() {
    # Purpose: Install shared library file and
    #          create the necessary links
    # Example: oe_soinstall libfoo.so.1.2.3 ${D}${libdir}
    libname=`basename $1`
    case "$libname" in
        *.so)
            bbfatal "oe_soinstall: Shared library must haved versioned
filename (e.g. libfoo.so.1.2.3)"
            ;;
    esac
    install -m 755 $1 $2/$libname
    sonamelink=`${HOST_PREFIX}readelf -d $1 | grep 'Library soname:' |
sed -e 's/.*\[\(.*\)\].*/\1/'`
    if [ -z $sonamelink ]; then
        bbfatal "oe_soinstall: $libname is missing ELF tag 'SONAME'."
    fi
    solink=`echo $libname | sed -e 's/\.so\..*/.so/'`
    ln -sf $libname $2/$sonamelink
    ln -sf $libname $2/$solink
}
```

The readers which don't know what the soname setting is may consider seeing the example on Section 9.2 to better understand it.

As reported in the comment of the function, we can use it to rewrite the do_install task above as shown below:

```
do_install () {
    install -d ${D}${libdir}
    oe_soinstall ${B}/libleak.so ${D}${libdir}
}
```

In this manner, we can be sure that everything is done correctly and also that the soname parameter is reliably checked, and the relative links are built.

However, the oe_soinstall() function works only with shared libraries, and in the case we need to install static libraries too, we can use a more generic utility named oe_libinstall(). It is defined in the same file as oe_soinstall(), and to see how it works, we can take a look at how it is defined:

```
$ cat poky/meta/classes/bin_package.bbclass
...
oe_libinstall() {
    # Purpose: Install a library, in all its forms
    # Example
    #
    # oe_libinstall libltdl ${STAGING_LIBDIR}/
    # oe_libinstall -C src/libblah libblah ${D}/${libdir}/
...
    while [ "$#" -gt 0 ]; do
        case "$1" in
                -C)
                        shift
                        dir="$1"
                        ;;
                -s)
                        silent=1
                        ;;
                -a)
                        require_static=1
                        ;;
                -so)
                        require_shared=1
                        ;;
                -*)
                        bbfatal "oe_libinstall: unknown option: $1"
                        ;;
                *)
                        break;
                        ;;
        esac
        shift
    done
```

```
    libname="$1"
    shift
    destpath="$1"
    if [ -z "$destpath" ]; then
        bbfatal "oe_libinstall: no destination path specified"
    fi
...
```

The function, by default, tries to install both shared and static libraries doing proper checks as oe_soinstall() does. However, it can be driven by using special option arguments to require shared or static library files (or error) and to specify an alternate directory where it must search for library files. A practical example is reported within the tcp-wrappers_7.6.bb recipe, as shown below:

```
$ cat poky/meta/recipes-extended/tcp-wrappers/tcp-wrappers_7.6.bb
...
do_install () {
    oe_libinstall -a libwrap ${D}${libdir}
    oe_libinstall -C shared -so libwrap ${D}${base_libdir}
...
```

The first line installs the static libraries libwrap taken from the directory pointed to by B, while the shared library files are taken from the directory ${B}/shared.

Note that oe_libinstall() creates the destination directory ${D}${libdir} by itself, while function oe_soinstall() does not.

The readers should note that what was said until now regarding the shared (or static) library installation is correct; however, to do a perfect job, we should also consider installing the header files among the binary ones. In fact, to be able to compile against libraries, we also need these files.

So a complete do_install task for libraries should be defined as done within the tcp-wrappers_7.6.bb recipe:

```
$ cat poky/meta/recipes-extended/tcp-wrappers/tcp-wrappers_7.6.bb
...
do_install () {
    oe_libinstall -a libwrap ${D}${libdir}
    oe_libinstall -C shared -so libwrap ${D}${base_libdir}
...
    install -d ${D}${includedir}
    install -m 0644 tcpd.h ${D}${includedir}/
...
}
```

After the binary files (man pages and other files), the recipe installs the tcpd.h header file into the directory pointed to by includedir.

6.5 Building Images

Until now, we have discussed recipes in general, without making any differences between *recipes for packages* and *recipes for images*. However, they are extremely diverse concepts!

Both of them are used by BitBake to build something, but recipes for packages hold instructions to generate one or more packages which hold programs, configuration files, and any other files required for a specified software to work, while recipes for images hold instructions to generate a binary image which holds a complete OS, that is, several programs, their configuration, and data files. Simply speaking, a recipe for images holds a list of packages.

Actually, recipes for images hold instructions to create a root filesystem. But thanks to some special settings, we can generate a final binary image with the root filesystem and the bootloaders, kernel, and whatever needed to be put on the mass storage to get a functional system.

6.5.1 The Core Image Recipe

If we recall what we did in Section 2.2, when we executed the file imx-setup-release.sh, we got something as below:

```
...
Welcome to Freescale Community BSP
...
You can now run 'bitbake <target>'

Common targets are:
    core-image-minimal
    meta-toolchain
    meta-toolchain-sdk
    adt-installer
    meta-ide-support
...
```

The core-image-minimal is the name of the minimal image recipe defined within the Poky meta layer, as shown below:

```
$ cat poky/meta/recipes-core/images/core-image-minimal.bb
SUMMARY = "A small image just capable of allowing a device to boot."

IMAGE_INSTALL = "packagegroup-core-boot ${CORE_IMAGE_EXTRA_INSTALL}"

IMAGE_LINGUAS = " "

LICENSE = "MIT"


inherit core-image

IMAGE_ROOTFS_SIZE ?= "8192"
IMAGE_ROOTFS_EXTRA_SPACE:append = "${@bb.utils.contains("DISTRO_FEATURE
S", "systemd", " + 4096", "", d)}"
```

As we can see, the recipe is elementary, and some variables are the same as for package recipes. However, what makes the difference here are the inherit core-image statement and all variables prefixed with the IMAGE_ string.

In order to know how it works, let's take a look at the **core-image class**. It is held into a quite short file divided into two main regions. The first region looks like this:

```
$ cat poky/meta/classes/core-image.bbclass
...
# IMAGE_FEATURES control content of the core reference images
#
# By default we install packagegroup-core-boot and
# packagegroup-base-extended packages; this gives us working (console
# only) rootfs.
#
# Available IMAGE_FEATURES:
#
# - weston             - Weston Wayland compositor
# - x11                - X server
# - x11-base           - X server with minimal environment
# - x11-sato           - OpenedHand Sato environment
# - tools-debug        - debugging tools
...
# - ssh-server-dropbear - SSH server (dropbear)
# - ssh-server-openssh  - SSH server (openssh)
# - hwcodecs           - Install hardware acceleration codecs
...
FEATURE_PACKAGES_weston = "packagegroup-core-weston"
FEATURE_PACKAGES_x11 = "packagegroup-core-x11"
FEATURE_PACKAGES_x11-base = "packagegroup-core-x11-base"
FEATURE_PACKAGES_x11-sato = "packagegroup-core-x11-sato"
FEATURE_PACKAGES_tools-debug = "packagegroup-core-tools-debug"
...
FEATURE_PACKAGES_ssh-server-dropbear = "packagegroup-core-ssh-dropbear"
FEATURE_PACKAGES_ssh-server-openssh = "packagegroup-core-ssh-openssh"
FEATURE_PACKAGES_hwcodecs = "${MACHINE_HWCODECS}"
...
```

Here are all the supported image features we can specify within the IMAGE_FEATURES variable with their respective explanations. The variable FEATURE_PACKAGES is used to define one or more packages to include in an image when a specific item is included in IMAGE_FEATURES. As in the example above, when we set its value, we must append the name of the feature, for example, if we set the following:

```
FEATURE_PACKAGES_foo = "package1 package2"
```

When foo were added to IMAGE_FEATURES, package1 and package2 would be included in the image.

Packages installed by features defined through the FEATURE_ PACKAGES variable are often package groups, which are recipes that bundle multiple packages together. Then, instead of having to explicitly specify each package in the IMAGE_INSTALL variable, we can simply specify the package group name. See Section 11.4 for further information on this topic.

Then the core-image class continues, and the second region looks like this:

```
...
# IMAGE_FEATURES_REPLACES_foo = 'bar1 bar2'
# Including image feature foo would replace the image features bar1 and
# bar2
IMAGE_FEATURES_REPLACES_ssh-server-openssh = "ssh-server-dropbear"
# Do not install openssh complementary packages if either
# packagegroup-core-ssh-dropbear or dropbear is installed to avoid
# openssh-dropbear conflict see [Yocto #14858] for more information
PACKAGE_EXCLUDE_COMPLEMENTARY:append = "${@bb.utils.contains_any('PACKA
GE_INSTALL', 'packagegroup-core-ssh-dropbear dropbear', 'openssh', '' ,
 d)}"
# IMAGE_FEATURES_CONFLICTS_foo = 'bar1 bar2'
# An error exception would be raised if both image features foo and
# bar1(or bar2) are included

MACHINE_HWCODECS ??= ""

CORE_IMAGE_BASE_INSTALL = '\
    packagegroup-core-boot \
    packagegroup-base-extended \
    \
    ${CORE_IMAGE_EXTRA_INSTALL} \
    '

CORE_IMAGE_EXTRA_INSTALL ?= ""

IMAGE_INSTALL ?= "${CORE_IMAGE_BASE_INSTALL}"

inherit image
```

The variables IMAGE_FEATURES_REPLACES and IMAGE_FEATURES_CONFLICTS can be used to manage the IMAGE_FEATURES settings, while with PACKAGE_EXCLUDE_COMPLEMENTARY we can prevent specific packages (by using a regular expression to match the packages we want to exclude) from being installed when we are installing complementary packages. In the above example, we ask the build system to not install openssh complementary packages if either packagegroup-core-ssh-dropbear or dropbear is installed to avoid openssh-dropbear conflicts.

In the end, we have the IMAGE_INSTALL variable which is used to specify the packages to install into an image through the **image class** (called with inherit image – see below).

However, when we use this core-image class, we should not directly set this variable; instead, we should use the CORE_IMAGE_BASE_INSTALL variable by appending more packages to be installed, as shown below:

```
CORE_IMAGE_BASE_INSTALL += "${@bb.utils.contains('DISTRO_FEATURES', 'x1
1', 'weston-xwayland matchbox-terminal', '', d)}"
```

Note that we can also use the variable CORE_IMAGE_EXTRA_INSTALL, which provides the same functionalities as CORE_IMAGE_BASE_INSTALL (i.e., specifying the list of extra packages to be added to the image), but it can be used in the local.conf configuration file.

At the end of the core-image-minimal.bb file, we can find the IMAGE_ROOTFS_SIZE and IMAGE_ROOTFS_EXTRA_SPACE variables, which can be used to define the size in Kbytes for the generated root filesystem image.

The final size of the generated image (final-rootfs-size) is computed as follows:

```
final-rootfs-size = image-du * IMAGE_OVERHEAD_FACTOR
if (final-rootfs-size) < IMAGE_ROOTFS_SIZE:
    final-rootfs-size = IMAGE_ROOTFS_SIZE
final-rootfs-size += IMAGE_ROOTFS_EXTRA_SPACE
```

where image-du is the returned value of the du command on the root filesystem image. These last variables are useful to add extra space in the final root filesystem if needed.

In order to prevent that the final-rootfs-size is too large for our embedded kit, we can use IMAGE_ROOTFS_MAXSIZE to specify a maximum value above which a build error occurs.

Moreover, with IMAGE_ROOTFS_ALIGNMENT, we can specify the alignment for the final image file in Kbytes. If the size of the image is not a multiple of this value, then the size is rounded up to the nearest multiple of the value (it defaults to 1).

OK, here is all about the core-image class. So what we have to do is just list the needed packages within CORE_IMAGE_BASE_INSTALL as the recipe core-image-weston.bb does:

```
$ cat poky/meta/recipes-graphics/images/core-image-weston.bb
SUMMARY = "A very basic Wayland image with a terminal"

IMAGE_FEATURES += "splash package-management ssh-server-dropbear hwcode
cs weston"

LICENSE = "MIT"

inherit core-image

CORE_IMAGE_BASE_INSTALL += "gtk+3-demo"
CORE_IMAGE_BASE_INSTALL += "${@bb.utils.contains('DISTRO_FEATURES', 'x1
1', 'weston-xwayland matchbox-terminal', '', d)}"
...
```

This recipe just inherits the core-image class and then uses the CORE_IMAGE_BASE_INSTALL variable to list the packages to be installed in the root filesystem.

6.5.2 The Image Class

It's quite obvious that image recipes are really different from normal package recipes, and all the ticks used to generate a binary image apart from a binary package are held into the file poky/meta/classes/image. bbclass.

This class is inherited by any other image class, and even if it can be used directly, it's quite usual that it is inherited when we use a derived image class (as the core-image class above). This implies that image recipes set IMAGE_INSTALL to specify the packages to install into an image through this class. However, the derived image class, usually referred to as *image helper* classes such as the core-image class seen in the previous section, can take lists used with IMAGE_FEATURES and turn them into auto-generated entries in IMAGE_INSTALL in addition to its default contents. For all these reasons, when we use this variable, it is best to use it as follows:

```
IMAGE_INSTALL:append = " package"
```

First, be sure to include the space between the quotation character and the start of the package name or names! Then, note that using the += operator to append packages to IMAGE_INSTALL is not recommended. In fact, core-image.bbclass (another image class) does the following setting:

```
IMAGE_INSTALL ?= "${CORE_IMAGE_BASE_INSTALL}"
```

Initializing a variable with the ?= operator, and then using a += operation against it, results in unexpected behavior when used within the local.conf. Furthermore, depending on the circumstances an image recipe may or may not work. In both these cases, the behavior is contrary to how most users expect the += operator to work.

To do its job, the image class redefines some tasks and disables/deletes others, as we can see within the file image.bbclass as shown below:

```
$ cat poky/meta/classes/image.bbclass
...
do_fetch[noexec] = "1"
do_unpack[noexec] = "1"
do_patch[noexec] = "1"
do_configure[noexec] = "1"
do_compile[noexec] = "1"
do_install[noexec] = "1"
deltask do_populate_lic
deltask do_populate_sysroot
do_package[noexec] = "1"
deltask do_package_qa
deltask do_packagedata
deltask do_package_write_ipk
deltask do_package_write_deb
deltask do_package_write_rpm
...
```

Smart readers should have noticed that some tasks are deleted, while others are simply disabled by setting the noexec flag. Because when we use the deltask directive, we mean that accidentally left in some task dependencies are no longer needed nor processed.

Moreover, new tasks are added, for example:

```
...
fakeroot python do_rootfs () {
    from oe.rootfs import create_rootfs
    from oe.manifest import create_manifest
    import logging
...
    # generate rootfs
    d.setVarFlag('REPRODUCIBLE_TIMESTAMP_ROOTFS', 'export', '1')
    create_rootfs(d, progress_reporter=progress_reporter, logcatcher=lo
gcatcher)
```

```
    progress_reporter.finish()
}
do_rootfs[dirs] = "${TOPDIR}"
do_rootfs[cleandirs] += "${IMAGE_ROOTFS} ${IMGDEPLOYDIR} ${S}"
do_rootfs[file-checksums] += "${POSTINST_INTERCEPT_CHECKSUMS}"
addtask rootfs after do_prepare_recipe_sysroot

fakeroot python do_image () {
    from oe.utils import execute_pre_post_process

    d.setVarFlag('REPRODUCIBLE_TIMESTAMP_ROOTFS', 'export', '1')
    pre_process_cmds = d.getVar("IMAGE_PREPROCESS_COMMAND")

    execute_pre_post_process(d, pre_process_cmds)
}
do_image[dirs] = "${TOPDIR}"
addtask do_image after do_rootfs
...
```

The do_image and do_rootfs tasks are used, respectively, to start the image generation process and to create the root filesystem (file and directory structure, the binary image is then generated later by other tasks; then the completion is due to the do_image_complete task, not reported here).

To well understand this difference, the readers should see the beautiful and really explicating image from the Yocto Reference Manual at https://docs.yoctoproject.org/dev/_images/image-generation.png describing the image generation process.

Just by taking a first look at that image, we can well understand how an image is generated. Below, we are going to do our best to describe these steps:

1. At the beginning, we have the *source mirrors* where BitBake takes the code, and, by using package recipes, it produces the *package feeds*, that is, the IPKG, RPM, or DEB packages.

316

2. Then, within the special task do_rootfs, it proceeds
    to create the target's root filesystem by doing the
    following steps:

    2.1. By reading IMAGES_ and PACKAGE_ variables,
          BitBake creates the final list of packages passed
          to the package manager for installation into the
          image (the list is held within the internal PACKAGE_
          INSTALL variable – see below in this section about
          how we can properly use this variable).

    2.2. Then the final root filesystem is created within the
          location addressed by the IMAGE_ROOTFS variable
          (this variable is not configurable, so we have not
          changed it).

    2.3. At this point, some post-processing tasks are
          executed. By default, there is an optimization
          stage and a Manifest generation (see Section 7.4.3
          for further information about the Manifest).

          Furthermore, via the ROOTFS_POSTPROCESS_
          COMMAND we can specify a list of functions
          separated by spaces to call once the Yocto
          build system has created the root filesystem:

```
ROOTFS_POSTPROCESS_COMMAND += "function;"
```

3. When the do_rootfs task has been finished, BitBake
   starts the do_image one, which has as main target
   the root filesystem binary image generation:

   3.1. In the same manner as above, by using the IMAGE_
        PREPROCESS_COMMAND variable, we can specify a
        list of functions separated by spaces to call before
        the Yocto build system creates the final image
        output files:

        ```
        IMAGE_PREPROCESS_COMMAND += "function;"
        ```

   3.2. At this point, according to the IMAGE_FSTYPES
        variable that specifies the formats the Yocto build
        system uses during the build when creating the
        root filesystem, several do_image_* tasks are
        executed to create the final root filesystem files.

   3.3. At the end, by using IMAGE_POSTPROCESS_
        COMMAND, we can specify a list of functions
        separated by spaces to call once the Yocto build
        system creates the final image output files:

        ```
        IMAGE_POSTPROCESS_COMMAND += "function;
        ```

Note that the right format to specify functions in these variables has
a final semicolon; also, it is safer to add our functions by using the +=
(or append) operator instead of the equal sign (=) as shown below:

```
IMAGE_POSTPROCESS_COMMAND += "function; ... "
IMAGE_PREPROCESS_COMMAND:append = "function; ... "
```

An example of IMAGE_PREPROCESS_COMMAND usage is reported in the following example:

```
$ cat meta-security/recipes-core/images/dm-verity-image-initramfs.bb
...
deploy_verity_hash() {
    install -D -m 0644 \
        ${STAGING_VERITY_DIR}/${DM_VERITY_IMAGE}.${DM_VERITY_IMAGE_TYPE
}.verity.env \
        ${IMAGE_ROOTFS}${datadir}/misc/dm-verity.env
}
IMAGE_PREPROCESS_COMMAND += "deploy_verity_hash;"
```

Note that the only way to precede the do_rootfs task is by using the addtask statement, as in the following example:

```
$ cat meta-virtualization/recipes-extended/images/xen-image-minimal.bb
...
do_check_xen_state() {
    if [ "${@bb.utils.contains('DISTRO_FEATURES', 'xen', ' yes', 'no',
d)}" = "no" ]; then
        die "DISTRO_FEATURES does not contain 'xen'"
    fi
}

addtask check_xen_state before do_rootfs
...
```

A final note on these variables is that they can also be used with overrides, as shown below:

```
$ cat meta-engicam-nxp/recipes-images/images/engicam-evaluation-image-m
x8.bb
...
ROOTFS_POSTPROCESS_COMMAND:append:mx8 = "fix_bcm43430;"

fix_bcm43430() {
    cd ${IMAGE_ROOTFS}/lib/firmware/brcm
    ln -sf brcmfmac43430-sdio.bin brcmfmac43430-sdio.engi,imx8-icore.bin
}
...
```

The readers should note that to pass the root filesystem path to the commands within the new functions, we can use the `IMAGE_ROOTFS` variable which points to the directory that becomes the root filesystem image (this variable is used also during the `do_rootfs` task, and it is not configurable, so we don't have to change it!).

Within the image class, we can also find other useful variables we can set to configure the Yocto image generation, for example, below is a list of the most used ones:

- `IMAGE_NAME`: Specifies the name of the output image files without the extension. It defaults to

  `"${IMAGE_BASENAME}-${MACHINE}${IMAGE_VERSION_SUFFIX}"`

  where `IMAGE_BASENAME` usually defaults to the recipe name (PN), and `IMAGE_VERSION_SUFFIX` defaults to the string `"-${DATETIME}"`.

  `IMAGE_LINK_NAME`: Is a symbolic link to `IMAGE_NAME` which does not include the version part (`IMAGE_VERSION_SUFFIX`) in its name; in fact, it defaults to `"${IMAGE_BASENAME}-${MACHINE}"`. It is usually useful to refer to the final image file by using a well-defined, and not variable, name.

- `IMAGE_FSTYPES`: Specifies the formats of the root filesystem. For example, by setting `IMAGE_FSTYPES = "ext4 tar.bz2"` we ask the build system to create the root filesystem using two formats: .ext4 and .tar.bz2.

  The complete list of supported image formats can be retrieved at `https://docs.yoctoproject.org/4.0.13/ref-manual/variables.html#term-IMAGE_TYPES`.

There are two recommendations in using this variable:

1) If a recipe uses the `inherit image` line, then it must set `IMAGE_FSTYPES` prior to this line.

2) Recipes must use the += operator only to add one or more options to the `IMAGE_FSTYPES` variable (using :append or :prepend may produce unexpected behaviors).

- `IMAGE_LINGUAS`: Specifies the list of locales to install into the image. It defaults to `"de-de fr-fr en-gb"` so, by default, packages `locale-base-de-ed`, `locale-base-fr-fr`, and `locale-base-en-gb` are installed.

- `IMAGE_MANIFEST`: Specifies the manifest file for the image. The name of the file defaults to

  `"${IMGDEPLOYDIR}/${IMAGE_NAME}${IMAGE_NAME_SUFFIX}.manifest"`

  where `IMGDEPLOYDIR` points to a temporary work area for deployed files, and `IMAGE_NAME_SUFFIX` defaults to `.rootfs` to distinguish the image file from other files created during image building.

  This variable holds a list of all the installed packages that make up the image. Each line of this file contains the package information: package name, package arch, and version. See Section 7.4.3 for a practical usage of this file.

There are many other variables in the image class, and curious readers may take a look into the `image.bbclass` file; as far as this book is concerned, the variables reported above are enough for our purposes.

6.5.3 Generating Initramfs

An **initial RAM filesystem** (usually referred to as **Initramfs**) is an optionally compressed (typically in cpio format) archive which is extracted by the Linux kernel into RAM in a special tmpfs instance, used as the initial root filesystem.

It is typically used for several reasons:

1) For mounting a root filesystem which cannot be mounted directly by the kernel. Typically, when the rootfs is encrypted.

2) For supporting system update or factory reset procedures. If we need to completely rewrite the rootfs, we can do it within an Initramfs and then move into the new root filesystem.

3) For doing something faster. As the root filesystem is extracted into RAM, accessing the first user-space applications is very fast, compared to having to initialize a block device (e.g., it allows displaying a splash screen very early on boot).

To create an Initramfs, we must, firstly, create a proper recipe to define what the build system has to put in it. A good example is shown below:

```
$ cat poky/meta/recipes-core/images/core-image-minimal-initramfs.bb
# Simple initramfs image. Mostly used for live images.
DESCRIPTION = "Small image capable of booting a device. The kernel \
includes the Minimal RAM-based Initial Root Filesystem (initramfs), \
which finds the first 'init' program more efficiently."

INITRAMFS_SCRIPTS ?= "\
                      initramfs-framework-base \
                      initramfs-module-setup-live \
                      initramfs-module-udev \
                      initramfs-module-install \
                      initramfs-module-install-efi \
                      "
```

```
PACKAGE_INSTALL = "${INITRAMFS_SCRIPTS} ${VIRTUAL-RUNTIME_base-utils} u
dev base-passwd ${ROOTFS_BOOTSTRAP_INSTALL}"

# Do not pollute the initrd image with rootfs features
IMAGE_FEATURES = ""

export IMAGE_BASENAME = "${MLPREFIX}core-image-minimal-initramfs"
IMAGE_NAME_SUFFIX ?= ""
IMAGE_LINGUAS = ""

LICENSE = "MIT"

IMAGE_FSTYPES = "${INITRAMFS_FSTYPES}"
inherit core-image

IMAGE_ROOTFS_SIZE = "8192"
IMAGE_ROOTFS_EXTRA_SPACE = "0"
...
```

First, we should note that when working with an Initramfs image, we
do not use the IMAGE_INSTALL variable to specify packages for installation.
Instead, we should use the PACKAGE_INSTALL variable, which allows the
initial RAM filesystem recipe to use a fixed set of packages and not be
affected by IMAGE_INSTALL.

Then we do other settings such as empty the IMAGE_FEATURES and
IMAGE_LINGUAS (used to specify the list of locales to install into the image)
to not pollute the Initramfs image with root filesystem features and
keep the size as small as possible. Moreover, we set IMAGE_FSTYPES as
INITRAMFS_FSTYPES (which defines the format for the output image of the
Initramfs) usually set up into a configuration file (it defaults to cpio.gz).

Now, to ask the build system to embed our new Initramfs into the
kernel, we should set the INITRAMFS_IMAGE_BUNDLE variable to 1 and put in
the INITRAMFS_IMAGE variable the name of the recipe for the Initramfs.

Typically, these operations are done in a configuration file (typically
the distro.conf), even if INITRAMFS_IMAGE can be set in a recipe file too.
An example can be as shown below:

```
INITRAMFS_IMAGE = "image-tiny-initramfs"
INITRAMFS_IMAGE_BUNDLE = "1"
```

Doing so causes the Initramfs image to be unpacked into the `${B}/usr/` directory which in turn is passed to the kernel's `Makefile` using the `CONFIG_INITRAMFS_SOURCE` variable, allowing the Initramfs image to be built into the kernel normally (a practical example about this setting is reported in Section 12.6).

6.6 Best Practices

Until now, we have seen how recipes are composed, and in Chapter 12 we are going to see some practical examples. However, before ending this chapter, we will list below some best practices every good Yocto developer should do when writing new recipes:

- Avoid overlapping entire recipes from other layers in our custom layer. In other words, we should not copy an entire recipe into our layer and then modify it. To customize a recipe, it is better to use an append file (`.bbappend`) to override only those parts of the original recipe we need to modify.

Note that during the build process, BitBake displays an error if it detects a `.bbappend` file that does not have a corresponding recipe with a matching name.

- Avoid duplicating include files. If we are introducing a new recipe that requires an included file from another layer, we should use the path relative to the original layer directory to refer to the file.

An example is in the `netcat` and "netcat-openbsd" recipes:

```
$ cat meta-openembedded/meta-networking/recipes-support/netcat/ne
tcat_0.7.1.bb
require netcat.inc
LICENSE = "GPL-2.0-only"
...
cat meta-openembedded/meta-networking/recipes-support/netcat/netc
at-openbsd_1.195.bb
require netcat.inc
SUMMARY = "OpenBSD Netcat"
HOMEPAGE = "http://ftp.debian.org"
LICENSE = "BSD-2-Clause"
...
```

Both recipes include the `netcat.inc` file for common settings, and then they define their own custom settings.

Inclusions should be done also in configuration files as shown below:

```
$ cat meta-freescale-3rdparty/conf/machine/imx7s-warp.conf
#@TYPE: Machine
#@NAME: WaRP7
#@SOC: i.MX7S
#@DESCRIPTION: Machine configuration for i.MX7S WaRP board.
#@MAINTAINER: Pierre-Jean Texier <texier.pj2@gmail.com>

MACHINEOVERRIDES =. "mx7:mx7d:"

require conf/machine/include/imx-base.inc
require conf/machine/include/arm/armv7a/tune-cortexa7.inc
...
```

These required files are located in other layers as shown below:

```
$ cd sources
find . -name imx-base.inc -o -name tune-cortexa7.inc
./meta-freescale/conf/machine/include/imx-base.inc
./poky/meta/conf/machine/include/arm/armv7a/tune-cortexa7.inc
```

- Place machine-specific files in machine-specific locations. When we have one or more files which change according to a specific machine setting, we can put them in different directories named for each machine. So we can make sure that a machine-specific file is used for a particular machine (see the example about the file /etc/fstab in Section 5.3.4).

- Use utility programs when possible. Instead of directly calling make, we should instead call oe_runmake(), or we should use install within the do_install task as seen above, etc.

- Use the COMPATIBLE_MACHINE variable to stop recipes from being built for machines with which the recipes are incompatible.

6.7 Summary

In this chapter, we have seen how recipes for building packages or complete Yocto images are composed.

We discovered which variables can be found in a recipe and the tasks we can use to build packages (or root filesystem). So now we are ready to move to the third part of this book, where we start doing practical examples about how to write a new layer, how to define new machines, and how to write new or customize old recipes.

CHAPTER 7

Generating and Managing Layers

Starting from this chapter, we enter the third part of this book, where we can see how to actually customize our newly installed Yocto system as released by the hardware supplier.

In this chapter, we are going to focus on the definition of a new layer where we can add new machines and new recipes (or customizing recipes from other layers) in order to customize an already running Yocto distribution working for an embedded kit. This will reduce the time to market for custom hardware.

7.1 A Typical Layout

As already introduced in Section 3.2, each layer provides different configuration types for a distribution (i.e., a machine or distro configuration, etc.), and best practices dictate that we should isolate these types of configurations into their layer.

© Rodolfo Giometti 2025
R. Giometti, *Yocto Project Customization for Linux*,
https://doi.org/10.1007/979-8-8688-1435-8_7

However, apart from these considerations, all layers usually look like below:

```
$ cd sources/meta-freescale
$ ls
COPYING.MIT   custom-licenses        recipes-dpaa         recipes-security
EULA          dynamic-layers         recipes-dpaa2        recipes-support
LICENSE       recipes-bsp            recipes-extended     scripts
README        recipes-connectivity   recipes-fsl          wic
SCR           recipes-core           recipes-graphics
classes       recipes-devtools       recipes-kernel
conf          recipes-downgrade      recipes-multimedia
```

Typically, a layer holds

- One or more license files: Usually named COPYING.MIT, EULA, LICENSE , etc. These files are located in the root directory of each layer or within specified directories (e.g., the meta-freescale layer stores additional license files under the custom-licenses directory).

- A README file: Even if not a must-have, it's best practice to add a README file in each layer which describes what the layer is for, its dependency layers, and other useful information regarding the layer. For example, within the above README file, we can see something as shown below:

```
$ cat README
OpenEmbedded/Yocto BSP layer for Freescale's platforms
======================================================

This layer provides support for Freescale's platforms for use with
OpenEmbedded and/or Yocto.

This layer depends on:

URI: git://git.openembedded.org/openembedded-core
branch: kirkstone
revision: HEAD

Contributing
------------
```

```
Please submit any patches against the meta-freescale layer by
using the GitHub pull-request feature.  Fork the repo, make a
branch, do the work, rebase from upstream, create the pull
request.

For some useful guidelines to be followed when submitting patches,
please refer to:
http://openembedded.org/wiki/Commit_Patch_Message_Guidelines

Pull requests will be discussed within the GitHub pull-request
infrastructure. If you want to get informed on new PRs and the
follow-up discussions please use the GitHub's notification system.

Mailing list:

    https://lists.yoctoproject.org/g/meta-freescale

Source code:

    https://github.com/Freescale/meta-freescale
```

- Class files: All .bbclass files are located within the classes subdirectory of the layer.

- Configuration files: All the .conf files are located in the conf subdirectory of the layer. In this directory, we find the configuration files for the layer (the conf/layer. conf file), optionally the machine (conf/machine/*. conf) and the distribution (conf/distro/*.conf) files, and any other useful configuration files and/or the include (.inc) files.

- Recipe files: Each recipe is stored within a dedicated directory with the name of the recipe itself, all grouped in directories named with the recipes- prefix. The contents within recipe directories can vary, and, generally, these directories contain recipe files (.bb), recipe append files (.bbappend), directories that are distro-specific for configuration files, and so forth. For example:

```
$ cd meta-freescale
$ ls recipes-devtools/
devregs  imx-usb-loader  qemu  qoriq-cst  utp-com  uuu
$ tree recipes-devtools/uuu/
recipes-devtools/uuu/
├── files
│   └── 0001-remove-unnecessary-libzip-dependency.patch
└── uuu_git.bb

1 directory, 2 files
```

- Specific custom directories: We can have several directories where we can find useful scripts or extra configuration files for custom tools of the layer, documentation files, etc.

To provide an example of what these last directories may look like, in this chapter we are going to define a custom `scripts` directory within our custom layer, where we will add our utility scripts.

7.2 Creating a New Layer

Even if it's not so difficult to create a new layer by hand (we have to create some directories and a few configuration files), creating a new layer with the `bitbake-layers` script with the `create-layer` subcommand is simpler and less error-prone.

The usage message is shown below:

```
$ bitbake-layers create-layer -h
NOTE: Starting bitbake server...
usage: bitbake-layers create-layer [-h] [--layerid LAYERID]
                                   [--priority PRIORITY]
                                   [--example-recipe-name EXAMPLERECIPE]
                                   [--example-recipe-version VERSION]
                                   layerdir
```

```
Create a basic layer

positional arguments:
  layerdir                Layer directory to create

options:
  -h, --help              show this help message and exit
  --layerid LAYERID, -i LAYERID
                          Layer id to use if different from layername
  --priority PRIORITY, -p PRIORITY
                          Priority of recipes in layer
  --example-recipe-name EXAMPLERECIPE, -e EXAMPLERECIPE
                          Filename of the example recipe
  --example-recipe-version VERSION, -v VERSION
                          Version number for the example recipe
```

So, for example, to create a new layer named meta-cy, we can execute the next command:

```
$ bitbake-layers create-layer ../sources/meta-cy
NOTE: Starting bitbake server...
Add your new layer with 'bitbake-layers add-layer ../sources/meta-cy'
```

Note that we use for layerdir the string ../sources/meta-cy due to the fact that we are executing bitbake-layers within the imx8mp-build directory, and every new layer should stay under the source's directory.

This is not a fixed rule, but by doing so, you can group all layers under the same parent directory.

Now if we take a look into the newly created layer directory, we should see something as below:

```
$ cd ../sources/meta-cy
$ ls
COPYING.MIT  README  conf  recipes-example
```

Here, the really important thing to note is in the `conf` directory:

```
$ ls conf/
layer.conf
```

In the `layer.conf file`, that is, the layer's configuration file, we should see something as below:

```
$ cat conf/layer.conf
# We have a conf and classes directory, add to BBPATH
BBPATH .= ":${LAYERDIR}"

# We have recipes-* directories, add to BBFILES
BBFILES += "${LAYERDIR}/recipes-*/*/*.bb \
            ${LAYERDIR}/recipes-*/*/*.bbappend"

BBFILE_COLLECTIONS += "meta-cy"
BBFILE_PATTERN_meta-cy = "^${LAYERDIR}/"
BBFILE_PRIORITY_meta-cy = "6"

LAYERDEPENDS_meta-cy = "core"
LAYERSERIES_COMPAT_meta-cy = "kirkstone"
```

A brief explanation of the meaning of the above settings is below:

- BBPATH: This variable adds the layer's root directory to BitBake's search path. By using this variable, it locates class files (`.bbclass`), configuration files (`.conf`), recipe files (`.bb` and `.bbappend`), and files that are included with include and require statements (`.inc`).

Note that BitBake uses the first file that matches the name found in BBPATH similarly to the way the PATH variable is used for binaries. So it is recommended that developers will use unique class and configuration filenames in their custom layers.

- BBFILES: It defines the location for all recipes in the layer. Usually, we don't need to alter this setting, since it is almost a standard that recipes and appended files are located under directories prefixed with the string recipes- and located within a directory under them.

- BBFILE_COLLECTIONS: It's used to list the names of configured layers within the Yocto build system. These names are used to find the other BBFILE_* variables reported below.

All the following variables must be suffixed with the name of the specific layer.

- BBFILE_PATTERN: It expands to match files from BBFILES in a particular layer, often addressed by LAYERDIR, as in the example above.

- BBFILE_PRIORITY: Establishes a priority to use for recipes in the layer when the build finds recipes of the same name in different layers. A larger value for the variable results in a higher precedence regardless of a recipe's version (PV variable). For example, a layer that has a recipe with a higher PV value but for which the BBFILE_PRIORITY is set to have a lower precedence still has a lower precedence.

- LAYERDEPENDS: Lists all layers, separated by spaces, on which the current depends (if any). Optionally, we can specify a specific layer version for a dependency by adding it to the end of the layer name. For example:

```
LAYERDEPENDS_layer = "layer2 (=3)"
```

Then we require version 3 of layer2, and an error is produced if the version numbers do not match (or if any dependency is missing).

- LAYERSERIES_COMPAT: Lists the Yocto Project releases for which the current version is compatible. This variable is a good way to detect when a layer is not well maintained (i.e., it has not been tested with new Yocto releases).

Furthermore, not reported in the above example due to the fact that they are optional, we may have

- LAYERVERSION: An optional variable to specify the version of a layer as a single number. Then, this number can be used within LAYERDEPENDS of another layer (in its conf/layer.conf file) in order to depend on a specific version of our layer.

- LAYERRECOMMENDS: Similarly to LAYERDEPENDS, it lists the layers, separated by spaces, recommended for use with the current layer.

Well, now that we know exactly what these variables are for, and since our layer should have the precedence over other layers, it's better to set the higher priority value for it. To do so, we can use the command bitbake-layers show-layers to find the highest value defined within the system and then properly set the BBFILE_PRIORITY_meta-cy value:

```
$ bitbake-layers show-layers
NOTE: Starting bitbake server...
layer                   path                                              priority
===================================================================
meta       .../imx-yocto-bsp/sources/poky/meta                5
meta-poky .../imx-yocto-bsp/sources/poky/meta-poky            5
meta-oe    .../imx-yocto-bsp/sources/meta-openembedded/meta-oe 5
...
meta-engicam-nxp .../imx-yocto-bsp/sources/meta-engicam-nxp    6
```

The above output has been reduced for better readability. In fact, all layers' path names are not truncated with **...** and are absolute path names, for example, /home/giometti/yocto/imx-yocto-bsp/sources/meta-openembedded/meta-oe.

Here, we can easily see that, in our example, we can safely use 15 as the higher priority.

Moreover, since our custom embedded system is derived from the Engicam development kit, it is better to notify the Yocto build system that our layer depends on the meta-engicam layer too.

So we, have to do the following modifications:

```
--- sources/meta-cy/conf/layer.conf
+++ sources/meta-cy/conf/layer.conf
@@ -7,7 +7,7 @@
 BBFILE_COLLECTIONS += "meta-cy"
 BBFILE_PATTERN_meta-cy = "^${LAYERDIR}/"
-BBFILE_PRIORITY_meta-cy = "6"
+BBFILE_PRIORITY_meta-cy = "15"

-LAYERDEPENDS_meta-cy = "core"
+LAYERDEPENDS_meta-cy = "core meta-engicam-nxp"
 LAYERSERIES_COMPAT_meta-cy = "kirkstone"
```

Then, our layer.conf file should look like this:

```
$ cat meta-cy/conf/layer.conf
# We have a conf and classes directory, add to BBPATH
BBPATH .= ":${LAYERDIR}"

# We have recipes-* directories, add to BBFILES
BBFILES += "${LAYERDIR}/recipes-*/*/*.bb \
            ${LAYERDIR}/recipes-*/*/*.bbappend"

BBFILE_COLLECTIONS += "meta-cy"
BBFILE_PATTERN_meta-cy = "^${LAYERDIR}/"
BBFILE_PRIORITY_meta-cy = "15"

LAYERDEPENDS_meta-cy = "core meta-engicam-nxp"
LAYERSERIES_COMPAT_meta-cy = "kirkstone"
```

Now everything is in place, and we are ready to add our new layer to the Yocto building system.

7.3 Adding a Layer

Every layer is located within a directory, and, to add it to the Yocto building system, we need the `bitbake-layers add-layer` command as shown below:

```
$ bitbake-layers add-layer ../sources/meta-cy
NOTE: Starting bitbake server...
```

Note that we have used a relative path name since we have executed the above command within the build directory.

Doing this operation will alter the `conf/bblayers.conf` within our building directory. To verify it, we just need to take a look at it:

```
$ cat conf/bblayers.conf
LCONF_VERSION = "7"

BBPATH = "${TOPDIR}"
BSPDIR := "${@os.path.abspath(os.path.dirname(d.getVar('FILE', True))
+ '/../..')}"
...
BBLAYERS += "/home/giometti/yocto/imx-yocto-bsp/sources/meta-cy"
```

Another useful way to check this new setting is also by using the `bitbake-layers show-layers` command, as reported below:

```
$ bitbake-layers show-layers
NOTE: Starting bitbake server...
layer                   path                                          priority
================================================================
meta      .../imx-yocto-bsp/sources/poky/meta                  5
meta-poky .../imx-yocto-bsp/sources/poky/meta-poky             5
meta-oe   .../imx-yocto-bsp/sources/meta-openembedded/meta-oe  5
...
meta-engicam-nxp .../imx-yocto-bsp/sources/meta-engicam-nxp    6
meta-cy   .../imx-yocto-bsp/sources/meta-cy                    15
```

Even here the output has been altered for better readability, as above! In fact, the readers may also have an entry for the workspace which is not reported here.

Here, we can also verify that we have the priority we set in the previous section. To quickly check the layer dependencies, we can use the `bitbake-layers layerindex-show-depends` command as below:

```
$ bitbake-layers layerindex-show-depends meta-cy
NOTE: Starting bitbake server...
ERROR: Missing dependency selinux (HEAD)
ERROR: Missing dependency webserver (HEAD)
Layer                                        Git repository (bran
ch)                              Subdirectory
=====================================================================
local:HEAD:openembedded-core                 https://git.yoctopro
ject.org/git/poky (HEAD)          meta
   required by: meta-cy meta-engicam-nxp
local:HEAD:meta-engicam-nxp                  https://github.com/e
ngicam-stable/meta-engicam-nxp.git (kirkstone)
   required by: meta-cy
local:HEAD:meta-cy                           file:///home/giomett
i/yocto/imx-yocto-bsp/sources/meta-cy (<unknown>)
```

The output of the above command is really vast; that's why we have rearranged some information in the above output. The readers may expect to get a different formatting on their systems.

In the above output, we have several additional information regarding the current setup of our building system. First, we notice that the dependencies we set are correctly set up, then we can see that the layers on which our new layer depends came from remote repositories, and we also

know their current branches. Our new layer has in field Git repository
(branch) the value file:///home/giometti/yocto/imx-yocto-bsp/
sources/meta-cy (<unknown>) since we have not created a git repository
on it yet. However, we can fix it by doing as below:

```
$ cd /home/giometti/yocto/imx-yocto-bsp/sources/meta-cy
$ git init
Initialized empty Git repository in /home/giometti/yocto/imx-yocto-bsp/
sources/meta-cy/.git/
```

On some system, after this command, the readers may get the
following warning message:

```
hint: Using 'master' as the name for the initial branch. This
hint: default branch name is subject to change. To configure the
hint: initial branch name to use in all of your new repositories,
hint: which will suppress this warning, call:
hint:
hint: git config --global init.defaultBranch <name>
hint:
hint: Names commonly chosen instead of 'master' are 'main', 'trunk'
hint: and 'development'. The just-created branch can be renamed via
hint: this command:
hint:
hint: git branch -m <name>
```

If so, we can simply follow what the hint message says to fix it.

However, in this book, we continue without doing it, and then our
default branch will still be named master.

However, to rename the branch, we can use the git branch
(-m | -M) [<oldbranch>] <newbranch> command.

Then we continue by adding all files in the current directory to the new
Git repository:

```
$ git add .
$ git commit -m "Initial commit"
[master 0828270] Initial commit
 Date: Fri Nov 17 10:47:42 2023 +0000
 4 files changed, 84 insertions(+)
 create mode 100644 COPYING.MIT
 create mode 100644 README
 create mode 100644 conf/layer.conf
 create mode 100644 recipes-example/example/example_0.1.bb
```

Now the local Git repository for our new layer is created, and then we can push it to a remote location by creating it on a remote host (in our example, we have a freshly created repository on https://github.com/giometti/meta-cy). Then we execute the next command:

```
$ git push -u origin master
Enumerating objects: 9, done.
Counting objects: 100% (9/9), done.
Delta compression using up to 24 threads
Compressing objects: 100% (6/6), done.
Writing objects: 100% (9/9), 1.81 KiB | 1.81 MiB/s, done.
Total 9 (delta 0), reused 0 (delta 0), pack-reused 0
To github.com:giometti/meta-cy.git
 * [new branch]      master -> master
Branch 'master' set up to track remote branch 'master' from 'origin'.
```

Now if we execute the bitbake-layers layerindex-show-depends command again, we notice that the line regarding our new layer is changed and the remote Git repository is reported:

```
$ bitbake-layers layerindex-show-depends meta-cy
...
local:HEAD:meta-cy                         ssh://git@github.com
:giometti/meta-cy.git (master)
```

Now, to verify that our new layer is up and running, we can try to compile the new example_0.1.bb recipe that has been added during the layer creation. To do so, we just need to execute bitbake to deploy the new example recipe as shown below:

```
$ bitbake example
```

If everything is OK, we should see that the building system will start compiling the recipe, and we should see something as below when finished:

```
...
NOTE: Executing Tasks
**********************************************
*                                            *
*  Example recipe created by bitbake-layers  *
*                                            *
**********************************************
NOTE: Tasks Summary: Attempted 747 tasks of which 731 didn't need to be
 rerun and all succeeded.
```

Great! The new layer is ready and functional!

7.4 Adding Custom Scripts

Now our new custom layer is ready, but before we start defining new machines or recipes, we should take a look at how we can add custom scripts to do useful and common tasks.

In a section above, we introduced the possibility for a layer to define custom directories, and one of these is the `scripts` one. So let's create it within our layer:

```
$ cd ../sources/meta-cy/
$ mkdir scripts
```

Then we can also add a tiny example program as shown below:

```
$ cat > scripts/cy-test << __EOF
#!/bin/bash
echo "\$(basename \$0): hello world!"
__EOF
$ chmod +x scripts/cy-test
```

This new script can be executed as reported below:

```
$ ./scripts/cy-test
cy-test: hello world!
```

However, doing it in this manner is not what we want! In fact, we would like that, once we entered within the Yocto environment, we can execute all scripts within this new directory just by writing their names. To do so, we should take a look at the `setup-environment` script which is the one that actually does this job; in particular, we can see the following code:

```
$ cat ../setup-environment
...
OEROOT=$PWD/sources/poky
if [ -e $PWD/sources/oe-core ]; then
    OEROOT=$PWD/sources/oe-core
fi

. $OEROOT/oe-init-build-env $CWD/$1 > /dev/null
...
```

Here, the `OEROOT` variable is set, so we can put here our special code to properly set up the `PATH` Bash's variable as reported below:

```
--- ../setup-environment
+++ ../setup-environment
@@ -138,6 +138,10 @@
     return 1
 fi

+# Add specific CY's defines and set the script directory in PATH
+export CY_METADIR="$PWD/sources/meta-cy"
+export PATH="$CY_METADIR/scripts:$PATH"
+
 OEROOT=$PWD/sources/poky
 if [ -e $PWD/sources/oe-core ]; then
    OEROOT=$PWD/sources/oe-core
```

Now we have to exit and then re-enter into the Yocto environment by closing the current terminal and then resourcing the file setup-environment, as shown below:

```
$ cd imx-yocto-bsp
$ source setup-environment imx8mp-build
```

Then the new variable should be available:

```
$ echo $CY_METADIR
/home/giometti/yocto/imx-yocto-bsp/sources/meta-cy
$ echo $PATH
/home/giometti/yocto/imx-yocto-bsp/sources/poky/scripts:/home/giometti/
yocto/imx-yocto-bsp/sources/poky/bitbake/bin:/home/giometti/yocto/imx-y
octo-bsp/sources/meta-cy/scripts:/sbin:/usr/sbin:...
```

And the cy-test program should be executable by just writing its name:

```
$ cy-test
cy-test: hello world!
```

At this point, we can consider adding another file where we can put all our utility functions. The new file (located in our meta layer meta-cy) is reported below:

```
$ cat scripts/cy-misc.inc
#!/bin/bash
#
if [[ "${BASH_SOURCE[0]}" = "${0}" ]] ; then
        echo "Don't call me directly! Just source me" >&2
        exit 1
fi

__RED='\033[0;31m'
__YELLOW="\e[33m"
__GREEN='\033[0;32m'
__NC='\033[0m' # No Color

# ********************************************************************
# * Exported API
# ********************************************************************

NAME=$(basename $0)

function fatal() {
        echo -e "$__RED$NAME$__NC: $@" >&2
        exit 1
}

function warn() {
        echo -e "$__YELLOW$NAME$__NC: $@"
}
```

```
function info() {
        echo -e "$__GREEN$NAME$__NC: $@"
}

function good() {
        echo -e "$__GREEN$@$__NC"
}

function bad() {
        echo -e "$__RED$@$__NC"
}

return 0
```

The file is elementary, and it defines some special functions to print nice strings on the terminal. It also defines a new Bash's variable named CY_METADIR which can be used within our new scripts to address the directory holding our new layer.

Another interesting and widely used environment variable defined by these init scripts is BUILDDIR; it points to the main build directory. In our example, we have

```
$ echo $BUILDDIR
/home/giometti/yocto/imx-yocto-bsp/imx8mp-build
```

See below in this section for some possible usages.

To use this new file, we can rewrite our cy-test program as shown below:

```
$ cat scripts/cy-test
#!/bin/bash

CY_MISC_SH_FILE="cy-misc.inc"
if ! . $(dirname $0)/$CY_MISC_SH_FILE ; then
        echo "$0: fatal error! Cannot source $CY_MISC_SH_FILE"
        exit 1
fi

info "hello world!"
info "CY_METADIR=$CY_METADIR"

exit 0
```

Now if we execute it again, we should get something as shown below:

```
$ cy-test
cy-test: hello world!
cy-test: CY_METADIR=/home/giometti/yocto/imx-yocto-bsp/sources/meta-cy
```

On terminals which support colors, the readers should see the prefix `cy-test` in green.

7.4.1 Inspecting Variables

Starting from Section 4.1.3, we discovered that to read a BitBake's variable from the command line, we can use the following command:

```
$ bitbake -e recipe | grep "VARIABLE="
```

where `recipe` is a recipe name (which can be optional if we wish to inspect a generic variable instead of a recipe's one), and `VARIABLE` is the variable name. However, a more complete schema is reported below:

```
$ bitbake -e recipe | grep "^\(export \)\?VARIABLE="
```

This is because, as seen in Section 5.1.1, some variables can be exported, and then, when listed, they are prepended with the string `export`.

So, for example, to get the value for the generic variable `DL_DIR`, we can do the following:

```
$ bitbake -e | grep "^\(export \)\?DL_DIR="
DL_DIR="/home/giometti/Projects/DL_ARCHIVES/yocto/"
```

while to get the value for `S` when the `devmem2` package is compiled, we can do as reported below:

```
$ bitbake -e devmem2 | grep "^\(export \)\?S="
S="/home/giometti/yocto/imx-yocto-bsp/imx8mp-build/tmp/work/armv8a-poky
-linux/devmem2/2.0-r0/git"
```

Another useful variable is IMAGE_ROOTFS which points to the directory where the root filesystem is built. For example, once the image engicam-evaluation-image-mx8 is built with the command:

```
$ bitbake engicam-evaluation-image-mx8
```

then we can inspect its value to see where the Yocto build system has created the root filesystem for our target machine:

```
$ bitbake -e engicam-evaluation-image-mx8 | \
                    grep "^\(export \)\?IMAGE_ROOTFS="
IMAGE_ROOTFS="/home/giometti/yocto/imx-yocto-bsp/imx8mp-build/tmp/work/
imx8mp_icore-poky-linux/engicam-evaluation-image-mx8/1.0-r0/rootfs"
$ ls /home/giometti/yocto/imx-yocto-bsp/imx8mp-build/tmp/work/imx8mp_ic
ore-poky-linux/engicam-evaluation-image-mx8/1.0-r0/rootfs
bin   dev  home  media  opt   run   srv  tmp            usr
boot  etc  lib   mnt    proc  sbin  sys  unit_tests     var
```

On the other hand, if we wish to see where the Yocto build system has generated the IPKG packages for a certain recipe, we can inspect the variable PKGWRITEDIRIPK as shown below:

```
$ bitbake -e devmem2 | grep "^\(export \)\?PKGWRITEDIRIPK="
PKGWRITEDIRIPK="/home/giometti/yocto/imx-yocto-bsp/imx8mp-build/tmp/wor
k/armv8a-poky-linux/devmem2/2.0-r0/deploy-ipks"
$ ls /home/giometti/yocto/imx-yocto-bsp/imx8mp-build/tmp/work/armv8a-po
ky-linux/devmem2/2.0-r0/deploy-ipks
armv8a
$ ls /home/giometti/yocto/imx-yocto-bsp/imx8mp-build/tmp/work/armv8a-po
ky-linux/devmem2/2.0-r0/deploy-ipks/armv8a/
devmem2-dbg_2.0-r0_armv8a.ipk  devmem2-src_2.0-r0_armv8a.ipk
devmem2-dev_2.0-r0_armv8a.ipk  devmem2_2.0-r0_armv8a.ipk
```

Note that, as for the image example above, the devmem2 package file must be deployed by using

```
$ bitbake devmem2
```

Note also that the IPKG files are usually located under a machine subdirectory equal to MACHINE, but not in all cases (this is one of such special cases).

All these considerations suggest that we create a new utility, which we can call `cy-vars`, which can inspect all these variables by using simple commands. A possible implementation is reported in the file `meta-cy/scripts/cy-vars` which can be retrieved from our Git repository at `https://github.com/Apress/Yocto-Project-Customization-for-Linux`.

If we execute the utility, we get the following output:

```
$ cy-vars
usage: cy-vars <group>|<var> [<recipe>]
where <group> can be:
        bitbake              - main bitbake\'s variables
        main                 - main Yocto\'s variables
        names                - package names
        dirs                 - package directories
        image                - final image's variables
        virtual              - virtual packages
```

So, to read the global BitBake's variables, we can execute the following command:

```
$ cy-vars bitbake
BBFILES=" /home/giometti/yocto/imx-yocto-bsp/sources/poky/meta/recipes-
*/*/*.bb /home/giometti/yocto/imx-yocto-bsp/sources/poky/meta-poky/reci
pe...
```

while to get the list of the main directory variables for the `devmem2` recipe, we can do as below:

```
$ cy-vars dirs devmem2
B="/home/giometti/yocto/imx-yocto-bsp/imx8mp-build/tmp/work/armv8a-poky
-linux/devmem2/2.0-r0/git"
D="/home/giometti/yocto/imx-yocto-bsp/imx8mp-build/tmp/work/armv8a-poky
-linux/devmem2/2.0-r0/image"
S="/home/giometti/yocto/imx-yocto-bsp/imx8mp-build/tmp/work/armv8a-poky
-linux/devmem2/2.0-r0/git"
T="/home/giometti/yocto/imx-yocto-bsp/imx8mp-build/tmp/work/armv8a-poky
-linux/devmem2/2.0-r0/temp"
export base_bindir="/bin"
export base_libdir="/lib"
export base_sbindir="/sbin"
export bindir="/usr/bin"
export datadir="/usr/share"
export docdir="/usr/share/doc"
export includedir="/usr/include"
```

```
...
export sysconfdir="/etc"
export systemd_system_unitdir="/lib/systemd/system"
export systemd_unitdir="/lib/systemd"
export systemd_user_unitdir="/usr/lib/systemd/user"
target_datadir="/usr/share"
```

The core part of this script is reported below:

```
$ cat scripts/cy-vars
...
case $varid in
bitbake)
        regex="BBPATH\|BBFILES\|BBLAYERS\|"
        regex+="BB_ENV_PASSTHROUGH\|BB_ENV_PASSTHROUGH_ADDITIONS\|BB_PRES
ERVE_ENV\|"
        regex+="BSPDIR\|"
        regex+="BB_DEFAULT_TASK\|BB_GENERATE_MIRROR_TARBALLS"
        ;;
...
dirs)
        regex="S\|B\|D\|T\|"
        regex+="base_bindir\|base_libdir\|base_sbindir\|"
        regex+="bindir\|datadir\|docdir\|includedir\|infodir\|libdir\|"
        regex+="libexecdir\|localedir\|localstatedir\|mandir\|sbindir\|"
        regex+="servicedir\|sharedstatedir\|sysconfdir\|"
        regex+="nonarch_base_libdir\|nonarch_libdir\|target_datadir\|"
        regex+="systemd_system_unitdir\|systemd_unitdir\|systemd_user_uni
tdir"
        ;;
...
esac

bitbake -e $recipe | grep --color "^\(export \)\?\($regex\)="

exit 0
```

where variable regex holds a regular expression according to the user input.

In later chapters, this command will be widely used, so the readers may understand how to use it in different situations.

7.4.2 Inspecting Packages

During development and so in this book, we may need to locate a
new package (a `.ipk` file), to see what a package holds in it, or to get
some information regarding it. In all these cases, we may use different
commands to solve the problem, but we can group them within a special
script we can call `cy-ipk`.

This can be got from our Git repository, and once executed it shows the
following message:

```
$ cy-ipk
usage:
        cy-ipk find <name> [<name> ...]
        cy-ipk recipe <name> [<name> ...]
        cy-ipk depends <name> [<name> ...]
        cy-ipk inspect|get-info <file.ipk>
```

By specifying the `find` subcommand, we simply call the `find` tool on
`BUILDDIR` which is an environment variable that points to the current build
directory:

```
find)
        info "searching in $BUILDDIR..."
        cd $BUILDDIR
        shift
        for n in $@ ; do
                find tmp/deploy/ipk/ -name "${n}*"
        done
        exit 0
        ;;
```

For example, the `devmem2` packages previously created can be found by
using the command below:

```
$ cy-ipk find devmem2
cy-ipk: searching in /home/giometti/yocto/imx-yocto-bsp/imx8mp-build...
tmp/deploy/ipk/armv8a/devmem2-dbg_2.0-r0_armv8a.ipk
tmp/deploy/ipk/armv8a/devmem2-dev_2.0-r0_armv8a.ipk
tmp/deploy/ipk/armv8a/devmem2_2.0-r0_armv8a.ipk
tmp/deploy/ipk/armv8a/devmem2-src_2.0-r0_armv8a.ipk
```

The recipe subcommand is used to find the recipe which provides the input package. For example, package devmem2 is provided by the same name recipe:

```
$ cy-ipk recipe devmem2
package devmem2 is provided by: devmem2
```

But, as we can see in the next chapters, the package python3-debugger is provided by the python3 recipe, as shown below:

```
$ cy-ipk recipe python3-debugger
package python3-debugger is provided by: python3
```

Recalling the command bitbake-layers show-recipes recipename presented in Section 4.2, the readers can see that if we execute

```
$ bitbake-layers show-recipes python3-debugger
```

we get no valid output, while if we execute the following command, we discover where the python recipe is also located:

```
$ bitbake-layers show-recipes python3
...
=== Matching recipes: ===
python3:
  meta                    3.10.7
```

The core of this subcommand is reported below:

```
recipe)
    shift
    for n in $@ ; do
        echo -n "package $n is provided by: "
        oe-pkgdata-util lookup-recipe $n
    done
    exit 0
    ;;
```

And we can see that the trick is using the oe-pkgdata-util lookup-recipe command.

Another useful information is the one about which are packages that a recipe depends on; for example, by using the next command, we list all package dependencies for the package named python3-debugger:

```
$ cy-ipk depends python3-debugger
package python3-debugger depends on: python3-core python3-pprint python
3-shell python3-stringold
```

Again, we combine oe-pkgdata-util list-pkgs and oe-pkgdata-util read-value RDEPENDS to resolve the problem:

```
depends)
    shift
    for n in $@ ; do
        if ! oe-pkgdata-util list-pkgs $n 2>/dev/null 1>&2 ; then
            warn "cannot find package $n!"
            continue
        fi
        echo -n "package $n depends on: "
        oe-pkgdata-util read-value RDEPENDS $n
    done
    exit 0
    ;;
```

The first command is used to verify the input data are valid packages' names, while the second is used to read the content of RDEPENDS for a desired package.

Now, the last two subcommands are inspect and get-info. The former can be used to see what there are within a .ipk file, as shown below:

```
$ cy-ipk inspect tmp/deploy/ipk/armv8a/devmem2_2.0-r0_armv8a.ipk
drwxr-xr-x root/root         0 2022-05-30 16:07 ./usr/
drwxr-xr-x root/root         0 2022-05-30 16:07 ./usr/bin/
-rwxr-xr-x root/root     10208 2022-05-30 16:07 ./usr/bin/devmem2
```

while by using the latter, we can read IPKG information:

```
$ cy-ipk get-info tmp/deploy/ipk/armv8a/devmem2_2.0-r0_armv8a.ipk
Package: devmem2
Version: 2.0-r0
Description: Program to read/write from/to any location in memory
 Program to read/write from/to any location in memory.
Section: base
Priority: optional
```

```
Maintainer: NXP <lauren.post@nxp.com>
License: GPL-2.0-or-later
Architecture: armv8a
OE: devmem2
Depends: libc6 (>= 2.35)
Source: devmem2_2.0.bb
```

Note that both subcommands require a file (and not just a package name); this is because they use the dpkg command to solve their duties, as reported below:

```
inspect)
    dpkg -c $BUILDDIR/$name
    exit 0
    ;;

get-info)
    dpkg -f $BUILDDIR/$name
    exit 0
    ;;
```

The readers should now be clear that IPKG format is just a (simplified) DEB-like format, and it can be managed by the dpkg utility. If we take a look at the dpkg usage message, we get that the -c option argument is used to get the DEB (and IPKG) file list, while the -f is used to get the package's information data:

```
$ dpkg --help
...
Use dpkg with -b, --build, -c, --contents, -e, --control, -I, --info,
  -f, --field, -x, --extract, -X, --vextract, --ctrl-tarfile,
  --fsys-tarfile
on archives (type dpkg-deb --help).
...
```

These option arguments are then used within our utility to get the needed information from a .ipk file.

7.4.3 Inspecting Images

Regarding the final Yocto image inspection, we can provide the cy-image tool:

```
$ cy-image
usage:
        cy-image find-path <image> <pathname> [<pathname> ...]
        cy-image chk-pkg <image> <package> [<package> ...]
```

The first subcommand can be used to find which package provides a desired path name. For example, if we wish to know which are the packages that provide files /etc/fstab, /var/lost.log, /usr/bin/vi, and /bin/zcat, we can use the command below:

```
$ cy-image find-path engicam-evaluation-image-mx8 /etc/fstab \
                          /var/lost.log /bin/vi /bin/zcat
cy-image: searching in /home/giometti/yocto/imx-yocto-bsp/imx8mp-build/
tmp/work/imx8mp_icore-poky-linux/engicam-evaluation-image-mx8/1.0-r0/ro
otfs...
pathname /etc/fstab is provided by: base-files
pathname /var/lost.log is provided by: not found
pathname /bin/vi is provided by: busybox [symlink: /bin/busybox.nosuid]
pathname /bin/zcat is provided by: gzip [symlink: /bin/zcat.gzip]
```

The subcommand is implemented as shown below:

```
find-path)
    # Read BitBake variables
    vars=$(cy-vars 'IMAGE_ROOTFS' $name)
    img_rootfs=$(get IMAGE_ROOTFS $vars)

    # Find packages
    [ -d $img_rootfs ] || \
        fatal "rootfs image directory $img_rootfs doesn't exist!" \
            "Please generate it with 'bitbake $name' and then rerun"
    info "searching in $img_rootfs..."
    for p in $@ ; do
        # Resolve any symlinks
        real_path=$(readlink ${img_rootfs}$p || true)
        [ -z "$real_path" ] && real_path=$p
```

```
        echo -n "pathname $p is provided by: "
        if n=$(oe-pkgdata-util find-path $real_path 2>&1) ; then
            good ${n%%:*} $([ "$real_path" != "$p" ] && echo " [symlink
: $real_path]")
        else
            bad not found
        fi
    done
    exit 0
    ;;
```

The readers should note here that we cannot just use the oe-pkgdata-util find-path command, since it cannot resolve symbolic links. In fact, the path names /bin/vi and /bin/zcat are both symbolic links to respectively /bin/busybox.nosuid and /bin/zcat.gzip files, and if we supply them to oe-pkgdata-util, instead of the files they link to, we will get nothing:

```
$ oe-pkgdata-util find-path /bin/vi
ERROR: Unable to find any package producing path /bin/vi
$ oe-pkgdata-util find-path /bin/zcat
ERROR: Unable to find any package producing path /bin/zcat
```

That's why we must first resolve the symbolic links and then pass real files to the oe-pkgdata-util find-path command.

We may get the following error message:

```
$ cy-image find-path engicam-evaluation-image-mx8 /etc/fstab \
                          /var/lost.log /bin/vi /bin/zcat
cy-image: rootfs image directory /home/giometti/yocto/imx-yocto-bsp/imx
8mp-build/tmp/work/imx8mp_icore-poky-linux/engicam-evaluation-image-mx8
/1.0-r0/rootfs doesn't exist! Please generate it with 'bitbake engicam-
evaluation-image-mx8' and then rerun
```

In this case, we just have to do what the error message itself suggests to us.

On the other hand, if we have to check if one or more packages (supplied on the command line) are present within an image, we can use the chk-pkg subcommand as in the following example:

```
$ cy-image chk-pkg engicam-evaluation-image-mx8 devmem2 \
                            python3-debugger python3-shell
```

```
cy-image: searching in /home/develop/Projects-OLD/packt/Customizing_Yoc
to/yocto/imx-yocto-bsp/imx8mp-build...
package devmem2 is present
package python3-debugger is not present
package python3-shell is present
```

The subcommand is implemented as below:

```
chk-pkg)
        # Read BitBake variables
        vars=$(cy-vars 'MACHINE\IMAGE_LINK_NAME' $name)
        machine=$(get MACHINE $vars)
        link_name=$(get IMAGE_LINK_NAME $vars)

        # Compose manifest pathname
        man_img="tmp/deploy/images/$machine/${link_name}.manifest"
        [ -f $BUILDDIR/$man_img ] || \
                fatal "manifest file $man_img doesn't exist!" \
                        "Please generate it with 'bitbake $name' and
 then rerun"
        info "searching in $BUILDDIR..."

        for p in $@ ; do
                echo -n "package $p is "
                if grep -q $p $BUILDDIR/$man_img ; then
                        good present
                else
                        bad not present
                fi
        done
        exit 0
        ;;
```

To do its duty, the subcommand uses the manifest file generated for each Yocto image. Each time we ask the Yocto build system to generate an image, it also generates this manifest file which holds all installed packages with some attached information, as shown below:

```
$ cat /home/giometti/yocto/imx-yocto-bsp/imx8mp-build/tmp/deploy/images
/imx8mp-icore/engicam-evaluation-image-mx8-imx8mp-icore.manifest
acl armv8a 2.3.1-r0
acl-dbg armv8a 2.3.1-r0
acl-dev armv8a 2.3.1-r0
adwaita-icon-theme-symbolic all 41.0-r0
alsa-conf armv8a-mx8mp 1.2.6.1-r0
```

```
alsa-plugins-dbg armv8a 1.2.6-r0
alsa-plugins-pulseaudio-conf armv8a 1.2.6-r0
alsa-state imx8mp_icore 0.2.0-r5
alsa-state-dbg imx8mp_icore 0.2.0-r5
alsa-states imx8mp_icore 0.2.0-r5
alsa-tools armv8a 1.2.5-r0
alsa-tools-dbg armv8a 1.2.5-r0
...
```

This is the file referred to by the IMAGE_MANIFEST variable presented in Section 6.5.2.

If a package has been installed within the image, then it is reported here with the compatible machine and the release. For example, the package alsa-state release 0.2.0-r5 is installed, and it is available just for the imx8mp_icore machine, while package acl is available for armv8a machines (which is compatible with imx8mp_icore), and the adwaita-icon-theme-symbolic package is compatible with all machines.

So, once the manifest file for an image is retrieved, we just have to verify whether a package name is (or not) in the list.

Even for this subcommand, we can get an error message as below:

```
$ cy-image chk-pkg engicam-evaluation-image-mx8 devmem2 \
                              python3-debugger python3-shell
cy-image: manifest file tmp/deploy/images/imx8mp-icore/engicam-evaluati
on-image-mx8-imx8mp-icore.manifest doesn't exist! Please generate it with
'bitbake engicam-evaluation-image-mx8' and then rerun
```

If so, as done before, we just have to follow the suggestion within the message and run 'bitbake engicam-evaluation-image-mx8' to create the manifest file.

7.4.4 Inspecting the Git Repositories

Since we are going to customize a Yocto image, we must be prudent in tracking whatever we change, and using Git is the Right-Thing. However, we have several Git repositories to track, and doing it by hand may be risky; that's why we developed the `cy-gitchk` utility.

This utility is tricky; we just need to execute it as shown below:

```
$ cy-gitchk
cy-gitchk: ====== base ======
cy-gitchk: ====== meta-browser ======
cy-gitchk: ====== meta-clang ======
cy-gitchk: ====== meta-cy ======
cy-gitchk: ====== meta-engicam-nxp ======
cy-gitchk: ====== meta-freescale ======
cy-gitchk: ====== meta-freescale-3rdparty ======
cy-gitchk: ====== meta-freescale-distro ======
cy-gitchk: ====== meta-imx ======
cy-gitchk: ====== meta-nxp-demo-experience ======
cy-gitchk: ====== meta-openembedded ======
cy-gitchk: ====== meta-qt6 ======
cy-gitchk: ====== meta-timesys ======
cy-gitchk: ====== meta-virtualization ======
cy-gitchk: ====== poky ======
```

If it just returns the above message, it means that everything is up to date within each repository. Also, we can get the list of all repositories within our Yocto distribution to check that the autodetection works correctly.

On the other hand, we made some modifications to our Yocto Project, so we should expect a different output! For example, at the time this book was written, the output for `cy-gitchk` looks like below:

```
$ cy-gitchk
cy-gitchk: ====== base ======
 M setup-environment
cy-gitchk: ====== meta-browser ======
cy-gitchk: ====== meta-clang ======
cy-gitchk: ====== meta-cy ======
AM scripts/cy-test
?? scripts/cy-gitchk
?? scripts/cy-image
?? scripts/cy-image.OK
```

```
?? scripts/cy-ipk
?? scripts/cy-misc.inc
?? scripts/cy-vars
cy-gitchk: ====== meta-engicam-nxp ======
 M conf/machine/imx8mp-icore.conf
?? classes/
?? recipes-example/
...
```

The readers should note that this output may vary according to how the meta-cy layer (and maybe others) has been altered during the reading of this book.

In the above output, we can see that within base the file setup-environment has been modified; this was when we added modifications in Section 7.4. Furthermore, we see that imx8mp-icore.conf has been modified too, and it was when we did our first build, and we changed the default machine configuration in Section 2.3 to set the right memory layout.

Regarding our custom layer meta-cy, we can see that the file cy-test is currently tracked by Git but has been changed, while other files marked with ?? are unknown to Git.

The readers may understand that, in this manner, they can get a quick and reliable look at all Git repositories' statuses. However, some of them may notice the fact that this feature is really similar to the one we already saw in Section 2.6 by using the repo command. However, they should consider what we already said there, that is, repo will show modifications in all layers in the manifest, while Engicam's layer is not there! So, this is a better solution which works in every condition.

7.5 Summary

In this chapter, we have seen how to create a custom meta layer where we can put all our customizations. And we have started to add some information to it, especially new utilities we can use in the next chapters of this book to do recursive tasks reliably.

However, our goal is not only to create a new layer or just add new recipes to it (which is anyway explained in Chapter 9 and following) but also to manage new machines.

In fact, compiling code for a development kit can be useful during initial development, but, before or later, we will need to test our code on our custom machine which is derived from the development kit. So let's move on to the next chapter to see how to do this important step.

CHAPTER 8

Adding New Hardware

Now that we have a new custom layer, and we have seen how BitBake and other Yocto components work, in this chapter, we are going to take a look at how a developer can define a new hardware by adding a new machine.

Thereafter, we will show how developers can customize the bootloader and kernel for their embedded system (and we will also spend a few words about how to customize the prebootloaders).

8.1 Adding a Machine

As already said in several parts of this book, usually a custom machine is designed by altering in some parts the schematic of an already functional development kit to suit specific needs. The result is a new machine which is very similar to the original development kit (frequently with few hardware differences) and with different peripherals.

In most cases, those changes are so small that, as a first step, we can use on the new hardware both the bootloader and kernel which run on the development kit! For example, we adopted such a solution in Section 2.3 where we altered the `UBOOT_CONFIG` variable within the `imx8mp-icore.conf` file in the `meta-engicam-nxp` layer from 2gb to 4gb.

© Rodolfo Giometti 2025
R. Giometti, *Yocto Project Customization for Linux*,
https://doi.org/10.1007/979-8-8688-1435-8_8

However, this solution is not the best because

1) It can be used for few and very limited settings.

2) All modifications regarding our custom hardware should be done within our layer, eventually by renaming the current machine name to fix our project (i.e., by using overrides).

So let's see some best-practice techniques we can use to add to our Yocto Project all the modifications we need to do to support our hardware.

The readers should note that we are not going to show how to create an entirely new machine from scratch, but just how we can modify an already running one to fix our hardware modifications! In order to see how to define a new machine, curious readers may take a look at `https://docs.yoctoproject.org/dev-manual/new-machine.html`.

8.1.1 By Including the Original machine.conf

The first step is to create a new machine name to be used in the `MACHINE` variable in place of the development kit machine's name. In our example, we have `MACHINE="imx8mp-icore"` (see Section 2.2) defined into the `meta-engicam-nxp` layer as shown below:

```
$ cat meta-engicam-nxp/conf/machine/imx8mp-icore.conf
#@TYPE: Machine
#@NAME: NXP i.MX 8M Plus i.core
#@SOC: i.MX8MP
#@DESCRIPTION: Machine configuration for Engicam imx8mp-icore SOM
#@MAINTAINER: <support@engicam.com>

require include/imx8mp-engicam.inc

KERNEL_DEVICETREE_BASENAME = "imx8mp-icore"
```

```
KERNEL_DEVICETREE:append:use-nxp-bsp = " \
        engicam/imx8mp-icore-starterkit.dtb \
        engicam/imx8mp-icore-ctouch2.dtb \
"

UBOOT_CONFIG_BASENAME = "imx8mp_icore"
UBOOT_CONFIG ??= "2gb"
UBOOT_CONFIG[1gb] = "${UBOOT_CONFIG_BASENAME}_1gb_defconfig,sdcard"
UBOOT_CONFIG[2gb] = "${UBOOT_CONFIG_BASENAME}_defconfig,sdcard"
UBOOT_CONFIG[4gb] = "${UBOOT_CONFIG_BASENAME}_4gb_defconfig,sdcard"

# Set DDR FIRMWARE
DDR_FIRMWARE_VERSION = "202006"
DDR_FIRMWARE_NAME = " \
        lpddr4_pmu_train_1d_dmem_${DDR_FIRMWARE_VERSION}.bin \
        lpddr4_pmu_train_1d_imem_${DDR_FIRMWARE_VERSION}.bin \
        lpddr4_pmu_train_2d_dmem_${DDR_FIRMWARE_VERSION}.bin \
        lpddr4_pmu_train_2d_imem_${DDR_FIRMWARE_VERSION}.bin \
"

IMXBOOT_TARGETS_BASENAME = "flash_evk"
IMX_DEFAULT_BSP = "nxp"

IMX_KERNEL_CONFIG_AARCH64 = "imx8_icore_defconfig"
```

As we can see, in this file there are the most important settings for the
SOM installed into our development kit, so we can create a new file into
the conf/machine directory within our layer holding the next content:

```
$ cd sources/meta-cy/
$ cat conf/machine/imx8mp-icore-cy.conf
#@TYPE: Machine
#@NAME: CY machine based on NXP i.MX 8M Plus i.core
#@SOC: i.MX8MP
#@DESCRIPTION: Machine configuration for custom CY imx8mp-icore SOM
#@MAINTAINER: <giometti@enneenne.com>

require conf/machine/imx8mp-icore.conf

UBOOT_CONFIG = "4gb"

MACHINEOVERRIDES =. "imx8mp-icore:"
```

Note that this is a dirty trick, since it is not usual to include a .conf file. All included files should end with .inc.

By doing so, we tell the Yocto build system that our machine imx8mp-icore-cy is derived from imx8mp-icore by some minor changes; the most important setting here is the one applied to the MACHINEOVERRIDES variable, which is used to specify that our machine needs all machine overrides needed by the parent machine imx8mp-icore (see Section 5.3.2).

Now to compile a Yocto image for our new machine, we can simply use the command below:

```
$ MACHINE=imx8mp-icore-cy bitbake engicam-evaluation-image-mx8
```

Before doing so, the readers should verify that the modification done in previous sections within the meta-engicam-nxp layer has been removed. To do so, we just need to use the command below:

```
$ cd sources/meta-engicam-nxp
$ git reset -hard
```

Moreover, we should take care of removing all non-tracked files. If everything has been removed, we should see something as below:

```
$ git status
On branch kirkstone
Your branch is up to date with 'origin/kirkstone'.

nothing to commit, working tree clean
```

If we take a look at the messages displayed by the above bitbake command, we can verify that now within the build configuration settings we get our new machine:

```
...
Build Configuration:
BB_VERSION           = "2.0.0"
BUILD_SYS            = "x86_64-linux"
NATIVELSBSTRING      = "universal"
TARGET_SYS           = "aarch64-poky-linux"
MACHINE              = "imx8mp-icore-cy"
...
```

When finished, we can try the new image as usual; however, now we must take the image from the newly created subdirectory tmp/deploy/ images/imx8mp-icore-cy within the build directory:

```
$ cd tmp/deploy/images/imx8mp-icore-cy
$ ls *.wic.zst
engicam-evaluation-image-mx8-imx8mp-icore-cy-20231128095310.rootfs.wic.
zst
engicam-evaluation-image-mx8-imx8mp-icore-cy.wic.zst
```

So, to test the new image, we have to rewrite the microSD used before by using the command below:

```
$ zstdcat engicam-evaluation-image-mx8-imx8mp-icore-cy.wic.zst | \
    sudo dd of=/dev/sdd bs=8M conv=fdatasync status=progress
```

Again, the readers should replace the /dev/ssd device used above with their block device.

Now on the serial console, we should get the following output:

```
U-Boot 2022.04-master+g05dea559b9 (Oct 26 2023 - 13:17:23 +0000)

CPU:   i.MX8MP[8] rev1.1 1600 MHz (running at 1200 MHz)
CPU:   Industrial temperature grade (-40C to 105C) at 20C
Reset cause: POR
Model: Engicam i.MX8MPlus iCore
DRAM:  4 GiB
...
```

OK, the system starts again, and we have the right amount of DRAM, while at the end of the booting stage we can verify that the machine name is changed, as it should be:

```
...
NXP i.MX Release Distro 5.15-kirkstone imx8mp-icore-cy ttymxc1

imx8mp-icore-cy login:
```

Now before moving on to the next section, we can alter the configuration file `conf/local.conf` in the build directory as shown below. This is to avoid prepending the setting `MACHINE=imx8mp-icore-cy` in all next `bitbake` (and any other Yocto) commands:

```
--- conf/local.conf
+++ conf/local.conf
@@ -1,4 +1,4 @@
-MACHINE ??= 'imx8mp-icore'
+MACHINE ??= 'imx8mp-icore-cy'
 DISTRO ?= 'fsl-imx-xwayland'
 PACKAGE_CLASSES ?= 'package_rpm'
 EXTRA_IMAGE_FEATURES ?= "debug-tweaks"
```

OK, now it's time to see another method to create a new machine configuration which clones the original `machine.conf` file, instead of including it.

8.1.2 By Cloning the Original machine.conf

If we decide to clone the original `machine.conf` file, we can do it by simply doing

```
$ cd sources/meta-cy/conf/machine/
$ cp ../../../meta-engicam-nxp/conf/machine/imx8mp-icore.conf \
      imx8mp-icore-cy.conf
```

then by modifying it to properly set the memory layout and to add the `MACHINEOVERRIDES` for the same reasons explained above:

```
--- imx8mp-icore-cy.conf
+++ imx8mp-icore-cy.conf
```

```
@@ -1,8 +1,8 @@
 #@TYPE: Machine
-#@NAME: NXP i.MX 8M Plus i.core
+#@NAME: CY machine based on NXP i.MX 8M Plus i.core
 #@SOC: i.MX8MP
-#@DESCRIPTION: Machine configuration for Engicam imx8mp-icore SOM
-#@MAINTAINER: <support@engicam.com>
+#@DESCRIPTION: Machine configuration for custom CY imx8mp-icore SOM
+#@MAINTAINER: <giometti@enneenne.com>

 require include/imx8mp-engicam.inc

@@ -14,7 +14,7 @@
 "

 UBOOT_CONFIG_BASENAME = "imx8mp_icore"
-UBOOT_CONFIG ??= "2gb"
+UBOOT_CONFIG ??= "4gb"
 UBOOT_CONFIG[1gb] = "${UBOOT_CONFIG_BASENAME}_1gb_defconfig,sdcard"
 UBOOT_CONFIG[2gb] = "${UBOOT_CONFIG_BASENAME}_defconfig,sdcard"
 UBOOT_CONFIG[4gb] = "${UBOOT_CONFIG_BASENAME}_4gb_defconfig,sdcard"
@@ -32,4 +32,6 @@
 IMXBOOT_TARGETS_BASENAME = "flash_evk"
 IMX_DEFAULT_BSP = "nxp"

-IMX_KERNEL_CONFIG_AARCH64 = "imx8_icore_defconfig"
+IMX_KERNEL_CONFIG_AARCH64 = "imx8_icore_defconfig"
+
+MACHINEOVERRIDES =. "imx8mp-icore:"
```

Now we may suppose that we are at the same conditions as the previous section, but it is not. In fact, if we try to generate the Yocto image, we get the following:

```
$ bitbake engicam-evaluation-image-mx8
ERROR: ParseError at /home/giometti/yocto/imx-yocto-bsp/sources/meta-cy
/conf/machine/imx8mp-icore-cy.conf:7: Could not include required file i
nclude/imx8mp-engicam.inc
```

This is because the include file imx8mp-engicam.inc is wrongly referred, as explained in Section 5.4.1. In fact, BitBake locates the first file it can find within BBPATH or the current directory, and using the require keyword as above is wrong since there is no include subdirectory within our layer! So, the best thing to do is to set it considering that in BBPATH all meta layer directories are reported and that the include directory is under meta-engicam-nxp/conf/machine. So we must do as shown below:

```
--- imx8mp-icore-cy.conf
+++ imx8mp-icore-cy.conf
@@ -4,7 +4,7 @@
 #@DESCRIPTION: Machine configuration for custom CY imx8mp-icore SOM
 #@MAINTAINER: <giometti@enneenne.com>

-require include/imx8mp-engicam.inc
+require conf/machine/include/imx8mp-engicam.inc

 KERNEL_DEVICETREE_BASENAME = "imx8mp-icore"
```

Now, if we try to generate the Yocto image engicam-evaluation-image-mx8, everything should work well as before.

Even if the first cloning method seen in the previous section is tricky and allows us to do very few modifications, this last method allows us to have a more complete control of the machine settings, especially if the original imx8mp-icore.conf will be changed in future releases by Engicam's developers.

At this point, we have a new machine within our Yocto build system, but this machine still uses the same bootloader and the kernel settings of Engicam's embedded kit, and usually this doesn't fit our needs! In fact, it is quite usual that derived hardware have several differences between development kits, so let's see how we can resolve this problem.

8.2 Customizing the Bootloader

Before continuing, we have to state that with the word *bootloader* we typically mean the U-Boot program and not all the various software packages needed to actually do a boot; in fact, in these days it is quite

usual that to boot a GNU/Linux system we require a prebootloader (as
the **ARM Trusted Firmware** – often named TF-A or ATF), with other
companion pieces of software (as the Open Portable Trusted Execution
Environment or **OP-TEE**), which loads the bootloader (i.e., U-Boot) and
then which loads the kernel (which is obviously Linux).

In this scenario, the readers can continue considering that when we
say *customizing the bootloader* we mean just the U-Boot program.

Some notes about these software programs and how to modify them
are reported in Section 8.3.

As every good developer knows, **U-Boot** supports different
architectures, but once compiled it can only run on the architecture
for which it was compiled (and the same rule applies to the kernel). So,
in this section (and the same will be for the section about the kernel
customization), we may do something specific to the i.MX8 CPUs.
However, we will do our best to keep the explanation as generic as
possible, and the readers should consider making minor changes to fix
their needs.

8.2.1 Understanding the U-Boot Configuration Variables

Before we start making changes in the U-Boot code and recipes, we should
introduce some variables from the uboot-config class, which is used to
simplify the U-Boot configuration for a machine. The class is defined
in poky/meta/classes/uboot-config.bbclass, and by looking at the
heading of this file we can find how to specify the machine configuration:

```
$ cat sources/poky/meta/classes/uboot-config.bbclass:
# Handle U-Boot config for a machine
#
```

```
# The format to specify it, in the machine, is:
#
# UBOOT_CONFIG ??= <default>
# UBOOT_CONFIG[foo] = "config,images,binary"
#
# or
#
# UBOOT_MACHINE = "config"
#
...
```

Each flag variable defines the values to be used for

- UBOOT_MACHINE: The default configuration file (the _defconfig file in the U-Boot world) passed to the make command line when building the U-Boot sources.

- IMAGE_FSTYPES: As already specified in Section 6.5.2, this variable specifies the formats the Yocto build system uses during the build when creating the root filesystem.

- UBOOT_BINARY: Specifies the name of the U-Boot binary image.

A real example from the meta-freescale layer is reported below:

```
UBOOT_CONFIG ??= "sdcard"
UBOOT_CONFIG[nor] = "P4080DS_config,,u-boot-with-dtb.bin"
UBOOT_CONFIG[sdcard] = "P4080DS_SDCARD_config,,u-boot.pbl"
UBOOT_CONFIG[spi] = "P4080DS_SPIFLASH_config,,u-boot.pbl"
```

In this example, each configuration specifies a _defconfig file to be used as UBOOT_MACHINE and an individual name for UBOOT_BINARY, while no configuration defines a second parameter for IMAGE_FSTYPES to be used for the U-Boot image. The UBOOT_CONFIG variable specifies by default one of three possible configurations (i.e., sdcard).

Note that, on simple settings, we can just set the UBOOT_MACHINE variable.

8.2.2 Customizing U-Boot by Hand

The first method to customize U-Boot is by doing all steps by hand and by defining a private repository (derived from the original development kit's one) where we can put all our changes.

This solution has the advantages that it works in every condition and allows developers to have full control over the bootloader sources and recipes.

Honestly speaking, the second solution presented in the next section can also be used to define a private repository, but (as the readers can see by reading this book) having the possibility to use a handmade technique can solve some situations where automated tools don't work.

To start our customization, we need to discover which is the recipe that the Yocto Project is using to generate the bootloader image; we can easily do it by checking who is providing the virtual/bootloader package by inquiring the PREFERRED_PROVIDER_virtual/bootloader variable, as reported below:

```
$ cy-vars PREFERRED_PROVIDER_virtual/bootloader
PREFERRED_PROVIDER_virtual/bootloader="u-boot-engicam"
```

Then to discover where the recipe u-boot-engicam is located, we can do as follows:

```
$ bitbake-layers show-recipes u-boot-engicam
...
=== Matching recipes: ===
u-boot-engicam:
  meta-engicam-nxp      2022.04
```

So, the recipe we have to consider is the one named u-boot-engicam which lies within the meta-engicam directory and specifically the file u-boot-engicam_2022.04.bb.

The important part to consider with this recipe is the value of SRC_URI and SRCREV variables, which are defined as below:

```
$ cd meta-engicam-nxp
$ cat recipes-bsp/u-boot-engicam/u-boot-engicam_2022.04.bb
# Copyright (C) 2013-2016 Freescale Semiconductor
# Copyright 2018 (C) O.S. Systems Software LTDA.
# Copyright 2017-2022 NXP

require recipes-bsp/u-boot/u-boot.inc

DESCRIPTION = "i.MX U-Boot supporting i.MX reference boards."
...
SRC_URI = "${UBOOT_SRC};branch=${SRCBRANCH}"
UBOOT_SRC = "git://github.com/engicam-stable/u-boot-engicam-nxp-2022.04
.git;protocol=https"
SRCBRANCH = "master"
SRCREV = "05dea559b91f3f41c47c23e895196299d4bac75f"
#SRCREV = "${AUTOREV}"
...
```

Here is straightforward to discover which is the repository where the source code lies and which is the commit to use; however, to be certain, we can ask BitBake to find out these values for us:

```
$ cy-vars 'SRC_URI\|SRCREV' u-boot-engicam
SRCREV="05dea559b91f3f41c47c23e895196299d4bac75f"
SRC_URI="git://github.com/engicam-stable/u-boot-engicam-nxp-2022.04.git
;protocol=https;branch=master"
```

So, in order to create our custom repository where we make all our changes, we can move into the parent yocto directory and execute the following command:

```
$ git clone https://github.com/engicam-stable/u-boot-engicam-nxp-2022.0
4.git
```

Then we can enter within the u-boot-engicam-nxp-2022.04 directory to create our custom branch master-cy starting on the commit ID 05dea559b91f3f41c47c23e895196299d4bac75f:

```
$ cd u-boot-engicam-nxp-2022.04/
$ git checkout -b master-cy 05dea559b91f3f41c47c23e895196299d4bac75f Switched
to a new branch 'master-cy'
```

```
$ git log --oneline -1
05dea559b9 (HEAD -> master-cy, origin/master, origin/HEAD, master) imx8m
p icore 2e: fixed i2c6 pin uboot
```

OK, now that we have a custom repository, we have to create a custom recipe for the bootloader; however, the best way to do it is to use a u-boot-engicam_2022.04.bbappend file which can be created in our custom layer within the recipes-bsp/u-boot-engicam directory, as shown below:

```
$ cd ../imx-yocto-bsp/sources/meta-cy/recipes-bsp/u-boot-engicam
$ cat u-boot-engicam_2022.04.bbappend
DESCRIPTION = "i.MX U-Boot supporting CY (i.MX8) reference boards."

UBOOT_SRC = "git:///home/giometti/yocto/u-boot-engicam-nxp-2022.04/"
SRCBRANCH = "master-cy"
SRCREV = "${AUTOREV}"
```

In the above .bbappend file, the variable UBOOT_SRC has been changed to address the newly created repository (and the readers should alter it according to their setup), and also the SRCBRANCH variable now points to the new branch. Regarding the SRCREV, we set it to ${AUTOREV} to get the U-Boot source code recompiled each time we do a new commit within our new repository.

Of course, these are not the final settings (we should use a remote Git repository and a well-fixed commit ID for SRCREV); however, for the moment we can leave them as is in order to well understand how a customization process works (in Section 13.2, we'll see how to fix a specific release).

Moreover, note that when SRCREV is set to ${AUTOREV} the devtool modify command presented below may fail!

Now to test if everything still works well, we can try to recompile U-Boot with our new recipe (via .bbappend). First, we clear the current state:

```
$ bitbake -c cleansstate u-boot-engicam
```

371

Then we can ask BitBake to recompile the code:

```
$ bitbake u-boot-engicam
...
NOTE: Executing Tasks
Setscene tasks: 196 of 196
Currently  1 running tasks (821 of 833)  98% |######################## |
0: u-boot-engicam-2022.04-r0 do_compile - 7s (pid 3778889)
```

OK, the compilation is still working, but now we have to really customize the bootloader by creating our custom machine within the U-Boot sources. To do so, we have to create a custom configuration file (i.e., a _defconfig file) and a custom device tree (i.e., a .dtb file).

To achieve this goal, let's review the U-Boot settings in our machine configuration file; we have the following:

```
$ cat meta-cy/conf/machine/imx8mp-icore-cy.conf
...
UBOOT_CONFIG_BASENAME = "imx8mp_icore"
UBOOT_CONFIG ??= "4gb"
UBOOT_CONFIG[1gb] = "${UBOOT_CONFIG_BASENAME}_1gb_defconfig,sdcard"
UBOOT_CONFIG[2gb] = "${UBOOT_CONFIG_BASENAME}_defconfig,sdcard"
UBOOT_CONFIG[4gb] = "${UBOOT_CONFIG_BASENAME}_4gb_defconfig,sdcard"
...
```

Here, we see that UBOOT_CONFIG is set to 4gb, then UBOOT_MACHINE will be set to imx8mp_icore_4gb_defconfig which is the configuration file of the development kit, while we wish to have our configuration file. As a first step, this file, which we will name imx8mp_icore_cy_4gb_defconfig, can be a copy of imx8mp_icore_4gb_defconfig (with little modifications), so we have to check under our new U-Boot repository where such file is located:

```
$ cd $BUILDDIR/../../u-boot-engicam-nxp-2022.04/
$ find . -name imx8mp_icore_4gb_defconfig
./configs/imx8mp_icore_4gb_defconfig
```

Then, within such a file, we can discover which is the default device tree file used to configure the U-Boot image. This is defined by the configuration entry CONFIG_DEFAULT_DEVICE_TREE, which is set as shown below:

```
$ grep CONFIG_DEFAULT_DEVICE_TREE configs/imx8mp_icore_4gb_defconfig
CONFIG_DEFAULT_DEVICE_TREE="imx8mp-icore"
```

So the default device tree file for the Engicam machine is imx8mp-icore.dtb, and we can find the corresponding dts file as below:

```
$ find . -name imx8mp-icore.dts
./arch/arm/dts/imx8mp-icore.dts
```

Well, now it should be clear what we have to do to add our custom machine; first, we have to create a dedicated _defconfig file by simply copying Engicam's one and then changing it as shown below:

```
$ cp configs/imx8mp_icore_4gb_defconfig \
      configs/imx8mp_icore_cy_4gb_defconfig
```

Once copied, the modifications are below:

```
--- configs/imx8mp_icore_cy_4gb_defconfig
+++ configs/imx8mp_icore_cy_4gb_defconfig
@@ -22,7 +22,7 @@
 CONFIG_SPL_DRIVERS_MISC=y
 CONFIG_SPL=y
 CONFIG_SPL_IMX_ROMAPI_LOADADDR=0x48000000
-CONFIG_DEFAULT_DEVICE_TREE="imx8mp-icore"
+CONFIG_DEFAULT_DEVICE_TREE="imx8mp-icore-cy"
 CONFIG_DISTRO_DEFAULTS=y
 CONFIG_SYS_LOAD_ADDR=0x40400000
 CONFIG_BOOTCOMMAND="run distro_bootcmd;run bsp_bootcmd"
```

Then we have to create a proper device tree file by doing something similar as above:

```
$ cp arch/arm/dts/imx8mp-icore.dts \
      arch/arm/dts/imx8mp-icore-cy.dts
$ cp arch/arm/dts/imx8mp-icore-u-boot.dtsi \
      arch/arm/dts/imx8mp-icore-cy-u-boot.dtsi
```

And the needed modifications are

```
--- ./arch/arm/dts/imx8mp-icore-cy.dts
+++ ./arch/arm/dts/imx8mp-icore-cy.dts
@@ -9,7 +9,7 @@
 #include "imx8mp.dtsi"

 / {
-        model = "Engicam i.MX8MPlus iCore";
+        model = "CY board i.MX8MPlus iCore";
         compatible = "fsl,imx8mp-evk", "fsl,imx8mp";

         chosen {
```

Note that we also have to copy the file `arch/arm/dts/imx8mp-icore-u-boot.dtsi` to have a valid SPL device file.

In this example, we have simply changed the model name, but, of course, in the case that our hardware needs further adjustments, we have to work a little more within U-Boot sources. However, these are the minimal steps we have to do to define our custom board based on the hardware vendor's one.

Now to enable these changes, we have to commit them with the following command:

```
$ git add configs/imx8mp_icore_cy_4gb_defconfig \
         arch/arm/dts/imx8mp-icore-cy.dts \
         arch/arm/dts/imx8mp-icore-cy-u-boot.dtsi
$ git commit -s -m "arm dts: add new board imx8mp-icore-cy"
[master-cy e82751c363] arm dts: add new board imx8mp-icore-cy
 Date: Tue Nov 28 17:09:26 2023 +0100
 3 files changed, 920 insertions(+)
 create mode 100644 arch/arm/dts/imx8mp-icore-cy-u-boot.dtsi
 create mode 100644 arch/arm/dts/imx8mp-icore-cy.dts
 create mode 100644 configs/imx8mp_icore_cy_4gb_defconfig
```

The modifications for the U-Boot sources are in place, but now we have to change the configuration of our machine `imx8mp-icore-cy` as follows to address the Yocto build system about how to configure the U-Boot compilation for our custom machine:

```
--- a/conf/machine/imx8mp-icore-cy.conf
+++ b/conf/machine/imx8mp-icore-cy.conf
@@ -13,7 +13,8 @@ KERNEL_DEVICETREE:append:use-nxp-bsp = " \
        engicam/imx8mp-icore-ctouch2.dtb \
 "

-UBOOT_CONFIG_BASENAME = "imx8mp_icore"
+UBOOT_CONFIG_BASENAME = "imx8mp_icore_cy"
+UBOOT_DTB_NAME = "imx8mp-icore-cy.dtb"
 UBOOT_CONFIG ??= "4gb"
 UBOOT_CONFIG[1gb] = "${UBOOT_CONFIG_BASENAME}_1gb_defconfig,sdcard"
 UBOOT_CONFIG[2gb] = "${UBOOT_CONFIG_BASENAME}_defconfig,sdcard"
```

In this manner, we notify the building system that now it must use a different configuration for the U-Boot package.

Notice that we have to set also the UBOOT_DTB_NAME to `imx8mp-icore-cy.dtb` due to the fact that within the Engicam layer it has been defined as below:

```
$ rgrep UBOOT_DTB_NAME \
    sources/meta-engicam-nxp/conf/machine/include/imx8mp-engicam.i
nc
UBOOT_DTB_NAME = "${KERNEL_DEVICETREE_BASENAME}.dtb"
```

This is a conceptual error done by Engicam developers, since whatever is related to the U-Boot recipe should not depend on other recipes and, specifically, not to the kernel one!

However, this is not a problem at all since, when we customize the kernel in the next section, we can easily fix it by changing the KERNEL_DEVICETREE_BASENAME variable accordingly.

The variable UBOOT_DTB_NAME is specific for the Freescale iMX family meta layers.

Then, to verify our changes, we should clean the current state of the U-Boot recipe and then recompile a new Yocto image by executing the next two commands in sequence:

```
$ bitbake -c cleansstate u-boot-engicam && \
  bitbake engicam-evaluation-image-mx8
```

During the compilation process, we should notice that the U-Boot sources are recompiled, and, at the end, we have to rewrite our microSD as usual. Then on the serial console, we should get something as below:

```
U-Boot SPL 2022.04-master-cy+ge82751c363 (Nov 29 2023 - 15:15:45 +0000)
DDRINFO: start DRAM init
DDRINFO: DRAM rate 4000MTS
DDRINFO:ddrphy calibration done
DDRINFO: ddrmix config done
SECO:  RNG instantiated
Normal Boot
Trying to boot from BOOTROM
Boot Stage: Primary boot
image offset 0x8000, pagesize 0x200, ivt offset 0x0
NOTICE:  BL31: v2.6(release):automotive-13.0.0_1.1.0-0-g3c1583ba0
NOTICE:  BL31: Built : 11:00:38, Nov 21 2022

U-Boot 2022.04-master-cy+ge82751c363 (Nov 29 2023 - 15:15:45 +0000)

CPU:   i.MX8MP[8] rev1.1 1600 MHz (running at 1200 MHz)
CPU:   Industrial temperature grade (-40C to 105C) at 20C
Reset cause: POR
Model: CY board i.MX8MPlus iCore
DRAM:  4 GiB
Core:  56 devices, 21 uclasses, devicetree: separate
MMC:   FSL_SDHC: 1, FSL_SDHC: 2
...
```

Yes, U-Boot is now using the new code, and we are sure about that because we can see the current branch and HEAD within the string 2022.04-master-cy+ge82751c363 and our custom model name in Model: CY board i.MX8MPlus iCore.

Starting from this point, each time we do a new commit, the Yocto build system will rebuild U-Boot with our changes. However, this implies that we *must* commit our changes even if they are not in their final form yet, or nothing will change. It could be acceptable, of course, but we can avoid doing it by using a simple trick.

As a first step, we must be sure that sources are in place by doing a new build:

```
$ bitbake -c build u-boot-engicam
```

Note that in this case, we can also use the `virtual/bootloader` target as below:

```
$ bitbake -c build virtual/bootloader
...
NOTE: Executing Tasks
Setscene tasks: 196 of 196
Currently  2 running tasks (819 of 833)   98% |################### |
0: u-boot-engicam-2022.04-r0 do_populate_lic - 0s (pid 2004837)
1: u-boot-engicam-2022.04-r0 do_deploy_source_date_epoch - 0s (pid
  2004836)
```

As we can see above, `bitbake` selects the right recipe.

Now we can move to the source's directory which is pointed to by the S variable (see Section 6.3.2) we can read as usual:

```
$ cy-vars dirs u-boot-engicam
...
S="/home/giometti/yocto/imx-yocto-bsp/imx8mp-build/tmp/work/imx8mp_icor
e_cy-poky-linux/u-boot-engicam/2022.04-r0/git"
...
```

So let's move to that directory and try to change something, for example, we can alter the `version` command in order to show a custom message as below:

```
--- a/cmd/version.c
+++ b/cmd/version.c
@@ -14,7 +14,7 @@
 #include <asm/cb_sysinfo.h>
 #endif
```

```
-#define U_BOOT_VERSION_STRING U_BOOT_VERSION " (" U_BOOT_DATE " - " \
+#define U_BOOT_VERSION_STRING "CY-" U_BOOT_VERSION " (" U_BOOT_DATE "
- " \
         U_BOOT_TIME " " U_BOOT_TZ ")" CONFIG_IDENT_STRING

 const char version_string[] = U_BOOT_VERSION_STRING;
```

Now we can check if everything is OK by trying to recompile the code:

```
$ bitbake -C compile -c compile u-boot-engicam
...
NOTE: Tainting hash to force rebuild of task /home/giometti/yocto/imx-y
octo-bsp/sources/meta-engicam-nxp/recipes-bsp/u-boot-engicam/u-boot-eng
icam_2022.04.bb, do_compile
WARNING: /home/giometti/yocto/imx-yocto-bsp/sources/meta-engicam-nxp/re
cipes-bsp/u-boot-engicam/u-boot-engicam_2022.04.bb:do_compile is tainte
d from a forced run
...
0: u-boot-engicam-2022.04-r0 do_compile - 7s (pid 1967968)
...
```

The -C option argument is needed to force a new compilation since we
changed the sources by hand, and we should use it each time we change
and then recompile the code.

Due to the usage of the -C option argument, now each time we
execute bitbake it's OK to see the do_<task> is tainted
from a forced run message.

When the code is in a suitable form to be tested on the machine, we
can deploy it by using the command below:

```
$ bitbake -C deploy u-boot-engicam
...
NOTE: Tainting hash to force rebuild of task /home/giometti/yocto/imx-y
octo-bsp/sources/meta-engicam-nxp/recipes-bsp/u-boot-engicam/u-boot-eng
icam_2022.04.bb, do_deploy
WARNING: /home/giometti/yocto/imx-yocto-bsp/sources/meta-engicam-nxp/re
cipes-bsp/u-boot-engicam/u-boot-engicam_2022.04.bb:do_compile is tainte
d from a forced run
```

```
WARNING: /home/giometti/yocto/imx-yocto-bsp/sources/meta-engicam-nxp/re
cipes-bsp/u-boot-engicam/u-boot-engicam_2022.04.bb:do_deploy is tainted
 from a forced run
...
```

This time, we didn't use the -c option argument since we wished to execute the default task.

Now we can try the new U-Boot code by regenerating a new microSD image as usual with the bitbake engicam-evaluation-image-mx8. If everything has been done correctly, when we execute the version command within the U-Boot prompt, we should see something as below:

```
u-boot=> version
CY-U-Boot 2022.04-master-cy+g272669822a (Nov 30 2023 - 08:36:04 +0000)

aarch64-poky-linux-gcc (GCC) 11.3.0
GNU ld (GNU Binutils) 2.38.20220708
```

Great! Now we can report all changes within our repository, being sure that what we have done is correct.

Now, before taking a look at the second way to alter U-Boot, we should spend a few words about how we can alter the U-Boot configuration.

Every U-Boot developer knows that there are two main ways to do so:

1) By altering the configs/<machine>.h file, which falls in the above example

2) By altering the .config file and, in turn, the _defconfig file, which is precisely what we are going to explain right now

Let's suppose we wish to add the uuid command to our U-Boot, then there are two possibilities: we know what to do within our machine's default configuration file (i.e., the file imx8mp_icore_cy_defconfig), or we can ask the build system to do it for us. In the first case, we can directly make the changes, but in the second case we can do as follows.

First, we need to execute the devshell:

```
$ bitbake -c devshell u-boot-engicam
```

And by doing this, we move within the directory where the build system holds the sources:

```
$ pwd
/home/giometti/yocto/imx-yocto-bsp/imx8mp-build/tmp/work/imx8mp_icore_c
y-poky-linux/u-boot-engicam/2022.04-r0/git
```

OK, it's the same directory we already discovered above, but unluckily it's not the right place to invoke the make menuconfig command (i.e., the command we have to use to call the U-Boot configuration menu), so we have to move where the .config file is held. To find it, we can do as shown below:

```
$ find .. -name .config
../build/imx8mp_icore_cy_4gb_defconfig/.config
```

As we can see, the build system has created a directory named as the default configuration file where such configuration has been applied, so let's move to that directory:

```
$ cd ../build/imx8mp_icore_cy_4gb_defconfig/
```

Now, before continuing, we should check if the current default configuration file has been reduced to its minimal form or not. To do so, we can generate a proper copy of the default configuration file and then check it against the current one; this means that we should generate the minimal default configuration by using the make savedefconfig command as shown below:

```
$ make savedefconfig
...
  HOSTCC  scripts/kconfig/conf.o
  HOSTLD  scripts/kconfig/conf
scripts/kconfig/conf  --savedefconfig=defconfig Kconfig
```

The minimal default configuration is named defconfig, and we can check it against the one within the configs directory as below:

```
$ diff -q ../../git/configs/imx8mp_icore_4gb_defconfig defconfig
Files ../../git/configs/imx8mp_icore_4gb_defconfig and defconfig differ
```

This is not optimal, since every _defconfig file should be into its minimal state (i.e., generated by the make savedefconfig command); however, we can just replace it with the newly generated defconfig file, or we try to get just the differences to be applied to the current version of the file imx8mp_icore_4gb_defconfig. In the first case, we can just do a proper commit within our custom U-Boot repository, while in the second case we can use the following trick: let's save the current version of the defconfig file as shown below:

```
$ cp defconfig defconfig.orig
```

Then we can proceed as normal by issuing the make menuconfig command to alter the U-Boot configuration:

```
$ make menuconfig
```

In the case we get the following error message when executing the above command:

```
*
* Unable to find the ncurses package.
* Install ncurses (ncurses-devel or libncurses-dev
* depending on your distribution).
*
make[3]: *** [/home/giometti/yocto/imx-yocto-bsp/imx8mp-build/tmp/
work/imx8mp_icore_cy-poky-linux/u-boot-engicam/2022.04-r0/git/scri
pts/kconfig/
Makefile:224: scripts/kconfig/.mconf-cfg] Error 1
make[2]: *** [/home/giometti/yocto/imx-yocto-bsp/imx8mp-build/tmp/
work/imx8mp_icore_cy-poky-linux/u-boot-engicam/2022.04-
r0/git/Makefile:574: menuconfig] Error 2
make[1]: *** [Makefile:177: sub-make] Error 2
make: *** [Makefile:15: __sub-make] Error 2
```

we can solve it by exiting the devshell and then executing the next command:

```
$ sudo apt install libncurses-dev
```

At this point, we can restart the devshell as above, and everything should properly work.

If everything works well, we should see the usual U-Boot configuration menu. To enable the uuid command, we have to navigate through the menu entries Command line interface, then Misc commands, and then mark the uuid, guid - generation of unique IDs entry as in Figure 8-1.

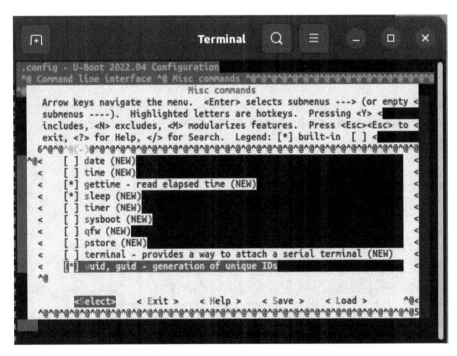

Figure 8-1. The U-Boot configuration menu

The ugly window's borders are due to some invalid terminal settings, so the readers can safely ignore them and use the menu configuration utility as usual.

Then we can save and exit. In the case the original _defconfig file was not into its minimal form (as in our case), we can get the differences due to our configuration changes by regenerating again the defconfig file and then using the diff command as shown below:

```
$ make savedefconfig
  GEN     Makefile
scripts/kconfig/conf  --savedefconfig=defconfig Kconfig
$ diff -u defconfig.orig defconfig
--- defconfig.orig      2024-02-07 12:24:56.564022695 +0000
+++ defconfig   2024-02-07 12:25:46.909785434 +0000
@@ -63,6 +63,7 @@
 CONFIG_CMD_TIME=y
 CONFIG_CMD_GETTIME=y
 CONFIG_CMD_TIMER=y
+CONFIG_CMD_UUID=y
 CONFIG_CMD_REGULATOR=y
 CONFIG_CMD_EXT4_WRITE=y
 CONFIG_OF_CONTROL=y
```

So, in this case, we just need to add the line CONFIG_CMD_UUID=y to our default configuration file. However, before doing it, we should check if everything is OK by recompiling U-Boot and then executing it on our devkit. So let's exit devshell, then execute the usual compiling and deploy commands as below:

```
$ bitbake -C compile -c compile u-boot-engicam
$ bitbake -C deploy u-boot-engicam
```

If we get no errors, we can rebuild the image binary:

```
$ bitbake engicam-evaluation-image-mx8
```

Finally, regenerate a new microSD. When we run the new U-Boot version, we should now have the `uuid` command as shown below:

```
u-boot=> uuid
62686d1d-127a-4fbc-9461-af3212443c0f
```

Now, to fix our changes, we can do a new commit within our custom U-Boot repository as below:

```
--- a/configs/imx8mp_icore_4gb_defconfig
+++ b/configs/imx8mp_icore_4gb_defconfig
@@ -153,4 +153,4 @@ CONFIG_OPTEE=y
 CONFIG_CMD_OPTEE_RPMB=y
 CONFIG_TEE=y
 CONFIG_FIT_SIGNATURE=y
-
+CONFIG_CMD_UUID=y
```

Then we just have to commit the changes:

```
$ git add configs/imx8mp_icore_4gb_defconfig
$ git commit -s -m "configs imx8mp_icore_4gb_defconfig: add uuid comman
d support"
[master-cy e0bb517601] configs imx8mp_icore_4gb_defconfig: add uuid com
mand support
 1 file changed, 1 insertion(+), 1 deletion(-)
```

Then we can try the new commit as usual by regenerating a new Yocto image. If we do so, as shown below, we should also notice that the U-Boot sources will be fetched again due to our last commit above:

```
$ bitbake engicam-evaluation-image-mx8
...
NOTE: Executing Tasks
Setscene tasks: 3839 of 3839
Currently  1 running tasks (2871 of 8909)   32% |#########         |
0: u-boot-engicam-2022.04-r0 do_fetch - 0s (pid 2706323) |<=>        |
...
```

Once finished, the readers can try the code on their systems and verify that everything is functional as desired.

8.2.3 Customizing U-Boot with devtool

What we saw in the previous section is a best practice to manage the
U-Boot sources to generate custom code for our boards; however, there is
another way to do so by using devtool and then by automatizing (quite) all
steps presented in the previous section.

To present this solution, we should temporarily revoke all settings we
did in the previous section to the U-Boot recipe. We can easily do it by
renaming the .bbappend file created above as follows:

```
$ cd sources/meta-cy/recipes-bsp/u-boot-engicam/
$ mv u-boot-engicam_2022.04.bbappend \
        u-boot-engicam_2022.04.bbappend.DISABLED
$ cd $BUILDDIR
```

Furthermore, we need to use the default settings for the Engicam
devkit, and, to do so, we can change the default MACHINE setting within
the conf/local.conf to MACHINE = 'imx8mp-icore' or execute all next
commands with the prepending MACHINE = "imx8mp-icore" setting, as
we have done below when we invoke the devtool utility to alter the U-Boot
sources:

```
$ MACHINE="imx8mp-icore" devtool modify virtual/bootloader
...
INFO: Mapping virtual/bootloader to u-boot-engicam
...
INFO: Source tree extracted to /home/giometti/yocto/imx-yocto-bsp/imx8m
p-build/workspace/sources/u-boot-engicam
INFO: Recipe u-boot-engicam now set up to build from /home/giometti/yoc
to/imx-yocto-bsp/imx8mp-build/workspace/sources/u-boot-engicam
```

As we can see above, the devtool utility correctly detects the right
recipe and creates a new entry named u-boot-engicam within the
workspace.

At this point, we can use the edit-recipe subcommand to alter the
current recipe:

```
$ MACHINE="imx8mp-icore" devtool edit-recipe virtual/bootloader
```

For our purposes, we don't need to alter this recipe; however, to do some modifications as an example, we can change the string for the DESCRIPTION variable by setting it to "i.MX U-Boot supporting CY (i.MX8) reference boards." (the same value we used in the previous section).

Now we should be able to compile the code as below:

```
$ MACHINE="imx8mp-icore" devtool build u-boot-engicam
...
NOTE: u-boot-engicam: compiling from external source tree /home/giomet
ti/yocto/imx-yocto-bsp/imx8mp-build/workspace/sources/u-boot-engicam
NOTE: Tasks Summary: Attempted 817 tasks of which 805 didn't need to b
e rerun and all succeeded.
```

As expected, now the build system is telling us that the u-boot-engicam recipe is now compiled from an external source tree. So we can now move to the directory workspace/sources/u-boot-engicam to do our modifications.

To mimic what we did in the previous section, we can just alter the model string within the device tree as below:

```
--- a/arch/arm/dts/imx8mp-icore.dts
+++ b/arch/arm/dts/imx8mp-icore.dts
@@ -9,7 +9,7 @@
 #include "imx8mp.dtsi"

 / {
-        model = "Engicam i.MX8MPlus iCore";
+        model = "CY board [devtool] i.MX8MPlus iCore";
         compatible = "fsl,imx8mp-evk", "fsl,imx8mp";

         chosen {
```

By doing so, we should get the following output when we inspect the repository status:

```
$ git status
On branch devtool
Changes not staged for commit:
  (use "git add <file>..." to update what will be committed)
```

```
(use "git restore <file>..." to discard changes in working directory)
      modified:   arch/arm/dts/imx8mp-icore.dts

no changes added to commit (use "git add" and/or "git commit -a")
```

The readers should notice that now the current branch is automatically changed to devtool to mark that we are using this tool to make our changes.

Now we build the code again to test that our modifications didn't break anything:

```
$ MACHINE="imx8mp-icore" devtool build u-boot-engicam
NOTE: Tasks Summary: Attempted 817 tasks of which 808 didn't need to be
 rerun and all succeeded.
```

The readers should notice that we didn't do any commit within the repository in the workspace, but the code has been correctly recompiled. Now to test our modifications on the embedded machine, we can use the build-image; however, before doing so, we must remember to correctly set the UBOOT_CONFIG variable within the imx8mp-icore.conf file in the Engicam layer. This is because we are using imx8mp-icore as MACHINE setting, and in our case we have to set UBOOT_CONFIG to 4gb as we did in Section 2.3.

OK, if everything is now in place, we can rebuild our U-Boot:

```
$ MACHINE="imx8mp-icore" devtool build u-boot-engicam
...
NOTE: u-boot-engicam: compiling from external source tree /home/giomett
i/yocto/imx-yocto-bsp/imx8mp-build/workspace/sources/u-boot-engicam
...
```

Note that devtool tells us that it is now compiling from an external source tree!

If no errors, we can try it by recompiling the whole image as usual:

```
$ MACHINE="imx8mp-icore" \
        devtool build-image engicam-evaluation-image-mx8
...
INFO: Building image engicam-evaluation-image-mx8 with the following ad
ditional packages: u-boot-engicam
...
```

The readers should notice above that devtool notifies us that the image engicam-evaluation-image-mx8 is now compiled with the u-boot-engicam additional package!

The readers should also notice that, in this case, the following command will lead to the same result:

```
$ MACHINE="imx8mp-icore" bitbake engicam-evaluation-image-mx8
```

However, there is a special case where the two commands don't work the same. In fact, with devtool all packages within the workspace will be added to the final image, even if they are not directly explicit within the IMAGE_INSTALL variable (and they can be skipped by using the -p option argument, as already shown in Section 4.5.3). On the other hand, by using the above command, this will not happen.

When finished, we can move the new Yocto image within the microSD and test the modifications to the U-Boot sources.

Warning   Since we used the MACHINE setting imx8mp-icore, we must put on the microSD the file engicam-evaluation-image-mx8-imx8mp-icore.wic.zst under tmp/deploy/images/imx8mp-icore/ and not the one we usually use for our example machine imx8mp-icore-cy!

If everything has been done correctly, we should see the booting messages below:

```
...
U-Boot 2022.04-master+g05dea559b9 (Feb 13 2024 - 13:40:00 +0000)

CPU:   i.MX8MP[8] rev1.1 1600 MHz (running at 1200 MHz)
CPU:   Industrial temperature grade (-40C to 105C) at 21C
Reset cause: POR
Model: CY board [devtool] i.MX8MPlus iCore
DRAM:  4 GiB
...
```

At this point, to save our changes, we can do a commit:

```
$ git add arch/arm/dts/imx8mp-icore.dts
$ git commit -s -m "arm imx8mp-icore.dts: rework to support CY board"
[devtool 85654bc5d5] arm imx8mp-icore.dts: rework to support CY board
 1 file changed, 1 insertion(+), 1 deletion(-)
```

This is just an example, so we have just one commit, but, of course, we can do whatever commits we need to save and document our job!

Now, before closing this part, we have to take a look at how we can operate to change the U-Boot configuration. This part needs some explanations due to the fact that it is not so clean as changing the code.

By using devtool, the usual way to alter a configuration could be by using the subcommand menuconfig; however, it is quite usual for U-Boot recipes to get the error below:

```
$ MACHINE="imx8mp-icore" devtool menuconfig u-boot-engicam
INFO: Launching menuconfig
...
make: *** No rule to make target 'menuconfig'.  Stop.
Command failed.
Press any key to continue...
```

This is because not all U-Boot recipes correctly support such a mode of operation. So we have to use a dirty trick to solve the problem!

A correct way to use the `devtool menuconfig` command will be explained in Section 8.4.3.

The trick is similar as before, that is, we have to alter the `.config` file within the build directory. The problem now is that our sources are under the workspace, then we cannot use the `find` command as done in the previous section; however, we can use `bitbake` to discover where the build directory is located, as shown below:

```
$ MACHINE="imx8mp-icore" cy-vars dirs u-boot-engicam
B="/home/giometti/yocto/imx-yocto-bsp/imx8mp-build/tmp/work/imx8mp_icor
e-poky-linux/u-boot-engicam/2022.04-r0/u-boot-engicam-2022.04/"
...
S="/home/giometti/yocto/imx-yocto-bsp/imx8mp-build/workspace/sources/u-
boot-engicam"
...
```

As we can see, the sources (pointed by S) are under the workspace, while the build directory (pointed by B) is not, so we can execute `devshell` and then directly move to that directory:

```
$ MACHINE="imx8mp-icore" bitbake -c devshell u-boot-engicam
$ pwd
/home/giometti/yocto/imx-yocto-bsp/imx8mp-build/workspace/sources/u-boo
t-engicam
$ cd /home/giometti/yocto/imx-yocto-bsp/imx8mp-build/tmp/work/imx8mp_icore-p
oky-linux/u-boot-engicam/2022.04-r0/u-boot-engicam-2022.04/
```

Now, as done in the previous section, we should move within the directory named as our default configuration file:

```
$ ls
imx8mp_icore_4gb_defconfig
$ cd imx8mp_icore_4gb_defconfig/
```

Now, as done before, we can generate a defconfig file to be saved for later use:

```
$ make savedefconfig
...
scripts/kconfig/conf  --savedefconfig=defconfig Kconfig
$ cp defconfig defconfig.orig
```

Then we can safely execute the make menuconfig command and do all the settings needed to enable the uuid command as in the previous section. Once finished, we can take a look at the configuration settings:

```
$ make savedefconfig
...
scripts/kconfig/conf  --savedefconfig=defconfig Kconfig
$ diff -u defconfig.orig defconfig
--- defconfig.orig       2024-02-14 11:26:12.387778204 +0000
+++ defconfig    2024-02-14 11:26:55.513158680 +0000
@@ -63,6 +63,7 @@
 CONFIG_CMD_TIME=y
 CONFIG_CMD_GETTIME=y
 CONFIG_CMD_TIMER=y
+CONFIG_CMD_UUID=y
 CONFIG_CMD_REGULATOR=y
 CONFIG_CMD_EXT4_WRITE=y
 CONFIG_OF_CONTROL=y
```

OK, now we can exit devshell and recompile the code. However, if we do as usual, we can notice that nothing will be compiled since the build system cannot recognize the changes! That's why we must do as in the previous section when we forced the recompilation:

```
$ MACHINE="imx8mp-icore" bitbake -C compile -c compile u-boot-engicam
```

In this manner, each time we execute the devtool build command as below, a new compilation is forced:

```
$ MACHINE="imx8mp-icore" devtool build u-boot-engicam
```

391

If everything compiles well, we can ask the Yocto build system to regenerate our Yocto image as usual:

```
$ MACHINE="imx8mp-icore" devtool build-image engicam-evaluation-image-mx8
```

Once finished, we can check if the new command has been correctly added:

```
U-Boot 2022.04-master+g05dea559b9 (Feb 14 2024 - 16:56:57 +0000)

CPU:   i.MX8MP[8] rev1.1 1600 MHz (running at 1200 MHz)
CPU:   Industrial temperature grade (-40C to 105C) at 25C
Reset cause: POR
Model: CY board [devtool] i.MX8MPlus iCore
DRAM:  4 GiB
...
Normal Boot
Hit any key to stop autoboot:  0
u-boot=> uuid
9750a803-0a3d-4c3e-ac14-e9905a6ef5ff
```

Great! Now we have to report all settings done to alter the default configuration as below:

```
--- a/configs/imx8mp_icore_4gb_defconfig
+++ b/configs/imx8mp_icore_4gb_defconfig
@@ -153,4 +153,4 @@ CONFIG_OPTEE=y
 CONFIG_CMD_OPTEE_RPMB=y
 CONFIG_TEE=y
 CONFIG_FIT_SIGNATURE=y
-
+CONFIG_CMD_UUID=y
```

And then we can do another commit to save this last setting within the devtool's Git repository:

```
$ git add configs/imx8mp_icore_4gb_defconfig
$ git commit -s -m "configs imx8mp_icore_4gb_defconfig: add uuid comman
d support"
[devtool 05699dab0b] configs imx8mp_icore_4gb_defconfig: add uuid comma
nd support
 1 file changed, 1 insertion(+), 1 deletion(-)
```

To force the execution of the do_configure task for the package, we can use the -c option argument of the devtool build subcommand, as shown below:

```
$ MACHINE="imx8mp-icore" devtool build -c u-boot-engicam
```

Then, we have to rebuild the package.

We can continue in this manner until we have added all the needed changes, and, when finished, we can take the full list by using the command below:

```
$ git log --oneline devtool-base..devtool
05699dab0b (HEAD -> devtool) configs imx8mp_icore_4gb_defconfig: add
uuid command support
85654bc5d5 arm imx8mp-icore.dts: rework to support CY board
```

When finished, we can use devtool to save all our works into our private layer as shown below:

```
$ MACHINE="imx8mp-icore" \
        devtool update-recipe --append $CY_METADIR u-boot-engicam
...
NOTE: Writing append file /home/giometti/yocto/imx-yocto-bsp/sources/me
ta-cy/recipes-bsp/u-boot-engicam/u-boot-engicam_2022.04.bbappend
NOTE: Copying 0001-arm-imx8mp-icore.dts-rework-to-support-CY-board.patc
h to /home/giometti/yocto/imx-yocto-bsp/sources/meta-cy/recipes-bsp/u-b
oot-engicam/u-boot-engicam/0001-arm-imx8mp-icore.dts-rework-to-support-
CY-board.patch
NOTE: Copying 0002-configs-imx8mp_icore_4gb_defconfig-add-uuid-command-
.patch to /home/giometti/yocto/imx-yocto-bsp/sources/meta-cy/recipes-bs
p/u-boot-engicam/u-boot-engicam/0002-configs-imx8mp_icore_4gb_defconfig
-add-uuid-command-.patch
```

By using this command, we ask BitBake to create a .bbappend file within our meta-cy layer, then the Yocto build system will create the following u-boot-engicam_2022.04.bbappend file:

```
$ cat sources/meta-cy/recipes-bsp/u-boot-engicam/u-boot-engicam_2022.04
.bbappend
FILESEXTRAPATHS:prepend := "${THISDIR}/${PN}:"

SRC_URI += "file://0001-arm-imx8mp-icore.dts-rework-to-support-CY-board.
patch file
://0002-configs-imx8mp_icore_4gb_defconfig-add-uuid-command-.patch"
```

Unluckily, the update-recipe subcommand didn't report our modification to the DESCRIPTION variable within the newly created .bbappend file due to the fact that, when we invoked the edit-recipe subcommand, the modification had been done within the original recipe. In fact, in the meta-engicam-nxp layer, we check it out:

```
$ cd sources/meta-engicam-nxp
$ git diff
diff --git a/conf/machine/imx8mp-icore.conf b/conf/machine/imx8mp-icore
.conf
index 06dba1e..f5c035c 100644
--- a/conf/machine/imx8mp-icore.conf
+++ b/conf/machine/imx8mp-icore.conf
@@ -14,7 +14,7 @@ KERNEL_DEVICETREE:append:use-nxp-bsp = " \
 "

 UBOOT_CONFIG_BASENAME = "imx8mp_icore"
-UBOOT_CONFIG ??= "2gb"
+UBOOT_CONFIG ??= "4gb"
 UBOOT_CONFIG[1gb] = "${UBOOT_CONFIG_BASENAME}_1gb_defconfig,sdcard"
 UBOOT_CONFIG[2gb] = "${UBOOT_CONFIG_BASENAME}_defconfig,sdcard"
 UBOOT_CONFIG[4gb] = "${UBOOT_CONFIG_BASENAME}_4gb_defconfig,sdcard"
diff --git a/recipes-bsp/u-boot-engicam/u-boot-engicam_2022.04.bb b/rec
ipes-bsp/u-boot-engicam/u-boot-engicam_2022.04.bb
index 194a938..2a34d12 100644
--- a/recipes-bsp/u-boot-engicam/u-boot-engicam_2022.04.bb
+++ b/recipes-bsp/u-boot-engicam/u-boot-engicam_2022.04.bb
@@ -4,7 +4,7 @@

 require recipes-bsp/u-boot/u-boot.inc

-DESCRIPTION = "i.MX U-Boot suppporting i.MX reference boards."
+DESCRIPTION = "i.MX U-Boot supporting CY (i.MX8) reference boards."

 LICENSE = "GPL-2.0-or-later"
 LIC_FILES_CHKSUM = "file://Licenses/gpl-2.0.txt;md5=b234ee4d69f5fce448
6a80fdaf4a4263"
```

What we can do here is to move all recipe modifications by hand to have everything within our layer.

When all modification has been done and everything is in place, we can free the workspace by using the following command:

```
$ MACHINE="imx8mp-icore" devtool reset u-boot-engicam
NOTE: Starting bitbake server...
INFO: Cleaning sysroot for recipe u-boot-engicam...
INFO: Leaving source tree /home/giometti/yocto/imx-yocto-bsp/imx8mp-bui
ld/workspace/sources/u-boot-engicam as-is; if you no longer need it the
n please delete it manually
```

Note that, by default, the directory where our sources have been held during the development was not removed, and in that case we have to do it by hand.

Before ending this section, we would like to underline a final note about the possibility to create a separate repository by using devtool. In fact, if we use the --mode srcrev option argument as shown below, we can ask bitbake to create a .bbappend file without adding patches but just updating the SRCREV variable in the recipe:

```
$ MACHINE="imx8mp-icore" devtool update-recipe \
        --mode srcrev --append $CY_METADIR u-boot-engicam
INFO: Updating SRCREV in recipe u-boot-engicam_2022.04.bb
NOTE: Writing append file /home/giometti/yocto/imx-yocto-bsp/sources/me
ta-cy/recipes-bsp/u-boot-engicam/u-boot-engicam_2022.04.bbappend
INFO: You will need to update SRC_URI within the recipe to point to a g
it repository where you have pushed your changes
```

Of course, the above command must be executed before the devtool reset, or we are going to get the error:

```
ERROR: No recipe named 'u-boot-engicam' in your workspace
```

Now, the file `u-boot-engicam_2022.04.bbappend` holds the following setting:

```
$ cat u-boot-engicam_2022.04.bbappend
SRCREV = "05699dab0b4130f57b1a715ea4241847deda19eb"
```

That is our last commit ID, while `devtool` suggests that we properly update the `SRC_URI` variable within the recipe (or better, within the `.bbappend` file) to point to a custom git repository where we have pushed our changes. Now what we have to do is to push all modifications to the original repository or just create a new one as already explained before.

8.3 Notes on the Prebootloaders

As already introduced in Section 8.2, modern CPUs usually use several software packages to actually do a boot; as an example, for the ARM platform, the prebootloader used to set up the DRAM (and other minor tasks) is named **ARM Trusted Firmware** (**ATF** or **TF-A**), and the companion software is named **Open Portable Trusted Execution Environment** (**OP-TEE**), which is used to execute some security-related tasks.

Typically, the RomBoot within the CPU loads the ATF, which in turn loads the bootloader (i.e., U-Boot) and the OP-TEE. Then U-Boot loads the kernel, while the OP-TEE sits down waiting for requests by the kernel (see further information about the OP-TEE and kernel interactions on `https://docs.kernel.org/tee/op-tee.html`).

During the customization process, it may be needed to modify the ATF (it may be needed in the case we heavily modify the peripherals used to do the boot), and the usual way to do so is to alter the sources of the package referred to by the `virtual/trusted-firmware-a` package.

In our example, if we try to use devtool to do the job, we get the following output:

```
$ devtool modify virtual/trusted-firmware-a
...
ERROR: Unable to find any recipe file matching "virtual/trusted-firmware
-a"
```

On recent Yocto releases (as for Scarthgap), we may get two versions of the Trusted Firmware, that is, the usual TF-A and the one named Trusted Firmware for Cortex-M (TF-M), which is an open source reference implementation of the runtime trusted execution environment operating system for Cortex-M hosted under www.trustedfirmware.org.

As an example, we can get these two implementations within the Yocto Scarthgap by ST, as shown below:

```
$ bitbake st-image-weston -e | grep 'virtual/trusted-firmware.*='
PREFERRED_PROVIDER_virtual/trusted-firmware-a="tf-a-stm32mp"
PREFERRED_PROVIDER_virtual/trusted-firmware-m="tf-m-stm32mp"
```

This is because the PREFERRED_PROVIDER_virtual/trusted-firmware-a variable was not properly set. We can verify it by using the bitbake command with our utility as shown below:

```
$ cy-vars virtual
PREFERRED_PROVIDER_virtual/bootloader="u-boot-engicam"
PREFERRED_PROVIDER_virtual/containerd="containerd-opencontainers"
PREFERRED_PROVIDER_virtual/crypt="libxcrypt"
PREFERRED_PROVIDER_virtual/docker="docker-ce"
PREFERRED_PROVIDER_virtual/egl="imx-gpu-viv"
PREFERRED_PROVIDER_virtual/gettext="gettext"
PREFERRED_PROVIDER_virtual/kernel="linux-engicam"
PREFERRED_PROVIDER_virtual/libc="glibc"
PREFERRED_PROVIDER_virtual/libgl="imx-gpu-viv"
PREFERRED_PROVIDER_virtual/libiconv="glibc"
```

```
PREFERRED_PROVIDER_virtual/libintl="glibc"
PREFERRED_PROVIDER_virtual/make="make"
PREFERRED_PROVIDER_virtual/mesa="mesa"
PREFERRED_PROVIDER_virtual/runc="runc-opencontainers"
PREFERRED_PROVIDER_virtual/xserver="xserver-xorg"
```

There are several virtual packages, but not one regarding the ATF. So we have to find the right package name by hand, and to do so we can use the bitbake-layers show-recipes command as shown below:

```
$ bitbake-layers show-recipes -r '*atf*'
...
=== Matching recipes: ===
atftp
imx-atf
imx-atf-boundary (skipped: incompatible with machine imx8mp-icore-cy (n
ot in COMPATIBLE_MACHINE))
p8platform
qoriq-atf (skipped: incompatible with machine imx8mp-icore-cy (not in C
OMPATIBLE_MACHINE))
qoriq-atf-tools
```

Note that we have used the -r option argument in the above command to have just a list of recipes instead of the normal output.

In this list, we can skip the packages atftp and qoriq-atf-tools since they are not ATFs at all. While for the others (which are ATFs instead), we can select the package imx-atf, due to the fact that BitBake tells us the other packages should be skipped for incompatibility with our machine!

Here is a beautiful example about why we should add the COMPATIBLE_MACHINE setting in our recipes!

OK, now that we know which is the ATF package to be altered, we can proceed as explained above:

```
$ devtool modify imx-atf
...
Currently  1 running tasks (91 of 93)  96% |######################## |
0: imx-atf-2.6+gitAUTOINC+3c1583ba0a-r0 do_unpack - 4s (pid 846945)
...
```

Note that at the end of the extraction, devtool says:

```
...
INFO: Source tree extracted to /home/giometti/yocto/imx-yocto-bsp/
imx8mp-build/workspace/sources/imx-atf
INFO: Using source tree as build directory since that would be the
 default for this recipe
INFO: Recipe imx-atf now set up to build from /home/giometti/yocto
/imx-yocto-bsp/imx8mp-build/workspace/sources/imx-atf
```

This message is displayed when the system detects that B and S variables point to the same directory; this can be checked out as shown below:

```
$ cy-vars dirs imx-atf
B="/home/develop/Projects-OLD/packt/Customizing_Yocto/yocto/imx-yo
cto-bsp/imx8mp-build/workspace/sources/imx-atf"
...
S="/home/develop/Projects-OLD/packt/Customizing_Yocto/yocto/imx-yo
cto-bsp/imx8mp-build/workspace/sources/imx-atf"
...
```

Now we can move to the directory under the workspace where the ATF sources have been extracted, and we can start doing all the needed modifications:

```
$ cd workspace/sources/imx-atf
$ ls
bl1    changelog.yaml  fdts          Makefile           readme.rst
bl2    common          include       make_helpers       services
bl2u   dco.txt         lib           package.json       tools
bl31   docs            license.rst   package-lock.json
bl32   drivers         licenses      plat
```

If altering ATF is not usual, altering the OP-TEE is even less usual. However, in the case we have to do it, we can do as done for the ATF but considering that the virtual package is named virtual/optee-os. If we do so in our example, we get

```
$ devtool modify virtual/optee-os
...
ERROR: Unable to find any recipe file matching "virtual/optee-os"
```

No luck, we got the same error as before. This was expected; in fact, if we take a look at the PREFERRED_PROVIDER list above, we can see that even the PREFERRED_PROVIDER_virtual/optee-os doesn't exist. So we have to find the right package by hand again:

```
$ bitbake-layers show-recipes -r '*optee*'
...
=== Matching recipes: ===
optee-client (skipped: missing required machine feature 'optee' (not in
 MACHINE_FEATURES))
optee-client-qoriq (skipped: incompatible with machine imx8mp-icore-cy
(not in COMPATIBLE_MACHINE))
optee-os (skipped: missing required machine feature 'optee' (not in MAC
HINE_FEATURES))
optee-os-qoriq (skipped: incompatible with machine imx8mp-icore-cy (not
 in COMPATIBLE_MACHINE))
optee-test (skipped: missing required machine feature 'optee' (not in M
ACHINE_FEATURES))
optee-test-qoriq (skipped: incompatible with machine imx8mp-icore-cy (n
ot in COMPATIBLE_MACHINE))
packagegroup-fsl-optee-imx
```

In this list, it is easy to find that the correct package should be optee-os; however, the tool tells us that it can't be selected because the optee option is not specified within the MACHINE_FEATURES. This means that our machine.conf file doesn't specify it, and if we wish to use the OP-TEE, we have to modify this setting.

The same conclusions can be achieved even if we use `devtool` to alter the OP-TEE recipe:

```
$ devtool modify optee-os
...
ERROR: optee-os is unavailable:
  optee-os was skipped: missing required machine feature 'optee' (not i
n MACHINE_FEATURES)
optee-os was skipped: missing required machine feature 'optee' (not in
MACHINE_FEATURES)
```

Curious readers can try to enable this feature in their settings and then try to modify the OP-TEE.

8.4 Customizing the Kernel

Linux is the kernel of our Yocto OS, and since it is the one which interfaces the hardware with the processes running in the OS, it must be modified to support all peripherals. That's why, if our embedded machine is different from the original development one, we must modify it.

To do so, we can do similarly as we did above for U-Boot.

8.4.1 Understanding the Linux Configuration Variables

Regarding the Linux configuration variables, the most important one is `KERNEL_DEVICETREE` (defined by the kernel-devicetree class) which is used to specify the name of the generated Linux kernel device tree (i.e., the `.dtb`) file.

However, other important variables to know are

- `KBUILD_DEFCONFIG`: Specifies the kernel configuration file to be used during the kernel build.

- `KERNEL_DEVICETREE_BUNDLE`: Allows the Linux kernel and the device tree binary to be bundled together in a single file when it is set to 1 (these settings should be enabled if the bootloader has been properly set up; otherwise, the boot may halt).

- `KERNEL_IMAGETYPE`: Specifies the kernel type to be built, and it is usually set in the `machine.conf` file. It defaults to `zImage`, but the other most used value is `fitImage` to obtain a flattened image tree image.

- `KERNEL_IMAGE_NAME` and `KERNEL_IMAGE_LINK_NAME`: Respectively, the name and the link name of the kernel image.

- `KERNEL_DTB_NAME` and `KERNEL_DTB_LINK_NAME`: Respectively, the name and the link name of the kernel device tree binary (`.dtb`).

  Note that when the flattened image tree (FIT) image is enabled (by setting `KERNEL_IMAGETYPE` to `fitImage`), then the kernel and DTB files are put in it, so the FIT image is referred to by `KERNEL_FIT_NAME` and `KERNEL_FIT_LINK_NAME`. These are, respectively, the name and the link name of the FIT image.

8.4.2 Customizing Linux by Hand

As seen for U-Boot, we can create a new repository to customize the kernel, and to do so we need to know which is the recipe used to compile our kernel. Without using `devtool`, we can use the `cy-vars` utility to inquire the `PREFERRED_PROVIDER_virtual/kernel` setting, as shown below:

```
$ cy-vars virtual
PREFERRED_PROVIDER_virtual/bootloader="u-boot-engicam"
PREFERRED_PROVIDER_virtual/containerd="containerd-opencontainers"
PREFERRED_PROVIDER_virtual/crypt="libxcrypt"
PREFERRED_PROVIDER_virtual/docker="docker-ce"
PREFERRED_PROVIDER_virtual/egl="imx-gpu-viv"
PREFERRED_PROVIDER_virtual/gettext="gettext"
PREFERRED_PROVIDER_virtual/kernel="linux-engicam"
...
```

So we have to change the recipe named linux-engicam within, of
course, Engicam's layer:

```
$ cd sources/
$ find meta-engicam-nxp/ -name 'linux-engicam*.bb'
meta-engicam-nxp/recipes-kernel/linux-engicam/linux-engicam_5.15.bb
```

Within the file linux-engicam_5.15.bb, we can see what is
reported below:

```
$ cat meta-engicam-nxp/recipes-kernel/linux-engicam/linux-engicam_5.15.
bb
...
KERNEL_SRC ?= "git://github.com/engicam-stable/linux-engicam-nxp.git;pr
otocol=http"
SRCBRANCH = "5.15.71"
SRC_URI = "${KERNEL_SRC};branch=${SRCBRANCH}"
SRCREV = "ac5854881745bdc06b48cb58670e0a98c0eaf3a6"
```

So, as done before for U-Boot, we can clone the kernel repository
within the parent directory yocto by using the following commands:

```
$ git clone https://github.com/engicam-stable/linux-engicam-nxp.git
```

Then we must create our custom branch 5.15.71-cy starting from the
commit ID ac5854881745bdc06b48cb58670e0a98c0eaf3a6:

```
$ cd linux-engicam-nxp/
$ git checkout -b 5.15.71-cy ac5854881745bdc06b48cb58670e0a98c0eaf3a6
Updating files: 100% (55830/55830), done.
Switched to a new branch '5.15.71-cy'
$ git log --oneline -1
ac5854881745 (HEAD -> 5.15.71-cy) imx6sx smarcore: added support for ks
z9021/ksz9031
```

Now we need a `.bbappend` file (within the new directory `recipes-kernel/linux-engicam` in our meta layer) to address the Yocto building system about what to do to compile our custom kernel. We can do it by adding the file `linux-engicam_5.15.bbappend` holding the content shown below:

```
$ cat recipes-kernel/linux-engicam/linux-engicam_5.15.bbappend
KERNEL_SRC = "git:///home/giometti/yocto/linux-engicam-nxp/"
SRCBRANCH = "5.15.71-cy"
SRCREV = "${AUTOREV}"
```

As for the bootloader above, we set `SRCREV` to `${AUTOREV}` to get the kernel sources recompiled each time we do a new commit within our kernel repository. Moreover, we have changed the `KERNEL_SRC` and `SRCBRANCH` variables in order to point to our newly created repository.

Now we have to check if everything still continues to compile correctly, so let's clear the current state of `linux-engicam` recipe and then recompile the code:

```
$ bitbake -c cleansstate linux-engicam && bitbake linux-engicam
...
NOTE: Executing Tasks
Setscene tasks: 172 of 172
Currently  1 running tasks (749 of 765)   97% |####################### |
0: linux-engicam-5.15.71+gitAUTOINC+ac58548817-r0 do_compile - 6s (pid
175644)
```

OK, now we can start defining our custom machine within the kernel sources. To do so, we just need to remember what we discovered in Section 8.1 within the file `imx8mp-icore.conf` in Engicam's layer, that is, the variable `KERNEL_DEVICETREE_BASENAME` is set to `imx8mp-icore`; so the device tree file should be based on the prefix `imx8mp-icore`. If we do a little search within kernel sources, we can easily verify it:

```
$ cd ../../linux-engicam-nxp/
$ find . -name imx8mp-icore*.dts
./arch/arm64/boot/dts/engicam/imx8mp-icore-fasteth-ctouch2-amp10.dts
./arch/arm64/boot/dts/engicam/imx8mp-icore-fasteth-ctouch2.dts
```

```
./arch/arm64/boot/dts/engicam/imx8mp-icore-starterkit.dts
...
./arch/arm64/boot/dts/engicam/imx8mp-icore-2e-ctouch3-yes7.dts
```

However, to discover which is the device tree file supplied to the kernel by the bootloader, we have to take a closer look at the bootloader configuration file; in fact, we can see the following:

```
$ cd ../u-boot-engicam-nxp-2022.04/
$ rgrep imx8mp-icore configs/imx8mp_icore_cy_4gb_defconfig
CONFIG_DEFAULT_DEVICE_TREE="imx8mp-icore-cy"
CONFIG_DEFAULT_FDT_FILE="imx8mp-icore-starterkit.dtb"
```

So the file to be cloned is imx8mp-icore-starterkit.dts. We can get it by doing as below:

```
$ cp arch/arm64/boot/dts/engicam/imx8mp-icore-starterkit.dts \
    arch/arm64/boot/dts/engicam/imx8mp-icore-cy-board.dts
```

Furthermore, we can alter it to simulate some modifications, as we did for the U-Boot sources:

```
--- a/arch/arm64/boot/dts/engicam/imx8mp-icore-cy-board.dts
+++ b/arch/arm64/boot/dts/engicam/imx8mp-icore-cy-board.dts
@@ -9,7 +9,7 @@
 #include "../freescale/imx8mp.dtsi"

 / {
-        model = "Engicam i.Core i.MX8MPlus";
+        model = "CY board i.Core i.MX8MPlus";
         compatible = "engi,imx8-icore", "fsl,imx8mp";

         chosen {
```

Again, the readers should consider that we have done a very minimal change to have a different model name, but, in the case of real hardware, more work must be done.

Then we can also add our new device tree file to the kernel Makefile as below:

```
--- a/arch/arm64/boot/dts/engicam/Makefile
+++ b/arch/arm64/boot/dts/engicam/Makefile
@@ -13,6 +13,7 @@ dtb-$(CONFIG_ARCH_MXC) += \
                          imx8mp-icore-2e-net-phy.dtb \
                          imx8mp-icore-2e-ctouch3-yes7.dtb \
                          imx8mp-icore-starterkit.dtb \
+                         imx8mp-icore-cy-board.dtb \
                          imx8mp-smarcore-multimedia-4k.dtb \
                          imx8mp-smarcore-xtouch2.dtb \
                          imx8mp-icore-fasteth-starterkit.dtb \
```

Then let's commit these modifications as below:

```
$ git add arch/arm64/boot/dts/engicam/Makefile arch/arm64/boot/dts/engi
cam/imx8mp-icore-cy-board.dts
$ git commit -s -m "arm dts: add new board imx8mp-icore-cy-board"
[5.15.71-cy d1c9a311f7ef] arm dts: add new board imx8mp-icore-cy-board
 2 files changed, 1030 insertions(+)
 create mode 100644 arch/arm64/boot/dts/engicam/imx8mp-icore-cy-board.d
ts
```

Now, as before, for our changes to get effective, we need both to alter the U-Boot default configuration and then alter a bit the machine configuration file.

The U-Boot sources must be changed as below:

```
--- a/configs/imx8mp_icore_cy_4gb_defconfig
+++ b/configs/imx8mp_icore_cy_4gb_defconfig
@@ -32,7 +32,7 @@ CONFIG_SPL_LOAD_FIT=y
 CONFIG_OF_BOARD_FIXUP=y
 CONFIG_OF_BOARD_SETUP=y
 CONFIG_OF_SYSTEM_SETUP=y
-CONFIG_DEFAULT_FDT_FILE="imx8mp-icore-starterkit.dtb"
+CONFIG_DEFAULT_FDT_FILE="imx8mp-icore-cy-board.dtb"
 CONFIG_ARCH_MISC_INIT=y
 CONFIG_BOARD_EARLY_INIT_F=y
 CONFIG_BOARD_LATE_INIT=y
```

Then we have to commit the changes:

```
$ git add configs/imx8mp_icore_cy_4gb_defconfig
$ git commit -s -m 'configs imx8mp_icore_cy_4gb_defconfig: set default
FDT file to imx8mp-icore-cy-board.dtb'
[master-cy 272669822a] configs imx8mp_icore_cy_4gb_defconfig: set defau
lt FDT file to imx8mp-icore-cy-board.dtb
 1 file changed, 1 insertion(+), 1 deletion(-)
```

In the end, the machine configuration within our meta layer must be changed as shown below:

```
--- a/conf/machine/imx8mp-icore-cy.conf
+++ b/conf/machine/imx8mp-icore-cy.conf
@@ -6,15 +6,16 @@

 require conf/machine/include/imx8mp-engicam.inc

-KERNEL_DEVICETREE_BASENAME = "imx8mp-icore"
+KERNEL_DEVICETREE_BASENAME = "imx8mp-icore-cy"

 KERNEL_DEVICETREE:append:use-nxp-bsp = " \
        engicam/imx8mp-icore-starterkit.dtb \
        engicam/imx8mp-icore-ctouch2.dtb \
+       engicam/imx8mp-icore-cy-board.dtb \
 "

 UBOOT_CONFIG_BASENAME = "imx8mp_icore_cy"
-UBOOT_DTB_NAME = "imx8mp-icore-cy.dtb"
+# UBOOT_DTB_NAME = "imx8mp-icore-cy.dtb"
 UBOOT_CONFIG ??= "4gb"
 UBOOT_CONFIG[1gb] = "${UBOOT_CONFIG_BASENAME}_1gb_defconfig,sdcard"
 UBOOT_CONFIG[2gb] = "${UBOOT_CONFIG_BASENAME}_defconfig,sdcard"
```

The readers should notice that now we have defined the KERNEL_ DEVICETREE_BASENAME variable to its right value, that is, imx8mp-icore-cy, so we can drop the settings done above for the UBOOT_ DTB_NAME.

However, instead of completely removing the line, we just prefer to comment it out to underline (and remember) this *imperfection*.

Now we have to recompile a new image with the usual `bitbake engicam-evaluation-image-mx8` and then rewrite the microSD. If everything works well now, we should get something as shown below:

```
...
Starting kernel ...
[    0.000000] Booting Linux on physical CPU 0x0000000000 [0x410fd034]
[    0.000000] Linux version 5.15.71+gd1c9a311f7ef (oe-user@oe-host) (a
arch64-poky-linux-gcc (GCC) 11.3.0, GNU ld (GNU Binutils) 2.38.20220708
) #1 SMP PREEMPT Wed Nov 29 17:06:47 UTC 2023
[    0.000000] Machine model: CY board i.Core i.MX8MPlus
...
```

Here, we can verify that our new custom kernel is running by considering the string `Machine model: CY board i.Core i.MX8MPlus`.

Regarding the kernel configuration, we can obviously alter the `imx8mp_icore_cy_4gb_defconfig` configuration file and then commit the changes to test our new setting. However, this is odd since we are committing just for testing and not for saving something stable. To avoid this procedure (which is not wrong, anyway), we can use the `bitbake` command as shown below:

```
$ bitbake -c menuconfig linux-engicam
```

This command asks BitBake to execute the `do_menuconfig` task, which in turn should open a new terminal, as in Figure 8-2.

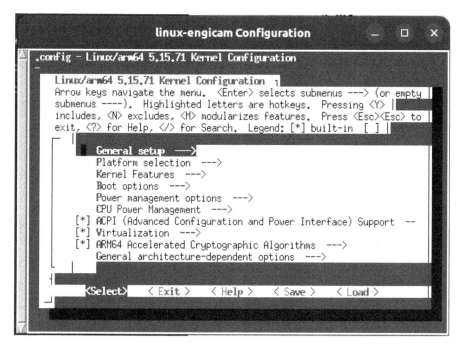

Figure 8-2. *The kernel's menuconfig window*

Now we can try to alter the current kernel configuration, and a simple example could be adding a testing kernel module, which usually is not compiled by default. We can move through Device Drivers, then PPS support, and select the Kernel timer client (Testing client, use for debug) entry, as shown in Figure 8-3.

The PPS support is a special kernel subsystem which provides a programming interface (API) to define in the system several PPS sources. PPS means *Pulse Per Second*, and a PPS source is just a device which provides a high-precision signal each second so that an application can use it to adjust system clock time.

See https://docs.kernel.org/driver-api/pps.html for further information.

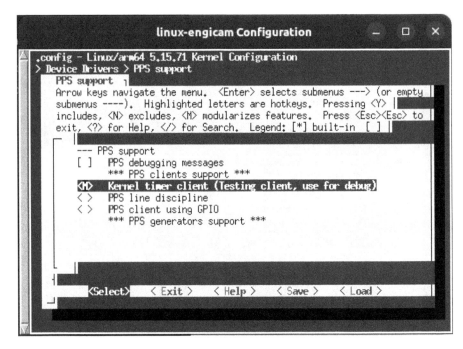

Figure 8-3. *Configuring the PPS support by adding the timer client*

Then we can exit and save the new configuration. Now to see what is changed, we should use bitbake again but asking for the do_ diffconfig task:

```
$ bitbake -c diffconfig linux-engicam
...
Config fragment has been dumped into:
 /home/giometti/yocto/imx-yocto-bsp/imx8mp-build/tmp/work/imx8mp_icore_
cy-poky-linux/linux-engicam/5.15.71+gitAUTOINC+d1c9a311f7-r0/fragment.c
fg
NOTE: Tasks Summary: Attempted 309 tasks of which 308 didn't need to be
 rerun and all succeeded.
```

Within the fragment.cfg file are our changes:

```
$ cat /home/giometti/yocto/imx-yocto-bsp/imx8mp-build/tmp/work/imx8mp_i
core_cy-poky-linux/linux-engicam/5.15.71+gitAUTOINC+d1c9a311f7-r0/fragm
ent.cfg
CONFIG_PPS_CLIENT_KTIMER=m
```

Just to explain a bit about a kernel configuration fragment, we can say that kernel configuration can be done conveniently by using **configuration fragments**. Configuration fragments are small files that contain kernel configuration options in the syntax of the original kernel's `.config` configuration file.

In our example above, we got the new setting:

```
CONFIG_PPS_CLIENT_KTIMER=m
```

which is the only modification we have to add to our kernel configuration file (i.e., the `.config`).

Now to test our modification, we have to move this file into our kernel recipe, and we can easily do it by using `recipetool` as shown below:

```
$ recipetool appendsrcfile -W $CY_METADIR/ linux-engicam \
      /home/giometti/yocto/imx-yocto-bsp/imx8mp-build/tmp/work/imx8mp_i
core_cy-poky-linux/linux-engicam/5.15.71+gitAUTOINC+d1c9a311f7-r0/fragm
ent.cfg pps_ktimer.cfg
...
NOTE: Writing append file /home/giometti/yocto/imx-yocto-bsp/sources/me
ta-cy/recipes-kernel/linux-engicam/linux-engicam_5.15.bbappend
NOTE: Copying /home/giometti/yocto/imx-yocto-bsp/imx8mp-build/tmp/work/
imx8mp_icore_cy-poky-linux/linux-engicam/5.15.71+gitAUTOINC+d1c9a311f7-
r0/fragment.cfg to /home/giometti/yocto/imx-yocto-bsp/sources/meta-cy/r
ecipes-kernel/linux-engicam/linux-engicam/pps_ktimer.cfg
```

Note that we have used the -W option argument within the above `recipetool` command because fragment files must be added into WORKDIR rather than into the S directory! See Section 4.3.

The fragment file has been renamed into the more appropriate and descriptive name pps_ktimer.cfg, and the linux-engicam_5.15. bbappend file has been updated with the new SRC_URI entry as shown below:

```
$ cat /home/giometti/yocto/imx-yocto-bsp/sources/meta-cy/recipes-kernel
/linux-engicam/linux-engicam_5.15.bbappend
...
SRCREV = "${AUTOREV}"
SRC_URI += "file://pps_ktimer.cfg"

FILESEXTRAPATHS:prepend := "${THISDIR}/${PN}:"
```

Before continuing, we have to check a possible bug within the meta-imx kernel recipe, which is still present at the time of the writing of this book. If not fixed, even if the fragment file has been added within SRC_URI, it will not be applied during the kernel recipe do_configure task!

To check it, we have to force the do_configure task and then check if the fragment has been processed. So:

```
$ bitbake -c configure -f linux-engicam
...
NOTE: Tainting hash to force rebuild of task /home/giometti/yocto/
imx-yocto-bsp/sources/meta-engicam-nxp/recipes-kernel/linux-engica
m/linux-engicam_5.15.bb, do_configure
WARNING: /home/giometti/yocto/imx-yocto-bsp/sources/meta-engicam-n
xp/recipes-kernel/linux-engicam/linux-engicam_5.15.bb:do_configure
 is tainted from a forced run
```

Now the .config file is in the directory addressed by the B variable, and its name can be retrieved with cy-vars as shown below:

```
$ cy-vars B linux-engicam
B="/home/giometti/yocto/imx-yocto-bsp/imx8mp-build/tmp/work/imx8mp
_icore_cy-poky-linux/linux-engicam/5.15.71+gitAUTOINC+d1c9a311f7-r
0/build"
```

So to check the new setting, we can use the following command:

```
$ grep CONFIG_PPS_CLIENT_KTIMER \
        /home/giometti/yocto/imx-yocto-bsp/imx8mp-build/tmp/work/
imx8mp_icore_cy-poky-linux/linux-engicam/5.15.71+gitAUTOINC+d1c9a3
11f7-r0/build/.config
# CONFIG_PPS_CLIENT_KTIMER is not set
```

The fragment hasn't been processed! To resolve this issue, we can add the following .bbappend file to our meta layer:

```
$ cat $CY_METADIR/recipes-kernel/linux-engicam/linux-engicam_%.bba
ppend
do_configure:append() {
    for i in ../*.cfg; do
        [ -f "$i" ] || break
        bbdebug 2 "applying $i file contents to .config"
        cat "$i" >> ${B}/.config
    done
}
```

By doing so, we just append a simple procedure to the do_configure task for the kernel recipe, which applies all .cfg files present into the build directory to the .config configuration file.

To test if now everything works correctly, we have to clean all generated files first:

```
$ bitbake -c cleanall linux-engicam
```

And then execute the do_configure task again:

```
$ bitbake -c configure linux-engicam
```

Now the fragments should be correctly applied:

```
$ grep CONFIG_PPS_CLIENT_KTIMER \
        /home/giometti/yocto/imx-yocto-bsp/imx8mp-build/tmp/work/
imx8mp_icore_cy-poky-linux/linux-engicam/5.15.71+gitAUTOINC+d1c9a3
11f7-r0/build/.config
# CONFIG_PPS_CLIENT_KTIMER is not set
CONFIG_PPS_CLIENT_KTIMER=m
```

The first entry is due to the default configuration file, while the second is due to the `pps_ktimer.cfg` fragment file.

Now we can regenerate our Yocto image:

```
$ bitbake engicam-evaluation-image-mx8
...
WARNING: /home/giometti/yocto/imx-yocto-bsp/sources/meta-engicam-nxp/re
cipes-kernel/linux-engicam/linux-engicam_5.15.bb:do_compile is tainted
from a forced run
...
```

We can verify that the `linux-engicam` recipe is rebuilt, and once finished we can check on the serial console if the new kernel module has been correctly added:

```
...
NXP i.MX Release Distro 5.15-kirkstone imx8mp-icore-cy ttymxc1

imx8mp-icore login: root
root@imx8mp-icore:~# echo 8 > /proc/sys/kernel/printk
root@imx8mp-icore:~# modprobe pps-ktimer
[   29.273506] pps pps0: new PPS source ktimer
[   29.277919] pps pps0: ktimer PPS source registered
root@imx8mp-icore:~# cat /sys/class/pps/pps0/name
ktimer
```

Great! The module is now present.

Note that if we have to add something else to the current kernel settings, for example, the `PPS line discipline` support (which is located in the same menu entry as before), we have to generate a new `fragment.cfg`. This must be appended to the previous one or added to `SRC_URI` as done before with `recipetool` (or just by editing the `.bbappend` file by hand).

The correct procedure to do so is to launch the `menuconfig`:

```
$ bitbake -c menuconfig linux-engicam
```

Then select the PPS line discipline as module (m), in the same manner as done before for the Kernel timer client entry (see Figure 8-4), and create the new configuration fragment with the do_diffconfig task:

```
$ bitbake -c diffconfig linux-engicam
...
Config fragment has been dumped into:
 /home/giometti/yocto/imx-yocto-bsp/imx8mp-build/tmp/work/imx8mp_icore_
cy-poky-linux/linux-engicam/5.15.71+gitAUTOINC+d1c9a311f7-r0/fragment.c
fg
NOTE: Tasks Summary: Attempted 309 tasks of which 308 didn't need to be
 rerun and all succeeded.
```

which holds just the last changes:

```
$ cat /home/giometti/yocto/imx-yocto-bsp/imx8mp-build/tmp/work/imx8mp_i
core_cy-poky-linux/linux-engicam/5.15.71+gitAUTOINC+d1c9a311f7-r0/fragm
ent.cfg
CONFIG_PPS_CLIENT_LDISC=m
```

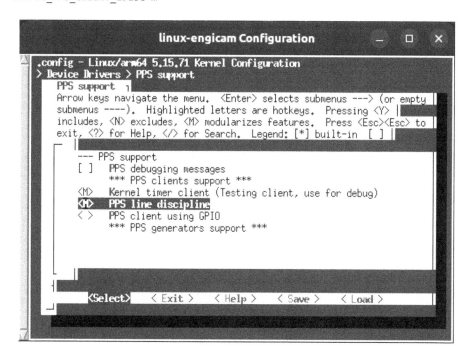

Figure 8-4. *Configuring the PPS support by adding the line discipline*

So developers should take it into account and do the following:

```
$ cat /home/giometti/yocto/imx-yocto-bsp/imx8mp-build/tmp/work/imx8mp_i
core_cy-poky-linux/linux-engicam/5.15.71+gitAUTOINC+d1c9a311f7-r0/fragm
ent.cfg >> $CY_METADIR/recipes-kernel/linux-engicam/linux-engicam/pps_k
timer.cfg
```

Or rather, define a new fragment file by using again `recipetool`, as shown below:

```
$ recipetool appendsrcfile -W $CY_METADIR/ linux-engicam \
      /home/giometti/yocto/imx-yocto-bsp/imx8mp-build/tmp/work/imx8mp_i
core_cy-poky-linux/linux-engicam/5.15.71+gitAUTOINC+d1c9a311f7-r0/fragment.
cfg pps_ldisc.cfg
...
NOTE: Writing append file /home/giometti/yocto/imx-yocto-bsp/sources/me
ta-cy/recipes-kernel/linux-engicam/linux-engicam_5.15.bbappend
NOTE: Copying /home/giometti/yocto/imx-yocto-bsp/imx8mp-build/tmp/work/
imx8mp_icore_cy-poky-linux/linux-engicam/5.15.71+gitAUTOINC+d1c9a311f7-
r0/fragment.cfg to /home/giometti/yocto/imx-yocto-bsp/sources/meta-cy/r
ecipes-kernel/linux-engicam/linux-engicam/pps_ldisc.cfg
```

This latter solution is preferable because we have a proper fragment file for each setting. The former solution is correct, but we should use a proper filename, for instance, `pps_settings.cfg` instead of `pps_ktimer.cfg`, to avoid misunderstandings. In this last case, the `linux-engicam_5.15.bbappend` becomes

```
$ cat $CY_METADIR/recipes-kernel/linux-engicam/linux-engicam_5.15.bbapp
end
...
SRCREV = "${AUTOREV}"
SRC_URI += "file://pps_ktimer.cfg \
            file://pps_ldisc.cfg \
            "

FILESEXTRAPATHS:prepend := "${THISDIR}/${PN}:"
```

8.4.3 Customizing Linux with devtool

Now, similarly to what was done in Section 8.2.3 for U-Boot, we can explain how to customize our kernel by using `devtool`.

As done before, we should temporarily revoke all settings we did in the previous section about the Linux and U-Boot recipes. Again, we can easily do it by renaming the .bbappend file created above. For the kernel, we have

```
$ cd ../sources/meta-cy/recipes-kernel/linux-engicam/
$ mv linux-engicam_5.15.bbappend linux-engicam_5.15.bbappend.DISABLED
$ cd $BUILDDIR
```

Furthermore, we need to use the default settings for the Engicam devkit by prepending the MACHINE="imx8mp-icore" setting to all next bitbake and devtool commands.

Then we can invoke the devtool utility to alter the Linux sources as usual:

```
$ MACHINE="imx8mp-icore" devtool modify virtual/kernel
...
INFO: Mapping virtual/kernel to linux-engicam
...
INFO: Copying kernel config to srctree
INFO: Source tree extracted to /home/giometti/yocto/imx-yocto-bsp/imx8m
p-build/workspace/sources/linux-engicam
INFO: Recipe linux-engicam now set up to build from /home/giometti/yoct
o/imx-yocto-bsp/imx8mp-build/workspace/sources/linux-engicam
```

As we can see above, the devtool utility correctly detects the right recipe and creates a new entry named linux-engicam within the workspace.

At this point, we can use the edit-recipe subcommand to alter the current recipe:

```
$ MACHINE="imx8mp-icore" devtool edit-recipe virtual/kernel
```

As for U-Boot, we don't need to alter this recipe; however, to do some modifications as an example, we can change the string for the SUMMARY variable by setting it to "Linux Kernel for CY board".

Now we should be able to compile the code as below:

```
$ MACHINE="imx8mp-icore" devtool build linux-engicam
...
NOTE: linux-engicam: compiling from external source tree /home/giometti
/yocto/imx-yocto-bsp/imx8mp-build/workspace/sources/linux-engicam
NOTE: Tasks Summary: Attempted 817 tasks of which 805 didn't need to be
 rerun and all succeeded.
```

As expected, now the build system is telling us that the linux-engicam recipe is now compiled from an external source tree. So we can now move to the directory workspace/sources/linux-engicam to do our modifications:

```
$ cd workspace/sources/linux-engicam/
```

To mimic what we did in the previous section, we can just alter the model string within the device tree as below:

```
--- a/arch/arm64/boot/dts/engicam/imx8mp-icore-starterkit.dts
+++ b/arch/arm64/boot/dts/engicam/imx8mp-icore-starterkit.dts
@@ -9,7 +9,7 @@
 #include "../freescale/imx8mp.dtsi"

 / {
-        model = "Engicam i.Core i.MX8MPlus";
+        model = "CY board [devtool] i.Core i.MX8MPlus";
         compatible = "engi,imx8-icore", "fsl,imx8mp";

         chosen {
```

At this point, our newly created repository should have something similar to the following status output:

```
$ git status
On branch 5.15.71
Your branch is behind 'origin/5.15.71' by 2 commits, and can be fast-fo
rwarded.
  (use "git pull" to update your local branch)

Changes not staged for commit:
  (use "git add <file>..." to update what will be committed)
  (use "git restore <file>..." to discard changes in working directory)
        modified:   arch/arm64/boot/dts/engicam/imx8mp-icore-starterkit.dts

no changes added to commit (use "git add" and/or "git commit -a")
```

The readers should notice that this time the current branch is not changed to `devtool`; however, we can still detect our next changes by using the tags `devtool-base` and `devtool-patched` as shown below:

```
$ git log --decorate --oneline -1
ac5854881745 (HEAD -> 5.15.71, tag: devtool-patched, tag: devtool
-base, devtool) imx6sx smarcore: added support for ksz9021/ksz9031
```

Now we should try to build the code again to test that our modifications still allow proper source compilation:

```
$ MACHINE="imx8mp-icore" devtool build linux-engicam
...
NOTE: Tasks Summary: Attempted 747 tasks of which 734 didn't need to be
 rerun and all succeeded.
```

Now to test our modifications on the embedded machine, we can use the `build-image` subcommand:

```
$ MACHINE="imx8mp-icore" devtool build u-boot-engicam
```

The readers should be sure that the UBOOT_CONFIG variable within the `sources/meta-engicam-nxp/conf/machine/imx8mp-icore.conf` file in the Engicam layer is properly set (see what's done in Section 8.2.3).

In case of no errors, we can move forward by recompiling the whole image as usual:

```
$ MACHINE="imx8mp-icore" devtool build-image engicam-evaluation-image-m
x8
...
WARNING: Skipping recipe linux-engicam as it doesn't produce a package
with the same name
WARNING: No recipes in workspace, building image engicam-evaluation-ima
ge-mx8 unmodified
...
```

The readers should notice above that this time `devtool` tells us that the recipe `linux-engicam` will be skipped due to the fact that it doesn't produce a package with the same name. This behavior is quite usual for a kernel recipe; we shouldn't worry about it.

When finished, we can move the new Yocto image within the microSD and then test the modifications to the Linux sources.

Don't forget to use the file `engicam-evaluation-image-mx8-imx8mp-icore.wic.zst` under the `tmp/deploy/images/imx8mp-icore/` directory and not the one we usually use for our example machine `imx8mp-icore-cy`!

If everything has been done correctly, we should see the booting messages below:

```
...
Starting kernel ...

[    0.000000] Booting Linux on physical CPU 0x0000000000 [0x410fd034]
[    0.000000] Linux version 5.15.71+gac5854881745 (oe-user@oe-host) (a
arch64-poky-linux-gcc (GCC) 11.3.0, GNU ld (GNU Binutils) 2.38.20220708
) #1 SMP PREEMPT Thu Feb 15 15:33:19 UTC 2024
[    0.000000] Machine model: CY board [devtool] i.Core i.MX8MPlus
...
```

Now, to save our changes, we can do a new commit:

```
$ git add arch/arm64/boot/dts/engicam/imx8mp-icore-starterkit.dts
$ git commit -s -m "arm64 imx8mp-icore-starterkit.dts: rework to suppor
t CY board"
[5.15.71 bd04d3ed43a4] arm64 imx8mp-icore-starterkit.dts: rework to sup
port CY board
 1 file changed, 1 insertion(+), 1 deletion(-)
```

OK, all source modifications are now in place, but what about how to change the Linux configuration? As already stated above for U-Boot, with devtool the usual way to alter a configuration is by using the subcommand menuconfig, so let's try to see if this time we are lucky:

```
$ MACHINE="imx8mp-icore" devtool menuconfig linux-engicam
INFO: Launching menuconfig
...
```

Great! This time, the command works, and Figure 8-5 shows an example of what we should see on our monitor.

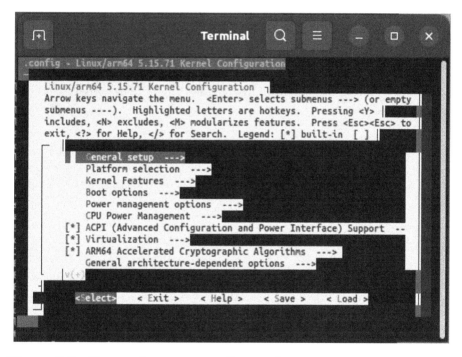

Figure 8-5. *Yet another menuconfig window*

This is precisely what we got in Figure 8-2. Now we can try to alter the current kernel configuration, as in the previous section, that is, by moving through Device Drivers, then PPS support, and selecting the Kernel timer client (Testing client, use for debug) entry.

Then we can exit and save the new configuration, and `devtool` should say the following:

```
...
INFO: Updating config fragment /home/giometti/yocto/imx-yocto-bsp/imx8m
p-build/workspace/sources/linux-engicam/oe-local-files/devtool-fragment
.cfg
```

This means that the kernel has been modified, and the new settings have been added as fragments within the file `devtool-fragment.cfg` file:

```
$ cat /home/giometti/yocto/imx-yocto-bsp/imx8mp-build/workspace/sources
/linux-engicam/oe-local-files/devtool-fragment.cfg
CONFIG_PPS_CLIENT_KTIMER=m
```

which is the only modification we have to add to our kernel configuration file (i.e., the `.config`).

Now to test our modification, we can ask the build system to regenerate our Yocto image:

```
$ MACHINE="imx8mp-icore" \
        devtool build-image engicam-evaluation-image-mx8
```

Once finished, we can check if the new kernel module has been correctly added:

```
...
NXP i.MX Release Distro 5.15-kirkstone imx8mp-icore ttymxc1

imx8mp-icore login: root
root@imx8mp-icore:~# echo 8 > /proc/sys/kernel/printk
root@imx8mp-icore:~# modprobe pps-ktimer
[   29.273506] pps pps0: new PPS source ktimer
[   29.277919] pps pps0: ktimer PPS source registered
root@imx8mp-icore:~# cat /sys/class/pps/pps0/name
ktimer
```

Great! The module has been added. Now, as done before, we can continue in this manner until we have added all the needed changes, and, when finished, we can take the full list by using the same command as in the example below:

```
$ git log --oneline devtool-base..HEAD
bd04d3ed43a4 (HEAD -> 5.15.71) arm64 imx8mp-icore-starterkit.dts: rewor
k to support CY board
```

When finished, we can use `devtool` to save all our job into our private layer as shown below:

```
$ MACHINE="imx8mp-icore" \
        devtool update-recipe --append $CY_METADIR linux-engicam
...
INFO: Updating config fragment
/tmp/devtoolvd8nmozw/tmpcqjp_1er/devtool-fragment.cfg
NOTE: Writing append file /home/giometti/yocto/imx-yocto-bsp/sources/me
ta-cy/recipes-kernel/linux-engicam/linux-engicam_5.15.bbappend
NOTE: Copying devtool-fragment.cfg to /home/giometti/yocto/imx-yocto-bs
p/sources/meta-cy/recipes-kernel/linux-engicam/linux-engicam/devtool-fr
agment.cfg
NOTE: Copying 0001-arm64-imx8mp-icore-starterkit.dts-rework-to-support-.
patch to /hom
e/giometti/yocto/imx-yocto-bsp/sources/meta-cy/recipes-kernel/linux-eng
icam/linux-engicam/0001-arm64-imx8mp-icore-starterkit.dts-rework-to-sup
port-.patch
```

Note that to save the kernel configuration, we can also do as follows:

```
$ MACHINE="imx8mp-icore" bitbake -c savedefconfig virtual/kernel
...
Saving defconfig to:
/home/giometti/yocto/imx-yocto-bsp/imx8mp-build/tmp/work/imx8mp_ic
ore-poky-linux/linux-engicam/5.15.71+git999-r0/linux-engicam-5.15.
71+git999/defconfig
NOTE: Tasks Summary: Attempted 445 tasks of which 444 didn't need
to be rerun and all succeeded.
```

Now we can overwrite the newly generated `defconfig` with the one specified in the original recipe within the kernel sources, for example:

```
$ cp /home/giometti/yocto/imx-yocto-bsp/imx8mp-build/tmp/work/imx8
mp_icore-poky-linux/linux-engicam/5.15.71+git999-r0/linux-engicam-
5.15.71+git999//defconfig \
        arch/arm64/configs/imx8_icore_defconfig
```

Now we can commit the imx8_icore_defconfig file as usual, and
then devtool will produce a patch for us (in the same manner as we
saw above for U-Boot).

By using this command, we ask bitbake to create a .bbappend file
within our meta-cy layer, so the following linux-engicam_5.15.bbappend
file is created:

```
$ cat sources/meta-cy/recipes-kernel/linux-engicam/linux-engicam_5.15.b
bappend
FILESEXTRAPATHS:prepend := "${THISDIR}/${PN}:"

SRC_URI += "file://devtool-fragment.cfg file://0001-arm64-imx8mp-icore-
starterkit.dts-rework-to-support-.patch"
```

As in the previous section, the update-recipe subcommand didn't
report our modification to the SUMMARY variable within the .bbappend file
due to the fact that, when we invoked the edit-recipe subcommand,
the modification has been done within the original recipe. In the meta-
engicam-nxp layer, we check it out:

```
$ cd sources/meta-engicam-nxp
$ git diff
diff --git a/conf/machine/imx8mp-icore.conf b/conf/machine/imx8mp-icore
.conf
index 06dba1e..f5c035c 100644
--- a/conf/machine/imx8mp-icore.conf
+++ b/conf/machine/imx8mp-icore.conf
@@ -14,7 +14,7 @@ KERNEL_DEVICETREE:append:use-nxp-bsp = " \
 "

 UBOOT_CONFIG_BASENAME = "imx8mp_icore"
-UBOOT_CONFIG ??= "2gb"
+UBOOT_CONFIG ??= "4gb"
 UBOOT_CONFIG[1gb] = "${UBOOT_CONFIG_BASENAME}_1gb_defconfig,sdcard"
 UBOOT_CONFIG[2gb] = "${UBOOT_CONFIG_BASENAME}_defconfig,sdcard"
 UBOOT_CONFIG[4gb] = "${UBOOT_CONFIG_BASENAME}_4gb_defconfig,sdcard"
diff --git a/recipes-kernel/linux-engicam/linux-engicam_5.15.bb b/recip
es-kernel/linux-engicam/linux-engicam_5.15.bb
index 499727d..2c6c091 100644
--- a/recipes-kernel/linux-engicam/linux-engicam_5.15.bb
```

```
+++ b/recipes-kernel/linux-engicam/linux-engicam_5.15.bb
@@ -5,7 +5,7 @@
 # SPDX-License-Identifier: MIT
 #
-SUMMARY = "Linux Kernel provided and supported by NXP"
+SUMMARY = "Linux Kernel for CY board"
 DESCRIPTION = "Linux Kernel provided and supported by NXP with focus o
n \
 i.MX Family Reference Boards. It includes support for many IPs such as
 GPU, VPU and IPU."
```

What we can do here is moving all recipe modifications by hand to have everything within our layer.

When all modification has been done and everything is in place, we can free the workspace by using the following command:

```
$ MACHINE="imx8mp-icore" devtool reset linux-engicam
NOTE: Starting bitbake server...
INFO: Cleaning sysroot for recipe linux-engicam...
INFO: Leaving source tree /home/giometti/yocto/imx-yocto-bsp/imx8mp-bui
ld/workspace/sources/linux-engicam as-is; if you no longer need it then
 please delete it manually
```

Note that, by default, the directory where our sources have been held during the development was not removed, and in that case we have to do it by hand.

As done in Section 8.2.3, we can also use the --mode srcrev option argument to create a .bbappend file without adding patches but just updating the SRCREV variable in the recipe:

```
$ MACHINE="imx8mp-icore" devtool update-recipe \
        --mode srcrev --append $CY_METADIR linux-engicam
...
INFO: Updating SRCREV in recipe linux-engicam_5.15.bb
INFO: Updating config fragment /tmp/devtool7j5vafre/tmp1shk4wo9/devtool
-fragment.cfg
NOTE: Writing append file /home/giometti/yocto/imx-yocto-bsp/sources/me
ta-cy/recipes-kernel/linux-engicam/linux-engicam_5.15.bbappend
```

```
NOTE: Copying devtool-fragment.cfg to /home/giometti/yocto/imx-yocto-bs
p/sources/meta-cy/recipes-kernel/linux-engicam/linux-engicam/devtool-fr
agment.cfg
INFO: You will need to update SRC_URI within the recipe to point to a g
it repository where you have pushed your changes
```

Now, the linux-engicam_5.15.bbappend holds the following setting:

```
$ cat linux-engicam_5.15.bbappend
SRCREV = "bd04d3ed43a46f260d61736b269dadc4c3939d6b"

FILESEXTRAPATHS:prepend := "${THISDIR}/${PN}:"

SRC_URI += "file://devtool-fragment.cfg"
```

And SRCDEV points to our last commit ID, while devtool suggests again that we properly update the SRC_URI variable within the recipe (or better, within the .bbappend file) to point to a custom git repository.

8.5 Summary

In this chapter, we learned how to add a new machine within our Yocto build system to support a new hardware derived from an already running embedded kit. We discovered how to alter U-Boot (with a note about prebootloaders) and how to modify the kernel.

Now that our new hardware is fully supported, we should take a look at adding new software to our Yocto OS in order to do all such tasks which our embedded machine has been designed for. So let's move on to the next chapter.

Starting from this point, until the end of the book, we are going to use the new machine imx8mp-icore-cy created in this chapter instead of Engicam's imx8mp-icore, but everything should continue to work with the original one.

CHAPTER 9

C Application Recipes

In Chapter 6, we saw what a recipe is and how we can use the *overlays* concept to alter it from different layers. Also, in Chapter 8, we discovered how to define a new machine derived from an already supported development kit. Now it's time to see how to create recipes for new software packages we wish to run on our embedded machine or how to alter already existing recipes in order to fix our specific embedded application.

In this chapter, we begin a series of examples about C-based projects (user space or kernel space projects and libraries); in the next chapter, we will see some examples of Python-based projects. Then, in the following chapters, we will continue in this presentation by proposing other miscellaneous examples of common real cases.

The readers should consider the fact that, even if we have cataloged each example, they can adapt what is suggested in a certain example to different problems; therefore, it is a good idea not to stop at the title of each section, but to read its contents to see if the proposed solution may solve their problem.

Before continuing, the readers should be sure that their embedded kits are reachable via the serial console and network interface as explained in Section 1.3.

© Rodolfo Giometti 2025
R. Giometti, *Yocto Project Customization for Linux*,
https://doi.org/10.1007/979-8-8688-1435-8_9

9.1 User Space Programs

Writing a recipe for a user space program is really a simple task. A good example of how to do it is reported within Yocto sources in the poky layer, as already introduced in Section 6.3 and reported again below:

```
$ cat poky/meta-skeleton/recipes-skeleton/hello-single/hello_1.0.bb
DESCRIPTION = "Simple helloworld application"
SECTION = "examples"
LICENSE = "MIT"
LIC_FILES_CHKSUM = "file://${COMMON_LICENSE_DIR}/MIT;md5=0835ade698e0bc
f8506ecda2f7b4f302"

SRC_URI = "file://helloworld.c"

S = "${WORKDIR}"

do_compile() {
        ${CC} ${LDFLAGS} helloworld.c -o helloworld
}

do_install() {
        install -d ${D}${bindir}
        install -m 0755 helloworld ${D}${bindir}
}
```

So, in order to do an elementary example of how to create a recipe for C projects we have developed ourselves on our machine, we can consider the hello-world C program reported below:

```
$ cd ~/yocto/examples/hello/
$ cat hello.c
#include <stdio.h>

int main(int argc, char *argv[])
{
        printf("hello world!\n");
        return 0;
}
```

Note that the `hello` directory can be everywhere within our filesystem and not necessarily under the build directory. In our example, we have a separate directory named `examples` which can be retrieved at `https://github.com/Apress/Yocto-Project-Customization-for-Linux`.

Now we can use the `recipetool` command as shown in Section 4.3 to create a custom recipe from the same directory:

```
$ recipetool create hello.c
NOTE: Starting bitbake server...
INFO: Fetching file:///home/giometti/yocto/examples/hello/hello.c...
...
NOTE: No setscene tasks
NOTE: Executing Tasks
NOTE: Tasks Summary: Attempted 2 tasks of which 0 didn't need to be rer
un and all succeeded.
INFO: Recipe hello.bb has been created; further editing may be required
 to make it fully functional
```

Now a new `hello.bb` recipe file has been created in the local directory with the following content:

```
$ cat hello.bb
# Recipe created by recipetool
# This is the basis of a recipe and may need further editing in order to
# be fully functional.
# (Feel free to remove these comments when editing.)

# Unable to find any files that looked like license statements. Check
# the accompanying documentation and source headers and set LICENSE and
# LIC_FILES_CHKSUM accordingly.
#
# NOTE: LICENSE is being set to "CLOSED" to allow you to at least start
# building - if this is not accurate with respect to the licensing of
# the software being built (it will not be in most cases) you must
# specify the correct value before using this recipe for anything other
# than initial testing/development!
LICENSE = "CLOSED"
LIC_FILES_CHKSUM = ""
```

```
SRC_URI = "file:///home/giometti/yocto/examples/hello/hello.c"

S = "${WORKDIR}/home"

# NOTE: no Makefile found, unable to determine what needs to be done

do_configure () {
        # Specify any needed configure commands here
        :
}
do_compile () {
        # Specify compilation commands here
        :
}
do_install () {
        # Specify install commands here
        :
}
```

So, the `recipetool` command has created the recipe `hello.bb` file with the following preset information:

- `LICENSE` set as `CLOSED` and `LIC_FILES_CHKSUM` set as an empty string – this is because we have specified no license at all.

- `SRC_URI` which points to the `hello.c` file, since it is the only source file for our project.

- And empty `do_configure`, `do_compile`, and `do_install` tasks that we have to fill with proper commands to compile our application.

In fact, the readers should note the following message in the above output:

```
# NOTE: no Makefile found, unable to determine what needs to be done
```

Well, we can fix this in two manners: by providing a compiling command within the do_compile() method as in the hello_1.0.bb example above, or we can add a Makefile as below:

```
$ cat Makefile
TARGET = hello

all: ${TARGET}

install:
        install -d ${DESTDIR}/usr/bin/
        install hello ${DESTDIR}/usr/bin/
```

OK, we can now delete the current hello.bb recipe and execute again the recipetool command:

```
$ rm hello.bb
$ recipetool create -N hello .
NOTE: Starting bitbake server...
...
INFO: Recipe hello.bb has been created; further editing may be required
 to make it fully functional
```

And within the hello.bb file, we should have the following contents:

```
$ cat hello.bb
# Recipe created by recipetool
...
# No information for SRC_URI yet (only an external source tree was
# specified)
SRC_URI = ""

# NOTE: this is a Makefile-only piece of software, so we cannot generate
# much of the recipe automatically - you will need to examine the
# Makefile yourself and ensure that the appropriate arguments are passed
# in.

do_configure () {
        # Specify any needed configure commands here
        :
}

do_compile () {
        # You will almost certainly need to add additional arguments here
        oe_runmake
}
```

```
do_install () {
        # This is a guess; additional arguments may be required
        oe_runmake install 'DESTDIR=${D}'
}
```

As we can see, now methods do_compile() and do_install() have some instructions added by recipetool which has detected our new Makefile, and it has auto-added the oe_runmake utility (see Section 3.3.2). However, this is not enough yet, since, in this case, recipetool cannot automatically set the SRC_URI variable (check the output above against what we have gotten in the first run).

It's obvious that we can manually add the needed entries in SRC_URI; however, to get a better result, we can move our project within a Git repository so that recipetool can use a smarter algorithm to automatically generate the recipe. To do so, we can follow the example below by removing the not good hello.bb file and then creating the repository:

```
$ rm hello.bb
$ git init
Initialized empty Git repository in /home/giometti/yocto/examples/hello
/.git/
$ git add .
$ git commit -m "Initial commit"
[master (root-commit) 81ec687] Initial commit
 2 files changed, 13 insertions(+)
 create mode 100644 Makefile
 create mode 100644 hello.c
```

Now that a Git repository is in place, we can use the prefix git:// in order to tell recipetool that the directory passed as an argument is not just a simple directory, but it's a Git repository. Doing this, the recipetool command line becomes

```
$ recipetool create git://$(pwd)
NOTE: Starting bitbake server...
INFO: Fetching git:///home/giometti/yocto/examples/hello;branch=master.
..
...
INFO: Recipe hello_git.bb has been created; further editing may be requ
ired to make it fully functional
```

Now the recipe's name has been set to hello_git.bb (this is because, as already explained in Section 6.1, the _git postfix is generally used to mark git managed projects), and it now has the following content:

```
$ cat hello_git.bb
# Recipe created by recipetool
# This is the basis of a recipe and may need further editing in order to
# be fully functional.
# (Feel free to remove these comments when editing.)

# Unable to find any files that looked like license statements. Check
# the accompanying documentation and source headers and set LICENSE and
# LIC_FILES_CHKSUM accordingly.
#
# NOTE: LICENSE is being set to "CLOSED" to allow you to at least start
# building - if this is not accurate with respect to the licensing of
# the software being built (it will not be in most cases) you must
# specify the correct value before using this recipe for anything other
# than initial testing/development!
LICENSE = "CLOSED"
LIC_FILES_CHKSUM = ""

SRC_URI = "git:///home/giometti/yocto/examples/hello;branch=master"

# Modify these as desired
PV = "1.0+git${SRCPV}"
SRCREV = "b3b4da551b6b25b56cc1fdad3f83ebfd88bcaeee"

S = "${WORKDIR}/git"

# NOTE: this is a Makefile-only piece of software, so we cannot generate
# much of the recipe automatically - you will need to examine the
# Makefile yourself and ensure that the appropriate arguments are passed
# in.

do_configure () {
        # Specify any needed configure commands here
        :
}

do_compile () {
        # You will almost certainly need to add additional arguments here
        oe_runmake
}
```

```
do_install () {
        # This is a guess; additional arguments may be required
        oe_runmake install 'DESTDIR=${D}'
}
```

This last version of our recipe is definitely better than before! By using a Git repository, we have got an (almost) complete recipe (and this is another good reason why every developer should use an SCM).

Now, to test it, we can move within our meta-cy layer and execute the following commands:

```
$ mkdir -p recipes-example/hello
$ mv /home/giometti/yocto/examples/hello/hello_git.bb \
        recipes-example/hello/
```

The recipe is now in place, and then we can try to compile the code by using bitbake as below:

```
$ bitbake hello
```

If everything works well, the compilation should end without any errors and a new IPKG package should be created as below:

```
$ cd $BUILDDIR
$ cy-ipk find hello
cy-ipk: searching in /home/giometti/yocto/imx-yocto-bsp/imx8mp-build...
tmp/deploy/ipk/armv8a/hello-dev_1.0+git0+b3b4da551b-r0_armv8a.ipk
tmp/deploy/ipk/armv8a/hello-src_1.0+git0+b3b4da551b-r0_armv8a.ipk
tmp/deploy/ipk/armv8a/hello_1.0+git0+b3b4da551b-r0_armv8a.ipk
tmp/deploy/ipk/armv8a/hello-dbg_1.0+git0+b3b4da551b-r0_armv8a.ipk
```

Now we just have to copy the file hello_1.0+git0+b3b4da551b-r0_armv8a.ipk to our target machine by using scp:

```
$ scp tmp/deploy/ipk/armv8a/hello_1.0+git0+b3b4da551b-r0_armv8a.ipk \
        root@192.168.32.132:
hello_1.0+git0+b3b4da551b-r0_armv8a.ipk    100% 2090     1.4MB/s   00:00
```

Note that if a new image has been installed on the microSD generated in the first chapters of this book, we can get the following error:

```
@@@@@@@@@@@@@@@@@@@@@@@@@@@@@@@@@@@@@@@@@@@@@@@@@@@@@@@@@@@@@
@    WARNING: REMOTE HOST IDENTIFICATION HAS CHANGED!    @
@@@@@@@@@@@@@@@@@@@@@@@@@@@@@@@@@@@@@@@@@@@@@@@@@@@@@@@@@@@@@
IT IS POSSIBLE THAT SOMEONE IS DOING SOMETHING NASTY!
Someone could be eavesdropping on you right now (man-in-the-middle
 attack)!
It is also possible that a host key has just been changed.
The fingerprint for the RSA key sent by the remote host is
SHA256:0b9AHYkwbkPpFjHqTmD5FUte7Axi5J1ZXIY397NaX8Q.
Please contact your system administrator.
Add correct host key in /home/giometti/.ssh/known_hosts to get rid
 of this message.
Offending RSA key in /home/giometti/.ssh/known_hosts:102
  remove with:
  ssh-keygen -f "/home/giometti/.ssh/known_hosts" -R "192.168.32.1
32"
Host key for 192.168.32.132 has changed and you have requested str
ict checking.
Host key verification failed.
lost connection
```

If so, we may recover just executing the suggested command as below:

```
$ ssh-keygen -f "/home/giometti/.ssh/known_hosts" -R "192.168.32.1
32"
# Host 192.168.32.132 found: line 102
/home/giometti/.ssh/known_hosts updated.
Original contents retained as /home/giometti/.ssh/known_hosts.old
```

And then re-executing the `scp` command:

```
$ scp tmp/deploy/ipk/armv8a/hello_1.0+git0+b3b4da551b-r0_armv8a.ip
k \
        root@192.168.32.132:
The authenticity of host '192.168.32.132 (192.168.32.132)' can't b
e established.
```

```
RSA key fingerprint is SHA256:Ob9AHYkwbkPpFjHqTmD5FUte7Axi5J1ZXIY3
97NaX8Q.
This key is not known by any other names
Are you sure you want to continue connecting (yes/no/[fingerprint])?
```

Now we have to answer yes, and the copy should start:

```
Warning: Permanently added '192.168.32.132' (RSA) to the list of k
nown hosts.
hello_1.0+gitO+b3b4da551b-rO_armv8a.ipk    100% 2090   1.3MB/s   00:00
```

And then install and execute it:

```
# opkg install hello_1.0+gitO+b3b4da551b-rO_armv8a.ipk
Installing hello (1.0+gitO+b3b4da551b) on root
Configuring hello.
root@imx8mp-icore-mbevx:~# hello
hello world
```

It may also happen that some readers get the following error during the package installation:

```
# opkg install hello_1.0+gitO+b3b4da551b-rO_armv8a.ipk
Installing hello (1.0+gitO+b3b4da551b) on root
 * check_data_file_clashes: Package hello wants to install file /u
sr/bin/hello
        But that file is already provided by package  * lmbench
To remove package debris, try opkg remove hello.
To re-attempt the install, try opkg install hello.
```

This situation can be recovered by using the following command:

```
# opkg install --force-overwrite hello_1.0+gitO+b3b4da551b-rO_armv
8a.ipk
Installing hello (1.0+gitO+b3b4da551b) on root
Configuring hello.
```

Of course, this is an exception, and we should avoid doing as above, but we should resolve the issue, for example, by changing some name or by using an alternative naming as explained in Section 6.3.4 regarding the ALTERNATIVE variable and its friends.

OK, now the code works on the target machine; however, a good recipe writer should not stop working here but should check that everything is correct. In fact, as explained in Section 6.3.1, we should set some descriptive variables too. By getting the package information, we can see the following result:

```
$ cy-ipk get-info tmp/deploy/ipk/armv8a/hello_1.0+git0+b3b4da551b-r0_ar
mv8a.ipk
Package: hello
Version: 1.0+git0+b3b4da551b-r0
Description: hello version 1.0+gitAUTOINC+b3b4da551b-r0
 hello version 1.0+gitAUTOINC+b3b4da551b-r0.
Section: base
Priority: optional
Maintainer: NXP <lauren.post@nxp.com>
License: CLOSED
Architecture: armv8a
OE: hello
Depends: libc6 (>= 2.35)
Source: hello_git.bb
```

So it's better to fix the package's description, section, license, and maintainer fields. Moreover, we can remove all unnecessary comments added by recipetool.

For example, we can rewrite our hello_git.bb recipe file as shown below:

```
$ cat $CY_METADIR/recipes-example/hello/hello_git.bb
SUMMARY = "Yet another hello world program"
DESCRIPTION = "A simple example about how to write a recipe for a user
space C program."
MAINTAINER = "Rodolfo Giometti <giometti@enneenne.com>"
SECTION = "examples"
LICENSE = "MIT"
```

```
LIC_FILES_CHKSUM = "file://${COMMON_LICENSE_DIR}/MIT;md5=0835ade698e0bc
f8506ecda2f7b4f302"

SRC_URI = "git:///home/giometti/yocto/examples/hello;branch=master"

PV = "1.0+git${SRCPV}"
SRCREV = "b3b4da551b6b25b56cc1fdad3f83ebfd88bcaeee"

S = "${WORKDIR}/git"

do_configure () {
        :
}

do_compile () {
        oe_runmake
}

do_install () {
        oe_runmake install 'DESTDIR=${D}'
}
```

Here, we should notice that LIC_FILES_CHKSUM uses the variable COMMON_LICENSE_DIR to specify the MIT license, since there is no license file within the sources.

Now, if we regenerate the package, we should get the following package's information:

```
$ cy-ipk get-info tmp/deploy/ipk/armv8a/hello_1.0+git0+b3b4da551b-r0_ar
mv8a.ipk
Package: hello
Version: 1.0+git0+b3b4da551b-r0
Description: Yet another hello world program
 A simple example about how to write a recipe for a user space C progra
m.
Section: examples
Priority: optional
Maintainer: Rodolfo Giometti <giometti@enneenne.com>
License: MIT
Architecture: armv8a
OE: hello
Depends: libc6 (>= 2.35)
Source: hello_git.bb
```

Now the recipe should be considered finished. However, before moving to the next section, as we saw in Section 4.5.1, we should consider that we can do the same thing done above by using devtool; so, for completeness, we will report below the equivalent devtool commands to add a new recipe for a user space program.

In order to not overwrite whatever is done above, we will use a different recipe name (i.e., hello2):

```
$ devtool add hello2 ~/yocto/examples/hello/
NOTE: Starting bitbake server...
INFO: Creating workspace layer in /home/giometti/yocto/imx-yocto-bsp/im
x8mp-build/workspace
NOTE: Starting bitbake server...
INFO: Using source tree as build directory since that would be the defa
ult for this recipe
INFO: Recipe /home/giometti/yocto/imx-yocto-bsp/imx8mp-build/workspace/
recipes/hello2/hello2.bb has been automatically created; further editin
g may be required to make it fully functional
```

Now, if we take a look at the workspace directory, we should see something as reported below:

```
$ tree workspace/
workspace/
├── appends
│   └── hello2.bbappend
├── conf
│   └── layer.conf
├── recipes
│   └── hello2
│       └── hello2.bb
└── README

4 directories, 4 files
```

Of course, the output may vary according to whatever the readers has done within their workspaces.

As expected, a new `hello2.bb` recipe has been created with the following content:

```
$ cat workspace/recipes/hello2/hello2.bb
# Recipe created by recipetool
# This is the basis of a recipe and may need further editing in order to
# be fully functional.
# (Feel free to remove these comments when editing.)
...
LICENSE = "CLOSED"
LIC_FILES_CHKSUM = ""

# No information for SRC_URI yet (only an external source tree was
# specified)
SRC_URI = ""

# NOTE: this is a Makefile-only piece of software, so we cannot generate
# much of the recipe automatically - you will need to examine the
# Makefile yourself and ensure that the appropriate arguments are passed
# in.

do_configure () {
        # Specify any needed configure commands here
        :
}

do_compile () {
        # You will almost certainly need to add additional arguments here
        oe_runmake
}

do_install () {
        # This is a guess; additional arguments may be required
        oe_runmake install 'DESTDIR=${D}'
}
```

We didn't report all content, since it's the same as the previous example generated with `recipetool`. This is also explicit by the note `Recipe created by recipetool` we can see in the output.

Furthermore, in the workspace, a new `.bbappend` file has been added:

```
$ cat workspace/appends/hello2.bbappend
inherit externalsrc
EXTERNALSRC = "/home/giometti/yocto/examples/hello"
EXTERNALSRC_BUILD = "/home/giometti/yocto/examples/hello"

# initial_rev: 58088a51b34db61e10ebab64e6cd7408a27ec8ca
```

Here are the settings to inform the build system (via the externalsrc class) that it has to get sources from a directory that is external to the Yocto build system (see Section 4.5.1).

Then we can edit the recipe by using the edit-recipe subcommand, as shown below:

```
$ devtool edit-recipe hello2
```

Note that the recipetool counterpart lets us see both the hello2. bb recipe file and the hello2.bbappend within the workspace, instead of just the recipe file, as devtool does. In fact, we have

```
$ recipetool edit hello2
...
2 files to edit
```

And then, within our preferred editor, we have both hello2.bb and hello2.bbappend!

Furthermore, to build the code, we can now use the build subcommand:

```
$ devtool build hello2
NOTE: Starting bitbake server...
...
NOTE: hello2: compiling from external source tree /home/giometti/yocto/
examples/hello
Setscene tasks: 168 of 168
Currently  2 running tasks (728 of 730)   99% |####################### |
0: hello2-1.0-r0 do_populate_sysroot - 0s (pid 139651)
1: hello2-1.0-r0 do_package - 0s (pid 139650)
```

Until now, there were few differences between this solution and the previous one with recipetool; however, now a really new and powerful command is available, that is, the devtool deploy-target command we can use to move generated code directly into the target machine! To do so, we can use the command below:

```
$ devtool deploy-target -s hello2 root@192.168.32.132
...
devtool_deploy.list                          100%   21     40.1KB/s    00:00
devtool_deploy.sh                            100% 1017      1.9MB/s    00:00
./
./usr/
./usr/bin/
./usr/bin/hello
INFO: Successfully deployed /home/giometti/yocto/imx-yocto-bsp/imx8mp-b
uild/tmp/work/armv8a-poky-linux/hello2/1.0-r0/image
```

Some readers may get the following extra messages during the deployment:

```
tar: ./usr/bin/hello: time stamp 2024-05-13 14:21:48 is 64407765.3
30864
25 s in the future
tar: ./usr/bin: time stamp 2024-05-13 14:21:48 is 64407765.3306766
25 s in the future
tar: ./usr: time stamp 2024-05-13 14:21:48 is 64407765.330483375 s
 in the future
tar: .: time stamp 2024-05-13 14:21:48 is 64407765.330399625 s in
the future
```

No problem, we can safely ignore these warnings.

Now we can directly test the code on the target machine without installing anything:

```
# hello
hello world!
```

Note that, even in this case, we should also add proper SUMMARY, DESCRIPTION, MAINTAINER, etc., variables as done before.

Before closing this section, it's really interesting to try to remove this package from our workspace. As seen in Section 4.5.4, we can just remove our package by using the devtool reset subcommand; however, if we try to do so on our current workspace, we get the following error message:

```
$ devtool reset hello2
...
NOTE: Starting bitbake server...
INFO: Cleaning sysroot for recipe hello2...
ERROR: Command 'bitbake -c clean hello2' failed, output:
...
NOTE: Running task 1 of 2 (/home/giometti/yocto/imx-yocto-bsp/imx8mp-bu
ild/workspace/recipes/hello2/hello2.bb:do_buildclean)
NOTE: recipe hello2-1.0-r0: task do_buildclean: Started
Log data follows:
| DEBUG: Executing shell function do_buildclean
| NOTE: make clean
| make: *** No rule to make target 'clean'.  Stop.
| ERROR: oe_runmake failed
| WARNING: exit code 1 from a shell command.
NOTE: recipe hello2-1.0-r0: task do_buildclean: Failed
NOTE: Tasks Summary: Attempted 1 tasks of which 0 didn't need to be rer
un and 1 failed.

Summary: 1 task failed:
  /home/giometti/yocto/imx-yocto-bsp/imx8mp-build/workspace/recipes/hello
2/hello2.bb:do_buildclean
Summary: There were 2 ERROR messages, returning a non-zero exit code.

If you wish, you may specify -n/--no-clean to skip running this command
 when resetting
```

This is because the subcommand tries to execute a cleaning action (i.e., a bitbake -c clean hello2 command), and our Makefile doesn't implement a clean target (i.e., we cannot execute a make clean). In this scenario, we have two possible solutions:

1) We can supply the missing target to clean up our working directory.

2) We can follow the above suggestion and then specify the -n (or --no-clean) option argument to skip this cleaning action.

443

Since we are not interested in doing the first solution, we can just do as follows:

```
$ devtool reset -n hello2
NOTE: Starting bitbake server...
INFO: Leaving source tree /home/giometti/yocto/examples/hello as-is; if
 you no longer need it then please delete it manually
```

Note that, this time, the working directory is not under workspace, so we have to carefully decide whether we have to remove the working directory or not!

9.2 Library Packages

Being able to compile packages for C programs is important, but as good embedded developers and C programmers, we know perfectly that being able to compile packages for C libraries is essential too.

To see how to do it, we can use a simple library code and a simple program which requests such a library. In this section, we are going to see how we should create our shared object and the related recipe to be used in the Yocto Project. Then in the next section, we will see how we can create a recipe for a C program that requires this library.

The code for a simple library is reported below:

```
$ cd examples/hellolib/
$ cat hello.c
#include <stdio.h>

int hello(void)
{
        printf("hello world!\n");
        return 0;
}
$ cat hello.h
#ifndef HELLO_H
#define HELLO_H

extern int hello(void);

#endif /* HELLO_H */
```

Our simple library (which is composed of the two files hello.c and hello.h) just defines a single function named hello(), and it can be compiled with the following Makefile:

```
$ cat Makefile
NAME = libhello.so
CFLAGS += -Wall -O2

MAJOR = 1
MINOR = 0
PATCH = 0
SONAME = ${NAME}.${MAJOR}
TARGET = ${SONAME}.${MINOR}.${PATCH}

all: ${TARGET}


${TARGET}: hello.o
        $(CC) $(CFLAGS) $(CPPFLAGS) $(LDFLAGS) \
                -shared -fPIC -Wl,-soname,${SONAME} -o $@ $^
install:
        install -d ${DESTDIR}/usr/lib/
        install ${TARGET} ${DESTDIR}/usr/lib/
        ln -rs ${DESTDIR}/usr/lib/${TARGET} ${DESTDIR}/usr/lib/${SONAME}
        ln -rs ${DESTDIR}/usr/lib/${SONAME} ${DESTDIR}/usr/lib/${NAME}
clean:
        rm -f ${TARGET} *.o
```

In this Makefile, the only relevant part is the one regarding the soname field, and we have to spend a few words on it in order to well understand how it should be managed.

In UNIX and UNIX-like operating systems, within a shared library, the soname field of data is a string which is used as a *logical name* describing the functionality of the object. It has the purpose to provide a level of indirection.

Typically, soname is equal to the filename of the library. For example, in the libbz2.so.1 library file the soname is set as shown below:

```
$ file libbz2.so*
libbz2.so:      symbolic link to /lib/x86_64-linux-gnu/libbz2.so.1.0
libbz2.so.1:    symbolic link to libbz2.so.1.0.4
```

```
libbz2.so.1.0:    symbolic link to libbz2.so.1.0.4
libbz2.so.1.0.4: ELF 64-bit LSB shared object, x86-64, version 1 (SYSV)
, dynamically linked, BuildID[sha1]=e56b62c27bcc7ace8f9be36b255bd7b31bf
de405, stripped
$ objdump -p libbz2.so.1.0.4 | grep SONAME
  SONAME                libbz2.so.1.0
```

The soname is used at compilation time by the linker to determine from the library file what is the actual target library version, and it is often used to provide version backward-compatibility information. In the example above, the so-called *real name* of the library is libbz2.so.1.0.4, while the soname is libbz2.so.1.0, and the so-called *linker name* is libbz2.so. When a program is created and then linked with the option argument -lbz2, the linker detects that libbz2.so contains the soname libbz2.so.1.0 and embeds the latter name inside the executable. In fact, the program bzcat requests the library file libbz2.so.1.0:

```
$ ldd $(which bzcat)
        linux-vdso.so.1 (0x00007ffd0bf99000)
        libbz2.so.1.0 => /lib/x86_64-linux-gnu/libbz2.so.1.0 (0x00007f743
533b000)
        libc.so.6 => /lib/x86_64-linux-gnu/libc.so.6 (0x00007f7435112000)
        /lib64/ld-linux-x86-64.so.2 (0x00007f743537a000)
```

These versioning numbers for a library can be thought of as libfoo. so.MAJOR.MINOR.PATCH where

- PATCH is incremented for changes that are both forward and backward compatible with other versions, for example, fixes from previous releases without API change.

- MINOR should be incremented if the new version of the library is source and binary compatible with the old version. Different minor versions are backward compatible, but not necessarily forward compatible, with each other. In this case, the new code may just

add a new function or define and deprecate existing
functions, but may not remove anything that is
externally exposed.

- MAJOR is incremented when a change is introduced
  that breaks the API or is otherwise incompatible with
  the previous version. In the new code, constants may
  be removed or changed (deprecated), functions may
  be removed, and, of course, any changes that would
  normally increment the MINOR or PATCH number.

So, in the above example, if the libbz2.so.1.0.4 is replaced by the
libbz2.so.1.0.5, the soname remains to libbz2.so.1.0 and bzcat is still
functional.

To verify what we have just stated, we can use the code within the
example/lhello directory:

```
$ cat ../lhello/lhello.c
#include <hello.h>

int main(int argc, char *argv[])
{
        return hello();
}
```

where the Makefile is done as follows:

```
$ cat ../lhello/Makefile
TARGET = lhello
CFLAGS += -Wall -O2
LDLIBS = -lhello

all: ${TARGET}

${TARGET}: ${TARGET}.o

install:
        install -d ${DESTDIR}/usr/bin/
        install ${TARGET} ${DESTDIR}/usr/bin/

clean:
        rm -f ${TARGET} ${TARGET}.o
```

Now we should verify that everything works as expected on the host, then we can see how to do the same on the target. So let's compile the library and install it on a temporary directory on the host as follows:

```
$ make
cc -Wall -O2    -c -o hello.o hello.c
cc -Wall -O2    \
        -shared -fPIC -Wl,-soname,libhello.so.1 -o libhello.so.1.0.0 hell
o.o
$ make install DESTDIR=/tmp/libhello/
install -d /tmp/libhello//usr/lib/
install libhello.so.1.0.0 /tmp/libhello//usr/lib/
ln -rs /tmp/libhello//usr/lib/libhello.so.1.0.0 \
          /tmp/libhello//usr/lib/libhello.so.1
ln -rs /tmp/libhello//usr/lib/libhello.so.1 \
          /tmp/libhello//usr/lib/libhello.so
$ file /tmp/libhello/usr/lib/*
/tmp/libhello/usr/lib/libhello.so:      symbolic link to libhello.so.1
.0.0
/tmp/libhello/usr/lib/libhello.so.1:    symbolic link to libhello.so.1
.0.0
/tmp/libhello/usr/lib/libhello.so.1.0.0: ELF 64-bit LSB shared object,
x86-64, version 1 (SYSV), dynamically linked, BuildID[sha1]=88c412833b0
950755ad55872c69b956009439f69, not stripped
$ objdump -p /tmp/libhello/usr/lib/libhello.so.1.0.0 | grep SONAME
  SONAME                libhello.so.1
```

OK, now we can try to compile the application which requires our new library:

```
$ CFLAGS="-I ../hellolib/" LDFLAGS="-L /tmp/libhello/usr/lib/" make
cc -I ../hellolib/ -Wall -O2    -c -o lhello.o lhello.c
cc -L /tmp/libhello/usr/lib/  lhello.o  -lhello -o lhello
```

Note that to do it we have to supply proper directories to the compiler and then to the linker to find the two files hello.h and libhello.so. Now, if we check what the linker has done, we can see that it has honored the soname:

```
$ LD_LIBRARY_PATH=/tmp/libhello/usr/lib/ ldd lhello
        linux-vdso.so.1 (0x00007ffd3b86d000)
        libhello.so.1 => /tmp/libhello/usr/lib/libhello.so.1 (0x00007fe53
e51f000)
        libc.so.6 => /lib/x86_64-linux-gnu/libc.so.6 (0x00007fe53e2d8000)
        /lib64/ld-linux-x86-64.so.2 (0x00007fe53e52b000)
```

The LD_LIBRARY_PATH is needed in order to tell the dynamic linker where to find the file libhello.so.1. And, if we try to execute it, we get the following:

```
$ LD_LIBRARY_PATH=/tmp/libhello/usr/lib/ ./lhello
hello world!
```

Great! Now let's see how we can create a recipe for the Yocto Project in order to compile all this stuff for our embedded machine. We can use again recipetool, but now specifying a proper name libhello due to the fact that all libraries in the Yocto Project should be called with the lib prefix:

```
$ cd examples/hellolib
$ recipetool create -N libhello git://$(pwd)
NOTE: Starting bitbake server...
INFO: Fetching git:///home/giometti/yocto/examples/hellolib;branch=mast
er...
...
INFO: Recipe libhello_git.bb has been created; further editing may be r
equired to make it fully functional
```

We have already created a Git repository in the hellolib directory, as done above.

The resulting recipe has a do_install() task which is not correct for a library, so it must be rewritten as follows:

```
do_install () {
        install -m 0755 -d ${D}${libdir}
        oe_soinstall ${S}/libhello.so.1.0.0 ${D}${libdir}
        install -d ${D}${includedir}
        install -m 0755 ${S}/*.h ${D}${includedir}
}
```

where we used the oe_soinstall utility, which installs the library file and then creates all needed links (see Section 6.4.5).

To test our new recipe, we can do as usual by creating a proper entry within our custom layer as shown below:

```
$ mkdir $CY_METADIR/recipes-example/libhello
$ mv libhello_git.bb $CY_METADIR/recipes-example/libhello/
```

Then we can invoke bitbake as below:

```
$ bitbake libhello
```

If everything works well, new packages should be created:

```
$ cy-ipk find libhello
cy-ipk: searching in /home/giometti/yocto/imx-yocto-bsp/imx8mp-build...
tmp/deploy/ipk/armv8a/libhello-src_1.0+git0+ce5c28efa3-r0_armv8a.ipk
tmp/deploy/ipk/armv8a/libhello1_1.0+git0+ce5c28efa3-r0_armv8a.ipk
tmp/deploy/ipk/armv8a/libhello-dev_1.0+git0+ce5c28efa3-r0_armv8a.ipk
tmp/deploy/ipk/armv8a/libhello-dbg_1.0+git0+ce5c28efa3-r0_armv8a.ipk
```

All files needed for the program's executions are held in the libhello1_1.0+git0+ce5c28efa3-r0_armv8a.ipk package file:

```
$ cy-ipk inspect tmp/deploy/ipk/armv8a/libhello1_1.0+git0+ce5c28efa3-r0
_armv8a.ipk
drwxr-xr-x root/root              0 2024-02-19 17:09 ./usr/
drwxr-xr-x root/root              0 2024-02-19 17:09 ./usr/lib/
lrwxrwxrwx root/root              0 2024-02-19 17:09 ./usr/lib/libhello.so.1
-> libhello.so.1.0.0
-rwxr-xr-x root/root           5968 2024-02-19 17:09 ./usr/lib/libhello.so.1
.0.0
```

while files needed for the program's compilation are held in the libhello-dev_1.0+git0+ce5c28efa3-r0_armv8a.ipk package file:

```
$ cy-ipk inspect tmp/deploy/ipk/armv8a/libhello-dev_1.0+git0+ce5c28efa3
-r0_armv8a.ipk
drwxr-xr-x root/root              0 2024-02-19 17:09 ./usr/
drwxr-xr-x root/root              0 2024-02-19 17:09 ./usr/include/
-rw-r--r-- root/root             79 2024-02-19 17:09 ./usr/include/hello.h
drwxr-xr-x root/root              0 2024-02-19 17:09 ./usr/lib/
lrwxrwxrwx root/root              0 2024-02-19 17:09 ./usr/lib/libhello.so -
> libhello.so.1.0.0
```

Now we have to generate the recipe for the hello program that requires our library, so as before we can use recipetool:

```
$ cd ../lhello/
$ recipetool create git://$(pwd)
NOTE: Starting bitbake server...
INFO: Fetching git:///home/giometti/yocto/examples/lhello;branch=master
...
...
INFO: Recipe lhello_git.bb has been created; further editing may be req
uired to make it fully functional
```

Again, the Git repository has already been created within the examples/lhello directory.

Then we add the recipe to the Yocto build system as before:

```
$ mkdir $CY_METADIR/recipes-example/lhello
$ mv lhello_git.bb $CY_METADIR/recipes-example/lhello/
```

And we compile the code:

```
$ bitbake lhello
...
NOTE: Executing Tasks
ERROR: lhello-1.0+gitAUTOINC+9bcdf085b9-r0 do_compile: oe_runmake failed
ERROR: lhello-1.0+gitAUTOINC+9bcdf085b9-r0 do_compile: ExecutionError('
/home/giometti/yocto/imx-yocto-bsp/imx8mp-build/tmp/work/armv8a-poky-li
nux/lhello/1.0+gitAUTOINC+9bcdf085b9-r0/temp/run.do_compile.771536', 1,
 None, None)
ERROR: Logfile of failure stored in: /home/giometti/yocto/imx-yocto-bsp
/imx8mp-build/tmp/work/armv8a-poky-linux/lhello/1.0+gitAUTOINC+9bcdf085
b9-r0/temp/log.do_compile.771536
...
| lhello.c:1:10: fatal error: hello.h: No such file or directory
|     1 | #include <hello.h>
|       |          ^~~~~~~~~
| compilation terminated.
| make: *** [<builtin>: lhello.o] Error 1
| ERROR: oe_runmake failed
| WARNING: exit code 1 from a shell command.
...
```

Here is the demonstration that to compile the code which needs our `libhello` library, we also need the header files. The error is because we forgot to add to the `lhello_git.bb` the DEPENDS setting, as reported below:

```
--- a/lhello_git.bb
+++ b/lhello_git.bb
@@ -14,6 +14,8 @@

 SRC_URI = "git:///home/giometti/yocto/examples/lhello;branch=master"

+DEPENDS = "libhello"
+
 # Modify these as desired
 PV = "1.0+git${SRCPV}"
 SRCREV = "${AUTOREV}"
```

After recipe modification, the `bitbake` command should execute correctly, and the new packages are created as shown below:

```
$ cy-ipk find lhello
cy-ipk: searching in /home/giometti/yocto/imx-yocto-bsp/imx8mp-build...
tmp/deploy/ipk/armv8a/lhello-dev_1.0+git0+9bcdf085b9-r0_armv8a.ipk
tmp/deploy/ipk/armv8a/lhello-src_1.0+git0+9bcdf085b9-r0_armv8a.ipk
tmp/deploy/ipk/armv8a/lhello_1.0+git0+9bcdf085b9-r0_armv8a.ipk
tmp/deploy/ipk/armv8a/lhello-dbg_1.0+git0+9bcdf085b9-r0_armv8a.ipk
```

And the package with the executable is ready to be installed:

```
$ cy-ipk inspect tmp/deploy/ipk/armv8a/lhello_1.0+git0+9bcdf085b9-r0_ar
mv8a.ipk
drwxr-xr-x root/root          0 2024-02-19 17:54 ./usr/
drwxr-xr-x root/root          0 2024-02-19 17:54 ./usr/bin/
-rwxr-xr-x root/root       6112 2024-02-19 17:54 ./usr/bin/lhello
```

Note also the package description has the correct dependencies:

```
$ cy-ipk get-info tmp/deploy/ipk/armv8a/lhello_1.0+git0+9bcdf085b9-r0_a
rmv8a.ipk
Package: lhello
Version: 1.0+git0+9bcdf085b9-r0
Description: lhello version 1.0+gitAUTOINC+9bcdf085b9-r0
...
Depends: libc6 (>= 2.35), libhello1 (>= 1.0+git0+ce5c28efa3)
Source: lhello_git.bb
```

So let's move the package and its needed library on our embedded kit:

```
$ scp $BUILDDIR/tmp/deploy/ipk/armv8a/lhello_1.0+git0+9bcdf085b9-r0_arm
v8a.ipk \
      $BUILDDIR/tmp/deploy/ipk/armv8a/libhello1_1.0+git0+ce5c28efa3-r0_
armv8a.ipk \
      root@192.168.32.132:/tmp/
lhello_1.0+git0+9bcdf085b9-r0_armv8a.ipk       100% 2086   3.0MB/s    00:00
libhello1_1.0+git0+ce5c28efa3-r0_armv8a.ipk    100% 2048   3.2MB/s    00:00
```

And install them as usual:

```
# opkg install /tmp/lhello_1.0+git0+9bcdf085b9-r0_armv8a.ipk \
               /tmp/libhello1_1.0+git0+ce5c28efa3-r0_armv8a.ipk
Installing libhello1 (1.0+git0+ce5c28efa3) on root
Installing lhello (1.0+git0+9bcdf085b9) on root
Configuring libhello1.
Configuring lhello.
```

Now we can execute our new program with the related library:

```
# lhello
hello world!
```

As done in the previous section, before going further, we should remove all unnecessary comments and fix the package's information. A possible solution for the libhello package can be as below:

```
$ cat $CY_METADIR/recipes-example/libhello/libhello_git.bb
SUMMARY = "Yet another hello world library"
DESCRIPTION = "A simple example about how to write a recipe for a user
space C library."
MAINTAINER = "Rodolfo Giometti <giometti@enneenne.com>"
SECTION = "libs"
LICENSE = "MIT"
LIC_FILES_CHKSUM = "file://${COMMON_LICENSE_DIR}/MIT;md5=0835ade698e0bc
f8506ecda2f7b4f302"
...
```

while for the `hello` package, we can do as below:

```
$ cat $CY_METADIR/recipes-example/lhello/lhello_git.bb
SUMMARY = "Yet another hello world program"
DESCRIPTION = "A simple example about how to write a recipe for a user
space C program which requires an external library."
MAINTAINER = "Rodolfo Giometti <giometti@enneenne.com>"
SECTION = "examples"
LICENSE = "MIT"
LIC_FILES_CHKSUM = "file://${COMMON_LICENSE_DIR}/MIT;md5=0835ade698e0bc
f8506ecda2f7b4f302"
...
```

Now we have to regenerate the packages:

```
$ bitbake lhello
```

Note that we don't need to explicitly recompile `libhello` due to the fact that `hello` depends on it and `bitbake` will correctly rebuild both.

Now we get the following information for the `hello` package:

```
$ cy-ipk get-info tmp/deploy/ipk/armv8a/lhello_1.0+git0+9bcdf085b9-r0_a
rmv8a.ipk
Package: lhello
Version: 1.0+git0+9bcdf085b9-r0
Description: Yet another hello world program
 A simple example about how to write a recipe for a user space C progra
m which requires an external library.
Section: examples
Priority: optional
Maintainer: Rodolfo Giometti <giometti@enneenne.com>
License: MIT
Architecture: armv8a
OE: lhello
Depends: libc6 (>= 2.35), libhello1 (>= 1.0+git0+ce5c28efa3)
Source: lhello_git.bb
```

And below is the information for `libhello`:

```
$ cy-ipk get-info tmp/deploy/ipk/armv8a/libhello1_1.0+git0+ce5c28efa3-r
0_armv8a.ipk
```

```
Package: libhello1
Version: 1.0+git0+ce5c28efa3-r0
Description: Yet another hello world library
 A simple example about how to write a recipe for a user space C
 library.
Section: libs
Priority: optional
Maintainer: Rodolfo Giometti <giometti@enneenne.com>
License: MIT
Architecture: armv8a
OE: libhello
Depends: libc6 (>= 2.35)
Provides: libhello
Source: libhello_git.bb
```

Now both recipes are completed.

9.3 Multi-packages

In previous sections, we saw how to generate a single package for a C program and for a C library; however, it may happen that within a single recipe, we can find both of them and maybe some tools and/or testing programs as well. In this last case, we should be able to produce several packages for each kind of code present in the source repository. To make a good example of how to do it, a suitable candidate is the Log2cb project available at https://gitlab.com/giometti/log2cb (Figure 9-1 shows a screenshot of the main project's page).

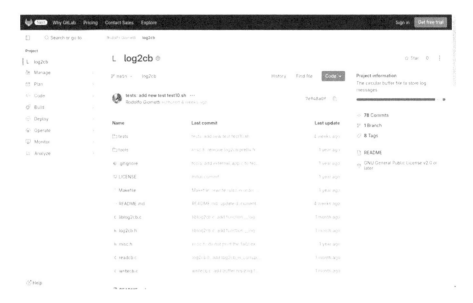

Figure 9-1. *The Log2cb home page*

This project implements a *basic circular buffer file* to store logging messages, and it has been specifically designed for embedded systems where saving (or being sure of a fixed amount of used) space for logging is crucial. Even if its main usage is with the syslog-ng daemon (see `https://github.com/syslog-ng/syslog-ng`), it exports some functions for C programs which want to define their own circular buffers. These functions are stored in a library with a well-defined API.

Before starting to write a proper recipe, it's better to understand how this project works, so we should first download the code on the host as reported on the main page at the Code menu (see Figure 9-2).

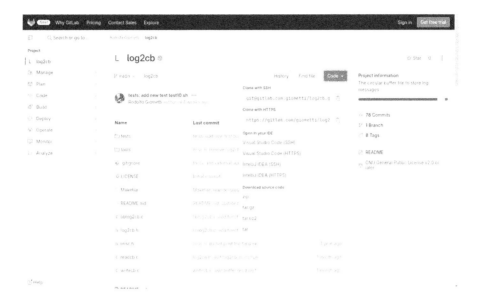

Figure 9-2. *How to download the Log2cb sources*

To clone the repository, we can use the suggested `git clone` command for HTTPS:

```
$ git clone https://gitlab.com/giometti/log2cb.git
Cloning into 'log2cb'...
remote: Enumerating objects: 327, done.
remote: Counting objects: 100% (327/327), done.
remote: Compressing objects: 100% (160/160), done.
remote: Total 327 (delta 216), reused 242 (delta 162), pack-reused 0
Receiving objects: 100% (327/327), 72.39 KiB | 36.19 MiB/s, done.
Resolving deltas: 100% (216/216), done.
```

Then we can go into the newly created directory `log2cb` and see what we have got:

```
$ cd log2cb/
$ ls
liblog2cb.c  log2cb.h  misc.h    README.md  tools
LICENSE      Makefile  readcb.c  tests      writecb.c
```

457

As we can read within the code or by reading the documentation file README.md, the file liblog2cb.c holds the library, while files readcb.c and writecb.c hold the basic programs to manage the circular buffer. Then in the tools directory, there are some utilities, and in tests there is a test suite composed of several Bash scripts.

When we compile the code on the host, we should get the following output:

```
$ make
gcc -c -O2 -Wall -D_GNU_SOURCE -D__VERSION=\"v1.5.0-0-g7e948a0f8c\" -MM
D       writecb.c \
        -o writecb.o
gcc -shared -fPIC -O2 -Wall -D_GNU_SOURCE -D__VERSION=\"v1.5.0-0-g7e948
a0f8c\" -MMD       liblog2cb.c -o liblog2cb.so
...
gcc -O2 -Wall -D_GNU_SOURCE -D__VERSION=\"v1.5.0-0-g7e948a0f8c\" -MMD
        tools/external_app.o -o tools/external_app  -L.  -llog2cb
```

Note that version numbers may vary. At the time of the writing of this book, the latest release is v1.5.0. So the readers may have to move to that release in order to be able to repeat all the above (and following) commands.

The generated library is named liblog2cb.so (which does not define the soname parameter as seen in Section 9.2), while the two main programs are named readcb and writecb, then the tools are named cbheader and external_app. The external_app, even if held within the tools directory, can be considered a testing program (curious readers can take a look at the code to verify it) so, in this scenario, it could be logic to generate four different packages: a library package named liblog2cb, a program package named log2cb holding readcb and writecb, a tool package named log2cb-tools holding cbheader, and finally a test package named log2cb-tests holding external_app. However, before doing it, we should be sure that our project can be compiled with the Yocto build system, then we can see how to get all the desired packages.

So, let's start by trying to download and compile it. To do so, we should take a look at stable releases; in fact, deciding to download the latest release is not always a good thing to do...

The available releases are reported in the Tags page, as shown in Figure 9-3.

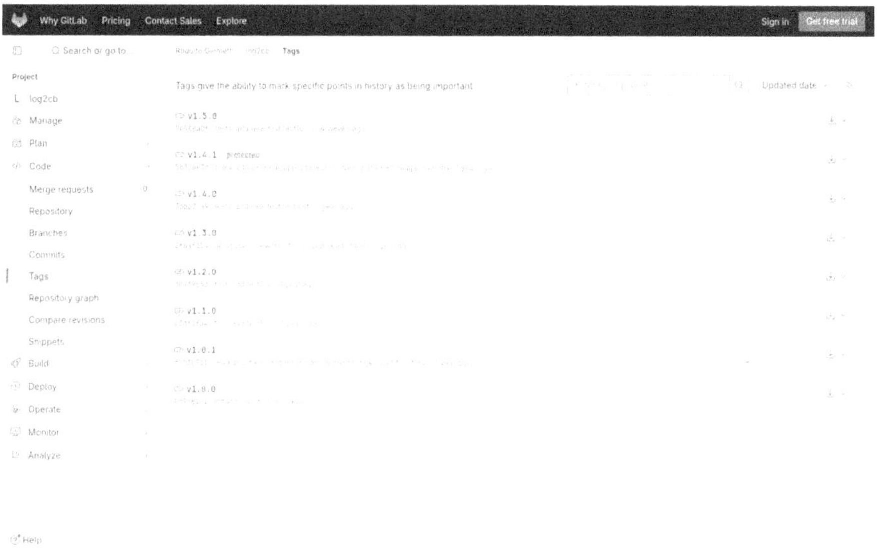

Figure 9-3. *Available Log2cb releases*

OK, we can use release v1.5.0, and to download and compile the code, this time we decide to use devtool by using the command line reported below:

```
$ devtool add --srcrev v1.5.0 --version 1.5.0 log2cb \
        "git://gitlab.com/giometti/log2cb.git;protocol=https"
NOTE: Starting bitbake server...
INFO: Fetching git://gitlab.com/giometti/log2cb.git;protocol=https;nobr
anch=1...
...
INFO: Using default source tree path /home/giometti/yocto/imx-yocto-bsp
/imx8mp-build/workspace/sources/log2cb
INFO: Using source tree as build directory since that would be the defa
ult for this recipe
```

```
INFO: Recipe /home/giometti/yocto/imx-yocto-bsp/imx8mp-build/workspace/
recipes/log2cb/log2cb_git.bb has been automatically created; further ed
iting may be required to make it fully functional
```

OK, the code is now under the workspace, and to see the newly generated recipe, we can use the edit-recipe subcommand as below:

```
$ devtool edit-recipe log2cb
```

The newly created recipe should look like this:

```
# Recipe created by recipetool
# This is the basis of a recipe and may need further editing in order to
# be fully functional.
# (Feel free to remove these comments when editing.)

# WARNING: the following LICENSE and LIC_FILES_CHKSUM values are best
# guesses - it is your responsibility to verify that the values are
# complete and correct.
LICENSE = "GPL-2.0-only"
LIC_FILES_CHKSUM = "file://LICENSE;md5=eb723b61539feef013de476e68b5c50a"

SRC_URI = "git://gitlab.com/giometti/log2cb.git;protocol=https;branch=m
ain"

# Modify these as desired
PV = "1.5.0+git${SRCPV}"
SRCREV = "v1.5.0"

S = "${WORKDIR}/git"


# NOTE: this is a Makefile-only piece of software, so we cannot generate
# much of the recipe automatically - you will need to examine the
# Makefile yourself and ensure that the appropriate arguments are passed
# in.

do_configure () {
        # Specify any needed configure commands here
        :
}

do_compile () {
        # You will almost certainly need to add additional arguments
        # here
        oe_runmake
}
```

```
do_install () {
        # NOTE: unable to determine what to put here - there is a
        # Makefile but no
        # target named "install", so you will need to define this
        # yourself
        :
}
```

First of all, we notice that the LICENSE file has been correctly guessed, so we can safely remove the comment above the variable in order to have the following listing:

```
...
# This is the basis of a recipe and may need further editing in order to
# be fully functional.
# (Feel free to remove these comments when editing.)

LICENSE = "GPL-2.0-only"
LIC_FILES_CHKSUM = "file://LICENSE;md5=eb723b61539feef013de476e68b5c50a"
...
```

Furthermore, we can safely remove the heading remarks about the fact that the recipe has been created by using recipetool, etc., and we can add the SUMMARY and DESCRIPTION variables, as below:

```
SUMMARY = "Basic circular buffer file manager log messages"
DESCRIPTION = "A basic circular buffer file creator and manager to store logging
messages for embedded systems. The goal is to limit the size of ever-growing log
to a maximum amount, losing in the process oldest entries if the amount is
exceeded."
HOMEPAGE = "https://gitlab.com/giometti/log2cb"

LICENSE = "GPL-2.0-only"
LIC_FILES_CHKSUM = "file://LICENSE;md5=eb723b61539feef013de476e68b5c50a"
...
```

Then we can drop the comments above and inside the basic compiling tasks to get a clean code:

```
...
S = "${WORKDIR}/git"

do_configure () {
        :
}
```

```
do_compile () {
        oe_runmake
}

do_install () {
        :
}
```

Since Log2cb doesn't need any configuration, the do_configure task can be left as is; also, the do_compile is correct since we just need to execute the make command to compile the code. What really needs a rework is the do_install() tasks, as reported below:

```
--- a/log2cb/log2cb_git.bb
+++ b/log2cb/log2cb_git.bb
@@ -31,7 +31,16 @@
 }

 do_install () {
-       :
+       # Install library files
+       install -m 0755 -d ${D}${libdir}
+       oe_soinstall ${S}/liblog2cb.so.1.5.0 ${D}${libdir}
+       install -d ${D}${includedir}
+       install -m 0755 ${S}/log2cb.h ${D}${includedir}
+
+       # Install programs files
+       install -d ${D}${bindir}
+       install readcb writecb ${D}${bindir}
+       install tools/cbheader tools/external_app ${D}${bindir}
 }
```

As the readers can see, we just used the installing code as done in previous sections for both programs and library files. Doing this, we assume that version 1.5.0 is generated in such a way that the major, minor, and patch values are assigned as for library versioning numbers according to the previous section. In this scenario, the library version could be set as 1.5.0, while the soname value can be set as 1.5.

> All these considerations should be properly done by the package maintainers, which have the task of verifying that everything is coherent. If not, they should resolve these issues eventually by proposing proper patches to the code author.
>
> For our example, we can assume that everything is correct, and we can go ahead as is.

OK, the above modifications may work, but having a fixed name for the generated library is not the best; what we would like to have is something configurable to be used for different releases. Simply speaking, we don't like having a fixed name as `liblog2cb.so.1.5.0`, so we can rework the code as below:

```
--- a/log2cb_git.bb
+++ b/log2cb_git.bb
@@ -8,8 +8,9 @@
 SRC_URI = "git://gitlab.com/giometti/log2cb.git;protocol=https;branch=
main"

 # Modify these as desired
-PV = "1.5.0+git${SRCPV}"
-SRCREV = "v1.5.0"
+LOG2CB_VERSION = "1.5.0"
+PV = "${LOG2CB_VERSION}+git${SRCPV}"
+SRCREV = "v${LOG2CB_VERSION}"

 S = "${WORKDIR}/git"


@@ -24,7 +25,7 @@
 do_install () {
     # Install library files
     install -m 0755 -d ${D}${libdir}
-    oe_soinstall ${S}/liblog2cb.so.1.5.0 ${D}${libdir}
+    oe_soinstall ${S}/liblog2cb.so.${LOG2CB_VERSION} ${D}${libdir}
     install -d ${D}${includedir}
     install -m 0755 ${S}/log2cb.h ${D}${includedir}
```

By doing so, we can simply properly set the new variable `LOG2CB_VERSION`, and a new release will be packaged!

Of course, still assuming that the VERSION numbers are always properly set by the author! But we may consider that it was true.

Now we are ready to try the code compilation; however, before continuing we have to rework the Makefile to fix the missing soname setting and other minor issues. The Makefile from the log2cb repository looks as below:

```
$ cat Makefile
TARGETS += writecb readcb
TARGETS += tools/cbheader
TARGETS += tools/external_app

# Set to n to generate statically linked files
DYNAMIC ?= y

# --------------------------------------------------------------------

all: $(TARGETS)

VERSION := $(shell git describe --tags --abbrev=10 \
                        --dirty --long --always 2> /dev/null || \
                            echo "v0.0.0")
CC := $(CROSS_COMPILE)gcc
AR := $(CROSS_COMPILE)ar
CFLAGS += -O2 -Wall -D_GNU_SOURCE -D__VERSION=\"$(VERSION)\"
CFLAGS += -MMD    # automatic .d dependency file generation
ifneq ($(DYNAMIC),y)
CFLAGS += -static
endif
# CFLAGS += -Werror

ifeq ($(DYNAMIC),y)
define lib_rules
$1: $(foreach n,$($(1)_LDLIBS),lib$n.so)
lib$(1).so: $($(1)_SOURCES)
        $(CC) -shared -fPIC $(CFLAGS) $($(1)_CFLAGS) $(CPPFLAGS) $($(1)_CPPFLAGS) \
                $($(1)_SOURCES) -o lib$(1).so \
                $(LDFLAGS) $($(1)_LDFLAGS) $(LDLIBS) $(foreach n,$($(1)_LDLIBS),-l$n)
-include $($(1)_SOURCES:%.c=%.d)
...
```

Firstly, we notice that it is better to force dynamic library generation, then a proper change could be

```
--- a/Makefile
+++ b/Makefile
@@ -3,7 +3,7 @@ TARGETS += tools/cbheader
 TARGETS += tools/external_app

 # Set to n to generate statically linked files
-DYNAMIC ?= y
+DYNAMIC = y

 # --------------------------------------------------------------------
```

Now is the best practice to create a commit to save and document the change:

```
$ git add Makefile
$ git commit -s -m "Makefile: force dynamic linked files"
[devtool a6441a0] Makefile: force dynamic linked files
 1 file changed, 1 insertion(+), 1 deletion(-)
```

Then, before making the changes to add the soname field, we should check how the VERSION variable is set, so we can do as reported below:

```
$ git describe --tags --abbrev=10 --dirty --long --always
devtool-base-1-ga6441a0487
```

Of course, this is not acceptable since we expected roughly 1.5.0. The easy way could be to replace the above command simply with the string 1.5.0, but, as done before, we like having something configurable, so we can notice the following:

```
$ git tag
devtool-base
v1.0.0
v1.0.1
v1.1.0
v1.2.0
v1.3.0
v1.4.0
v1.4.1
v1.5.0
```

And we can ask the git describe command to filter all tags in the form v*X*. *Y*. *Z*, as shown below:

```
$ git describe --tags --match 'v*' | cut -c2- | cut -d - -f 1
1.5.0
```

The git describe command is used to find the most recent tag that is reachable from a commit. See the man pages of the man git-describe command.

Then we can alter the Makefile as reported below:

```
--- a/Makefile
+++ b/Makefile
@@ -9,12 +9,12 @@ DYNAMIC = y

 all: $(TARGETS)

-VERSION := $(shell git describe --tags --abbrev=10 \
-                          --dirty --long --always 2> /dev/null || \
-                       echo "v0.0.0")
+VERSION := $(shell git describe --tags --match 'v*' | cut -c2- | cut -d
 - -f 1)
+SOVER   := $(shell echo $(VERSION) | cut -d '.' -f 1-2)
+
 CC := $(CROSS_COMPILE)gcc
 AR := $(CROSS_COMPILE)ar
-CFLAGS += -O2 -Wall -D_GNU_SOURCE -D__VERSION=\"$(VERSION)\"
+CFLAGS += -O2 -Wall -D_GNU_SOURCE -D__VERSION=\"v$(VERSION)\"
 CFLAGS += -MMD    # automatic .d dependency file generation
 ifneq ($(DYNAMIC),y)
 CFLAGS += -static
@@ -23,16 +23,19 @@ endif

 ifeq ($(DYNAMIC),y)
 define lib_rules
-$1: $(foreach n,$($(1)_LDLIBS),lib$n.so)
-lib$(1).so: $($(1)_SOURCES)
+$1: $(foreach n,$($(1)_LDLIBS),lib$n.so.$(VERSION))
+lib$(1).so.$(VERSION): $($(1)_SOURCES)
        $(CC) -shared -fPIC $(CFLAGS) $($(1)_CFLAGS) $(CPPFLAGS)
 $($(1)_CPPFLAGS) \
```

```
-                    $($(1)_SOURCES) -o lib$(1).so \
+                    -Wl,-soname,lib$(1).so.$(SOVER) \
+                    $($(1)_SOURCES) -o lib$(1).so.$(VERSION) \
                     $(LDFLAGS) $($(1)_LDFLAGS) $(LDLIBS) $(foreach n,$($(1)_
LDLIBS),-l$n)
+        ln -s lib$(1).so.$(VERSION) lib$(1).so
+        ln -s lib$(1).so.$(VERSION) lib$(1).so.$(SOVER)
 -include $($(1)_SOURCES:%.c=%.d)

-lib$(1).so_clean:
-        rm -rf lib$(1).so $($(1)_SOURCES:.c=.o) $($(1)_SOURCES:.c=.d)
-clean: lib$(1).so_clean
+lib$(1).so.$(VERSION)_clean:
+        rm -rf lib$(1).so* $($(1)_SOURCES:.c=.o) $($(1)_SOURCES:.c=.d)
+clean: lib$(1).so.$(VERSION)_clean
 endef
 else
 define lib_rules
@@ -49,7 +52,7 @@ endif

 define prog_rules
 ifeq ($(DYNAMIC),y)
-$1: $(foreach n,$($(1)_LDLIBS),lib$n.so)
+$1: $(foreach n,$($(1)_LDLIBS),lib$n.so.$(VERSION))
 else
 $1: $(foreach n,$($(1)_LDLIBS),lib$n.a)
 endif
```

This patch is quite complex, so the readers should carefully check the final result.

The above modifications first redefine VERSION as seen above, then deduce SOVER from it and replace all lib$n.so instances with the proper lib$n.so.$(VERSION). Finally, as we have seen in the previous section, it fixes __VERSION within the CFLAGS variable and creates proper links to lib$(1).so.$(VERSION) named lib$(1).so and lib$(1).so.$(SOVER).

As done before, now we should commit the changes:

```
$ git add Makefile
$ git commit -s -m "Makefile: add soname support for dynamic libraries"
[devtool 5efb495] Makefile: add soname support for dynamic libraries
 1 file changed, 14 insertions(+), 11 deletions(-)
```

OK, now we can try to compile the code:

```
$ devtool build log2cb
...
NOTE: log2cb: compiling from external source tree /home/giometti/yocto/
imx-yocto-bsp/imx8mp-build/workspace/sources/log2cb
ERROR: log2cb-1.5.0+git999-r0 do_populate_sysroot: Fatal errors occurre
d in subprocesses:
Command '['aarch64-poky-linux-strip', '--remove-section=.comment', '--r
emove-section=.note', '--strip-unneeded', '/home/giometti/yocto/imx-yoc
to-bsp/imx8mp-build/tmp/work/armv8a-poky-linux/log2cb/1.5.0+git999-r0/s
ysroot-destdir/usr/lib/liblog2cb.so.1.5.0']' returned non-zero exit sta
tus 1.
Subprocess output:aarch64-poky-linux-strip: Unable to recognise the for
mat of the input file `/home/giometti/yocto/imx-yocto-bsp/imx8mp-build/
tmp/work/armv8a-poky-linux/log2cb/1.5.0+git999-r0/sysroot-destdir/usr/l
ib/liblog2cb.so.1.5.0'
...
```

Something went wrong. In order to easily debug what happened, we
can try using devshell as below:

```
$ bitbake -c devshell log2cb
```

Within the devshell, we can try to recompile from a clean situation by
using the make clean command before the usual make:

```
$ make clean
rm -rf liblog2cb.so* liblog2cb.o liblog2cb.d
rm -rf writecb writecb.o writecb.d
rm -rf readcb readcb.o readcb.d
rm -rf tools/cbheader tools/cbheader.o tools/cbheader.d
rm -rf tools/external_app tools/external_app.o tools/external_app.d
$ make
gcc -c  -O2 -pipe -g -feliminate-unused-debug-types
...
```

The last make command didn't return an error, but we noticed
that the wrong compiler was used! In fact, make called gcc instead of
aarch64-poky-linux-gcc as stated within the CC variable in the current
environment:

```
$ echo $CC
aarch64-poky-linux-gcc -march=armv8-a+crc+crypto -fstack-protector-stro
ng -O2 -D_FORTIFY_SOURCE=2 -Wformat -Wformat-security -Werror=format-se
curity --sysroot=/home/giometti/yocto/imx-yocto-bsp/imx8mp-build/tmp/wo
rk/armv8a-poky-linux/log2cb/1.5.0+git999-r0/recipe-sysroot
```

As reported in Section 4.4, when we use `devshell` all compiling variables are correctly set in the environment to be able to compile the code for the target as we were on the target itself.

So the problem is here:

```
$ cat Makefile
...
CC := $(CROSS_COMPILE)gcc
AR := $(CROSS_COMPILE)ar
...
```

By using the `:=` operator, the environment CC variable is overwritten, so we have to make the following changes:

```
--- a/Makefile
+++ b/Makefile
@@ -12,8 +12,8 @@ all: $(TARGETS)
 VERSION := $(shell git describe --tags --match 'v*' | cut -c2- | cut -
d - -f 1)
 SOVER   := $(shell echo $(VERSION) | cut -d '.' -f 1-2)

-CC := $(CROSS_COMPILE)gcc
-AR := $(CROSS_COMPILE)ar
+CC ?= $(CROSS_COMPILE)gcc
+AR ?= $(CROSS_COMPILE)ar
 CFLAGS += -O2 -Wall -D_GNU_SOURCE -D__VERSION=\"v$(VERSION)\"
 CFLAGS += -MMD    # automatic .d dependency file generation
 ifneq ($(DYNAMIC),y)
```

469

Now if we retry to compile as done above, we should get the following:

```
$ make clean
...
$ make
aarch64-poky-linux-gcc  -march=armv8-a+crc+crypto -fstack-protector-str
ong  -O2
...
```

OK, now we can exit devshell and retry the compilation with devtool:

```
$ devtool build log2cb
...
NOTE: log2cb: compiling from external source tree /home/giometti/yocto/
imx-yocto-bsp/imx8mp-build/workspace/sources/log2cb
NOTE: Tasks Summary: Attempted 730 tasks of which 725 didn't need to be
 rerun and all succeeded.
```

Great! Now the compilation succeeded, and so we can commit this last changes too:

```
$ git add Makefile
$ git commit -s -m "Makefile: fix wrong CC and AR assignment"
[devtool 3985d1c] Makefile: fix wrong CC and AR assignment
 1 file changed, 2 insertions(+), 2 deletions(-)
```

OK, now it's time to verify the code running on our target. To do so, we can use the deploy-target subcommand:

```
$ devtool deploy-target -s log2cb root@192.168.32.132
...
./
./usr/
./usr/include/
./usr/include/log2cb.h
./usr/bin/
./usr/bin/external_app
./usr/bin/writecb
./usr/bin/readcb
./usr/lib/
./usr/lib/liblog2cb.so
./usr/lib/liblog2cb.so.1.5.0
./usr/lib/liblog2cb.so.1.5
INFO: Successfully deployed /home/giometti/yocto/imx-yocto-bsp/imx8mp-b
uild/tmp/work/armv8a-poky-linux/log2cb/1.5.0+git999-r0/image
```

Note that getting some warning messages as below is normal if the target's clock is not correctly set. So, we can safely ignore them:

```
tar: ./usr/include/log2cb.h: time stamp 2024-02-22 15:45:22 is 574
48605.422320375 s in the future
...
tar: ./usr/include: time stamp 2024-02-22 15:45:22 is 57448605.422
128125 s in the future
...
tar: ./usr/bin/external_app: time stamp 2024-02-22 15:45:22 is 574
48605.421556125 s in the future
...
```

Now we can try to execute the readcb command directly on the target:

```
# readcb -h
usage: readcb [-h | --help] [-v | --version] [-d | --debug]
              [-t | --print-time]
              [ -f ] [ --last | -l <n> ] <logfile>
```

It seems everything is OK, so we can remove this code from the target and go further in order to get different packages. To do so, let's use the undeploy-target subcommand to safely remove all code:

```
$ devtool undeploy-target -s log2cb root@192.168.32.132
NOTE: Starting bitbake server...
devtool_undeploy.sh                      100%  614    613.6KB/s   00:00
INFO: Successfully undeployed log2cb
```

Now we have a working recipe, so let's move it within our custom layer with the finish subcommand as reported below:

```
$ devtool finish log2cb $CY_METADIR/recipes-example/
NOTE: Starting bitbake server...
ERROR: Source tree is not clean:

?? liblog2cb.so.1.5
?? liblog2cb.so.1.5.0

Ensure you have committed your changes or use -f/--force if you are sure
there's nothing that needs to be committed
```

The above warning is because the Git repository is not clean; in fact, we have the following:

```
$ git status
On branch devtool
Untracked files:
  (use "git add <file>..." to include in what will be committed)
        liblog2cb.so.1.5
        liblog2cb.so.1.5.0

nothing added to commit but untracked files present (use "git add" to t
rack)
```

To solve the issue, we can clean the repository or follow the suggestion by devtool and then use the -f option argument. We decided to use this latter solution:

```
$ devtool finish -f log2cb $CY_METADIR/recipes-example/
NOTE: Starting bitbake server...
WARNING: Source tree is not clean, continuing as requested by -f/--force
...
INFO: Adding new patch 0001-Makefile-force-dynamic-linked-files.patch
INFO: Adding new patch 0002-Makefile-add-soname-support-for-dynamic-lib
raries.patch
INFO: Adding new patch 0003-Makefile-fix-wrong-CC-and-AR-assignment.pat
ch
INFO: Updating recipe log2cb_git.bb
INFO: Moving recipe file to /home/giometti/yocto/imx-yocto-bsp/sources/
meta-cy/recipes-example/log2cb
INFO: Leaving source tree /home/giometti/yocto/imx-yocto-bsp/imx8mp-bui
ld/workspace/sources/log2cb as-is; if you no longer need it then please
 delete it manually
```

Now within the meta-cy/recipes-example/log2cb directory, we should have the following status:

```
$ cd $CY_METADIR/recipes-example/log2cb
$ tree
.
├── log2cb
│   ├── 0001-Makefile-force-dynamic-linked-files.patch
│   ├── 0002-Makefile-add-soname-support-for-dynamic-libraries.patch
│   └── 0003-Makefile-fix-wrong-CC-and-AR-assignment.patch
└── log2cb_git.bb

1 directory, 4 files
```

Now, if we try to use `bitbake` to compile our new recipe, we get just one package as expected:

```
$ bitbake log2cb
...
$ cy-ipk find log2cb
cy-ipk: searching in /home/giometti/yocto/imx-yocto-bsp/imx8mp-build...
tmp/deploy/ipk/armv8a/log2cb-dbg_1.5.0+git0+7e948a0f8c-r0_armv8a.ipk
tmp/deploy/ipk/armv8a/log2cb-src_1.5.0+git0+7e948a0f8c-r0_armv8a.ipk
tmp/deploy/ipk/armv8a/log2cb_1.5.0+git0+7e948a0f8c-r0_armv8a.ipk
tmp/deploy/ipk/armv8a/log2cb-dev_1.5.0+git0+7e948a0f8c-r0_armv8a.ipk
```

And if we inspect the package's contents, we can see that it holds all installed files:

```
$ cy-ipk inspect tmp/deploy/ipk/armv8a/log2cb_1.5.0+git0+7e948a0f8c-r0_
armv8a.ipk
drwxr-xr-x root/root           0 2024-01-22 17:36 ./usr/
drwxr-xr-x root/root           0 2024-01-22 17:36 ./usr/bin/
-rwxr-xr-x root/root       14472 2024-01-22 17:36 ./usr/bin/cbheader
-rwxr-xr-x root/root       10376 2024-01-22 17:36 ./usr/bin/external_app
-rwxr-xr-x root/root       14496 2024-01-22 17:36 ./usr/bin/readcb
-rwxr-xr-x root/root       18688 2024-01-22 17:36 ./usr/bin/writecb
drwxr-xr-x root/root           0 2024-01-22 17:36 ./usr/lib/
lrwxrwxrwx root/root           0 2024-01-22 17:36 ./usr/lib/liblog2cb.so.
1.5 -> liblog2cb.so.1.5.0
-rwxr-xr-x root/root       22448 2024-01-22 17:36 ./usr/lib/liblog2cb.so.
1.5.0
```

However, at the beginning of this section, we said that we wish to get more packages, so let's see how we can split this package into all the desired packages: `liblog2cb`, `log2cb`, `log2cb-tools`, and `log2cb-tests`. To do so, we have to add these names to the `PACKAGES` variable as reported below:

```
PACKAGES += "lib${PN} ${PN}-tools ${PN}-tests"
```

Then we have to assign proper files to these packages by using the `FILES` variable as shown below:

```
FILES:${PN} = " \
    ${bindir}/readcb \
    ${bindir}/writecb \
"
```

```
FILES:lib${PN} = " \
    ${libdir}/liblog2cb.so* \
    ${includedir}/log2cb.h \
"

FILES:${PN}-tools = " \
    ${bindir}/cbheader \
"

FILES:${PN}-tests = " \
    ${bindir}/external_app \
"
```

All these modifications are temporary ones, so the readers should keep reading to have a definitive version they can also try on their machines.

Now, if we rebuild the recipe, we get the following:

```
$ bitbake log2cb
...
$ cy-ipk find '*log2cb'
cy-ipk: searching in /home/giometti/yocto/imx-yocto-bsp/imx8mp-build...
tmp/deploy/ipk/armv8a/log2cb-dbg_1.5.0+git0+7e948a0f8c-r0_armv8a.ipk
tmp/deploy/ipk/armv8a/log2cb-src_1.5.0+git0+7e948a0f8c-r0_armv8a.ipk
tmp/deploy/ipk/armv8a/log2cb-tools_1.5.0+git0+7e948a0f8c-r0_armv8a.ipk
tmp/deploy/ipk/armv8a/liblog2cb1.5_1.5.0+git0+7e948a0f8c-r0_armv8a.ipk
tmp/deploy/ipk/armv8a/log2cb_1.5.0+git0+7e948a0f8c-r0_armv8a.ipk
tmp/deploy/ipk/armv8a/log2cb-dev_1.5.0+git0+7e948a0f8c-r0_armv8a.ipk
tmp/deploy/ipk/armv8a/log2cb-tests_1.5.0+git0+7e948a0f8c-r0_armv8a.ipk
```

Great! All expected packages are now available. And if we inspect some of them, we should see something as below:

```
$ cy-ipk inspect tmp/deploy/ipk/armv8a/liblog2cb1.5_1.5.0+git0+7e948a0f
8c-r0_armv8a.ipk
drwxr-xr-x root/root          0 2024-01-22 17:36 ./usr/
drwxr-xr-x root/root          0 2024-01-22 17:36 ./usr/lib/
lrwxrwxrwx root/root          0 2024-01-22 17:36 ./usr/lib/liblog2cb.so.
1.5 -> liblog2cb.so.1.5.0
-rwxr-xr-x root/root      22448 2024-01-22 17:36 ./usr/lib/liblog2cb.so.
1.5.0
```

```
$ cy-ipk inspect tmp/deploy/ipk/armv8a/log2cb_1.5.0+git0+7e948a0f8c-r0_
armv8a.ipk
drwxr-xr-x root/root          0 2024-01-22 17:36 ./usr/
drwxr-xr-x root/root          0 2024-01-22 17:36 ./usr/bin/
-rwxr-xr-x root/root      14496 2024-01-22 17:36 ./usr/bin/readcb
-rwxr-xr-x root/root      18688 2024-01-22 17:36 ./usr/bin/writecb
$ cy-ipk inspect tmp/deploy/ipk/armv8a/log2cb-tools_1.5.0+git0+7e948a0f
8c-r0_armv8a.ipk
drwxr-xr-x root/root          0 2024-01-22 17:36 ./usr/
drwxr-xr-x root/root          0 2024-01-22 17:36 ./usr/bin/
-rwxr-xr-x root/root      14472 2024-01-22 17:36 ./usr/bin/cbheader
$ cy-ipk inspect tmp/deploy/ipk/armv8a/log2cb-tests_1.5.0+git0+7e948a0f
8c-r0_armv8a.ipk
drwxr-xr-x root/root          0 2024-01-22 17:36 ./usr/
drwxr-xr-x root/root          0 2024-01-22 17:36 ./usr/bin/
-rwxr-xr-x root/root      10376 2024-01-22 17:36 ./usr/bin/external_app
```

which is precisely what we expected.

However, our job is not finished yet because if we read the information for the library package, we get

```
$ cy-ipk get-info tmp/deploy/ipk/armv8a/liblog2cb1.5_1.5.0+git0+7e948a0
f8c-r0_armv8a.ipk
Package: liblog2cb1.5
Version: 1.5.0+git0+7e948a0f8c-r0
Description: Basic circular buffer file manager log messages
 A basic circular buffer file creator and manager to store logging
 messages for embedded systems. The goal is to limit the size of
 ever-growing log to a maximum amount, loosing in the process oldest
 entries if the amount is exceeded.
Section: base
Priority: optional
Maintainer: NXP <lauren.post@nxp.com>
License: GPL-2.0-only
Architecture: armv8a
OE: log2cb
Homepage: https://gitlab.com/giometti/log2cb
Depends: libc6 (>= 2.35)
Provides: liblog2cb
Source: log2cb_git.bb
```

which are similar information to the ones from the tools package:

```
$ cy-ipk get-info tmp/deploy/ipk/armv8a/log2cb-tools_1.5.0+git0+7e948a0
f8c-r0_armv8a.ipk
Package: log2cb-tools
Version: 1.5.0+git0+7e948a0f8c-r0
Description: Basic circular buffer file manager log messages
 A basic circular buffer file creator and manager to store logging
 messages for embedded systems. The goal is to limit the size of
 ever-growing log to a maximum amount, loosing in the process oldest
 entries if the amount is exceeded.
Section: base
Priority: optional
Maintainer: NXP <lauren.post@nxp.com>
License: GPL-2.0-only
Architecture: armv8a
OE: log2cb
Homepage: https://gitlab.com/giometti/log2cb
Depends: libc6 (>= 2.35), liblog2cb1.5 (>= 1.5.0+git0+7e948a0f8c)
Source: log2cb_git.bb
```

Note that the Depends field in the above package has been correctly set by the Yocto build system; however, this is not always true. In this case, we have to properly set the DEPENDS or RDEPENDS variables (see below for an example).

This is odd, and it could be more correct if we consider setting the section libs for the library package and utils for the other to provide custom description for each package and, maybe, to fix the maintainer. Moreover, we would like the tools package depending on the log2cb one.

To do so, we can do the following modifications:

```
--- a/log2cb_git.bb
+++ b/log2cb_git.bb
@@ -1,6 +1,8 @@
 SUMMARY = "Basic circular buffer file manager log messages"
 DESCRIPTION = "A basic circular buffer file creator and manager to store logging
messages for embedded systems. The goal is to limit the size of ever-growing log
to a maximum amount, losing in the process oldest entries if the amount is
exceeded."
```

```
 HOMEPAGE = "https://gitlab.com/giometti/log2cb"
+MAINTAINER = "Rodolfo Giometti <giometti@enneenne.com>"
+SECTION = "utils"

 LICENSE = "GPL-2.0-only"
 LIC_FILES_CHKSUM = "file://LICENSE;md5=eb723b61539feef013de476e68b5c50
a"
@@ -11,6 +13,8 @@
             file://0003-Makefile-fix-wrong-CC-and-AR-assignment.patch \
             "

+PACKAGES += "lib${PN} ${PN}-tools ${PN}-tests"
+
 # Modify these as desired
 LOG2CB_VERSION = "1.5.0"
 PV = "${LOG2CB_VERSION}+git${SRCPV}"
@@ -39,3 +43,25 @@
         install tools/cbheader tools/external_app ${D}${bindir}
 }

+FILES:${PN} = " \
+    ${bindir}/readcb \
+    ${bindir}/writecb \
+"
+
+FILES:lib${PN} = " \
+    ${libdir}/liblog2cb.so* \
+    ${includedir}/log2cb.h \
+"
+SUMMARY:lib${PN} = "Libraries for basic circular buffer file manager l
og messages"
+SECTION:lib${PN} = "libs"
+
+FILES:${PN}-tools = " \
+    ${bindir}/cbheader \
+"
+SUMMARY:${PN}-tools = "Tools for basic circular buffer file manager lo
g messages"
+RDEPENDS:${PN}-tools = "${PN}"
+
+FILES:${PN}-tests = " \
+    ${bindir}/external_app \
+"
+SUMMARY:${PN}-tools = "Tests for basic circular buffer file manager lo
g messages"
```

In these modifications, we added the MAINTAINER and SECTION variables as default for each package, then at the end of the recipe we added the FILES variables for each package by overrides. In the same manner, that is, by overriding, we also redefine the SUMMARY and SECTION variables properly for each package.

Now, if we reread the package's information as before, we get the following output:

```
$ cy-ipk get-info tmp/deploy/ipk/armv8a/liblog2cb1.5_1.5.0+git0+7e948a0
f8c-r0_armv8a.ipk
Package: liblog2cb1.5
Version: 1.5.0+git0+7e948a0f8c-r0
Description: Libraries for basic circular buffer file manager log messages
 A basic circular buffer file creator and manager to store logging
 messages for embedded systems. The goal is to limit the size of ever-
 growing log to a maximum amount, losing in the process oldest entries
 if the amount is exceeded.
Section: libs
Priority: optional
Maintainer: Rodolfo Giometti <giometti@enneenne.com>
License: GPL-2.0-only
Architecture: armv8a
OE: log2cb
Homepage: https://gitlab.com/giometti/log2cb
Depends: libc6 (>= 2.35)
Provides: liblog2cb
Source: log2cb_git.bb
```

The library package now has its description and proper section, while the tools package looks like below:

```
$ cy-ipk get-info tmp/deploy/ipk/armv8a/log2cb-tools_1.5.0+git0+7e948a0
f8c-r0_armv8a.ipk
Package: log2cb-tools
Version: 1.5.0+git0+7e948a0f8c-r0
Description: Tests for basic circular buffer file manager log messages
 A basic circular buffer file creator and manager to store logging
 messages for embedded systems. The goal is to limit the size of ever-
 growing log to a maximum amount, losing in the process oldest entries
 if the amount is exceeded.
Section: utils
Priority: optional
Maintainer: Rodolfo Giometti <giometti@enneenne.com>
```

```
License: GPL-2.0-only
Architecture: armv8a
OE: log2cb
Homepage: https://gitlab.com/giometti/log2cb
Depends: libc6 (>= 2.35), liblog2cb1.5 (>= 1.5.0+git0+7e948a0f8c), log2
cb
Source: log2cb_git.bb
```

Package `log2cb-tools` now depends on the library package, as before, but also on the `log2cb` package, which is what we expected.

9.4 External Dependencies

In previous sections, we have seen how to create recipes for packages which need a library (or other similar code) to work. But what can we do if the project we wish to compile needs some code which is not provided by us, or it is within the project itself?

In order to make an example of how to generate a recipe for a software which depends on another software (in our example, a library) which is not provided in the project, we can consider what is available at `https://github.com/giometti/umrp`.

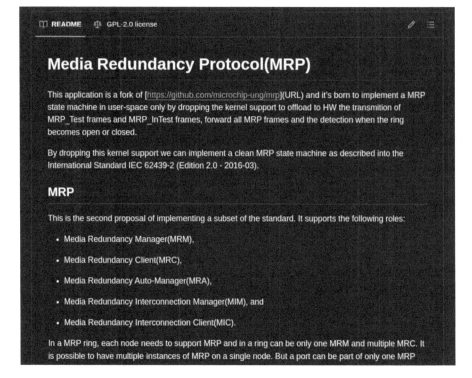

Figure 9-4. *The user space MRP protocol implementation home page*

This project implements a Media Redundancy Protocol (MRP) state machine (see `https://en.wikipedia.org/wiki/Media_Redundancy_ Protocol` for further information about the protocol) as described in the International Standard IEC 62439-2, where all code runs in user space only. MRP allows rings of Ethernet switches to overcome any single failure with recovery time much faster, and especially in a more reliable manner, than achievable with other more common protocols, such as the Spanning Tree Protocol (STP). For these reasons, the MRP is suitable for most industrial Ethernet applications with real-time needs.

As a first step, we can start by adding the sources to our workspace with the devtool add command as shown below:

```
$ devtool add umrp https://github.com/giometti/umrp
...
INFO: Fetching git://github.com/giometti/umrp;protocol=https;branch=mas
ter...
...
NOTE: Tasks Summary: Attempted 2 tasks of which 0 didn't need to be rer
un and all succeeded.
INFO: Using default source tree path /home/giometti/yocto/imx-yocto-bsp
/imx8mp-build/workspace/sources/umrp
INFO: Recipe /home/giometti/yocto/imx-yocto-bsp/imx8mp-build/workspace/
recipes/umrp/umrp_git.bb has been automatically created; further editin
g may be required to make it fully functional
```

Then, we should take a look at the auto-generated recipe by using the edit-recipe subcommand:

```
$ devtool edit-recipe umrp
```

We should get something as below:

```
# Recipe created by recipetool
# This is the basis of a recipe and may need further editing in order to
# be fully functional.
# (Feel free to remove these comments when editing.)

# WARNING: the following LICENSE and LIC_FILES_CHKSUM values are best
# guesses - it is your responsibility to verify that the values are
# complete and correct.
LICENSE = "GPL-2.0-only"
LIC_FILES_CHKSUM = "file://LICENSE;md5=b234ee4d69f5fce4486a80fdaf4a4263"

SRC_URI = "git://github.com/giometti/umrp;protocol=https;branch=master"

# Modify these as desired
PV = "1.0+git${SRCPV}"
SRCREV = "fb193eac1a2df51fe42e19d4ea36bb0157bda09f"

S = "${WORKDIR}/git"
```

```
# NOTE: unable to map the following CMake package dependencies: DBus1
# NOTE: the following library dependencies are unknown, ignoring: ev
# cfm_netlink nl-genl nl
#        (this is based on recipes that have previously been built and packaged)
DEPENDS = "libnl libmnl"

inherit cmake

# Specify any options you want to pass to cmake using EXTRA_OECMAKE:
EXTRA_OECMAKE = ""
```

Note that devtool has detected that this project must be compiled by
using cmake, so it added the inherit cmake statement (to load the cmake
class) and proposed the EXTRA_OECMAKE variable we can use to pass extra
arguments to cmake (refer to Sections 6.4.3 and 6.4.4).

As a first step, we should drop all comments and add proper
description variables as in the following example:

```
SUMMARY = "User space implementation of MRP state machine"
DESCRIPTION = "A user space implementation of the Media Redundancy Protocol
(MRP) state machine as described into the International Standard IEC 62439-2."
MAINTAINER = "Rodolfo Giometti <giometti@enneenne.com>"
SECTION = "net"
LICENSE = "GPL-2.0-only"
LIC_FILES_CHKSUM = "file://LICENSE;md5=b234ee4d69f5fce4486a80fdaf4a4263"
```

The remaining part of the recipe can be left as is, then we can try
to compile the project by executing the devtool build subcommand
as below:

```
$ devtool build umrp
NOTE: Starting bitbake server...
...
NOTE: Executing Tasks
ERROR: umrp-1.0+git999-r0 do_configure: ExecutionError('/home/giometti/
yocto/imx-yocto-bsp/imx8mp-build/tmp/work/armv8a-poky-linux/umrp/1.0+gi
t999-r0/temp/run.do_configure.70537', 1, None, None)
...
| CMake Error at CMakeLists.txt:50 (message):
|   Could not find libev.
|
|
```

```
| -- Configuring incomplete, errors occurred!
| See also "/home/giometti/yocto/imx-yocto-bsp/imx8mp-build/tmp/work/ar
mv8a-poky-linux/umrp/1.0+git999-r0/umrp-1.0+git999/CMakeFiles/CMakeOutp
ut.log".
...
Summary: There was 1 ERROR message, returning a non-zero exit code.
```

This error is quite obvious since if we read carefully the README.adoc
file in the project's repository, we should see the following statement:

```
$ cat workspace/sources/umrp/README.adoc
...
## Dependencies

It depends on the following libs 'libnl', 'libev', 'libmnl' and
'libcfm' and on a kernel that has MRP support (at least v5.8). This last
...
```

while devtool has set only the following dependencies:

```
DEPENDS = "libnl libmnl"
```

So the libev dependency has not been detected when the recipe
has been generated, and the build system has reported the missing
dependency. To solve this problem, we can try to search for this library
within the Yocto build system as shown below:

```
$ bitbake-layers show-recipes libev
...
=== Matching recipes: ===
libev:
  meta-oe               4.33
```

Great! So let's add libev in the dependencies list by setting DEPENDS as
reported below:

```
DEPENDS = "libnl libmnl libev"
```

Now, if we execute again the build command, we should see that the system is now downloading the `libev` library. However, we are still not lucky, and another error arises:

```
...
| CMake Error at CMakeLists.txt:61 (message):
|   Could not find libcfm_netlink.
|
|
| -- Configuring incomplete, errors occurred!
| See also "/home/giometti/yocto/imx-yocto-bsp/imx8mp-build/tmp/work/ar
mv8a-poky-linux/umrp/1.0+git999-r0/umrp-1.0+git999/CMakeFiles/CMakeOutp
ut.log".
...
Summary: There was 1 ERROR message, returning a non-zero exit code.
```

The problem now is the missing of the library named `libcfm_netlink`, so we can try to do the same as above by trying to search the library within the build system:

```
$ bitbake-layers show-recipes libcfm-netlink
NOTE: Starting bitbake server...
Loading cache: 100% |################################| Time: 0:00:00
Loaded 4759 entries from dependency cache.
Parsing recipes: 100% |################################| Time: 0:00:01
Parsing of 3216 .bb files complete (3211 cached, 5 parsed). 4764 target
s, 295 skipped, 3 masked, 0 errors.
```

Note that we used the name `libcfm-netlink` instead of `libcfm_netlink` as suggested in the error message because underscore characters are forbidden within the recipe's names.

This time, we got no available recipes. So we can read again into the `README.adoc` file, where we read the following information:

```
$ cat workspace/sources/umrp/README.adoc
...
CFM can be found here: https://github.com/microchip-ung/cfm
...
```

So we should try to add such a library package before continuing in compiling our main project. To do so, let's use again the `devtool add` command against the URL reported above:

```
$ devtool add libcfm-netlink https://github.com/microchip-ung/cfm
...
INFO: Fetching git://github.com/microchip-ung/cfm;protocol=https;branch
=master...
...
INFO: Recipe /home/giometti/yocto/imx-yocto-bsp/imx8mp-build/workspace/
recipes/libcfm-netlink/libcfm-netlink_git.bb has been automatically cre
ated; further editing may be required to make it fully functional
```

OK, now we can take a look at the new recipe with the `edit-recipe` subcommand as before:

```
$ devtool edit-recipe libcfm-netlink
```

As per uMRP, we drop all comments and just add description variables to get the final version of the recipe as below:

```
SUMMARY = "Implementation of Connectivity Fault Management protocol"
DESCRIPTION = "A user space implementation of the Connectivity Fault Management
(CFM) protocol as defined in 802.1Q section 12.14."
MAINTAINER = "Rodolfo Giometti <giometti@enneenne.com>"
SECTION = "libs/network"
LICENSE = "GPL-2.0-only"
LIC_FILES_CHKSUM = "file://LICENSE;md5=b234ee4d69f5fce4486a80fdaf4a4263"

SRC_URI = "git://github.com/microchip-ung/cfm;protocol=https;branch=mas
ter"

PV = "1.0+git${SRCPV}"
SRCREV = "2b431096fc280fab8cc5c4d636b09be217eb9965"

S = "${WORKDIR}/git"

DEPENDS = "libev libmnl libnl"

inherit cmake

EXTRA_OECMAKE = ""
```

Now we feel lucky and then we try to build it:

```
$ devtool build libcfm-netlink
...
NOTE: libcfm-netlink: compiling from external source tree /home/giomett
i/yocto/imx-yocto-bsp/imx8mp-build/workspace/sources/libcfm-netlink
NOTE: Tasks Summary: Attempted 796 tasks of which 787 didn't need to be
 rerun and all succeeded.
```

Great! Everything went well, so we can come back to the umrp program
and update the DEPENDS variable as below:

```
DEPENDS = "libnl libmnl libev libcfm-netlink"
```

Then we can retry to compile the uMRP sources again:

```
$ devtool build umrp
...
NOTE: Executing Tasks
NOTE: libcfm-netlink: compiling from external source tree /home/giomett
i/yocto/imx-yocto-bsp/imx8mp-build/workspace/sources/libcfm-netlink
NOTE: umrp: compiling from external source tree /home/giometti/yocto/im
x-yocto-bsp/imx8mp-build/workspace/sources/umrp
NOTE: Tasks Summary: Attempted 805 tasks of which 793 didn't need to be
 rerun and all succeeded.
```

Great! Now our new uMRP daemon is ready. However, it's still not
enough for a complete usage; in fact, if we take a look at the project's
README.adoc file, we can read the following compilation instructions:

```
$ cat workspace/sources/umrp/README.adoc
...
### Enable DBus support

If you wish using DBus support to remotely signal a port state change, just add
the string -DMRP_HAVE_DBus1=ON to the cmake command line as below:


```
cmake -B build/ -S . -DMRP_HAVE_DBus1=ON
```

By default all Dbus messages are sent to the path /org/mrp/Event by the
interface org.mrp.Event, but you may alter these defaults by using a command
line as below:
```

```
```
cmake -B build/ -S . -DMRP_HAVE_DBus1=ON -DMRP_DBUS_PATH="/org/act/mrp" -
DMRP_DBUS_IFACE="org.act.mrp"
```
```

```
**Note:** to successfully compile the code you may need to install the DBus
library code (for instance on Debian based system you can use the command sudo
apt install libdbus-1-dev).
...
```

And, of course, we wish to enable the DBus support, so we must supply extra parameters to cmake. To do so, we should redefine the EXTRA_OECMAKE variable as below:

```
EXTRA_OECMAKE = "-DMRP_HAVE_DBus1=ON"
```

Then we can try to recompile the project:

```
$ devtool build umrp
...
| CMake Error at CMakeLists.txt:66 (find_package):
|   By not providing "FindDBus1.cmake" in CMAKE_MODULE_PATH this project
|   has asked CMake to find a package configuration file provided by
|   "DBus1", but CMake did not find one.
|
|   Could not find a package configuration file provided by "DBus1" with
|   any of the following names:
|
|     DBus1Config.cmake
|     dbus1-config.cmake
|
|   Add the installation prefix of "DBus1" to CMAKE_PREFIX_PATH or set
|   "DBus1_DIR" to a directory containing one of the above files.  If
|   "DBus1" provides a separate development package or SDK, be sure it
|   has been installed.
|
|
| -- Configuring incomplete, errors occurred!
...
```

Now bitbake is telling us that it cannot find the DBus1 package, which is, of course, related to the new setting for cmake. To try to resolve this issue, we can do as before and ask bitbake-layers:

```
$ bitbake-layers show-recipes '*dbus*'
...
=== Matching recipes: ===
dbus:
  meta                 1.14.0
dbus-broker:
  meta-oe              29
dbus-cxx:
  meta-oe              2.1.0
dbus-daemon-proxy:
  meta-oe              0.0.0+gitrAUTOINC+1226a0a137
dbus-glib:
  meta                 0.112
dbus-wait:
  meta                 0.1+gitAUTOINC+6cc6077a36
...
```

It's clear that we have to add dbus to DEPENDS as shown below:

```
DEPENDS = "libnl libmnl libev libcfm-netlink dbus"
```

OK, now let's try again the compilation:

```
$ devtool build umrp
...
| -- Could NOT find PkgConfig (missing: PKG_CONFIG_EXECUTABLE)
| CMake Error at /home/giometti/yocto/imx-yocto-bsp/imx8mp-build/tmp/wo
rk/armv8a-poky-linux/umrp/1.0+git999-r0/recipe-sysroot-native/usr/share
/c
make-3.22/Modules/FindPackageHandleStandardArgs.cmake:230 (message):
|   Could NOT find DBus1 (missing: DBus1_LIBRARY DBus1_ARCH_INCLUDE_DIR)
| Call Stack (most recent call first):
|   /home/giometti/yocto/imx-yocto-bsp/imx8mp-build/tmp/work/armv8a-pok
y-linux/umrp/1.0+git999-r0/recipe-sysroot-native/usr/share/cmake-3.22/M
odules/FindPackageHandleStandardArgs.cmake:594 (_FPHSA_FAILURE_MESSAGE)
|   /home/giometti/yocto/imx-yocto-bsp/imx8mp-build/tmp/work/armv8a-pok
y-linux/umrp/1.0+git999-r0/recipe-sysroot/usr/lib/cmake/DBus1/DBus1Conf
ig
.cmake:62 (find_package_handle_standard_args)
|   CMakeLists.txt:66 (find_package)
|
|
| -- Configuring incomplete, errors occurred!
...
```

No luck; however, this time the problem is clear: we need the PkgConfig support. The Yocto Project has a proper class to operate with PkgConfig, so we have to inherit it as shown below:

```
inherit pkgconfig cmake
```

In this manner, we ask to inherit both pkgconfig.bbclass and cmake. bbclass class files. Now the compilation finally works correctly:

```
$ devtool build umrp
...
NOTE: umrp: compiling from external source tree /home/giometti/yocto/i
mx-yocto-bsp/imx8mp-build/workspace/sources/umrp
NOTE: Tasks Summary: Attempted 1596 tasks of which 1589 didn't need to
 be rerun and all succeeded.
```

To recap all the changes made to the recipe for umrp, the final recipe in the workspace is reported below:

```
$ cat $BUILDDIR/workspace/recipes/umrp/umrp_git.bb
SUMMARY = "User space implementation of MRP state machine"
DESCRIPTION = "A user space implementation of the Media Redundancy Proto
col (MRP) state machine as described into the International Standard IEC
62439-2."
MAINTAINER = "Rodolfo Giometti <giometti@enneenne.com>"
SECTION = "net"
LICENSE = "GPL-2.0-only"
LIC_FILES_CHKSUM = "file://LICENSE;md5=b234ee4d69f5fce4486a80fdaf4a4263"

SRC_URI = "git://github.com/giometti/umrp;protocol=https;branch=master"

PV = "1.0+git${SRCPV}"
SRCREV = "fb193eac1a2df51fe42e19d4ea36bb0157bda09f"

S = "${WORKDIR}/git"

DEPENDS = "libnl libmnl libev libcfm-netlink dbus"

inherit pkgconfig cmake

EXTRA_OECMAKE = "-DMRP_HAVE_DBus1=ON"
```

while for the imported library `libcfm-netlink`, we have the following code:

```
$ cat $BUILDDIR/workspace/recipes/libcfm-netlink/libcfm-netlink_git.bb
SUMMARY = "Implementation of Connectivity Fault Management protocol"
DESCRIPTION = "A user space implementation of the Connectivity Fault
Management (CFM) protocol as defined in 802.1Q section 12.14."
MAINTAINER = "Rodolfo Giometti <giometti@enneenne.com>"
SECTION = "libs/network"
LICENSE = "GPL-2.0-only"
LIC_FILES_CHKSUM = "file://LICENSE;md5=b234ee4d69f5fce4486a80fdaf4a4263"

SRC_URI = "git://github.com/microchip-ung/cfm;protocol=https;branch=mas
ter"

PV = "1.0+git${SRCPV}"
SRCREV = "2b431096fc280fab8cc5c4d636b09be217eb9965"

S = "${WORKDIR}/git"


DEPENDS = "libev libmnl libnl"


inherit cmake


EXTRA_OECMAKE = ""
```

Now we can try our new MRP daemon with `devtool` by using the `deploy-target` subcommand; however, we prefer to generate the IPKG files and then install them on the embedded machine. So let's create the recipes for `libcfm-netlink` and `umrp` projects:

```
$ mkdir $CY_METADIR/recipes-networking/
$ devtool finish -f libcfm-netlink $CY_METADIR/recipes-networking
...
INFO: Updating SRCREV in recipe libcfm-netlink_git.bb
INFO: Moving recipe file to /home/giometti/yocto/imx-yocto-bsp/sources/
meta-cy/recipes-networking/libcfm-netlink
INFO: Leaving source tree /home/giometti/yocto/imx-yocto-bsp/imx8mp-bui
ld/workspace/sources/libcfm-netlink as-is; if you no longer need it the
n please delete it manually
$ rm -rf $BUILDDIR/workspace/sources/libcfm-netlink
```

Note that we have to execute a `mkdir` command to create the `recipes-networking` directory under our meta layer. We used the `-f` option argument to force the `finish` subcommand to execute because we got a warning:

```
ERROR: Source tree is not clean:

 M cfm_server.c
 M include/uapi/linux/cfm_bridge.h

Ensure you have committed your changes or use -f/--force if you ar
e sure there's nothing that needs to be committed
```

And those modifications are because

```
$ git -C $BUILDDIR/workspace/sources/libcfm-netlinkdiff
diff --git a/cfm_server.c b/cfm_server.c
old mode 100755
new mode 100644
diff --git a/include/uapi/linux/cfm_bridge.h b/include/uapi/linux/
cfm_bridge.h
old mode 100755
new mode 100644
```

And they can be safely dropped.

```
$ devtool finish umrp $CY_METADIR/recipes-networking/
...
INFO: Updating SRCREV in recipe umrp_git.bb
INFO: Moving recipe file to /home/giometti/yocto/imx-yocto-bsp/sources/
meta-cy/recipes-networking/umrp
INFO: Leaving source tree /home/giometti/yocto/imx-yocto-bsp/imx8mp-bui
ld/workspace/sources/umrp as-is; if you no longer need it then please d
elete it manually
$ rm -rf $BUILDDIR/imx8mp-build/workspace/sources/umrp
```

Now we can generate the IPKG files by simply doing

```
$ bitbake umrp
```

During the compilation, the readers should notice that packages for
libcfm-netlink are not built! In fact, by using cy-ipk we can verify that
only packages for umrp are present:

```
$ cy-ipk find umrp libcfm-netlink
cy-ipk: searching in /home/giometti/yocto/imx-yocto-bsp/imx8mp-build...
tmp/deploy/ipk/armv8a/umrp-dbg_1.0+git0+fb193eac1a-r0_armv8a.ipk
tmp/deploy/ipk/armv8a/umrp-dev_1.0+git0+fb193eac1a-r0_armv8a.ipk
tmp/deploy/ipk/armv8a/umrp-src_1.0+git0+fb193eac1a-r0_armv8a.ipk
tmp/deploy/ipk/armv8a/umrp_1.0+git0+fb193eac1a-r0_armv8a.ipk
```

This is a first demonstration of the difference between DEPENDS and
RDEPENDS; in fact, libcfm-netlink has been used to generate the umrp
package, but it is not needed for umrp installation on the root filesystem, so
no .ipk files have been generated. We can inspect the package information
to verify it:

```
$ cy-ipk get-info tmp/deploy/ipk/armv8a/umrp_1.0+git0+fb193eac1a-r0_arm
v8a.ipk
Package: umrp
Version: 1.0+git0+fb193eac1a-r0
Description: User space implementation of MRP state machine
 A user space implementation of the Media Redundancy Protocol (MRP)
 state machine as described into the International Standard IEC 62439-2.
Section: net
Priority: optional
Maintainer: Rodolfo Giometti <giometti@enneenne.com>
License: GPL-2.0-only
Architecture: armv8a
OE: umrp
Depends: libc6 (>= 2.35), libdbus-1-3 (>= 1.14.0), libev4 (>= 4.33), li
bmnl0 (>= 1.0.4)
Source: umrp_git.bb
```

However, in our example, we wish to state that libcfm-netlink is also
needed when we install umrp; to do so, we have to alter the umrp recipe as
shown below:

```
--- a/recipes-networking/umrp/umrp_git.bb
+++ b/recipes-networking/umrp/umrp_git.bb
@@ -13,6 +13,7 @@
 S = "${WORKDIR}/git"
```

```
DEPENDS = "libnl libmnl libev libcfm-netlink dbus"
+RDEPENDS:${PN} = "libev libcfm-netlink dbus"

inherit pkgconfig cmake
```

Note that we have also set dbus into RDEPENDS due to the fact that it is needed on the root filesystem too.

Now if we try to generate umrp with the command below, the libcfm-netlink packages are generated too:

```
$ bitbake umrp
```

In fact, now we have

```
$ cy-ipk find umrp libcfm-netlink
cy-ipk: searching in /home/develop/Projects-OLD/packt/Customizing_Yocto
/yocto/imx-yocto-bsp/imx8mp-build...
tmp/deploy/ipk/armv8a/umrp-dbg_1.0+git0+fb193eac1a-r0_armv8a.ipk
tmp/deploy/ipk/armv8a/umrp-dev_1.0+git0+fb193eac1a-r0_armv8a.ipk
tmp/deploy/ipk/armv8a/umrp-src_1.0+git0+fb193eac1a-r0_armv8a.ipk
tmp/deploy/ipk/armv8a/umrp_1.0+git0+fb193eac1a-r0_armv8a.ipk
tmp/deploy/ipk/armv8a/libcfm-netlink-staticdev_1.0+git0+2b431096fc-r0_a
rmv8a.ipk
tmp/deploy/ipk/armv8a/libcfm-netlink-dev_1.0+git0+2b431096fc-r0_armv8a.
ipk
tmp/deploy/ipk/armv8a/libcfm-netlink_1.0+git0+2b431096fc-r0_armv8a.ipk
tmp/deploy/ipk/armv8a/libcfm-netlink-dbg_1.0+git0+2b431096fc-r0_armv8a.
ipk
tmp/deploy/ipk/armv8a/libcfm-netlink-src_1.0+git0+2b431096fc-r0_armv8a.
ipk
```

And if we inspect the umrp package's information, now we get

```
$ cy-ipk get-info tmp/deploy/ipk/armv8a/umrp_1.0+git0+fb193eac1a-r0_arm
v8a.ipk
Package: umrp
Version: 1.0+git0+fb193eac1a-r0
Description: User space implementation of MRP state machine
 A user space implementation of the Media Redundancy Protocol (MRP)
 state machine as described into the International Standard IEC 62439-2.
Section: net
Priority: optional
```

```
Maintainer: Rodolfo Giometti <giometti@enneenne.com>
License: GPL-2.0-only
Architecture: armv8a
OE: umrp
Depends: dbus, libc6 (>= 2.35), libcfm-netlink, libdbus-1-3 (>= 1.14.0)
, libev4 (>= 4.33), libmnl0 (>= 1.0.4)
Source: umrp_git.bb
```

OK, now we are ready to install umrp on the target machine, and we can move the .ipk file on the target with scp:

```
$ scp tmp/deploy/ipk/armv8a/umrp_1.0+git0+fb193eac1a-r0_armv8a.ipk \
     root@192.168.32.132:/tmp/
```

So let's install it on our target machine:

```
# opkg install /tmp/umrp_1.0+git0+fb193eac1a-r0_armv8a.ipk
 * Solver encountered 1 problem(s):
 * Problem 1/1:
 *   - conflicting requests
 *   - nothing provides libcfm-netlink needed by umrp-1.0+git0+fb193eac1
a-r0.armv8a
 *
 * Solution 1:
 *   - do not ask to install umrp-1.0+git0+fb193eac1a-r0.armv8a
```

Perfect; as expected, we need the libcfm-netlink, so let's move the package in the target:

```
$ scp tmp/deploy/ipk/armv8a/libcfm-netlink_1.0+git0+2b431096fc-r0_armv8
a.ipk \
     root@192.168.32.132:/tmp/
```

And then install it:

```
# opkg install /tmp/libcfm-netlink_1.0+git0+2b431096fc-r0_armv8a.ipk
 * Solver encountered 1 problem(s):
 * Problem 1/1:
 *   - conflicting requests
 *   - nothing provides libev4 >= 4.33 needed by libcfm-netlink-1.0+git
0+2b431096fc-r0.armv8a
 *
 * Solution 1:
 *   - do not ask to install libcfm-netlink-1.0+git0+2b431096fc-r0.armv8a
```

OK, another dependency can be found below:

```
$ cy-ipk find libev4
cy-ipk: searching in /home/giometti/yocto/imx-yocto-bsp/imx8mp-build...
tmp/deploy/ipk/armv8a/libev4_4.33-r0_armv8a.ipk
```

The libev4 package is precisely what we are looking for, so let's move it on the target as usual:

```
$ scp tmp/deploy/ipk/armv8a/libev4_4.33-r0_armv8a.ipk \
    root@192.168.32.132:/tmp/
```

Now we can install everything as shown below:

```
# opkg install /tmp/libev4_4.33-r0_armv8a.ipk
Installing libev4 (4.33) on root
Configuring libev4.
# opkg install /tmp/libcfm-netlink_1.0+git0+2b431096fc-r0_armv8a.ipk
Installing libcfm-netlink (1.0+git0+2b431096fc) on root
Configuring libcfm-netlink.
# opkg install /tmp/umrp_1.0+git0+fb193eac1a-r0_armv8a.ipk
Installing umrp (1.0+git0+fb193eac1a) on root
Configuring umrp.
```

Now everything is in place.

Curious readers may try to execute the uMRP daemon, but they must properly configure the DBus to be able to execute the `mrp_server` program. These settings are out of the scope of this book, so we leave this job as an exercise.

9.5 Kernel Modules

Knowing how to produce recipes for user space applications is useful, since most applications are developed within this environment. However, in the embedded world, we may have to develop kernel applications for several reasons: we need new device drivers to support new hardware, new networking protocols (in kernel space), new filesystems support, etc.

Of course, we can implement all these things directly within the kernel sources, but a better and cleaner way to do so is also by using out-of-tree kernel modules. This solution is also useful when our main target is to create kernel code which should be compatible with many kernel releases or when we are not interested in having our code included in the vanilla kernel (i.e., the Linux repository). So we need to write a recipe for these objects.

Kernel modules are out of the scope of this book; however, we should spend a few words about what they are and how they look like, in order to be clear for the readers what we are talking about.

A kernel module is a piece of code that can be dynamically loaded within the kernel to add a new functionality to it (e.g., a new device driver or a networking communication protocol or whatever needs to be placed inside the kernel).

The readers should keep in mind that, once loaded, the kernel code within a module works in the same manner as it was in the kernel at the boot time. So, regarding the code execution, once loaded, our module is loaded it runs as it was loaded with the kernel at boot time.

Well, we can now add a new kernel module to our Yocto image by writing a simple kernel code, as shown below:

```
$ cat examples/khello/khello.c
#define pr_fmt(fmt) "%s:%s: " fmt, KBUILD_MODNAME, __func__
#include <linux/module.h>

static int __init khello_init(void)
{
        pr_info("khello loaded\n");
        return 0;
}

static void __exit khello_exit(void)
{
        pr_info("khello unloaded\n");
}
```

```
module_init(khello_init);
module_exit(khello_exit);

MODULE_LICENSE("GPL");
MODULE_AUTHOR("Rodolfo Giometti <giometti@enneenne.com>");
MODULE_DESCRIPTION("khello: example kernel module");
```

Even if the readers are not kernel developers, they can easily understand what we are going to do. The above example is usually the first kernel code; every book speaking about Linux programming usually presents as the first example, and without going deeper into the details, we can say that the main things to know here are as follows:

- With the module_init(), we specify the function to be executed in kernel space at module insertion.

- With the module_exit(), we specify the function to be executed in kernel space at module removal.

- The function pr_info() is equivalent to the printf() within the kernel.

- MODULE_LICENSE(), MODULE_AUTHOR(), and MODULE_ DESCRIPTION() are just used for description (their usage will be more clear below in this section).

Knowing that, it should be clear that once loaded our module should display the message khello loaded and, of course, the message khello unloaded when unloaded.

Before taking a look at the recipe, we should spend a few words about the Makefile needed to compile a kernel module, which is reported below:

```
$ cat examples/khello/Makefile
obj-m += khello.o
SRC := $(shell pwd)

all:
        $(MAKE) -C $(KERNEL_SRC) M=$(SRC) modules

modules_install:
        ${MAKE} -C $(KERNEL_SRC) M=$(SRC) modules_install
```

To get compiled, a kernel module must use a `Makefile` which defines the variable `obj-m` used to list all modules to be compiled and then at least two targets used to compile (`all`) and to install (`modules_install`) the new module. The trick here is calling `make` within the directory where kernel sources are held (addressed by the variable `KERNEL_SRC`) and passing to it the variable `M` pointing to the directory where our module resides. `KERNEL_SRC` is set by the Yocto building system, while `M` is computed by `make` at execution time.

Now we are ready to create our new recipe. Firstly, we need a git repository, so let's create it:

```
$ git init
Initialized empty Git repository in /home/giometti/yocto/examples/khell
o/.git/
$ git add .
$ git commit -s -m "Initial commit"
[master 57fe9a7] Initial commit
 Date: Fri Jan 12 17:33:26 2024 +0100
 2 files changed, 28 insertions(+)
 create mode 100644 Makefile
 create mode 100644 khello.c
```

Now we can use, for example, `recipetool` to create the recipe as shown below:

```
$ cd examples/khello/
$ recipetool create git://$(pwd)
NOTE: Starting bitbake server...
INFO: Fetching git:///home/giometti/yocto/examples/khello;branch=master
...
...
NOTE: Tasks Summary: Attempted 2 tasks of which 0 didn't need to be rer
un and all succeeded.
INFO: Recipe khello_git.bb has been created; further editing may be req
uired to make it fully functional
```

The new recipe looks like below (all comments have been removed):

```
$ cat khello_git.bb
LICENSE = "CLOSED"
LIC_FILES_CHKSUM = ""

SRC_URI = "git:///home/giometti/yocto/examples/khello;branch=master"
```

498

```
PV = "1.0+git${SRCPV}"
SRCREV = "57fe9a7f816aa34ba88a759812d188dd82dc0175"

S = "${WORKDIR}/git"
```

```
inherit module
```

What is fascinating here is the last line, that is, the `inherit module` statement. By using this statement, the recipe states that all needed rules to create a kernel module should be used from the module class (located within the file `module.bbclass` in the poky layer).

Now, to test if everything has been done correctly, we should move the recipe to our meta layer by creating a proper directory under `recipes-kernel` (yes, we know, it is just an example, but the recipe is kernel related, so we prefer to move it under this directory):

```
$ mkdir -p $CY_METADIR/recipes-kernel/khello/
$ mv khello_git.bb $CY_METADIR/recipes-kernel/khello/
```

Now, before trying to compile our new kernel module, we should add some information variables as shown below:

```
--- a/khello_git.bb
+++ b/khello_git.bb
@@ -1,5 +1,9 @@
-LICENSE = "CLOSED"
-LIC_FILES_CHKSUM = ""
+SUMMARY = "Yet another hello world kernel module"
+DESCRIPTION = "A simple example about how to write a recipe for a kern
el space C module."
+MAINTAINER = "Rodolfo Giometti <giometti@enneenne.com>"
+SECTION = "kernel"
+LICENSE = "GPL-2.0-only"
+LIC_FILES_CHKSUM = "file://${COMMON_LICENSE_DIR}/GPL-2.0-
only;md5=801f80980d171dd642561083
3a22dbe6"

 SRC_URI = "git:///home/giometti/yocto/examples/khello;branch=master"
```

Now we are ready to generate the module by using `bitbake` as shown below:

```
$ bitbake khello
```

If everything goes well, we should get the following packages:

```
$ cy-ipk find khello
cy-ipk: searching in /home/giometti/yocto/imx-yocto-bsp/imx8mp-build...
tmp/deploy/ipk/imx8mp_icore_cy/khello-dbg_1.0+git0+57fe9a7f81-r0_imx8mp
_icore_cy.ipk
tmp/deploy/ipk/imx8mp_icore_cy/khello_1.0+git0+57fe9a7f81-r0_imx8mp_ico
re_cy.ipk
tmp/deploy/ipk/imx8mp_icore_cy/khello-src_1.0+git0+57fe9a7f81-r0_imx8mp
_icore_cy.ipk
tmp/deploy/ipk/imx8mp_icore_cy/khello-dev_1.0+git0+57fe9a7f81-r0_imx8mp
_icore_cy.ipk
```

However, before moving anything to the target machine, we should try to inspect the package:

```
$ cy-ipk inspect tmp/deploy/ipk/imx8mp_icore_cy/khello_1.0+git0+57fe9a7
f81-r0_imx8mp_icore_cy.ipk
```

It's empty!? And, in order to understand what happens, let's read its package information:

```
$ cy-ipk get-info tmp/deploy/ipk/imx8mp_icore_cy/khello_1.0+git0+57fe9a
7f81-r0_imx8mp_icore_cy.ipk
Package: khello
Version: 1.0+git0+57fe9a7f81-r0
Description: Yet another hello world kernel module
 A simple example about how to write a recipe for a kernel space C
 module.
Section: kernel
Priority: optional
Maintainer: Rodolfo Giometti <giometti@enneenne.com>
License: GPL-2.0-only
Architecture: imx8mp_icore_cy
OE: khello
Depends: kernel-module-khello-5.15.71+gd1c9a311f7ef
Source: khello_git.bb
```

As we can note, our package depends on the package named kernel-module-khello which is where our module really resides. In fact, we have the following:

```
$ cy-ipk find kernel-modules
cy-ipk: searching in /home/giometti/yocto/imx-yocto-bsp/imx8mp-build...
tmp/deploy/ipk/imx8mp_icore_cy/kernel-modules_5.15.71+git0+d1c9a311f7-r0_
imx8mp_icore_cy.ipk
$ cy-ipk inspect tmp/deploy/ipk/imx8mp_icore_cy/kernel-module-khello-5.15
.71+gd1c9a311f7ef_1.0+git0+57fe9a7f81-r0_imx8mp_icore_cy.ipk
drwxr-xr-x root/root          0 2024-05-17 13:10 ./lib/
drwxr-xr-x root/root          0 2024-05-17 13:10 ./lib/modules/
drwxr-xr-x root/root          0 2024-05-17 13:10 ./lib/modules/5.15.71+gd1
c9a311f7ef/
drwxr-xr-x root/root          0 2024-05-17 13:10 ./lib/modules/5.15.71+gd1
c9a311f7ef/extra/
-rw-r--r-- root/root       4480 2024-05-17 13:10 ./lib/modules/5.15.71+gd1
c9a311f7ef/extra/khello.ko
```

This is because the Yocto build system names all kernel module packages by prepending the kernel-module- prefix; however, we can refer to our code by simply using its name, which in turn depends on the package that really holds the module. So, in our example, we can refer to the khello package, for example, in the image recipes, and automatically the kernel-module-khello package will also be installed.

So, now we can move our kernel module to the target machine for testing:

```
$ scp /tmp/deploy/ipk/imx8mp_icore_cy/kernel-module-khello-5.15.71+gd1c
9a311f7ef_1.0+git0+57fe9a7f81-r0_imx8mp_icore_cy.ipk \
      root@192.168.32.132:/tmp/
```

On the target, we should be sure that all kernel messages will be shown on the serial console, so let's use the next command to enable all kernel messages on our embedded kit:

```
# echo 8 > /proc/sys/kernel/printk
```

Note that if we execute this command on an SSH connection, we get
nothing! We must use the serial console to see kernel messages at
runtime or use the dmesg command.

Then we can install the new package:

```
# opkg install /tmp/kernel-module-khello-5.15.71+gd1c9a311f7ef_1.0+git0
+57fe9a7f81-r0_imx8mp_icore_cy.ipk
Installing kernel-module-khello-5.15.71+gd1c9a311f7ef (1.0+git0+57fe9a7
f81) on root
Configuring kernel-module-khello-5.15.71+gd1c9a311f7ef.
```

OK, now we are to load the module within the kernel:

```
# modprobe khello
[ 2863.982403] khello: loading out-of-tree module taints kernel.
[ 2863.989410] khello:khello_init: khello loaded
```

The message loading out-of-tree module taints kernel
is just a warning for kernel developers to indicate that the kernel has
been tainted by some mechanism (in this case, by an out-of-tree
module). In this case, when we try to ask for any help, they may not
wish to support us.

Great, the module has been loaded. To unload it, we can just use the
modprobe command again:

```
# modprobe -r khello
[ 2871.846010] khello:khello_exit: khello unloaded
```

9.6 Summary

In this chapter, we have seen how to create new recipes for several C-based projects. We have seen how to manage user space programs with their libraries and how to write recipes that produce different packages in order to better categorize the software. Furthermore, at the end, we have seen how we can manage a kernel module (even if elementary).

Now it's time to move on to the next chapter, where we can see how we can manage Python-based packages.

CHAPTER 10

Python Application Recipes

In the embedded world, the C language is (maybe) the predominant programming language; however, the Python language is without doubt in the second position. So it could be useful to know how we can operate in the case we need to add Python code to our embedded system.

In this chapter, we are going to see some examples about what developers can do in order to add their packages to their embedded applications.

Before continuing, the readers should be sure that their embedded kits are reachable via the serial console and network interface as explained in Section 1.3.

10.1 Adding Python Applications (for Development)

Firstly, in order to add Python code to our system, we can consider using the pip3 (or pip for Python 2.x code) command. Within our embedded kit, the pip3 command should be already installed:

© Rodolfo Giometti 2025
R. Giometti, *Yocto Project Customization for Linux*,
https://doi.org/10.1007/979-8-8688-1435-8_10

```
# which pip3
/usr/bin/pip3
# pip3 -h

Usage:
  pip3 <command> [options]

Commands:
  install       Install packages.
  download      Download packages.
  uninstall     Uninstall packages.
  freeze        Output installed packages in requirements format.
  list          List installed packages.
  show          Show information about installed packages.
  check         Verify installed packages have compatible dependencies.
  config        Manage local and global configuration.
  search        Search PyPI for packages.
  cache         Inspect and manage pip's wheel cache.
  index         Inspect information available from package indexes.
  wheel         Build wheels from your requirements.
  hash          Compute hashes of package archives.
  completion    A helper command used for command completion.
  debug         Show information useful for debugging.
  help          Show help for commands.
...
```

If not, we can easily install it by using the package python3-pip as reported by the `oe-pkgdata-util` command:

```
$ oe-pkgdata-util find-path /usr/bin/pip3
python3-pip: /usr/bin/pip3
```

However, the problem with using this tool is that we cannot use it during an image generation. That is, `pip3` is really useful during development, but when we have to generate an image from scratch, we can't count on it! This means that we must have a proper recipe for each Python package we wish to add to our image via the `IMAGE_INSTALL` variable (and its friends; see Section 6.5 for further information about image generation).

Easily speaking, it means that even if a package can be installed by using pip3, it doesn't mean that the same package has a ready-to-use recipe with BitBake. That's why the usage of this tool without knowing what we are doing is discouraged.

OK, once this concept is clear, we can move further to show two different ways to create recipes for Python-based packages, which should (hopefully) cover most cases.

10.2 Using the setuptools3 Build System

As reported on the Yocto Reference Manual at https://docs. yoctoproject.org/ref-manual/classes.html#setuptools3:

> *The setuptools3 class supports Python version 3.x extensions that use build systems based on setuptools (e.g. only have a setup.py and have not migrated to the official pyproject.toml format). If your recipe uses these build systems, the recipe needs to inherit the setuptools3 class.*

So all projects which use the setup.py utility for the installation are good candidates, and one of these is the project pynmea2 at https:// github.com/Knio/pynmea2, as shown in Figure 10-1.

Figure 10-1. *The pynmea2 home page*

By taking a look at the project's home page, we can notice that the
setup.py file is present, and also the latest release is 1.18.0. In this
situation, a good command to easily add our new recipe is by using
devtool as shown below:

```
$ devtool add -S 1.18.0 python3-pynmea2 \
        https://github.com/Knio/pynmea2.git
NOTE: Starting bitbake server...
INFO: Fetching git://github.com/Knio/pynmea2.git;protocol=https;nobranc
h=1...
...
INFO: Scanning paths for packages & dependencies: pynmea2, pynmea2/type
s, pynmea2/types/proprietary
INFO: Using default source tree path /home/giometti/yocto/imx-yocto-bsp
/imx8mp-build/workspace/sources/python3-pynmea2
...
INFO: Using source tree as build directory since that would be the defa
ult for this recipe
INFO: Recipe /home/giometti/yocto/imx-yocto-bsp/imx8mp-build/workspace/
recipes/python3-pynmea2/python3-pynmea2_git.bb has been automatically c
reated; further editing may be required to make it fully functional
```

The readers should notice that, in this case, we didn't use the simpler name `pynmea2` just because it's best practice to prepend a `python-` string or, even better for Python 3.x projects, the `python3-` string to every Python-based project.

As usual, `devtool` tells us that a new recipe `python3-pynmea2_git.bb` has been created within the `workspace` and that we have to check it before continuing. So let's take a look at the new recipe by using the `edit-recipe` subcommand:

```
# Recipe created by recipetool
# This is the basis of a recipe and may need further editing in order to
# be fully functional.
# (Feel free to remove these comments when editing.)

SUMMARY = "Python library for the NMEA 0183 protcol"
HOMEPAGE = "https://github.com/Knio/pynmea2"
# WARNING: the following LICENSE and LIC_FILES_CHKSUM values are best
# guesses - it is your responsibility to verify that the values are
# complete and correct.
LICENSE = "MIT"
LIC_FILES_CHKSUM = "file://LICENSE;md5=bb5e173bc54080cb25079199959ba6b6"

SRC_URI = "git://github.com/Knio/pynmea2.git;protocol=https;branch=mast
er"

# Modify these as desired
PV = "1.0+git${SRCPV}"
SRCREV = "1.18.0"

S = "${WORKDIR}/git"

inherit setuptools3

# WARNING: the following rdepends are determined through basic analysis
# of the python sources, and might not be 100% accurate.
RDEPENDS:${PN} += "python3-core python3-datetime python3-numbers"
```

The relevant parts in the above recipe are

- The `inherit setuptools3` statement, which is needed in order to add all variables and functions needed to be able to install Python packages based on the `setuptools3` build system

- The `RDEPENDS` variable, which has been initialized through basic analysis of the project sources and that we have to accurately review

In our case, everything seems correct, so we can remove all not necessary comments, add some descriptive variables as done in the previous chapter, and then just try to generate the new package by still using `devtool` as shown below:

```
$ devtool build python3-pynmea2
NOTE: Starting bitbake server...
...
NOTE: pynmea2: compiling from external source tree /home/giometti/yocto
/imx-yocto-bsp/imx8mp-build/workspace/sources/python3-pynmea2
NOTE: Tasks Summary: Attempted 939 tasks of which 931 didn't need to be rerun
and all succeeded.
```

The recipe should look like this:

```
SUMMARY = "Python library for the NMEA 0183 protocol"
MAINTAINER = "Rodolfo Giometti <giometti@enneenne.com>"
SECTION = "console/network"
HOMEPAGE = "https://github.com/Knio/pynmea2"
LICENSE = "MIT"
LIC_FILES_CHKSUM = "file://LICENSE;md5=bb5e173bc54080cb25079199959ba6b6"

SRC_URI = "git://github.com/Knio/pynmea2.git;protocol=https;branch=mast
er"

PV = "1.0+git${SRCPV}"
SRCREV = "c546442d1ba38e488f47ef8a190eb5e890260aa2"

S = "${WORKDIR}/git"

inherit setuptools3

RDEPENDS:${PN} += "python3-core python3-datetime python3-numbers"
```

OK, now we can try to deploy the code on the target to test it on the embedded machine:

```
$ devtool deploy-target -s python3-pynmea2 root@192.168.32.132
...
devtool_deploy.list                          100% 3579       2.7MB/s    00:00
devtool_deploy.sh                            100% 1017       1.9MB/s    00:00
./
./usr/
./usr/lib/
./usr/lib/python3.10/
...
./usr/lib/python3.10/site-packages/pynmea2/nmea.py
...
```

The output here is quite long, so it has been broken up for space reasons. However, the readers may verify that all the files are in place on their systems.

Now, to test the code, we can use the example in the README.md file. So let's start the Python interpreter:

```
# python3
Python 3.10.7 (main, Sep  5 2022, 13:12:31) [GCC 11.3.0] on linux
Type "help", "copyright", "credits" or "license" for more information.
>>>
```

Then we can use the following command to load the new module and then use one of its exported methods:

```
>>> import pynmea2
>>> msg = pynmea2.parse("$GPGGA,184353.07,1929.045,S,02410.506,E,1,04,2
.6,100.00,M,-33.9,M,,0000*6D")
>>> print(msg)
$GPGGA,184353.07,1929.045,S,02410.506,E,1,04,2.6,100.00,M,-33.9,M,,0000
*6D
```

OK, everything seems to work correctly, so let's go ahead and create the corresponding package. Firstly, we have to remove the code by using the undeploy-target subcommand:

```
$ devtool undeploy-target python3-pynmea2 root@192.168.32.132
NOTE: Starting bitbake server...
INFO: Successfully undeployed python3-pynmea2
```

Then we have to create a proper recipe under the recipes-python directory as shown below:

```
$ mkdir $CY_METADIR/recipes-python
$ devtool finish python3-pynmea2 $CY_METADIR/recipes-python/
INFO: Updating SRCREV in recipe python3-pynmea2_git.bb
INFO: Moving recipe file to /home/giometti/yocto/imx-yocto-bsp/sources/
meta-cy/recipes-python/python3-pynmea2
INFO: Leaving source tree /home/giometti/yocto/imx-yocto-bsp/imx8mp-bui
ld/workspace/sources/python3-pynmea2 as-is; if you no longer need it then
please delete it manually
```

OK, now we can generate the package with BitBake:

```
$ bitbake python3-pynmea2
```

And the newly generated packages are shown below:

```
$ cy-ipk find python3-pynmea2
cy-ipk: searching in /home/giometti/yocto/imx-yocto-bsp/imx8mp-build...
tmp/deploy/ipk/armv8a/python3-pynmea2-dbg_1.0+git0+c546442d1b-r0_armv8a
.ipk
tmp/deploy/ipk/armv8a/python3-pynmea2-dev_1.0+git0+c546442d1b-r0_armv8a
.ipk
tmp/deploy/ipk/armv8a/python3-pynmea2_1.0+git0+c546442d1b-r0_armv8a.ipk
```

Now we can check the package's information:

```
$ cy-ipk get-info tmp/deploy/ipk/armv8a/python3-pynmea2_1.0+git0+c54644
2d1b-r0_armv8a.ipk
Package: python3-pynmea2
Version: 1.0+git0+c546442d1b-r0
Description: Python library for the NMEA 0183 protocol
 Python library for the NMEA 0183 protcol.
Section: console/network
Priority: optional
```

```
Maintainer: Rodolfo Giometti <giometti@enneenne.com>
License: MIT
Architecture: armv8a
OE: python3-pynmea2
Homepage: https://github.com/Knio/pynmea2
Depends: python3-core, python3-datetime, python3-numbers
Source: python3-pynmea2_git.bb
```

Everything seems to be in place, so we can move the package to the
embedded machine:

```
$ scp tmp/deploy/ipk/armv8a/python3-pynmea2_1.0+git0+c546442d1b-r0_armv
8a.ipk \
     root@192.168.32.132:/tmp/
```

And then we can proceed to install the package:

```
# opkg install /tmp/python3-pynmea2_1.0+git0+c546442d1b-r0_armv8a.ipk
Installing python3-pynmea2 (1.0+git0+c546442d1b) on root
Configuring python3-pynmea2.
```

In order to be sure that everything is running, we can redo the above
little test:

```
# python3
Python 3.10.7 (main, Sep  5 2022, 13:12:31) [GCC 11.3.0] on linux
Type "help", "copyright", "credits" or "license" for more information.
>>> import pynmea2
>>> msg = pynmea2.parse("$GPGGA,184353.07,1929.045,S,02410.506,E,1,04,2.6
,100.00,M,-33.9,M,,0000*6D")
>>> print(msg)
$GPGGA,184353.07,1929.045,S,02410.506,E,1,04,2.6,100.00,M,-33.9,M,,0000*6D
```

We got the same results as above, so our job has been done correctly.

10.3 Using the pypi Build System

As in the previous section, still looking in the Yocto Reference
Manual at https://docs.yoctoproject.org/ref-manual/classes.
html#pypi, we read

> *The pypi class sets variables appropriately for recipes that build Python modules from PyPI, the Python Package Index. By default it determines the PyPI package name based upon BPN (stripping the "python-" or "python3-" prefix off if present), however in some cases you may need to set it manually in the recipe by setting PYPI_PACKAGE.*

The **Python Package Index** is a repository of software for the Python programming language available at `https://pypi.org/`, and we can find there a lot of useful software packages.

In order to show how we can create recipes for these packages, we can consider two main cases: in assisted mode by using `devtool` as usual and by using the pypi class manually.

10.3.1 The Assisted Mode

As seen in the previous chapter, using `devtool` is quite straightforward, and in order to find a suitable candidate to show a practical example, we can choose the project **memory profiler** at `https://pypi.org/project/memory-profiler`, as reported in Figure 10-2.

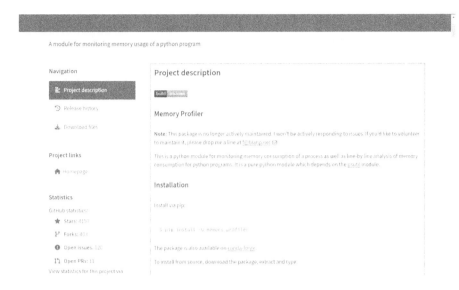

Figure 10-2. *The memory profiler home page*

Within the Download files link, we can get a list of available releases ready for the download. At the time of the writing of this book, the situation is as shown in Figure 10-3.

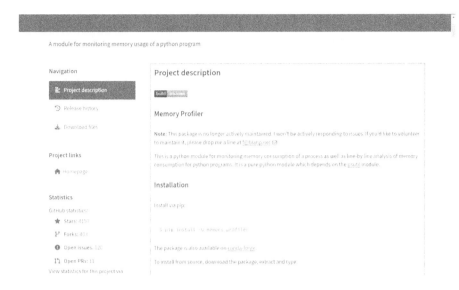

Figure 10-3. *The memory profiler download page*

So we can start our job by using devtool again, as shown below, where we use the URL to download the file memory_profiler-0.61.0.tar.gz from the above web page:

```
$ devtool add python3-memory-profiler \
        https://files.pythonhosted.org/packages/b2/88/e1907e1ca3488f2
d9507ca8b0ae1add7b1cd5d3ca2bc8e5b329382ea2c7b/memory_profiler-0.61.0.ta
r.gz
NOTE: Starting bitbake server...
INFO: Fetching https://files.pythonhosted.org/packages/b2/88/e1907e1ca3
488f2d9507ca8b0ae1add7b1cd5d3ca2bc8e5b329382ea2c7b/memory_profiler-0.61
.0.tar.gz...
...
INFO: Scanning paths for packages & dependencies: .
INFO: Please add the following line for 'COPYING' to a 'lib/recipetool/
licenses.csv' and replace `Unknown` with the license:
cde4ca348bb7feea790673481be0d980,Unknown
INFO: Using default source tree path /home/giometti/yocto/imx-yocto-bsp
/imx8mp-build/workspace/sources/python3-memory-profiler
INFO: Using source tree as build directory since that would be the defa
ult for this recipe
INFO: Recipe /home/giometti/yocto/imx-yocto-bsp/imx8mp-build/workspace/
recipes/python3-memory-profiler/python3-memory-profiler_0.61.0.bb has b
een automatically created; further editing may be required to make it f
ully functional
```

The readers should notice that, as we did in the previous section for every Python 3.x–based project, the package name has been prepended with the python3- prefix.

As in the previous section, devtool does its job, but this time we notice the note:

```
Please add the following line for 'COPYING' to a 'lib/recipetool/licens
es.csv' and replace `Unknown` with the license:
cde4ca348bb7feea790673481be0d980,Unknown
```

This is because devtool can't recognize the project's license, and it asks us to add this new license to the list of known licenses. However, we know perfectly which is the project's license, due to the fact that it is reported on the project's home page, and it is stated as BSD License (BSD), then we can easily fix it.

So let's start by removing not necessary comments (we have left the comments on dependencies anyway) and by editing the new recipe as usual with the edit-recipe subcommand. We should get something as below:

```
SUMMARY = "A module for monitoring memory usage of a python program"
MAINTAINER = "Rodolfo Giometti <giometti@enneenne.com>"
SECTION = "devel/python"
HOMEPAGE = "https://github.com/pythonprofilers/memory_profiler"
LICENSE = "BSD-3-Clause"
LIC_FILES_CHKSUM = "file://COPYING;md5=cde4ca348bb7feea790673481be0d980"

SRC_URI = "https://files.pythonhosted.org/packages/b2/88/e1907e1ca3488f
2d9507ca8b0ae1add7b1cd5d3ca2bc8e5b329382ea2c7b/memory_profiler-${PV}.ta
r.gz"
SRC_URI[md5sum] = "5fe93d5035288095c4f86ef69ee19f37"
SRC_URI[sha1sum] = "116c32efa5ea3612b616e269676e05c1fab86581"
SRC_URI[sha256sum] = "4e5b73d7864a1d1292fb76a03e82a3e78ef934d06828a698d
9dada76da2067b0"
SRC_URI[sha384sum] = "7a9b686739ac1dd76c6778d9d820b8bde5d27f5294932cc14
6abe62bb79b3ac4ef316a4f2acc92273389a3473b6b144c"
SRC_URI[sha512sum] = "b4b4629133221252ad336871781225688ba704c8c19ef3238
5672e4f18e8a160e7d68b640bde8a34bafe212d9501f1b7f24ba742cfe29d5785196695
9ef3800a"

S = "${WORKDIR}/memory_profiler-${PV}"

inherit setuptools3

# WARNING: the following rdepends are from setuptools install_requires.
# These upstream names may not correspond exactly to bitbake package
# names.
RDEPENDS:${PN} += "python3-psutil"

# WARNING: the following rdepends are determined through basic analysis
# of the python sources, and might not be 100% accurate.
RDEPENDS:${PN} += "python3-asyncio python3-core python3-debugger python
3-distutils python3-logging python3-misc python3-multiprocessing python
3-numpy python3-shell"
```

```
# WARNING: We were unable to map the following python package/module
# dependencies to the bitbake packages which include them:
#    IPython
#    IPython.core.error
#    IPython.core.magic
#    IPython.core.page
#    IPython.genutils
#    IPython.ipapi
#    IPython.ipstruct
#    IPython.utils.ipstruct
#    matplotlib
#    pylab
```

Regarding the license, the best guessed value appears to be OK, and the relevant part of the recipe is the one about the package's dependencies.

The first dependency detected is `python3-psutil`, which `devtool` has correctly extracted from the `setuptools install_requires` section (as reported in the above comment). In fact, if we take a look at the file `setup.cfg` in the project root directory, we can see the following settings:

```
[options]
py_modules =
    memory_profiler
    mprof
python_requires = >=3.7
install_requires = psutil
```

The other dependencies detected, even not 100% accurate, are

```
RDEPENDS:${PN} += "python3-asyncio python3-core python3-debugger python
3-distutils python3-logging python3-misc python3-multiprocessing python
3-numpy python3-shell"
```

In this case, as reported in the above comment, they have been detected via basic analysis of the python sources, so we should carefully review them (even if `devtool` works very well).

However, some problems may arise on the last (un)detected dependencies, as in the note below:

```
# WARNING: We were unable to map the following python package/module
# dependencies to the bitbake packages which include them:
#    IPython
```

```
#    IPython.core.error
#    IPython.core.magic
#    IPython.core.page
#    IPython.genutils
#    IPython.ipapi
#    IPython.ipstruct
#    IPython.utils.ipstruct
#    matplotlib
#    pylab
```

When we get a warning message as above, we have to investigate a bit in order to understand if we have to add more RDEPENDS entries, or we can go ahead without worries. We are not Python gurus, but in this case, we may safely think to remove the warning and go on expecting to see which error may arise during the package generation.

Well, after all considerations and after all modifications are in place, the final recipe state should be as reported below:

```
SUMMARY = "A module for monitoring memory usage of a python program"
MAINTAINER = "Rodolfo Giometti <giometti@enneenne.com>"
SECTION = "devel/python"
HOMEPAGE = "https://github.com/pythonprofilers/memory_profiler"
LICENSE = "BSD-3-Clause"
LIC_FILES_CHKSUM = "file://COPYING;md5=cde4ca348bb7feea790673481be0d980"

SRC_URI = "https://files.pythonhosted.org/packages/b2/88/e1907e1ca3488f
2d9507ca8b0ae1add7b1cd5d3ca2bc8e5b329382ea2c7b/memory_profiler-${PV}.ta
r.gz"
SRC_URI[md5sum] = "5fe93d5035288095c4f86ef69ee19f37"
SRC_URI[sha1sum] = "116c32efa5ea3612b616e269676e05c1fab86581"
SRC_URI[sha256sum] = "4e5b73d7864a1d1292fb76a03e82a3e78ef934d06828a698d
9dada76da2067b0"
SRC_URI[sha384sum] = "7a9b686739ac1dd76c6778d9d820b8bde5d27f5294932cc14
6abe62bb79b3ac4ef316a4f2acc92273389a3473b6b144c"
SRC_URI[sha512sum] = "b4b4629133221252ad336871781225688ba704c8c19ef3238
5672e4f18e8a160e7d68b640bde8a34bafe212d9501f1b7f24ba742cfe29d5785196695
9ef3800a"

S = "${WORKDIR}/memory_profiler-${PV}"

inherit setuptools3
```

519

```
RDEPENDS:${PN} += "python3-psutil"
RDEPENDS:${PN} += "python3-asyncio python3-core python3-debugger python
3-distutils python3-logging python3-misc python3-multiprocessing python
3-numpy python3-shell"
```

OK, now we can try to build the package as usual:

```
$ devtool build python3-memory-profiler
...
NOTE: python3-memory-profiler: compiling from external source tree /hom
e/giometti/yocto/imx-yocto-bsp/imx8mp-build/workspace/sources/python3-m
emory-profiler
NOTE: Tasks Summary: Attempted 939 tasks of which 931 didn't need to be
 rerun and all succeeded.
```

Great! Everything worked well, so we can try to deploy the code to test it on the target machine:

```
$ devtool deploy-target -s python3-memory-profiler root@192.168.32.132
...
./
./usr/
./usr/bin/
./usr/bin/mprof
./usr/lib/
./usr/lib/python3.10/
...
./usr/lib/python3.10/site-packages/memory_profiler.py
...
```

As before, the output here is quite long, so it has been broken up for space reasons. However, the readers may verify that all the files are in place on their systems.

Now, as written in the package's documentation, we should be able to execute the mprof command, so let's try it as reported below:

```
# mprof
Traceback (most recent call last):
  File "/usr/bin/mprof", line 5, in <module>
    from mprof import main
```

```
  File "/usr/lib/python3.10/site-packages/mprof.py", line 17, in <modul
e>
    import memory_profiler as mp
  File "/usr/lib/python3.10/site-packages/memory_profiler.py", line 20,
 in <module>
    import pdb
ModuleNotFoundError: No module named 'pdb'
```

This time, we have no luck, since it appears that some runtime dependencies are missing, so we have to check if all packages listed within the RDEPENDS variable are present in our current image. To easily do so, we can use our utility cy-image as shown below:

```
$ cy-image chk-pkg engicam-evaluation-image-mx8 python3-psutil \
    python3-asyncio python3-core python3-debugger python3-distutils \
    python3-logging python3-misc python3-multiprocessing python3-numpy \
    python3-shell
cy-image: searching in /home/giometti/yocto/imx-yocto-bsp/imx8mp-build.
..
package python3-psutil is not present
package python3-asyncio is present
package python3-core is present
package python3-debugger is not present
package python3-distutils is present
package python3-logging is present
package python3-misc is not present
package python3-multiprocessing is present
package python3-numpy is not present
package python3-shell is present
```

The missing packages are python3-psutil, python3-debugger, python3-misc, and python3-numpy, so let's see which recipes provide them. Again, we can use our utility cy-ipk:

```
$ cy-ipk recipe python3-psutil python3-debugger python3-misc python3-num
py
package python3-psutil is provideb by... python3-psutil
package python3-debugger is provideb by... python3
package python3-misc is provideb by... python3
package python3-numpy is provideb by... python3-numpy
```

Great! So `python3-debugger` and `python3-misc` are already provided by the core Python recipe, and we simply have to generate the other two packages by using BitBake:

```
$ bitbake python3-psutil python3-numpy
```

Now all needed packages should be in place, and we can easily find them by using again `cy-ipk` as below:

```
$ cy-ipk find python3-psutil python3-debugger python3-misc python3-numpy
cy-ipk: searching in /home/giometti/yocto/imx-yocto-bsp/imx8mp-build...
tmp/deploy/ipk/armv8a/python3-psutil_5.9.0-r0_armv8a.ipk
tmp/deploy/ipk/armv8a/python3-psutil-tests_5.9.0-r0_armv8a.ipk
tmp/deploy/ipk/armv8a/python3-psutil-dev_5.9.0-r0_armv8a.ipk
tmp/deploy/ipk/armv8a/python3-psutil-dbg_5.9.0-r0_armv8a.ipk
tmp/deploy/ipk/armv8a/python3-psutil-src_5.9.0-r0_armv8a.ipk
tmp/deploy/ipk/armv8a/python3-debugger_3.10.7-r0_armv8a.ipk
tmp/deploy/ipk/armv8a/python3-misc_3.10.7-r0_armv8a.ipk
tmp/deploy/ipk/armv8a/python3-numpy_1.22.3-r0_armv8a.ipk
tmp/deploy/ipk/armv8a/python3-numpy-dbg_1.22.3-r0_armv8a.ipk
tmp/deploy/ipk/armv8a/python3-numpy-src_1.22.3-r0_armv8a.ipk
tmp/deploy/ipk/armv8a/python3-numpy-dev_1.22.3-r0_armv8a.ipk
tmp/deploy/ipk/armv8a/python3-numpy-ptest_1.22.3-r0_armv8a.ipk
tmp/deploy/ipk/armv8a/python3-numpy-staticdev_1.22.3-r0_armv8a.ipk
```

Once identified the package files, we can easily move them on the target machine via `scp`:

```
$ scp tmp/deploy/ipk/armv8a/python3-psutil_5.9.0-r0_armv8a.ipk \
      tmp/deploy/ipk/armv8a/python3-debugger_3.10.7-r0_armv8a.ipk \
      tmp/deploy/ipk/armv8a/python3-misc_3.10.7-r0_armv8a.ipk \
      tmp/deploy/ipk/armv8a/python3-numpy_1.22.3-r0_armv8a.ipk \
        root@192.168.32.132:/tmp/
```

And then we can proceed with the installation via `opkg`:

```
# opkg install /tmp/*.ipk
 * Solver encountered 3 problem(s):
 * Problem 1/3:
 *   - conflicting requests
 *   - nothing provides python3-audio needed by python3-misc-3.10.7-r0.
armv8a
 *
 * Solution 1:
```

```
*   - do not ask to install python3-misc-3.10.7-r0.armv8a

* Problem 2/3:
*   - conflicting requests
*   - nothing provides python3-doctest needed by python3-numpy-1.22.3-
r0.armv8a
*
* Solution 1:
*   - do not ask to install python3-numpy-1.22.3-r0.armv8a

* Problem 3/3:
*   - conflicting requests
*   - nothing provides python3-resource needed by python3-psutil-5.9.0
-r0.armv8a
*
* Solution 1:
*   - do not ask to install python3-psutil-5.9.0-r0.armv8a
```

Still no luck! We need more packages. So let's find them:

```
$ cy-ipk find python3-audio python3-doctest python3-resource
cy-ipk: searching in /home/giometti/yocto/imx-yocto-bsp/imx8mp-build...
tmp/deploy/ipk/armv8a/python3-audio_3.10.7-r0_armv8a.ipk
tmp/deploy/ipk/armv8a/python3-doctest_3.10.7-r0_armv8a.ipk
tmp/deploy/ipk/armv8a/python3-resource_3.10.7-r0_armv8a.ipk
```

Then let's move them to the target machine:

```
$ scp tmp/deploy/ipk/armv8a/python3-audio_3.10.7-r0_armv8a.ipk \
      tmp/deploy/ipk/armv8a/python3-doctest_3.10.7-r0_armv8a.ipk \
      tmp/deploy/ipk/armv8a/python3-resource_3.10.7-r0_armv8a.ipk \
         root@192.168.32.132:/tmp/
```

And try again to install all packages:

```
# opkg install /tmp/*.ipk
* Solver encountered 2 problem(s):
* Problem 1/2:
*   - conflicting requests
*   - nothing provides python3-codecs needed by python3-misc-3.10.7-r0
.armv8a
*
* Solution 1:
*   - do not ask to install python3-misc-3.10.7-r0.armv8a

* Problem 2/2:
*   - package python3-numpy-1.22.3-r0.armv8a requires python3-misc, but
```

```
* none of the providers can be installed
*    - conflicting requests
*    - nothing provides python3-codecs needed by python3-misc-3.10.7-r0
.armv8a
*
* Solution 1:
*    - do not ask to install python3-numpy-1.22.3-r0.armv8a
```

No way. However, this time it should be the last missing dependency, since both errors are about the missing python3-codecs package. So let's find and move it on the target machine as usual:

```
$ cy-ipk find python3-codecs
cy-ipk: searching in /home/giometti/yocto/imx-yocto-bsp/imx8mp-build...
tmp/deploy/ipk/armv8a/python3-codecs_3.10.7-r0_armv8a.ipk
$ scp tmp/deploy/ipk/armv8a/python3-codecs_3.10.7-r0_armv8a.ipk \
      root@192.168.32.132:/tmp/
```

OK, let's try again to install all the packages:

```
# opkg install /tmp/*.ipk
Installing python3-debugger (3.10.7) on root
Installing python3-codecs (3.10.7) on root
Installing python3-audio (3.10.7) on root
Installing python3-resource (3.10.7) on root
Installing python3-doctest (3.10.7) on root
Installing python3-misc (3.10.7) on root
Installing python3-psutil (5.9.0) on root
Installing python3-numpy (1.22.3) on root
Configuring python3-debugger.
Configuring python3-audio.
Configuring python3-codecs.
Configuring python3-misc.
Configuring python3-doctest.
Configuring python3-numpy.
Configuring python3-resource.
Configuring python3-psutil.
```

Great! Now we get it. Now we can try to execute the new tool as we did before, hoping this time everything will work good:

```
# mprof
Usage: mprof <command> <options> <arguments>

Available commands:
```

```
    run      run a given command or python file
    attach   alias for 'run --attach': attach to an existing process b
y pid or name
    rm       remove a given file generated by mprof
    clean    clean the current directory from files created by mprof
    list     display existing profiles, with indices
    plot     plot memory consumption generated by mprof run
    peak     print the maximum memory used by an mprof run

Type mprof <command> --help for usage help on a specific command.
For example, mprof plot --help will list all plotting options.
```

Now we are ready to generate the recipe, so let's use devtool with the finish subcommand as shown below:

```
$ devtool finish python3-memory-profiler $CY_METADIR/recipes-python/
NOTE: Starting bitbake server...
ERROR: Source tree is not clean:

?? build/

Ensure you have committed your changes or use -f/--force if you are sur
e there's nothing that needs to be committed
```

The tool correctly recognized that our source tree is not clean, but we know that the build directory has been generated during the package building, so we can safely use the -f option argument, as suggested above:

```
$ devtool finish -f python3-memory-profiler $CY_METADIR/recipes-python/
NOTE: Starting bitbake server...
WARNING: Source tree is not clean, continuing as requested by -f/--forc
e...
INFO: No patches or files need updating
INFO: Moving recipe file to /home/giometti/yocto/imx-yocto-bsp/sources/
meta-cy/recipes-python/python3-memory-profiler
INFO: Leaving source tree /home/giometti/yocto/imx-yocto-bsp/imx8mp-bui
ld/workspace/sources/python3-memory-profiler as-is; if you no longer ne
ed it then please delete it manually
```

Now the recipe is in place:

```
$ cd $CY_METADIR
$ tree recipes-python/python3-memory-profiler/
recipes-python/python3-memory-profiler/
└── python3-memory-profiler_0.61.0.bb

0 directories, 1 file
```

And we can use the `bitbake` command to generate the relative package file:

```
$ bitbake python3-memory-profiler
```

In the end, the package is ready:

```
$ cy-ipk find python3-memory-profiler
cy-ipk: searching in /home/giometti/yocto/imx-yocto-bsp/imx8mp-build...
tmp/deploy/ipk/armv8a/python3-memory-profiler-dev_0.61.0-r0_armv8a.ipk
tmp/deploy/ipk/armv8a/python3-memory-profiler_0.61.0-r0_armv8a.ipk
tmp/deploy/ipk/armv8a/python3-memory-profiler-dbg_0.61.0-r0_armv8a.ipk
```

And also the package's information are set correctly:

```
$ cy-ipk get-info tmp/deploy/ipk/armv8a/python3-memory-profiler_0.61.0-
r0_armv8a.ipk
Package: python3-memory-profiler
Version: 0.61.0-r0
Description: A module for monitoring memory usage of a python program
 A module for monitoring memory usage of a python program.
Section: devel/python
Priority: optional
Maintainer: Rodolfo Giometti <giometti@enneenne.com>
License: BSD-3-Clause
Architecture: armv8a
OE: python3-memory-profiler
Homepage: https://github.com/pythonprofilers/memory_profiler
Depends: python3-asyncio, python3-core, python3-debugger, python3-distu
tils, python3-logging, python3-misc, python3-multiprocessing, python3-n
umpy, python3-psutil, python3-shell
Source: python3-memory-profiler_0.61.0.bb
```

Now we can do as before and test the package installation on the embedded kit; however, we left this job to the readers as an exercise.

10.3.2 The Manual Way

If we take a look at the recipe just written in the section above for the `python3-memory-profiler` package, we should notice that we didn't use the pypi class at all! In fact, in the recipe, there is no `inherit pypi` call. So what is this class for? Well, we can use this class to write a recipe manually without using `devtool` or in the case where `devtool` fails.

In order to show what we are talking about, let's consider the package **fastecdsa** at `https://pypi.org/project/fastecdsa/`. Figure 10-4 shows the screenshot of the software download page.

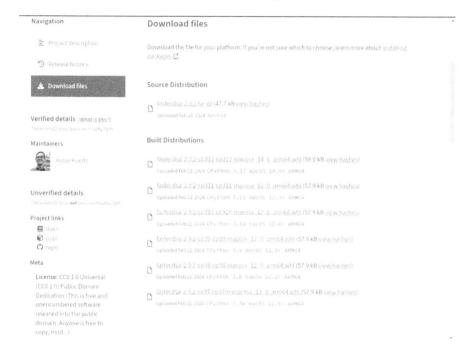

Figure 10-4. *The fastecdsa download page*

In the case we decide to create a package for release 2.3.2, we can get the URL of the corresponding archive file `fastecdsa-2.3.2.tar.gz` and execute the command reported below:

```
$ devtool add python3-fastecdsa \
        https://files.pythonhosted.org/packages/fc/21/d5585856169c59
5d99a596dd8000afae40053f9f5c955d8ec8fb2ec3247c/fastecdsa-2.3.2.tar.gz
```

However, this time, we have no luck since the output of the above command should be something as shown below:

```
...
  File "/home/giometti/yocto/imx-yocto-bsp/sources/poky/meta/lib/oe/lic
ense.py", line 62, in get_elements
    raise InvalidLicense(element)
oe.license.InvalidLicense: invalid characters in license 'This-is-free-
and-unencumbered-software-released-into-the-public-domain.
--------
--------Anyone-is-free-to-copy,-modify,-publish,-use,-compile,-sell,-or
--------distribute-this-software,-either-in-source-code-form-or-as-a
--------compiled-binary,-for-any-purpose,-commercial-or-non-commercial,
--------and-by-any-means.
...
--------For-more-information,-please-refer-to-<http://unlicense.org/>
'
ERROR: Command 'script -e -q -c "recipetool --color=always create –devt
ool -o /tmp/devtoolqp80pxf_ 'https://files.pythonhosted.org/packages/fc
/21/d5585856169c595d99a596dd8000afae40053f9f5c955d8ec8fb2ec3247c/fastec
dsa-2.3.2.tar.gz'  -x /home/giometti/yocto/imx-yocto-bsp/imx8mp-build/w
orkspace/sources/devtoolsrc8855cvb1 -N python3-fastecdsa" /dev/null' fa
iled
...
```

In this case, no recipes are created, and the only thing to do is writing our recipes by hand using the pypi class. In this scenario, we can move within our meta layer and start creating the recipe manually:

```
$ cd $CY_METADIR
$ mkdir recipes-python/python3-fastecdsa
```

We can use the following skeleton:

```
SUMMARY = " "
MAINTAINER = " "
SECTION = " "
HOMEPAGE = " "
LICENSE = " "
LIC_FILES_CHKSUM = " "

PYPI_PACKAGE = "fastecdsa"

inherit pypi ...
```

In order to know what to write within the several empty variables above, we can take a look at the project page at `https://pypi.org/project/fastecdsa` or at the project repository at `https://github.com/AntonKueltz/fastecdsa` to get useful information. So the first part of the recipe can be filled as below:

```
SUMMARY = "A module for fast elliptic curve cryptography"
MAINTAINER = "Rodolfo Giometti <giometti@enneenne.com>"
SECTION = "devel/python"
HOMEPAGE = "https://github.com/AntonKueltz/fastecdsa"
```

Regarding the license, in the repository we see a file named `LICENSE` which can be inspected as shown below:

```
$ git clone https://github.com/AntonKueltz/fastecdsa.git
$ cd fastecdsa
$ cat LICENSE
This is free and unencumbered software released into the public domain.

Anyone is free to copy, modify, publish, use, compile, sell, or
distribute this software, either in source code form or as a compiled
binary, for any purpose, commercial or non-commercial, and by any
means.
...
For more information, please refer to <http://unlicense.org/>
```

Moreover, in the project home page at pypi.org, we see that the license is classified as *CC0 1.0 Universal (CC0 1.0) Public Domain Dedication*. By doing a quick search within the `licenses.conf` file in the poky meta layer, we can see that this is a known license:

```
$ grep 'CC0.1\.0' poky/meta/conf/licenses.conf
DATA_LICENSE = "CC0-1.0"
```

So we can fill the license information as shown below:

```
LICENSE = "CC0-1.0"
LIC_FILES_CHKSUM = "file://LICENSE;md5=7246f848faa4e9c9fc0ea91122d6e680"
```

529

where the checksum is obtained by using the `md5sum` command on the `LICENSE` file:

```
$ md5sum LICENSE
7246f848faa4e9c9fc0ea91122d6e680   LICENSE
```

Now, considering that the package has the `setup.py` file, which means that it uses the `setuptools` utility to get installed, we must add the `setuptools3` class at the `inherit` statement. Finally, our recipe should look like this:

```
$ cat recipes-python/python3-fastecdsa/python3-fastecdsa_2.3.2.bb
SUMMARY = "A module for fast elliptic curve cryptography"
MAINTAINER = "Rodolfo Giometti <giometti@enneenne.com>"
SECTION = "devel/python"
HOMEPAGE = "https://github.com/AntonKueltz/fastecdsa"
LICENSE = "CC0-1.0"
LIC_FILES_CHKSUM = "file://LICENSE;md5=7246f848faa4e9c9fc0ea91122d6e680"

PYPI_PACKAGE = "fastecdsa"

inherit pypi setuptools3
```

OK, now let's execute `bitbake` on it:

```
$ bitbake python3-fastecdsa
...
NOTE: Executing Tasks
ERROR: python3-fastecdsa-2.3.2-r0 do_fetch: No checksum specified for '
/home/giometti/Projects/DL_ARCHIVES/yocto/fastecdsa-2.3.2.tar.gz', plea
se add at least one to the recipe:
SRC_URI[sha256sum] = "f35255a6d3e41109166b5d4b08866d5acbb99f2e1e64d3a7e
74c774664cda842"
ERROR: python3-fastecdsa-2.3.2-r0 do_fetch: Bitbake Fetcher Error:
NoChecksumError('Missing SRC_URI checksum', 'https://files.pythonhosted
.org/packages/source/f/fastecdsa/fastecdsa-2.3.2.tar.gz')
...
```

We got the above error, which is expected because we didn't specify a proper value for SRC_URI[`sha256sum`]. So let's do what is suggested, altering the recipe as shown below:

```
--- a/recipes-python/python3-fastecdsa/python3-fastecdsa_2.3.2.bb
+++ b/recipes-python/python3-fastecdsa/python3-fastecdsa_2.3.2.bb
```

```
@@ -6,5 +6,6 @@
 LIC_FILES_CHKSUM = "file://LICENSE;md5=7246f848faa4e9c9fc0ea91122d6e68
0"

 PYPI_PACKAGE = "fastecdsa"
+SRC_URI[sha256sum] = "f35255a6d3e41109166b5d4b08866d5acbb99f2e1e64d3a7
e74c774664cda842"

 inherit pypi setuptools3
```

Then we can execute `bitbake` again:

```
$ bitbake python3-fastecdsa
...
NOTE: Executing Tasks
ERROR: python3-fastecdsa-2.3.2-r0 do_compile: 'python3 setup.py bdist_w
heel ' execution failed.
ERROR: python3-fastecdsa-2.3.2-r0 do_compile:
ExecutionError('/home/giometti/yocto/imx-yocto-bsp/imx8mp-build/tmp/wor
k/armv8a-poky-linux/python3-fastecdsa/2.3.2-r0/temp/run.do_compile.1217
193', 1, None, None)
ERROR: Logfile of failure stored in: /home/giometti/yocto/imx-yocto-bsp/imx8mp-
build/tmp/work/armv8a-poky-li
nux/python3-fastecdsa/2.3.2-r0/temp/log.do_compile.1217193
Log data follows:
| DEBUG: Executing shell function do_compile
| running bdist_wheel
| running build
| running build_ext
| building 'fastecdsa.curvemath' extension
...
-I/home/giometti/yocto/imx-yocto-bsp/imx8mp-build/tmp/work/armv8a-poky-
linux/python3-fastecdsa/2.3.2-r0/recipe-sysroot/usr/include/python3.10
-c src/curve.c -o build/temp.linux-x86_64-3.10/src/curve.o -O2
| In file included from src/curve.c:1:
| src/curve.h:4:10: fatal error: gmp.h: No such file or directory
|     4 | #include "gmp.h"
|       |          ^~~~~~~
| compilation terminated.
...
```

Here, we have to investigate the code a bit, and then we can discover that what we need here is the *GNU multiprecision arithmetic library* which is provided by the gmp package. So we should add the following dependency:

```
--- a/recipes-python/python3-fastecdsa/python3-fastecdsa_2.3.2.bb
+++ b/recipes-python/python3-fastecdsa/python3-fastecdsa_2.3.2.bb
@@ -5,6 +5,8 @@
 LICENSE = "CC0-1.0"
 LIC_FILES_CHKSUM = "file://LICENSE;md5=7246f848faa4e9c9fc0ea91122d6e680"

+DEPENDS += "gmp"
+
 PYPI_PACKAGE = "fastecdsa"
 SRC_URI[sha256sum] = "f35255a6d3e41109166b5d4b08866d5acbb99f2e1e64d3a7
e74c774664cda842"
```

Now, if we execute bitbake again, we should come to a successful end. In fact, the package is now compiled, and new package files have been created as shown below:

```
$ cy-ipk find python3-fastecdsa
cy-ipk: searching in /home/giometti/yocto/imx-yocto-bsp/imx8mp-build...
tmp/deploy/ipk/armv8a/python3-fastecdsa-dbg_2.3.2-r0_armv8a.ipk
tmp/deploy/ipk/armv8a/python3-fastecdsa-dev_2.3.2-r0_armv8a.ipk
tmp/deploy/ipk/armv8a/python3-fastecdsa_2.3.2-r0_armv8a.ipk
tmp/deploy/ipk/armv8a/python3-fastecdsa-src_2.3.2-r0_armv8a.ipk
```

And all package information is correctly set:

```
$ cy-ipk get-info tmp/deploy/ipk/armv8a/python3-fastecdsa_2.3.2-r0_armv
8a.ipk
Package: python3-fastecdsa
Version: 2.3.2-r0
Description: A module for fast elliptic curve cryptography
 A module for fast elliptic curve cryptography.
Section: devel/python
Priority: optional
Maintainer: Rodolfo Giometti <giometti@enneenne.com>
License: CC0-1.0
Architecture: armv8a
OE: python3-fastecdsa
Homepage: https://github.com/AntonKueltz/fastecdsa
Depends: libc6 (>= 2.35), libgmp10 (>= 6.2.1), python3-core
Source: python3-fastecdsa_2.3.2.bb
```

However, if we take a look at the files stored in the package, something is not correct:

```
$ cy-ipk inspect tmp/deploy/ipk/armv8a/python3-fastecdsa_2.3.2-r0_armv8
a.ipk
drwxr-xr-x root/root       0 2024-02-22 19:34 ./usr/
drwxr-xr-x root/root       0 2024-02-22 19:34 ./usr/lib/
drwxr-xr-x root/root       0 2024-02-22 19:34 ./usr/lib/python3.10/
drwxr-xr-x root/root       0 2024-02-22 19:34 ./usr/lib/python3.10/site-
packages/
drwxr-xr-x root/root       0 2024-02-22 19:34 ./usr/lib/python3.10/site-
packages/UNKNOWN-0.0.0.dist-info/
-rw-r--r-- root/root    1211 2024-02-22 19:34 ./usr/lib/python3.10/site-
packages/UNKNOWN-0.0.0.dist-info/LICENSE
-rw-r--r-- root/root     154 2024-02-22 19:34 ./usr/lib/python3.10/site-
packages/UNKNOWN-0.0.0.dist-info/METADATA
-rw-r--r-- root/root     729 2024-02-22 19:34 ./usr/lib/python3.10/site-
packages/UNKNOWN-0.0.0.dist-info/RECORD
-rw-r--r-- root/root     105 2024-02-22 19:34 ./usr/lib/python3.10/site-
packages/UNKNOWN-0.0.0.dist-info/WHEEL
-rw-r--r-- root/root      10 2024-02-22 19:34 ./usr/lib/python3.10/site-
packages/UNKNOWN-0.0.0.dist-info/top_level.txt
drwxr-xr-x root/root       0 2024-02-22 19:34 ./usr/lib/python3.10/site-
packages/fastecdsa/
-rwxr-xr-x root/root   18680 2024-02-22 19:34 ./usr/lib/python3.10/site-
packages/fastecdsa/_ecdsa.cpython-310-aarch64-linux-gnu.so
-rwxr-xr-x root/root   14384 2024-02-22 19:34 ./usr/lib/python3.10/site-
packages/fastecdsa/curvemath.cpython-310-aarch64-linux-gnu.so
```

In fact, there are no Python files (`.py` files), and the directory `UNKNOWN-0.0.0.dist-info` is not correct. This happens because this package is not compatible with the *Python wheel packaging standard* (named also *bdist_wheel* – see `https://wheel.readthedocs.io/en/stable/`), so we have to move to the setuptools3 legacy support, as shown below:

```
--- a/python3-fastecdsa_2.3.2.bb
+++ b/python3-fastecdsa_2.3.2.bb
@@ -10,4 +10,4 @@
 PYPI_PACKAGE = "fastecdsa"
 SRC_URI[sha256sum] =
"f35255a6d3e41109166b5d4b08866d5acbb99f2e1e64d3a7e74c774664cda842"

-inherit pypi setuptools3
+inherit pypi setuptools3_legacy
```

The setuptools3 legacy support is provided by the `setuptools3_legacy.bbclass` within the poky meta layer. The readers should also note that at the beginning of the file, there is the following disclaimer:

```
$ cat poky/meta/classes/setuptools3_legacy.bbclass
# This class is for packages which use the deprecated setuptools
# behaviour, specifically custom install tasks which don't work
# correctly with bdist_wheel.
# This behaviour is deprecated in setuptools[1] and won't work in
# the future, so all users of this should consider their options:
# pure Python modules can use a modern Python tool such as
# build[2], or packages which are doing more (such as installing
# init scripts) should use a fully-featured build system such as
# Meson.
#
# [1] https://setuptools.pypa.io/en/latest/history.html#id142
# [2] https://pypi.org/project/build/
```

In Yocto Scarthgap, the class is still present.

If we execute `bitbake` again, then the package should hold the following files:

```
$ cy-ipk inspect tmp/deploy/ipk/armv8a/python3-fastecdsa_2.3.2-r0_armv8
a.ipk
...
drwxr-xr-x root/root        0 2024-02-22 19:34 ./usr/lib/python3.10/site-
packages/UNKNOWN-0.0.0-py3.10.egg-info/
-rw-r--r-- root/root      154 2024-02-22 19:34 ./usr/lib/python3.10/site-
packages/UNKNOWN-0.0.0-py3.10.egg-info/PKG-INFO
-rw-r--r-- root/root      294 2024-02-22 19:34 ./usr/lib/python3.10/site-
packages/UNKNOWN-0.0.0-py3.10.egg-info/SOURCES.txt
...
-rwxr-xr-x root/root    18680 2024-02-22 19:34 ./usr/lib/python3.10/site-
packages/fastecdsa/_ecdsa.cpython-310-aarch64-linux-gnu.so
-rwxr-xr-x root/root    14384 2024-02-22 19:34 ./usr/lib/python3.10/site-
packages/fastecdsa/curvemath.cpython-310-aarch64-linux-gnu.so
```

Still no luck, so we should try to investigate more by using the devshell as shown in Section 4.4:

```
$ bitbake -c devshell python3-fastecdsa
```

Now we can inspect the working directory:

```
$ ls
fastecdsa           MANIFEST.in     README.rst  src
fastecdsa.egg-info  PKG-INFO        setup.cfg   UNKNOWN.egg-info
LICENSE             pyproject.toml  setup.py
```

Two egg-info directories have been created, but the valid one is fastecdsa.egg-info. Also, within the fastecdsa, there are all other files we should have into the final package:

```
$ ls fastecdsa
benchmark.py  ecdsa.py   __init__.py  point.py  util.py
curve.py      encoding   keys.py      tests
```

So a possible solution should be to append some code to the do_install task in order to drop the invalid egg-info directory, install the correct one, and add all missing files. The needed modifications are reported below:

```
--- a/python3-fastecdsa_2.3.2.bb
+++ b/python3-fastecdsa_2.3.2.bb
@@ -11,3 +11,14 @@
 SRC_URI[sha256sum] = "f35255a6d3e41109166b5d4b08866d5acbb99f2e1e64d3a7
e74c774664cda842"

 inherit pypi setuptools3_legacy
+
+do_install:append() {
+       # Remove invalid UNKNOWN-0.0.0-py3.10.egg-info directory
+       rm -r ${D}${PYTHON_SITEPACKAGES_DIR}/UNKNOWN-0.0.0-py3.10.egg-info
+
+       # Install valid egg-info information
+       cp -r ${S}/fastecdsa.egg-info ${D}${PYTHON_SITEPACKAGES_DIR}/fast
ecdsa-${PV}-py${PYTHON_BASEVERSION}.egg-info
+
+       # Add all missing files
+       cp -r ${S}/fastecdsa ${D}${PYTHON_SITEPACKAGES_DIR}/
+}
```

At this point, if we re-execute `bitbake` we get something better than before:

```
$ cy-ipk inspect tmp/deploy/ipk/armv8a/python3-fastecdsa_2.3.2-r0_armv8
a.ipk
...
drwxr-xr-x root/root       0 2024-02-22 19:34 ./usr/lib/python3.10/site-
packages/fastecdsa-2.3.2-py3.10.egg-info/
-rw-r--r-- root/root   17798 2024-02-22 19:34 ./usr/lib/python3.10/site-
packages/fastecdsa-2.3.2-py3.10.egg-info/PKG-INFO
-rw-r--r-- root/root    1195 2024-02-22 19:34 ./usr/lib/python3.10/site-
packages/fastecdsa-2.3.2-py3.10.egg-info/SOURCES.txt
...
-rw-r--r-- root/root       0 2024-02-22 19:34 ./usr/lib/python3.10/site-
packages/fastecdsa/__init__.py
-rwxr-xr-x root/root   18680 2024-02-22 19:34 ./usr/lib/python3.10/site-
packages/fastecdsa/_ecdsa.cpython-310-aarch64-linux-gnu.so
-rw-r--r-- root/root    1135 2024-02-22 19:34 ./usr/lib/python3.10/site-
packages/fastecdsa/benchmark.py
-rw-r--r-- root/root   13920 2024-02-22 19:34 ./usr/lib/python3.10/site-
packages/fastecdsa/curve.py
...
-rw-r--r-- root/root    4878 2024-02-22 19:34 ./usr/lib/python3.10/site-
packages/fastecdsa/tests/test_brainpool_ecdh.py
-rw-r--r-- root/root    1121 2024-02-22 19:34 ./usr/lib/python3.10/site-
packages/fastecdsa/tests/test_key_export_import.py
-rw-r--r-- root/root     615 2024-02-22 19:34 ./usr/lib/python3.10/site-
packages/fastecdsa/tests/test_key_recovery.py
...
```

Now all the needed files are present; however, we notice that there are also present files within the `tests` directory we can move into a proper package named `python3-fastecdsa-tests` since they are useful only for testing purposes. To do so, we can alter the recipe as shown below:

```
--- a/python3-fastecdsa_2.3.2.bb
+++ b/python3-fastecdsa_2.3.2.bb
@@ -22,3 +22,8 @@
        # Add all missing files
        cp -r ${S}/fastecdsa ${D}${PYTHON_SITEPACKAGES_DIR}/
 }
```

```
+
+PACKAGES =+ "${PN}-tests"
+FILES:${PN}-tests = "${PYTHON_SITEPACKAGES_DIR}/fastecdsa/tests/"
+
+RDEPENDS:${PN}-tests = "${PN}"
```

Now, when we ask BitBake to process the python3-fastecdsa.bb recipe, we get the new package as expected:

```
$ bitbake python3-fastecdsa
$ cy-ipk find python3-fastecdsa
cy-ipk: searching in /home/giometti/yocto/imx-yocto-bsp/imx8mp-build...
tmp/deploy/ipk/armv8a/python3-fastecdsa-dbg_2.3.2-r0_armv8a.ipk
tmp/deploy/ipk/armv8a/python3-fastecdsa-dev_2.3.2-r0_armv8a.ipk
tmp/deploy/ipk/armv8a/python3-fastecdsa_2.3.2-r0_armv8a.ipk
tmp/deploy/ipk/armv8a/python3-fastecdsa-src_2.3.2-r0_armv8a.ipk
tmp/deploy/ipk/armv8a/python3-fastecdsa-tests_2.3.2-r0_armv8a.ipk
```

OK, now we have to do the last step: that is, moving the package to our embedded kit to test if everything works well:

```
$ scp tmp/deploy/ipk/armv8a/python3-fastecdsa_2.3.2-r0_armv8a.ipk \
        root@192.168.32.132:/tmp/
```

Now we can install the new package:

```
# opkg install /tmp/python3-fastecdsa_2.3.2-r0_armv8a.ipk
Installing python3-fastecdsa (2.3.2) on root
Configuring python3-fastecdsa.
```

To test the code, we can just execute the keys.gen_keypair() function as reported below in order to create a key pair:

```
# python3
Python 3.10.7 (main, Sep  5 2022, 13:12:31) [GCC 11.3.0] on linux
Type "help", "copyright", "credits" or "license" for more information.
>>> from fastecdsa import keys, curve
>>> priv_key, pub_key = keys.gen_keypair(curve.P521)
>>> print(pub_key)
X: 0x13feefa2bb3d1f868cca8c09a67c43fd316025da645a4c16a27b9865eaab390190
59aefa76bc535a7f46e193bdd611c128de05b40b7c6590493c84e489e0e614d4c
Y: 0x1a3ab43c7c6d25893e2010ad88ab97e12f4ffad99af6f2c3ed9d401f97a62135b2
8748621ff8f7d51ce7650f3e727c397c606301385b73c07f43e9bdbd648726ded
(On curve <P521>)
>>>
```

Great, everything is OK.

Note that, if we need to use this package to generate code for
another package, we can add (as the last line of the recipe) the
following setting:

```
BBCLASSEXTEND = "native"
```

Doing so, we can call the native version of this package within
another recipe, just adding the following dependency in the DEPENDS
variable:

```
DEPENDS += "python3-fastecdsa-native"
```

In this manner, we can use the fastecdsa functions on the host
(an exhaustive example about how to use native packages is in
Section 11.6).

10.4 Summary

In this chapter, we have seen how a Python package can be created by
using two different techniques. Embedded developers now have a way to
add powerful programs to their systems; however, adding new C or Python
packages is not the only thing a Yocto developer can do, and in the next
chapter we will see several practical examples of package manipulation.

CHAPTER 11

Miscellaneous Recipes

In this chapter, we are going to see some other examples of Yocto recipes, covering several common problems in embedded computing which don't fit in the previous two chapters.

Before continuing, the readers should be sure that their embedded kits are reachable via the serial console and network interface as explained in Section 1.3.

11.1 Adding System Services

When the kernel has finished the boot, it starts the first process with PID equal to 1, which is responsible for getting the system ready for its first login prompt and, to some extent, helps manage some processes afterward.

In particular, this so-called **init process** (or simply **init**) is responsible for starting all needed services in the system, and as every good embedded developer knows, in every embedded application there is at least a service running on the embedded machine. So it's essential to know how developers can add a new service to their Yocto systems.

© Rodolfo Giometti 2025
R. Giometti, *Yocto Project Customization for Linux*,
https://doi.org/10.1007/979-8-8688-1435-8_11

Nowadays, there are two major implementations of this init process: Initd and Systemd. The Yocto Project supports both of them, so, in this book, we are going to present both, even if we focus on the newer and most used one, that is, Systemd.

11.1.1 Notes on Initd

If some of our readers are still using Initd in their systems, we can suggest them to take a look at the service recipe in the poky meta layer:

```
$ cd sources/poky/meta-skeleton/recipes-skeleton/service
$ tree
.
├── service
│   ├── COPYRIGHT
│   ├── skeleton
│   └── skeleton_test.c
└── service_0.1.bb

1 directory, 4 files
```

As we can see, the recipe holds whatever is needed to build a dummy service based on Init; in fact, a simple daemon is defined within the skeleton_test.c file, as shown below:

```
$ cat service/skeleton_test.c
#include <unistd.h>

/* This demo does nothing except for testing /etc/init.d/skeleton */

int main(int argc, char *argv[])
{
        daemon(0, 0);
        while (1) {
                sleep(1);
        }
        return 0;
}
```

while the recipe file `service_0.1.bb` is defined as shown below:

```
$ cat service_0.1.bb
SUMMARY = "The canonical example of init scripts"
SECTION = "base"
DESCRIPTION = "This recipe is a canonical example of init scripts"
LICENSE = "GPL-2.0-only"
LIC_FILES_CHKSUM = "file://${WORKDIR}/COPYRIGHT;md5=349c872e0066155e181
8b786938876a4"

SRC_URI = "file://skeleton \
           file://skeleton_test.c \
           file://COPYRIGHT \
           "

do_compile () {
        ${CC} ${CFLAGS} ${LDFLAGS} ${WORKDIR}/skeleton_test.c -o ${WORKDI
R}/skeleton-test
}

do_install () {
        install -d ${D}${sysconfdir}/init.d
        cat ${WORKDIR}/skeleton | \
          sed -e 's,/etc,${sysconfdir},g' \
              -e 's,/usr/sbin,${sbindir},g' \
              -e 's,/var,${localstatedir},g' \
              -e 's,/usr/bin,${bindir},g' \
              -e 's,/usr,${prefix},g' > ${D}${sysconfdir}/init.d/skeleton
        chmod a+x ${D}${sysconfdir}/init.d/skeleton

        install -d ${D}${sbindir}
        install -m 0755 ${WORKDIR}/skeleton-test ${D}${sbindir}/
}

RDEPENDS:${PN} = "initscripts"

CONFFILES:${PN} += "${sysconfdir}/init.d/skeleton"
```

The interesting things to underline here are as follows:

- `LIC_FILES_CHKSUM` points to a custom license file which is located in the project sources; that's why its definition uses the `WORKDIR` to instruct the build system where to look for the license text.

In this situation, in order to compute the checksum for a custom license text file we can use the `md5sum` command as shown below:

```
$ md5sum service/COPYRIGHT
349c872e0066155e1818b786938876a4  service/COPYRIGHT
```

The generated checksum is equal to the one specified above in the recipe.

- Since the project doesn't have a `Makefile`, the `do_compile` task holds the command line to compile the daemon; also, in the `do_install`, proper `install` calls are used to install it.

- Inside the `do_install`, there is also the installation of the `skeleton` service file (see below) under the `${sysconfdir}/init.d/skeleton` directory (note that the `sysconfdir` variable usually resolves in `/etc`).

- The recipe depends on the `initscripts` package which provides the basic system startup initialization (and shutdown reverse) scripts for the system (see recipe `poky/meta/recipes-core/initscripts/initscripts_1.0.bb`).

- The `CONFFILES` variable setting which is used to specify the package's configuration file as described in Section 6.3.4.

Since every service usually runs as a daemon (even if some exceptions exist), we need a way to stop, start, or inquire the service's status; to do so, Initd uses special files, usually called the service itself, which are defined in a special format, and `skeleton` is implemented in that way.

If we take a look at the file structure, we can see the following code:

```
$ cat service/skeleton
#! /bin/sh
### BEGIN INIT INFO
# Provides:          skeleton
# Required-Start:    $local_fs
# Should-Start:
# Required-Stop:     $local_fs
# Should-Stop:
# Default-Start:     2 3 4 5
# Default-Stop:      0 1 6
# Short-Description: Example initscript
# Description:       This file should be used to construct scripts to be
#                    placed in /etc/init.d
### END INIT INFO
...
```

Even if explaining Initd's internals is out of the scope of this book, we can spend a few words explaining how it works afterward. In the above descriptive part, we notify the *initscripts* (i.e., all the scripts used to manage Initd's services) that our service should run into runlevels 2, 3, 4, and 5 at startup and in 0, 1, and 6 during the shutdown. Moreover, the service requires that the local filesystems be mounted before running or stopping stages.

A runlevel is a preset operating state, defined as a single integer that could range from zero to six, in a Unix-like OS. Each operating state determines which programs can execute after the OS boots up.

Then the file continues as reported below:

```
...
# The definition of actions: (From LSB 3.1.0)
# start        start the service
# stop         stop the service
# restart      stop and restart the service if the service is already
#              running, otherwise start the service
# try-restart  restart the service if the service is already running
```

```
# reload              cause the configuration of the service to be reloaded
#                     without actually stopping and restarting the service
# force-reload  cause the configuration to be reloaded if the service
#                     supports this, otherwise restart the service if it is
#                     running
# status              print the current status of the service

# The start, stop, restart, force-reload, and status actions shall be
# supported by all init scripts; the reload and the try-restart actions
# are optional
...
```

Here is some information regarding the default actions, that is, what the service should do when we ask our service to stop, start, restart, etc. These actions are parsed and then executed in the ending part of the file, as reported below:

```
...
case "$1" in
start)
        do_start
        ;;
stop)
        do_stop || exit $?
        ;;
status)
        status_of_proc
        ;;
restart)
        # Always start the service regardless the status of do_stop
        do_stop
        do_start
        ;;
try-restart|force-reload)
        # force-reload is the same as reload or try-restart according
        # to its definition, the reload is not implemented here, so
        # force-reload is the alias of try-restart here, but it should
        # be the alias of reload if reload is implemented.
        #
        # Only start the service when do_stop succeeds
        do_stop && do_start
        ;;
#reload)
```

```
        # If the "reload" action is implemented properly, then let the
        # force-reload be the alias of reload, and remove it from
        # try-restart|force-reload)
        #
        #do_reload
        #;;
*)
        echo "Usage: $0 {start|stop|status|restart|try-
restart|force-relo
ad}" >&2
        exit 3
        ;;
esac
```

As an example, users can ask the initscripts to start or stop our service by using the two commands below:

```
# /etc/init.d/skeleton start
# /etc/init.d/skeleton stop
```

And these are also the same commands that Initd executes during the boot or shutdown procedure.

11.1.2 A Systemd Simple Example

The scope of this section is to provide a new service for Systemd, which does the same job as Initd, but in an entirely different manner. And this is also confirmed by how a recipe for Systemd has to be implemented.

Within our meta layer, we can add a new recipe as shown below:

```
$ cd $CY_METADIR
$ tree recipes-daemons/service/
recipes-daemons/service/
├── service
│   ├── COPYRIGHT
│   ├── skeleton.service
│   └── skeleton_test.c
└── service_0.2.bb

1 directory, 4 files
```

Even if it appears that nothing changes, actually there are plenty of differences starting from the daemon implementation. In fact, we have the following:

```
$ cd recipes-daemons/service/
$ cat service/skeleton_test.c
#include <unistd.h>

/* This demo does nothing except for testing the Systemd skeleton.servi
ce */
int main(int argc, char *argv[])
{
        while (1) {
                sleep(1);
        }
        return 0;
}
```

In the code above, we have no daemon() function since Systemd has the ability to turn every process into a daemon and then run it. However, how to execute a specific service is defined within the skeleton.service file, which completely defines the new service. Below is an example of our demo code:

```
$ cat service/skeleton.service
[Unit]
Description=The skeleton service

[Service]
Type=simple
Restart=always
RestartSec=1
ExecStart=/usr/sbin/skeleton-test

[Install]
WantedBy=multi-user.target
```

A file whose name ends in .service encodes information about a process controlled and supervised by Systemd, that is, how to start or stop the service, under which circumstances it should be automatically started or stopped, and the dependency and ordering information for related software. It is called *unit configuration.* How to write these files and all possible configuration settings is out of the scope of this book, and the readers may see the complete documentation at `https://www.freedesktop.org/software/systemd/man/latest/systemd.service.html`; however, here we should explain at least what we have put within our service file above.

The common configuration items are configured in the generic `Unit` and `Install` sections, while the service-specific configuration options are configured in the `Service` section.

With `Description` we set a short human-readable title of the unit. Note that since Systemd uses it as a user-visible label for the unit, this string should identify the unit rather than describe it, despite the name.

In `WantedBy`, which can be used more than once, we can specify a space-separated list of unit names which want that this service is running before they start. It is the most common way to specify how a unit should be enabled. Simply speaking, this option is used to specify dependencies within the Systemd environment (see `https://www.freedesktop.org/software/systemd/man/latest/systemd.unit.html`).

Apart from these two sections, the interesting part in order to understand how a service can be defined within Systemd is within the `Service` section above. Here, we can specify several directives to define how our service works.

The most important are

- Type: Categorizes services by their process and daemonizing behavior, and it is important because it tells Systemd how to manage the service correctly and find out its state. The `Type` directive supports several settings; however, the most important ones for our purposes are

  - `simple`: Specifies that the main process of the service executes as a normal process and that the service is stopped when the process halts.

547

- forking: Specifies that the main process of the service forks a child process, exiting the parent process almost immediately. So, the opposite of what simple does, this tells Systemd that the process is still running even though the parent exited (this is the way a daemon should be executed).

- oneshot: It is used for one-off tasks. In fact, this type indicates that the process will be short-lived and that Systemd should wait for the process to exit before continuing on with other units.

- Restart: Indicates when Systemd will attempt to restart the service automatically. This can be set to values like always, on-success, on-failure, etc. These will trigger a restart according to the way that the service was stopped.

- RestartSec: Specifies the amount of time in seconds to wait before attempting to restart the service when the automatic service restarting is enabled.

- ExecStart: Specifies the full path and the arguments of the command to be executed to start the process. This may only be specified once (except for oneshot services), and if the path to the command is preceded by a dash character (-), nonzero exit statuses will be accepted without marking the unit activation as failed.

- ExecStop: As opposed to ExecStart, it indicates the command needed to stop the service. If this is not given, the process will be killed immediately when the service is stopped.

- • ExecReload: This is an optional directive which indicates the command necessary to reload the configuration of the service, if available.

Other interesting (and useful) directives are also ExecStartPre, ExecStartPost, and ExecStopPost which can be used to execute some commands before or after start and stop operations. However, they have not been reported here for space reasons, but the readers may read how they work at https://www.freedesktop.org/software/systemd/man/latest/systemd.service.html.

Now it should be clear why we have used the above settings to define our new Systemd service.

OK, now as the last step, we have to define a proper recipe into a .bb file to generate our new service. A possible implementation is reported below:

```
$ cat service_0.2.bb
SUMMARY = "Simple example of systemd service"
DESCRIPTION = "A simple example of the skeleton daemon installed as a s
ystemd service"
MAINTAINER = "Rodolfo Giometti <giometti@enneenne.com>"
SECTION = "base"
LICENSE = "GPL-2.0-only"
LIC_FILES_CHKSUM = "file://${WORKDIR}/COPYRIGHT;md5=349c872e0066155e181
8b786938876a4"

inherit systemd

SYSTEMD_AUTO_ENABLE = "enable"
SYSTEMD_SERVICE:${PN} = "skeleton.service"

SRC_URI = " \
        file://skeleton.service \
        file://skeleton_test.c \
        file://COPYRIGHT \
"
```

```
do_compile () {
        ${CC} ${CFLAGS} ${LDFLAGS} ${WORKDIR}/skeleton_test.c -o ${WORK
DIR}/skeleton-test

}

do_install() {
        install -d ${D}/${systemd_unitdir}/system
        cat ${WORKDIR}/skeleton.service | \
          sed -e 's,/etc,${sysconfdir},g' \
              -e 's,/usr/sbin,${sbindir},g' \
              -e 's,/var,${localstatedir},g' \
              -e 's,/usr/bin,${bindir},g' \
              -e 's,/usr,${prefix},g' > \
                ${D}/${systemd_unitdir}/system/skeleton.service

        install -d ${D}/${sbindir}
        install -m 0700 ${WORKDIR}/skeleton-test ${D}/${sbindir}/skelet
on-test
}
FILES:${PN} += "${systemd_unitdir}/system/skeleton.service"
```

The description part of our recipe is quite obvious, while the interesting things start at the `inherit systemd` directive, where we ask BitBake to load the `systemd` class. This class uses several variables to specify how the new service should work. In particular, we have

- SYSTEMD_AUTO_ENABLE: Specifies whether the specified service in SYSTEMD_SERVICE should start automatically or not. It defaults to `enable`, and we can disable the service by setting the variable to `disable` instead.

- SYSTEMD_DEFAULT_TARGET: Sets the default unit that Systemd starts at boot up. Usually, this is either `multi-user.target` or `graphical.target`, and it is set within an image recipe, not in a package recipe.

- SYSTEMD_PACKAGES: Is used to list the packages in which the build system can find the Systemd unit files when they are not found in the main recipe's package.

In fact, the SYSTEMD_PACKAGES variable is set such that the Systemd unit files are assumed to reside in the recipe's main package, as shown below:

```
SYSTEMD_PACKAGES ?= "${PN}"
```

- SYSTEMD_SERVICE: Specifies the Systemd service name for a package. To use it, we must use a package name override to indicate the package to which the value applies. In this case, multiple services can be specified, each one separated by a space.

As a final note, we should not forget to set the FILES variable properly to add our skeleton.service file; otherwise, the build system will raise an error.

OK, now everything is in place, and we can start generating our new service by executing bitbake as shown below:

```
$ bitbake service
...
Currently  2 running tasks (734 of 746)  98% |####################### |
0: service-0.2-r0 do_prepare_recipe_sysroot - 0s (pid 941612)
1: service-0.2-r0 do_patch - 0s (pid 941625)
```

If everything works well, the new service-0.2 recipe is processed, and the new packages are generated as shown below:

```
$ cy-ipk find service
cy-ipk: searching in /home/giometti/yocto/imx-yocto-bsp/imx8mp-build...
tmp/deploy/ipk/armv8a/service-dev_0.2-r0_armv8a.ipk
tmp/deploy/ipk/armv8a/service_0.2-r0_armv8a.ipk
tmp/deploy/ipk/armv8a/service-src_0.2-r0_armv8a.ipk
tmp/deploy/ipk/armv8a/service-dbg_0.2-r0_armv8a.ipk
```

In order to see the package's information, we can use our cy-ipk tool as usual:

```
$ cy-ipk get-info tmp/deploy/ipk/armv8a/service_0.2-r0_armv8a.ipk
Package: service
Version: 0.2-r0
```

```
Description: Simple example of systemd service
 A simple example of the skeleton daemon installed as a systemd service
Section: base
Priority: optional
Maintainer: Rodolfo Giometti <giometti@enneenne.com>
License: GPL-2.0-only
Architecture: armv8a
OE: service
Depends: libc6 (>= 2.35)
Source: service_0.2.bb
```

Then we can move the new package within our embedded kit:

```
$ scp $BUILDDIR/tmp/deploy/ipk/armv8a/service_0.2-r0_armv8a.ipk \
        root@192.168.32.132:/tmp/
```

On the target machine, we can install it by using the opkg tool:

```
# opkg install /tmp/service_0.2-r0_armv8a.ipk
Installing service (0.2) on root
Configuring service.
```

During the package installation, we may get several messages from Systemd's subsystem as below:

```
[   78.221247] systemd-sysv-generator[916]: SysV service '/etc/ini
t.d/umountfs' lacks a native systemd unit file. Automatically gene
rating a unit file for compatibility. Please update package to inc
lude a native systemd unit file, in order to make it more safe and
 robust.
```

They can be safely ignored.

Then we can ask Systemd to display our new service status by using the systemctl utility:

```
# systemctl -l --no-pager status skeleton
* skeleton.service - The skeleton service
    Loaded: loaded (8;;file://imx8mp-icore-cy/lib/systemd/system/skele
ton.service/lib/systemd/system/skeleton.service8;;; enabled; vendor pre
set: enabled)
```

```
    Active: active (running) since Thu 2022-04-28 18:03:09 UTC; 10s ago
  Main PID: 919 (skeleton-test)
     Tasks: 1 (limit: 3197)
    Memory: 132.0K
    CGroup: /system.slice/skeleton.service
            `- 919 /usr/sbin/skeleton-test

Apr 28 18:03:09 imx8mp-icore-cy systemd[1]: Started The skeleton servic
e.
```

OK, everything is in place, but before ending this section we should also verify that the service will start at boot. So let's restart our machine by issuing a reboot command, and then let's take a look at booting messages; we should see something as reported below:

```
...
[ OK  ] Started ISP i.MX 8Mplus daemon.
         Starting IPv6 Packet Filtering Framework...
         Starting IPv4 Packet Filtering Framework...
         Starting Network Time Service (one-shot ntpdate mode)...
         Starting Telephony service...
[ OK  ] Started The skeleton service.
...
```

Our new service has been correctly started! And we can verify it by using again the systemctl tool after we have logged in as root:

```
# systemctl -l --no-pager status skeleton
* skeleton.service - The skeleton service
     Loaded: loaded (8;;file://imx8mp-icore-
cy/lib/systemd/system/skeleton.service/lib/sys
temd/system/skeleton.service8;;; enabled; vendor preset: disabled)
     Active: active (running) since Fri 2022-04-29 11:14:46 UTC; 1min
56s ago
   Main PID: 261 (skeleton-test)
     Tasks: 1 (limit: 3197)
    Memory: 140.0K
    CGroup: /system.slice/skeleton.service
            `- 261 /usr/sbin/skeleton-test

Apr 29 11:14:46 imx8mp-icore-cy systemd[1]: Started The skeleton servic
e.
```

Our new service has been correctly started at boot.

11.2 Getting Newer (or Older) Releases

Another usual problem in managing a complex OS is the need to update a package to fix some bugs or to have new functionalities. In this scenario, the Yocto build system gives us good tools to easily update a package to a newer (or older if needed) release.

The first tool is a subcommand of devtool named check-upgrade-status:

```
$ devtool check-upgrade-status -h
NOTE: Starting bitbake server...
usage: devtool check-upgrade-status [-h] [--all] [recipe ...]

Prints a table of recipes together with versions currently provided by
Recipes, and latest upstream versions, when there is a later version
available

arguments:
  recipe      Name of the recipe to report (omit to report upgrade info
              for all recipes)
...
```

Here is a partial example table that reports on all the recipes:

```
$ devtool check-upgrade-status
...
INFO: bind        9.16.20  9.16.21 Armin Kuster <akuster808@gmail.com
>
INFO: inetutils   2.1      2.2     Tom Rini <trini@konsulko.com>
INFO: iproute2    5.13.0   5.14.0  Changhyeok Bae <changhyeok.bae@gma
il.com>
INFO: openssl     1.1.1l   3.0.0   Alexander Kanavin <alex.kanavin@gm
ail.com>
INFO: base-passwd 3.5.29   3.5.51 Anuj Mittal <anuj.mittal@intel.com
> cannot be updated due to: Version 3.5.38 requires cdebconf for update
-passwd utility
...
```

Note the reason for not upgrading the base-passwd recipe. In this example, while a new version is available upstream, you would rather not use it because the dependency on cdebconf is not easily satisfied.

Maintainers can express the reason that is shown by adding the RECIPE_ NO_UPDATE_REASON variable to the corresponding recipe. See the base-passwd.bb recipe in the poky layer for an example:

```
$ cat poky/meta/recipes-core/base-passwd/base-passwd_3.5.29.bb
SUMMARY = "Base system master password/group files"
DESCRIPTION = "The master copies of the user database files (/etc/passw
d and /etc/group).  The update-passwd tool is also provided to keep the
 system databases synchronized with these master files."
HOMEPAGE = "https://launchpad.net/base-passwd"
SECTION = "base"
LICENSE = "GPL-2.0-only"
LIC_FILES_CHKSUM = "file://COPYING;md5=eb723b61539feef013de476e68b5c50a"

RECIPE_NO_UPDATE_REASON = "Version 3.5.38 requires cdebconf for update-
passwd utility"
...
```

However, we exactly know which is the package we have to update, and we can use the latest-version subcommand as shown below:

```
$ devtool latest-version -h
NOTE: Starting bitbake server...
usage: devtool latest-version [-h] recipename

Queries the upstream server for what the latest upstream release is (for
git, tags are checked, for tarballs, a list of them is obtained, and one
with the highest version number is reported)

arguments:
  recipename  Name of recipe to query (just name - no version, path or
              extension)
...
```

Note that this subcommand doesn't recognize the RECIPE_NO_ UPDATE_REASON as the check-upgrade-status above. In fact, if we execute it on base-passwd, we get no warning:

```
$ devtool latest-version base-passwd
...
INFO: Current version: 3.5.29
INFO: Latest version: 3.6.3
```

So it's best practice to use both tools before starting a package update.

For example, we can get the latest version for the dropbear package, as shown below:

```
$ devtool latest-version dropbear
...
URL transformed to HTTPS due to an HSTS policy
--2024-03-18 14:35:32--  https://matt.ucc.asn.au/dropbear/releases/
Resolving matt.ucc.asn.au (matt.ucc.asn.au)... 104.26.8.126, 104.26.9.1
26, 172.67.72.143, ...
Connecting to matt.ucc.asn.au (matt.ucc.asn.au)|104.26.8.126|:443... co
nnected.
HTTP request sent, awaiting response... 200 OK
Length: unspecified [text/html]
Saving to: '/tmp/wget-index-g4al2_73/wget-listing-3k45ri9r'

    OK .......... ...                                        483K=0.03s

2024-03-18 14:35:33 (483 KB/s) - '/tmp/wget-index-g4al2_73/wget-listing
-3k45ri9r' saved [13441]

INFO: Current version: 2020.81
INFO: Latest version: 2022.83
```

OK, now that we know which is the latest release of a package, we should see how we can proceed to do the real update. And to do so, we can use the upgrade subcommand, as shown below:

```
$ devtool upgrade -h
NOTE: Starting bitbake server...
usage: devtool upgrade [-h] [--version VERSION] [--srcrev SRCREV]
                       [--srcbranch SRCBRANCH] [--branch BRANCH]
                       [--no-patch]
                       [--no-overrides] [--same-dir | --no-same-dir]
                       [--keep-temp] [--keep-failure]
                       recipename [srctree]

Upgrades an existing recipe to a new upstream version. Puts the upgraded
recipe file into the workspace along with any associated files, and
extracts the source tree to a specified location (in case patches need
rebasing or adding to as a result of the upgrade).

arguments:
  recipename              Name of recipe to upgrade (just name - no
                          version, path or extension)
```

```
  srctree               Path to where to extract the source tree. If not
                        specified, a subdirectory of /home/giometti/yoct
                        o/imx-yocto-bsp/imx8mp-build/workspace/sources
                        will be used.

options:
  -h, --help            show this help message and exit
  --version VERSION, -V VERSION
                        Version to upgrade to (PV). If omitted, latest
                        upstream version will be determined and used, if
                        possible.
  --srcrev SRCREV, -S SRCREV
                        Source revision to upgrade to (useful when
                        fetching from an SCM such as git)
  --srcbranch SRCBRANCH, -B SRCBRANCH
                        Branch in source repository containing the
                        revision to use (if fetching from an SCM such as
                        git)
  --branch BRANCH, -b BRANCH
                        Name for new development branch to checkout
                        (default "devtool")
  --no-patch            Do not apply patches from the recipe to the new
                        source code
  --no-overrides, -O    Do not create branches for other override
                        configurations
  --same-dir, -s        Build in same directory as source
  --no-same-dir         Force build in a separate build directory
  --keep-temp           Keep temporary directory (for debugging)
  --keep-failure        Keep failed upgrade recipe and associated files
                        (for debugging)
```

By using this tool, we can (hopefully) easily update a package since it puts the upgraded recipe file into the workspace along with any associated files. Then the sources are extracted, and, in the case of patches, a rebasing is automatically invoked.

Simply speaking, if we are lucky, the procedure may terminate automatically; otherwise, some reworks should be done by us.

In order to do a practical example of how to do a real upgrade, let's use the devtool upgrade command on the dropbear package to move to the release 2022.83. The current recipe is in the poky meta layer:

```
$ cat ./poky/meta/recipes-core/dropbear/dropbear_2020.81.bb
```

```
require dropbear.inc

SRC_URI[sha256sum] = "48235d10b37775dbda59341ac0c4b239b82ad6318c31568b9
85730c788aac53b"
```

To see the content of the SRC_URI variable, we have to take a look into the required file dropbear.inc:

```
$ cat ./poky/meta/recipes-core/dropbear/dropbear.inc
SUMMARY = "A lightweight SSH and SCP implementation"
...
SRC_URI = "http://matt.ucc.asn.au/dropbear/releases/dropbear-${PV}.tar.bz2 \
           file://0001-urandom-xauth-changes-to-options.h.patch \
           file://init \
           file://dropbearkey.service \
           file://dropbear@.service \
           file://dropbear.socket \
           file://dropbear.default \
           ${@bb.utils.contains('DISTRO_FEATURES', 'pam', '${PAM_SRC_UR
I}', '', d)} \
           ${@bb.utils.contains('PACKAGECONFIG', 'disable-weak-ciphers'
, 'file://dropbear-disable-weak-ciphers.patch', '', d)} "
...
```

Some patch files are listed, so we may get problems in applying them to the new release. However, we are optimistic, and we decide to proceed. To start the updating procedure, we execute the devtool upgrade command with the -V option argument specifying the release we wish to obtain (note that sometimes we don't need the latest release, and the -V option argument comes to help):

```
$ devtool upgrade -V 2022.83 dropbear
...
INFO: Fetching http://matt.ucc.asn.au/dropbear/releases/dropbear-2022.8
3.tar.bz2...
...
INFO: Rebasing devtool onto 069d4ed47544b121abc70022804066026beb629f
WARNING: Command 'git rebase 069d4ed47544b121abc70022804066026beb629f'
failed:
Auto-merging default_options.h
CONFLICT (content): Merge conflict in default_options.h

You will need to resolve conflicts in order to complete the upgrade.
INFO: Upgraded source extracted to /home/giometti/yocto/imx-yocto-bsp/i
```

```
mx8mp-build/workspace/sources/dropbear
INFO: New recipe is /home/giometti/yocto/imx-yocto-bsp/imx8mp-build/wor
kspace/recipes/dropbear/dropbear_2022.83.bb
```

The devtool subcommand has downloaded the right sources and
started the rebasing to try to apply all patches in the old recipe. However,
we had no luck, and the rebase failed. So we have to resolve the issues. To
do so, we have to move where the source has been placed:

```
$ cd $BUILDDIR/workspace/sources/dropbear
```

Then we have to restart the rebasing as done by devtool:

```
$ git rebase 069d4ed47544b121abc70022804066026beb629f
Auto-merging default_options.h
CONFLICT (content): Merge conflict in default_options.h
error: could not apply af4067b... dropbear: new feature: disable-weak-c
iphers
hint: Resolve all conflicts manually, mark them as resolved with
hint: "git add/rm <conflicted_files>", then run "git rebase --continue".
hint: You can instead skip this commit: run "git rebase --skip".
hint: To abort and get back to the state before "git rebase", run "git
hint: rebase --abort".
Could not apply af4067b... dropbear: new feature: disable-weak-ciphers
```

**Note that the commit ID may vary. The readers should consider what
they get into the above message at these lines:**

```
...
INFO: Rebasing devtool onto 069d4ed47544b121abc70022804066026beb62
9f
WARNING: Command 'git rebase 069d4ed47544b121abc70022804066026beb6
29f' failed:
...
```

The rebase stopped returning the same error as above, then we have to
inspect the conflict:

```
$ git diff
diff --cc default_options.h
index 33238ec,4bd7bd4..0000000
```

```
--- a/default_options.h
+++ b/default_options.h
@@@ -192,8 -162,8 +192,13 @@@ IMPORTANT: Some options will require "m

   * Small systems should generally include either curve25519 or ecdh f
or performance.
   * curve25519 is less widely supported but is faster
++<<<<<<< HEAD
 + */
 +#define DROPBEAR_DH_GROUP14_SHA1 1
++=======
+  */
+ #define DROPBEAR_DH_GROUP14_SHA1 0
++>>>>>>> af4067b (dropbear: new feature: disable-weak-ciphers)
   #define DROPBEAR_DH_GROUP14_SHA256 1
   #define DROPBEAR_DH_GROUP16 0
   #define DROPBEAR_CURVE25519 1
```

The issue is trivial, and the following patch should resolve it:

```
--- a/default_options.h
+++ b/default_options.h
@@ -193,7 +193,7 @@ IMPORTANT: Some options will require "make clean" after
changes */
   * Small systems should generally include either curve25519 or ecdh fo
r performance.
   * curve25519 is less widely supported but is faster
   */
-#define DROPBEAR_DH_GROUP14_SHA1 1
+#define DROPBEAR_DH_GROUP14_SHA1 0
 #define DROPBEAR_DH_GROUP14_SHA256 1
 #define DROPBEAR_DH_GROUP16 0
 #define DROPBEAR_CURVE25519 1
```

Then, to close the conflict, we have to add the modifications to the index and then call git rebase --continue in order to move to the next step:

```
$ git add default_options.h
$ git rebase --continue
ACCEPT commit text
[detached HEAD a8559da] dropbear: new feature: disable-weak-ciphers
 Author: Joseph Reynolds <joseph.reynolds1@ibm.com>
 1 file changed, 1 insertion(+), 1 deletion(-)
```

560

```
Successfully rebased and updated refs/heads/devtool.
```

Great! Other patches applied, and now the rebase is complete. So we can finish our updating procedure by asking devtool to move our new updated package to our meta layer, as shown below:

```
$ devtool finish dropbear meta-cy
...
INFO: Updating patch 0001-urandom-xauth-changes-to-options.h.patch
INFO: Updating patch 0005-dropbear-enable-pam.patch
INFO: Updating patch dropbear-disable-weak-ciphers.patch
INFO: Moving recipe file to /home/giometti/yocto/imx-yocto-bsp/sources/
meta-cy/recipes-core/dropbear
INFO: Leaving source tree /home/giometti/yocto/imx-yocto-bsp/imx8mp-bui
ld/workspace/sources/dropbear as-is; if you no longer need it then plea
se delete it manually
```

Now we can take a look at the new recipe sources by moving within our meta layer:

```
$ tree recipes-core/dropbear
recipes-core/dropbear
├── dropbear
│   ├── 0001-urandom-xauth-changes-to-options.h.patch
│   ├── 0005-dropbear-enable-pam.patch
│   ├── 0006-dropbear-configuration-file.patch
│   ├── dropbear
│   ├── dropbear.default
│   ├── dropbear-disable-weak-ciphers.patch
│   ├── dropbearkey.service
│   ├── dropbear@.service
│   ├── dropbear.socket
│   └── init
├── dropbear_2022.83.bb
└── dropbear.inc

1 directory, 12 files
```

To test the code, we do as usual; we should generate the new package first to check that everything still properly works:

```
$ bitbake dropbear
...
0: dropbear-2022.83-r0 do_compile - 0s (pid 965341)
```

...

And, in case of no errors, we can generate a new Yocto image which should now include our new dropbear package:

```
$ bitbake engicam-evaluation-image-mx8
```

Here, we can also use our image cy-evaluation-image-mx8 to test the new recipe.

Now we can rewrite our microSD with the new image; however, to be sure that the new version has really been installed, we can take a look within the manifest file as explained in Section 7.4.3:

```
$ grep dropbear $BUILDDIR/tmp/deploy/images/imx8mp-icore-cy/engicam-eva
luation-image-mx8-imx8mp-icore-cy.manifest
dropbear armv8a 2022.83-r0
packagegroup-core-ssh-dropbear all 1.0-r1
```

OK, it's the right release. Now, as the last step, we have to execute our new image and verify that everything is still running. When the boot has been ended, we have to log in as root and check again the dropbear's release, as shown below:

```
# dropbear -V
Dropbear v2022.83
```

In case the network settings have been lost, we should restore the default settings as explained in Section 1.3.2, then we have to try an SSH connection:

```
$ ssh root@192.168.32.132
@@@@@@@@@@@@@@@@@@@@@@@@@@@@@@@@@@@@@@@@@@@@@@@@@@@@@@@@@@@@@@@
@    WARNING: REMOTE HOST IDENTIFICATION HAS CHANGED!     @
@@@@@@@@@@@@@@@@@@@@@@@@@@@@@@@@@@@@@@@@@@@@@@@@@@@@@@@@@@@@@@@
IT IS POSSIBLE THAT SOMEONE IS DOING SOMETHING NASTY!
Someone could be eavesdropping on you right now (man-in-the-middle atta
```

```
ck)!
It is also possible that a host key has just been changed.
The fingerprint for the RSA key sent by the remote host is
SHA256:LzmhIlYZuOPOqGYGHOegNycfNUju/8VgCImJh/7ACsg.
Please contact your system administrator.
Add correct host key in /home/giometti/.ssh/known_hosts to get rid of t
his message.
Offending RSA key in /home/giometti/.ssh/known_hosts:104
  remove with:
  ssh-keygen -f "/home/giometti/.ssh/known_hosts" -R "192.168.32.132"
Host key for 192.168.32.132 has changed and you have requested strict c
hecking.
Host key verification failed.
```

This is expected due to the fact that we have reprogrammed the microSD with a new image, so we just need to remove the offending keys from our list and retry the connection:

```
$ ssh-keygen -f "/home/giometti/.ssh/known_hosts" -R "192.168.32.132"
# Host 192.168.32.132 found: line 104
/home/giometti/.ssh/known_hosts updated.
Original contents retained as /home/giometti/.ssh/known_hosts.old
$ ssh root@192.168.32.132
The authenticity of host '192.168.32.132 (192.168.32.132)' can't be est
ablished.
RSA key fingerprint is SHA256:LzmhIlYZuOPOqGYGHOegNycfNUju/8VgCImJh/7AC
sg.
This key is not known by any other names
Are you sure you want to continue connecting (yes/no/[fingerprint])? yes
Warning: Permanently added '192.168.32.132' (RSA) to the list of known
hosts.
root@imx8mp-icore-cy:~#
```

Great, now our image has a newer dropbear release.

11.3 Editing (or Appending) Existing Recipes

There are several ways to easily edit an existing recipe, and in this section we are going to see some of them, starting from the usage of the recipetool command introduced in Section 4.3.

11.3.1 Adding Custom Files

The simpler command to use when we wish to edit an existing recipe is the following:

```
$ recipetool edit hello
```

By doing so, we ask the Yocto build system to use our preferred editor to show us the recipe for our hello package (the command will open the main recipe and all the related .bbappend files!). Then we can proceed in altering the original file; however, as already said, altering a recipe which is not in our custom layer is not the better way to solve the problem, but it is better to use the .bbappend solution. Then we should use the next command:

```
$ recipetool newappend $CY_METADIR devmem2
NOTE: Starting bitbake server...
...
/home/giometti/yocto/imx-yocto-bsp/sources/meta-cy/recipes-support/devm
em2/devmem2_2.0.bbappend
```

In this manner, we get an empty devmem2_2.0.bbappend file within our custom layer that we can use to do all our needed modifications to the recipe without altering the original recipe file.

Note that in the example, we get a versioned `.bbappend` file, and in order to get a file to apply to any recipe version, we can add the `-w` option argument as below:

```
$ recipetool newappend -w $CY_METADIR devmem2
NOTE: Starting bitbake server...
...
/home/giometti/yocto/imx-yocto-bsp/sources/meta-cy/recipes-support
/devmem2/devmem2_%.bbappend
```

On the other hand, if we just wish to alter the recipe to add a new source file, for example, a simple custom utility to call the devmem2 tool above, we can use the appendsrcfiles subcommand as below:

```
$ recipetool appendsrcfiles $CY_METADIR devmem2 cy_devmem2
NOTE: Starting bitbake server...
...
NOTE: Writing append file /home/giometti/yocto/imx-yocto-bsp/sources/me
ta-cy/recipes-support/devmem2/devmem2_2.0.bbappend
NOTE: Copying cy_devmem2 to /home/giometti/yocto/imx-yocto-bsp/sources/
meta-cy/recipes-support/devmem2/devmem2/cy_devmem2
```

To add just a single file, we can also use the `appendsrcfile` subcommand for `recipetool`; however, the multiple version is more general.

Moreover, notice that in some circumstances, we may prefer to add the file into WORKDIR instead of S, and to do so we can use the `-W` option argument. The readers should remember that the S directory is where the sources are placed, while WORKDIR is where the recipe is being built. So choosing this last option may result in something we don't want.

where the file cy_devmem2 should be already present, and in this example it holds the following code:

```
$ cat cy_devmem2
#!/bin/sh
echo "$0 - CY release"
devmem2 $@
```

Now within our custom layer, we get the following new directory structure:

```
$ cd $CY_METADIR
$ tree recipes-support/devmem2/
recipes-support/devmem2/
├── devmem2
│   └── cy_devmem2
└── devmem2_2.0.bbappend

1 directory, 2 files
```

where the new file devmem2_2.0.bbappend holds the following code:

```
$ cat $CY_METADIR/recipes-support/devmem2/devmem2_2.0.bbappend
SRC_URI += "file://cy_devmem2;subdir=git"

FILESEXTRAPATHS:prepend := "${THISDIR}/${PN}:"
```

Note that, as above, to have a .bbappend which is valid for any recipe version, we can use the -w option argument.

Now, in order to have the file cy_devmem2 properly installed within the root filesystem, we have to add a proper installation procedure. To do so, we have to append proper instructions in the do_install() function by adding the following lines to devmem2_2.0.bbappend:

```
--- a/devmem2/devmem2_2.0.bbappend
+++ b/devmem2/devmem2_2.0.bbappend
@@ -4,3 +4,7 @@

 PACKAGE_ARCH = "${MACHINE_ARCH}"
```

```
+do_install:append() {
+    install -d ${D}${bindir}
+    install cy_devmem2 ${D}${bindir}
+}
```

In this manner, `bitbake` will execute the recipe's default `do_install()` function and then our custom one which adds the program `my_devmem2` to the root filesystem.

Now to test if everything works well, we can try to generate the `.ipk` file for devmem2 by using the next command:

```
$ bitbake devmem2
```

The new package now should have been generated:

```
$ cy-ipk find devmem2
cy-ipk: searching in /home/giometti/yocto/imx-yocto-bsp/imx8mp-build...
tmp/deploy/ipk/imx8mp_icore_cy/devmem2-src_2.0-r0_imx8mp_icore_cy.ipk
tmp/deploy/ipk/imx8mp_icore_cy/devmem2_2.0-r0_imx8mp_icore_cy.ipk
tmp/deploy/ipk/imx8mp_icore_cy/devmem2-dbg_2.0-r0_imx8mp_icore_cy.ipk
tmp/deploy/ipk/imx8mp_icore_cy/devmem2-dev_2.0-r0_imx8mp_icore_cy.ipk
```

Now, to verify that the new command has been added, we can use our `cy-ipk` tool as usual:

```
$ cy-ipk inspect tmp/deploy/ipk/imx8mp_icore_cy/devmem2_2.0-r0_imx8mp_i
core_cy.ipk
drwxr-xr-x root/root          0 2022-05-30 16:07 ./usr/
drwxr-xr-x root/root          0 2022-05-30 16:07 ./usr/bin/
-rwxr-xr-x root/root         44 2022-05-30 16:07 ./usr/bin/cy_devmem2
-rwxr-xr-x root/root      10208 2022-05-30 16:07 ./usr/bin/devmem2
```

OK, everything is in place. So we can install the file package within our embedded kit by copying the file on it:

```
$ scp tmp/deploy/ipk/imx8mp_icore_cy/devmem2_2.0-r0_imx8mp_icore_cy.ipk
  \
      root@192.168.32.132:/tmp/
```

then by installing the package:

```
# opkg install /tmp/devmem2_2.0-r0_imx8mp_icore_cy.ipk
Installing devmem2 (2.0) on root
Configuring devmem2.
```

567

Note that, in the case the package devmem2 release 2.0-r0 is already present on the system, we'll get the following error:

```
* opkg_prepare_file_for_install: Refusing to load file '/tmp/devme
m2_2.0-r0_imx8mp_icore_cy.ipk' as it matches the installed version
 of devmem2 (2.0-r0).
```

In this case, we can resolve by using the --force-reinstall option argument as shown below:

```
# opkg install --force-reinstall /tmp/devmem2_2.0-r0_imx8mp_icore_
cy.ipk
```

Now we should have our new custom file:

```
# cy_devmem2
/usr/bin/cy_devmem2 - CY release

Usage:  devmem2 { address } [ type [ data ] ]
        address : memory address to act upon
        type    : access operation type : [b]yte, [h]alfword, [w]ord,
[l]ong
        data    : data to be written
```

At this point, the readers should notice the -m option argument for the recipetool appendsrcfiles command. This can be used when the new files we wish to add to our recipe should be reserved for a specific machine only or if we have to install different versions of the file according to the current MACHINE value.

In this case, we can use a modified version of the command to obtain that the new file is added when the package is generated for the machine imx8mp-icore-cy only. However, before running recipetool again, we have to delete what's already done, or the new execution will not run successfully:

```
$ rm -rf $CY_METADIR/recipes-support/devmem2
```

Then we can use the next command:

```
$ recipetool appendsrcfiles -m imx8mp-icore-cy $CY_METADIR \
        devmem2 cy_devmem2
NOTE: Starting bitbake server...
...
NOTE: Writing append file /home/giometti/yocto/imx-yocto-bsp/sources/me
ta-cy/recipes-support/devmem2/devmem2_2.0.bbappend
NOTE: Copying cy_devmem2 to /home/giometti/yocto/imx-yocto-bsp/sources/
meta-cy/recipes-support/devmem2/devmem2/imx8mp-icore-cy/cy_devmem2
```

Note that `cy_devmem2` must be in the current working directory.

Now, the file devmem2_2.0.bbappend holds the following content:

```
$ cat $CY_METADIR/recipes-support/devmem2/devmem2_2.0.bbappend
SRC_URI += "file://cy_devmem2;subdir=git"

FILESEXTRAPATHS:prepend := "${THISDIR}/${PN}:"

PACKAGE_ARCH = "${MACHINE_ARCH}"
```

To get a functional recipe, the readers should remember to add again the do_install:append() function, as done before.

The file `cy_devmem2` is now copied within a special directory as below:

```
$ tree recipes-support/devmem2/
recipes-support/devmem2/
├── devmem2
│   └── imx8mp-icore-cy
│       └── cy_devmem2
└── devmem2_2.0.bbappend
```

If we regenerate the package, we should get the same result. However, there could be a problem; in fact, if we try to generate the devmem2 package for another machine, we may get the following error:

```
$ MACHINE=imx8mp-icore bitbake devmem2
...
WARNING: /home/giometti/yocto/imx-yocto-bsp/sources/meta-openembedded/m
eta-oe/recipes-support/devmem2/devmem2_2.0.bb: Unable to get checksum f
or devmem2 SRC_URI entry cy_devmem2: file could not be found
...
WARNING: devmem2-2.0-r0 do_fetch: Failed to fetch URL file://cy_devmem2
;subdir=git, attempting MIRRORS if available
ERROR: devmem2-2.0-r0 do_fetch: Fetcher failure: Unable to find file fi
le://cy_devmem2;subdir=git anywhere. The paths that were searched were:
/home/giometti/yocto/imx-yocto-bsp/sources/meta-cy/recipes-support/devm
em2/devmem2/fsl
...  /home/giometti/yocto/imx-yocto-bsp/sources/meta-cy/recipes-support/d
evmem2/devmem2/imx8mp-icore
...  /home/giometti/yocto/imx-yocto-bsp/sources/meta-cy/recipes-support/d
evmem2/devmem2/
...  /home/giometti/yocto/imx-yocto-bsp/sources/meta-openembedded/meta-oe
/recipes-support/devmem2/files/
    /home/giometti/Projects/DL_ARCHIVES/yocto/
ERROR: devmem2-2.0-r0 do_fetch: Bitbake Fetcher Error: FetchError('Unab
le to fetch URL from any source.', 'file://cy_devmem2;subdir=git')
ERROR: Logfile of failure stored in: /home/giometti/yocto/imx-yocto-bsp
/imx8mp-build/tmp/work/imx8mp_icore-poky-linux/devmem2/2.0-r0/temp/log.
do_fetch.1456494
ERROR: Task (/home/giometti/yocto/imx-yocto-bsp/sources/meta-openembedd
ed/meta-oe/recipes-support/devmem2/devmem2_2.0.bb:do_fetch) failed with
 exit code '1'
NOTE: Tasks Summary: Attempted 732 tasks of which 731 didn't need to be
 rerun and 1 failed.

Summary: 1 task failed:
...
```

This is because the Yocto build system is trying to locate the file cy_devmem2 in several directories (see above what is reported within the error message) with no success. When we generated the package for our machine, it checked successfully under the directory sources/meta-cy/ recipes-support/devmem2/devmem2/imx8mp-icore-cy, where the file lies. But now under sources/meta-cy/recipes-support/devmem2/devmem2/ imx8mp-icore, there is nothing, nor under the parent directory (which is one of the locations where the system searches on)!

One possible solution is to add a generic version of the file cy_devmem2 under the directory recipes-support/devmem2/devmem2, as shown below:

```
$ cp recipes-support/devmem2/devmem2/imx8mp-icore-cy/cy_devmem2 \
        recipes-support/devmem2/devmem2/
$ tree recipes-support/devmem2/
recipes-support/devmem2/
├── devmem2
│   ├── imx8mp-icore-cy
│   │   └── cy_devmem2
│   └── cy_devmem2
└── devmem2_2.0.bbappend

2 directories, 3 files
```

But this implies that the file will be added also for other machines that, maybe, are not interested in using it! So, if we wish the modification to apply just to our machine only, we can use some overrides within our .bbappend file, as reported below:

```
--- a/devmem2_2.0.bbappend
+++ b/devmem2_2.0.bbappend
@@ -4,7 +4,7 @@

 PACKAGE_ARCH = "${MACHINE_ARCH}"

-do_install:append() {
+do_install:append:imx8mp-icore-cy() {
     install -d ${D}${bindir}
     install cy_devmem2 ${D}${bindir}
 }
```

In this scenario, the overrides will take place with the imx8mp-icore-cy machine only.

11.3.2 Changing the Default Configuration

Another really useful way to alter a recipe is by using the recipetool appendfile subcommand.

Let's suppose we need to change the current configuration of the ptpd daemon because, within our custom hardware, the data arrives from the eth1 device instead of the eth0. The current content of the file, as we can see on our embedded kit, is the following:

```
# cat /etc/default/ptpd
#
# PTPD Configuration
#
# See man ptpd2 for arguments.
#
# Example arguments
PTPDARGS="-d 1 -i eth0"
```

To alter it, we can simply create a new custom_ptpd file with the right settings (i.e., having PTPDARGS="-d 1 -i eth1") and then use the command below:

```
$ recipetool appendfile $CY_METADIR /etc/default/ptpd custom_ptpd
NOTE: Starting bitbake server...
...
NOTE: Writing append file /home/giometti/yocto/imx-yocto-bsp/sources/me
ta-cy/recipes-daemons/ptpd/ptpd_2.3.1.bbappend
NOTE: Copying custom_ptpd to /home/giometti/yocto/imx-yocto-bsp/sources
/meta-cy/recipes-daemons/ptpd/ptpd/ptpd.conf
```

Note that the command may fail in the case recipetool cannot determine which recipe is providing the file and how to overwrite it with our version. The readers should be sure that the file /etc/default/ptpd is present within their final root filesystem. See below in this section.

As we can see above, the command has installed our file with the right name so that it will be used to build the package for our system. Within our meta layer, we now have the following new subdirectory:

```
$ cd $CY_METADIR
$ tree recipes-daemons/ptpd
recipes-daemons/ptpd
├── ptpd
│   └── ptpd.conf
└── ptpd_2.3.1.bbappend

1 directory, 2 files
```

where the .bbappend file holds the following setting:

```
$ cat recipes-daemons/ptpd/ptpd_2.3.1.bbappend
FILESEXTRAPATHS:prepend := "${THISDIR}/${PN}:"
```

while the new configuration file is exactly our file:

```
$ cat recipes-daemons/ptpd/ptpd/ptpd.conf
#
# PTPD Configuration - CY version
#
# See man ptpd2 for arguments.
#
# Example arguments
PTPDARGS="-d 1 -i eth1"
```

Now to see if everything works well, we can regenerate a new image and verify the result.

On some system, we may get the following error message:

```
$ recipetool appendfile $CY_METADIR /etc/default/ptpd custom_ptpd
NOTE: Starting bitbake server...
...
ERROR: Unable to find any package producing path /etc/default/ptp
d - this may be because the recipe packaging it has not been buil
t yet
```

This is because, as reported in the error message, the package has not been built yet; so, if we know which is the package, we can build it:

```
$ bitbake ptpd
```

And then execute again the above command.

11.3.3 Changing a Variable

Before ending this section, it could be interesting to take a look at another recipetool subcommand, that is, setvar.

Suppose we wish to change the default value (currently to 100) for the variable ALTERNATIVE_PRIORITY within the i2c-tools in the poky meta layer. It is set as reported below:

```
$ grep ALTERNATIVE_PRIORITY \
        sources/poky/meta/recipes-devtools/i2c-tools/i2c-tools_4.3.bb
ALTERNATIVE_PRIORITY = "100"
```

And we can change it by just using the command below:

```
$ recipetool setvar -r \
        sources/poky/meta/recipes-devtools/i2c-tools/i2c-tools_4.3.bb \
        ALTERNATIVE_PRIORITY '200'
```

Note the -r option argument to be sure that the variable is not set in any include file, if present.

However, this will change a file outside our custom layer (which is not what we want), so we can first create a void .bbappend file:

```
$ recipetool newappend $CY_METADIR i2c-tools
NOTE: Starting bitbake server...
...
/home/giometti/yocto/imx-yocto-bsp/sources/meta-cy/recipes-devtools/i2c
-tools/i2c-tools_4.3.bbappend
```

And then set there the desired value:

```
$ recipetool setvar -r \
        $CY_METADIR/recipes-devtools/i2c-tools/i2c-tools_4.3.bbappend \
        ALTERNATIVE_PRIORITY '200'
```

Now, the new .bbappend file holds the following:

```
$ cat $CY_METADIR/recipes-devtools/i2c-tools/i2c-tools_4.3.bbappend
ALTERNATIVE_PRIORITY = "200"
```

We can verify that the new setting is active by taking a look at its value using `cy-vars` as shown below:

```
$ cy-vars ALTERNATIVE_PRIORITY i2c-tools
ALTERNATIVE_PRIORITY="200"
```

The variable is set to the expected value.

11.4 Adding Custom Package Groups

Package groups are recipes with the sole purpose of creating dependencies to simplify image creation. In fact, a package group recipe bundles multiple packages together, and then, instead of having to explicitly specify each package in the `IMAGE_INSTALL` variable, we can simply specify the package group name.

For example, if we recall what was seen in Section 6.5.1 where we mentioned the `core-image-minimal.bb` recipe in the poky meta layer, we have seen a setting as shown below:

```
$ cat poky/meta/recipes-core/images/core-image-minimal.bb
SUMMARY = "A small image just capable of allowing a device to boot."

IMAGE_INSTALL = "packagegroup-core-boot ${CORE_IMAGE_EXTRA_INSTALL}"
...
```

As we can see, `IMAGE_INSTALL` is initialized with the *package* `packagegroup-core-boot`, but if we take a look at its recipe we can see that it is not a normal package recipe:

```
$ cat poky/meta/recipes-core/packagegroups/packagegroup-core-boot.bb
#
# Copyright (C) 2007 OpenedHand Ltd.
#

SUMMARY = "Minimal boot requirements"
DESCRIPTION = "The minimal set of packages required to boot the system"
PR = "r17"
```

```
PACKAGE_ARCH = "${MACHINE_ARCH}"

inherit packagegroup
...
RDEPENDS:${PN} = "\
    base-files \
    base-passwd \
    ${VIRTUAL-RUNTIME_base-utils} \
    ${@bb.utils.contains("DISTRO_FEATURES", "sysvinit", "${SYSVINIT_SCR
IPTS}", "", d)} \
    ${@bb.utils.contains("MACHINE_FEATURES", "keyboard", "${VIRTUAL-RUN
TIME_keymaps}", "", d)} \
    ${@bb.utils.contains("MACHINE_FEATURES", "efi", "${EFI_PROVIDER} ke
rnel", "", d)} \
    netbase \
    ${VIRTUAL-RUNTIME_login_manager} \
    ${VIRTUAL-RUNTIME_init_manager} \
    ${VIRTUAL-RUNTIME_dev_manager} \
    ${VIRTUAL-RUNTIME_update-alternatives} \
    ${MACHINE_ESSENTIAL_EXTRA_RDEPENDS}"

RRECOMMENDS:${PN} = "\
    ${VIRTUAL-RUNTIME_base-utils-syslog} \
    ${MACHINE_ESSENTIAL_EXTRA_RRECOMMENDS}"
```

The above recipe inherits the packagegroup class and then defines a
list of RDEPENDS and RRECOMMENDS.

Note that the recipe also redefines the PACKAGE_ARCH variable,
which is used to set the architecture of the resulting packages.
As suggested by the Yocto Reference Manual at https://
docs.yoctoproject.org/ref-manual/variables.
html?highlight=kernel_devicetree_bundle#term-
PACKAGE_ARCH, if our packages are built specific to the target
machine rather than generally for the architecture of the machine, we
should do the same PACKAGE_ARCH setting.

However, a good example of a package group recipe is the
packagegroup-base.bb recipe which is located, among other package
group recipes, within the poky meta layer in the directory recipes-core/
packagegroups:

```
$ cat poky/meta/recipes-core/packagegroups/packagegroup-base.bb
SUMMARY = "Merge machine and distro options to create a basic machine t
ask/package"
PR = "r83"

#
# packages which content depend on MACHINE_FEATURES need to be
# MACHINE_ARCH
#
PACKAGE_ARCH = "${MACHINE_ARCH}"

inherit packagegroup

PACKAGES = ' \
            packagegroup-base \
            packagegroup-base-extended \
            packagegroup-distro-base \
            packagegroup-machine-base \
            \
            ${@bb.utils.contains("MACHINE_FEATURES", "acpi", "packagegr
oup-base-acpi", "",d)} \
            ${@bb.utils.contains("MACHINE_FEATURES", "alsa", "packagegr
oup-base-alsa", "", d)} \
...
#
# packagegroup-base contain stuff needed for base system (machine
# related)
#
RDEPENDS:packagegroup-base = "\
    packagegroup-distro-base \
    packagegroup-machine-base \
    \
    module-init-tools \
    ${@bb.utils.contains('MACHINE_FEATURES', 'apm', 'packagegroup-base-
apm', '',d)} \
    ${@bb.utils.contains('MACHINE_FEATURES', 'acpi', 'packagegroup-base
-acpi', '',d)} \
...
```

```
RRECOMMENDS:packagegroup-base = "\
    kernel-module-nls-utf8 \
    kernel-module-input \
    kernel-module-uinput \
    kernel-module-rtc-dev \
    kernel-module-rtc-proc \
    kernel-module-rtc-sysfs \
    kernel-module-unix"
...
```

Looking at the recipe, we can see that the PACKAGES variable lists the package group packages to produce. Then the inherit packagegroup statement sets appropriate default values and automatically adds -dev, -dbg, and -ptest packages for each package specified in the PACKAGES statement.

This sequence is crucial: the inherit packagegroup line should be located near the top of the recipe, certainly before the PACKAGES statement.

For each package we specify in PACKAGES, we can use RDEPENDS and RRECOMMENDS entries to provide a list of packages the parent task package should contain.

Note also how the recipe uses the bb.utils.contains() functions to selectively add more packages to the RDEPENDS list according to the settings in MACHINE_FEATURES.

Another interesting setting to consider in the above recipe is reported below:

```
...
#
# packages added by distribution
#
SUMMARY:packagegroup-distro-base = "${DISTRO} extras"
DEPENDS_packagegroup-distro-base = "${DISTRO_EXTRA_DEPENDS}"
RDEPENDS:packagegroup-distro-base = "${DISTRO_EXTRA_RDEPENDS}"
RRECOMMENDS:packagegroup-distro-base = "${DISTRO_EXTRA_RRECOMMENDS}"
```

```
#
# packages added by machine config
#
SUMMARY:packagegroup-machine-base = "${MACHINE} extras"
SUMMARY:packagegroup-machine-base = "Extra packages required to fully support
${MACHINE} hardware"
RDEPENDS:packagegroup-machine-base = "${MACHINE_EXTRA_RDEPENDS}"
RRECOMMENDS:packagegroup-machine-base = "${MACHINE_EXTRA_RRECOMMENDS}"
...
```

Above it is a fascinating example of how we can use the variables
DISTRO, MACHINE, and their siblings to define dependencies for the
packagegroup-distro-base and packagegroup-machine-base package
groups which are related to the current distribution and machine settings.

OK, now it's time to build a custom packagegroup recipe. Below is a
simple example:

```
$ cat $CY_METADIR/recipes-core/packagegroup/packagegroup-cy.bb
SUMMARY = "Custom CY Package Groups"
MAINTAINER = "Rodolfo Giometti <giometti@enneenne.com>"

inherit packagegroup

PACKAGES = " \
    ${PN}-examples \
    ${PN}-apps \
"

SUMMARY:${PN}-examples = "Custom CY Examples Package Groups"
SECTION:${PN}-examples = "examples"
RDEPENDS:${PN}-examples = "\
    hello \
    lhello \
"

SUMMARY:${PN}-apps = "Custom CY Applications Package Groups"
SECTION:${PN}-apps = "utils"
RDEPENDS:${PN}-apps = "\
    log2cb \
    umrp \
"
```

Two packagegroup packages are created with their dependencies. To build an image using these packagegroup packages, we need to add packagegroup-cy-examples and/or packagegroup-cy-apps to IMAGE_ INSTALL.

However, as a first step, let's generate the packages:

```
$ bitbake packagegroup-cy
```

If everything works well, we should get our new packages as shown below:

```
$ cy-ipk find packagegroup-cy
cy-ipk: searching in /home/giometti/yocto/imx-yocto-bsp/imx8mp-build...
tmp/deploy/ipk/all/packagegroup-cy-examples-ptest_1.0-r0_all.ipk
tmp/deploy/ipk/all/packagegroup-cy-apps-ptest_1.0-r0_all.ipk
tmp/deploy/ipk/all/packagegroup-cy-apps-dbg_1.0-r0_all.ipk
tmp/deploy/ipk/all/packagegroup-cy-apps_1.0-r0_all.ipk
tmp/deploy/ipk/all/packagegroup-cy-examples-dev_1.0-r0_all.ipk
tmp/deploy/ipk/all/packagegroup-cy-examples_1.0-r0_all.ipk
tmp/deploy/ipk/all/packagegroup-cy-apps-dev_1.0-r0_all.ipk
tmp/deploy/ipk/all/packagegroup-cy-examples-dbg_1.0-r0_all.ipk
```

Furthermore, we can take a look at package information to verify that everything has been set up correctly:

```
$ cy-ipk get-info tmp/deploy/ipk/all/packagegroup-cy-examples_1.0-r0_al
l.ipk
Package: packagegroup-cy-examples
Version: 1.0-r0
Description: Custom CY Examples Package Groups
 Custom CY Package Groups.
Section: examples
Priority: optional
Maintainer: Rodolfo Giometti <giometti@enneenne.com>
License: MIT
Architecture: all
OE: packagegroup-cy
Depends: hello, lhello
Source: packagegroup-cy.bb
$ cy-ipk get-info tmp/deploy/ipk/all/packagegroup-cy-apps_1.0-r0_all.ipk
Package: packagegroup-cy-apps
Version: 1.0-r0
Description: Custom CY Applications Package Groups
```

```
 Custom CY Package Groups.
Section: utils
Priority: optional
Maintainer: Rodolfo Giometti <giometti@enneenne.com>
License: MIT
Architecture: all
OE: packagegroup-cy
Depends: log2cb, umrp
Source: packagegroup-cy.bb
```

The readers should notice that there are no files within the IPKG file archives:

```
$ cy-ipk inspect tmp/deploy/ipk/all/packagegroup-cy-examples_1.0-r0_al
l.ipk
$ cy-ipk inspect tmp/deploy/ipk/all/packagegroup-cy-apps_1.0-r0_all.ipk
```

The output of both commands was empty. This is because they don't need to install something but define their dependency packages! So their real usage is when they are used within an image recipe in the IMAGE_INSTALL variable.

11.5 Adding Binary Packages

Binary packages usually are used to hold precompiled code or binary images that should be installed verbatim (i.e., with no compilation and the same directory structure).

These special packages can be created by using the bin-package class already introduced in Section 6.4.5, and an example is reported in the wireless-regdb (Wireless Central Regulatory Domain Database) recipe in the poky meta layer:

```
$ cat poky/meta/recipes-kernel/wireless-regdb/wireless-regdb_2022.08.12
.bb
SUMMARY = "Wireless Central Regulatory Domain Database"
HOMEPAGE = "https://wireless.wiki.kernel.org/en/developers/regulatory/c
rda"
SECTION = "net"
```

```
LICENSE = "ISC"
LIC_FILES_CHKSUM = "file://LICENSE;md5=07c4f6dea3845b02a18dc00c8c87699c"

SRC_URI = "https://www.kernel.org/pub/software/network/${BPN}/${BP}.tar
.xz"
SRC_URI[sha256sum] = "59c8f7d17966db71b27f90e735ee8f5b42ca3527694a8c5e6
e9b56bd379c3b84"

inherit bin_package allarch

do_install() {
    install -d -m0755 ${D}${nonarch_libdir}/crda
    install -d -m0755 ${D}${sysconfdir}/wireless-regdb/pubkeys
    install -m 0644 regulatory.bin ${D}${nonarch_libdir}/crda/regulator
y.bin
    install -m 0644 sforshee.key.pub.pem ${D}${sysconfdir}/wireless-reg
db/pubkeys/sforshee.key.pub.pem

    install -m 0644 -D regulatory.db ${D}${nonarch_base_libdir}/firmwar
e/regulatory.db
    install -m 0644 regulatory.db.p7s ${D}${nonarch_base_libdir}/firmwa
re/regulatory.db.p7s
}
...
```

The recipe just downloads the archive file holding the binary files and then overloads the do_install task to fit its needs. However, in order to do a little example, we can consider the following archive file which holds some made-up binary files:

```
$ tar tf examples/bindata/bindata-1.2.tar.gz
usr/
usr/share/
usr/share/bindata/
usr/share/bindata/data3.bin
usr/share/bindata/data2.bin
usr/share/bindata/data0.bin
usr/share/bindata/data1.bin
```

We can assume that all path names are correct, and then we just need to create a package with the same tree. To do so, we can recall the usage message for the recipetool create command:

```
$ recipetool create -h
...
  -b, --binary            Treat the source tree as something that should
                          be installed verbatim (no compilation, same
                          directory structure)
...
```

In this scenario, the command we should use is shown below:

```
$ recipetool create -b examples/bindata/bindata-1.2.tar.gz
NOTE: Starting bitbake server...
INFO: Fetching file:///home/giometti/yocto/examples/bindata/bindata-1.2
.tar.gz;subdir=${BPN}...
...
INFO: Recipe bindata_1.2.bb has been created; further editing may be re
quired to make it fully functional
```

The newly created recipe holds the following settings:

```
$ cat bindata_1.2.bb
...
LICENSE = "CLOSED"
LIC_FILES_CHKSUM = ""

SRC_URI = "file:///home/giometti/yocto/examples/bindata/bindata-${PV}.t
ar.gz;subdir=${BPN}"

inherit bin_package

INSANE_SKIP:${PN} += "already-stripped"
```

The code is elementary; however, we should spend some time talking about the INSANE_SKIP variable. This variable, used in the insane class (see the class file poky/meta/classes/insane.bbclass), specifies the Questions/Answers (QA for short) checks to skip for a specific package within a recipe.

There are several tests done by this class which are listed in the Yocto Reference Manual at https://docs.yoctoproject.org/ref-manual/classes.html#insane.

In our example, the `already-stripped` test is used to verify that
produced binaries have not already been stripped before the build system
extracting debug symbols. In fact, it is common for upstream software
projects to default to stripping debug symbols for output binaries, and in
order for debugging to work on the target using the -dbg packages, this
stripping must be disabled.

Since in our example, stripping debug symbols is nonsense, we must
disable this check too.

Now to test our new recipe, we have to move it into our meta layer and
then execute bitbake as done below:

```
$ mkdir -p $CY_METADIR/recipes-example/bindata
$ mv bindata_1.2.bb $CY_METADIR/recipes-example/bindata/
$ cd $BUILDDIR/
$ bitbake bindata
...
NOTE: Executing Tasks
ERROR: bindata-1.2-r0 do_install: bin_package has nothing to install. B
e sure the SRC_URI unpacks into S.
ERROR: bindata-1.2-r0 do_install: ExecutionError('/home/giometti/yocto/
imx-yocto-bsp/imx8mp-build/tmp/work/armv8a-poky-linux/bindata/1.2-r0/te
mp/run.do_install.17833', 1, None, None)
...
Summary: 1 task failed:
  /home/giometti/yocto/imx-yocto-bsp/sources/meta-cy/recipes-example/bi
ndata/bindata_1.2.bb:do_install
```

We got the error because, as suggested by the above message, the
archive pointed to by SRC_URI doesn't unpack into S. In fact, we have

```
$ cy-vars S bindata
S="/home/giometti/yocto/imx-yocto-bsp/imx8mp-build/tmp/work/armv8a-poky
-linux/bindata/1.2-r0/bindata-1.2"
```

And in this directory, there is nothing:

```
$ ls /home/giometti/yocto/imx-yocto-bsp/imx8mp-build/tmp/work/armv8a-po
ky-linux/bindata/1.2-r0/bindata-1.2
```

All files have been exploded in

```
$ cd $BUILDDIR/tmp/work/armv8a-poky-linux/bindata/1.2-r0
$ tree bindata
bindata
└── usr
    └── share
        └── bindata
            ├── data0.bin
            ├── data1.bin
            ├── data2.bin
            └── data3.bin

3 directories, 4 files
```

So the recipe should be reworked as shown below:

```
--- a/recipes-example/bindata/bindata_1.2.bb
+++ b/recipes-example/bindata/bindata_1.2.bb
@@ -1,7 +1,7 @@
 LICENSE = "CLOSED"
 LIC_FILES_CHKSUM = ""

-SRC_URI = "file:///home/giometti/yocto/examples/bindata/bindata-${PV}.
tar.gz;subdir=${BPN}"
+SRC_URI = "file:///home/giometti/yocto/examples/bindata/bindata-${PV}.
tar.gz;subdir=${BPN}-${PV}"

 inherit bin_package
```

This is because the expression ${BPN}-${PV} resolves in bindata-1.2 which is also the correct prefix to use to avoid problems in case we decide to build different releases.

Now we can retry in executing BitBake:

```
$ bitbake bindata
...
NOTE: Tasks Summary: Attempted 746 tasks of which 731 didn't need to be
 rerun and all succeeded.
...
```

OK, now we can verify that the package has been created:

```
$ cy-ipk find bindata
cy-ipk: searching in /home/giometti/yocto/imx-yocto-bsp/imx8mp-build...
tmp/deploy/ipk/armv8a/bindata-dev_1.2-r0_armv8a.ipk
tmp/deploy/ipk/armv8a/bindata-dbg_1.2-r0_armv8a.ipk
tmp/deploy/ipk/armv8a/bindata_1.2-r0_armv8a.ipk
```

and that it holds the right data files:

```
$ cy-ipk inspect tmp/deploy/ipk/armv8a/bindata_1.2-r0_armv8a.ipk
drwxr-xr-x root/root    0 2024-08-21 14:11 ./usr/
drwxr-xr-x root/root    0 2024-08-21 14:11 ./usr/share/
drwxr-xr-x root/root    0 2024-08-21 14:11 ./usr/share/bindata/
-rw-r--r-- root/root 4096 2024-08-21 14:11 ./usr/share/bindata/data0.bin
-rw-r--r-- root/root 4096 2024-08-21 14:11 ./usr/share/bindata/data1.bin
-rw-r--r-- root/root 4096 2024-08-21 14:11 ./usr/share/bindata/data2.bin
-rw-r--r-- root/root 4096 2024-08-21 14:11 ./usr/share/bindata/data3.bin
```

which is precisely what we wanted.

11.6 Notes on Native Recipes

Some projects may have complex compiling procedures. For example, if we think of language parsers, we may have a first stage where the parser generator (as Bison or YACC) reads the language syntax and generates the C program file (.c file) holding the language parser which decodes that syntax. Then a second stage does the real compilation to generate the final executable.

In general, whenever we need one or more stages to be executed on the build host, before the final compilation for the target may run, we must rely on **native recipes**.

The *native* suffix identifies recipes (and variants of recipes) that produce files intended for the build host, instead of the target machine.

In this section, we are going to present two examples of native recipes, one recipe for a C program and one for a Python program.

11.6.1 Native C Code

A real and very simple example of how to generate native code for a C program is reported in the following code:

```
$ cat $CY_METADIR/recipes-example/cy-nat/files/cy-tool.c
#include <stdio.h>
#include <stdlib.h>
#include <unistd.h>
#include <errno.h>

int main(int argc, char *argv[]) {
        const size_t len = sysconf(_SC_PAGESIZE);
        char buf[len], *ptr;
        int nread, nwritten;

        while ((nread = read(STDIN_FILENO, buf, len)) > 0) {
            ptr = buf;
            while (nread > 0) {
                    nwritten = write(STDOUT_FILENO, ptr, nread);
                    if (nwritten < 0) {
                            perror("write:");
                            exit(EXIT_FAILURE);
                    }
                    nread -= nwritten;
                    ptr += nwritten;
            }
        }
        if (nread < 0) {
            perror("read:");
            exit(EXIT_FAILURE);
        }

        return 0;
}
```

This is a C program that reads some data from its stdin and then writes this data to its stdout stream. Simply speaking, it is another cat implementation.

However, we can suppose that it must be used to generate a new program for the target machine in this way:

```
$ cy-tool < cy-tool.c > cy-target.c
```

That is, when executed on the host, it takes the `cy-tool.c` file and transforms it into `cy-target.c`, then this last file can be compiled and executed on the target.

In order to solve this problem, we can use the following recipe:

```
$ cat $CY_METADIR/recipes-example/cy-nat/cy-nat_0.1.bb
LICENSE = "CLOSED"

SRC_URI = "file://cy-tool.c"

S = "${WORKDIR}"

do_install() {
    install -d ${D}${bindir}
}

do_compile:class-native() {
    ${CC} ${CFLAGS} ${LDFLAGS} cy-tool.c -o cy-tool
}

do_install:append:class-native() {
    install cy-tool ${D}${bindir}
}

DEPENDS:class-target = "cy-nat-native"

do_compile:append:class-target() {
    cy-tool < cy-tool.c > cy-target.c
    ${CC} ${CFLAGS} ${LDFLAGS} cy-target.c -o cy-target
}

do_install:append:class-target() {
    install cy-target ${D}${bindir}
}

BBCLASSEXTEND = "native"
```

The recipe may seem complex, but actually is not. First of all, we should notice the setting of the BBCLASSEXTEND variable at the end. It allows us to extend a recipe so that it builds variants of the software too.

In our example, by setting it to `native`, we ask the build system to generate a variant of our recipe as *native* like `cy-nat-native`, which is a copy of `cy-nat` but compiled to run on the build system.

We can use several variants, such as `crosses` which generate packages that run on the host machine but produce binaries that run on the target (e.g., the cross-compiler). The readers can get further information starting at `https://docs.yoctoproject.org/ref-manual/variables.html#term-BBCLASSEXTEND`.

The trick used internally by the BBCLASSEXTEND mechanism is to rewrite variable values and apply overrides in order to do different actions and to get different results. For example, the variable `bindir`, where we should install our binaries, changes according to the fact that we are compiling for the host or for the target machine. Moreover, special overrides as `class-native` and `class-target` can be used to distinguish between settings or procedures for the host or for the target machine.

In this scenario, it should be obvious why we have defined the two `do_install` tasks as above. In fact, when we do

```
do_install:append:class-native() {
    install cy-tool ${D}${bindir}
}
```

we ask the build system to install the `cy-tool` executable within the directory addressed by `bindir` for the build machine, while when we do

```
do_install:append:class-target() {
    install cy-target ${D}${bindir}
}
```

we ask the Yocto build system to install the `cy-target` executable within the directory addressed by `bindir` for the target machine (which, of course, points to another path!).

On the other hand, when we create the `bindir` we can use a default task as below:

```
do_install() {
    install -d ${D}${bindir}
}
```

589

Note that we must use variables as `bindir`, etc., to address specific directories to avoid unexpected behaviors!

In fact, if we look at how the `do_install` task is defined for the target, we have

```
$ cat $BUILDDIR/tmp/work/armv8a-poky-linux/cy-nat/0.1-r0/temp/run.
do_install
...
# line: 7, file: /home/giometti/yocto/imx-yocto-bsp/sources/meta-c
y/recipes-example/cy-nat/cy-nat_0.1.bb
do_install() {
    install -d /home/giometti/yocto/imx-yocto-bsp/imx8mp-build/tmp
/work/armv8a-poky-linux/cy-nat/0.1-r0/image/usr/bin
    install cy-target /home/giometti/yocto/imx-yocto-bsp/imx8mp-bu
ild/tmp/work/armv8a-poky-linux/cy-nat/0.1-r0/image/usr/bin
}
...
```

while for the host, we have

```
$ cat $BUILDDIR/tmp/work/x86_64-linux/cy-nat-native/0.1-r0/temp/ru
n.do_install
...
# line: 7, file: /home/giometti/yocto/imx-yocto-bsp/sources/meta-c
y/recipes-example/cy-nat/cy-nat_0.1.bb
do_install() {
    install -d /home/giometti/yocto/imx-yocto-bsp/imx8mp-build/tmp
/work/x86_64-linux/cy-nat-native/0.1-r0/image/home/giometti/yocto/
imx-yocto-bsp/imx8mp-build/tmp/work/x86_64-linux/cy-nat-native/0.1
-r0/recipe-sysroot-native/usr/bin
    install cy-tool /home/giometti/yocto/imx-yocto-bsp/imx8mp-buil
d/tmp/work/x86_64-linux/cy-nat-native/0.1-r0/image/home/giometti/y
octo/imx-yocto-bsp/imx8mp-build/tmp/work/x86_64-linux/cy-nat-nativ
e/0.1-r0/recipe-sysroot-native/usr/bin
}
```

Now, in order to make everything work, we need to specify that the target package depends on the native one, and we can do it with the line reported below:

```
DEPENDS:class-target = "cy-nat-native"
```

In this manner, the Yocto build system knows that, before compiling the `cy-nat` package, it must compile the `cy-nat-native` one.

OK, within our meta layer, we should have something as below:

```
$ cd $CY_METADIR
$ tree recipes-example/cy-nat/
recipes-example/cy-nat/
├── files
│   └── cy-tool.c
└── cy-nat_0.1.bb

1 directory, 2 files
```

Then we can try our recipe as usual:

```
$ bitbake cy-nat
```

If everything works well, we should obtain our final package as shown below:

```
$ cy-ipk find cy-nat
cy-ipk: searching in /home/giometti/yocto/imx-yocto-bsp/imx8mp-build...
tmp/deploy/ipk/armv8a/cy-nat-dev_0.1-r0_armv8a.ipk
tmp/deploy/ipk/armv8a/cy-nat-dbg_0.1-r0_armv8a.ipk
tmp/deploy/ipk/armv8a/cy-nat-src_0.1-r0_armv8a.ipk
tmp/deploy/ipk/armv8a/cy-nat_0.1-r0_armv8a.ipk
```

And looking into the package, we should see that only the `cy-target` program is present as expected:

```
$ cy-ipk inspect tmp/deploy/ipk/armv8a/cy-nat_0.1-r0_armv8a.ipk
drwxr-xr-x root/root          0 2011-04-05 23:00 ./usr/
drwxr-xr-x root/root          0 2011-04-05 23:00 ./usr/bin/
-rwxr-xr-x root/root       6120 2011-04-05 23:00 ./usr/bin/cy-target
```

Our tool `cy-tool` (compiled for the host) is placed within the Yocto build system, in a proper directory, where other tools are saved:

```
$ ls $BUILDDIR/tmp/work/armv8a-poky-linux/cy-nat/0.1-r0/recipe-sysroot-n
ative/usr/bin/
aarch64-poky-linux    infocmp          pseudo
arfile.py             infotocap        pseudodb
...
```

```
curl              lzma              rpmdb.real
curl-config       lzmadec           rpmgraph
cy-tool           lzmainfo          rpmgraph.real
...
```

11.6.2 Native Python Code

In order to show how a Python-native recipe can be written, we can use a simple C program that is generated by a Python script. In the examples/ ecdemo directory, we can find the following files:

```
$ cd ~/yocto/examples/ecdemo/
$ ls
Makefile  gen_data.py  key.h  print_key.c
```

where within the Makefile we have the following instructions:

```
$ cat Makefile
TARGET = print_key
CFLAGS = -Wall -O2
PYTHON ?= python3

all: $(TARGET)

$(TARGET): print_key.c key.c

key.c:
        $(PYTHON) gen_data.py

clean:
        rm -f *.o $(TARGET) key.c

PHONY: all clean
```

The target file print_key is an executable obtained by compiling the two .c files named print_key.c and key.c.

The readers should notice that the key.c file is generated with the following command:

```
$(PYTHON) gen_data.py
```

In fact, to execute gen_data.py, we need to invoke the Python interpreter, but, as we did in Chapter 9 to call the C compiler, we didn't call the python program directly, but we use the environment variable PYTHON to be sure that the correct program is called by bitbake. However, since this variable is not defined by default in a normal Bash environment as the CC variable, we need the special setting PYTHON ?= python3 to be sure that a default value is used.

The content of gen_data.py that generates the key.c file holds the following code:

```
$ cat gen_data.py
import os
import sys
import getopt
import struct

from fastecdsa import keys, curve

NAME = os.path.basename(sys.argv[0])

def c_print(file, name, data):
    file.write('uint8_t %s[SIGN_PUB_KEY_SIZE] = {\n' % name)
    for counter, v in enumerate(data):
        if counter % 8 == 0:
            file.write('\t');
        file.write('0x%02x, ' % v)
        if counter % 8 == 7:
            file.write('\n');
    file.write('\n};\n')

#
# Main
#

try:
    f = open("key.c", "w+")
except err:
    print(str(err))
    os.exit(1)

# generate a keypair (i.e. both keys) for curve P521
priv_key, pub_key = keys.gen_keypair(curve.P521)
```

```
print("pub x:", hex(pub_key.x))
print("pub y:", hex(pub_key.y))

xl = struct.unpack('B' * 66, pub_key.x.to_bytes(66, 'big'))
yl = struct.unpack('B' * 66, pub_key.y.to_bytes(66, 'big'))

f.write('#include "key.h"\n\n')
f.write('/*** Warning: auto-generated file! Do not modify ***/\n\n')
c_print(f, "pub_key_x", xl)
c_print(f, "pub_key_y", yl)

exit(0)
```

What this code does is simple: it generates a key pair and then generates a C code that copies the public key into two byte arrays. Then these arrays are read by the code into print_key.c and printed in hexadecimal form on the standard output. This file just holds the following simple code:

```
$ cat print_key.c
#include <stdio.h>

#include "key.h"

void print_data(char *label, uint8_t *data)
{
        int i;

        printf("%s ", label);
        for (i = 0; i < SIGN_PUB_KEY_SIZE; i++)
                printf("%02x", data[i]);
        printf("\n");
}

int main(void)
{
        print_data("pub x: ", pub_key_x);
        print_data("pub y: ", pub_key_y);

        return 0;
}
```

while within file key.h we have

```
$ cat key.h
#ifndef _KEY_H
#define _KEY_H

#include <stdint.h>

#define SIGN_PUB_KEY_SIZE      66

extern uint8_t pub_key_x[SIGN_PUB_KEY_SIZE];
extern uint8_t pub_key_y[SIGN_PUB_KEY_SIZE];

#endif
```

Now, to have an idea about what this code performs, we can compile and execute it:

```
$ make
python3 gen_data.py
pub x: 0x18f73632029f79088fcdfb6672d77d75a00ff15ebb0afb26d538db17866a06
8555ee859b5c77f658e72435bc25cc77a205b797e4873258fd903f9b7122fe5996b2f
pub y: 0x1a0d3430e4a908fc9720f675bd1e2409350aba4730955267dcc0017e3f2303
29705e3d0941c2bc28302294deba456136890fd62145f0f7b0976786ff5e645d80156
cc -Wall -O2    print_key.c key.c    -o print_key
```

In the case we get the following error, it means that our system lacks the fastecdsa support (see Section 10.3.2):

```
Traceback (most recent call last):
  File "/home/giometti/yocto/examples/ecdemo/gen_data.py", line 6,
 in <module>
    from fastecdsa import keys, curve
ModuleNotFoundError: No module named 'fastecdsa'
make: *** [Makefile:10: key.c] Error 1
```

We can solve this issue by using the following command to install the package into our host system:

```
$ pip3 install fastecdsa
```

Note also that it is useful to be able to use fastecdsa functions within the Yocto build system, where we need the native version of the package.

The generated file holds the following code:

```
$ cat key.c
#include "key.h"

/*** Warning: auto-generated file! Do not modify ***/

uint8_t pub_key_x[SIGN_PUB_KEY_SIZE] = {
        0x01, 0x8f, 0x73, 0x63, 0x20, 0x29, 0xf7, 0x90,
        0x88, 0xfc, 0xdf, 0xb6, 0x67, 0x2d, 0x77, 0xd7,
        0x5a, 0x00, 0xff, 0x15, 0xeb, 0xb0, 0xaf, 0xb2,
        0x6d, 0x53, 0x8d, 0xb1, 0x78, 0x66, 0xa0, 0x68,
        0x55, 0x5e, 0xe8, 0x59, 0xb5, 0xc7, 0x7f, 0x65,
        0x8e, 0x72, 0x43, 0x5b, 0xc2, 0x5c, 0xc7, 0x7a,
        0x20, 0x5b, 0x79, 0x7e, 0x48, 0x73, 0x25, 0x8f,
        0xd9, 0x03, 0xf9, 0xb7, 0x12, 0x2f, 0xe5, 0x99,
        0x6b, 0x2f,
};
uint8_t pub_key_y[SIGN_PUB_KEY_SIZE] = {
        0x01, 0xa0, 0xd3, 0x43, 0x0e, 0x4a, 0x90, 0x8f,
        0xc9, 0x72, 0x0f, 0x67, 0x5b, 0xd1, 0xe2, 0x40,
        0x93, 0x50, 0xab, 0xa4, 0x73, 0x09, 0x55, 0x26,
        0x7d, 0xcc, 0x00, 0x17, 0xe3, 0xf2, 0x30, 0x32,
        0x97, 0x05, 0xe3, 0xd0, 0x94, 0x1c, 0x2b, 0xc2,
        0x83, 0x02, 0x29, 0x4d, 0xeb, 0xa4, 0x56, 0x13,
        0x68, 0x90, 0xfd, 0x62, 0x14, 0x5f, 0x0f, 0x7b,
        0x09, 0x76, 0x78, 0x6f, 0xf5, 0xe6, 0x45, 0xd8,
        0x01, 0x56,
};
```

The bytes into the arrays are the ones composing the generated public key. So, if we execute the print_key program, we should get the following output:

```
$ ./print_key
pub x:   018f73632029f79088fcdfb6672d77d75a00ff15ebb0afb26d538db17866a06
8555ee859b5c77f658e72435bc25cc77a205b797e4873258fd903f9b7122fe5996b2f
pub y:   01a0d3430e4a908fc9720f675bd1e2409350aba4730955267dcc0017e3f2303
29705e3d0941c2bc28302294deba456136890fd62145f0f7b0976786ff5e645d80156
```

Now that we know how this demo project works, we are ready to generate the corresponding recipe with devtool as usual:

```
$ devtool add ecdemo git:///home/giometti/yocto/examples/ecdemo/
...
INFO: Recipe /home/giometti/yocto/imx-yocto-bsp/imx8mp-
build/workspace/recipes/ecdem
o/ecdemo_git.bb has been automatically created; further editing may be
required to make it fully functional
```

Now we can edit the generated recipe with the command devtool
edit-recipe ecdemo in order to be similar to the code reported below:

```
LICENSE = "MIT"
LIC_FILES_CHKSUM = "file://${COMMON_LICENSE_DIR}/MIT;md5=0835ade698e0bcf
8506ecda2f7b4f302"

SRC_URI = "git:///home/giometti/yocto/examples/ecdemo/;branch=master"

PV = "1.0+git${SRCPV}"
SRCREV = "64af940badaa46fd4b5eb3b176aeddfc980db611"

S = "${WORKDIR}/git"

do_configure () {
        :
}

do_compile () {
        oe_runmake
}

do_install () {
        install -d ${D}/${bindir}
        install print_key ${D}/${bindir}/
}
```

In the above code, we just fixed the license and the do_install task;
the remaining parts have been left untouched.

Now, if we ask devtool to build the recipe, we should get the
following output:

```
$ devtool build ecdemo
...
NOTE: ecdemo: compiling from external source tree /home/giometti/yocto/
imx-yocto-bsp/imx8mp-build/workspace/sources/ecdemo
...
| DEBUG: Executing shell function do_compile
```

```
| NOTE: make -j 2
| /home/giometti/yocto/imx-yocto-bsp/imx8mp-build/tmp/work/armv8a-poky-
linux/ecdemo/1.0+git999-r0/recipe-sysroot-native/usr/bin/python3-native
/python3 gen_data.py
| Traceback (most recent call last):
|   File "/home/giometti/yocto/imx-yocto-bsp/imx8mp-build/workspace/sou
rces/ecdemo/gen_data.py", line 6, in <module>
|     from fastecdsa import keys, curve
| ModuleNotFoundError: No module named 'fastecdsa'
| make: *** [Makefile:9: key.c] Error 1
| ERROR: oe_runmake failed
| WARNING: exit code 1 from a shell command.
...
```

> The readers should notice that the variable PYTHON expands into the correct path name for the Yocto Project's Python interpreter.

The error was expected, since the package depends on the fastecdsa package we already prepared in Section 10.3.2. However, we need the native version of such package, so we should change the recipe as follows to support the native package generation:

```
--- a/python3-fastecdsa_2.3.2.bb
+++ b/python3-fastecdsa_2.3.2.bb
@@ -10,7 +10,7 @@
 PYPI_PACKAGE = "fastecdsa"
 SRC_URI[sha256sum] = "f35255a6d3e41109166b5d4b08866d5acbb99f2e1e64d3a7
e74c774664cda842"

-inherit pypi setuptools3_legacy
+inherit pypi setuptools3_legacy python3native

 do_install:append() {
         # Remove invalid UNKNOWN-0.0.0-py3.10.egg-info directory
@@ -27,3 +27,5 @@
 FILES:${PN}-tests = "${PYTHON_SITEPACKAGES_DIR}/fastecdsa/tests/"

 RDEPENDS:${PN}-tests = "${PN}"
+
+BBCLASSEXTEND = "native"
```

The setting for BBCLASSEXTEND is something similar to the one done in the previous section, while the inherit of the class python3native is needed to be sure that all Python-related variables are properly set. In fact, in the file python3native.bbclass we can see the PYTHON setting:

```
$ cat poky/meta/classes/python3native.bbclass
inherit python3-dir

PYTHON="${STAGING_BINDIR_NATIVE}/python3-native/python3"
EXTRANATIVEPATH += "python3-native"
DEPENDS:append = " python3-native "
...
```

Now we can ask BitBake to build the python3-fastecdsa-native recipe to be sure that everything still compiles correctly:

```
$ bitbake python3-fastecdsa-native
```

Then we can update the recipe for the ecdemo package to explicitly add the compiling dependency:

```
--- a/workspace/recipes/ecdemo/ecdemo_git.bb
+++ b/workspace/recipes/ecdemo/ecdemo_git.bb
@@ -1,6 +1,8 @@
 LICENSE = "CLOSED"
 LIC_FILES_CHKSUM = ""

+DEPENDS = "python3-fastecdsa-native"
+
 SRC_URI = "git:///home/develop/Projects-OLD/packt/Customizing_Yocto/yo
cto/examples/ecdemo/;branch=master"
```

Now the build command should execute successfully. Then, to test the code, we can deploy it:

```
$ devtool deploy-target -s ecdemo root@192.168.32.132
...
./
./usr/
./usr/bin/
./usr/bin/print_key
INFO: Successfully deployed /home/giometti/yocto/imx-yocto-bsp/imx8mp-b
uild/tmp/work/armv8a-poky-linux/ecdemo/1.0+git999-r0/image
```

Then on the target, the output should be something as shown below:

```
# print_key
pub x:  009445b538e4af441c24622eceb46fab5db927435806b3c04e5acbc905ef61f
cd5b54b0d049e263f4658a955924a94be7a6f0667d39b5668b7a918fac6019b9d9e5c
pub y:  00e01d18911e9649a04b6c62e51e07ff0bd0d449f092aa35c3be74acdd82d32
5f558158598b8864f782371932a192fc109d10494338a099e3485b1814d531b9805d7
```

Now to create the recipe, we can use `devtool finish` as shown below:

```
$ devtool finish -f ecdemo $CY_METADIR/recipes-example
...
INFO: Updating SRCREV in recipe ecdemo_git.bb
INFO: Moving recipe file to /home/giometti/yocto/imx-yocto-bsp/sources/
meta-cy/recipes-example/ecdemo
INFO: Leaving source tree /home/giometti/yocto/imx-yocto-bsp/imx8mp-bui
ld/workspace/sources/ecdemo as-is; if you no longer need it then please
 delete it manually
```

The recipe is now into our meta layer:

```
$ cd $CY_METADIR
$ tree recipes-example/ecdemo/
recipes-example/ecdemo/
└── ecdemo_git.bb

0 directories, 1 file
```

11.7 Summary

In this chapter, we have seen other examples of writing recipes in order to solve usual tasks in embedded system development. With Chapters 9 and 10, we should have covered almost all the usual problems an embedded developer may encounter in writing their recipes; however, a last step is missing: writing recipes for images.

So it's time to move on to the next chapter where we can learn how to do so with several practical examples.

CHAPTER 12

Image Recipes

Now that we know perfectly how to write recipes for several kinds of packages, we need to see how to write another important kind of recipe: the image recipes. In fact, this kind of recipe is a bit different from the others seen in the previous chapters because they don't generate packages, but, instead, they use packages to generate root filesystem images!

In this chapter, we are going to see how to manage recipes that produce root filesystem images.

12.1 Custom Recipe Files

As already seen in Section 6.5, we can define a .bb file to be an image recipe by inheriting the core-image class and properly defying the IMAGE_INSTALL. Simply speaking, an image recipe can be done as shown below:

```
$ cat $CY_METADIR/recipes-images/images/cy-image-minimal.bb
SUMMARY = "A small image just capable of allowing a device to boot."
LICENSE = "MIT"

IMAGE_INSTALL = "packagegroup-core-boot"
IMAGE_LINGUAS = " "

inherit core-image

IMAGE_ROOTFS_SIZE ?= "8192"
```

© Rodolfo Giometti 2025
R. Giometti, *Yocto Project Customization for Linux*,
https://doi.org/10.1007/979-8-8688-1435-8_12

Defining the software using a custom recipe gives us total control over the contents of the image, but we have to properly instruct the build system in order to be able to get a runnable image. In fact, we can generate the image by using the following BitBake command:

```
$ bitbake cy-image-minimal
...
0: cy-image-minimal-1.0-r0 do_rootfs - 2s (pid 128164)   0% |         |
...
```

And the final result will be

```
$ basename -a $BUILDDIR/tmp/deploy/images/imx8mp-icore-cy/cy-image-mini
mal*
cy-image-minimal.env
cy-image-minimal-imx8mp-icore-cy-20240523130749.rootfs.manifest
cy-image-minimal-imx8mp-icore-cy-20240523130749.rootfs.tar.zst
cy-image-minimal-imx8mp-icore-cy-20240523130749.rootfs.wic.bmap
cy-image-minimal-imx8mp-icore-cy-20240523130749.rootfs.wic.zst
cy-image-minimal-imx8mp-icore-cy-20240523130749.testdata.json
cy-image-minimal-imx8mp-icore-cy.manifest
cy-image-minimal-imx8mp-icore-cy.tar.zst
cy-image-minimal-imx8mp-icore-cy.testdata.json
cy-image-minimal-imx8mp-icore-cy.wic.bmap
cy-image-minimal-imx8mp-icore-cy.wic.zst
cy-image-minimal-imx-imx-boot-bootpart.wks
```

However, it is not certain that the result will be moved to the target machine and that it will work. That's why, usually, it's quite common that to customize an image recipe, developers prefer using one of the methods we are going to present in the next sections.

On the other hand, this example is fascinating since it can be used to show to the readers how we can alter the root filesystem by properly changing an image recipe. So let's take a look at the root filesystem by exploding the newly generated archive:

```
$ mkdir /tmp/cy-image-minimal && \
    tar -xf $BUILDDIR/tmp/deploy/images/imx8mp-icore-cy/cy-image-minima
l-imx8mp-icore-cy.tar.zst \
        -C /tmp/cy-image-minimal
```

In the temporary directory /tmp/cy-image-minimal, we can inspect the archive content:

```
$ cd /tmp/cy-image-minimal && ls
bin   dev home  media  proc sbin  sys  usr
boot  etc lib   mnt    run  srv   tmp  var
```

And, for example, we can read a file content as in the following example:

```
$ cat etc/issue
NXP i.MX Release Distro 5.15-kirkstone
```

Furthermore, we can look for a specified file:

```
$ ls usr/bin/strace
ls: cannot access 'usr/bin/strace': No such file or directory
```

Now we can proceed to alter our cy-image-minimal recipe to change the issue file and to add the strace command. To add strace, we should modify the recipe as reported below:

```
--- cy-image-minimal.bb
+++ cy-image-minimal.bb
@@ -2,6 +2,7 @@
 LICENSE = "MIT"

 IMAGE_INSTALL = "packagegroup-core-boot"
+IMAGE_INSTALL += "strace"
 IMAGE_LINGUAS = " "

 inherit core-image
```

while to alter the issue file, we have two possibilities:

1) We can try to discover which is the package that provides the /etc/issue file by using the oe-pkgdata-util command as shown below:

```
$ oe-pkgdata-util find-path /etc/issue
base-files: /etc/issue
```

Then we can generate a proper .bbappend file for the base-files to do a file override.

2) Or, we can use `ROOTFS_POSTPROCESS_COMMAND`
    to alter the file just after the root filesystem is
    generated by adding the following code:

```
--- cy-image-minimal.bb
+++ cy-image-minimal.bb
@@ -8,3 +8,9 @@
 inherit core-image

 IMAGE_ROOTFS_SIZE ?= "8192"
+
+CURR_DATE = "${@time.strftime('%Y%m%d%H%M%S', time.gmtime())}"
+fix_issue() {
+    echo "=== CY rootfs IMAGE [${CURR_DATE}] ===\n" >> ${IMAGE_R
OOTFS}${sysconfdir}/issue
+}
+ROOTFS_POSTPROCESS_COMMAND = "fix_issue; "
```

The function `fix_issue` is executed after the root
filesystem has been generated, and it simply alters
the `issue` file.

In our example, we choose this second way, and then, after all the
modifications, we generate again the image:

```
$ bitbake cy-image-minimal
```

Then, to verify if everything works well, we have to re-explode the root
filesystem archive:

```
$ rm -rf /tmp/cy-image-minimal
$ tar -xf $BUILDDIR/tmp/deploy/images/imx8mp-icore-cy/cy-image-minimal-
imx8mp-icore-cy.tar.zst \
        -C /tmp/cy-image-minimal
```

Now the `strace` program is present:

```
$ find /tmp/cy-image-minimal/ -name strace
/tmp/cy-image-minimal/usr/bin/strace
```

And the `issue` file is altered as requested:

```
$ cat /tmp/cy-image-minimal/etc/issue
NXP i.MX Release Distro 5.15-kirkstone \n \l

=== CY rootfs IMAGE [20240523144953] ===
```

OK, all steps presented here have resolved our problems, but, as already said before, if we have to modify a recipe which is not in our meta layer, we should consider using an append file. So let's move to the next section.

12.2 Customizing by bbappend(ing)

The other method for creating a custom image (which is generally considered as better practice) is to base it on an existing image. In fact, we may wish to add specific packages to specific images or just alter already existing settings, then we can use the already existing recipe and change it via a `.bbappend` file to be placed into our custom layer.

As a basic example, in order to show this technique, we can consider the well-known core-image-minimal.bb recipe reported below:

```
$ cat sources/poky/meta/recipes-core/images/core-image-minimal.bb
SUMMARY = "A small image just capable of allowing a device to boot."

IMAGE_INSTALL = "packagegroup-core-boot ${CORE_IMAGE_EXTRA_INSTALL}"

IMAGE_LINGUAS = " "

LICENSE = "MIT"

inherit core-image

IMAGE_ROOTFS_SIZE ?= "8192"
IMAGE_ROOTFS_EXTRA_SPACE:append = "${@bb.utils.contains("DISTRO_FEATURE
S", "systemd", " + 4096", "", d)}"
```

To generate it as is, we can do as shown below:

```
$ bitbake core-image-minimal
```

At the end, we can inspect the root filesystem content as done in the section above:

```
$ mkdir /tmp/core-image-minimal && \
    tar -xf $BUILDDIR/tmp/deploy/images/imx8mp-icore-cy/core-image-mini
mal-imx8mp-icore-cy.tar.zst \
        -C /tmp/core-image-minimal
$ cd /tmp/core-image-minimal && ls
bin    dev  home  media  proc  sbin  sys  usr
boot   etc  lib   mnt    run   srv   tmp  var
```

Now, if we wish to add the strace command to the image and alter the /etc/issue file in the same manner as done in the previous section, we can use a .bbappend file as shown below:

```
$ cat $CY_METADIR/recipes-images/images/core-image-minimal.bbappend
IMAGE_INSTALL:append = " strace"

CURR_DATE = "${@time.strftime('%Y%m%d%H%M%S', time.gmtime())}"
fix_issue() {
    echo "=== CY-version rootfs IMAGE [${CURR_DATE}] ===\n" >> ${IMAGE_R
OOTFS}${sysconfdir}/issue
}
ROOTFS_POSTPROCESS_COMMAND = "fix_issue; "
```

This time, we have used the :append operator to add the strace package to the IMAGE_INSTALL variable, while the fix_issue function is defined as before.

The readers should notice the leading space after the opening quote and before the package name. This space is required since the :append operator does not add the space.

Now we can regenerate the image:

```
$ bitbake core-image-minimal
```

And then verify that everything is in place, so we have to clean the previous image version and then explode the archive again:

```
$ rm -rf /tmp/core-image-minimal/
$ mkdir /tmp/core-image-minimal && \
    tar -xf $BUILDDIR/tmp/deploy/images/imx8mp-icore-cy/core-image-mini
mal-imx8mp-icore-cy.tar.zst \
        -C /tmp/core-image-minimal
```

Moreover, we can verify that everything is in place in the same manner as before:

```
$ find /tmp/core-image-minimal/ -name strace
/tmp/core-image-minimal/usr/bin/strace
$ cat /tmp/core-image-minimal/etc/issue
NXP i.MX Release Distro 5.15-kirkstone \n \l

=== CY-version rootfs IMAGE [20240524083824] ===
```

Now we can move to the next section to see another way to generate an image recipe by cloning an already existing one.

12.3 Cloning and Renaming

By using the `.bbappend` solution, we can solve most common customization problems. However, sometimes changes are so many that it may be easier to create an image based on an already present one, by cloning the recipe file into our custom layer and renaming it.

Just to make a simple example, we can clone the engicam-evaluation-image-mx8.bb recipe by copying it under our meta layer (and providing a proper new name):

```
$ cp meta-engicam-nxp/recipes-images/images/engicam-evaluation-image-mx
8.bb \
        $CY_METADIR/recipes-images/images/cy-evaluation-image-mx8.bb
```

Then we can alter the recipe content according to our needs:

```
--- recipes-images/images/cy-evaluation-image-mx8.bb
+++ recipes-images/images/cy-evaluation-image-mx8.bb
@@ -1,8 +1,9 @@
 # Copyright (C) 2015 Freescale Semiconductor
 # Copyright 2017-2019 NXP
+# Copyright 2024 Rodolfo Giometti <giometti@enneenne.com>
 # Released under the MIT license (see COPYING.MIT for the terms)

-DESCRIPTION = "Engicam evaluation image"
+DESCRIPTION = "CY evaluation image"
 LICENSE = "MIT"

 inherit core-image
@@ -14,6 +15,13 @@
    ln -sf brcmfmac43430-sdio.bin brcmfmac43430-sdio.engi,imx8-icore.bin
 }

+ROOTFS_POSTPROCESS_COMMAND:append = "fix_issue;"
+CURR_DATE = "${@time.strftime('%Y%m%d%H%M%S', time.gmtime())}"
+
+fix_issue() {
+   echo "=== CY rootfs IMAGE [${CURR_DATE}] ===\n" >> ${IMAGE_ROOTFS}${s
ysconfdir}/issue
+}
+
 ## Select Image Features
 IMAGE_FEATURES += " \
        debug-tweaks \
```

Now we can generate the new image as shown below:

```
$ bitbake cy-evaluation-image-mx8
...
Currently  1 running tasks (8898 of 8909)  99% |###################### |
0: cy-evaluation-image-mx8-1.0-r0 do_rootfs - 3s (pid 274357)
...
```

If everything works well, we should get the following files in the deployment space:

```
$ basename -a $BUILDDIR/tmp/deploy/images/imx8mp-icore-cy/cy-evaluation
-image-mx8*
cy-evaluation-image-mx8.env
cy-evaluation-image-mx8-imx8mp-icore-cy-20240524090658.rootfs.manifest
```

```
cy-evaluation-image-mx8-imx8mp-icore-cy-20240524090658.rootfs.tar.zst
cy-evaluation-image-mx8-imx8mp-icore-cy-20240524090658.rootfs.wic.bmap
cy-evaluation-image-mx8-imx8mp-icore-cy-20240524090658.rootfs.wic.zst
cy-evaluation-image-mx8-imx8mp-icore-cy-20240524090658.testdata.json
cy-evaluation-image-mx8-imx8mp-icore-cy.manifest
cy-evaluation-image-mx8-imx8mp-icore-cy.tar.zst
cy-evaluation-image-mx8-imx8mp-icore-cy.testdata.json
cy-evaluation-image-mx8-imx8mp-icore-cy.wic.bmap
cy-evaluation-image-mx8-imx8mp-icore-cy.wic.zst
cy-evaluation-image-mx8-imx-imx-boot-bootpart.wks
```

OK, now to test the newly created image, we have to rewrite our microSD as shown below:

```
$ zstdcat tmp/deploy/images/imx8mp-icore-cy/cy-evaluation-image-mx8-imx
8mp-icore-cy.wic.zst | \
    sudo dd of=<DISK> bs=8M conv=fdatasync status=progress
```

Don't forget to replace <DISK> with your microSD block device!

Once the microSD is ready, we can check if everything works as expected. If we boot the system, on the serial console, we should get the output reported below:

```
...
[  OK  ] Reached target Graphical Interface.
        Starting Record Runlevel Change in UTMP...
[  OK  ] Finished Record Runlevel Change in UTMP.

NXP i.MX Release Distro 5.15-kirkstone imx8mp-icore-cy ttymxc1

=== CY rootfs IMAGE [20240822105421] ===

imx8mp-icore-cy login:
```

Great! Now we have our own customized root filesystem. So we can move to the next section in order to see how to add more customizations.

12.4 Customizing by Configuration Files

Another interesting way to customize an image is to add a package via the local.conf configuration file (or by any other available configuration file). This method generally only allows developers to add packages and is not as flexible as creating our own customized image as seen in previous customization examples.

Furthermore, we should consider that when we add packages using local variables this way, these variable changes are in effect for every build and consequently affect all images, which might not be what we require.

For example, if we add the line below to our local.conf file, we can add the strace package to all images:

```
IMAGE_INSTALL:append = " strace"
```

However, it is possible to extend the syntax so that the variable applies to a specific image only, as in the following example:

```
IMAGE_INSTALL:append:pn-cy-evaluation-image-mx8 = " strace"
```

This example adds strace to our cy-evaluation-image-mx8 image only.

Note that to add a package via IMAGE_INSTALL to our image using the local configuration file, we should use the :append operator. In fact, using the += operator to append packages to IMAGE_INSTALL is not recommended because core-image.bbclass (another image class) does the following setting:

```
IMAGE_INSTALL ?= "${CORE_IMAGE_BASE_INSTALL}"
```

Initializing a variable with ?= and then using a += operation against it results in unexpected behavior when used within the local.conf (or any other configuration files) and also within an image recipe may or may not succeed depending on the specific situation. In both these cases, the behavior is contrary to how most users expect the += operator to work.

Another way to differentiate a configuration by using configuration files can be accomplished via bitbake with the -R option argument. If we recall what was seen in Section 4.1.2, by specifying the -R option argument we can tell bitbake to read an additional configuration file after the bitbake.conf:

```
$ bitbake -h
...
 -R POSTFILE, --postread=POSTFILE
                      Read the specified file after bitbake.conf.
...
```

So we can compile our image as in the following example:

```
$ bitbake -R conf/cy-evaluation-image.conf cy-evaluation-image-mx8
```

where in the file conf/cy-evaluation-image.conf we can put all settings we wish to supply for the specified target image. Simply by changing the .conf file, we can change the final image configuration (a practical example of this technique is reported in Section 13.1).

In the end, we should mention IMAGE_FEATURES. Typically, we configure this variable in an image recipe to select the list of features to include in an image, but we can use it from our local.conf file (even if best practices dictate that we do not, use EXTRA_IMAGE_FEATURES instead).

As already introduced in Sections 6.3.4 and 6.5.1, we can think of IMAGE_FEATURES (and EXTRA_IMAGE_FEATURES) as a variable containing a list of switches that tells the build system to automatically append a given set of packages, and/or different package configurations, to the IMAGE_INSTALL variable. Depending on the base class of the target image, we have a set of features we can select in order to be added or not to our final image. Recipes can check (and append) for specific features in this variable to change its default configuration/build process accordingly.

For example, we can image to selectively enable debugging tools according to the recipe image as shown below:

```
EXTRA_IMAGE_FEATURES:append:pn-cy-evaluation-image-mx8 = " tools-debug"
```

Please keep in mind the extra space at the beginning of the tools-debug string!

As a simple example, we can alter our `local.conf` in order to do so:

```
--- a/conf/local.conf
+++ b/conf/local.conf
@@ -23,6 +23,7 @@ ACCEPT_FSL_EULA = "1"
 PACKAGE_CLASSES = "package_ipk"
 EXTRA_IMAGE_FEATURES += "package-management"
 #EXTRA_IMAGE_FEATURES += "dbg-pkgs"
+EXTRA_IMAGE_FEATURES:append:pn-cy-evaluation-image-mx8 = " tools-debug"

 # Limiting HW resources
 BB_NUMBER_THREADS = "4"
```

Now, if we check the content of `EXTRA_IMAGE_FEATURES` when we generate the `cy-evaluation-image-mx8`, we should get the following output:

```
$ cy-vars EXTRA_IMAGE_FEATURES cy-evaluation-image-mx8
EXTRA_IMAGE_FEATURES="debug-tweaks package-management tools-debug"
```

On the other hand, if we do the same while generating the `engicam-evaluation-image-mx8` image, we get

```
$ cy-vars EXTRA_IMAGE_FEATURES engicam-evaluation-image-mx8
EXTRA_IMAGE_FEATURES="debug-tweaks package-management"
```

So we got exactly the expected behavior.

12.5 Changing the System Configuration

Once we have defined our custom image (in our example, we have
cy-evaluation-image-mx8), it could be interesting to see some
common (and useful) techniques to modify some global settings, for
example, adding system's users (and their passwords) or the networking
configuration, etc.

12.5.1 Adding Users

In the case we need more users than the ones defined by default in an
image recipe, we can consider the "useradd" sampling recipe in the poky
meta layer:

```
$ cat poky/meta-skeleton/recipes-skeleton/useradd/useradd-example.bb
SUMMARY = "Example recipe for using inherit useradd"
DESCRIPTION = "This recipe serves as an example for using features fro
m useradd.bbclass"
SECTION = "examples"
...
```

The interesting part of this recipe is reported below:

```
...
PACKAGES =+ "${PN}-user3"

EXCLUDE_FROM_WORLD = "1"

inherit useradd

# You must set USERADD_PACKAGES when you inherit useradd. This
# lists which output packages will include the user/group
# creation code.
USERADD_PACKAGES = "${PN} ${PN}-user3"

# You must also set USERADD_PARAM and/or GROUPADD_PARAM when
# you inherit useradd.

# USERADD_PARAM specifies command line options to pass to the
# useradd command. Multiple users can be created by separating
# the commands with a semicolon. Here we'll create two users,
```

```
# user1 and user2:
USERADD_PARAM:${PN} = "-u 1200 -d /home/user1 -r -s /bin/bash user1; -u
 1201 -d /home/user2 -r -s /bin/bash user2"

# user3 will be managed in the useradd-example-user3 pacakge:
# As an example, we use the -P option to set clear text password for
# user3
USERADD_PARAM:${PN}-user3 = "-u 1202 -d /home/user3 -r -s /bin/bash -P
'user3' user3"

# GROUPADD_PARAM works the same way, which you set to the options
# you'd normally pass to the groupadd command. This will create
# groups group1 and group2:
GROUPADD_PARAM:${PN} = "-g 880 group1; -g 890 group2"

# Likewise, we'll manage group3 in the useradd-example-user3 package:
GROUPADD_PARAM:${PN}-user3 = "-g 900 group3"
...
```

In addition to the variable EXCLUDE_FROM_WORLD which can be used to exclude a recipe from world builds (i.e., bitbake world), we see that in PACKAGES the useradd-example-user3 extra package is appended. Then both packages are added to USERADD_PACKAGES to list to the Yocto build system, which output packages will include the user/group creation code.

The variable USERADD_PARAM specifies command-line options to pass to the useradd command. In our example, two users are created, and to specify the commands for each user we separate the commands with a semicolon. Note also that, by using an override, we specify different commands for each package.

However, to do a practical example, we should rework a bit the above example recipe as shown below:

```
$ cat $CY_METADIR/recipes-core/useradd/useradd-example.bb
SUMMARY = "Example recipe for using inherit useradd"
DESCRIPTION = "This recipe serves as an example for using features from
 useradd.bbclass"
SECTION = "examples"
...
# USERADD_PARAM specifies command line options to pass to the
# useradd command. Multiple users can be created by separating
# the commands with a semicolon. Here we'll create two users,
# user1 and user2:
```

```
USERADD_PARAM:${PN} = "-u 200 -d /home/user1 -r -s /bin/bash user1; -u
201 -d /home/user2 -r -s /bin/bash user2"

# user3 will be managed in the useradd-example-user3 pacakge:
# As an example, we use the -p option to set a password for user3
# obtained by using the command:
#     mkpasswd -m sha-512 'cY!pass1'
#     $6$E8OGB11MDb1xon3p$Hwhz.yRgjcW33qIaOVksyckbwX7UxLqUXsfscAuGbfkM6
IYjlnnPoNHUdpQJYkEDNwLVjpm3xt1GKtWFmTnNv/
USERADD_PARAM:${PN}-user3 = "-u 202 -d /home/user3 -r -s /bin/bash -p '
\$6\$E8OGB11MDb1xon3p\$Hwhz.yRgjcW33qIaOVksyckbwX7UxLqUXsfscAuGbfkM6IYj
lnnPoNHUdpQJYkEDNwLVjpm3xt1GKtWFmTnNv/' user3"

# GROUPADD_PARAM works the same way, which you set to the options
# you'd normally pass to the groupadd command. This will create
# groups group1 and group2:
GROUPADD_PARAM:${PN} = "-g 880 group1; -g 890 group2"

# Likewise, we'll manage group3 in the useradd-example-user3 package:
GROUPADD_PARAM:${PN}-user3 = "-g 900 group3"
```

In the above recipe, we redefined the users' home pages as /home/
user1, /home/user2, and /home/user3, and also we used the command
mkpasswd to properly generate a password suitable for latest useradd
command releases. In fact, the useradd command doesn't accept the -P
option argument anymore to set a user's password.

The readers should notice that the output of mkpasswd is as
shown below:

```
$ mkpasswd -m sha-512 'cY!pass1'
$6$E8OGB11MDb1xon3p$Hwhz.yRgjcW33qIaOVksyckbwX7UxLqUXsfscAuGbfkM6I
YjlnnPoNHUdpQJYkEDNwLVjpm3xt1GKtWFmTnNv/
```

while the value passed to the -p option argument is

```
'\$6\$E8OGB11MDb1xon3p\$Hwhz.yRgjcW33qIaOVksyckbwX7UxLqUXsfscAuGbf
kM6IYjlnnPoNHUdpQJYkEDNwLVjpm3xt1GKtWFmTnNv/'
```

In the above string, all $ characters are escaped as \$.

OK, now we can generate our new packages:

```
$ bitbake useradd-example
```

And, if everything works well, we should get something as reported below:

```
$ cy-ipk find useradd-example
cy-ipk: searching in /home/giometti/yocto/imx-yocto-bsp/imx8mp-build...
tmp/deploy/ipk/armv8a/useradd-example_1.0-r1_armv8a.ipk
tmp/deploy/ipk/armv8a/useradd-example-dbg_1.0-r1_armv8a.ipk
tmp/deploy/ipk/armv8a/useradd-example-dev_1.0-r1_armv8a.ipk
tmp/deploy/ipk/armv8a/useradd-example-user3_1.0-r1_armv8a.ipk
```

If we get a look inside the new packages, we get the following output:

```
$ cy-ipk inspect tmp/deploy/ipk/armv8a/useradd-example_1.0-r1_armv8a.ipk
drwxr-xr-x root/root         0 2011-04-05 23:00 ./usr/
drwxr-xr-x root/root         0 2011-04-05 23:00 ./usr/share/
drwxr-xr-x user1/group1      0 2011-04-05 23:00 ./usr/share/user1/
-rw-r--r-- user1/group1      0 2011-04-05 23:00 ./usr/share/user1/file1
-rw-r--r-- user1/group1      0 2011-04-05 23:00 ./usr/share/user1/file2
drwxr-xr-x user2/group2      0 2011-04-05 23:00 ./usr/share/user2/
-rw-r--r-- user2/group2      0 2011-04-05 23:00 ./usr/share/user2/file2
-rw-r--r-- user2/group2      0 2011-04-05 23:00 ./usr/share/user2/file3
$ cy-ipk inspect tmp/deploy/ipk/armv8a/useradd-example-user3_1.0-r1_arm
v8a.ipk
drwxr-xr-x root/root         0 2011-04-05 23:00 ./usr/
drwxr-xr-x root/root         0 2011-04-05 23:00 ./usr/share/
drwxr-xr-x user3/group3      0 2011-04-05 23:00 ./usr/share/user3/
-rw-r--r-- user3/group3      0 2011-04-05 23:00 ./usr/share/user3/file3
-rw-r--r-- user3/group3      0 2011-04-05 23:00 ./usr/share/user3/file4
```

which is precisely what we expected it to be. OK, now we can add these packages to our image as shown below:

```
--- recipes-images/images/cy-evaluation-image-mx8.bb
+++ recipes-images/images/cy-evaluation-image-mx8.bb
@@ -102,6 +102,8 @@
        ${ENGICAM_PKG} \
        ${EXTRA_PACKAGE_INSTALL} \
        ${G2D_SAMPLES} \
+        \
+       useradd-example useradd-example-user3 \
     "

  IMAGE_INSTALL += " \
```

Then we have to regenerate the image:

```
$ bitbake cy-evaluation-image-mx8
```

When finished, we have to rewrite our microSD as done above to update our image, and then we can verify that all new users are in place:

```
imx8mp-icore-cy login: root
root@imx8mp-icore-cy:~# id user1
uid=200(user1) gid=200(user1) groups=200(user1)
root@imx8mp-icore-cy:~# id user2
uid=201(user2) gid=201(user2) groups=201(user2)
root@imx8mp-icore-cy:~# id user3
uid=202(user3) gid=202(user3) groups=202(user3)
```

We can also try to log in via SSH to test the user3's password we set to cY!pass1 as shown below:

```
$ ssh user3@192.168.32.132
user3@192.168.32.132's password:
user3@imx8mp-icore-cy:~$
```

The readers should remember to reset their host key by using this command:

```
$ ssh-keygen -f "/home/giometti/.ssh/known_hosts" -R "192.168.32.1
32"
```

Great, the login works as expected. Then we can check the user's home:

```
user3@imx8mp-icore-cy:~$ whoami
user3
user3@imx8mp-icore-cy:~$ pwd
/home/user3
user3@imx8mp-icore-cy:~$ ls -l
total 0
-rw-r--r-- 1 user3 group3 0 Mar  9  2018 file3
-rw-r--r-- 1 user3 group3 0 Mar  9  2018 file4
```

OK, everything is in place.

12.5.2 Changing Root's Settings

If we need to alter (or set) a password for the root user, we can do as shown below:

```
inherit extrausers

EXTRA_USERS_PARAMS = " \
    ${@bb.utils.contains('IMAGE_FEATURES', 'debug-tweaks', '', "usermod
 -p '\$6\$VXgIp2C84GuR9Hjo\$NNHWN/RINO.qQLyOON2CIKN7f28SAMsgQ8hacDg59ig
6p6gHJVRMo/iybK81VRFwRZSj.B9qD3EcAnsQy.dLE.' root;", d)} \
"
```

The setting is very similar as in the above section, but this time we first check the IMAGE_FEATURES variable for the debug-tweaks settings, then we set EXTRA_USERS_PARAMS to hold the usermod command. When inheriting the extrausers class, this variable provides image-level user and group operations. This is a more global method of providing user and group configurations as compared to using the useradd class, which ties user and group configurations to a specific recipe.

If we look in the extrausers.bbclass in the poky meta layer, we get the list of commands we can configure using the EXTRA_USERS_PARAMS:

```
$ cat poky/meta/classes/extrausers.bbclass
# This bbclass is used for image level user/group configuration.
# Inherit this class if you want to make EXTRA_USERS_PARAMS effective.

# Below is an example showing how to use this functionality.
# IMAGE_CLASSES += "extrausers"
# EXTRA_USERS_PARAMS = "\
#     useradd -p '' tester; \
#     groupadd developers; \
#     userdel nobody; \
#     groupdel -g video; \
#     groupmod -g 1020 developers; \
#     usermod -s /bin/sh tester; \
# "
...
```

In the case we wish to change the root's home directory, we can use the ROOT_HOME variable. It defaults to

```
$ bitbake -e cy-evaluation-image-mx8
...
#
# $ROOT_HOME
#   set /home/giometti/yocto/imx-yocto-bsp/sources/poky/meta/conf/bitbak
e.conf:87
#      [_defaultval] "/home/root"
ROOT_HOME="/home/root"
...
```

This unusual default value, instead of the more common /root, is likely used because some embedded solutions prefer a read-only root filesystem and prefer to keep writable data in one place.

We can override the default by setting the variable in any layer or in the local.conf file.

12.5.3 Setting a Custom Hostname

By default, the configured hostname (i.e., the name in /etc/hostname) in an image is the same as the machine name; in fact, if we take a look into the base-files recipe, we see the following settings:

```
$ cat sources/poky/meta/recipes-core/base-files/base-files_3.0.14.bb
...
# By default the hostname is the machine name. If the hostname is unset
# then a /etc/hostname file isn't written, suitable for environments
# with dynamic hostnames.
#
# The hostname can be changed outside of this recipe by using
# hostname:pn-base-files = "my-host-name".
hostname = "${MACHINE}"
...
```

As reported above, we can customize this name by altering the value of the `hostname` variable in the `base-files` recipe using either an append file or a configuration file. In the former case, we can do as shown below:

```
hostname = "myhostname"
```

while in the latter case, we should have the next setting which uses an override:

```
hostname:pn-base-files = "myhostname"
```

This setting can be useful, for example, to fix a generic hostname detached from the machine's name or to append something meaningful as below:

```
hostname:append:pn-base-files = "${@'-devel' if d.getVar('DEVELOPMENT'
) == '1' else ''}"
```

In the case that `DEVELOPMENT` is set to 1, then `hostname` becomes `${MACHINE}-devel` (this topic will be better explained in Section 13.1).

12.5.4 Setting the Default Network Configuration

As already seen from the initial chapters (see Section 2.5), the default network configuration may have wrong settings; in fact, we needed to manually add the following file to force Systemd to properly set up our network configuration:

```
# cat > /etc/systemd/network/50-eth0.network <<__EOF
[Match]
Name=eth0

[Network]
Address=192.168.32.132/24
Gateway=192.168.32.2
DNS=192.168.32.2
__EOF
```

However, we would like to have an already fixed network configuration within our custom image, so let's see how we can do so.

The main problem here is not how to configure Systemd, since we already know that we have to add the above 50-eth0.network file, but which is the recipe to alter to fix our needs.

As a first step, we can take a look at files within the /etc/systemd/ network/ directory:

```
# ls -l /etc/systemd/network/
total 4
-rw-r--r-- 1 root root 37 Mar  9  2018 89-unmanage.network
lrwxrwxrwx 1 root root  9 Mar  9  2018 99-default.link -> /dev/null
```

So we can try to ask the build system which is the package which produces such file:

```
$ oe-pkgdata-util find-path /etc/systemd/network/89-unmanage.network
systemd: /etc/systemd/network/89-unmanage.network
```

Then we can take a look at systemd's recipe files:

```
$ bitbake-layers show-appends systemd
...
=== Matching recipes: ===
systemd:
  meta                1:250.5
```

However, there is nothing there about the 89-unmanage.network file, so let's try within some .bbappend file:

```
$ bitbake-layers show-appends systemd
...
=== Matched appended recipes ===
systemd_250.5.bb:
  /home/giometti/yocto/imx-yocto-bsp/sources/meta-imx/meta-bsp/recipes-
core/systemd/systemd_%.bbappend
```

Great! Now we got it:

```
$ cat /home/giometti/yocto/imx-yocto-bsp/sources/meta-imx/meta-bsp/reci
pes-core/systemd/systemd_%.bbappend
FILESEXTRAPATHS:prepend := "${THISDIR}/${BPN}:"
```

```
SRC_URI += " \
            file://0001-systemd-udevd.service.in-Set-PrivateMounts-to-n
o-to-.patch \
            file://0020-logind.conf-Set-HandlePowerKey-to-ignore.patch \
            file://89-unmanage.network \
"

PACKAGECONFIG[unmanaged-network] = ""

do_install:append () {

    # Disable the assignment of the fixed network interface name
    install -d ${D}${sysconfdir}/systemd/network
    ln -s /dev/null ${D}${sysconfdir}/systemd/network/99-default.link

    # Configure the network as unmanaged
    if [ "${@bb.utils.filter('PACKAGECONFIG', 'unmanaged-network', d)}"
 ]; then
        install -Dm 0644 ${WORKDIR}/89-unmanage.network ${D}${sysconfdi
r}/systemd/network/
    fi
...
```

So, we may imagine putting here our modifications; however, for
Systemd the proper way to do so is by using the `systemd-conf` package.
In fact, if we look into its recipe file, we should see something as
reported below:

```
$ bitbake-layers show-recipes -f systemd-conf
...
=== Matching recipes: ===
/home/giometti/yocto/imx-yocto-bsp/sources/poky/meta/recipes-core/syste
md/systemd-conf_1.0.bb
$ cat /home/giometti/yocto/imx-yocto-bsp/sources/poky/meta/recipes-core
/systemd/systemd-conf_1.0.bb
SUMMARY = "Systemd system configuration"
DESCRIPTION = "Systemd may require slightly different configuration \
for different machines. For example, qemu machines require a longer \
DefaultTimeoutStartSec setting."
LICENSE = "MIT"
LIC_FILES_CHKSUM = "file://${COREBASE}/meta/COPYING.MIT;md5=3da9cfbcb78
8c80a0384361b4de20420"

PE = "1"

PACKAGECONFIG ??= "dhcp-ethernet"
PACKAGECONFIG[dhcp-ethernet] = ""
```

```
SRC_URI = "\
    file://journald.conf \
    file://logind.conf \
    file://system.conf \
    file://system.conf-qemuall \
    file://wired.network \
"

do_install() {
    install -D -m0644 ${WORKDIR}/journald.conf ${D}${systemd_unitdir}
/journald.conf.d/00-${PN}.conf
    install -D -m0644 ${WORKDIR}/logind.conf ${D}${systemd_unitdir}/l
ogind.conf.d/00-${PN}.conf
    install -D -m0644 ${WORKDIR}/system.conf ${D}${systemd_unitdir}/s
ystem.conf.d/00-${PN}.conf

        if ${@bb.utils.contains('PACKAGECONFIG', 'dhcp-ethernet', 'true
', 'false', d)}; then
                install -D -m0644 ${WORKDIR}/wired.network ${D}${systemd_un
itdir}/network/80-wired.network
        fi
}
...
```

As we can see above, this package does several configuration settings for Systemd; in particular, we should notice that if dhcp-ethernet is specified in PACKAGECONFIG, then the wired.network file is installed. This file holds the following settings:

```
$ cat /home/giometti/yocto/imx-yocto-bsp/sources/poky/meta/recipes-core
/systemd/systemd-conf/wired.network
[Match]
Type=ether
Name=!veth*
KernelCommandLine=!nfsroot
KernelCommandLine=!ip

[Network]
DHCP=yes

[DHCP]
UseMTU=yes
RouteMetric=10
ClientIdentifier=mac
```

which are the proper settings for using the DHCP protocol on all Ethernet interfaces in the system. So, what we can do here is to create an empty .bbappend file for systemd-conf as shown below:

```
$ recipetool newappend $CY_METADIR systemd-conf
...
/home/giometti/yocto/imx-yocto-bsp/sources/meta-cy/recipes-core/systemd
/systemd-conf_1.0.bbappend
```

Then we can add a new file named eth0.network:

```
$ mkdir $CY_METADIR/recipes-core/systemd/systemd-conf/
$ cat > $CY_METADIR/recipes-core/systemd/systemd-conf/eth0.network <<__
EOF
[Match]
Name=eth0

[Network]
Address=192.168.32.132/24
Gateway=192.168.32.2
DNS=192.168.32.2
__EOF
```

Now we can prepare the .bbappend in order to add the new file with the proper name as shown below:

```
$ cat $CY_METADIR/recipes-core/systemd/systemd-conf_1.0.bbappend
FILESEXTRAPATHS:prepend := "${THISDIR}/systemd-conf:"

SRC_URI += " \
    file://eth0.network \
"

FILES:${PN} += " \
    ${sysconfdir}/systemd/network/50-eth0.network \
"

do_install:append() {
    install -d ${D}${sysconfdir}/systemd/network
    install -m 0644 ${WORKDIR}/eth0.network ${D}${sysconfdir}/systemd/n
etwork/50-eth0.network
}
```

The readers should note that the file /etc/systemd/network/50-eth0. network is a new file we must also add into the FILES variable.

Now we can regenerate the binary image to verify that everything works well:

```
$ bitbake cy-evaluation-image-mx8
```

Once we have reprogrammed the microSD as usual, we should get something as below after a new boot:

```
# ip addr show dev eth0
4: eth0: <BROADCAST,MULTICAST,UP,LOWER_UP> mtu 1500 qdisc mq state UP g
roup default qlen
1000
    link/ether ca:1a:ab:a1:8e:d4 brd ff:ff:ff:ff:ff:ff
    inet 192.168.32.132/24 brd 192.168.32.255 scope global eth0
       valid_lft forever preferred_lft forever
    inet6 fe80::c81a:abff:fea1:8ed4/64 scope link
       valid_lft forever preferred_lft forever
```

which is the default configuration we wished to have at boot.

12.5.5 automount fstab

Another useful setting is about which mass storages should be automatically mounted at boot. For example, on our machine, which boots from the microSD, we have the following mounting table:

```
# mount | grep mmcblk
/dev/mmcblk1p2 on / type ext4 (rw,relatime)
/dev/mmcblk2p1 on /run/media/boot-mmcblk2p1 type vfat (rw,relatime,gid=
6,fmask=0007,dmask=0007,allow_utime=0020,codepage=437,iocharset=iso8859
-1,shortname=mixed,errors=remount-ro)
/dev/mmcblk2p2 on /run/media/root-mmcblk2p2 type ext4 (rw,relatime)
/dev/mmcblk1p1 on /run/media/boot-mmcblk1p1 type vfat (rw,relatime,gid=
6,fmask=0007,dmask=0007,allow_utime=0020,codepage=437,iocharset=iso8859
-1,shortname=mixed,errors=remount-ro)
```

The first entry is about the root filesystem (and we are not going to change it), while the other entries are about the partitioning of the microSD (/dev/mmcblk1) and the onboard eMMC (dev/mmcblk2). Below are the current settings:

```
# fdisk -l /dev/mmcblk1
Disk /dev/mmcblk1: 7.51 GiB, 8068792320 bytes, 15759360 sectors
...
Device          Boot  Start     End  Sectors  Size Id Type
/dev/mmcblk1p1 *     16384  186775   170392 83.2M  c W95 FAT32 (LBA)
/dev/mmcblk1p2       196608 11777285 11580678  5.5G 83 Linux
# fdisk -l /dev/mmcblk2
Disk /dev/mmcblk2: 14.56 GiB, 15634268160 bytes, 30535680 sectors
...
Device          Boot  Start     End  Sectors  Size Id Type
/dev/mmcblk2p1 *     16384  186775   170392 83.2M  c W95 FAT32 (LBA)
/dev/mmcblk2p2       196608 10228353 10031746  4.8G 83 Linux
```

What we would like to have here is having the first partition of the microSD to be mounted on /boot at boot time, and to do so we have to alter the /etc/fstab file which is currently set as shown below:

```
# cat /etc/fstab
# stock fstab - you probably want to override this with a machine specific one

/dev/root     /                         auto      defaults              1  1
proc          /proc                     proc      defaults              0  0
devpts        /dev/pts                  devpts    mode=0620,ptmxmode=0666,g
id=5       0  0
tmpfs         /run                      tmpfs     mode=0755,nodev,nosuid,st
rictatime 0  0
tmpfs         /var/volatile             tmpfs     defaults              0  0

# uncomment this if your device has a SD/MMC/Transflash slot
#/dev/mmcblk0p1       /media/card              auto       defaults,sync,noa
uto  0  0
```

As we can see above, this is the default fstab file which is provided by the base-files recipe as we can easily verify as shown below:

```
$ oe-pkgdata-util find-path /etc/fstab
base-files: /etc/fstab
```

So, the easy way to alter it is by using a proper .bbappend file. First of all, we can get the current fstab file and modify it in order to fit our needs, so we can get the file from the directory IMAGE_ROOTFS where the root filesystem is locally generated:

```
$ cy-vars image cy-evaluation-image-mx8
...
IMAGE_ROOTFS="/home/giometti/yocto/imx-yocto-bsp/imx8mp-build/tmp/work/
imx8mp_icore_cy-poky-linux/cy-evaluation-image-mx8/1.0-r0/rootfs"
...
```

Then we can copy the file into a temporary one:

```
$ cp $BUILDDIR/tmp/work/imx8mp_icore_cy-poky-linux/cy-evaluation-image-
mx8/1.0-r0/rootfs/etc/fstab \
        /tmp/fstab
```

And finally, we can change the file in order to fix our needs, as shown below:

```
$ cat /tmp/fstab
# fstab for CY image

/dev/root       /                       auto    defaults            1  1
proc            /proc                   proc    defaults            0  0
devpts          /dev/pts                devpts  mode=0620,ptmxmode=0666,g
id=5     0  0
tmpfs           /run                    tmpfs   mode=0755,nodev,nosuid,st
rictatime 0  0
tmpfs           /var/volatile           tmpfs   defaults            0  0
/dev/mmcblk1p1 /boot                    auto    ro                  0  0
```

Then we have to generate the .bbappend file by using the recipetool appendfile command, as shown below:

```
$ recipetool appendfile $CY_METADIR /etc/fstab /tmp/fstab
...
NOTE: Writing append file /home/giometti/yocto/imx-yocto-bsp/sources/me
ta-cy/recipes-core/base-files/base-files_3.0.14.bbappend
NOTE: Copying fstab to /home/giometti/yocto/imx-yocto-bsp/sources/meta-
cy/recipes-core/base-files/base-files/fstab
```

The new .bbappend file should have the following content:

```
$ cat /home/giometti/yocto/imx-yocto-bsp/sources/meta-cy/recipes-core/b
ase-files/base-files_3.0.14.bbappend
FILESEXTRAPATHS:prepend := "${THISDIR}/${PN}:"
```

627

This is to tell BitBake to use our version of the `fstab` file. Now we can regenerate our image to test our modifications:

```
$ bitbake cy-evaluation-image-mx8
```

Once we have rewritten the microSD, at boot we should have the following status:

```
# cat /etc/fstab
# fstab for CY image

/dev/root       /                       auto    defaults            1  1
proc            /proc                   proc    defaults            0  0
devpts          /dev/pts                devpts  mode=0620,ptmxmode=0666,g
id=5       0  0
tmpfs           /run                    tmpfs   mode=0755,nodev,nosuid,st
rictatime 0  0
tmpfs           /var/volatile           tmpfs   defaults            0  0
/dev/mmcblk1p1 /boot                    auto    ro                  0  0
```

The first partition of the microSD is now correctly mounted on /boot:

```
# mount | grep mmcblk
/dev/mmcblk1p2 on / type ext4 (rw,relatime)
/dev/mmcblk1p1 on /boot type vfat (ro,relatime,fmask=0022,dmask=0022,co
depage=437,iocharset=iso8859-1,shortname=mixed,errors=remount-ro)
/dev/mmcblk2p1 on /run/media/boot-mmcblk2p1 type vfat (rw,relatime,gid=
6,fmask=0007,dmask=0007,allow_utime=0020,codepage=437,iocharset=iso8859
-1,shortname=mixed,errors=remount-ro)
/dev/mmcblk2p2 on /run/media/root-mmcblk2p2 type ext4 (rw,relatime)
# ls /boot/
Image  imx8mp-icore-ctouch2.dtb  imx8mp-icore-cy-board.dtb  imx8mp-icore-
starterkit.dtb
```

Another useful setting regarding the mount table can be the ability to block some automount which are done by udev. In fact, the default rule is to automount all mass storage devices connected to our system; on our system, we have the eMMC partitions automounted on /run/media/boot-mmcblk2p1 and /run/media/root-mmcblk2p2, as reported above. So, to block this behavior, we can use the /etc/udev/mount.ignorelist file which looks like below:

```
# cat /etc/udev/mount.ignorelist
/dev/loop
/dev/ram
/dev/mtdblock
/dev/md
/dev/dm-*
```

Here, we can specify the new pattern /dev/mmcblk* to block the automount for all MMC devices. We have two possibilities:

1) We can alter this file within the package that provides it, which can be retrieved as shown below:

```
$ oe-pkgdata-util find-path /etc/udev/mount.ignorelist
udev-extraconf: /etc/udev/mount.ignorelist
```

Note that, as for Systemd, we should not alter the udev package directly, but its associate configuration package.

---

2) We can add a single file named mmcblk.list into the /etc/udev/mount.ignorelist.d/ directory.

The first solution is similar as above, while to do the second one, we have to create a new file holding the exclude pattern and then execute the recipetool newappend command to create an empty .bbappend file. For example, we can do as follow:

```
$ recipetool newappend $CY_METADIR udev-extraconf
...
/home/giometti/yocto/imx-yocto-bsp/sources/meta-cy/recipes-core/udev/ud
ev-extraconf_1.1.bbappend
$ mkdir $CY_METADIR/recipes-core/udev/udev-extraconf/
echo '/dev/mmcblk*' > $CY_METADIR/recipes-core/udev/udev-extraconf/mmcb
lk.exclude.list
```

Now we have to add mmcblk.exclude.list to SRC_URI and then write a proper installation procedure. The .bbappend file should look like this:

```
$ cat $CY_METADIR/recipes-core/udev/udev-extraconf_1.1.bbappend
FILESEXTRAPATHS:prepend := "${THISDIR}/${PN}:"
```

```
SRC_URI += "file://mmcblk.exclude.list"

do_install:append() {
    install -m 0644 ${WORKDIR}/mmcblk.exclude.list \
                    ${D}${sysconfdir}/udev/mount.ignorelist.d/mmcblk.list
}
```

Now we can regenerate the image:

```
$ bitbake cy-evaluation-image-mx8
```

and then rewrite the microSD to test if everything is in place and properly
working:

```
# mount | grep mmcblk
/dev/mmcblk1p2 on / type ext4 (rw,relatime)
/dev/mmcblk1p1 on /boot type vfat (ro,relatime,fmask=0022,dmask=0022,cod
epage=437,iocharset=iso8859-1,shortname=mixed,errors=remount-ro)
```

Now only entries in /etc/fstab have been mounted, while others
matching the pattern /dev/mmcblk* are correctly ignored.

12.5.6 Getting Logs and tmp Files As Nonvolatile

Occasionally, it may be useful that system's logs stored in /var/log or even
temporary files in /tmp were persistent across system reboots. In fact, by
default, these directories are mounted on a tmpfs so that, after a reboot,
whatever stored in them is lost. This happens because variables VOLATILE_
LOG_DIR and VOLATILE_TMP_DIR are set to yes, which implies that /var/
log and /tmp are located as shown below:

```
# ls -l /var/log
lrwxrwxrwx  1 root root 12 Mar  9  2018 /var/log -> volatile/log
drwxrwxrwt  4 root root   80 Apr 28 17:42 volatile
# mount | egrep /tmp\|volatile
tmpfs on /tmp type tmpfs (rw,nosuid,nodev,size=1859012k,nr_inodes=10485
76)
tmpfs on /var/volatile type tmpfs (rw,relatime)
```

However, we can override such behavior by setting something as shown below, within our `distro.conf` configuration file. To test these settings, we can create our distro configuration file by cloning the current distro file `fsl-imx-xwayland.conf`. The final result is reported below:

```
$ cd $CY_METADIR
$ cat conf/distro/cy-xwayland.conf
# i.MX DISTRO for Wayland with X11

include conf/distro/include/fsl-imx-base.inc
include conf/distro/include/fsl-imx-preferred-env.inc

DISTRO = "cy-xwayland"

# Remove conflicting backends
DISTRO_FEATURES:remove = "directfb "
DISTRO_FEATURES:append = " x11 wayland pam"
```

Now the needed modifications for `VOLATILE_LOG_DIR` and `VOLATILE_TMP_DIR` are

```
--- a/conf/distro/cy-xwayland.conf
+++ b/conf/distro/cy-xwayland.conf
@@ -8,3 +8,7 @@ DISTRO = "fsl-imx-xwayland"
 # Remove conflicting backends
 DISTRO_FEATURES:remove = "directfb "
 DISTRO_FEATURES:append = " x11 wayland pam"
+
+# Set logs and tmp files as non-volatile
+VOLATILE_LOG_DIR = "no"
+VOLATILE_TMP_DIR = "no"
```

Everything is now in place, but to make the changes effective, we need to alter the `local.conf` settings as shown below:

```
--- a/conf/local.conf
+++ b/conf/local.conf
@@ -1,5 +1,5 @@
 MACHINE ??= 'imx8mp-icore-cy'
-DISTRO ?= 'fsl-imx-xwayland'
+DISTRO ?= 'cy-xwayland'
 PACKAGE_CLASSES ?= 'package_rpm'
 USER_CLASSES ?= "buildstats"
 PATCHRESOLVE = "noop"
```

Now we can re-execute `bitbake` and check that the new DISTRO setting
is correct:

```
$ bitbake cy-evaluation-image-mx8
...
Build Configuration:
BB_VERSION           = "2.0.0"
BUILD_SYS            = "x86_64-linux"
NATIVELSBSTRING      = "universal"
TARGET_SYS           = "aarch64-poky-linux"
MACHINE              = "imx8mp-icore-cy"
DISTRO               = "cy-xwayland"
DISTRO_VERSION       = "5.15-kirkstone"
TUNE_FEATURES        = "aarch64 armv8a crc crypto"
TARGET_FPU           = ""
...
```

Now, after the microSD reprogramming as usual, we get the following:

```
root@imx8mp-icore:~# ls -l /var/log
total 340
drwxr-xr-x 2 root root    4096 Apr 29 09:02 ConsoleKit
lrwxrwxrwx 1 root root      39 Apr 28 17:42 README -> ../../usr/share/doc/
systemd/README.logs
-rw-r--r-- 1 root root    1481 Apr 29 09:04 auth.log
-rw-rw---- 1 root utmp       0 Apr 28 17:42 btmp
-rw-r--r-- 1 root root   81413 Apr 29 09:03 kern.log
-rw-rw-r-- 1 root utmp     296 Apr 29 09:04 lastlog
-rw-r--r-- 1 root root       0 Apr 29 09:02 mail.err
-rw-r--r-- 1 root root       0 Apr 29 09:02 mail.log
-rw-r--r-- 1 root root   80769 Apr 29 09:03 messages
drwx------ 2 root root    4096 Apr 28 17:42 private
-rw-r--r-- 1 root root  152525 Apr 29 09:04 syslog
-rw-rw-r-- 1 root utmp    8800 Apr 29 09:04 wtmp
root@imx8mp-icore:~# ls -l /tmp
total 76
-rw-r--r-- 1 root root 58435 Apr 29 08:58 g2d_opencl_kernel.bin
drwx------ 3 root root  4096 Apr 29 09:02 systemd-private-f5b7ef58804545
f0b2d207da0824936a-ninfod.service-RNkUrc
drwx------ 3 root root  4096 Apr 29 09:02 systemd-private-f5b7ef58804545
f0b2d207da0824936a-rdisc.service-jIkXyI
drwx------ 3 root root  4096 Apr 29 09:02 systemd-private-f5b7ef58804545
f0b2d207da0824936a-systemd-logind.service-CGiXIe
drwx------ 3 root root  4096 Apr 28 17:42 systemd-private-f5b7ef58804545
f0b2d207da0824936a-systemd-timesyncd.service-Vj2XyN
```

This supports both sysvinit- and systemd-based systems.

In Yocto 5.0 Scarthgap, these variables are still present, but in the next release 5.1 (codename styhead) they are not. To do the job of these variables, we will use the new variable FILESYSTEM_PERMS_ TABLES which, by default, contains the value files/fs-perms- volatile-log.txt and files/fs-perms-volatile-tmp. txt, which means, respectively, that volatile log and volatile tmp are enabled. Users can disable the volatile log or tmp by removing the value files/fs-perms-volatile-log.txt or files/fs- perms-volatile-tmp.txt.

12.6 Adding an Initramfs

In Section 6.5.3, we introduced how we can manage Yocto settings in order to obtain an Initramfs from a recipe image. In this section, we are going to apply what was said before to our embedded kit to get a practical example of how to effectively add a fully customized initramfs.

There are several ready-to-run initramfs recipes in the Yocto Project, but in the case we need a fully customizable and really compact Initramfs, we can use a recipe as shown below:

```
$ cat $CY_METADIR/recipes-initramfs/images/image-tiny-initramfs.bb
SUMMARY = "CY initramfs"
DESCRIPTION = "Embedded Linux initramfs [CY version]"
LICENSE = "MIT"
LIC_FILES_CHKSUM ?= "file://${COMMON_LICENSE_DIR}/MIT;md5=0835ade698e0b
cf8506ecda2f7b4f302"

# Do not pollute the initrd image with rootfs features
IMAGE_FEATURES = ""
IMAGE_LINGUAS = ""

# Set image properties
IMAGE_FSTYPES = "${INITRAMFS_FSTYPES}"
```

```
IMAGE_ROOTFS_SIZE = "8192"
IMAGE_ROOTFS_EXTRA_SPACE = "0"

inherit core-image

# Packages to be installed
VIRTUAL-RUNTIME_dev_manager ?= "busybox-mdev"
PACKAGE_INSTALL = " \
        ${VIRTUAL-RUNTIME_base-utils} \
        ${VIRTUAL-RUNTIME_dev_manager} \
        ${ROOTFS_BOOTSTRAP_INSTALL} \
        tiny-initramfs \
"

BAD_RECOMMENDATIONS += "busybox-syslog"
```

This image recipe just installs the minimal required packages to boot plus the package tiny-initramfs, defined as shown below:

```
$ cat $CY_METADIR/recipes-initramfs/tiny-initramfs/tiny-initramfs_1.0.bb
SUMMARY = "CY tiny initramfs framework"
LICENSE = "MIT"
LIC_FILES_CHKSUM = "file://${COREBASE}/meta/COPYING.MIT;md5=3da9cfbcb78
8c80a0384361b4de20420"

PR = "r0"
S = "${WORKDIR}"

SRC_URI = " \
        file://fstab \
        file://init \
"

do_install() {
        install -d ${D}/tmp
        install -d ${D}/mnt
        install -d ${D}/dev
        mknod -m 622 ${D}/dev/console c 5 1

        install -d ${D}/proc
        install -d ${D}/sys

        install -d ${D}/etc
        install ${WORKDIR}/fstab ${D}/etc/fstab

        install -m 0755 ${WORKDIR}/init ${D}/init
}
```

```
FILES:${PN} = " \
        /dev /dev/console \
        /proc /sys /tmp /mnt \
        /etc /etc/fstab \
        /init \
"
```

This recipe just needs the shell interpreter provided by the image-tiny-initramfs to run, plus two extra files; the first one, the fstab file, is to define the minimal mount points to be used:

```
$ cat $CY_METADIR/recipes-initramfs/tiny-initramfs/tiny-initramfs/fstab
devtmpfs      /dev          devtmpfs      defaults      0       0
proc          /proc         proc          defaults      0       0
sysfs         /sys          sysfs         defaults      0       0
tmpfs         /tmp          tmpfs         defaults      0       0
```

And the second one, the init script, simply does the following steps:

```
$ cat $CY_METADIR/recipes-initramfs/tiny-initramfs/tiny-initramfs/init
#!/bin/sh

export PATH=/usr/bin:/bin:/usr/sbin:/sbin


#
# Defines
#

NAME="init"
ROOT_DIR="/mnt/root"
ROOT_DEV="/dev/mmcblk1p2"
...
#
# Main
#

echo "$NAME: ***** Initramfs started *****"

# Mount filesystems into /etc/fstab
mount -a

# Do symlink for /etc/mtab
ln -s /proc/self/mounts /etc/mtab

init=$(get_cmdline_value init)
mkdir -p $ROOT_DIR
wait_for_blockdev $ROOT_DEV || fatal "no block device!"
```

635

```
mount $ROOT_DEV $ROOT_DIR || fatal "cannot mount real rootfs!"

echo "$NAME: booting real rootfs..."
move_mountpoint /dev /proc /sys /tmp
exec switch_root -c /dev/console $ROOT_DIR ${init:-/sbin/init}

# Something goes wrong? Time to die...
fatal "System hangs!"

# Can't happen
exit 1
```

The function get_cmdline_value returns the value set within the
kernel command line for the init variable (usually not defined or
defaulted to /sbin/init), while the function wait_for_blockdev is used
to wait for a while before attempting to mount the block device holding the
real root filesystem to use; this is because some devices, for example, the
USB ones, need a while before becoming operational.

Then, function move_mountpoint just does the following steps to
properly move the specified mount points in the new root filesystem:

```
move_mountpoint() {
        for mp in $* ; do
                mount -o move $mp $ROOT_DIR$mp
        done
}
```

However, the core steps in the above file are as follows:

1) The mkdir command is used to create the /mnt/
   root directory where the real root filesystem is
   temporarily mounted.

2) The mount $ROOT_DEV $ROOT_DIR command, which
   effectively does the real root filesystem mount
   operation.

3) The switch_root command that switches to
   another filesystem as the root of the mount tree
   and then starts the init process in the real root
   filesystem.

Our example is elementary, but on real production systems we can add several operations, such as doing updates or factory resets, mounting encrypted root filesystems, etc., before executing the above steps.

OK, now to test our Initramfs, we need to properly set the variables INITRAMFS_IMAGE and INITRAMFS_IMAGE_BUNDLE as described in Section 6.5.3. To do so, we define a new distro.conf file as shown below:

```
$ cat $CY_METADIR/conf/distro/cy-xwayland-initramfs.conf
require conf/distro/fsl-imx-xwayland.conf

INITRAMFS_IMAGE_BUNDLE = "1"
INITRAMFS_IMAGE = "image-tiny-initramfs"
```

So, we get a distribution equal to the one described by fsl-imx-xwayland.conf but with our Initramfs between the kernel booting and the root filesystem cy-evaluation-image-mx8 execution.

To generate the correct kernel image, we need to change the DISTRO variable within our conf/local.conf file:

```
--- conf/local.conf
+++ conf/local.conf
@@ -1,5 +1,5 @@
 MACHINE ??= 'imx8mp-icore-cy'
-DISTRO ?= 'fsl-imx-xwayland'
+DISTRO ?= 'cy-xwayland-initramfs'
 PACKAGE_CLASSES ?= 'package_rpm'
 USER_CLASSES ?= "buildstats"
 PATCHRESOLVE = "noop"
```

Then we can execute bitbake as usual:

```
$ bitbake cy-evaluation-image-mx8
...
Build Configuration:
BB_VERSION           = "2.0.0"
BUILD_SYS            = "x86_64-linux"
NATIVELSBSTRING      = "universal"
TARGET_SYS           = "aarch64-poky-linux"
MACHINE              = "imx8mp-icore-cy"
DISTRO               = "cy-xwayland-initramfs"
DISTRO_VERSION       = "5.15-kirkstone"
TUNE_FEATURES        = "aarch64 armv8a crc crypto"
TARGET_FPU           = ""
...
```

In the command output, we can verify that DISTRO is set correctly. When the image generation is finished, we should get the following files:

```
$ ls $BUILDDIR/tmp/deploy/images/imx8mp-icore-cy/
Image
Image--5.15.71+git0+d1c9a311f7-r0-imx8mp-icore-cy-20240822151742.bin
Image-imx8mp-icore-cy.bin
Image-initramfs--5.15.71+git0+d1c9a311f7-r0-imx8mp-icore-cy-20240822151
742.binImage-initramfs-imx8mp-icore-cy.bin
...
image-tiny-initramfs-imx8mp-icore-cy-20240822151742.rootfs.cpio.gz
image-tiny-initramfs-imx8mp-icore-cy-20240822151742.rootfs.manifest
image-tiny-initramfs-imx8mp-icore-cy-20240822151742.testdata.json
image-tiny-initramfs-imx8mp-icore-cy.cpio.gz
image-tiny-initramfs-imx8mp-icore-cy.manifest
image-tiny-initramfs-imx8mp-icore-cy.testdata.json
...
```

The file image-tiny-initramfs-imx8mp-icore-cy.cpio.gz holds our Initramfs, and other files with the same prefix name are related to it (note the .manifest file), while the file Image-initramfs-imx8mp-icore-cy.bin is the kernel image as Image-imx8mp-icore-cy.bin but with the bundled Initramfs. So, to test if everything works well, we can simply replace the Image file in the microSD boot partition with the file Image-initramfs-imx8mp-icore-cy.bin:

```
$ ls /media/giometti/boot/
Image                        imx8mp-icore-cy-board.dtb
imx8mp-icore-ctouch2.dtb  imx8mp-icore-starterkit.dtb
$ cp $BUILDDIR/tmp/deploy/images/imx8mp-icore-cy/Image-initramfs-imx8mp
-icore-cy.bin \
        /media/giometti/boot/Image
```

The readers should consider that the directory where their system mounts the boot partition will differ from /media/giometti/boot. So they should rewrite the command above to fit their needs.

Once the Image file has been properly replaced, we can do a new boot, and when the kernel has finished its boot, we should see something as reported below:

```
...
[    3.859587] Freeing unused kernel memory: 10880K
[    3.870595] Run /init as init process
init: ***** Initramfs started *****
[    4.410349] EXT4-fs (mmcblk1p2): recovery complete
[    4.477331] EXT4-fs (mmcblk1p2): mounted filesystem with ordered dat
a mode. O
pts: (null). Quota mode: none.
init: booting real rootfs...
[    5.122593] systemd[1]: System time before build time, advancing clo
ck.
[    5.171162] systemd[1]: systemd 250.5+ running in system mode (+PAM
-AUDIT -S
...
```

We can see that the kernel runs our /init script, which in turn mounts and executes the real root filesystem as before.

It may happen that while u-boot is loading the kernel, it displays the following error message:

```
...
59437 bytes read in 5 ms (11.3 MiB/s)
## Flattened Device Tree blob at 43000000
   Booting using the fdt blob at 0x43000000
ERROR: FDT image overlaps OS image (OS=0x40400000..0x430e0000)
u-boot=>
```

This is because the loading addresses for the kernel and device tree images are not fixed well. Our new kernel image with the bundled Initramfs is too large to fit in memory, so we resolve the issue by executing the following command:

```
u-boot=> setenv fdt_addr_r 0x44000000
```

Then we can continue the boot with the boot command:

```
u-boot=> boot
```

When the real root filesystem finishes booting, everything will work as usual.

12.7 Summary

In this chapter, we have seen several practical examples of how to write image recipes. We can now write our image recipe from scratch or by simply cloning an already written one. We also know how to alter some common system configurations and how to add an Initramfs to do special operations before booting our real root filesystem.

Now we can move on to the last chapter of this book in order to see how to do some Yocto optimizations or customizations and some best practices for the Yocto embedded development.

CHAPTER 13

Optimizations and Best Practices

In this last chapter of this book, we are going to see some useful optimizations and best practices a good Yocto developer may use.

13.1 Development and Production Releases

Every good developer knows the importance of having the ability to easily switch between development and production releases while developing a new software. And for a Yocto distribution, it is the same. In fact, during the development, we may need some packages that can be removed in production in order to save space and/or not pollute our final image with not needed (or dangerous/not secure) tools. For example, in a production image, tools such as `i2cdetect`, `perf`, or `valgrind` should be removed; also, having the ability to log in as root without a password should be avoided.

For all these reasons, in this section we are going to propose some possible configurations that developers can easily use to produce a development or a production image.

To customize an image recipe, there are two main places where we can operate: within the configuration files (`.conf`) or directly into the recipe file. So we must carefully check our configuration files and, especially, the `conf/local.conf` one.

© Rodolfo Giometti 2025
R. Giometti, *Yocto Project Customization for Linux*,
https://doi.org/10.1007/979-8-8688-1435-8_13

Before we start doing our modifications, let's check if the current `local.conf` setting looks like the following:

```
$ cat $BUILDDIR/conf/local.conf
MACHINE ??= 'imx8mp-icore-cy'
DISTRO ?= 'fsl-imx-xwayland'
PACKAGE_CLASSES ?= 'package_rpm'
EXTRA_IMAGE_FEATURES ?= "debug-tweaks"
USER_CLASSES ?= "buildstats"
PATCHRESOLVE = "noop"
BB_DISKMON_DIRS ??= "\
    STOPTASKS,${TMPDIR},1G,100K \
    STOPTASKS,${DL_DIR},1G,100K \
    STOPTASKS,${SSTATE_DIR},1G,100K \
    STOPTASKS,/tmp,100M,100K \
    HALT,${TMPDIR},100M,1K \
    HALT,${DL_DIR},100M,1K \
    HALT,${SSTATE_DIR},100M,1K \
    HALT,/tmp,10M,1K"
PACKAGECONFIG:append:pn-qemu-system-native = " sdl"
CONF_VERSION = "2"

DL_DIR = "/home/giometti/Projects/DL_ARCHIVES/yocto/"
ACCEPT_FSL_EULA = "1"

# Switch to IPKG packaging and include package-management in the image
PACKAGE_CLASSES = "package_ipk"
EXTRA_IMAGE_FEATURES += "package-management"
#EXTRA_IMAGE_FEATURES += "dbg-pkgs"

# Limiting HW resources
BB_NUMBER_THREADS = "4"
PARALLEL_MAKE = "-j 2"
```

So the first thing to do is to remove the `debug-tweaks` within the `EXTRA_IMAGE_FEATURES` variable, since this setting should be done according to the fact that we are building a development or a production image. In fact, as reported in Section 3.4.1, such setting is used to make an image suitable for development, and so ssh root access has a blank password. So the needed modifications are shown below:

```
--- conf/local.conf
+++ conf/local.conf
@@ -1,7 +1,6 @@
```

```
 MACHINE ??= 'imx8mp-icore-cy'
 DISTRO ?= 'fsl-imx-xwayland'
 PACKAGE_CLASSES ?= 'package_rpm'
-EXTRA_IMAGE_FEATURES ?= "debug-tweaks"
 USER_CLASSES ?= "buildstats"
 PATCHRESOLVE = "noop"
 BB_DISKMON_DIRS ??= "\
```

Now, we can alter our custom image recipe cy-evaluation-image-mx8.bb to select the image features according to a new CY_DEVELOPMENT variable:

```
--- cy-evaluation-image-mx8.bb
+++ cy-evaluation-image-mx8.bb
@@ -6,6 +6,9 @@
 DESCRIPTION = "CY evaluation image"
 LICENSE = "MIT"

+CY_DEVELOPMENT ?= "0"
+OVERRIDES .= "${@bb.utils.contains('CY_DEVELOPMENT', '1', ':cy_develop
ment', '', d)}"
+
 inherit core-image

 ROOTFS_POSTPROCESS_COMMAND:append:mx8 = "fix_bcm43430;"
@@ -17,17 +20,19 @@

 ## Select Image Features
 IMAGE_FEATURES += " \
-        debug-tweaks \
-        tools-profile \
         splash \
-        tools-debug \
         ssh-server-dropbear \
-        tools-testapps \
         hwcodecs \
         ${@bb.utils.contains('DISTRO_FEATURES', 'wayland', 'weston', \
                 bb.utils.contains('DISTRO_FEATURES', 'x11', 'x11-base x11-s
ato', '', d), d)} \
 "
```

```
+IMAGE_FEATURES:append:cy_development = " \
+          debug-tweaks \
+          tools-profile \
+          tools-debug \
+          tools-testapps \
+"

 G2D_SAMPLES = ""
 G2D_SAMPLES:imxgpu2d = "imx-g2d-samples"
```

In this manner, when we set the default value for CY_DEVELOPMENT, we get the following settings:

```
$ cy-vars 'OVERRIDES\|IMAGE_FEATURES' cy-evaluation-image-mx8
IMAGE_FEATURES="hwcodecs package-management splash ssh-server-dropbear
weston"
OVERRIDES="runtime-gnu:toolchain-gcc:linux:aarch64:pn-cy-evaluation-ima
gE-mx8:imx8mp-icore:aarch64:armv8a:use-nxp-bsp:imx-generic-bsp:imx-nxp-
bsP:imxdrm:imxvpu:imxgpu:imxgpu2d:imxgpu3d:imxvulkan:mx8-generic-bsp:mx
8-nXp-bsp:mx8m-generic-bsp:mx8m-nxp-bsp:mx8mp-generic-bsp:mx8mp-nxp-bsp
:imx8mp-icore-cy:fsl:class-target:libc-glibc:forcevariable"
```

And the IMAGE_FEATURES variable just holds the minimal features needed to run our application, while when we set CY_DEVELOPMENT to 1, we get the following alternate settings:

```
$ cy-vars 'OVERRIDES\|IMAGE_FEATURES' cy-evaluation-image-mx8
IMAGE_FEATURES="debug-tweaks hwcodecs package-management splash ssh-ser
ver-dropbear tools-debug tools-profile tools-testapps weston"
OVERRIDES="runtime-gnu:toolchain-gcc:linux:aarch64:pn-cy-evaluation-ima
ge-mx8:imx8mp-icore:aarch64:armv8a:use-nxp-bsp:imx-generic-bsp:imx-nxp-
Bsp:imxdrm:imxvpu:imxgpu:imxgpu2d:imxgpu3d:imxvulkan:mx8-generic-bsp:mx
8-nxp-bsp:mx8m-generic-bsp:mx8m-nxp-bsp:mx8mp-generic-bsp:mx8mp-nxp-bsp
:imx8mp-icore-cy:fsl:class-target:libc-glibc:forcevariable:cy_developme
nt"
```

Now we can see that OVERRIDES holds the cy_development overrides, and this appends to IMAGE_FEATURES all the development features normally disabled.

> Note that to set CY_DEVELOPMENT, we can alter the .bb file and set
>
> ```
> CY_DEVELOPMENT = "1"
> ```
>
> But we can also leave the above setting in the .bb file and then change it by using a .bbappend file!

This solution is quite elegant, but has a disadvantage: it applies to the image recipe only! In fact, if we build a single package, the setting is lost.

In order to have a global setting, that is, that it works each time we execute bitbake for every recipe, we have to move the OVERRIDES setting from the cy-evaluation-image-mx8.bb into a special configuration file. So we should have

```
--- cy-evaluation-image-mx8.bb
+++ cy-evaluation-image-mx8.bb
@@ -17,17 +17,19 @@

 ## Select Image Features
 IMAGE_FEATURES += " \
-        debug-tweaks \
-        tools-profile \
         splash \
-        tools-debug \
         ssh-server-dropbear \
-        tools-testapps \
         hwcodecs \
         ${@bb.utils.contains('DISTRO_FEATURES', 'wayland', 'weston', \
                 bb.utils.contains('DISTRO_FEATURES', 'x11', 'x11-base x11-s
ato', '', d), d)} \
 "

+IMAGE_FEATURES:append:cy_development = " \
+        debug-tweaks \
+        tools-profile \
+        tools-debug \
+        tools-testapps \
+"

 G2D_SAMPLES = ""
 G2D_SAMPLES:imxgpu2d = "imx-g2d-samples"
```

And then create a new configuration file named `development.conf`
with the following content:

```
$ cat conf/development.conf
# Define the "development" override to enable special configuration
# settings in the form XXXXXX:development or XXXXXX:append:development.
OVERRIDES =. "development:"
```

Now, if we execute `bitbake` as usual, we get

```
$ bitbake -e | grep '^OVERRIDES='
OVERRIDES="runtime-gnu:toolchain-gcc:linux:aarch64:pn-defaultpkgname:im
X8mp-icore:aarch64:armv8a:use-nxp-bsp:imx-generic-bsp:imx-nxp-bsp:imxdr
M:imxvpu:imxgpu:imxgpu2d:imxgpu3d:imxvulkan:mx8-generic-bsp:mx8-nxp-bsp
:mx8m-generic-bsp:mx8m-nxp-bsp:mx8mp-generic-bsp:mx8mp-nxp-bsp:imx8mp-i
core-cy:fsl:class-target:libc-glibc:forcevariable"
```

while if we use the `-R` option argument to ask `bitbake` to read the
specified file after `bitbake.conf`, we get

```
$ bitbake -e -R conf/development.conf | grep '^OVERRIDES='
OVERRIDES="runtime-gnu:toolchain-gcc:development:linux:aarch64:pn-defau
ltpkgname:imx8mp-icore:aarch64:armv8a:use-nxp-bsp:imx-generic-bsp:imx-n
xp-bsp:imxdrm:imxvpu:imxgpu:imxgpu2d:imxgpu3d:imxvulkan:mx8-generic-bsp
:mx8-nxp-bsp:mx8m-generic-bsp:mx8m-nxp-bsp:mx8mp-generic-bsp:mx8mp-nxp-
bsp:imx8mp-icore-cy:fsl:class-target:libc-glibc:forcevariable"
```

So, if we build our image recipe as usual, we get a production image:

```
$ bitbake -e cy-evaluation-image-mx8 | grep '^IMAGE_FEATURES='
IMAGE_FEATURES="hwcodecs package-management splash ssh-server-dropbear
weston"
```

On the other hand, if we supply the `conf/development.conf`
configuration file, we get the development version:

```
$ bitbake -e -R conf/development.conf cy-evaluation-image-mx8 | \
      grep '^IMAGE_FEATURES='
IMAGE_FEATURES="debug-tweaks hwcodecs package-management splash ssh-ser
ver-dropbear tools-debug tools-profile tools-testapps weston"
```

Note that this trick can be used within all recipes defined into the
meta layer.

However, this is still not enough; in fact, in some circumstances, we may need to do something as reported below to conditionally set a variable flag:

```
UBOOT_CONFIG[sd] = "imx8mq_var_dart${@'_devel' if d.getVar('DEVELOPMENT
') == '1' else ''}_config,sdcard"
```

This special setting is used to define as the default U-Boot's configuration the file imx8mq_var_dart_config or imx8mq_var_dart_devel_config, according to the fact that the DEVELOPMENT variable is set to 1 or not.

To automatically define this behavior, the final version of the development.conf file should be

```
$ cat conf/development.conf
# Define the "development" override to enable special configuration
# settings in the form XXXXXX:development or XXXXXX:append:development.
OVERRIDES =. "development:"

# Define the DEVELOPMENT variable to "1" in case of development mode to
# be used to enable special configuration settings in the form
# VARIABLE[flag] = "${@'true_setting' if d.getVar('DEVELOPMENT') == '1'
# else 'false_setting'}"
DEVELOPMENT:development = "1"
```

In this manner, DEVELOPMENT is properly set to 1 each time the file is included in the configuration file list for BitBake.

For completeness, recalling what we said in Section 12.5.3, we can also add the hostname rewriting, so the final version for conf/development.conf can result in

```
$ cat conf/development.conf
# Define the "development" override to enable special configuration
# settings in the form XXXXXX:development or XXXXXX:append:development.
OVERRIDES =. "development:"

# Define the DEVELOPMENT variable to "1" in case of development mode to
# be  used to enable special configuration settings in the form
# VARIABLE[flag] = "${@'true_setting' if d.getVar('DEVELOPMENT') == '1'
# else 'false_setting'}"
DEVELOPMENT:development = "1"
```

647

```
# Rewrite the hostname to signal the development release
hostname:append:pn-base-files = "${@'-devel' if d.getVar('DEVELOPMENT'
) == '1' else ''}"
```

Doing so, the hostname changes to `${MACHINE}-devel` during the development stage.

13.2 Fixing All Package Revision

In Section 6.2, we have noticed that each package has its own fixed version which is stated in the recipe name. For example, within our meta layer we have the recipes `python3-memory-profiler_0.61.0.bb`, `dropbear_2022.83.bb`, and `example_0.1.bb` which refer to specific and well-defined versions. However, it's quite usual to use a Git repository to hold the sources, and in this case, recipes have the `_git` postfix as our `python3-pynmea2_git.bb`, `umrp_git.bb`, and `lhello_git.bb`. Here, the revision number is written in the recipe in the SRCREV variable:

```
$ grep SRCREV $CY_METADIR/recipes-python/python3-pynmea2/python3-pynmea2_git.bb
SRCREV = "c546442d1ba38e488f47ef8a190eb5e890260aa2"
$ grep SRCREV $CY_METADIR/recipes-networking/umrp/umrp_git.bb
SRCREV = "fb193eac1a2df51fe42e19d4ea36bb0157bda09f"
$ grep SRCREV $CY_METADIR/recipes-example/lhello/lhello_git.bb
SRCREV = "9bcdf085b9b24794706d25f17ec814f05afdc3d2"
```

If the code is in its final state, everything can be left untouched. However (especially during the development of a custom software), we may need `bitbake` to take the latest commit within a branch each time we build the recipe so that we can proceed with our tests. To do so, we have to put the value `${AUTOREV}` into SRCREV, as shown below:

```
SRCREV = "${AUTOREV}"
```

The readers should remember what we have said previously in this book about the above setting and the `devtool` command: having such a setting in a recipe may cause the command to fail! So it must be used carefully.

Doing so may result in having several packages in this situation around our meta layer. When we are ready to move from the development stage to the production one, we have to put all the correct commit IDs in every SRCREV set to ${AUTOREV}. This operation can be annoying and error-prone, so it would be better doing it automatically by using the **Build History**.

The Yocto Project's Build History can help us to highlight unexpected and possibly unwanted changes in the build output by automatically recording information about the contents of each package and image, then committing that information to a local Git repository where we can examine the information.

The scope of this section is not to explain in detail the Build History framework, but just those parts we can use to resolve our problem of automatically setting the SRCREV variable. However, some words must be spent on it in order to explain a bit to the readers how it works.

Firstly, to enable the Build History, we must inherit the `buildhistory` class and then set a few variables within the `conf/local.conf` file, as shown below:

```
--- conf/local.conf
+++ conf/local.conf
@@ -26,3 +26,8 @@
 # Limiting HW resources
 BB_NUMBER_THREADS = "4"
 PARALLEL_MAKE = "-j 2"
+
+# Enable the Build History data
+INHERIT += "buildhistory"
+BUILDHISTORY_COMMIT = "1"
+BUILDHISTORY_FEATURES="image package task"
```

The INHERIT variable is used to enable inheritance within a configuration file (see Section 5.4.3), while for the other variables we can say that

- BUILDHISTORY_COMMIT is used to enable the committing of the build history output in a local Git repository. When set to 1, this local repository will be maintained automatically by the buildhistory class (stored in poky/meta/classes/buildhistory.bbclass), and a commit will be created on every build for changes to each top-level subdirectory of the build history output (according to the settings in BUILDHISTORY_FEATURES). It defaults to 1.

- BUILDHISTORY_FEATURES defaults to the string image package sdk, and it is used to specify the build history features to be enabled as a space-separated list. Available values are

  - image: Enables analysis of the contents of images (e.g., the list of installed packages)

  - package: Enables analysis of the contents of individual packages

  - sdk: Enables analysis of the contents of the Software Development Kit (not covered in this book)

  - task: Saves one file per task and lists the SHA-256 checksums for each file staged

In our example, we just used these two variables; however, there are others we can use to customize the Build History functioning. The most interesting are as follows:

- BUILDHISTORY_COMMIT_AUTHOR specifies the author to use for each Git commit in the form of name <email@host>. It defaults to buildhistory <buildhistory@${DISTRO}>.

- BUILDHISTORY_DIR specifies the directory in which build history information is kept. It defaults to ${TOPDIR}/buildhistory.

OK, once we have enabled the Build History mechanism, we must regenerate the image as shown below to force the image's build history data generation:

```
$ bitbake -c cleanall cy-evaluation-image-mx8 && \
    bitbake cy-evaluation-image-mx8
```

When the build is finished, the new directory buildhistory should be created with the following content:

```
$ tree buildhistory/
buildhistory/
├── images
│   └── imx8mp_icore_cy
│       └── glibc
│           └── cy-evaluation-image-mx8
│               ├── image-files
│               │   └── etc
│               │       ├── group
│               │       └── passwd
│               ├── build-id.txt
│               ├── depends.dot
│               ├── depends-nokernel.dot
│               ├── depends-nokernel-nolibc.dot
│               ├── depends-nokernel-nolibc-noupdate.dot
│               ├── depends-nokernel-nolibc-noupdate-nomodules.dot
│               ├── files-in-image.txt
│               ├── image-info.txt
│               ├── installed-package-info.txt
│               ├── installed-package-names.txt
│               ├── installed-package-sizes.txt
│               └── installed-packages.txt
```

```
├──  task
│   ├──  output
│   │   ├──  cy-evaluation-image-mx8.image_complete
│   │   └──  cy-evaluation-image-mx8.image_qa
│   └──  tasksigs.txt
└──  metadata-revs

8 directories, 18 files
```

Under `buildhistory/task` are stored all task output and signatures (the readers are invited to navigate around this directory), while under `buildhistory/images/imx8mp_icore_cy` are stored all information regarding our machine, and in the subdirectory `glibc/cy-evaluation-image-mx8` are all information about our image. So let's move into it:

```
$ cd $BUILDDIR/buildhistory/images/imx8mp_icore_cy/glibc/cy-evaluation-
image-mx8/
$ ls
build-id.txt
depends.dot
depends-nokernel.dot
depends-nokernel-nolibc.dot
depends-nokernel-nolibc-noupdate.dot
depends-nokernel-nolibc-noupdate-nomodules.dot
files-in-image.txt
image-files
image-info.txt
installed-package-info.txt
installed-package-names.txt
installed-package-sizes.txt
installed-packages.txt
```

Within `image-info.txt`, there is some useful information about our image:

```
$ cat image-info.txt
DISTRO = fsl-imx-xwayland
DISTRO_VERSION = 5.15-kirkstone
USER_CLASSES = buildstats meta-virt-cfg meta-virt-k8s-cfg meta-virt-xen
-cfg meta-virt-hosts
IMAGE_CLASSES = image_types_fsl license_image
IMAGE_FEATURES = debug-tweaks hwcodecs package-management splash ssh-se
rver-dropbear tools-debug tools-profile tools-testapps weston
IMAGE_LINGUAS = en-us en-gb
```

```
IMAGE_INSTALL = packagegroup-core-boot packagegroup-base-extended packa
gegroup-core-full-cmdline packagegroup-tools-bluetooth firmwared weston
-xwayland xterm alsa-utils brcm-patchram-plus cantest canutils devmem2
dosfstools e2fsprogs e2fsprogs-resize2fs engicam-emmc-tools ethtool evt
est firmware-imx-hdmi i2c-tools iproute2 ldd libgpiod libgpiod-tools li
nux-firmware-bcm43430 linux-firmware minicom parted serialtools usbutil
s zstd stress-ng packagegroup-fsl-tools-audio packagegroup-fsl-tools-gp
u packagegroup-fsl-tools-gpu-external packagegroup-fsl-tools-testapps p
ackagegroup-fsl-tools-benchmark packagegroup-imx-isp packagegroup-fsl-g
streamer1.0 packagegroup-fsl-gstreamer1.0-full imx-g2d-samples useradd-
example useradd-example-user3 tzdata jailhouse
BAD_RECOMMENDATIONS =
NO_RECOMMENDATIONS =
PACKAGE_EXCLUDE =
ROOTFS_POSTPROCESS_COMMAND = write_package_manifest; license_create_man
ifest;    ssh_allow_empty_password; ssh_allow_root_login; postinst_e
nable_logging;  rootfs_update_timestamp;   write_image_test_data;  set_
systemd_default_target; systemd_create_users; empty_var_volatile;   sor
t_passwd; rootfs_reproducible;
IMAGE_POSTPROCESS_COMMAND = buildhistory_get_imageinfo ;
IMAGESIZE = 3419400
```

while within `files-in-image.txt` there is the complete list of all files held in the root filesystem:

```
$ head -20 files-in-image.txt
drwxr-xr-x root   root      4096 ./bin
-rwxr-xr-x root   root     22496 ./bin/arping
lrwxrwxrwx root   root        19 ./bin/ash -> /bin/busybox.nosuid
lrwxrwxrwx root   root        25 ./bin/base32 -> /usr/bin/base32.coreutils
lrwxrwxrwx root   root        25 ./bin/base64 -> /usr/bin/base64.coreutils
-rwxr-xr-x root   root   1284224 ./bin/bash.bash
lrwxrwxrwx root   root        14 ./bin/bash -> /bin/bash.bash
lrwxrwxrwx root   root        14 ./bin/busybox -> busybox.nosuid
-rwxr-xr-x root   root    690840 ./bin/busybox.nosuid
-rwsr-xr-x root   root     75840 ./bin/busybox.suid
lrwxrwxrwx root   root        18 ./bin/cat -> /bin/cat.coreutils
-rwxr-xr-x root   root     43328 ./bin/cat.coreutils
lrwxrwxrwx root   root        21 ./bin/chattr -> /bin/chattr.e2fsprogs
-rwxr-xr-x root   root     14328 ./bin/chattr.e2fsprogs
lrwxrwxrwx root   root        20 ./bin/chgrp -> /bin/chgrp.coreutils
-rwxr-xr-x root   root     76056 ./bin/chgrp.coreutils
lrwxrwxrwx root   root        20 ./bin/chmod -> /bin/chmod.coreutils
-rwxr-xr-x root   root     67872 ./bin/chmod.coreutils
lrwxrwxrwx root   root        20 ./bin/chown -> /bin/chown.coreutils
-rwxr-xr-x root   root     80152 ./bin/chown.coreutils
```

653

This is really useful to easily check which files are present or not within the root filesystem, while in `installed-package-sizes.txt` we have the list of all installed packages ordered by size:

```
$ head -20 installed-package-sizes.txt
815208      KiB      imx-gpu-sdk
360086      KiB      ltp
276669      KiB      linux-firmware
155101      KiB      linux-firmware-iwlwifi-misc
143500      KiB      linux-firmware-netronome
140275      KiB      boost-dev
74751       KiB      libnn-imx
74098       KiB      imx-test
43090       KiB      linux-firmware-ath11k
41191       KiB      kernel-image-image-5.15.71+gd1c9a311f7ef
37185       KiB      imx-gpu-viv-demos
36977       KiB      go-runtime
28782       KiB      libicudata70
24867       KiB      linux-firmware-liquidio
24116       KiB      vulkan-validationlayers
21979       KiB      linux-firmware-i915
21680       KiB      libc6-dbg
21679       KiB      valgrind
16049       KiB      linux-firmware-ibt-misc
16019       KiB      libvsc-imx
```

Moreover, in `installed-packages.txt` there is a list of installed packages with full package filenames and ordered by name:

```
$ head -20 installed-packages.txt
acl_2.3.1-r0_armv8a.ipk
acl-dev_2.3.1-r0_armv8a.ipk
adwaita-icon-theme-symbolic_41.0-r0_all.ipk
alsa-conf_1.2.6.1-r0_armv8a-mx8mp.ipk
alsa-plugins-pulseaudio-conf_1.2.6-r0_armv8a.ipk
alsa-state_0.2.0-r5_imx8mp_icore_cy.ipk
alsa-states_0.2.0-r5_imx8mp_icore_cy.ipk
alsa-tools_1.2.5-r0_armv8a.ipk
alsa-topology-conf_1.2.5.1-r0_all.ipk
alsa-ucm-conf_1.2.6.3-r0_all.ipk
alsa-utils-aconnect_1.2.6-r0_armv8a.ipk
alsa-utils-alsactl_1.2.6-r0_armv8a.ipk
alsa-utils-alsaloop_1.2.6-r0_armv8a.ipk
alsa-utils-alsamixer_1.2.6-r0_armv8a.ipk
alsa-utils-alsatplg_1.2.6-r0_armv8a.ipk
```

```
alsa-utils-alsaucm_1.2.6-r0_armv8a.ipk
alsa-utils_1.2.6-r0_armv8a.ipk
alsa-utils-amixer_1.2.6-r0_armv8a.ipk
alsa-utils-aplay_1.2.6-r0_armv8a.ipk
alsa-utils-aseqdump_1.2.6-r0_armv8a.ipk
```

Finally, the depends.dot file holds the complete dependency list of all packages in the image in the GraphViz DOT file format (see https:// graphviz.org/). Since this format is human-readable, we can easily discover, for example, all dependencies of the packagegroup-base-alsa package just by using the grep command:

```
$ grep packagegroup-base-alsa depends.dot
"packagegroup-base-alsa" -> "alsa-state"
"packagegroup-base-alsa" -> "alsa-utils-alsactl"
"packagegroup-base-alsa" -> "alsa-utils-amixer"
"packagegroup-base-alsa" -> "kernel-module-snd-mixer-oss" [style=dotted]
"packagegroup-base-alsa" -> "kernel-module-snd-pcm-oss" [style=dotted]
"packagegroup-base" -> "packagegroup-base-alsa"
```

Here, we can see that the package packagegroup-base depends on packagegroup-base-alsa, which in turn depends on alsa-state, alsa-utils-alsactl, alsa-utils-amixer, kernel-module-snd-mixer-oss, and kernel-module-snd-pcm-oss packages.

OK, now that we know a bit better what the Build History is, we can use it to list all those packages that use AUTOREV within their SRCREV variables. The command to be used is buildhistory-collect-srcrevs, which has the following usage message:

```
$ buildhistory-collect-srcrevs  -h
Usage:
    buildhistory-collect-srcrevs [options]

Collects the recorded SRCREV values from buildhistory and reports on them.

Options:
  -h, --help             show this help message and exit
  -a, --report-all       Report all SRCREV values, not just ones where
                         AUTOREV has been used
  -f, --forcevariable    Use forcevariable override for all output lines
```

```
-p BUILDHISTORY_DIR, --buildhistory-dir=BUILDHISTORY_DIR
                    Specify path to buildhistory directory (defaults
                    to buildhistory/ under cwd)
```

Firstly, we must note that the `buildhistory` directory must be within the current working directory (`cwd`), so we must execute it within the `BUILDDIR` or with the `-p` command argument (with a proper argument). Then the `-a` (or `--report-all`) option argument can be used to get all `SRCREV` values stored within the `buildhistory` directory and not just ones where `AUTOREV` is used, while the `-f` (or `--forcevariable`) option argument can be used to append the `forcevariable` overrides to each output line, in the case we need to be sure that other overrides applied elsewhere, which may lead to unwanted settings.

In this last case, the output is in the form

```
$ buildhistory-collect-srcrevs -f
# armv8a-poky-linux
SRCREV:pn-umrp:forcevariable = "fb193eac1a2df51fe42e19d4ea36bb0157
bda09f"
```

Note the usage of the `forcevariable` override.

OK, to show a simple example about how we can use this command, we should modify our `umrp_git.bb` recipe, as shown below:

```
--- a/recipes-networking/umrp/umrp_git.bb
+++ b/recipes-networking/umrp/umrp_git.bb
@@ -8,7 +8,7 @@ LIC_FILES_CHKSUM = "file://LICENSE;md5=b234ee4d69f5fce4
486a80fdaf4a4263"
 SRC_URI = "git://github.com/giometti/umrp;protocol=https;branch=master"

 PV = "1.0+git${SRCPV}"
-SRCREV = "fb193eac1a2df51fe42e19d4ea36bb0157bda09f"
+SRCREV = "${AUTOREV}"

 S = "${WORKDIR}/git"
```

And then we can add the package to our image by simply adding it to the IMAGE_INSTALL variable as below:

```
--- recipes-images/images/cy-evaluation-image-mx8.bb
+++ recipes-images/images/cy-evaluation-image-mx8.bb
@@ -100,6 +100,7 @@

 IMAGE_INSTALL += " \
         tzdata \
+        umrp \
 "

 IMAGE_INSTALL:append:mx8m = "\
```

Now we should clean all umrp's building data and then regenerate our image:

```
$ bitbake -c cleanall umrp && bitbake cy-evaluation-image-mx8
...
0: umrp-1.0+gitAUTOINC+fb193eac1a-r0 do_compile - 0s (pid 1311053)   23
% |##          |
...
```

As we can see, umrp is regenerated, and, once the building is finished, a new directory packages under the buildhistory directory has been created regarding the umrp package:

```
$ tree buildhistory
buildhistory
├── images
│   └── imx8mp_icore_cy
...
├── packages
│   └── armv8a-poky-linux
│       └── umrp
│           ├── umrp
│           │   └── latest
│           ├── umrp-dbg
│           │   └── latest
│           ├── umrp-dev
│           │   └── latest
│           ├── umrp-doc
│           │   └── latest
│           ├── umrp-locale
│           │   └── latest
```

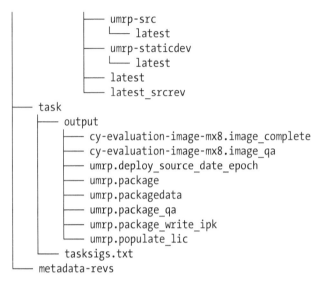

```
                  ├── umrp-src
                  │   └── latest
                  ├── umrp-staticdev
                  │   └── latest
                  ├── latest
                  └── latest_srcrev
    ├── task
    │   ├── output
    │   │   ├── cy-evaluation-image-mx8.image_complete
    │   │   ├── cy-evaluation-image-mx8.image_qa
    │   │   ├── umrp.deploy_source_date_epoch
    │   │   ├── umrp.package
    │   │   ├── umrp.packagedata
    │   │   ├── umrp.package_qa
    │   │   ├── umrp.package_write_ipk
    │   │   └── umrp.populate_lic
    │   └── tasksigs.txt
    └── metadata-revs

18 directories, 33 files
```

Note also that within `task/output` some new files regarding `umrp` tasks have been added too.

Now we can execute the `buildhistory-collect-srcrevs` command:

```
$ buildhistory-collect-srcrevs
# armv8a-poky-linux
SRCREV:pn-umrp = "fb193eac1a2df51fe42e19d4ea36bb0157bda09f"
```

Note that if we execute `buildhistory-collect-srcrevs` with also the -a option argument, the output doesn't change due to the fact that we didn't regenerate all packages, and then no Build History data has been created yet.

This output can be used, once the development stage has been finished, to properly set the SRCREV values of all our custom packages, by putting it within a dedicated configuration file as shown below:

```
$ buildhistory-collect-srcrevs > conf/srcrev.conf
```

Then we can ask bitbake to read it by using the -R option argument:

```
$ bitbake -R conf/srcrev.conf cy-evaluation-image-mx8
```

or by including it via the local.conf file, as shown below:

```
--- conf/local.conf
+++ conf/local.conf
@@ -31,3 +31,6 @@
 INHERIT += "buildhistory"
 BUILDHISTORY_COMMIT = "1"
 BUILDHISTORY_FEATURES="image package task"
+
+# Include SRCREV information (if present)
+include srcrev.conf
```

Doing so, even if in the recipes AUTOREV is specified for the SRCREV variables, we can set them to a fixed commit ID.

The include directive doesn't require that the specified file exist, so the file srcrev.conf can be safely deleted according to our needs.

Note that, once the image is regenerated with these settings, the output of buildhistory-collect-srcrevs is empty again! And we must remove the conf/srcrev.conf file and then regenerate the umrp package again in order to get some output:

```
$ rm conf/srcrev.conf
$ bitbake -c cleanall umrp && bitbake umrp
$ buildhistory-collect-srcrevs
# armv8a-poky-linux
SRCREV:pn-umrp = "fb193eac1a2df51fe42e19d4ea36bb0157bda09f"
```

So we must be sure to create this file at the end of the development stage, or we must reset it properly to avoid some misconfigurations.

13.3 Downloading Everything

In Section 2.3, we have introduced the DL_DIR variable which can be used to specify a common download directory where all builds can download their sources and where they can check to find already downloaded code. However, during a build, BitBake will also obtain sources from remote repositories managed by a revision control tool, for example, Git or SVN. By default, BitBake doesn't store these sources in the DL_DIR for performance reasons.

In the case we wish to have all the code locally, we can instruct BitBake to create an archive for each source that it checks out in the download directory, by adding the following settings within the conf/local.conf file:

```
BB_GENERATE_MIRROR_TARBALLS = "1"
```

Doing so, for subsequent builds, if the source is needed, BitBake will first look in the download directory for an archive before attempting to fetch it via a source control manager.

Note that, by enabling this setting, we may require several gigabytes of disk space to save all needed sources to build even one small image!

Using these settings for DL_DIR and BB_GENERATE_MIRROR_TARBALLS can improve the time it takes to build the Yocto Project by reducing the amount of time taken to obtain sources from the Internet. Moreover, it assures the reliability and reproducibility of builds in the case that, for example, a server pointed to by SRC_URI is temporarily unavailable.

In fact, this mode of operation is effectively an offline build, and we can use it to simply download all the sources needed to build our image, thus providing a way to populate the DL_DIR without having to build anything. This can be done by using the --runonly option argument in the bitbake command, as shown below:

```
$ bitbake --runonly=fetch cy-evaluation-image-mx8
```

To test that we have downloaded all the required sources for a build, we can add the BB_NO_NETWORK option to our local.conf file and then rebuild our image, as shown below:

```
$ echo 'BB_NO_NETWORK = "1"' >> conf/local.conf
$ bitbake cy-evaluation-image-mx8
```

This disables network access and thus results in an error if a source is needed that is not already downloaded.

13.4 Creating a Custom Repo Manifest

In this section, we are going to see in detail how the repo command works and how a **repo Manifest** can be used to be sure that we can generate immutable releases.

Note that, to be sure to be able to regenerate an image from scratch, we should also consider downloading all sources as explained in the previous section.

Firstly, we should spend some words explaining how a repo Manifest is done and how we can alter it in order to fix our needs. To do so, we are going to create a custom repo Manifest by starting from the NXP one, where we will add first the Engicam meta layer and then our custom meta layer.

The first step is to clone the NXP manifest, and to do so we can execute the following commands:

```
$ cd /home/giometti/yocto
$ mkdir manifest && cd manifest
$ git clone https://github.com/nxp-imx/imx-manifest cy-manifest
Cloning into 'cy-manifest'...
remote: Enumerating objects: 2330, done.
remote: Counting objects: 100% (567/567), done.
remote: Compressing objects: 100% (160/160), done.
remote: Total 2330 (delta 463), reused 486 (delta 405), pack-reused 1763
Receiving objects: 100% (2330/2330), 612.75 KiB | 2.88 MiB/s, done.
Resolving deltas: 100% (1548/1548), done.
```

Then we have to check out the initial release. If we recall what we did in Section 2.1, we have to work on branch imx-linux-kirkstone as shown below:

```
$ cd cy-manifest/
$ git checkout -b cy-linux-kirkstone origin/imx-linux-kirkstone
Branch 'cy-linux-kirkstone' set up to track remote branch 'imx-linux-ki
rkstone' from 'origin'.
Switched to a new branch 'cy-linux-kirkstone'
$ git branch 'imx-linux-kirkstone'
```

In this manner, we have a custom branch named cy-linux-kirkstone and a reference one named imx-linux-kirkstone.

This last branch will be used to easily display our modifications against the NXP original manifest.

The command we used to get NXP's code was

```
$ repo init -u https://github.com/nxp-imx/imx-manifest -b imx-linux-kirks
tone -m imx-5.15.71-2.2.0.xml
```

So, the NXP Manifest is in the file imx-5.15.71-2.2.0.xml, and to clone it we can do as shown below:

```
$ cp imx-5.15.71-2.2.0.xml cy-5.15.71-2.2.0.xml
$ git add cy-5.15.71-2.2.0.xml
$ git commit -s -m "Clone NXP manifest and create CY one"
```

Our new Manifest file should look like this:

```
$ cat cy-5.15.71-2.2.0.xml
<?xml version="1.0" encoding="UTF-8"?>
<manifest>

  <default sync-j="2"/>

  <remote fetch="https://github.com/nxp-imx" name="nxp-imx"/>
  <remote fetch="https://github.com/OSSystems" name="OSSystems"/>
  <remote fetch="https://code.qt.io/yocto"  name="QT6"/>
  <remote fetch="https://github.com/TimesysGit"  name="Timesys"/>
  <remote fetch="https://github.com/kraj" name="clang"/>
  <remote fetch="https://github.com/Freescale" name="community"/>
  <remote fetch="https://github.com/openembedded" name="oe"/>
  <remote fetch="https://git.yoctoproject.org/git" name="yocto"/>
  <remote fetch="https://github.com/nxp-imx-support" name="imx-
support"
/>

  <project name="fsl-community-bsp-base" path="sources/base" remote="co
mmunity" revision="60f79f7af60537146298560079ae603260f0bd14" upstream="
kirkstone">
    <linkfile dest="README" src="README"/>
    <linkfile dest="setup-environment" src="setup-environment"/>
  </project>
  <project name="meta-browser" path="sources/meta-browser" remote="OSSy
stems" revision="e232c2e21b96dc092d9af8bea4b3a528e7a46dd6"/>
  <project name="meta-clang" path="sources/meta-clang" remote="clang" r
evision="c728c3f9168c8a4ed05163a51dd48ca1ad8ac21d" upstream="kirkstone"
/>
  <project name="meta-freescale" path="sources/meta-freescale" remote="
community" revision="c82d4634e7aba8bc0de73ce1dfc997b630051571" upstream
="kirkstone"/>
  <project name="meta-freescale-3rdparty" path="sources/meta-freescale-
3rdparty" remote="community" revision="5977197340c7a7db17fe3e02a4e014ad
997565ae" upstream="kirkstone"/>
  <project name="meta-freescale-distro" path="sources/meta-freescale-di
stro" remote="community" revision="d5bbb487b2816dfc74984a78b67f7361ce40
4253" upstream="kirkstone"/>
```

```
  <project name="meta-imx" path="sources/meta-imx" remote="nxp-imx" rev
ision="refs/tags/rel_imx_5.15.71_2.2.0" upstream="kirkstone-5.15.71-2.2
.0">
    <linkfile dest="imx-setup-release.sh" src="tools/imx-setup-release.
sh"/>
    <linkfile dest="README-IMXBSP" src="README"/>
  </project>

  <project name="meta-nxp-demo-experience" path="sources/meta-nxp-demo-
experience" remote="imx-support" revision="52eaf8bf42f8eda2917a1c8c0460
03c8c2c8f629" upstream="kirkstone-5.15.71-2.2.0"/>
  <project name="meta-openembedded" path="sources/meta-openembedded" re
mote="oe" revision="744a4b6eda88b9a9ca1cf0df6e18be384d9054e3" upstream=
"kirkstone"/>
  <project name="meta-qt6" path="sources/meta-qt6" remote="QT6" revisio
n="ed785a25d12e365d1054700d4fc94a053176eb14" upstream="6.3"/>
  <project name="meta-timesys" path="sources/meta-timesys" remote="Time
sys" revision="d1ad27bfacc937048e7f9084b17f4d7c917d2004" upstream="mast
er"/>
  <project name="meta-virtualization" path="sources/meta-virtualization
" remote="yocto" revision="9482648daf0bb42ff3475e7892542cf99f3b8d48" up
stream="master"/>
  <project name="poky" path="sources/poky" remote="yocto" revision="24a
3f7b3648185e33133f5d96b184a6cb6524f3d" upstream="kirkstone"/>
</manifest>
```

This XML file is simple to read: within the `manifest` element, there is the Manifest definition divided into several elements as

- `default`: Used to set some default settings by using several attributes as

  - `remote`: Specifies the default remote value for those project elements lacking a remote attribute of their own

  - `revision`: Specifies the default revision value for those project elements lacking a revision attribute of their own

  - `sync-j`: Specifies the default number of parallel jobs to use when synching (if not defined within the command line)

- `remote`: Specifies a Git URL shared by one or more projects. This element supports the following attributes:

  - `fetch`: Specifies the Git URL prefix, and the `name` attribute in each `project` element is appended to this prefix to form the actual URL used to clone the project.

  - `name`: Specifies a short name unique to this Manifest file for the remote source. Projects can refer to it to point to their remote Git server.

- `project`: Specifies a single Git repository to be cloned into the repo client workspace. It supports the following attributes:

  - `name`: Specifies a unique name for this project, which is appended onto its remote's fetch URL to generate the actual URL from where to fetch sources. The URL is generated as `<remote>/<name>.git`, so it cannot be empty or an absolute path or use `.` or `..` path components.

  - `path`: Specifies a path relative to the top directory of the repo client, where the Git working directory for this project should be placed.

  - This parameter is optional, and, if so, the project `name` attribute is used. If specified, it should not be an absolute path or use `.` or `..` path components.

  - `remote`: Addresses a previously defined remote element by referring to its `name`.

  - `revision`: Specifies the name of the Git branch the Manifest wants to track for this project.

However, it is often used to specify the tag (in the form refs/tags/*tag_name*) or commit ID (as explicit SHA-1) to be fetched. It is useful to fix a specific version of all sources within our Yocto build system.

- upstream: The name of the Git reference (usually a branch name) in which the tag or commit ID specified in revision above can be found.

- copyfile: This element can be specified as children of a project element, and it is used to copy the src file to the dest place during the repo sync command.

   File src is project relative, while the dest file is relative to the top of the tree, and directories or symlinks are not allowed in these arguments. Furthermore, copying from paths outside the project or to paths outside the repo client is not allowed either.

- linkfile: This element works the same as copyfile and runs at the same time, but instead of copying, it creates a symlink.

This element and attribute list is not exhaustive, so for a complete description of the repo Manifest format, the readers should refer to https://gerrit.googlesource.com/git-repo/+/HEAD/docs/manifest-format.md.

In order to do some explanations about the repo Manifest format, we can analyze some definitions done by our Manifest file. For example:

```
<project name="meta-browser" path="sources/meta-browser" remote="OSSys
tems" revision="e232c2e21b96dc092d9af8bea4b3a528e7a46dd6"/>
```

This project entry refers to the remote entry OSSystems, so that the Git URL is https://github.com/OSSystems/meta-browser.git, and sources from commit ID e232c2e21b96dc092d9af8bea4b3a528e7a46dd6 will be fetched into the sources/meta-browser directory. In fact, we have

```
$ git -C sources/meta-browser/ log -1 --oneline
e232c2e (HEAD, m/imx-linux-kirkstone) cbindgen: upgrade to 0.23.0
```

Another example can be the entry:

```
<project name="meta-imx" path="sources/meta-imx" remote="nxp-imx" revis
ion="refs/tags/rel_imx_5.15.71_2.2.0" upstream="kirkstone-5.15.71-2.2.0
">
```

Here, the project entry refers to the remote entry nxp-imx, so that the Git URL is https://github.com/nxp-imx/meta-imx.git, and sources from tag rel_imx_5.15.71_2.2.0 in branch kirkstone-5.15.71-2.2.0 will be fetched into the sources/meta-imx directory. In fact, we have

```
$ git -C sources/meta-imx/ log -1 --oneline
9174c61f4d (HEAD, tag: rel_imx_5.15.71_2.2.0, nxp-imx/kirkstone-5.15.71
-2.2.0, m/imx-linux-kirkstone) Fix Yocto syntax error of i.MX 8M AB2 bo
ards [YOCIMX-7250]
```

Finally, a fascinating example is the following entry:

```
<project name="fsl-community-bsp-base" path="sources/base" remote="comm
unity" revision="60f79f7af60537146298560079ae603260f0bd14" upstream="ki
rkstone">
    <linkfile dest="README" src="README"/>
    <linkfile dest="setup-environment" src="setup-environment"/>
</project>
```

Here, as before, the project entry refers to the remote entry community, so that the Git URL is https://github.com/Freescale/fsl-community-bsp-base.git, and sources from commit ID 60f79f7af60537146298560079ae603260f0bd14 in branch kirkstone will be fetched into the sources/base directory. In fact, we have

```
$ git -C sources/base/ log -1 --oneline
60f79f7 (HEAD, m/imx-linux-kirkstone, community/kirkstone, community/ho
nister) setup-environment: Update NXP EULA reference
```

However, this time, the structure of the project is a bit more complex than before since two `linkfile` elements have been specified too. This will cause, once the sources have been fetched, two symlinks named README and `setup-environment` to be created at the top of the tree pointing to the same name files into the project local directory (i.e., `sources/base`). In fact, in the `imx-yocto-bsp` directory, we have

```
$ cd imx-yocto-bsp
$ ls -l README setup-environment
lrwxrwxrwx 1 giometti giometti 19 Nov 24  2023 README -> sources/base/R
EADME
lrwxrwxrwx 1 giometti giometti 30 Nov 24  2023 setup-environment -> sou
rces/base/setup-environment
```

OK, now that we know perfectly how a Manifest file works, adding the Engicam meta layer is simple. All needed modifications are reported below:

```
--- a/cy-5.15.71-2.2.0.xml
+++ b/cy-5.15.71-2.2.0.xml
@@ -12,6 +12,7 @@
   <remote fetch="https://github.com/openembedded" name="oe"/>
   <remote fetch="https://git.yoctoproject.org/git" name="yocto"/>
   <remote fetch="https://github.com/nxp-imx-support" name="imx-support"/>
+  <remote fetch="https://github.com/engicam-stable" name="engicam-supp
ort"/>

   <project name="fsl-community-bsp-base" path="sources/base" remote="c
ommunity" revision="60f79f7af60537146298560079ae603260f0bd14" upstream=
"kirkstone">
      <linkfile dest="README" src="README"/>
@@ -34,4 +35,5 @@
   <project name="meta-timesys" path="sources/meta-timesys" remote="Tim
esys" revision="d1ad27bfacc937048e7f9084b17f4d7c917d2004" upstream="mas
ter"/>
   <project name="meta-virtualization" path="sources/meta-virtualizatio
n" remote="yocto" revision="9482648daf0bb42ff3475e7892542cf99f3b8d48" u
pstream="master"/>
   <project name="poky" path="sources/poky" remote="yocto" revision="24
a3f7b3648185e33133f5d96b184a6cb6524f3d" upstream="kirkstone"/>
+  <project name="meta-engicam-nxp" path="sources/meta-engicam-nxp" rem
ote="engicam-support" revision="983ed77473c8567045d88165a33c81c4ac8b4e8
9" upstream="kirkstone"/>
 </manifest>
```

In the above patch, we added a new remote element to address Engicam's support URL and then a new project element to specify the remote repository's name, the commit ID, and where the sources should be placed into.

To test if everything works well, we need to commit our changes as shown below:

```
$ git add cy-5.15.71-2.2.0.xml
$ git commit -s -m "cy-5.15.71-2.2.0.xml: add Engicam meta layer"
[cy-linux-kirkstone a8540b0] cy-5.15.71-2.2.0.xml: add Engicam meta lay
er
 1 file changed, 2 insertions(+)
```

Now we can try to regenerate our Yocto build system as shown below:

```
$ mkdir /tmp/manifest-test && cd /tmp/manifest-test
$ repo init -u /home/giometti/yocto/manifest/cy-manifest/ \
        -b cy-linux-kirkstone -m cy-5.15.71-2.2.0.xml
Downloading Repo source from https://gerrit.googlesource.com/git-repo

Your identity is: Rodolfo Giometti <giometti@enneenne.com>
If you want to change this, please re-run 'repo init' with --config-name

repo has been initialized in /tmp/manifest-test
```

Note that, as already said in Section 2.1, if we get a warning message as below:

```
... A new version of repo (2.45) is available.
... New version is available at: /tmp/manifest-test/.repo/repo/rep
o
... The launcher is run from: /usr/bin/repo
!!! The launcher is not writable.  Please talk to your sysadmin or
 distro
!!! to get an update installed.
```

we can update our `repo` application or just continue with the current version.

669

```
$ repo sync
...
Fetching:  0% (0/14) 0:05 | 2 jobs | 0:04 meta-freescale @ sources/meta
-freescale
...
```

The readers should notice that when executing the `repo init` command

- With the `-u` option argument, we supplied the directory where our custom manifest is stored.

- With the `-b` option argument, we used our custom branch.

- With the `-m` option argument, we used our manifest XML file.

while during the execution of the `repo sync` command, two concurrent jobs have been started as defined into the `sync-j` attribute in the `default` element.

Now we can check that everything is in place:

```
$ ls
imx-setup-release.sh  README  README-IMXBSP  setup-environment  sources
$ ls sources/
base                  meta-freescale-3rdparty  meta-qt6
meta-browser          meta-freescale-distro    meta-timesys
meta-clang            meta-imx                 meta-virtualization
meta-engicam-nxp      meta-nxp-demo-experience  poky
meta-freescale        meta-openembedded
```

We can also check that the right commit ID has been used to fetch Engicam's sources:

```
$ git -C sources/meta-engicam-nxp/ log -1 --oneline
983ed77 (HEAD, m/cy-linux-kirkstone) Updated UBoot SRCREV
```

OK, now we need to add our custom meta layer. However, before doing so, we need to save our modification within `setup-environment` done in Section 7.4:

```
$ cd $CY_METADIR
$ mkdir tools
$ cp ../../setup-environment tools/
$ git add tools/setup-environment
$ git commit -s -m "tools: add our custom setup-environment"
[master 66f43fc] tools: add our custom setup-environment
 1 file changed, 278 insertions(+)
 create mode 100755 tools/setup-environment
```

Our meta layer is now finished, so we can push all changes into our
GitHub repository:

```
$ git push -f -u origin
Enumerating objects: 215, done.
Counting objects: 100% (215/215), done.
Delta compression using up to 24 threads
Compressing objects: 100% (177/177), done.
Writing objects: 100% (215/215), 42.04 KiB | 4.20 MiB/s, done.
Total 215 (delta 48), reused 0 (delta 0), pack-reused 0
remote: Resolving deltas: 100% (48/48), done.
To github.com:giometti/meta-cy.git
 + 0828270...66f43fc master -> master
Branch 'master' set up to track remote branch 'master' from 'origin'.
```

Considering what we have said above about the Manifest files, the
needed modifications to add our meta layer are reported below:

```
$ git diff
diff --git a/cy-5.15.71-2.2.0.xml b/cy-5.15.71-2.2.0.xml
index 38063d0..79da148 100644
--- a/cy-5.15.71-2.2.0.xml
+++ b/cy-5.15.71-2.2.0.xml
@@ -13,10 +13,10 @@
   <remote fetch="https://git.yoctoproject.org/git" name="yocto"/>
   <remote fetch="https://github.com/nxp-imx-support" name="imx-support"/>
   <remote fetch="https://github.com/engicam-stable" name="engicam-support"/>
+  <remote fetch="https://github.com/giometti" name="cy-support"/>

   <project name="fsl-community-bsp-base" path="sources/base" remote="community" revision="60f79f7af60537146298560079ae603260f0bd14" upstream="kirkstone">
     <linkfile dest="README" src="README"/>
-    <linkfile dest="setup-environment" src="setup-environment"/>
   </project>
```

671

```
    <project name="meta-browser" path="sources/meta-browser" remote="OSS
ystems" revision="e232c2e21b96dc092d9af8bea4b3a528e7a46dd6"/>
    <project name="meta-clang" path="sources/meta-clang" remote="clang"
revision="c728c3f9168c8a4ed05163a51dd48ca1ad8ac21d" upstream="kirkstone
"/>
@@ -36,4 +37,7 @@
    <project name="meta-virtualization" path="sources/meta-virtualizatio
n" remote="yocto" revision="9482648daf0bb42ff3475e7892542cf99f3b8d48" u
pstream="master"/>
    <project name="poky" path="sources/poky" remote="yocto" revision="24
a3f7b3648185e33133f5d96b184a6cb6524f3d" upstream="kirkstone"/>
    <project name="meta-engicam-nxp" path="sources/meta-engicam-nxp" rem
ote="engicam-support" revision="983ed77473c8567045d88165a33c81c4ac8b4e8
9" upstream="kirkstone"/>
+   <project name="meta-cy" path="sources/meta-cy" remote="cy-support" r
evision="4cca1f0aae0d545114776308e1b1b857c3e0a406" upstream="kirkstone">
+     <linkfile dest="setup-environment" src="tools/setup-environment"/>
+   </project>
 </manifest>
```

In the above patch, we should notice that we have removed the line:

```
-      <linkfile dest="setup-environment" src="setup-environment"/>
```

This is because we wish to use our custom `setup-environment` file, instead of the one within the `fsl-community-bsp-base` repository.

Now we just need to commit the changes:

```
$ git add cy-5.15.71-2.2.0.xml
$ git commit -s -m "cy-5.15.71-2.2.0.xml: add CY meta layer"
[cy-linux-kirkstone 5759997] cy-5.15.71-2.2.0.xml: add CY meta layer
 1 file changed, 4 insertions(+)
```

To test our new Manifest, we should recreate the temporary directory used before:

```
$ cd /tmp/
$ rm -rf manifest-test/
$ mkdir manifest-test && cd manifest-test
```

Then we can execute again the repo init and sync commands as done before:

```
$ repo init -u /home/giometti/yocto/manifest/cy-manifest/ -b cy-linux-k
irkstone -m cy-5.15.71-2.2.0.xml
$ repo sync
```

Once the synchronization has been finished, we can check if everything is in place:

```
$ ls
imx-setup-release.sh  README  README-IMXBSP  setup-environment  sources
$ ls sources/
base                meta-freescale          meta-openembedded
meta-browser        meta-freescale-3rdparty meta-qt6
meta-clang          meta-freescale-distro   meta-timesys
meta-cy             meta-imx                meta-virtualization
meta-engicam-nxp    meta-nxp-demo-experience poky
```

Everything is as before, but now we also have our meta-cy layer! We can also verify that it is at the correct commit:

```
$ git -C sources/meta-cy/ log -1 --oneline
66f43fc (HEAD, m/cy-linux-kirkstone, cy-support/master) tools: add our
custom setup-environment
```

We can also check if the setup-environment holds our modifications:

```
$ grep CY_METADIR setup-environment
export CY_METADIR="$PWD/sources/meta-cy"
export PATH="$CY_METADIR/scripts:$PATH"
```

Great! Now everything seems to be in place... but something is still missing! In fact, if we try to generate our custom CY Yocto image by using the commands below, we get

```
$ DISTRO=cy-xwayland MACHINE=imx8mp-icore-cy source imx-setup-release.s
h -b imx8mp-build
...
Your build environment has been configured with:

    MACHINE=imx8mp-icore-cy
    SDKMACHINE=i686
    DISTRO=cy-xwayland
    EULA=
```

```
BSPDIR=
BUILD_DIR=.
meta-freescale directory found
```

Note that, this time, we have specified our `cy-xwayland` distro and `imx8mp-icore-cy` machine. Then if we try to build an image as usual, the following error will arise:

```
$ bitbake core-image-minimal
...
ERROR:  OE-core's config sanity checker detected a potential misconfigu
ration.
    Either fix the cause of this error or at your own risk disable the
checker (see sanity.conf).
    Following is the list of potential problems / advisories:

    DISTRO 'cy-xwayland' not found. Please set a valid DISTRO in your l
ocal.conf
MACHINE=imx8mp-icore-cy is invalid. Please set a valid MACHINE in your
local.conf, environment or other configuration file.
...
```

This is because if we take a look at the `conf/bblayers.conf` file, both our meta layer and the Engicam one are missing. To quickly address this issue, we can use the `bitbake-layers add-layer` command as seen in this book, but we wish having everything already fixed by `repo`. To do so, we need to clone and modify the `imx-setup-release.sh` script as we did for the `setup-environment` one:

```
$ cd $CY_METADIR
$ cp ../meta-imx/tools/imx-setup-release.sh tools/
```

Then we have to alter the script as reported below to add the Engicam meta layer and our layer:

```
--- a/tools/imx-setup-release.sh
+++ b/tools/imx-setup-release.sh
@@ -188,6 +188,10 @@
 # Enable docker for mx8 machines
 echo "BBLAYERS += \"\${BSPDIR}/sources/meta-virtualization\"" >> conf/
bblayers.conf
```

```
+# Add Engicam and CY meta layers
+echo "BBLAYERS += \"\${BSPDIR}/sources/meta-engicam-nxp\"" >> conf/bbl
ayers.conf
+echo "BBLAYERS += \"\${BSPDIR}/sources/meta-cy\"" >> conf/bblayers.conf
+
 echo BSPDIR=$BSPDIR
 echo BUILD_DIR=$BUILD_DIR
```

Now we have to commit our modifications to be referenced by the manifest:

```
$ git add tools/imx-setup-release.sh
$ git commit -m "tools: add custom imx-setup-release.sh"
[master 4cca1f0] tools: add custom imx-setup-release.sh
 1 file changed, 208 insertions(+)
 create mode 100755 tools/imx-setup-release.sh
```

The manifest file should now be modified as reported below:

```
--- a/cy-5.15.71-2.2.0.xml
+++ b/cy-5.15.71-2.2.0.xml
@@ -25,7 +25,6 @@
   <project name="meta-freescale-distro" path="sources/meta-freescale-distro"
remote="community" revision="d5bbb487b2816dfc74984a78b67f7361ce404253"
upstream="kirkstone"/>

   <project name="meta-imx" path="sources/meta-imx" remote="nxp-imx" re
vision="refs/tags/rel_imx_5.15.71_2.2.0" upstream="kirkstone-5.15.71-2.2.0">
-     <linkfile dest="imx-setup-release.sh" src="tools/imx-setup-release.sh"/>
      <linkfile dest="README-IMXBSP" src="README"/>
   </project>

@@ -36,7 +35,8 @@
   <project name="meta-virtualization" path="sources/meta-virtualization"
remote="yocto" revision="9482648daf0bb42ff3475e7892542cf99f3b8d48"
upstream="master"/>
   <project name="poky" path="sources/poky" remote="yocto" revision="24
a3f7b3648185e33133f5d96b184a6cb6524f3d" upstream="kirkstone"/>
   <project name="meta-engicam-nxp" path="sources/meta-engicam-nxp" rem
ote="engicam-support" revision="983ed77473c8567045d88165a33c81c4ac8b4e8
9" upstream="kirkstone"/>
-  <project name="meta-cy" path="sources/meta-cy" remote="cy-support" r
evision="dcd463f76dc7fceb0b01e6cc8a03d78ab9abcef7" upstream="master">
+  <project name="meta-cy" path="sources/meta-cy" remote="cy-support" r
```

```
evision="4cca1f0aae0d545114776308e1b1b857c3e0a406" upstream="master">
     <linkfile dest="setup-environment" src="tools/setup-environment"/>
+    <linkfile dest="imx-setup-release.sh" src="tools/imx-setup-release.sh"/>
   </project>
 </manifest>
```

In the above patch, we replaced the commit ID for the meta-cy layer, and we replaced the symbolic link for imx-setup-release.sh in order to point to our custom one.

At this point, if we retry to execute repo against our new manifest as above, we should get the following status after the repo sync:

```
$ ls -l
...
lrwxrwxrwx  1 giometti giometti   42 Dec 29 11:17 imx-setup-release.sh
-> sources/meta-cy/tools/imx-setup-release.sh
lrwxrwxrwx  1 giometti giometti   39 Dec 29 11:17 setup-environment ->
sources/meta-cy/tools/setup-environment
...
```

When we execute again the command:

```
$ DISTRO=cy-xwayland MACHINE=imx8mp-icore-cy source \
        imx-setup-release.sh -b imx8mp-build
```

Now our custom script is executed and the bblayers.conf file is correctly created:

```
$ cat conf/bblayers.conf
...
BBLAYERS += "${BSPDIR}/sources/meta-virtualization"
BBLAYERS += "${BSPDIR}/sources/meta-engicam-nxp"
BBLAYERS += "${BSPDIR}/sources/meta-cy"
```

If we try to generate an image, everything should work well:

```
$ bitbake core-image-minimal
...
Build Configuration:
BB_VERSION        = "2.0.0"
BUILD_SYS         = "x86_64-linux"
NATIVELSBSTRING   = "ubuntu-22.04"
```

```
TARGET_SYS          = "aarch64-poky-linux"
MACHINE             = "imx8mp-icore-cy"
DISTRO              = "cy-xwayland"
...
```

And the build can continue without errors.

13.5 Checking for Common Vulnerabilities and Exposures (CVEs)

Good embedded developers should be able to write wonderful code and to manage and configure programs; however, they should also be able to fix possible vulnerabilities. In this scenario, the cve-check class can come to help.

This class looks for known CVEs (Common Vulnerabilities and Exposures from https://nvd.nist.gov/vuln) while building with BitBake. To enable it, we have to use the INHERIT variable from a configuration file (e.g., in the local.conf):

```
--- a/conf/local.conf
+++ b/conf/local.conf
@@ -35,5 +35,10 @@
 BUILDHISTORY_COMMIT = "1"
 BUILDHISTORY_FEATURES="image package task"

+# Add CVE checks
+INHERIT += "cve-check"
+CVE_CHECK_SHOW_WARNINGS = "0"
+include cve-extra-exclusions.inc
+
 # Then include SRCREV information (if present)
 include srcrev.conf
```

where the CVE_CHECK_SHOW_WARNINGS can be used to specify whether the cve-check class should generate warning messages on the console when unpatched CVEs are found (the default value is 1; that's why we have set it to 0 to suppress them).

The include `cve-extra-exclusions.inc` statement is used to filter out obsolete CVE database entries which are known not to impact software from Poky.

Now, if we regenerate our image, we should see that `bitbake` is downloading the CVE database:

```
$ bitbake cy-evaluation-image-mx8
...
1: cve-update-db-native-1.0-r0 do_fetch - 1s (pid 3881116)  13% |#      |
...
Complete CVE report summary created at: /home/giometti/yocto/imx-yocto-
bsp/imx8mp-build/tmp/log/cve/cve-summary
NOTE: Generating JSON CVE summary
Complete CVE JSON report summary created at: /home/giometti/yocto/imx-y
octo-bsp/imx8mp-build/tmp/log/cve/cve-summary.json
...
```

After building, as shown above, CVE check output reports are available in `tmp/deploy/cve` as both text and JSON files and image-specific summaries in `tmp/deploy/images/MACHINE/DISTRO*.cve` or `tmp/deploy/images/MACHINE/DISTRO*.json` files. In our example, we have

```
$ ls tmp/deploy/images/imx8mp-icore-cy/cy-evaluation-image-mx8*.{cve,js
on}
...
tmp/deploy/images/imx8mp-icore-cy/cy-evaluation-image-mx8-imx8mp-icore-
cy.cve
tmp/deploy/images/imx8mp-icore-cy/cy-evaluation-image-mx8-imx8mp-icore-
cy.json
...
```

We can also look for vulnerabilities in specific packages by passing the option argument `-c cve_check` to BitBake. For example:

```
$ bitbake -c cve_check strace
...
Complete CVE report summary created at: /home/giometti/yocto/imx-y
octo-bsp/imx8mp-build/tmp/log/cve/cve-summary
NOTE: Generating JSON CVE summary
Complete CVE JSON report summary created at: /home/giometti/yocto/
```

```
imx-yocto-bsp/imx8mp-build/tmp/log/cve/cve-summary.json
$ cat tmp/log/cve/cve-summary
LAYER: meta
PACKAGE NAME: strace
PACKAGE VERSION: 5.16
CVE: CVE-2000-0006
CVE STATUS: Unpatched
CVE SUMMARY: strace allows local users to read arbitrary files via
 memory mapped file names.
CVSS v2 BASE SCORE: 2.6
CVSS v3 BASE SCORE: 0.0
VECTOR: LOCAL
MORE INFORMATION: https://nvd.nist.gov/vuln/detail/CVE-2000-0006
```

Note that this output has overwritten the previous one, so we have to execute again the `bitbake cy-evaluation-image-mx8` command to restore the previous content.

When building, the CVE checker will emit build-time warnings for any detected issues which are in the state:

- `Unpatched`: Which means that the CVE issue seems to affect the software component and version being compiled, and no patches have been applied to address the issue.

- `Patched`: Which means that a patch to address the issue is already applied instead.

- `Ignored`: Which means that the issue can be ignored.

We can see these values for our `cy-evaluation-image-mx8` by using the following command:

```
$ grep 'CVE STATUS:' tmp/deploy/images/imx8mp-icore-cy/cy-evaluation-im
age-mx8-imx8mp-icore-cy.cve | sort | uniq
CVE STATUS: Ignored
CVE STATUS: Patched
CVE STATUS: Unpatched
```

The Patched state of a CVE vulnerability is detected from patch files with the format CVE-YYYY-XXXXX.patch in the SRC_URI variable and using CVE metadata of format CVE: CVE-YYYY-XXXXX in the commit message of the patch file. In our Yocto sources, we have, for example

```
$ cd ../sources/
$ find . -name 'CVE-*.patch' | head -5
./meta-virtualization/recipes-containers/podman/podman/CVE-2022-27649.p
atch
./meta-openembedded/meta-networking/recipes-support/wireshark/files/CVE
-2022-3190.patch
./meta-openembedded/meta-networking/recipes-support/ntopng/files/CVE-20
21-36082.patch
./meta-openembedded/meta-networking/recipes-netkit/netkit-rsh/netkit-rs
h/CVE-2019-7282-and-CVE-2019-7283.patch
./meta-openembedded/meta-networking/recipes-netkit/netkit-telnet/files/
CVE-2020-10188.patch
```

So, CVE issue CVE-2020-10188 is marked as patched by the patch named CVE-2020-10188.patch in the meta-openembedded layer for the package netkit-telnet, as shown below:

```
$ cat ./meta-openembedded/meta-networking/recipes-netkit/netkit-telnet/
files/CVE-2020-10188.patch
From 6ab007dbb1958371abff2eaaad2b26da89b3c74e Mon Sep 17 00:00:00 2001
From: Yi Zhao <yi.zhao@windriver.com>
Date: Fri, 24 Apr 2020 09:43:44 +0800
Subject: [PATCH] telnetd/utility.c: fix CVE-2020-10188

Upstream-Status: Backport
[Fedora: https://src.fedoraproject.org/rpms/telnet/raw/master/f/telnet-
0.17-overflow-exploit.patch]

CVE: CVE-2020-10188

Signed-off-by: Yi Zhao <yi.zhao@windriver.com>
---
 telnetd/utility.c | 32 ++++++++++++++++++++++++-----------
 1 file changed, 21 insertions(+), 11 deletions(-)
...
```

where we can also find the line with the tag CVE: CVE-2020-10188 and, if we do a CVE check, get

```
$ bitbake -c cve_check netkit-telnet
...
Complete CVE report summary created at: /home/giometti/yocto/imx-yocto-
bsp/imx8mp-build/tmp/log/cve/cve-summary
...
$ cat $BUILDDIR/tmp/log/cve/cve-summary
LAYER: meta-networking
PACKAGE NAME: netkit-telnet
PACKAGE VERSION: 0.17
CVE: CVE-2020-10188
CVE STATUS: Patched
...
```

On the other hand, if the recipe lists the CVE-YYYY-XXXXX ID in the CVE_CHECK_IGNORE variable, then the CVE state is reported as ignored (multiple CVEs can be listed separated by spaces). For example, in the glibc recipe, we have

```
$ grep CVE_CHECK_IGNORE poky/meta/recipes-core/glibc/glibc_2.35.bb
CVE_CHECK_IGNORE += "CVE-2020-10029 CVE-2021-27645"
CVE_CHECK_IGNORE += "CVE-2019-1010022 CVE-2019-1010023 CVE-2019-1010024"
CVE_CHECK_IGNORE += "CVE-2019-1010025"
```

Before closing this section, we should remark that this CVE check may report false positives or false negatives! This is not a perfect tool. In this case, these issues may be resolved in recipes by adjusting the CVE product name using the CVE_PRODUCT and CVE_VERSION variables. For example, the recipe for the TIFF library states:

```
$ cat poky/meta/recipes-multimedia/libtiff/tiff_4.3.0.bb
SUMMARY = "Provides support for the Tag Image File Format (TIFF)"
...
CVE_PRODUCT = "libtiff"
...
# Tested with check from
# https://security-tracker.debian.org/tracker/CVE-2015-7313 and 4.3.0
# doesn't have the issue
CVE_CHECK_IGNORE += "CVE-2015-7313"
# These issues only affect libtiff post-4.3.0 but before 4.4.0,
```

```
# caused by 3079627e and fixed by b4e79bfa.
CVE_CHECK_IGNORE += "CVE-2022-1622 CVE-2022-1623"

# Issue is in jbig which we don't enable
CVE_CHECK_IGNORE += "CVE-2022-1210"
...
```

Here, the recipe redefines the default value for CVE_PRODUCT (which is set to the plain recipe name, i.e., the value in BPN) which moves the checks against the CVE database to the string libtiff instead of tiff.

Specifically, in the variable CVE_PRODUCT, both vendor and product pairs can be specified using the following syntax:

```
CVE_PRODUCT = "tuxera:ntfs-3g"
```

where, for the recipe ntfs-3g-ntfsprogs_2022.5.17.bb, the string tuxera is the CVE database vendor name, and ntfs-3g is the product name.

Similarly, if the default recipe version PV does not match the version numbers of the package in upstream releases or the CVE database, then the CVE_VERSION variable can be used to set the CVE database compatible version number.

Regarding the reliability of this tool, the readers should notice the warning reported at the Yocto Project Documentation site at https://docs.yoctoproject.org/ref-manual/classes. html#cve-check where they can read:

Users should note that security is a process, not a product, and thus also CVE checking, analyzing results, patching and updating the software should be done as a regular process. The data and assumptions required for CVE checker to reliably detect issues are frequently broken in various ways. These can only be detected by reviewing the details of the issues and iterating over the generated reports, and following what happens in other Linux distributions and in the greater open source community.

More details in the *Checking for Vulnerabilities* section in the Development Tasks Manual at `https://docs.yoctoproject.org/dev-manual/vulnerabilities.html#checking-for-vulnerabilities`.

Now, in order to do a simple example about how we can fix a detected vulnerability, we can consider the following report:

```
$ cat tmp/deploy/images/imx8mp-icore-cy/cy-evaluation-image-mx8-imx8mp-
icore-cy.cve
...
LAYER: meta
PACKAGE NAME: libarchive
PACKAGE VERSION: 3.6.1
CVE: CVE-2022-36227
CVE STATUS: Unpatched
CVE SUMMARY: In libarchive before 3.6.2, the software does not check for an
error after calling calloc function that can return with a NULL pointer if the
function fails, which leads to a resultant NULL pointer dereference. NOTE:
the discoverer cites this CWE-476 remark but third parties dispute the code-
execution impact: "In rare circumstances, when NULL is equivalent to the 0x0
memory address and privileged code can access it, then writing or reading
memory is possible, which may lead to code execution."
CVSS v2 BASE SCORE: 0.0
CVSS v3 BASE SCORE: 9.8
VECTOR: NETWORK
MORE INFORMATION: https://nvd.nist.gov/vuln/detail/CVE-2022-36227
...
```

In this scenario, we can take a look at the suggested URL `https://nvd.nist.gov/vuln/detail/CVE-2022-36227` where, after a deep (and not easy) quest, we discover that a patch can be downloaded at `https://github.com/obiwac/libarchive/commit/` `bff38efe8c110469c5080d387bec62a6ca15b1a5`. To get the raw patch from that website, we can use the command below:

```
$ wget https://github.com/obiwac/libarchive/commit/bff38efe8c110469c508
0d387bec62a6ca15b1a5.patch -O /tmp/CVE-2022-36227.patch
...
Saving to: '/tmp/CVE-2022-36227.patch'
...
```

Once downloaded, the patch looks like this:

```
$ cat /tmp/CVE-2022-36227.patch
From bff38efe8c110469c5080d387bec62a6ca15b1a5 Mon Sep 17 00:00:00 2001
From: obiwac <obiwac@gmail.com>
Date: Fri, 22 Jul 2022 22:41:10 +0200
Subject: [PATCH] libarchive: Handle a `calloc` returning NULL (fixes #1754)

---
 libarchive/archive_write.c | 8 ++++++++
 1 file changed, 8 insertions(+)
...
```

Then we can add it to the recipe via a `.bbappend` file:

```
$ recipetool appendsrcfile $CY_METADIR libarchive \
        /tmp/CVE-2022-36227.patch
...
NOTE: Writing append file /home/giometti/yocto/imx-yocto-bsp/sources/me
ta-cy/recipes-extended/libarchive/libarchive_3.6.1.bbappend
NOTE: Copying CVE-2022-36227.patch to /home/giometti/yocto/imx-yocto-bs
p/sources/meta-cy/recipes-extended/libarchive/libarchive/CVE-2022-36227
.patch
```

And our meta layer should now have a new directory as shown below:

```
$ cd $CY_METADIR
$ tree recipes-extended/
recipes-extended/
└── libarchive
    ├── libarchive
    │   └── CVE-2022-36227.patch
    └── libarchive_3.6.1.bbappend

2 directories, 2 files
```

Then, if we rebuild the package and we redo a rebuild with CVE check, we should get

```
$ bitbake -c cleanall libarchive && bitbake libarchive
...
Complete CVE report summary created at: /home/giometti/yocto/imx-yocto-
bsp/imx8mp-build/tmp/log/cve/cve-summary
$ cat $BUILDDIR/tmp/log/cve/cve-summary
...
LAYER: meta
PACKAGE NAME: libarchive
PACKAGE VERSION: 3.6.1
CVE: CVE-2022-36227
CVE STATUS: Patched
...
```

as expected.

We used the target clean_all just to force a complete download and rebuild of the package, but we can omit it for a normal rebuild.

Before closing this section, we should mention that, starting from Yocto Scarthgap, this tool has changed. In particular, when preparing the patch file, we must add to the original patch the CVE: CVE-YYYY-XXXXX, and it is also recommended to add the Upstream-Status: tag with a link to the original patch and sign-off by people working on the backport.

For example, for the package yasm in the meta-oe layer, in Scarthgap we have the following patch file:

```
$ cat meta-openembedded/meta-oe/recipes-devtools/yasm/yasm/CVE-2023-319
75.patch
From b2cc5a1693b17ac415df76d0795b15994c106441 Mon Sep 17 00:00:00 2001
From: Katsuhiko Gondow <gondow@cs.titech.ac.jp>
Date: Tue, 13 Jun 2023 05:00:47 +0900
Subject: [PATCH] Fix memory leak in bin-objfmt (#231)

Upstream-Status: Backport [https://github.com/yasm/yasm/commit/b2cc5a16
93b17ac415df76d0795b15994c106441]
```

```
CVE: CVE-2023-31975
---
 modules/objfmts/bin/bin-objfmt.c | 4 ++++
 1 file changed, 4 insertions(+)
```

A good practice is to include the CVE identifier in the patch filename, the patch file commit message, and optionally in the recipe commit message.

On the other hand, if we notice that the CVE can be marked as ignored, we must use the new variable CVE_STATUS with an appropriate reason. As example, in Scarthgap we can read something as shown below:

```
$ cat meta-openembedded/meta-oe/recipes-support/atop/atop_2.4.0.bb
SUMMARY = "Monitor for system resources and process activity"
...
CVE_STATUS[CVE-2011-3618] = "fixed-version: The CPE in the NVD database
 doesn't reflect correctly the vulnerable versions."
...
```

If there are many CVEs with the same status and reason, those can be shared by using the CVE_STATUS_GROUPS variable, as the glibc recipe does:

```
$ cat openembedded-core/meta/recipes-core/glibc/glibc_2.39.bb
...
require glibc.inc
require glibc-version.inc

# glibc https://web.nvd.nist.gov/view/vuln/detail?vulnId=CVE-2019-10100
22
# glibc https://web.nvd.nist.gov/view/vuln/detail?vulnId=CVE-2019-10100
23
# glibc https://web.nvd.nist.gov/view/vuln/detail?vulnId=CVE-2019-10100
24
CVE_STATUS_GROUPS = "CVE_STATUS_RECIPE"
CVE_STATUS_RECIPE = "CVE-2019-1010022 CVE-2019-1010023 CVE-2019-1010024"
CVE_STATUS_RECIPE[status] = "disputed: \
Upstream glibc maintainers dispute there is any issue and have no plans
 to address it further. \
this is being treated as a non-security bug and no real threat."
...
```

Finally, recipes can be completely skipped by CVE check by including the list of package names (i.e., the PN variable) in the CVE_CHECK_SKIP_ RECIPE variable.

13.6 Summary

In this chapter, we have seen how to optimize and customize our Yocto distributions and also some best practices to manage our code. In the end, we have shown how to generate a custom repo Manifest to be able to fix and reproduce from scratch a complete Yocto image and then how to detect and resolve possible Common Vulnerabilities and Exposures (CVEs).

We are now ready to get the best results from every Yocto system we need to work on!

Enjoy.

Index

A

ACCEPT_FSL_EULA, 40
add and modify recipe, workspace
    add new recipe, 163
    appends, 163
    attic, 163
    BBLAYERS, 157
    bblayers.conf, 156
    conf, 163
    devmem2, 161, 162
    devtool output, 159
    devtool add command, 159
    edit-recipe subcommand, 165
    EXTERNALSRC_BUILD
        variable, 165
    EXTERNALSRC variable, 164
    extract the source, 160
    FILESEXTRAPATHS
        variable, 164
    FILESPATH variable, 164
    layer.conf, 156
    meta-openembedded/
        meta-oe, 166
    nettest, 165
    nettestc (the client), 158
    nettests (the server), 158
    no-extract (or-n), 161
    private environment, 161
    README file, 155
    recipes, 163
    rename subcommand, 159
    S and B variables, 164
    same-dir (or-s), 161
    sources, 163
    status, 155, 161
    SUMMARY variable, 166
    usage command, 161
add-layer, 135
appendfile, 143
Append files, 72
appendsrcfile, 146
ARM Trusted Firmware
    (ATF/TF-A), 396–400
Authentication, 277
Automount fstab
    bbappend file, 627
    eMMC partitions, 628
    fstab file, 626
    microSD, 626, 628, 630
    MMC devices, 629
    mmcblk.exclude.list, 629
    recipetool newappend, 629
    root filesystem, 625
autotools class, 75
autotools-brokensep
    class, 181

B

D

K

L

M

Y, Z

www.ingramcontent.com/pod-product-compliance
Lightning Source LLC
LaVergne TN
LVHW051634050326
832903LV00022B/758